THE GREENWOOD ENCYCLOPEDIA OF

CLOTHING THROUGH AMERICAN HISTORY 1900 TO THE PRESENT

THE GREENWOOD ENCYCLOPEDIA OF

CLOTHING THROUGH AMERICAN HISTORY 1900 TO THE PRESENT

VOLUME 2
1950-PRESENT

José Blanco F., Scott Leff,
Ann T. Kellogg, and Lynn W. Payne

Ann T. Kellogg, General Editor

GREENWOOD PRESS
Westport, Connecticut • London

Library of Congress Cataloging-in-Publication Data

The Greenwood encyclopedia of clothing through American history 1900 to the present /
Amy T. Peterson, general editor [v. 1], Ann T. Kellogg, general editor [v. 2].
    p. cm.
  Includes bibliographical references and index.
   ISBN 978-0-313-35855-5 ((set) : alk. paper)—ISBN 978-0-313-33395-8 ((vol. 1) :
alk. paper)—ISBN 978-0-313-33417-7 ((vol. 2) : alk. paper)
   1. Clothing and dress—United States—History—20th century. I. Peterson, Amy T.
II. Kellogg, Ann T., 1968–
  GT615.G74 2008
  391.0097309'04—dc22   2008024624

British Library Cataloguing in Publication Data is available.

Library of Congress Catalog Card Number: 2008024624
ISBN: 978-0-313-35855-5 (set)
     978-0-313-33395-8 (vol. 1)
     978-0-313-33417-7 (vol. 2)

First published in 2008

Greenwood Press, 88 Post Road West, Westport, CT 06881
An imprint of Greenwood Publishing Group, Inc.
www.greenwood.com

Printed in the United States of America

The paper used in this book complies with the
Permanent Paper Standard issued by the National
Information Standards Organization (Z39.48-1984).

10   9   8   7   6   5   4   3   2   1

Contents

Preface   *ix*

Chronology of World and Fashion Events, 1950 to the Present   *xiii*

Part I: The Social Significance of Dress   1

Chapter 1: The United States from 1950 to the Present:
An Overview   *3*

    Politics in America   *4*

    Ethnicity in America   *6*

    Arts and Entertainment   *7*

    Daily Life   *9*

    The Changing Role of Women   *11*

    Sexuality and Morality   *12*

    Growing Up in America   *13*

    Fashion   *14*

Chapter 2: Political and Cultural Events   *17*

    The 1950s   *19*

    The 1960s   *24*

    The 1970s   *30*

    The 1980s   *35*

    The 1990s and 2000s   *40*

Chapter 3: Arts and Entertainment   *49*

    The 1950s   *51*

    The 1960s   *58*

    The 1970s   *67*

    The 1980s   *74*

    The 1990s and 2000s   *83*

Chapter 4: Daily Life   *95*
  The 1950s   *96*
  The 1960s   *100*
  The 1970s   *104*
  The 1980s   *108*
  The 1990s and 2000s   *112*

Chapter 5: The Individual and Family   *119*
  The 1950s   *121*
  The 1960s   *126*
  The 1970s   *134*
  The 1980s   *142*
  The 1990s and 2000s   *148*

Part II: Fashion and the Fashion Industry, 1950–2008   157

Chapter 6: The Business of Fashion   *159*
  Haute Couture   *160*
  Ready-to-Wear   *164*
  Retail Operations   *167*
  Fashion Communication   *170*
  Fashion Technology   *174*

Chapter 7: Women's Fashions   *179*
  The 1950s   *180*
  The 1960s   *192*
  The 1970s   *204*
  The 1980s   *215*
  The 1990s   *227*
  The 2000s   *236*

Chapter 8: Men's Fashions   *247*
  The 1950s   *249*
  The 1960s   *258*
  The 1970s   *268*
  The 1980s   *277*
  The 1990s   *287*
  The 2000s   *297*

Chapter 9: Children's Fashions   *305*
  The 1950s   *306*
  The 1960s   *319*
  The 1970s   *332*
  The 1980s   *347*
  The 1990s and 2000s   *360*

Glossary, 1950 to the Present   *375*

Resource Guide, 1950 to the Present   *381*

    Print and Online Publications   *381*

    Films and Video Media   *388*

    Museums, Organizations, Special Collections, and Useful Websites   *390*

Cumulative Index   *397*

About the Contributors   *427*

Unnumbered photo essay appears following page 220.

Preface

Fashion is influenced by society, and, in turn, fashion influences society. Changes in appearance, however subtle or minimal, reflect changes in society. As society changes and evolves, so does fashion. Fashion is not the exclusive purview of the social elite, nor can it be summarily dismissed as mere vanity. It is much more complex than just wearing the latest styles. We use fashion to express who we are and what we think, to project an image, bolster our confidence, and attract partners. Fashion crosses all strata of society and is tightly interwoven into each individual's identity. Undeniably, fashion "… is an essential part of the human experience" (Damhorst, Miller, and Michelman 1999, p. xi).

Clothing through American History 1900 to the Present examines the relationship between social, cultural, and political developments and fashion in the United States of America. Volume One discusses the culture, clothing, and fashion in America from 1900 to 1949, and Volume Two discusses the culture, clothing, and fashion in America from 1950 to the present, about midway through 2008 at this writing. Both volumes in this set are structured to provide two levels of information to the reader: what people wore and, more important, why they wore it. In addition to chapters on fashion trends, this work contains chapters specifically dedicated to examining the impact that politics, culture, arts and entertainment, daily life, and family structures have on fashion and how fashion can serve as an impetus for change in society. This set also examines the history of the fashion industry and the communication of fashion information in print, in movies and television, and across the Internet.

Research for this work was conducted through numerous primary and secondary resources on fashion and history, which can be found in the chapter references and in the Resource Guide at the end of each volume, particularly in the "Print and Online Publications" section. Not all historical or current events, art movements, or sociocultural theories were considered in the development of this book; the scope was limited only to those areas the authors believe directly impacted fashion trends. Nor is this book a comprehensive guide to subculture or alternative fashion movements; the focus is on the mainstream, common fashion trends that were adopted by the majority of Americans.

To guide the reader, a chronology of key historical events and fashion trends is provided at the beginning of each volume. Illustrations of significant fashion trends for both men and women are included to supplement the descriptive text, as does a glossary of fashion terms, which will assist the reader with terminology. An extensive resource guide of numerous articles, books, videos, and films that demonstrate fashion of certain eras, and a substantial listing of authoritative websites, including those for museums and special collections, round out the selected resources provided.

THE TWENTIETH AND TWENTY-FIRST CENTURIES

The birth of the twentieth century marked the beginning of the new, modern era that was more open, expressive, and progressive than the reserved and sober nineteenth-century Victorian era. Changes in society were rapidly taking place. The telephone, electricity, automobiles, and cameras, at first technological marvels, became commonplace items. Over the course of the century, mass-produced ready-to-wear clothing replaced custom-made hand-tailored clothing, allowing new fashions to be rapidly reproduced and distributed in large volumes simultaneously across the entire country. First store catalogs, and then the Internet, made fashions immediately accessible to individuals in even the most remote parts of the country.

After World War II, the economic prosperity experienced by most of the United States resulted in a population shift from urban to suburban, and fashion followed suit with the development of the shopping mall. The last half of the twentieth century was marked by space exploration, activism, and civil unrest. Whereas the ultra-hip donned vinyl dresses with metallic details, African Americans explored their origins and adopted traditional forms of African dress to express their identity. Primarily middle-class youths became involved in numerous social protest movements against the establishment, and dubbed "hippies," chose to differentiate themselves from their parents by rejecting Jackie-O dresses with high heels and Brooks Brother suits and adopting ethnic dress, long hair, and beards.

As the final decades of the twentieth century approached, the social consciousness of the 1960s and 1970s was replaced by conspicuous consumption in the 1980s. Instead of reflecting allegiance with a social movement, fashion now reflected one's material worth and station. Status symbols were prominently displayed on all apparel, as well as on many household goods. Bigger was better, and indulging in luxury was the message broadcast across society.

In response to the excesses of the 1980s, the 1990s appeared almost generic. Most forms of self-expressions and status symbols in fashions faded: designer labels were reduced in size or eliminated. Khakis and white T-shirts became the norm and were considered acceptable dress for almost every occasion. Even the workplace began to dress down, implementing "business casual" and "casual Fridays" instead of the standard suit and tie for men or tailored outfits for women. Whereas the 1980s screamed self-indulgence, the 1990s quietly and calmly, in a more understated manner, closed out the century.

From the Chambre Syndicale de la Couture Parisienne to mass merchandisers, from Nordstrom's to Overstock.com, the rapid (and now global) dissemination of fashion information is a potent agent for change in society. Fashion and society are inextricably intertwined, each influencing the other. This book attempts to identify those connections and not just document the fashions of this time, but to give context to them. As we progress through the twenty-first-century, we will have to wait until enough time has passed to look back and read how fashion influenced twenty-first-century society and how the events of this new century are registered in the fashions we all wear.

We thank our friends, family, and colleagues for their support and encouragement throughout the course of this project. We are grateful for the assistance and reassurance that you each provided.

Ann T. Kellogg

Amy T. Peterson

REFERENCE

Damhorst, M. L., Miller, K. A., Michelman, S. O. (1999) *The Meanings of Dress.* New York: Fairchild Publications.

Chronology of World and Fashion Events, 1950 to the Present

1950   Senator Joseph McCarthy gives speech identifying Communists in the State Department.

1950   The Korean War escalates.

1950   Charles Shultz introduces the Peanuts cartoon on October 2.

1950   Paris decrees hemlines to be sixteen inches from the ground.

1950   Club Med is founded.

1950   Color TV becomes available.

1950   Consumer credit card introduced.

1951   *The King and I* debuts on Broadway.

1951   Lucille Ball and Desi Arnaz appear in the first *I Love Lucy* episode on October 15.

1951   Computers are sold commercially.

1951   Balmain opens ready-to-wear boutique in New York City.

1951   Balenciaga shows a waistless dress in autumn collection.

1951   Coaxial cable reaches from coast to coast.

1952   The term "wash-and-wear" is coined.

1952   *Ozzy and Harriet* and *American Bandstand* debut on network television.

1952   Dwight D. Eisenhower is elected president.

1952   Givenchy shows his first collection.

1952   Mr. Potato Head is the first toy to be advertised on television.

1952   Car seat belts are introduced.

1952   Polio vaccine is created.

1952   Sony introduces transistor radios.

1952   Flutter hem is introduced.

1952   Telephone area codes are introduced.

1952   Immigration and Naturalization Act passes to remove racial and ethnic barriers to entering the United States.

1953   Coronation of Queen Elizabeth II on June 2.

1953   The gray flannel suit becomes the businessman's uniform.

1953   Hugh Heffner opens his first Playboy Club.

1955   *Rebel Without a Cause* is released.

1955   Disneyland opens on July 17.

1955   *Gunsmoke* debuts on television.

1955   Rosa Parks is arrested in Montgomery, Alabama, on December 1 for not giving up her bus seat to a white person.

1955   First rock 'n' roll hit by Bill Haley and His Comets, *Rock Around the Clock*, goes to number one on the music charts.

1955   Music records are recorded in stereo.

1955   Mary Quant opens boutique in London aimed at women under 25 years of age.

1956   Grace Kelly marries Prince Rainier on April 19.

1956   The Interstate Highway system was approved.

1956   Elvis Presley appeared on *The Ed Sullivan Show* on September 9.

1956   First major Italian fashion show takes place in New York.

1956   *My Fair Lady* opens on Broadway.

1956   Velcro is introduced.

1956   Video tape recorders are introduced.

1956   The television remote control is invented.

1956   Baby-doll pajamas become popular.

1957   Eisenhower appears at his inauguration on January 21 in a homburg rather than a top hat, signaling the beginning of less formal attire.

1957   Soviet Union successfully launched Sputnik I on October 4.

1957   Givenchy shows the "sack" dress.

1957   Berry Gordy founds Motown Records.

1957   4.3 million baby boomers were born.

1957   Dr. Seuss introduces *The Cat in the Hat*.

1957   *The Music Man* opens on Broadway.

1958   The Explorer I rocket is successfully launched by the United States on January 31.

1958   Yves St. Laurent introduces the "trapeze line."

1958   The National Aeronautical and Space Administration (NASA) is created for space exploration.

1958   Paris decrees hemlines above the knee.

1958   The Beat movement begins.

1958   Sweet 'N Low artificial sweetener is introduced.

1959   Plane crash kills Buddy Holly, The Big Bopper, and Richie Valens on February 2.

1959   *Bonanza* becomes the first television series to be broadcast in color.

1959   The Barbie doll is introduced.

1959   Alaska and Hawaii become states.

1959   The microchip is invented.

1959   Xerox introduces a plain paper copier.

1959   *The Sound of Music* opens on Broadway.

1960   Sit-in at Greensboro, South Carolina, lunch counter sparks civil-rights movement on February 1.

1960   The Food and Drug Administration (FDA) approves "The Pill" for use but only with a prescription and only to married women on May 11.

1961   United States-backed invasion of Cuban exiles at the Bay of Pigs fails.

1961   Construction begins on the Berlin Wall on August 13.

1962   Johnny Carson becomes host of *The Tonight Show* on October 1.

1963   Coca-Cola debuts its first diet drink, Tab, on May 1.

1963   At the March on Washington, the Rev. Martin Luther King Jr. delivers the "I Have A Dream" speech on August 28.

1963   President John F. Kennedy is assassinated in Dallas, Texas, on November 22; Lyndon Johnson is sworn in as president.

1964   Yves St. Laurent opens the first ready-to-wear boutique in Paris under the label Rive Gauche.

1964   André Courrèges shows his Space Age Collection.

1964   Inaugural Sports Illustrated swimsuit issue comes out on January 24.

1964   The Beatles appear on *The Ed Sullivan Show* for the first time on February 9, sparking the British Invasion

1964   U.S. Congress passes the Gulf of Tonkin resolution, marking the official start of United States' involvement in Vietnam

1965   Mary Quant credited with launching the miniskirt.

1965   Malcolm X is assassinated in New York City on February 21.

1966   Acid Test takes place at the Fillmore in San Francisco, California.

1966   The National Organization for Women (NOW) is founded in Washington, DC, on June 30.

1967   It is the "Summer of Love" in San Francisco.

1968   American designer Ken Scott shows hippie-gypsy look.

1968   The Tet Offensive begins, with Viet Cong forces launching attacks on South Vietnam.

1968	Martin Luther King Jr. is assassinated in Memphis, Tennessee, on April 4, sparking riots in cities throughout the country.
1968	Robert F. Kennedy is assassinated at the Ambassador Hotel in Los Angeles, California, on June 5.
1969	The Stonewall Riots occur in New York City and mark the start of the gay-rights movement on June 28.
1969	Neil Armstrong and Buzz Aldrin land on the moon on July 20.
1969	500,000 people attend the Woodstock Music Festival, which promises three days of peace, love, and music.
1969	The Manson family, orchestrated by Charles Manson, goes on a killing spree in Los Angeles.
1970	First Earth Day is held to draw attention to the environment on April 22.
1970	Ohio National Guard opens fire on Kent State students protesting the Vietnam War; four are killed.
1971	Coco Chanel dies.
1971	The *New York Times* begins publishing "The Pentagon Papers," a classified document leaked by Daniel Ellsberg that detailed U.S. plans in Vietnam.
1972	Congress passes Title IX of the Education Amendments of 1972, outlawing discrimination for any program receiving federal assistance.
1972	Palestinian terrorists storm athletes' village at the Munich Olympics, killing eleven Israeli athletes.
1973	Supreme Court ruling on *Roe v. Wade* results in the legalization of abortion on January 22.
1973	Billie Jean King defeats Bobby Riggs in "Battle of the Sexes" tennis match on September 23.
1974	President Richard M. Nixon resigns on August 8.
1975	Saigon falls to North Vietnamese forces.
1975	*Jaws* is released in movie theaters on June 20.
1976	The United States celebrates its bicentennial.
1977	Zandra Rhodes popularizes punk fashions.
1977	The miniseries *Roots* airs on CBS and draws 130 million viewers.
1977	*Star Wars* hits movie theaters on May 5.
1977	Elvis Presley dies in Memphis, Tennessee, on August 16.
1978	Gloria Vanderbilt introduces designer jeans.
1978	Jim Jones and followers of the People's Temple church commit mass suicide in Jonestown, Guyana.
1979	Three Mile Island nuclear-power crisis occurs.

1979   U.S. embassy in Tehran is stormed, marking the beginning of the Iran hostage crisis on November 4.

1980   Lech Walesa leads the first Polish worker strike in Poland.

1980   Iraq invades Iran in the start of an eight-year war between the two countries on September 22.

1980   *American Gigolo* debuts, helping popularize Armani's suits for men on February 8.

1980   Brooke Shields is featured in controversial Calvin Klein Jeans advertising campaign.

1981   *Dynasty* debuts on ABC on January 12.

1981   Ronald Reagan becomes the fortieth president of the United States.

1981   American hostages held at the U.S. embassy in Iran since November 4, 1979, are released on January 20.

1981   Sandra Day O'Connor is appointed to the Supreme Court on August 19.

1981   MTV (Music Television) airs for the first time on August 1.

1981   Prince Charles marries Diana Spencer on July 29. The event is considered the wedding of the decade.

1981   MS-DOS operating system is released.

1981   First cases of AIDS (acquired immunodeficiency syndrome) are reported.

1982   Compact discs (CDs) are introduced by Sony.

1982   Legislation for the creation of the Dr. Martin Luther King Holiday is approved.

1983   The United States invades the small island nation of Grenada.

1983   *Flashdance* debuts in theaters on April 15, popularizing street gym wear

1984   The 23rd Olympic Games are held in Los Angeles.

1984   *Miami Vice* debuts on NBC on September 16.

1985   Donna Karan shows her first women's collection.

1985   World Health Organization declares AIDS an epidemic.

1985   Mikhail Gorbachev becomes Soviet general secretary of the Soviet Union's communist party.

1985   Madonna stars in *Desperately Seeking Susan* on March 29; teenage girls or "wannabees" imitate her style.

1985   A hole in the ozone layer is detected over Antarctica.

1985   Windows 1.0 software released.

1986   Uprising in the Philippines overthrows Ferdinand Marcos.

1986   Nuclear disaster occurs in Chernobyl, Soviet Union.

1987   American stock market drops 508 points on "Black Monday," October 19.

1987   The film *Wall Street* showcases "yuppie" fashion styles.

1989   George Bush becomes the forty-first president of the United States.

1989   The Berlin Wall falls on November 9.

1989   Chinese army crushes a student protest in Tiananmen Square.

1989   The United States invades Panama to arrest Manuel Noriega.

1989   Iraq invades Kuwait; the Gulf War begins on August 2.

1989   East Germany and West Germany are reunited as one country.

1990   Madonna's *Blond Ambition* tour features designs by Jean-Paul Gaultier.

1991   The Soviet Union is dissolved and replaced by the Commonwealth of Independent States on December 25.

1992   Socialist Federal Republic of Yugoslavia is dissolved.

1992   Maastricht Treaty is signed, creating the European Union on February 7.

1992   There are riots in Los Angeles after the acquittal of Los Angeles police officers involved in the beating of Rodney King.

1993   Bill Clinton becomes the forty-second president of the United States.

1993   Terrorists attack the World Trade Center on February 26.

1993   Czechoslovakia separates into the Czech Republic and Slovakia.

1994   North American Free Trade Agreement (NAFTA) goes into effect on January 1.

1994   The MP3 encoder is released.

1994   Robert Altman's *Prêt-à-Porter* (Ready-to-Wear), a film about the fashion world, is released.

1994   *Friends* debuts on NBC.

1994   The Republican Party wins the majority in both houses of Congress.

1994   Body-scanning method introduced by Levi's to improve fit.

1994   The Wonderbra is introduced.

1995   The Alfred P. Murrah Federal Building in Oklahoma City is bombed on April 19.

1995   *Unzipped*, a film about a day in the life of American designer Isaac Mizrahi, is released.

1996   The Opening Ceremony for the 1996 Summer Olympic Games takes place in Atlanta, Georgia.

1997   The British rule over Hong Kong ends.

1998   The Asian bond market collapses.

1999   The massacre at Columbine High School in Colorado is on April 20.

1999   Wal-Mart becomes the first retailer to reach the $150 million mark in sales around the world.

1999   Bill Clinton is acquitted of perjury and obstruction of justice by the U.S. Senate.

1999   Euro currency is introduced in the European Union.

2001   George W. Bush becomes the forty-third president of the United States.

2001   A terrorist attack destroys the World Trade Center towers in New York and damages the Pentagon in Washington, DC, on September 11.

2001   U.S. and British forces invade Afghanistan.

2001   Apple launches iPod.

2002   The FDA approves the use of Botox in cosmetic procedures.

2002   Kmart files for bankruptcy on January 22, the biggest bankruptcy ever for an American retailer.

2003   The invasion of Iraq begins on March 20.

2003   Lauren Weisberger's novel *The Devil Wears Prada* is released.

2003   *Queer Eye for the Straight Guy* debuts on Bravo network on July 15.

2004   Massachusetts issues first gay marriage licenses.

2004   Ronald Reagan dies.

2004   *Project Runway* debuts on Bravo network on December 1.

2004   There is a terrorist attack in Madrid on March 11.

2005   There is a terrorist attack in London on July 7.

2005   Hurricane Katrina destroys New Orleans on August 29.

2006   Hamas is elected to the majority in the Palestinian Authority Legislative Council.

2006   Israel invades Lebanon.

2006   Saddam Hussein is executed on December 29.

2007   Thirty-two people die in the Virginia Tech school shooting.

2007   Al Gore wins the Nobel Peace Prize.

2007   Ralph Lauren celebrates the fortieth anniversary of his business.

2007   *Rolling Stone* magazine celebrates its fortieth anniversary.

2008   Decline in housing market creates fears of recession or even economic depression.

PART I

The Social Significance of Dress

1

The United States from 1950 to the Present: An Overview

The United States entered the greatest period of economic growth it ever experienced after World War II (WWII). The population of the United States grew by 28 million between 1950 and 1960, representing the second-highest decade of population increase during the century. With a U.S. population of about 150 million in 1950, the postwar housing shortage for returning G.I.s (for "government issue") and their new families gave way to a new style of living, the suburbs. The suburbs offered newer housing, more open space, and usually better schools. However, prosperity did not reach all population groups. Many Americans, including a high percentage of African Americans, continued to live in poverty.

President Lyndon Baines Johnson (LBJ) declared a "war on poverty" in 1964 with his "Great Society" program. As a result, unemployment dropped from 5.5 percent in 1960 to 3.5 percent in 1969 (Kurian 1994, 75), and the number of U.S. citizens living below the poverty line decreased from 22.4 percent in 1960 to 14.7 percent in 1966. However, these gains were only temporary, and soon the United States faced extreme inflation, a recession, oil embargoes, and gas shortages. Unemployment rose steadily throughout the 1970s, peaking at 7.7 percent in 1976 (Kurian 1994, 75). By many measures, the average American's life had become much more difficult: interest rates were nearing 20 percent, and, from 1974 to 1975 alone, the number of poor grew by 10 percent (Zinn 1995, 545).

In response to the economic downturn of the 1970s, the nation elected Ronald Reagan president in 1980, and, over the next nine years, personal income grew at a rapid rate, increasing approximately 85 percent (Berkin 1995, 964). The last half of the twentieth century closed with the U.S. population almost doubling the 1950 level; more than 281 million people now resided in the United States. The world population also boomed at the close of the century to reach 6 billion. The United States, as part of an overpopulated world, now faced ever-increasing challenges dealing with poverty, crime, immigration, and environmental concerns.

POLITICS IN AMERICA

To many, the 1950s conjure an image of an idyllic and peaceful America; however, the reality was quite different from the image. The utopia everyone believed in was supported by the election of the "perfect president," Dwight D. Eisenhower, in 1952. Eisenhower was a war hero and supported the building of federal highways and the St. Lawrence Seaway for commerce. However, behind the "perfect" façade was a president planning not for a utopia but for nuclear war against the escalating communist threat; his support for federal highways was actually a plan to provide a network of emergency runways in case of Soviet attack. The eight years of the Eisenhower administration were marked by economic growth and innovation as well as the escalation of the Cold War and the threat of nuclear war that left Americans uneasy about the future.

When John Fitzgerald Kennedy (JFK) was sworn in as the thirty-fifth president of the United States in January 1961, it signaled an awakening in America. In his inaugural speech, JFK stated that "the torch has been passed to a new generation of Americans." The assassination of President Kennedy in Dallas on November 22, 1963, brought a tragic end to an administration that had captured the public's imagination. His successor, LBJ, capitalized on residual goodwill toward the fallen president to pass many of JFK's social programs as well as to champion his own.

The great strides that LBJ's administration made on social issues were overshadowed by the United States' involvement in the Vietnam War. Now, with the Vietnam conflict as an impetus, many groups were chafing against the established order: "There was general revolt against oppressive, artificial, previously unquestioned ways of living. It touched every aspect of personal life: childbirth, childhood, love, sex, marriage, dress, music, art, sports, language, food, housing, religion, literature, death, schools" (Zinn 1995, 526).

The presidential election of 1968 signaled the end of an era. By electing Richard Nixon, who had first gained notoriety during the Red Scare of the 1950s, the U.S. public signaled that it was fatigued by the upheaval of the 1960s and longed for someone to restore order. Driven in part by the growing antiwar movement, President Nixon began a de-escalation of U.S. forces in Vietnam. Although Nixon's policy toward the war contributed to his reelection in 1972, his administration would soon be overwhelmed by scandal. In the midst of the country's economic challenges, a political firestorm erupted over allegations of obstruction of justice and conspiracy by the Nixon administration. By June 1973, when 67 percent of the public believed that the president had been involved or had lied to cover up his involvement in the Watergate scandal (Zinn 1995, 532), the president had no choice but to take an unprecedented step: resign from office.

President Gerald Ford, who succeeded Richard Nixon after his resignation, was a decent, honest man who, in the opinion of many, was not capable of healing the nation and setting it on the right course. Jimmy Carter defeated Ford in the 1976 election, but to many, he seemed similarly unable to restore the country's faith in the presidency and government as a whole.

The presidency of Ronald Reagan was not only marked by increased wealth in the United States and a move toward conservatism but also by a commitment to a strong foreign policy. From the Middle East to Grenada, the message seemed clear: America had claimed a place as a superpower and worked to unite the world.

The economic and world policies established by Reagan were to be continued through the presidency of George Bush. However, two years after Bush's election in 1988, the United States faced both an economic recession and a war in the Persian Gulf. By 1992, Bush's approval rating had dropped to 40 percent, paving the way for the election of Bill Clinton. Clinton's agenda called for a stronger domestic policy, with a focus on education and healthcare. Even after facing several personal scandals and possible impeachment, Clinton remained one of the most popular American presidents, serving two terms. However, the 2000 election night would send Americans to bed without knowing who their next president would be, George W. Bush or Al Gore. Voter irregularities, especially in Florida, meant that Americans had to wait for an entire month for the final results naming George W. Bush the next president.

George W. Bush reinstated a strong foreign policy, which became more focused after the terrorist attacks of September 11, 2001. His presidency led the United States into another war in the Middle East, this one focused on eliminating terrorist activities and bringing democracy to Iraq. Reelected for a second term in 2004, Bush has presided over a nation divided in terms of war, morality, scientific research, the economy, and international affairs. President Bush's approval rate had plummeted to 25 percent in October of 2007. Illegal immigration and an ailing economy on the verge of recession were the top debate issues during the primary elections in the spring of 2008, issues that continued to be debated during the general election by Democratic candidate Barack Obama and Republican candidate John McCain.

ETHNICITY IN AMERICA

A redistribution of the population began in the 1950s. African Americans migrated to the north as postwar industry expansions created new jobs. As economical housing sprang up to meet the needs of young families after the war, the "white flight" to the suburbs began. Housing discrimination was prevalent, keeping African Americans and Puerto Ricans out of many growing neighborhoods.

Although a weak Civil Rights Act had been passed by Congress in 1957, blacks were no longer content to wait for the federal government to address the injustices they faced on a daily basis and began staging sit-ins to protest segregation. After many years of protest, the Civil Rights Act of 1964 was passed, outlawing segregation in public places and prohibiting racial discrimination in employment and education. The Voting Rights Act was passed one year later, removing many of the barriers that had been used to keep blacks from voting in state and national elections. The success of the civil rights movement at bringing about changes in the federal government's policies led many white students to become activists in the cause. However, the movement suffered a major blow when, in April of 1968, Martin Luther King Jr. was assassinated in Memphis.

The "melting pot" of American culture was further diversified toward the end of the twentieth century by the arrival of new immigrant groups from Central America, the Middle East, and the Far East. The concepts of "diversity" and "multiculturalism" became trendy ideals; however, racial and ethnic tension was still palpable in the country. Legal efforts to end discrimination continued, but programs such as affirmative action were criticized by some as creating a "reversed discrimination." At the close of the twentieth century and into the twenty-first, society became more pluralistic, allowing individuals, regardless of origin, to be recognized for their contributions to the greater society.

ARTS AND ENTERTAINMENT

The first thing to come to mind when reflecting on the 1950s is often rock 'n' roll. Developed from a blend of Southern blues and gospel music, this type of music was popular with teenagers who were trying to break out of the mainstream conservative American middle-class mold. Popular artists such as Bill Haley, Elvis Presley, and Jerry Lee Lewis were promoted on radio and influenced popular music worldwide.

Arriving on the music scene in 1964, the Beatles brought a fresh sound and hip new look to the American pop music scene. In tandem with the pop music scene, the burgeoning folk music movement, led by Bob Dylan, was gaining popularity because it provided the soundtrack for the ongoing civil rights movement with songs that dealt with race, prejudice, and protest.

Music also fueled the 1960s counterculture movement, which promoted experimentation and rejected the traditional approaches of mainstream society. The most notable events of 1960s counterculture were the "Summer of Love" in 1967 and the Woodstock Music and Arts Festival in 1969. Both events contained groundbreaking performances, but, more importantly, both were captured in documentary films that chronicled the scene surrounding the events, offering many people in other parts of the country their first glimpse of the counterculture.

By the mid-1970s, the emergence of a gay culture and the rising popularity of multiethnic gay dance clubs resulted in the opening of discotheques (or discos) throughout the country. The music that was played in these clubs reflected the eclectic audience and was engineered to keep people dancing all night. Black funk music was the template, but it was quickly co-opted by ethnically mixed bands, white groups, and female vocalists.

In the 1980s, disco and classic rock no longer dominated the music scene. Several new musical styles, often influenced by ethnic groups, were introduced, including rap, hip-hop, new wave, punk, and grunge. No one form of music dominated the 1980s or 1990s, but music videos soon took dominance over radio. MTV (Music Television) aired for the first time on August 1, 1981, with the appropriately titled *Video Killed the Radio Star*.

Rap, urban, and hip-hop music became widespread, spawning a new dance style: break dancing, a mixture between dance and acrobatics. Begun by young African Americans in the inner-city streets of the United States, the dance movements required specialized clothing that provided protection to the knees and elbows, design elements that were quickly adopted into mainstream fashions.

Although more popular in Europe than America, the extreme and rebellious styles of new wave and punk music became widespread among teenagers and college students in the 1980s. Groups from England, such as Duran Duran, epitomized the new wave movement, and the Clash made punk music more mainstream. In tandem with rap, new wave, and punk, American pop music was personified by individuals such as Cindy Lauper and Madonna. In response to the excessive and exaggerated 1980s, the 1990s gave birth to the Seattle-based grunge movement, led by bands such as Nirvana, whose followers donned flannel shirts and unkempt hair.

Perhaps the most far-reaching change in the last half of the twentieth century was the advancement in television broadcasting. Television played a crucial role in magnifying, publicizing, and personalizing the day's events. During the 1950s, television became the dominant mass media as people brought television into their homes in greater numbers and hours than ever before. By the mid-1960s, the number of households with television sets had risen to more than 50 million, from 4 million in 1950 (Rielly 2003, 40).

For most people in the United States, television was their primary source of news and entertainment. Sitcoms, variety shows, and soap operas featured popular characters whose lives thousands of viewers watched and copied. Television both reflected popular culture and shaped it at the same time. News broadcasting evolved from simply reading the news to broadcasting live events happening around the world. When Edward R. Murrow began offering his weekly radio program (called *Hear It Now*) on TV as *See It Now*, the world of news broadcasting was irrevocably changed. Events such as JFK's inauguration speech, his assassination and funeral, and the Apollo XI lunar landing were all televised "live." The civil rights movement, the women's movement, the war in Vietnam, and the demonstrations and protests against it, were all affected profoundly by the broadcast medium.

Television experienced yet another revolution when the video cassette recorder (VCR) was introduced in 1981. The ability to record a favorite show allowed the American public to personalize their television experience. There was a wide range of options, including television shows such as *The Cosby Show* and *Family Ties* that were praised for presenting strong family groups. Soap operas remained a staple of daytime television, but it was the primetime soap opera phenomenon that had the strongest influence in American pop culture. Week after week, *Dynasty* and *Dallas* presented the glamorous lifestyle of wealthy Americans.

The popularity of cable television in the 1990s created a never-before-seen market segmentation with programming targeting distinct populations. Programming such as *Barney*, *Teletubbies*, and *Dora the Explorer* was specifically targeted toward younger children and reenforced with products and merchandising. Teenagers, a particularly lucrative market, were catered to with new programming such as *Beverly Hills 90210*, *Melrose Place*, and *Party of Five*. Single women were also targeted through HBO's new fashion-conscious *Sex and the City*.

Despite the popularity of television, plays, musicals, and movies were still very well received by the general public. However, in the 1950s, with the Cold War brewing, McCarthyism took hold of the entertainment industry. Senator Joseph McCarthy was convinced that communists had infiltrated the government, and he was determined to flush out the traitors. McCarthy made Hollywood a focus of his investigations, and many Hollywood actors and producers were "blacklisted" as suspected communists and not allowed to work.

The combination of music, psychedelics, and the movie industry helped to produce a film that would usher in a new era in film that reflected what was happening in youth culture. In 1969, the release of *Easy Rider* created a sensation by telling the story of two bikers who travel across the country, with Steppenwolf and the Byrds providing the soundtrack. In addition to being the first major commercial film targeted to the counterculture, it also hastened the demise of the studio system and the rise of director-driven projects, paving the way during the 1970s for one of the richest periods in American cinema. Freed from the restrictiveness of the studio system, writers and directors, including such future legends as Francis Ford Coppola, Martin Scorsese, and Steven Spielberg, were creating movies with soaring narratives and coaxing indelible performances from their actors.

In the 1980s, Hollywood reached a worldwide market with high-budget productions packed with special effects and famous movie stars. Movies also used the same niche marketing strategy as television programming. Films such as *Sixteen Candles* and *Pretty in Pink* catered to teenage audiences, whereas *Working Girl* targeted the new female white-collar labor force.

The 1990s saw a proliferation of product placement in Hollywood movies, and blockbuster films became more commercial. The success of the big studio system was challenged with the popularity of independent and foreign films. These movies contributed to increase the exposure of the American public to foreign cultures and alternative subcultures.

DAILY LIFE

Daily life in the 1950s made every attempt to mimic what was seen on television. The typical middle- to upper-class suburban housewife of the 1950s' weekly routine included playing bridge, a rotating coffee klatch, an appointment at the beauty parlor, attending teas and luncheons, and volunteering at church. The sprouting of suburbia meant that moms were driving kids to activities as well as to the shopping center, dry cleaner's, and grocery store.

Weekends were for neighborhood activities and corporate parties. Mom would watch the kids by the country club pool while Dad took care of his corporate obligations on the golf course. Attending cocktail parties and formal receptions were a must to climb the corporate ladder, and the "perfect wife" had to also be the quintessential hostess.

With greater disposable income, people spent more money on leisure activities. With more cars on the road and more people driving greater distances, interstate road systems sprang up all over the country. The family was now the center of focus for daily life and recreation. Family-themed entertainment became commercialized, with Disneyland opening in 1955 and national parks becoming family friendly.

The second half of the twentieth century began with a focus on the family and ended with a focus on the individual. The 1980s became known as the "me" decade, and well-off men and women in their twenties and thirties, known as "yuppies" (for young urban professionals), seemed to dominate popular culture and trends. The obsession with wealth in the 1980s was matched only with the desire to look one's best. "Light" foods with low-fat content became popular, and more Americans made a visit to the gym a component of their daily routines. The American lifestyle became marked by an almost obsessive search for new diets, diet pills, and exercise routines. Toward the end of the century, cosmetic surgery became commonplace, and, if the pounds could not be dieted away, they could be removed via liposuction.

American life in the last part of the twentieth century was primarily defined by the availability and constant improvement of technology. In 1979, Americans experienced the flexibility of the newly introduced Walkman. Toward the end of the millennium, not only were Walkmans outdated by portable compact disc (CD) players, but, soon thereafter, the CD player was replaced by the seemingly all-powerful iPod and MP3 players.

Gaming devices became the favorite form of entertainment for American teens and preteens. Atari and Pac-Man video games of the 1980s, once considered "high-tech," gave way to the multimedia Game Boy and Sony PlayStations in the 1990s and the wireless-controlled Nintendo Wii in the 2000s. However, the most important toy to alter American life was the personal computer. The functionality and capability that the American public found on the computer was unparalleled. The advent of the information superhighway, or the Internet, in 1990 radically changed the way the world obtained information, communicated, and shopped. The World

Wide Web witnessed more than 10 million computers connected via the Internet by the end of the 1990s. During the first decade of the twenty-first century, the Internet had become a crucial tool for social networking through sites such as Facebook and My Space, whereas cellular telephones and Black-Berry devices incorporated technology, allowing consumers to access the Internet at numerous locations through wireless networks.

THE CHANGING ROLE OF WOMEN

The generation of women in the fifties, whose purpose seemed solely to give birth, created the aptly named "baby boom" when 3,845,000 babies were born in 1951 alone. Women were seen only in terms of their sex, and social barriers to participation in the workplace and government were erected. Women's magazines did little to promote alternatives; instead, they offered tips such as having another baby or dyeing hair blond to get over the feeling of depression and housewife blues.

The image of the ideal housewife kept many women at home and out of the workforce. Betty Freidan's *The Feminine Mystique* articulated the need of women to be defined by something more than being a dutiful wife or mother. Women reading this book realized they were not alone in feeling there had to be more to life than the role to which they had succumbed.

By 1969, women made up 40 percent of the entire workforce (Zinn 1995, 496). LBJ signed an executive order in 1967 banning sexual discrimination in federally connected employment. The entry of this new segment into the workforce resulted in women becoming more economically independent, increasing female attendance at colleges and universities, increasing the number of unmarried women under the age of twenty-four one third by 1970, and increasing the divorce rate by two thirds by 1970 for women under the age of forty-five.

On a political level, women participated in government in ever-growing numbers throughout the 1970s. The most vivid demonstration of this trend was the effort to pass the Equal Rights Amendment (ERA), which sought a constitutional amendment to guarantee protection against discrimination on the basis of sex. Although the bill stalled three states short of the number needed to amend the Constitution, it helped draw attention to women's issues and proved to be a rallying point for people across the nation.

Although women continued to gain greater economic and personal freedom in the 1980s and 1990s, they also strove to obtain more balance between their family life, personal life, and careers. American women "wanted it all" but strove for balance. At the turn of the twenty-first century, as the popular show *Sex and the City* seemed to indicate, women have been able to enjoy life by embracing their freedom of choice and sexuality as guaranteed by their long struggle for equality. In 2007, Democrat Hillary Clinton became the first female to seriously seek the nomination of a major party for the presidential campaign. There was much discussion and some criticism in the news and entertainment media of her fashion style, especially of the tailored pantsuits she wore during the campaign, as well as observations that the male candidates did not receive such scrutiny or remarks about their clothing choices.

SEXUALITY AND MORALITY

The conservatism of the 1950s meant subscribing to the rules of Dr. Spock, Billy Graham, and Norman Vincent Peale. Sexuality was kept private, not discussed in public or insinuated through advertising or programming. Married TV couples always had twin beds, and unmarried couples shared no more than an arm around a shoulder. This oppression gave birth to a small group of free thinkers, who were unwilling to buy into the mainstream corporate world and checked out to form the "Beat" subculture. As the movement grew, it eventually transformed into the free-love culture of the hippie movement in the 1960s.

On February 29, 1960, Hugh Hefner opened the first Playboy Club in Chicago. Hefner had published the first issue of Playboy in 1953, and, by 1960, the circulation was well over 1 million copies. Hugh Hefner became a symbol of a new approach to sexuality, marriage, and social mores. Although few feminists would argue that the publication did much to further the idea that women were more than just sexual objects, its rejection of Puritanism in society challenged established mores regarding sex outside the marital relationship and roles of men and women in society. The introduction of the new birth-control pill in the 1960s, along with publications such as the *Human Sexual Response* in 1966 and *The Joy of Sex*, pushed the boundaries further by discussing sexual gratification as a natural human impulse and helped to bring about "the sexual revolution."

The gay rights movement also found its birth in the 1960s. Gay groups lobbied government institutions to gain equal protection under the law and sought to have their sexual orientation and culture openly acknowledged and celebrated. However, the majority of the population was not prepared to accept the gay culture, and many smaller towns across the country repealed anti-discrimination laws passed during the civil rights movement because of the protection these measures afforded homosexuals. The sexual liberation of the 1970s was followed by a much more conservative period in the 1980s, in part attributable to the discovery, and initial confusion, of the acquired immunodeficiency syndrome (AIDS) epidemic and human immunodeficiency virus (HIV) infections. Americans found comfort in marriage and family. Talking openly about sex, however, was only fully embraced by American society as long as it was in the hands of a seemingly harmless personality such as Dr. Ruth Westheimer, a physician who managed to discuss every possible topic related to sexuality in her syndicated talk show.

In the 1990s, issues of morality continued dividing the country. Pro-life and pro-choice groups faced each other openly. Pro- and anti-gay marriage promoters were both influential in the first state and federal elections of the twenty-first century. The televangelists of the 1980s worked to promote a conservative moral agenda, whereas the entertainment industry and subcultures responded by becoming more daring and open about their lifestyle choices. When Janet Jackson exposed a breast during the 2004 Super Bowl, an entire nation went into crisis mode, and new measures were adopted to prevent sexuality from widely reaching American popular culture. It was obvious then that the United States still faced the challenge on reconciling a plethora of views on sexuality and morality.

GROWING UP IN AMERICA

In the 1950s, citizens were proud to be American. Conservatism and anti-communist feelings helped to define the 1950s. The phrase "under God" was added to the Pledge of Allegiance. Fathers were the unquestioned authority on everything surrounding the family. Children were to stay out of trouble and do well in school. Middle- and upper-class families supported children in their scholastic efforts and counted on them to go to college. Gender roles were strongly upheld: girls played with Barbie dolls and tea sets, and boys played sheriff and army.

Until 1950, the term "teenager" had never been heard. Teenagers were now defined as a separate generation and were represented by Elvis Presley and James Dean. This new marketing group was influenced by movies, TV, magazines, and rock 'n' roll. Food service and retail stores soon began to cater to this new source of revenue. This phenomenon ushered the beginning of the generation gap between parents and their children.

The 1960s saw the emergence of teenagers as an economic and sociopolitical force. By 1964, 18-year-olds were the largest cohort in U.S. society, and businesses targeted the segment with consumer products. By mid-decade, the youth movement was making itself heard through protests against the Vietnam War, the counterculture (including experimentation with drugs and sex), and a constant challenging of rules and traditions.

Although the 1960s protest movement did not continue as strongly through the 1970s, sex, drugs, and rock 'n' roll were as popular as ever. Sports such as skateboarding exemplified the onset of a new type of subculture and embodied all facets of the evolving teen experience. More significant was the development of a singles culture: as an increasing number of women spent more of their adult years single before getting married, the college years and the time immediately after graduation became a time of experimentation and independence.

In the 1980s and 1990s, American families enjoyed several opportunities to spend time together as entertainment and community programs emphasized family-oriented activities. However, more and more children were becoming "latch-key kids," supervising themselves after school because both parents now worked outside the home. Additionally, the ever-increasing divorce rate radically changed family dynamics, creating more single-parent homes and "weekend dads."

The emphasis on cultural diversity and multiculturalism, paired with the accessibility of information on the Internet, allowed American children of the 1990s to be exposed to other cultures, languages, and ideas. Access to information and more time alone meant teens were growing up faster, and schools had to compensate by including drug abuse prevention programs and sex education in school programming. Likewise, the ever-increasing immigrant populations meant the education system had to commit itself to providing assistance to students with limited proficiency in English. With more access to education, by 1999, more than 80 percent of Americans earned a high-school degree, as opposed to just over 40 percent in 1960.

FASHION

Parisian haute couture continued to dictate the fashionable silhouette through the 1950s and 1960s. However, American fashion designers played an ever-increasing role in dictating trends from the 1970s forward. As society became less formal, there was less demand for formal evening-wear and more demand for casual sportswear. Additionally, the increasing number of women entering the workforce created a new niche market, one for which Paris had never designed.

American designers were better at interpreting the fashion needs of the working woman and individuals with active lifestyles. Furthermore, with ongoing declines in the U.S. economy, there were fewer elite clients who could afford custom couture, and even those who could were no longer interested in spending time flying to Europe for lengthy fittings. As such, American ready-to-wear came to dominate the last half of the twentieth century.

Communication of what is considered "fashionable" permeates every aspect of society. From daytime soap operas to primetime family shows, not only the stars of the programming but all of the commercials exhibit the latest fashion trends that the fashion-conscious consumer should be wearing. Catalogs and Internet websites provide the opportunity to review and order the latest fashions, no matter where one lives. Simplicity, McCall's, Butterick, and Vogue translate trendy couture into sewing patterns for the frugal-minded consumer.

Fashion magazines continued to increase in number during the last half of the twentieth century because both housewives and working women needed to stay abreast of the latest trends. Whereas some magazines, such as *Vogue*, *Mademoiselle*, and *Glamour*, are exclusively dedicated to communicating fashion information, others, such as *People* and *Life*, add newsworthy articles to the brilliant photographs of movie stars and politicians.

One of the most significant innovations in fashion publications of the twentieth century was niche publishing. Teen magazines, such as *Seventeen* and *Tiger Beat*, were targeted to young girls aged 12 to 20. These magazines featured their favorite young movie stars and musicians and gave tips on fashion and makeup. Fashion magazines, such as *GQ*, also started targeting men. These publications communicate advice on fashion and grooming to men in the same manner that *Vogue* does for women.

In the 1950s, Hollywood once again portrayed women as they "should look." The elegant hourglass figure was considered the "perfect shape." Grace Kelly was the elegant glamour girl of the screen, with sloping shoulder line accenting the curve of the bust, rib cage, hip, and pelvis, high heels accenting the ankle and calf, and an understated hat with partial veil, gloves, and small handbag. Over the next fifty years, how women "should look" would shift several times. The 1960s saw a preference for the pencil-thin waif, whereas the 1970s opted for a more natural, relaxed figure. In the 1980s, bigger was better, and that included broad shoulders, full bust, and full hips for women. By the 1990s, a natural, athletic look was popular and continues.

Every period has its own ideal of beauty, shaped by the political, social, and cultural events of its time. Taken out of context, fashion can often appear ludicrous. Only when examined as an element of an era can fashion be understood. The second half of the twentieth century was as marked by numerous significant political and cultural changes: war, civil unrest, fluctuations in immigrant populations, and changes to family life, all of which manifested themselves in the fashions worn by men, women, and children. Society was transformed, changing the way people viewed the world around them, and fashion reflected those changes.

REFERENCES

Berkin, C., Miller, C. L., Cherny, R. W., Gormly, J. L. (1995) *Making America: A History of the United States.* Boston: Houghton Mifflin.

Kurian, G. T. (1994) *Datapedia of the United States, 1790–2000.* Lanham, MD: Bernan Press.

Rielly, E. J. (2003) *The 1960s.* Westport, CT: Greenwood Press.

Zinn, H. (1995) *A People's History of the United States.* New York: Harpers Perennial.

2

Political and Cultural Events

Post-WWII America was dominated by Cold War paranoia and Cold War spies, as well as science and space exploration. The 1950s were characterized by a massive migration to the suburbs, which created a modern consumer culture, an emphasis on gender roles that put women back in the home, and the emergence of the civil rights movement. The arms race and race to space brought a new fascination of science into everyday life. School science curricula shifted from rote memorization to inquiry and discovery. Empirical verification and the accumulation of knowledge entered mainstream American life.

A rapidly expanding economy in the 1950s provided more opportunity for men in business and industry. To ensure that men were positioned for success, the government, industry, and advertising together bombarded the American woman from all angles, proclaiming that her most important role was as a mother and homemaker. Emphasis on appropriate gender roles was found everywhere, from Dr. Spock's revolutionary child-rearing concepts to children's toys and television programs. In response to this acculturation, the civil rights movement and modern feminism had planted their roots firmly in the 1950s.

JFK's narrow defeat of then-Vice President Nixon in 1960 ushered in a new era not just in American politics but in American life. He was the first U.S. president to have been born in the twentieth century, a fact not lost on the millions of younger Americans for whom JFK represented a new optimism for what an individual and a country could accomplish. As the decade drew to a close, the optimism and liberalism that had fueled movements, both political and social, was in decline.

The growing antiwar movement forced President Nixon to de-escalate the presence of U.S. forces in Vietnam: in 1968, 500,000 combat troops were there; by 1972, less than 150,000 remained. Nixon continued several important Great Society programs in the 1970s that were initiated by LBJ in the 1960s, expanded the welfare system, and created a food stamp program. However, his political and personal views on most social issues were quite conservative and a noted departure from his predecessor, LBJ. The 1970s were marked by a deep recession experience during the presidency of Jimmy Carter and the loss of confidence in the political leaders. In tandem with the economic downturn were many exciting social and cultural developments that made lasting social, political, and artistic statements and changed the way people viewed the world around them.

The 1980s was defined by the presidency of Ronald Reagan. Consumerism became the watch word and greed was flaunted openly. Often called the "me generation," Americans in the 1980s focused on the obtainment of wealth and the display of status symbols. Conservatism gripped the country. From the Middle East to Grenada, the message seemed clear: America had claimed a place as a true world superpower.

During the 1990s, the United States witnessed an ever-changing world through the rise of the Internet and the twenty-four-hour television networks. The Cold War was over, but the fall of the Soviet Union left a convoluted European continent. Conflict in the Middle East escalated in such a way that the United States was involved in a war in the Persian Gulf in 1991 and then again at the turn of the twenty-first century. The United States faced the globalization challenges by implementing free-trade agreements such as the North American Free Trade Agreement (NAFTA) and by working with nations such as China, which by the end of the century had become a powerhouse in the manufacturing business, particularly for fashion goods.

The United States, as part of an overpopulated world, faced challenges dealing with poverty, crime, immigration, and environmental concerns. Words such as diversity and multiculturalism became trendy; however, racial and ethnic tensions were still palpable in the country. Legal efforts to end discrimination continued to be implemented, but programs such as affirmative action were criticized by some as creating a sort of reversed discrimination. The rising visibility of ethnic groups was fundamental in alerting the American public about the many cultures and subcultures that composed the United States. At the end of the twentieth century, the United States struggled to truly become the melting pot it claimed to be.

THE
1950s

GOVERNMENT AND POLITICAL MOVEMENTS

Before WWII, the United States had pursued a foreign policy of isolationism. However, the role the United States played in WWII forced America into the spotlight to take her place as a superpower amongst other countries. With much of Europe and Britain devastated from the war, only the United States was left to stand against the increasing spread of communism.

Many different schools of thought dominated government in the 1950s. Senator Robert A. Taft defined conservatism as a non-interventionist foreign policy (also known as "isolationism"), a small federal government of limited powers, states' rights, and scrupulous observance of the law. However, William F. Buckley and other conservatives accepted the need for large, proactive military and extensive foreign alliances to counter the threat of Soviet communism. Yet another group believed that free markets and free trade were the best paths to national prosperity.

Over the course of the decade, communism spread across the Soviet Union, into China, Cuba, North Korea, and North Vietnam, repeatedly placing the United States at direct opposition with the Soviet Union. President Harry Truman approved production of the hydrogen bomb in 1950 and sent both the Air Force and Navy to Korea in June of that year. Having so recently ended WWII, Americans were afraid the conflict in Korea would escalate and ultimately end in a stalemate with no victory. Between fighting a communist Korea and the Cold War with communist Soviet Union, the fear of communism was embedded deeply into the American psyche. The media thrived on the spy cases involving Alger Hiss and Julius and Ethel Rosenberg, especially when the Rosenbergs were electrocuted for their involvement with espionage in WWII.

Conservatism in the 1950s created a constant state of paranoia. America's former ally in WWII, the Soviet Union, was now considered an enemy that could not be trusted. With the possibility of atomic warfare, people went to extremes to prevent "infiltration" of industry, government, and even Hollywood. McCarthyism cast a broad and dark shadow over the political landscape. While the Korean conflict was escalating, Senator

Joe McCarthy from Wisconsin was convinced that communists had infiltrated the government and was determined to flush out the traitors. He began his communist witch hunt by announcing during a speech in 1950 that he had a list of fifty-seven people in the State Department known to be members of the American Communist Party.

Economic sanctions were imposed against those believed to have communist ties, and many thousands of people lost their jobs. McCarthy's Government Committee on Operations of the Senate investigated various government departments and questioned a large number of people regarding their political past. "Blacklists" of supposed communists soon appeared, and the only way to clear one's name from the list was by naming others. Many Hollywood actors and producers never recovered from the "blacklist." The McCarran Act, otherwise known as the Communist Control Act, was passed, giving the government the power to intern suspected communists.

Social issues began to take the center stage, with many conservatives fearing a trend toward liberalism. The Immigration and Naturalization Act of 1952 was intended to remove racial and ethnic barriers toward becoming a U.S. citizen. However, U.S. citizens were fighting for their own civil rights. Although racial segregation was ruled unconstitutional in public schools by the Supreme Court in *Brown v. Board of Education of Topeka* in 1954, it continued to thrive in the other venues in the south. Rosa Parks, who was lawfully seated in the black section of a public bus, refused to give up her seat to a white man, resulting in her arrest in Montgomery, Alabama, in 1955.

ECONOMIC TRENDS

During a period of "white flight," suburban land values increased as middle-class whites continued to leave cities for the suburbs. In the 1940s, only 15 percent of the U.S. population lived in suburbs, a number that rose to 23 percent by 1950 and 30 percent by 1960, whereas the percentage of the U.S. population living in cities remained flat at 32 percent across the same period (Hobbs and Stoops 2002, 33). Only 11 percent of the workforce now worked on farms. Even southern blacks had left the farms for factory work in the north. Economic expansion continued, fueled primarily by a fear of worldwide communism. Military buildup, missiles, aircraft, and highways provided jobs in the new emerging industries.

During the postwar economic boom, unemployment fell to record lows of 4 percent (Dolfman and McSweeney 2006, 21). The demand for workers was high, and, despite the preference for women to stay at home, 19 percent of married women worked outside the home (Dolfman and McSweeney 2006, 21), and women made up one-third of the total workforce (Dolfman and McSweeney 2006, 25). Average household income was $4,237.00 in 1950, nearly 200 percent higher that it had been during the Great Depression of the 1930s (Dolfman and McSweeney 2006, 25). This drastic increase in family income allowed 48 percent of the population to own their own home (Dolfman and McSweeney 2006, 25) while still having a surplus of discretionary spending for shopping and family holidays.

This increase in disposable income provided the perfect support for the development of the suburban shopping mall. Retail malls opened in suburbs across the United States so that families would not have to venture into the city to purchase clothing and household goods. Regular trips to the mall became a mainstay of the American wife's day as the 1950s placed a strong emphasis on always having the "perfect outfit" with matching accessories. With a strong emphasis on social gatherings, whether backyard cookouts, family camping trips, or cocktail parties, American women and their children all required proper attire.

The number of people earning a middle-class income increased substantially in the postwar period. More jobs, better-paying jobs, the G.I. bill, expansion of credit, and low-cost housing developments, like Levittown, allowed more people to realize the American Dream. Home ownership, cars in the driveway, college education, and upward mobility were symbols of "making it." The media and advertisers worked to convince Americans that all was right with the world and that they were safe, despite the looming atomic threat.

Families had vacation for the first time in a long time. With new cars and new highways, American families hit the road. Motels and restaurants began to spring up across the country. Holiday Inn, Howard Johnson, and McDonald's started new trends in chains and franchising. Fueled by new products and inventions such as transistor radios, videotape, frozen TV dinners, and the IBM 701 computer, the Dow Jones Industrial hit an all-time high since 1929.

INTERNATIONAL DEVELOPMENTS

Americans were put on alert on October 4, 1957, when the Soviet Union successfully launched Sputnik I. Taking about ninety-eight minutes to orbit the Earth on its elliptical path, the world's first artificial satellite was about the size of a basketball and weighed only 183 pounds. New political, military, technological, and scientific developments were generated from that crucial launch. When the Soviet Union launched Sputnik in 1957, orbiting the first satellite launched into space over the United States, the space race between the United States and the Soviet Union began.

However, the space race actually began many years earlier, when, in October of 1954, the International Council of Scientific Unions adopted a resolution calling for artificial satellites to be launched during the International Geophysical Year (IGY) to map the Earth's surface. Soliciting proposals from various government research agencies to undertake development, the White House announced in 1955 that it would launch an Earth-orbiting satellite for the IGY. The Naval Research Laboratory's Vanguard proposal was selected:

> "The Sputnik launch changed everything. As a technical achievement, Sputnik caught the world's attention and the American public off-guard. Its size was more impressive than Vanguard's intended 3.5-pound payload. In addition, the public feared that the Soviets' ability to launch satellites also translated into the capability to launch ballistic missiles that could carry nuclear weapons from Europe to the U.S." (NASA)

The U.S. Defense Department responded immediately to the political furor by approving funding for another U.S. satellite project. Work began on the Explorer project Redstone Arsenal. Congress passed the National Aeronautics and Space Act in 1958, which created the National Aeronautical and Space Administration (NASA) from the National Advisory Committee for Aeronautics and other government agencies.

The fear of communism and dominance by the Soviet Union was fueled on the ground as well as in space when the Soviet Union announced it had capabilities to produce atomic bombs. Additionally, the announcement of an alliance between the Soviet Union and China was additional cause for concern when the two allies signed a treaty naming Japan and the United States as enemies. The Soviet Union's refusal to unify Germany helped the Soviets retain a communist foothold in East Germany and was a final insult to the utopia the United States hoped to achieve. In fear of worldwide communism, the United States continued to escalate the production of atomic weapons to ensure the peace and safety of the nation, including carrying out nuclear tests at the Bikini Atoll, resulting in radioactive fallout on Micronesia.

Other critical events on the international landscape include the Korean conflict and the precursor to the Vietnam War. North Korea invaded South Korea, capturing Seoul three days later. The United Nations (UN) resolved to intervene on behalf of South Korea, and President Truman ordered American troops to the peninsula. After landing at Inchon and retaking Seoul, the UN resolved to invade North Korea, take Pyongyang, and reach the Yalu River. After North Korean troops were pushed back to the border, China entered the Korean War by sending 300,000 troops to help the North Koreans fight UN forces. At a Geneva Conference of the world's top powers, Vietnam was divided into two separate nations. Ho Chi Minh was named the president of the communist North; Ngo Dinh Diem took power in South Vietnam. France looked to other nations for help in preventing communist forces from entering Dien Bien Phu, and the U.S. responded with money and troops.

ETHNICITY IN AMERICA

Greater interracial understanding and cooperation emerged in the 1950s as a result of changing attitudes in America. In 1954, the Supreme Court ruled in *Brown v. Board of Education of Topeka* to end segregation in public schools. However, this did not abolish segregation in other public areas, such as restaurants and restrooms, nor did it require desegregation of public schools by a specified time. It did, however, declare the permissive or mandatory segregation that existed in twenty-one states unconstitutional.

Unfortunately, despite being classified as "unconstitutional," racial segregation continued in many parts of the south. In 1955, Rosa Parks was arrested in Montgomery, Alabama, for refusing to give up her seat on a public bus to a white person. The same year, fourteen-year-old Emmett Till, while visiting family in Mississippi, was lynched by two white men for allegedly talking to a white woman. The federal government attempted to provide greater equality of opportunity for all ethnic groups through continued legislation, including a 1956 Supreme Court ruling that outlawed racial segregation on intrastate public transportation. However, formal court rulings and legislative acts were insufficient to eliminate decades of discrimination. Racial conflicts were intense, and discrimination prevailed throughout the decade.

Federal subsidies for suburban housing and the postwar Montgomery G.I. Bill helped to create class mobility, for whites or those who could pass as white. Exclusion and discrimination continued at work, in public facilities, in housing segregation, and at other social institutions such as clubs and associations. Immigration laws were also reformed during the 1950s. The McCarran-Walter Act removed the ban on Asian and African immigration in 1952; however, it left small, restrictive quotas in place.

THE
1960s

GOVERNMENT AND POLITICAL MOVEMENTS

JFK's narrow victory over Richard Nixon in the 1960 presidential election signaled a new direction for the country. JFK was the youngest candidate, at forty-three, to win the presidency and, with his wife, Jacqueline Kennedy, captured the hearts, if not the political support, of the entire country. The Kennedys were the ideal American couple: attractive, refined, and graceful.

While JFK worked at governing the country, Jacqueline Kennedy worked at spreading culture. She supported museums, the restoration of the White House, and the arts. Her support of the arts extended to the fledging American fashion industry through her insistence on wearing only U.S. fashions. Her patronage of designer Oleg Cassini and Halston not only established *the* look of the early 1960s but brought increased international recognition to American designers.

President John F. Kennedy and Jackie Kennedy. The first lady wears a sheath dress; her fashion style was widely copied. [Courtesy of Photofest]

JFK inherited a nation on the upswing economically but with foreign-policy challenges and difficulties on the home front. Much of what JFK proposed—tax cuts, civil rights legislation, and putting a man on the moon—would be enacted and accomplished in subsequent administrations. His assassination in Dallas, Texas, on November 22, 1963, brought a sudden end to an all-too-brief presidency.

His successor, LBJ, used the residual goodwill of the nation to push many of JFK's programs through Congress. He built on these early successes and expanded them to include a wide array of legislation that would be referred to as The Great Society. LBJ declared a war on poverty and expanded the scope of the federal government to extend assistance to those parts of society that had been ignored in the past. Congress passed civil rights legislation in both 1964 and 1965; the latter, the Voting Rights Act, eliminated discriminatory practices that had denied minorities the right to vote.

The momentum of LBJ's presidency was slowed by the escalation of the Vietnam War. The Gulf of Tonkin Resolution in August of 1964 marked the active engagement of U.S. troops in Vietnam. By the time he decided not to seek reelection in 1968, the American public had turned against the war effort. Demonstrations, sit-ins, and protests, especially on college campuses, were daily activities. American youths distinguished themselves from the establishment by adopting jeans, T-shirts, and long hair, for both men and women, for their protests. Dubbed "hippies," these individuals were immediately recognizable alongside their suited and white-gloved counterparts. Richard Nixon defeated Hubert Humphrey by a narrow margin in 1968, primarily on the strength of Nixon's campaign promise to end the war.

Both JFK and LBJ had to contend with a growing dissatisfaction among certain segments of the population. The sit-ins in Greensboro, North Carolina, had reawakened the civil rights movement. The Southern Christian Leadership Council, led by Martin Luther King Jr., and the Student Nonviolent Coordinating Committee were among the groups that organized boycotts and marches to draw attention to the racial discrimination that existed in all facets of society. The civil rights movement was further strengthened by the adoption of traditional African dress by both blacks and whites. Dashikis, kaftans, and tunics were worn for both work and casual wear to provide solidarity for the cause. Men and women grew their hair into afros or braided it into "cornrows."

Despite several victories, for instance, James Meredith's integration of the University of Mississippi, violence against blacks continued: the Sixteenth Street Baptist Church was bombed in 1963, and three civil rights workers from the north were killed in Philadelphia, Mississippi. The passage by Congress of legislation to address these issues could not solve many of these problems, and race riots broke out in cities across the country from 1964 to 1969, with 1967 being the most violent year. The assassination of Martin Luther King Jr. in Memphis on April 4, 1968, fractured the fragile unity of the movement.

As the Vietnam War escalated, so did the antiwar protests. A large contingent of the antiwar movement had been involved in either the civil rights protests or the free-speech demonstrations at places such as Berkeley. No community in the country was left untouched by the war or the protests of it. The Tet Offensive, an attack on Saigon by the Viet Cong, shattered the illusion that the United States was winning the war, and the public backlash and demonstrations that resulted forced the government to alter its policies and begin a gradual de-escalation of the war.

Economic Trends

The fiscal and economic policies of the JFK and LBJ administrations had one goal: to jump-start the U.S. economy. The massive tax cut that LBJ championed and that Congress passed in 1964 gave Americans more money to invest and spend. At the same time, laws beneficial to companies led to expansion in the corporate sector. Most significant, federal programs under LBJ's Great Society expanded the scope of the government and extended assistance to those segments of the population that were most in need.

The effects of these measures were substantial. The economy grew every month from 1961 to 1969, unemployment dropped from 5.5 percent in 1960 to just 3.5 percent in 1969 (Kurian 1994, 75), and the median income of families rose from $5,620 in 1960 to $9,433 in 1969 (Kurian 1994, 111). As the U.S. workforce grew to 86 million people in 1970, from 72 million in 1960, the economy was able to grow enough to employ this influx of new workers. Furthermore, Americans spent more than $36 billion on recreation (up from $18 billion in 1960) (Kurian 1994, 152). All of these figures translated into more personal income, disposable income, and discretionary spending on nonessential items. By 1970, three-quarters of all Americans owned their own homes (at an average price of $23,000) (Rielly 2003, 4), and items such as automobiles, televisions, and appliances were no longer luxuries. When people could not afford to buy goods with their salaries, they borrowed money; short- and intermediate-term consumer credit climbed from $56 billion in 1960 to more than $122 billion in 1970.

This sustained economic growth made it possible for LBJ to undertake a number of legislative initiatives, most notably the war on poverty. Its goal, according to historian Robert M. Collins, was "not simply to enrich the poor but to change them so that they too could contribute to the national goal of increased growth" (Farber 1994, 24). By increasing the minimum wage from $1.15 in 1960 to $1.60 in 1968, those on the lower rungs of society were able to raise their standard of living: the percentage of the population living below the poverty line declined from 22.4 percent in 1960 to 14.7 percent by 1966 (Farber 1994, 19). Expenditures by the federal government on social programs grew from 25.4 percent of the budget in 1964 to 41.3 percent in 1972, and by 1970 national welfare rolls increased by 225 percent (Carroll 1982, 58).

For blacks and other minorities, who had historically been left out of previous booms, the new prosperity lifted their prospects as well. The combination of economic expansion and federal initiatives helped to reduce the number of people below the poverty line from more than 20 percent in the late 1950s to less than 12 percent by the early 1970s (Schulman 2001, 5). Furthermore, in 1960, only one-third of the people eligible to receive welfare benefits were actually doing so; by the early 1970s, the total was increased to around 90 percent (Schulman 2001, 33).

As the decade wore on, the Vietnam War and the Great Society programs were causing record federal budget deficits, and LBJ and the Congress were forced to make choices. LBJ had pursued a "guns-and-butter" strategy in an attempt to avoid raising taxes to support the war effort. The result was that, by 1969, spending on social programs was growing at just half the rate of 1965, marking the beginning of the end for the war on poverty.

INTERNATIONAL DEVELOPMENTS

United States relations with the Soviet Union, already tense because of the competition between the two nations following the end of WWII, worsened considerably in the early part of the decade. A U.S. spy plane was downed inside of Russia on May 1, 1960. President Eisenhower initially denied that the United States was engaged in any surveillance but eventually acknowledged the truth. After JFK became president, the U.S. government backed an attempted coup of Fidel Castro's communist regime by Cuban expatriates in April of 1961. The operation's failure, and the involvement of the United States, further eroded any remaining goodwill with Russia. In August of that year, Russia finished construction on the Berlin Wall, which served to unmistakably separate Germany into two separate countries.

The Cold War, which involved escalating nuclear stockpiles between the United States and the Soviet Union, was an ever-present worry for the American public. By 1962, JFK had more than 2,000 nuclear warheads capable of reaching Russia. Nikita Khrushchev, the Soviet premier, had about 340 intercontinental nuclear warheads. In October of 1962, Russia attempted to transport and install missiles in Cuba. JFK put the country on high alert and took his case to the UN in an effort to force Khrushchev's hand. After thirteen days, the Soviet Union backed down and the issue was resolved, but the event demonstrated how tenuous international politics were throughout the 1960s.

One area in which the competition between the United States and Russia resulted in positive escalation was through the space race. After the latter country launched Sputnik in 1957, the United States realized it needed to commit significant energy and resources to its own space program. JFK, in his inaugural address, had pledged to put a man on the moon by the end of the decade. NASA saw its budget grow from less than $1 billion in 1961 to $5.1 billion by 1964 (Farber 1994, 20). U.S. astronauts orbited the moon aboard Apollo 13 in August of 1968, and, on July 20, 1969, an enthralled nation watched Neil Armstrong become the first person to walk on the moon.

The United States' involvement in the Vietnam War would have far-reaching repercussions. The impetus for U.S. entry into this Asian country was to stem the advance of communism in other nations. As Dwight Eisenhower articulated the threat in 1954, "You have a row of dominoes set up and you knock over the first one, and what will happen to the last one is the certainty that it will go over very quickly." Because Russia and China were providing aid to the North Vietnamese, the United States felt compelled to lend its support to South Vietnam. The Tonkin Gulf Resolution, following an alleged attack on U.S. ships off the coast of Vietnam, marked the official entry of the United States into the war, and a rapid escalation of troops followed. By 1965, 200,000 U.S. troops had been deployed; the total number reached more than 500,000 three years later (Zinn 1995, 467). More than 40,000 soldiers had been killed and 250,000 wounded by the end of 1968. As it became apparent that the United States was not making progress in the war, despite its growing commitment of money and manpower, public sentiment turned against the effort. Richard Nixon was elected in large part to bring an end to the campaign, and he oversaw a drawdown of the military effort in Vietnam; by the end of the decade, less than 40,000 U.S. troops still remained there.

ETHNICITY IN AMERICA

The experience of blacks in U.S. society was radically different from that of their white counterparts. Although the Supreme Court had ruled in

1954 that schools could no longer be racially segregated, blacks had access to neither the means by which to improve their lot nor to some basic rights and freedoms, such as the right to vote, that were supposed to be guaranteed by the U.S. Constitution. As a result, blacks, who comprised 11 percent of the population and 92 percent of nonwhites, had to fight for every inch of progress that they made in the 1960s (Rielly 2003, 40).

Their efforts were undertaken on a number of fronts. Pressure from a number of civil rights groups helped force the government to enact the Civil Rights Acts of 1964 and 1965. Persistent and coordinated efforts by protest groups slowly loosened the grip of Jim Crow, an informal system of discrimination, on states in the South. The programs of the Great Society had an overwhelmingly positive effect on blacks, who as a group occupied the lower rungs of the economy. LBJ issued an executive order that required federal agencies to promote equal employment opportunities for all civilian employees (Bailey 2004, 58). By doing so, he helped champion the concept of affirmative action.

By the end of the decade, 40 percent of black families owned their own home, and half owned at least one car. As manufacturing jobs promised a better life, a great migration of southern blacks to northern cities continued throughout the 1960s. By 1965, 80 percent of all blacks lived in urban areas, 50 percent of which were in the north.

The decade was notable for the rise of the influence and visibility of blacks in entertainment and culture. Cassius Clay (known as Muhammad Ali after his conversion to Islam) dominated boxing and was an outspoken and charismatic figure. His opposition to the Vietnam War, his refusal to serve in the military, and his subsequent jail sentence made him a hero to blacks across the nation. The rise of Motown Records, with its stable of artists and groups who had a crossover appeal with white audiences, dominated music in the early 1960s. Sports stars such as Willie Mays, Jim Brown, Gale Sayers, and Wilt Chamberlain were some of the top performers within their respective leagues, and on television, Bill Cosby became the first black actor to get equal billing with a white co-star in the program *I Spy*. His success paved the way for shows such as *The Mod Squad*, which featured an integrated cast, and *Julia*, which starred Diahann Carroll. These shows reflected not only a recognition of blacks as a viewing audience but also the appeal of black stars to whites.

By 1960, there were 800,000 Native Americans in the United States, equally distributed between Indian reservations and towns and cities. A group of Native Americans took control of Alcatraz Island in November 1969 and occupied it for the next nineteen months to protest federal policies toward Indians. The flow of immigrants, many of whom were

Hispanic, increased from 1961 to 1980 with more than 8 million new arrivals entering the United States. Cesar Chavez, a Hispanic labor leader and devoted follower of the tenets of nonviolent demonstration, was instrumental in winning concessions from the agriculture industry and big business to improve the conditions for migrant farm workers.

THE
1970s

GOVERNMENT AND POLITICAL MOVEMENTS

Whereas the 1960s are remembered as a time of unbridled optimism, positive social movements, and an expanding economy, the 1970s are primarily regarded as a period when idealism gave way to pessimism and society as a whole searched for answers not from its elected officials but instead turned its collective focus inward. Indeed, President Richard Nixon's administration came to embody much of what was wrong with politics and government.

Nixon had won a landslide reelection over George McGovern in 1972, carrying 60 percent of the popular vote, but his second term was beset with scandal. Burglars financed by the Committee to Re-elect the President broke into Democratic National Headquarters, at the Watergate Hotel in Washington, DC, on June 17, 1972. Nixon denied any involvement and attempted to cover up any connections his administration had to the incident. As news organizations uncovered information that indicated the president was not being truthful, his support plummeted: by June of 1973, 67 percent of the American public believed that Nixon had something to do with the break-in or had lied to cover it up (Zinn 1995, 532). After exhausting his legal maneuvers to withhold information from the special prosecutor investigating the administration and having lost the support of his own party, Richard Nixon resigned the presidency on August 8, 1974.

The leadership vacuum in the Oval Office was indicative of the disconnect between government and the public. To cite one example, in 1969, Congress passed the National Environmental Policy Act, which called for the federal and state governments to file impact reports on all public projects, and the Endangered Species Act, which protected animals and wildlife from global extinction. On April 22, 1970, environmentalists sponsored the first Earth Day to draw attention to a wide range of environmental issues. On that same day, Nixon's interior secretary approved the construction of an 800-mile oil pipeline through the Alaskan wilderness.

The public's trust was further tested by the publication of the Pentagon Papers, a classified document in which the Department of Defense gave an assessment of the Vietnam War that was grossly at odds with the official government stance. After the Watergate scandal and inept leadership on the part of successive presidents and the Congress, a poll found that public confidence in these institutions had fallen to just 13 percent (Zinn 1995, 544–5).

Vice President Gerald Ford became president after Nixon's resignation and immediately set off a political firestorm by pardoning Nixon without consulting with Congress. Although a man of high integrity, he spent the remaining years of his term struggling to convey a sense of leadership and purpose. In the 1976 presidential campaign, Jimmy Carter, the governor of Georgia, defeated Ford by just 2 percent of the popular vote.

Although the public had been attracted to Carter by his vows to restore morality and honesty to the presidency, he too had problems outlining an agenda that connected with the public. Furthermore, Carter was an outsider who had trouble convincing the Washington establishment, including members of his own Democratic party, to support his programs. Faced with sinking poll numbers, on July 17, 1979, he delivered a speech outlining what he called a "crisis of confidence" that was afflicting the nation. He enjoyed a short-lived resurgence, but, as the decade drew to a close he faced a tough road: both economic woes and foreign-policy challenges would ultimately derail his quest for a second term.

ECONOMIC TRENDS

The impressive economic expansion of the 1960s, fueled primarily by government spending on the Vietnam War and social programs, came to end in the 1970s, in part because of LBJ's refusal to raise taxes to pay for the war. As a result, during the 1970s, the economy struggled to regain its footing. The runaway spending of the previous decade led to inflation that took a toll on the average consumer: $1 in 1967 was worth just 68¢ cents by 1974. In 1973 alone, the rate of inflation was 6.2 percent (14.5 percent for food items) (Carroll 1982, 131). Furthermore, an energy shortage, sparked by a decrease in oil production by the Organization of Petroleum Exporting Countries (OPEC), made things worse by raising the cost of consumer items. The Nixon administration tried to combat these woes by instituting price controls in an effort to get inflation under control. Despite these actions, the country sank into a recession that would last from 1974 through 1975.

The fallout was far reaching and severe: sectors such as agriculture, manufacturing, and construction were the hardest hit. The farm population, which stood at nearly 10 million people in 1970, had dropped to just over 6 million by the close of the decade (Kurian 1994, 177). The inroads that had been made as part of LBJ's war on poverty were largely reversed: the number of Americans who were legally poor rose 10 percent, to 25.9 million, during the 1974–1975 recession (Zinn 1995, 545). Unemployment rates, just 4.9 percent in 1970, hit 7.7 percent by 1976 (Kurian 1994, 75). To address the problems of the poor, the government continued to increase its spending on social programs. In the first five years of the decade, social-welfare expenditures nearly doubled, to $289 billion (Kurian 1994, 129).

Many of the government's measures intending to get the economy back on track ended up having the opposite effect. Congress passed legislation to boost the minimum wage and extended financial aid and price supports to ailing industries such as steel and agriculture to help them weather the economic downturn. These policies and a depreciated dollar combined to usher in another downturn in the late 1970s. Another round of gas shortages further dragged the economy down, and interest rates spiraled out of control. Inflation, driven by rising costs for fuel and consumer goods, rose from 6 percent in 1977 to 13 percent in 1979 (Carroll 1982, 222). General Motors, one of the Big Three automakers and a major employer, was pushed to the brink of bankruptcy in 1979.

One development that helped consumers cope with the economic upheaval was the invention of the Visa credit card and authorization system by Dee Hock in 1973. Credit card spending totaled $14 billion that year but increased to $66 billion by 1982. Inflation has rising so rapidly that it was actually more cost effective to pay for an item with credit, and many consumers took advantage of this dynamic (Schulman 2001, 13).

INTERNATIONAL DEVELOPMENTS

The Vietnam War was the primary focus for the U.S. government during the first half of the decade. President Nixon had run in 1968 on a message of achieving peace in Vietnam, and, although he did pursue a policy of "Vietnamization" (shifting the burden of fighting the ground war to South Vietnamese troops), he also approved an expansion of the war through bombing operations in Laos and Cambodia. In December of 1971, the military undertook a massive bombing campaign (dubbed the Christmas bombings) of North Vietnamese targets, with little effect. The Paris Peace Accord was reached in January of 1973 and ended the involvement of U.S. troops in ground operations, yet the war dragged on for another two years. The United States pulled out of the country in April of 1975, and two weeks later Saigon fell to North Vietnamese forces, thus ending the war.

Another event that had widespread repercussions was the Yom Kippur War in 1973. A dispute between Israel and Egypt escalated to a full-scale military assault on Israel by Egypt and Syria, with help from Saudi Arabia, Syria, Iraq, and the Soviet Union. The United States belatedly came to the aid of Israel, and a UN resolution instituted a cease-fire after sixteen days of fighting. In retaliation for the United States' support of Israel, OPEC instituted an embargo on oil shipments to the United States. The resulting fuel shortages in combination with rising grain prices helped to spur inflation and recession, and the economic downturn within the United States began to affect countries around the world.

The Carter administration's support of the Shah of Iran's dictatorial regime in the face of widespread resentment among Iranians also had grave implications. When the Shah was overthrown in 1979, he was offered refuge in the United States. In November of 1979, a group of student militants stormed the U.S. embassy in Teheran and took fifty-two employees hostage. The standoff would last for 444 days, and a commando mission to rescue the hostages failed. Public support of Carter and morale overall plummeted, because the United States seemed powerless to bring about a speedy resolution to the crisis. The hostages were finally released the day that Ronald Reagan took office on January 20, 1981.

Despite the numerous foreign-policy failures of the Nixon administration and its successors, some notable progress was made during the decade. President Nixon helped to thaw relations with China by visiting that country in February of 1972. Seven years later, President Carter extended formal diplomatic relations to China and terminated the mutual defense treaty between the United States and Taiwan. Carter also returned control of the Panama Canal to Panama in 1977, a move that resulted in widespread outcry within the United States. He also worked tirelessly to forge a peace accord between Egypt and Israel; his efforts resulted in the 1978 Camp David Accords, which laid out a path for achieving peace in the Middle East. President Carter also signed a strategic arms limitation treaty with the Soviet Union in 1979.

ETHNICITY IN AMERICA

Despite all of the economic and political progress that minorities collectively made in the 1960s, an overwhelming majority of individuals in minority groups still struggled with the same problems of poverty and a lack of economic opportunity. In 1973, the minority population in the United States, including blacks, Hispanics, American Indians, and others, stood at 15.4 percent. That same year, the income of average black families was just 58 percent for that of white households, and 42 percent of all black households were categorized as poor (Carroll 1982, 110). Mexican families fared a bit better, earning 71 percent of white income levels, but a bit more than one-quarter were below the poverty line (Carroll 1982, 107). Because minorities still occupied the lower rungs of the economy, the severe downturns that occurred in the 1970s disproportionately affected these groups. In 1977, the Department of Labor calculated unemployment among black youths at 34.8 percent, and 6 million blacks were unemployed the following year.

There were several trends at work behind these figures. The Immigration and Naturalization Act, passed by Congress in 1965, led to a pronounced increase in immigration that was felt most acutely in the following decade. The overall population grew by 11 percent in the 1970s, with immigrants coming primarily from Asia and Mexico. Indeed, 4 million people entered the country over the course of the decade, and the Asian-American population increased by 141 percent (Bailey 2004, 59). This constant influx of families meant that, as more people moved up the ladder, more were there to take their place at the bottom.

For blacks, the problems were of a different nature. Despite all of the progress that the civil rights movement made in raising the profile of the challenges blacks faced, little of these gains had translated to concrete economic improvements. The movement had largely splintered after Martin Luther King Jr. was assassinated in 1968, and blacks lost a powerful ally when LBJ decided not to run for reelection that year. The Nixon administration had fashioned a "Southern strategy" for the 1968 campaign that sought to reassure white voters who had felt threatened by the civil rights movement.

His victory freed him from any allegiance to help blacks, and his administration's policies bear this out. Despite an increase in overall spending on social-welfare programs, Nixon's policy of "benign neglect"—acknowledging the problems blacks faced but doing little to address them—had an effect. In fact, Nixon sought to discontinue many of LBJ's programs that were designed to foster racial progress and equality. Nixon unsuccessfully lobbied Congress to discontinue school desegregation but was able to abolish the Office of Racial Equality. In 1973, just 26 percent of black-owned business exceeded revenues of $5 million (Carroll 1982, 48). As Vernon Jordan, a lawyer and leader of the National Urban League, noted, "We're seeing a national backlash against the movement

toward economic and racial equality, a backlash fueled by selfish vindic-
tiveness that threatens to fragment our society" (Carroll 1982, 263). One
example of this trend was the Supreme Court ruling for *Bakke v. California*, in which the court found that a quota system for minority applicants
violated the Fourteenth Amendment and Title XI of the 1964 Civil
Rights Act. The ruling scaled back the reach of affirmative-action programs designed to address the effects of prejudice and social injustice.

Important developments among other minority groups included the
creation of the American Indian Movement (AIM), an organization dedicated to fighting police brutality and persecution of Native Americans.
For Hispanics and other immigrants, the emergence of Cesar Chavez,
who founded the United Farm Workers, as a labor organizer had a profound positive impact. Chavez devoted his life to improving the conditions of migrant workers through unionization and by staging hunger
strikes to draw attention to the plight of these workers at the lowest rung
of the economy. His achievements in the 1970s included securing higher
wages for grape and lettuce growers.

THE
1980s

GOVERNMENT AND POLITICAL MOVEMENTS

Ronald Reagan's presidency from 1981 to 1989 was marked by a strong
anticommunist policy and a concern with defense, which led to an
increase of the military budget. Reagan was particularly insistent on aug-
menting military spending for nuclear weapons and aircraft through his
Strategic Defense Initiative, commonly known as "Star Wars." The American invasion of the small island nation of Grenada in 1983 clearly
reflected the United States' low tolerance toward the expansion of communism. Reagan's liberal economy and free-market policies advocated
reduced government spending and tax reductions for the upper class. His
strategy was considered successful by many when economists declared an
end to the recession in 1983, with inflation down to 4 percent and unemployment marked at 7.5 percent (Berkin 1995, 981). The national debt,
conversely, increased as a result of the lack of appropriate revenue.

Nancy Reagan was readily considered the most fashion-conscious first
lady since Jackie Kennedy. She patronized designers such as Adolfo, James
Galanos, Oscar de la Renta, and Bill Blass. Mrs. Reagan was always
impeccably groomed; her trademark color was often referred to as

"Reagan Red." Her classic and elegant style was admired by many and criticized by others as an unnecessary display of wealth and consumption that aligned her with the new American aristocracy of the 1980s and their penchant to flaunt wealth and luxury (Silverman 1986, 41).

The cultural prominence of the "new right" was evident through the media emergence of Evangelical Christian groups and their televangelists denouncing that liberal views were on the verge of "destroying morality in America" (Berkin 1995, 979). Jerry Falwell founded the "Moral Majority," a group that functioned as the custodian of strict moral values. Falwell also called for a political war against homosexuality, communism, and abortion. Jim Bakker and Tammy Faye Bakker's show *Praise the Lord* was another popular outlet for such conservative agenda. Jim Bakker was eventually sentenced to prison in 1987 under charges of fraud and conspiracy after being accused of forcing women in his church to engage in sexual activities with him (Berkin 1995, 979). Tammy Faye, known for her extreme use of mascara, remained a powerful presence in American pop culture well into the twenty-first century, even making appearances on reality television shows.

Reagan's accomplishments included the 1981 liberation of American hostages held at the embassy in Iran and the appointment that same year of Sandra Day O'Connor, the first woman to sit on the Supreme Court. He was, however, criticized for his slow reaction to the first reports on

Nancy Reagan's Fashion Interests. Nancy Reagan gave up her own film acting career when she married Ronald Reagan in the 1950s, but her tenure at the White House during the 1980s brought her into the spotlight of gossip columns and popular magazines. Reagan was heavily criticized for expensive redecoration of the White House and for hosting numerous elegant formal events. The first lady drew even stronger criticism for her interest in haute couture and for allegedly accepting free items from fashion designers, including expensive jewelry pieces and fur accessories. Her "Queen Nancy" persona was created by political opponents and used to criticize the conspicuous consumption that shaped the Reagan administration. The issue was more pressing during the early years of the Reagan administration with the country facing an economic recession and high unemployment rates. Among the designers favored by Mrs. Reagan were Bill Blass, Oscar de la Renta, Adolfo, Carolina Herrera, and James Galanos, the designer of her inaugural gowns.

AIDS, even after the World Health Organization declared the disease an epidemic in 1985.

In 1984, Democrat candidate Walter Mondale nominated Geraldine Ferraro as his running mate. She was the first woman to ever be selected for the post, but the team failed to defeat Reagan, who was elected for a second term with 59 percent of the vote.

ECONOMIC TRENDS

The 1980s are remembered as an era of opulence and luxury with conspicuous consumption in many sectors of American society. The display of exuberant fashion and other personal possessions was often considered the perfect sign of economic achievement. The upper strata of society was certainly enjoying an increase in disposable income resulting in part from government policies designed to produce growth in the affluent segment, hoping that this wealth would "trickle down" to all levels of American economy. Often known as "Reaganomics," this economic policy also freed business and corporations from certain regulations and reduced the power of labor unions.

The reemergence of a worldwide elite class in the 1980s maintained haute couture as a vital business. Wealthy Americans benefited from the strength of the dollar and spent large amounts of money in apparel created by exclusive fashion designers in Paris (Mendes and de la Haye 1999, 232). American yuppies supported elegant fashion and "power dressing" outfits created by American designers such as Perry Ellis and Donna Karan, who continued developing a sense of American, and particularly New York, style in fashion. The worldwide success of capitalism

Branding Begins. Brand recognition became a crucial tool for the American fashion industry in the 1950s when corporate design first began playing an important part in the creation of a company's public image. The 1980s obsession with brands, however, brought corporate design to the forefront of the business. Brand recognition was essential for the success of any American manufacturer, designer, and retailer. Target markets were often completely defined by loyalty to specific brands. Corporate logos and brands were placed in prominent areas in most garments and textile products. Such brands as Izod, Ralph Lauren, Guess, and others became sought-after labels and logos on garments and handbags in the 1980s, continuing to the present.

and the early developments in globalization of the economy provided American designers with a perfect platform to export the American casual sportswear look to markets abroad.

Technology and real estate also brought economic success to many Americans. Computer mogul Bill Gates founded Microsoft, the largest worldwide software corporation, in 1975, but achieved greater success with the development of the operating system MS-DOS in the 1980s. Gates went on to become a popular figure in American pop culture, along with other entrepreneurs such as Ted Turner and Lee Iacocca. Active and clever self-promotion also made real estate guru Donald Trump and his famed comb-over an icon of American pop culture. His first wife, Ivana Trump, was admired in the 1980s for her beauty, fashionable apparel, and, particularly, for her appetite for jewels and furs (Seeling 2000, 517).

On October 19, 1987, the American stock market dropped 508 points, or 22 percent of its value, marking the largest decline ever in American history. This day, often known as "Black Monday," memorably coincided with the opening of Christian Lacroix's New York store. Some fashion historians saw great irony in the synchronicity of these two events. At the time, Lacroix was one of the most popular designers among the American opulent sectors and was often considered the epitome of excess and class separation (Steele 1997, 109). The market crash became a clear indicator that the age of greed was over. The last few years of the 1980s were the end of the shopping spree that had occupied Americans for a long period.

INTERNATIONAL DEVELOPMENTS

Unprecedented changes since the end of WWII modified the European political and geographical landscape in the late 1980s and early 1990s. In 1980, Lech Walesa led the first Polish worker strike with Solidarnosc, the workers syndicate, advancing Poland toward democracy and finally free elections in 1989. Mikhail Gorbachev became Soviet premier in 1985 and soon thereafter started "Perestroika," an initiative for government restructuring and economic reform, as well as "Glasnost," an open discussion of social problems leading to freedom of thought. Both initiatives proposed by Gorbachev signaled the end of communism as the ruling philosophy of the Soviet Union. The Soviet Union had lost control of its hold on Eastern Europe. The Soviet Union dissolved and was replaced by the Commonwealth of Independent States, winning Gorbachev the Nobel Peace Prize in 1990 in recognition for his efforts.

The changes in the Soviet Union had strong repercussions around the world, such as the 1989 uprising of Chinese students in Tiananmen

Square, which ended in the unfortunate death of over 2,000 demonstrators after the government decided to promptly dispel the protest. The most significant outcome of the collapse of the Soviet Union was the fall of the Berlin Wall in 1989. In November of that year, the German borders were opened, and, after years of separation resulting from WWII, East Germany and West Germany were reunited in 1990.

In the late 1970s, Japan emerged as a world superpower, a leader on technology development, and a new force in the apparel industry. Japanese fashion designers such as Issey Miyake and Kenzo began showing their collections in Europe in the late 1970s and early 1980s, opening the doors for a number of successful Japanese ventures to follow. The 1980s also reaped the benefits of the opening of the People's Republic of China to the Western world in the 1970s. China was now a strong competitor in the manufacturing business. China also signed a treaty with the United Kingdom in 1984, agreeing to the end of British rule over Hong Kong in 1997.

An uprising in the Philippines in 1986, after allegations of fraudulent elections, forced President Ferdinand Marcos to flee the country. His wife, Imelda, known worldwide as a conspicuous consumer, had famously amassed a collection of 2,700 pairs of shoes. Corazón Aquino assumed the presidency, becoming the first woman in Asia to ever hold such a post. Two years later, Benazir Bhutto became the second woman to hold that distinction after she was elected president of Pakistan (only to be assassinated in late 2007 when she ran for the presidency again).

Environmental concerns grew around the world in the last two decades of the twentieth century, particularly after acid rain affected the forests of Europe in 1981 and a hole in the ozone layer over Antarctica was detected in 1985. Adding to such concerns was the 1986 Chernobyl disaster in the Soviet Union, the largest nuclear disaster to date. Responses around the world included research into solar power and environmentally safe industry, but, in the United States, early attempts to fully fund initiatives for the use of alternative fuels often did not find proper support at the government level (Berkin 1995, 971). In the fashion industry, the 1980s were distinguished by a strong anti-fur movement led by People for the Ethical Treatment of Animals, with a strong campaign exposing cruel practices and promoting the closure of fur farms. Also significant were regulations on the importation of products such as tortoise shell, ivory, crocodile skin, and other products derived from animals in the endangered species list that had previously been used in accessories (Tortora 2005, 502). Sustainable or "green" products were developed using materials such as bamboo, hemp, and naturally colored or organic cotton. Green fabrics were also developed, including Polartec, a thermal fleece made from recycled plastic bottles, and Tencel, made from wood pulp (Lomas 2000, 29).

ETHNICITY IN AMERICA

By the end of the 1980s, the U.S. population was estimated at 248,709,873 (Buchanan 2005, 161). In 1986, the U.S. Congress passed the Immigration Reform and Control Act, easing regulations and allowing some illegal immigrants to seek amnesty (Buchanan 2005, 140). The American ideal of beauty and style began to change as myriad influences from world cultures, national ethnic groups, and subcultures became more prominent.

During the 1980s, Vanessa Williams became the first black woman to be crowned as Miss America (1983), the highly popular *Cosby Show* debuted (1984), Martin Luther King Day was celebrated for the first time (1986), and Colin Powell was appointed as National Security advisor (1987–1989), becoming the first African American to function as Chairman of the Joint Chiefs of Staff (1989–1993). In that same decade, however, the Reagan administration actively opposed affirmative action and racial quotas, although federal minority hiring quotas were upheld in 1980 by the Supreme Court (Berkin 1995, 1007).

THE
1990s AND 2000s

GOVERNMENT AND POLITICAL MOVEMENTS

In 1989, George Bush became president of the United States after serving as vice president for the Reagan administration. Bush had announced that he would occupy himself mostly with domestic affairs. His government, however, was forced to deal with global events such as the fall of the Berlin Wall and the Panama invasion in 1989, as well as the 1991 Persian Gulf War. Toward the end of Bush's presidency, the country experienced an economic recession and increased unemployment.

Bill Clinton was elected in 1992 as the forty-second president of the United States and was reelected for a second term in 1996. During his presidential campaign, Clinton used television shows as a political tool, famously appearing on the *Arsenio Hall Show* playing the saxophone. First lady Hillary Clinton, a successful lawyer in her own right, played an active role in her husband's administration. In 1993, the president appointed her to lead a task force on national health reform. Mrs. Clinton was also a strong supporter of women's rights and children's issues. She often made public appearances at fashion shows but kept her style simple and conservative, with skirt and pantsuits in earth tones and her trademark rope pearl necklaces. Her husband often wore creations by American designers such as Ralph Lauren and Tommy Hilfiger.

Clinton oversaw the 1993 approval of NAFTA, which aimed to eliminate trade barriers and reduce tariffs among Canada, Mexico, and the United States over a period of fifteen years. During Clinton's presidency, Americans experienced the abrupt appearance of violence with the 1993 terrorist attack on the World Trade Center, the 1995 bombing of the Alfred P. Murrah Federal Building in Oklahoma, and the 1999 massacre at Columbine High School in Colorado.

After results of the 2000 election were officially announced, Democratic candidate Al Gore was ahead in the popular vote, but Republican candidate George W. Bush was slightly ahead in the electoral vote. After a long controversy and manual recount of votes in the state of Florida, George W. Bush was declared president of the United States. Bush's presidency was distinguished by his radical foreign policy in reaction to the September 11, 2001, terrorist attacks on the United States. The United States invaded Afghanistan in 2001 and formed a coalition with other nations to invade Iraq in 2003. Bush was reelected for a second term in 2004, defeating Democratic candidate John Kerry. By 2008, Bush's approval rate had plummeted because of public concerns with the lengthening war in Iraq and domestic wiretapping of communications without court approval. Issues at the forefront during the 2007–2008 primary campaigns included problems with illegal immigration, general discontent with the results of the Iraq War, and an ailing economy, marked by a crisis in the home-buying market and rising fuel prices.

ECONOMIC TRENDS

The 1990s were distinguished by the introduction of portable CD players, cellular telephones, and portable game devices. The greatest technology story of the 1990s, however, was the fast development of the World Wide Web, with a rapidly increasing number of computers connected to the Internet in the United States. This information highway changed not only the way humans around the globe communicated but also the buying practices of those with access to online stores' websites.

The early 1990s' economic recession was distinguished by lower consumer spending and high unemployment. There was immediately a

Commemorating 9/11 in Clothing. On September 11, 2001, the United States was the target of a major terrorist attack that resulted in the destruction of the World Trade Center twin towers in New York and the death of nearly 3,000 civilians. Concerns with future terrorist attacks and particularly with chemical poisoning and the threat of anthrax led several manufacturers and retailers to create product lines offering protective clothing and accessories to general consumers. Retailers offered gas masks, chemical suits, protective gear, escape hoods, specialized gloves, and radiation detection devices. Although not many Americans purchased these products, the 9/11 terrorist attacks prompted a craze for patriotic apparel and accessories featuring colors and symbols associated with the United States or commemorating the New York City Fire Department, or FDNY. In the months after the attack, the Star Spangled Banner was prominently featured in many apparel items, as were the colors red, white, and blue. Other American symbols incorporated into apparel included bald eagles, the Statue of Liberty, the Liberty Bell, and the great seal of the United States.

negative reaction against the conspicuous consumption practices of the previous decade (Mendes and de la Haye 1999, 252). The motto for the fashionista in this new decade seemed to be "less is more." Clothing customers found alternatives in a fashionably restrained style dominated by socially accepted minimalist tendencies (Seelig 2000, 550).

The 1990s are also known in American history as the age of mergers and acquisitions. Mergers became a common business strategy seeking to bring together two strong companies, such as the 1985 merger of Revlon and Pantry Pride. During acquisitions, a large corporate institution acquires other firms by either agreement or stock takeover. The retail industry saw the merger of Sears and Kmart, announced in 2004 after Kmart had filed for bankruptcy in 2002. At that time, Kmart's total assets were estimated at over $17 billion, making the event the biggest bankruptcy ever for an American retailer.

By 1992, there were more than 35,000 malls in the United States, or approximately eighteen square feet of retail area per person, a nearly three times increase from 1972 (Agins 1999, 181). Manufacturers also faced strong competition from strengthening economies in Asia and the Middle East, which motivated many American companies to outsource production and services away from the United States. The elimination of export quotas to the United States and Europe in 2005 further opened possibilities for large economies such as China and India to compete in manufacturing with countries such as Indonesia and Sri Lanka, which had been partners with American companies with facilities abroad. In 1998, the Asian market collapsed, freezing spending by individuals in Asia, especially discretionary spending on Parisian haute couture (Agins 1999, 50). At that time, the United States was experiencing an economic rebirth mostly fueled by the success of the information technology sector.

During the Clinton administration, the gross domestic product expanded by 38 percent, and unemployment rates were reduced considerably. The year 2000, however, marked the start of another recession period. President George W. Bush replicated Reagan's approach by once again reducing taxes and restrictions for large companies and wealthy individuals. The economy gained some strength at the dawn of the twenty-first century, but the national debt continued expanding mostly as a result of the expense of the 2001 Afghanistan invasion and the 2003 war in Iraq. As the twenty-first century progressed, the American economy continued experiencing changes as it was forced to adapt to the globalization of culture and communications and the further integration of the international economic system. In early 2008, the country feared a potential recession as consumer spending continued slowing down.

INTERNATIONAL DEVELOPMENTS

The 1992 Maastricht meeting was organized to establish a treaty to create the European Union. The European Union became effective in 1993, debuting a new era in Europe as the continent became politically aligned and financially unified through a common currency, the euro, in 1998. Trade, finance, and manufacturing in the Western world were also intrinsically merged with Middle Eastern and Asian economies as individuals and companies from those areas invested large amounts in Western enterprises. American and European manufacturers outsourced production to developing countries where concerns arose related to the proper care of the environment and labor conditions in "sweatshops."

Communication outlets also became global, initially through cable television and later by satellite radio and the Internet. The information super-highway created by the World Wide Web had an effect on the globalization and standardization of fashion styles. Designers from several nontraditional countries such as Hong Kong, New Zealand, and Venezuela were able to enjoy worldwide fame thanks to the Internet.

The first Democratic elections in Russia were held in 1996, and some Eastern European countries went through a peaceful transition to a new political structure. Such was the case of Czechoslovakia where playwright Václav Havel became president in 1989 after a bloodless struggle, often dubbed as the "velvet revolution." The country peacefully split in 1993 into the Czech Republic and Slovakia. In 1989, a popular rebellion overthrew the Socialist regime in Romania, and, in 1991, the former Yugoslavia was dissolved after four of its republics, Macedonia, Croatia, Slovenia, and Bosnia, along with Herzegovina, seceded in 1992.

Instability continued reigning in the Middle East through the dawn of the twenty-first century. In 1990, Iraq invaded Kuwait, taking control of the country's oil reserves and sea access. Sadam Hussein ignored sanctions and timelines imposed by the UN, prompting armed conflict in the Persian Gulf in 1991 when a coalition of nations led by the United States liberated Kuwait. The war was televised in detail around the world by reporters who followed the conflict traveling with troops, initiating a new trend in war coverage seen again in the 2003 invasion of Iraq.

Trade between the West and the Middle East was considerably affected by the Gulf War confrontations. European fashion houses and perfume manufacturers, for instance, lost fortunes when trade with some Middle Eastern countries was halted (Mendes and de la Haye 1999, 252). Sanctions imposed on Iraq after the war increased tension with the United States and negatively affected the Iraqi economy in the following years. After terrorist attacks hit the United States in 2001, American and British troops led a coalition of countries that invaded Iraq to overthrow Hussein and stop his alleged development of weapons of mass destruction. Other terrorist attacks in Madrid in 2004 and London in 2005 motivated several countries to increase security measures and immigration controls.

Tension between Palestine and Israel continued during most of the period, particularly after the Palestine Liberation Organization proclaimed a Palestinian state in 1988. Leaders from both sides met in 1993 and 1995 to sign agreements over the Gaza Strip and the West Bank. In 1994, as part of the Oslo accords, the Palestinian National Authority was created as an interim organization for administration of the area. By the start of the new millennium, many Palestinians were unhappy with progress made in the resolution of conflicts, even after the Israeli government handed control of several West Bank cities to the Palestinian Authority in 2005. In 2006, Hamas, a militant Islamic organization that openly called for the destruction of Israel, was elected to the majority of seats in the Palestinian Authority Legislative Council, further complicating the peace process in the region.

ETHNICITY IN AMERICA

The 2000 census indicated an increase of 32.7 million residents in America, mostly attributable to immigration (Buchanan 2005, 161). The 2000 census was also the first time a census allowed citizens to identify themselves as multiracial, revealing that one in every forty Americans felt they fit into that category. Of the 281 million inhabitants, approximately 195 million were non-Hispanic whites (69.4 percent), 34 million were non-Hispanic blacks (12.1 percent), 35 million considered themselves of Hispanic descent (12.5 percent), 13 million were Asian, Native American, or other (4.6 percent), and 4.6 million defined themselves as mixed race (Denton and Tolnay 2002, 6). Overall, the census made evident the decline in the number of whites while Hispanic and Asian percentages rose, with Hispanics becoming the largest minority group in the nation.

By 2006, a heated debate over illegal immigration was occupying the nation. Many individuals and business sectors hoped for a moderate solution or even an amnesty program, whereas other groups asked for increased border safety and criminalization of illegal immigration. Latin America, the Caribbean, and Asia dominated immigration in the United States in the last quarter of the twentieth century. New immigrants in the late 1990s came mostly from Asia (32.2 percent), the Caribbean (11 percent), and Spanish-speaking areas such as Mexico (19.8 percent), South America (6.8 percent), and Central America (5.4 percent) (Denton and Tolnay 2002, 10).

As opposed to past immigrant groups, many Latin Americans maintained strong ties and often traveled back and forth to their nation of origin. This was particularly true for Mexican nationals, the largest and most visual group of Latin-American migrants. Improved communication and transportation systems allowed many Mexicans to travel freely between the United States and Mexico, often keeping ties and jobs in both countries and creating a new type of transnational migration (Barlow 2003, 70).

Presidents Bill Clinton and George W. Bush supported an increase in Border Patrol, and, in 2005, the "Minuteman Project" was created by volunteer citizens to patrol the Arizona-Mexico border. Adding to the controversy of border patrols was information revealing that thousands of people had died attempting illegal border crossings. In 2004, President George W. Bush presented his Guest Worker Plan by characterizing the United States, once again, as a country of immigrants. In 2006, such initiatives were still under debate.

African Americans continued playing an active and recognizable role in American life. Their accomplishments were important in many fields, and a highlight of the period was the awarding of the 1993 Nobel Prize for Literature to Toni Morrison. In the twenty-first century, Colin Powell and Condoleezza Rice became the highest-ranking African American government officials in the history of the country, both holding the position of Secretary of State. In 2008, Barack Obama, son of an African father and a white American mother, became the first African American to outstrip other Democratic primary candidates in a run for the presidency of the United States.

Hispanics struggled to maintain their identity, customs, and language whether they were new immigrants or had lived in the country for generations. By the end of the twentieth century, they were a strong presence in the movie and music business, and more of them were being elected as government officials, including mayors and members of Congress. Many American universities included not just African-American or black studies programs but also Latin-American and Caribbean studies. Spanish, used as a secondary language by many companies, became the most popular foreign language in most universities and could be heard on television as a result of the popularity of Spanish-speaking networks such as Univision and Telemundo. Hispanic fashion designers such as Carolina Herrera, Oscar de la Renta, and Narciso Rodriguez also enjoyed widespread popularity, but other Hispanics, such as farm workers, faced stern challenges. Farm workers continued working long hours under harsh conditions and fighting for health and education access, including overcoming barriers such as the 1994 passing of Proposition 187 in California that aimed to ban undocumented children from schools.

Asian Americans gained prominence in American politics at the end of the century. Individuals, such as Gary Locke, governor of Washington in 1996; Mike Honda, U.S. Congressman in 2000; and Elaine Chao, Secretary of Labor in 2001, were three of the first Asian Americans to hold such offices. Asian Americans also became more prominent in movies and literature (*Joy Luck Club* by Amy Tan), sports (Michelle Kwan in the winter Olympics), music (Yo-Yo Ma, the classical cellist), and fashion design (Vera Wang).

REFERENCES

Agins, T. (1999) *The End of Fashion: How Marketing Changed the Clothing Business Forever.* New York: William Morrow.

Bailey, B., Farber, D., eds. (2004) *America in the '70s.* Lawrence, KS: University Press of Kansas.

Barlow, A. L. (2003) *Between Fear and Hope: Globalization and Race in the United States.* Lanham, MD: Rowman & Littlefield.

Berkin, C., Miller, C. L., Cherny, R. W., Gormly, J. L. (1995) *Making America: A History of the United States.* Boston: Houghton Mifflin.

Buchanan, P. D. (2005) *Race Relations in the United States: A Chronology, 1896–2005.* Jefferson, NC: McFarland & Co.

Carroll, P. N. (1982) *It Seemed Like Nothing Happened.* New York: Holt, Rinehart, and Winston.

Denton, N. A., Tolnay, S. E., eds. (2002) *American Diversity: A Demographic Challenge for the Twenty-First Century.* Albany, NY: State University of New York Press.

Dolfman, M. L., McSweeney, D. M. (2006) *100 Years of U.S. Consumer Spending: Data for the Nation, New York City, and Boston.* BLS Report 991. Bureau of Labor Statistics.

Farber, D. (1994) *The Sixties: From Memory to History.* Chapel Hill, NC: The University of North Carolina Press.

Hobbs, F., Stoops, N. (2002) *Demographic Trends in the 20th Century.* U.S. Department of Commerce.

Kurian, G. T. (1994) *Datapedia of the United States, 1790–2000.* Lanham, MD: Bernan Press.

Lomas, C. (2000) *The '80s & '90s: Power Dressing to Sportswear.* Milwaukee, WI: Gareth Stevens Publishing.

Mendes, V., de la Haye, A. (1999) *20th Century Fashion.* London: Thames and Hudson.

NASA. *History of Sputnik,* http://www.hq.nasa.gov/office/pao/History/sputnik/.

Rielly, E. J. (2003) *The 1960s.* Westport, CT: Greenwood Press.

Schulman, B. J. (2001) *The Seventies: The Great Shift in American Culture, Society, and Politics.* Cambridge, MA: Da Capo Press.

Seeling, C., et al. (2000) *Fashion: The Century of the Designer 1900–1999.* English edition. Cologne, Germany: Könemann.

Silverman, D. (1986) *Selling Culture: Bloomingdale's, Diana Vreeland, and the New Aristocracy of Taste in Reagan's America.* 1st edition. New York: Pantheon Books.

Steele, V. (1997) *Fifty Years of Fashion: New Look to Now.* New Haven, CT: Yale University Press.

Tortora, P. G., Eubank, K. (2005) *Survey of Historic Costume: A History of Western Dress.* 4th edition. New York: Fairchild Publications.

Zinn, H. (1995) *A People's History of the United States.* New York: Harpers Perennial.

3

Arts and Entertainment

Fashion, art, and entertainment have a direct, almost symbiotic relationship. Trends in art, movies, television, and music all influence fashion, either directly or indirectly. Conversely, without fashion, the themes in art, movies, television, and music would be missing a vital communication vehicle. Furthermore, through movies and television, not only are fashion trends introduced, but they are launched virtually simultaneously around the world.

In art, artists broke away from accepted conventions in both technique and subject matter. Abstract expressionism, op art, pop art, minimalism, and postmodernism formed the new vocabulary of art through the last half of the twentieth century. The shapes, forms, colors, and textures of each movement were reflected in the fashions of each era. The optical illusions of op art were translated into textile designs for the "psychedelic '60s." The pop art movement not only elevated Campbell's soup cans to art but opened the door for the placement of logos, such as Guinness beer, and cartoon characters, such as Beavis and Butthead, on T-shirts.

The twentieth century also saw the birth of rock 'n' roll and its many genres: funk, punk, new wave, heavy metal, mod, glam, and disco. Through rock 'n' roll, in all its forms, youths created a generational gap that angered their parents and the establishment. Each genre, whether punk or new wave, metal or disco, rock or folk, had its costume to visually convey messages and identify subscribers. If hippies had dressed in suits

At this 1966 fashion show, a model wears a black and white op art beachshift and "happy glasses," which have colored interchangeable lenses held in position by magnetized frames. [AP / Wide World Photos]

and ties instead of donning jeans, T-shirts, and long hair, would their antiestablishment message have been heard?

Television was perhaps the greatest communication tool of the twentieth century. From Elvis performing on *The Ed Sullivan Show* to the moon landing, from the assassination of a president to the shooting of J. R. Ewing, from the Vietnam War to the unification of Germany, every celebration and every tragedy was broadcast for the world to see. When JFK did not wear a hat for his inauguration, the world took note and did the same. When Don Johnson wore shoes without socks on *Miami Vice*, again the world took note and did the same.

Movies repeatedly told the stories of our hopes, our fears, and our conflicts, reflected changes in women's roles, and got us all dancing. Cold War espionage played out in James Bond films, the impact of the Vietnam War was depicted in *The Deer Hunter*, the hippie revolution was recorded in the *Woodstock* documentary, and the rise of corporate America can be seen in *Wall Street*. Films such as *Desk Set*, *Working Girl*, and *Baby Boom*

Models pose in "mod" designs from Mary Quant's collection on a street in London, England, in 1969. [AP / Wide World Photos]

reflected women's ever-evolving role as wife, mother, and employee, whereas movies such as *Beach Blanket Bingo*, *Saturday Night Fever*, and *Flashdance* launched dance crazes as well as fashion trends. Whether leisure suits, power suits, or legwarmers, movies helped us learn what to wear.

THE
1950s

ART MOVEMENTS

The major artistic movement of the 1950s was abstract expressionism. The main concentration of artists working in this style was in New York City, where the Museum of Modern Art served as an incubator for the new artistic movement. This movement, which ranged from the unique to the bizarre, was dominated by existentialist thought, which placed importance on the act of creating, not on the finished object. The execution of the existential framework was applied differently by each artist, the cohesion of the movement being through a shared philosophy, not a brush stroke or color palette.

The primary interpretations of abstract expressionisms were color-field painting, gesture, op art, and minimalism, two of which, although they did not greatly influence fashions in their era, found their way into apparel fashions of the 1960s. Color-field painting, a technique developed in the early 1950s, focused on the effects of large areas of color. Color-field (or color-block) paintings by Mondrian in the 1950s served as inspiration for the "mod" or modern fashions of designer Yves Saint Laurent (YSL) and others in the 1960s in which garments were cordoned off into sections, each of a different color. Op art, an abstract movement begun in the mid-1950s, used surface kinetics to create optical illusions. Artists used colors, lines, and shapes to create perceived movements, flashes, vibrations, swells, or warps. The geometric patterns and visual effects created by op art became widely adopted in 1960s psychedelic fashions.

Pop art adapted images from advertising and comic books, and, most memorably, Campbell's soup cans and elevated everyday objects to the status of art. Considered as a counterattack against nonrepresentational abstract expressionism, pop art marked a return to figurative painting, in which objects were accurately represented by the artist. The pop art concept of elevating the ordinary, although not influential in fashions of the 1950s, greatly shaped fashion design in the 1960s. The most notable example of pop art fashion influence was when, in 1967, Geoffrey Beene designed a floor-length, sequined evening dress that looked like a football jersey, complete with numbers on the chest.

MUSIC

Rock 'n' roll will forever be the synonymous with the 1950s. The phrase rock 'n' roll was coined by Cleveland radio disc jockey Alan Freed when he dubbed his afternoon radio program *Alan Freed's Moon Dog Rock 'n' Roll House Party*. Rock 'n' roll was a hybrid of African-American rhythm & blues (R&B) and country music that combined a strong back beat with simple, repetitive rhythm and chords. The resulting sound provided American teenagers with a unique soundtrack to underscore the widening generation gap.

Early rockers such as Bill Haley, Jerry Lee Lewis, Buddy Holly, Ritchie Valens, The Big Bopper, and Elvis Presley laid the foundation for generations of rock 'n' roll artists. "Rock Around the Clock" by Bill Haley and His Comets became the first rock 'n' roll song to hit number one (July of 1955) and later became the best-selling record of the year.

Another early pioneer, Chuck Berry, exemplified the guitar sound and showmanship that would come to define the rock 'n' roll genre. His energy and charisma on songs such as "Maybellene" was contagious.

Elvis Presley entered the rock 'n' roll scene with his first number one hit, "Heartbreak Hotel," in 1956. With swiveling and gyrating hips, Elvis' overtly sexual stage presence had young girls screaming in the audience. Elvis not only gave youths a unique sound but also a unique look. His widespread fame, bad-boy look (blue jeans, T-shirts, D.A. haircut [short for duck's ass], and leather coat), and sexual aura had parents living in fear of teenage sex and rebellion. The Elvis image was in direct conflict and competition with the prevailing conservative values of the time. Elvis' performances were so controversial that, in 1957 when he was invited to perform on television's *The Ed Sullivan Show*, the cameramen were instructed to film him only from the waist up during his performance.

In an effort to advance record sales and make rock 'n' roll acceptable to mainstream white America, the music industry manipulated the music by whitewashing the lyrics. Every song was carefully reviewed, and any racy lyrics were rewritten to conform to generally accepted subjects and beliefs. Appealing to the new teen market, Dick Clark and American Bandstand promoted an assemblage of clean-cut teen idol "crooners," including Paul Anka, Frankie Avalon, Bobby Rydell, Bobby Darin, and Fabian. Clad in chinos, button-down shirts, and cardigan sweaters, these young crooners gave the younger crowd an updated version of their parents' idols: Frank Sinatra, Dean Martin, and Perry Como.

America, still a racially divided society in the 1950s, was uncomfortable with the mixture of cultures and races that rock 'n' roll engendered. Berry Gordy, son of a black entrepreneur who promoted the upward

Polite Early Rockers. Rock 'n' roll, transistor radios, television, and beach movies worked together to create an image for teens and young adults in the fifties. Elvis Presley's swiveling hips and Chuck Berry's electrifying guitar were not well received by parents, but they were an instant hit with teenagers. To be accepted by parents, early rockers needed to be polite, well groomed, and conservatively dressed. Performing in suits, button-down shirts, skinny neckties, and crew cuts, Buddy Holly, Ritchie Valens, and other top musicians projected the image of clean-cut, wholesome American teenagers and young adults, while changing the sound of popular music forever.

mobility of blacks, founded Motown Records in 1957. His support of young black artists ensured they fit the mold of respectable professionals. Gordy was intent on grooming and cultivating streetwise teens from Detroit, transforming them into polished professionals. He had a very strict dress code and code of conduct and indoctrinated all of his artists through participation in his charm school. His goal was to eliminate the old stereotype of musicians as lewd drug fiends.

Other sounds of the 1950s included doo-wop and California surf sounds. Doo-wop vocal groups such as the Mills Brothers and the Ink Spots blended jazz and pop for a smooth sound. The Platters, the Coasters, the Drifters, and the Four Seasons with Frankie Valli blended R&B, gospel, and falsetto voices to create unique sounds. The Southern California lifestyle was glamorized with Hollywood films such as *Gidget* and the beach party movies of Frankie Avalon and Annette Funicello, Elvis Presley, and other "dreamy" stars. The California surf sound that evolved in tandem with these movies featured hot-rod car- and beach-themed lyrics. Leading the pack with his trademark electric guitar sound was Duane Eddy, followed by the Ventures, Dick Dale and His Del-Tones, the Chantays, and the Surfaris.

LITERATURE

Much of the literature published in the 1950s reflected themes of isolationism, nuclear doom, contempt for war, and dreams of a better life. Works such as Truman Capote's *Breakfast at Tiffany's* stressed the theme of finding your proper place, whereas J. D. Salinger's *The Catcher in the Rye* reflected on the alienation of youth. Although conformity was the rule of the land in the 1950s, some authors chose to voice their concern over the loss of individuality through their works. David Riesman's *The Lonely Crowd*, John Kenneth Galbraith's *The Affluent Society*, William H. Whyte's *The Organization Man*, Ayn Rand's *Atlas Shrugged*, and Sloan Wilson's *The Man in the Gray Flannel Suit* all warned against the dangers of the loss of individual thought. Other classics of the era included Tennessee Williams' *The Roman Spring of Mrs. Stone*, Carl Sandberg's *Complete Poems*, Herman Wouk's *The Caine Mutiny*, John Steinbeck's *East of Eden*, Edna Ferber's *Giant*, James Michener's *Hawaii*, and Langston Hughes' *Laughing to Keep from Crying*.

A group of authors emerged during the 1950s preaching antiestablishment messages through literature and poetry. This group, known as beatniks, was lead by Jack Kerouac and his book *On the Road* (1957). The "beat" philosophy of anti-materialistic, open-mindedness, and self-reflection captured the minds of young readers and fueled the counterculture movement that was to come in the 1960s. The work of Kerouac, along with Allen Ginsberg's *Howl* (1956) and William S. Burroughs' *Naked Lunch* (1959), came to symbolize a generation searching for answers outside the norms of society. Amongst the clean-cut, pressed-shirt image of the 1950s, beatniks differentiated themselves visually in a head-to-toe black wardrobe, as well as intellectually, from the mainstream.

THEATER

Theatrical plays dealt with themes similar to those in literature during this period. The effects of war, the trappings of success, and the desire to escape one's lot in life ran were themes that ran through Tennessee Williams' *A Streetcar Named Desire*, Arthur Miller's *Death of a Salesman*, and Tennessee Williams' *Cat on a Hot Tin Roof*. Another important production of the 1950s was *A Raisin in the Sun* by Lorraine Hansberry. Hansberry, the first African-American woman to produce a play on Broadway, won the New York Drama Critics Circle Award in 1959 for this work, which examined the growing racial tensions that provided a subtext to the 1950s complacency.

Whereas plays and literature dealt with the harsh realities of life, Broadway musicals provided an escape. The musical genius of Rodgers & Hammerstein, Irving Berlin, Leonard Bernstein, and Jerome Kern gave birth to music and lyrics that are as memorable today as when they were first written. Musicals such as *Guys and Dolls*, *The King and I*, *Porgy and Bess*, *My Fair Lady*, *West Side Story*, *Singin' in the Rain*, and *The Sound of Music* brought music and theater together for a complete entertainment experience. The productions were lavish spectacles of set design and costume. The songs topped the pop charts and became classics for generations to come. Musicals produced during the 1950s, to this day, form the core of each season's theater production schedule.

MOVIES

The 1950s mark the end of the "golden age" of cinema in America, and, for the first time since its inception, Hollywood had to make a concerted effort to attract viewers. The increased popularity and accessibility of television meant that Hollywood had to compete with the novel new medium for entertainment budgets. Hollywood capitalized on new inventions and novelties such as three-dimensional effects, Cinemascope, and, briefly, Smell-O-Vision to draw viewers from their living rooms to the theaters.

Hollywood films of the 1950s relied on epic tales, space exploration, and teen angst for much of their subject matter. Lavish productions of *Ben Hur*, *20,000 Leagues Under the Sea*, and *War and Peace* were the cornerstone of the big studios. Epic pictures such as these were often three hours or more in length, recounting stories of heroism and triumph. The increased interest in space exploration and fear of the Cold War also gave filmmakers plenty of material for attracting audiences in the 1950s. Science fiction films such as *When Worlds Collide* and *The Day the Earth Stood Still* and Alfred Hitchcock's suspense thrillers *The Man Who Knew Too Much* and *North by Northwest* played on the prevailing fears of covert operations, spy rings, and the destruction of the earth.

Hollywood began marketing more and more films directly to teen and preteen audiences. Often referred to as "B movies" because of their low budgets, horror movies and science fiction movies were the first to leverage special effects, or gimmicks, to attract young viewers. Movies such as *The House of Wax*, *The Creature from the Black Lagoon*, and *It Came from Outer Space* all made use of three-dimensional goggles to bring the action from the screen to the viewer's chair. The popularity of Western-themed television shows also led to the creation of numerous Western-themed movies. *Shane*, *The Man from Laramie*, *Gunfight at the O.K. Corral*, and *Rio Bravo* were targeted specifically at young boys whose mothers would drop them at the movie theater for the afternoon. Drive-in movies were also popular with American youths and couples with small children in the 1950s. The B-movie genre dominated drive-in offerings, with movies such as *The Blob*, *Invasion of the Body Snatchers*, and *The Incredible Shrinking Man*.

In contrast to the B-movie offerings for teens, Hollywood also focused on films about anguished and rebellious youths. *The Wild One* with Marlon Brando and *Rebel Without a Cause* with James Dean both depicted the decay of the younger generation as a warning to society about the effects of bad parenting. In opposition to such heavy

James Dean sports the "biker look," with zipped jacket and white T-shirt, in the 1955 film *Rebel Without a Cause*. [Courtesy of Photofest]

subject matter, comic farces filled with sexual innuendo and the pursuit of the "good life" featuring Marilyn Monroe represented the cocktail culture of the period. *The Seven Year Itch*, *Gentlemen Prefer Blondes*, and *How to Marry a Millionaire* featured iconic performances by Monroe, including the song "Diamonds are a Girl's Best Friend" and the famous white dress blown upward by a subway train grate.

RADIO

The development of the transistor radio in 1954 helped spread rock 'n' roll and other forms of music. Transistor radios made music portable, so it became possible to hear music anywhere there was a signal. The increased popularity of camping, spending the day at the beach, and backyard cookouts increased the demand for music. This demand was answered by the emergence of more radio stations with greater broadcast capacity.

During the 1950s, many radio programs, such as *Guiding Light*, *Flash Gordon*, and *The Lone Ranger*, moved to television. Radio could not compete with the new visual medium for drama and comedy programming. Instead, radio began to focus its programming on sports, news, and music, developing the formats that are still in place today.

TELEVISION

Television was perhaps the most significant change in communications worldwide. TV quickly became the dominant mass medium, replacing radio, and most households considered TV as essential as a refrigerator. People believed what they saw and heard on TV and trusted it as a source of information.

For the first time, through the medium of television, individuals could be visually transported directly to where news was being made. Newsmen no longer simply read the news; instead, verbal information was supplemented by film and pictures of events that occurred all over the world. Coaxial cable, developed in 1951, provided microwave relays from coast to coast for real-time transmission of images. Edward R. Murrow's weekly radio program called *Hear It Now* became *See It Now* on television, and news broadcasting was changed forever.

The ideal family living in the ideal neighborhood with children at the ideal school was portrayed on television in a way that everyone wanted to believe was reality. Television programming stressed themes of family values, depicting the "average family," with polite children and stay-at-home mothers. Family shows such as *I Love Lucy*, *The Honeymooners*, *Father Knows Best*, *Lassie*, and *The Adventures of Ozzie and Harriet* brought families together for "TV time" and indoctrinated society with middle-class conservative values. When father returned home from a "hard day at the office," his lovely wife was waiting, freshly dressed in high heels, a strand of pearls, and a crisply pressed shirtwaist dress, complete with petticoat. Dinner was on the table, and the wife hung onto every word her husband uttered.

Variety shows such as *Disneyland* (later known as *The Wonderful World of Disney*), *Arthur Godfrey's Talent Scouts*, and *The Ed Sullivan Show* provided music, comedy, and fantasy for the entire family. Stars such as Pat Boone, the McGuire Sisters, Eddie Fisher, Tony Bennett, and Elvis Presley were broadcast into the privacy of the family living room. Western-themed programs were also extremely popular for family viewing. In 1950, Gene Autry became the first major movie star to move to television. Over the next five years, Autry produced and starred in ninety-one half-hour episodes of *The Gene Autry Show* for CBS Television. He was so successful with his own show that he began to produce other Western-themed hits for TV, such as *Annie Oakley*, *The Range Rider*, *Buffalo Bill Jr.*, and the first thirty-nine episodes of *Death Valley Days*.

Niche programming for television was introduced in the 1950s. Daytime serials such as *Guiding Light* gave housewives a storyline to follow while advertisers took advantage of the opportunity to sell many products to the homemakers of America, while "after school" or Saturday programming such as *The Howdy Doody Show*; *Kukla, Fran and Ollie*; and *Mighty Mouse Playhouse* was targeted to young children, complete with cereal and toy commercials.

The ultimate niche program of the decade was *American Bandstand*. The Philadelphia daily locally televised rock 'n' roll dance show called *American Bandstand* became nationally syndicated in 1957 with Dick Clark. Showcasing up-and-coming rock 'n' roll musicians and the latest dance crazes, *American Bandstand* was an instant national phenomenon. Clark performed a minor miracle by infusing rebellious rock 'n' roll music with a clean-cut image. Watched for the latest fashions as well as the music, *American Bandstand* instantly broadcast the latest trends in dance, music, and fashion across the country to America's teens.

THE
1960s

ART MOVEMENTS

As with many parts of society, art in the 1960s was characterized by a reaction to the popular styles of the previous decade and a radical departure from the status quo. Nowhere is this pattern more evident than in the pop art movement. Claes Oldenburg, Allan Kaprow, Lucas Samaras, and Andy Warhol were some of the influential artists that aspired to blur the lines between art and life. The first three helped popularize "happenings," which combined the visual arts, performance, and audience participation. Yoko Ono's "Cut Piece," for example, involved members of the audience cutting away parts of her clothing with scissors. Andy Warhol, along with Roy Lichtenstein and others, co-opted images from popular culture and society to comment on the disposability of consumerism. Warhol's famous silk screens of Campbell's soup cans, Marilyn Monroe, and Jackie Kennedy, and Lichtenstein's use of cartoon and comic styles are just some examples.

Moreover, pop artists, in contrast to their predecessors, not only understood the power of mass media but also eagerly courted it. The impact was twofold: people who were not normally interested in art were exposed to the works of these artists (thus bypassing New York's art critics), and the artists became well known in their own right. Andy Warhol was able to branch out into films ("Sleep" consisted of six hours of a person sleeping) and multimedia events, such as his work with Nico and the Velvet Underground, a Greenwich Village art rock band.

On the heels of pop art came minimalism, an additional deconstruction of the concept of what constitutes art. Painters such as Frank Stella, Robert Mangold, and Al Held produced works that were characterized by very simple lines and colors; in some cases, just one color on a canvas. In the area of sculpture, minimalism used works that utilized geometric shapes and repetition of simple themes. Often the emphasis of minimalist art was to challenge the audience's perception of the work against its surroundings. Donald Judd, for instance, had an installation of hollow concrete boxes placed around and throughout a small town in Texas.

Eccentric abstraction and anti-form continued the deconstruction of the traditional concept of art. The former used flexible materials to form curved shapes and stressed the visceral, sensual reaction to the pieces (Phillips 1999, 181). Anti-form used lead, rubber, neon, and other components; sometimes the pieces were so large that they could not be housed in galleries. The Earthworks movement was the next logical step in the progression. Robert Smithson's *Spiral Jetty* was a 1,500-foot rock pathway constructed in a lake in Utah. Christo and Jeanne-Claude covered more than 1 million square feet of coastline in Sydney, Australia, with fabric. For obvious reasons, photographs became the only surviving representation of these works. Toward the end of the decade, conceptual art, which often combined text with painting or sculpture, refocused the emphasis on the art itself rather than the spectacle surrounding it.

The government played an important role in the art world during the 1960s by dedicating funds to the cause. JFK instituted a program to commission mosaics, tapestries, and sculpture for new federal buildings. LBJ championed legislation to create the National Endowment for the Arts and the National Endowment for the Humanities, both important organizations in the support of artists.

MUSIC

The 1960s was one of the most creative, exciting periods in popular music. The early part of the decade was dominated by the emergence of Berry Gordy's Motown Records, featuring such acts as Smokey Robinson and the Miracles, the Supremes, Marvin Gaye, the Temptations, and Martha and the Vandellas. These groups appealed to white and black audiences alike and were major influences on the white bands that would follow them up the pop charts. Beyond Motown, Sam Cooke was fusing the sacred and the secular to forge a sound that would be dubbed soul music. After Cooke's death in 1964, Otis Redding and Aretha Franklin emerged as the major artists in this vein. Redding benefited greatly from exposure to white audiences at the Fillmore West and the Monterey Pop Festival, and Franklin's version of "Respect" was a massive hit with all audiences. By the end of the decade, soul was giving way to funk music, with James Brown and Sly and the Family Stone leading the way.

For many, the arrival of the Beatles to the United States in 1964 was the event that marked the beginning of modern rock 'n' roll. The group became a pop culture phenomenon with the help of television and feature films. Not only was their music revolutionary, but so was their appearance. The mod look, cultivated in London, was imported to America along with the Beatles. Men wore their hair longer, slim tapered pants, multicolored striped jackets, velvet jackets, and ankle boots, and women wore mini-skirts to signify their approval of the new sound and distinguish themselves from their parents' generation.

Their success paved the way for the bands of the British Invasion, including the Rolling Stones, the Who, and the Kinks. At the same time, the Beach Boys' songs about surfing, cars, and girls helped introduce the rest of the country to the California aesthetic. To distinguish themselves from the mods and the rockers, the casual, easy-going surfer look focused

The cast of the Broadway musical *Hair* shows a typical array of hippie styles, including African influences. [Courtesy of Photofest]

Fashion Diversifies by the End of the 1960s. The progression of popular music and the styles the artists wore during the 1960s reflected the growing liberalization of society and the transition from uniformity and conformity to individuality. Popular acts such as the Temptations and the Beatles, who wore matching suits and conventional hairstyles, were sporting more daring styles and haircuts by the end of the decade, reflecting the influence of the counterculture and psychedelia. The trajectory of the Beatles from mop tops in matching suits to long hair, beards, granny glasses, and individual ensembles is another example of this trend. Similarly, the rise of black musicians such as Jimi Hendrix and Aretha Franklin and their image of black power and independence also translated into the introduction of traditional African patterns and apparel forms.

New revolutionary Crimplene fashions for men, reminiscent of the Regency days, are shown in London, 1970. [AP / Wide World Photos]

on board shorts, Hawaiian print shirts, and sandals with tousled blond hair.

By mid-decade, the West Coast, and specifically San Francisco, was percolating with a mix of social, musical, and pharmaceutical elements that helped push the boundaries even further. The psychedelic sound, exemplified by Jefferson Airplane, the Grateful Dead, Janis Joplin, and the Doors, and characterized by drug use (particularly LSD [for lysergic acid diethylamide]) spread across the country and had a great impact on the appearance and attitude of adolescents. The festivals of the late 1960s, most notably the Monterey Pop Festival, Woodstock, and Altamont (and the subsequent movies that chronicled these events), cemented the sound and image of rock music into the public's consciousness. The eclectic ethnic hippie look deepened the generation gap, sending an immediately identifiable visual message to the establishment. Blue jeans, long hair, beads, and peasant tops that captured the Eastern philosophies were the wardrobe of the counterculture as people "tuned out" of the commercial mass-produced world and "tuned in" to nature.

LITERATURE

Some enduring works of literature were published during this time. The events of the decade had a major impact on works of both fiction and non-fiction. Harper Lee's *To Kill a Mockingbird* addressed the issues of racism and justice in the rural South. Similarly, readers of Joseph Heller's *Catch-22* and Kurt Vonnegut's *Slaughterhouse-Five* could not help but think of the Vietnam War. Nonfiction offerings such as Norman Mailer's *The Armies of the Night* (an account of the 1967 peace march on Washington, DC) and Truman Capote's *In Cold Blood* broke new ground in the literary treatment of real people and events. Works that seemed to speak directly to the counterculture, such as Ken Kesey's *One Flew Over the Cuckoo's Nest*, Thomas Wolfe's *The Electric Kool-Aid Acid Test*, and Hunter S. Thompson's *Hell's Angels: A Strange and Terrible Saga*, also enjoyed immense popularity. The experience of women and minorities also produced seminal literary works, including Alex Haley's *The Autobiography of Malcolm X*.

THEATER

In the 1960s, theater was competing not only with movies for the public's entertainment dollars but also with television. Although the number of annual productions on Broadway dwindled from seventy in 1960 to just thirty-four in 1970, the "Great White Way" was still home to dynamic playwrights, emerging stars, and incredibly popular productions. Neil Simon cemented a reputation for delivering plays that were consistently well received, with *The Odd Couple* being the most popular of his works. Standout debut productions included Edward Albee's *Who's Afraid of Virginia Woolf*, James Goldman's *The Lion in Winter*, Woody Allen's *Play It Again, Sam*, and Tom Stoppard's *Rosencrantz and Guildenstern Are Dead*.

Broadway in the 1960s proved to be a fertile ground for actors and career-defining performances. Zero Mostel originated roles in both *A Funny Thing Happened on the Way to the Forum* and *Fiddler on the Roof*. Barbra Streisand garnered rave reviews for her work as Fanny Brice in *Funny Face*, as did Carol Channing for her performance in *Hello, Dolly*.

Of all of the forms of entertainment, theater probably reflected current events and the social upheaval the least. Indeed, many of the offerings were fairly traditional. Several playwrights did address social issues, however. William Sackler's *The Great White Hope* and Charles Gordone's *No Place To Be Somebody* both dealt with questions of race in society. The counterculture musical *Hair*, originally staged off-Broadway in 1967,

Geraldine Chaplin and Omar Sharif wear thick fur hats and coats in the 1965 film *Dr. Zhivago,* a film that inspired Romantic fashion. [Courtesy of Photofest]

featured rock music, hippies, and nudity. It moved to Broadway in 1968 and enjoyed a long, successful run.

MOVIES

The progression of movies in the 1960s mirrored society in that, as the decade went on, the way films were produced as well as their subject matter became much less traditional. The studio system, in which the large movie studios produced the majority of the content, was still going strong early in the 1960s. Such popular, mainstream films as *The Sound of Music, Lawrence of Arabia,* and *My Fair Lady* were all adored by moviegoers. David Lean's *Dr. Zhivago* was both loved and criticized, but, more importantly, it had a lasting impact on 1960s fashions, popularizing fur-trimmed coats and hats for women. The industry on the whole did not reflect the turmoil of the early and mid-1960s, although offerings such as Stanley Kubrick's *Dr. Strangelove,* John Frankenheimer's *The Manchurian Candidate,* and Stanley Kramer's *Guess Who's Coming To Dinner?* did take on the subjects of nuclear war, politics, and racism.

Two notable developments in the late 1960s would result in a sea change in the film industry. The first was the Motion Picture Association of America's relaxing of the ratings code. Adopted in 1968, the new ratings guidelines gave filmmakers more freedom in what they could depict; subsequently, R-rated movies would include more profanity and nudity. Indeed, John Schlesinger's *Midnight Cowboy* was rated X but, despite this classification, won the Academy Award for best motion picture in 1969.

The second development was the rise of independently produced movies. In 1968, just eighteen independent motion pictures were released in the United States; by 1972, the number had risen to 100 (Karney 1995, 18). The most infamous and influential independent movie of the 1960s was *Easy Rider* (featuring Dennis Hopper, Peter Fonda, and Jack Nicholson), a story about and geared toward the counterculture. However, it was not just members of the counterculture who lined up for tickets. Made for just $500,000, it would go on to gross more than $19 million and demonstrate the marketability of films aimed at the youth segment as well as the influence of movies on fashions. The studios were still in the game, however: *Herbie the Love Bug* was the top-grossing film of 1969.

The decade also saw the emergence of a number of enduring, talented actors. Paul Newman (*Hud*, *The Hustler*, and *Butch Cassidy and the Sundance Kid*), Steve McQueen (*The Great Escape*), Sidney Poitier (*Guess Who's Coming To Dinner?* and *In the Heat of the Night*), and Dustin Hoffman (*The Graduate* and *Midnight Cowboy*) all enjoyed considerable success. Standout actresses included Natalie Wood (*West Side Story*), Audrey Hepburn (*My Fair Lady* and *Breakfast at Tiffany's*), and Jane Fonda (*Barbarella*).

Audrey Hepburn's association with French couturier Hubert de Givenchy was one of the most notable film-fashion collaborations of any era. Givenchy, trained as a traditional couturier, was more interested in youthful fashions and separates than his counterparts in France. His work was classic yet incorporated bright colors and bold patterns. Audrey Hepburn was slim, exuberant, and chic, creating the ideal for beauty for the 1960s. First paired together in *Sabrina* in 1954, Givenchy went on to design costumes for many of her other films, including the quintessential 1960s film *Breakfast at Tiffany's* (1961), as well as much of her personal wardrobe. Through their relationship and films, Hepburn and Givenchy together had a strong impact on the direction of women's fashions throughout the 1960s.

RADIO

The country was still ruled by the AM radio at the beginning of the decade. The format consisted of fifteen to twenty Top 40 hits played in regular rotation, interrupted only by news reports. The popularity of AM radio effectively restricted the length and type of songs that audiences could hear. In a landmark ruling, the Federal Communications Commission in 1965 mandated that AM stations must broadcast separate programming on the FM radio frequency. The effects of this regulatory change were many: by the end of 1965, 1,343

Audrey Hepburn models a pale lavender organza gown by Paris couturier Hubert de Givenchy, 1958. [AP / Wide World Photos]

FM radio stations were broadcasting, and there would be more than 2,000 FM stations by the end of the decade. Although the FM frequency was not as far reaching as the AM signal, the sound quality was much better: stations could broadcast in stereo, for instance. The proliferation of new stations meant that more content was needed to fill the airtime. Furthermore, the DJs played a wider variety of music than just Top 40, so bands were able to make music without worrying about conforming to the hit-single template. All of these factors helped establish FM radio as the soundtrack for American youths.

TELEVISION

If radio became more fragmented and localized in the 1960s, television became the common source of news, information, and entertainment for the entire country. Whereas in 1950 just 4 million households owned a television set, by the middle of the 1960s, the total has risen to 50 million (Rielly 2003, 40). Technological breakthroughs, such as lightweight, portable cameras, videotape, and communications satellites, revolutionized the scope and immediacy of the programming. News events such as the Kennedy-Nixon debate of 1960, the assassination and state funeral of JFK in 1963, the riots of 1968, and coverage of the war in Vietnam all became a shared experience through television. The lunar landing and moonwalk in 1969, for instance, was watched by 96.1 percent of U.S. households (MacDonald 1990, 165). The power of television to portray everyday events as well as influence the attitudes of people across the country would only grow as the decade went on.

The three national networks, ABC, CBS, and NBC, offered soap operas during the day, news around dinner time, and situation comedies and dramas in the evenings. As the networks expanded the amount of content they broadcast throughout the day, new types of programs were developed. Professional and collegiate athletic events were one of the beneficiaries of television's expansion. In 1962, the three networks committed more than $80 million to broadcast sports contests, and this money and exposure fueled the rise of professional sports, particularly that of football and basketball, as spectator sports. As a result, the professional leagues expanded and added new franchises across the country. Similarly, the 1968 summer and winter Olympics were the first to be broadcast live, and events such as downhill skiing and track and field received a boost in popularity.

As television became part of the U.S. public's daily routine, the networks all profited handsomely: the combined profits of the three broadcasting companies totaled $2.5 billion in 1968 (MacDonald 1990, 150).

As television extended its reach in U.S. society, other entertainment, such as movies and the theater, saw a drop off in their revenues.

THE
1970s

ART MOVEMENTS

The 1970s witnessed exciting and distinct movements in both traditional and nontraditional art forms. In the realm of painting and sculpture, the pattern and design movement integrated materials often associated with crafts, such as fabrics, wallpaper, and flower designs, into collages that bridged the gap between crafts and fine art. Pattern painting introduced the art world to non-Western influences. Artists such as Ree Morton, Robert Kushner, and Kim MacConnel brought a visceral, narrative, and personal approach to their art, whereas the "Chicago Imagists," led by Roger Brown, drew on street art and comic books to challenge mainstream art.

The emergence of female artists who had been heavily influenced by the feminist movement and who took on certain topics from this perspective was one of the most important developments in the art world during the 1970s. Women began to form their own art co-ops and collectives in cities across the country: for example, Judy Chicago and Miriam Shapiro started a women's arts program at the California Institute for the Arts. The influence of feminism was also seen in the area of performance art. Carolee Schneemann's *Interior Scroll*, for instance, involved her pulling a paper scroll from her vagina and reading from it. Eleanor Antin documented, in *Carving: A Traditional Sculpture*, her eleven-and-a-half-pound weight loss with 148 pictures of her naked body.

A number of artists used performance art to document their personal exploration. Often the goal was to remove the distinction between life and art and make the observer's experience more immediate and graphic. Vito Acconci's *Seedbed* involved the artist masturbating under a wooden ramp so that he was unseen but still audible. Chris Burden pushed two live wires into his chest in *Doorway to Heaven* and also got shot in the arm crawling over broken glass. Gilbert and George, two British artists, covered their hands and faces with paint to become "continuous sculpture."

This emphasis on experience and realism extended to not just the media that were chosen by artists but also in the way the media were used to create art. In the area of photography, technological innovation lent photography a new credibility and respect. Art based on photography, called photorealism, rose in prominence. Leading practitioners were William Eggleston, Stephen Shore, and Joel Meyerowitz. Often American landscape was the basis for commentary and was used to heighten the viewer's awareness of ecological and environmental issues. Photorealism was also applied to textile design during the 1970s. Large photographic prints of animals, such as tigers or lions, and nature scenes, such as the beach or rain forest, were reproduced on women's skirts and dresses, as well as T-shirts for both men and women.

The integration of video into art also became more common: Bruce Nauman, for instance, used multiple styles and media, including sculpture, photography, performance, and video. The urban street culture also began to make its way into art. In New York City, the mix of art and music helped create an energy and creativity that gave rise to a number of dynamic artists. Keith Haring used the city as a canvas for murals that reflected the hyperkinetic energy of the city. Robert Mapplethrope gained notoriety for his explicit photographs of subjects drawn from within the homosexual enclaves.

Toward the end of the decade, there was a return to traditional painting but with a twist. Photorealism and the new perceptualism were two such movements. Duane Hanson, a photorealist, would cast subjects in polyester resin, paint the casts down to the last detail, and then add accessories to complete the piece. New perceptualists were heavily influenced by photorealism and marked a return to still-life paintings. Artists such as Janet Fish and Rackstraw Downes produced works that focused on the ordinary settings and landscapes.

Music

Although the 1970s are often blamed for the emergence of disco and bland corporate rock, in fact the decade was one of the most vital and creative periods for popular music. Aided by the maturation of the music industry as a whole, rock and pop music expanded to encompass a dizzying array of styles and genres. Although the Beatles disbanded in 1970, other bands of the British Invasion, such as the Who and the Rolling Stones, enjoyed immense popularity. Led Zeppelin emerged as one of the biggest acts, releasing a string of successful albums and selling out stadiums around the country. Established acts such as Bob Dylan and the Band, along with newcomers such as the Eagles, Peter Frampton, and Bruce Springsteen, were just a sampling of the successful rock acts aimed at white audiences.

Other genres of music, such as heavy metal (Black Sabbath and Deep Purple), glam (David Bowie), and theatrical (Queen, Alice Cooper, and Kiss) also emerged as popular music forms and, more specifically, with specialized wardrobes. Glam music, best exemplified by David Bowie's alter ego Ziggy Stardust, featured sequin and lamé costumes and theatrical makeup. The outfits resembled a cross between spacesuits and dance leotards and gave the wearer an androgynous look that was popular briefly in the early 1970s. Costumes donned by Ziggy Stardust and Queen paved the way for the even more theatrical fashions of Kiss and Alice Cooper. Although glam and theatrical music influenced fashion design, especially the concoctions worn to discos like Studio 54 in New York City, the extreme nature of the costumes and makeup did not lend themselves to be literally incorporated into mainstream fashions.

At the same time, black musicians were producing music that combined traditional soul grooves with political and social commentary. Marvin Gaye's "What's Going On?" and Curtis Mayfield's "Superfly" (the soundtrack to the blaxploitation film of the same name) are two standouts. The funk sound that James Brown had pioneered in the 1960s was expanded on by Sly and the Family Stone and Parliament Funkadelic; when mainstream bands adopted these grooves, the result was disco. Slickly produced bands such as the Bee Gees, KC and the Sunshine Band, and a multitude of others flooded the airwaves with music tailored to the discotheques that had sprung up around the country. The popularity of discotheques with young Americans resulted in the need for a new category of clothing: dance clothes. Whereas historically an "evening out" meant dressing up in formal attire, now an evening out meant "shaking your groove thang." Stiff formal dresses would not suffice. The clothing had to move with the body, emphasizing the fluid, sexually charged gyrations of disco dancing.

Punk music was the direct result of the backlash against staid, bloated corporate rock. Raw bands, some of whom could barely play their instruments, produced stripped-down music that tapped into teen aggression and disenfranchisement. The Ramones, the Sex Pistols, and the Clash were some of the most popular punk bands of the era, whereas Blondie, fronted by Deborah Harry, demonstrated how to make punk music commercially successful. Punk music also had a strong influence in fashion, particularly in cities such as San Francisco, New York, and Los Angeles, where more people embraced some of the outrageous fashion styles seen in the London stage during the 1970s. Punk musicians embraced anarchic anti-fashion styles aiming to shock their audiences. Their apparel was often composed of bargain items, "do-it-yourself" garments, torn clothes, and historical accessories such as cravats and pirate garb.

LITERATURE

The literature of the 1970s also exhibited some of the same traits as the music business. Popular books coexisted with more significant works. The best-selling book of the decade was *The Late, Great Planet Earth*, in which author Hal Lindsey imagined the apocalypse and interpreted the Book of Revelation. Jim Bouton's *Ball Four*, a chronicle of his 1969 season in major league baseball, created the genre of the sports tell-all and became the best-selling sports book in publishing history.

On a more substantive level, Carl Bernstein and Bob Woodward's chronicle of the Nixon administration and Watergate, *All the President's Men*, and Alexander Solzhenitsyn's *The Gulag Archipelago* were exemplary works of nonfiction. Vincent Bugliosi's account of the murders by the Manson Family and the subsequent trial and conviction of Charles Manson, *Helter Skelter*, was also very popular. Noted novelists producing acclaimed works included John Irving (*The World According to Garp*), Stephen King (his first novel, *Carrie*), and Erich Segal (*Love Story*).

The feminist movement and the role of women in society were also reflected in literature. Gloria Steinem launched *Ms.* magazine in 1971, and two years later the Boston Women's Collective published *Our Bodies, Ourselves*, the first guide to women's health written by and expressly for a female audience. Black female writers such as Toni Morrison, Zora Neale Hurston, and Alice Walker also contributed strong works, and the rise of feminism helped to shine a light on them.

THEATER

As the decade opened, the mood on the theater scene was dreary. Attendance was down as a result of the economy and the Vietnam War. The openings of several popular shows received critical acclaim and commercial success, including *Grease* (a high-school love story set to music from the 1950s), *Jesus Christ Superstar* (a rock musical), and *Pippin*. Productions of shows from the late 1960s, including *Hair* and *Fiddler on the Roof*, helped to prop up business somewhat.

The middle of the decade saw box office receipts rebound. *The Wiz*, a musical updating of the *Wizard of Oz*, won the Tony Award for best musical in 1975 and enjoyed a long run on Broadway. Other standouts from the latter part of the decade were *A Chorus Line* and *Oh Calcutta!* The musical *Annie* (based on the comic strip *Little Orphan Annie*) also made its debut.

One of the more significant developments in theater occurred far off Broadway. Second City, an improvisational theater troupe run by Del

Close and based in Chicago, hit its stride in the 1970s and began to produce a large stable of comedic actors. Among the troupe's performers to rise to prominence were John Belushi, John Candy, Gilda Radner, and Eugene Levy.

MOVIES

The 1970s was one of the best periods in U.S. film history, as the list of iconic movies that were released during this period bears out: *The Godfather* (*I* and *II*) and *The Conversation*, directed by Francis Ford Coppola, *Taxi Driver* and *Mean Streets*, by Martin Scorscese, *Nashville* and *McCabe and Mrs. Miller*, by Robert Altman, and *Chinatown*, by Roman Polanski, were all products of directors who wrote and shaped the stories themselves. Woody Allen released several of his classic movies, including *Bananas*, *Sleeper*, and *Annie Hall*.

Annie Hall, winner of the Oscar for best picture in 1977, revolutionized women's wardrobes in the late 1970s. Modern, liberated Annie Hall co-opted the traditional men's ensembles of vests, ties, button-down shirts, and fedoras as an outward sign of her independence, and so did the women who saw the film. Surprisingly, despite the impact on fashion, *Annie Hall* was not nominated for an Oscar for costume design.

Films began to push the social boundaries by taking on subjects that had previously been considered taboo, at least for commercial movies. *Carnal Knowledge*, directed by Mike Nichols and starring Jack Nicholson and Art Garfunkel, was indicative of a new realism in films regarding sex.

Two New Looks: Disco and Annie Hall. As the movie industry expanded beyond the studio system to embrace independent film makers with a range of voices, the impact on popular culture and styles was reflected in some of the most popular movies of the decade. *Saturday Night Fever*, one of the most successful movies of the '70s, introduced the country to the disco movement, both musically and visually. The white suit John Travolta wore in the movie became emblematic of the styles favored in clubs and created a new genre of clothing: the "going out" ensembles worn by single men and women who required trendy looks for a night on the town rather than the more formal looks for dating. The success of Woody Allen's *Annie Hall*, featuring Diane Keaton sporting traditional men's styles (vests, ties, blazers, and pants) also expanded the boundaries of popular fashion for the modern woman.

Kramer vs. Kramer, with Dustin Hoffman and Meryl Streep, took on the dynamics of sex and divorce. Blaxploitation films (movies from black directors that combined overtly racial and political storylines with music from top black artists) also emerged, beginning with Melvin Van Peebles' *Sweet Sweetback's Badasssss Song* and *Shaft, Superfly,* and *Cleopatra Jones.*

From a commercial standpoint, the emergence of the blockbuster movie signaled a shift in how the studios produced and marketed films. Before 1975, studios had released films in a small number of theaters and then distributed them to the rest of the country, hoping that critics' reviews and word of mouth would contribute to a movie's success. That all changed with Steven Spielberg's *Jaws,* in 1975. The movie opened in hundreds of theaters at once and relied on advertising, rather than critical acclaim, to attract audiences. The proliferation of Cineplexes, theaters with multiple screens that showed movies several times a day, made such a distribution approach more effective. When *Star Wars* hit theaters in 1979, accompanied by a marketing campaign that included product tie-ins, the era of the "event" movie had officially arrived. Disaster movies such as *The Poseidon Adventure* and *Airport '77* also capitalized on this trend.

Movies that combined the latest musical and cultural trends also enjoyed success, the best example being *Saturday Night Fever,* in 1977. The film centered on the disco culture in New York City and made a movie star out of John Travolta. However, the true star of the film was its music: the Bee Gees provided a soundtrack steeped in disco and dance music, and the popularity of the music (the album was one of the biggest sellers of all time) attracted a whole new audience to the movie theaters. The white three-piece suit donned by John Travolta in the 1970s became *the* look for men, and the wrap dress, tube tops, and strappy platform sandals became a must for every disco diva.

Radio

The FM radio format was the main distribution channel for rock music during the 1970s. Although the rise of FM radio began in the mid-1960s, it had become entrenched by the early 1970s. The main model for FM radio was the college radio station, and even the major FM stations strove to create and maintain a countercultural image: DJs often programmed their own music and would sometimes play whole albums without commercial breaks. As music evolved throughout the decade, FM radio, which was populated largely by white programmers and DJs, ignored most black forms of music. With the exception of crossover artists such as Stevie Wonder, the majority of black groups were consigned to the AM dial, thus effectively segregating the airwaves and the listeners. The backlash by conventional radio against disco toward the end of the decade, represented by the "disco sucks" rallying cry and highlighted by the disco demolition night at a White Sox game at Chicago's Comiskey Park, was emblematic of FM radio's resistance to new groups and sounds.

TELEVISION

Situation comedies (or sitcoms) were among the most popular shows of the decade. *M*A*S*H*, *Barney Miller*, and *The Bob Newhart Show* stood out for quality and popularity. Much as in the film industry, television began to offer more diverse and realistic forms of entertainment that mirrored some of the social and political fissures in 1970s society. Producer Norman Lear was responsible for bringing several of the shows to the networks, and the most popular was *All in the Family*. Centered on a family in New York City, the show became a platform for exploring and commenting on social issues through comedy. Topics such as the Vietnam War, gun control, homosexuality, and racism provided the subject matter for each episode. Equally progressive at the time was the *Mary Tyler Moore Show*. The show featured a single professional woman in Minneapolis and included a character who was a divorcee, a first for television. The success of these shows demonstrated the public's hunger for entertainment that addressed current issues and trends in society.

The representation of minorities on television during the 1970s also increased significantly. The groundbreaking eight-part miniseries *Roots*, based on Alex Haley's chronicle of his ancestors, aired in 1977 and drew 130 million viewers. The response of critics and viewers alike proved that programming dealing with race and historical issues such as slavery could meet with mass acceptance. Other shows that featured minority actors and storylines included *The Jeffersons* (debuting in 1975), which featured the first interracial couple on television; *Good Times*, which focused on a poor working black family in Chicago; and *Chico and the Man*, starring the Hispanic comedian Freddie Prinze.

Several programming trends in the latter part of the decade were notable for their lack of substance and social awareness. *Charlie's Angels*, which revolved around attractive female detectives, was one of the most popular yet least substantive shows on television in the 1970s. The show's breakout star, Farrah Fawcett, became a pop culture icon overnight, thanks in part to the sales of millions of posters of the actress wearing a swimsuit, and her frosted, feathered hairstyle was emulated by millions of women. Other shows, such as *Three's Company*, which featured two single women living with a single man, focused on placing opposite-sex individuals in social and sexually awkward situations. The weak themes and scantily clad women helped these shows earn the moniker of "jiggle television" by the critics.

On a related note, ABC began to skew much of its programming to younger viewers in an effort to capture that increasingly lucrative market. Offerings such as *The Brady Bunch*, *The Partridge Family*, *Happy Days*, *Laverne and Shirley*, and *Mork and Mindy* tapped into the family niche. Two shows, *The Brady Bunch* and *The Partridge Family*, were important for mainstreaming hippie and mod fashion trends. The whitewashed versions of more extreme trends were adapted for these middle-class, wholesome television families, including hot pants, miniskirts, and fringed leather vests.

Last, *Saturday Night Live* debuted in 1975 and immediately transformed late-night weekend programming by giving mature viewers something to watch during a time slot that had largely been a wasteland. The show was seen as cutting edge and pushed the envelope for network television by having performers such as George Carlin and Richard Pryor as hosts in the first season.

THE
1980s

ART MOVEMENTS

Postmodernism dominated the world of art during the last decades of the twentieth century. The term, first used by many critics to describe trends in art and literature that began in the late 1960s, became widely used during this time. Postmodern art was defined by an adventurous sense of experimentation, often expressed in the appropriation and mixing of elements from different styles, historic periods, or cultures. The new postmodern aesthetic also proclaimed no real division between good design and kitsch art, high and popular culture, or form and function. The exploration of unusual materials, both organic and inorganic, as well as the curiosity for modern technology, as evident in installation work based on video and computer technology, defined the movement.

Postmodern experimentation also extended to architecture. The motto of the period—"The house is finished. In which style do you want it?"—clearly illustrates that architects often built basic structures that could be customized at will. One of the most important American architects during this period was Charles Moore, designer of the famous Piazza d'Italia in New Orleans (1976–1979), a work often considered the epitome of postmodern architecture in the United States. Other prominent architects experimenting with form and materials included Helmuth Jahn (United Airlines Terminal at Chicago O'Hare Airport in 1987), John Portman (Los Angeles Bonaventure Hotel atrium and the Detroit Renaissance Center), and John Burgee and Philip Johnson (the Crystal Cathedral in California, the Lipstick in New York, and the AT&T building in New York). Experimental design was also crucial in theme parks and restaurants, casinos, and innovative stores.

American artists expanded the genre of contemporary art in the 1980s. Jean Michel Basquiat, who started as a graffiti artist in New York City, became influential in the neo-expressionist art movement of the late 1970s and mid-1980s. The neo-expressionist art movement was characterized by vibrant colors and strong emotions and became extremely popular during the early and mid-1980s thanks to aggressive marketing strategies by art dealers and gallery owners. Another movement, neo-pop, an extension of the pop art movement of the 1960s, continued to elevate everyday objects to the status of art. Keith Haring, a leader of the movement, was known for his simple yet intricate flat plain-line art images of babies, dogs, and people and bold use of color.

MUSIC

Music remained a big business in America during the 1980s with increased revenue from large concerts and touring festivals. Rock musicians toured the world with individual and group concerts playing venues as large as football stadiums. The 1980s was one of the most diverse periods of music in history. A wide range of musical styles were equally popular in the 1980s, including pop, heavy metal, new wave, punk, country, and rap. Each genre had its own sound and look.

Cable television made music a visual art in the 1980s. MTV aired for the first time in 1981. The first video ever played was the Buggles' "Video Killed the Radio Star," a title that foretold the tremendous impact music videos would have in the following decades. By the end of the decade, music videos had become mandatory for a song to rise on the charts, and music video had become an art form. Led by Michael Jackson's *Thriller*, music videos had to tell a story, not just show the band playing instruments. In the years following the debut of MTV, other music channels also appeared on cable targeting country music fans (CMT), African-American audiences (BET), and yuppies (VH1).

Michael Jackson in the early 1980s. [Courtesy of Photofest]

Music genres and images varied greatly during the decade. Heavy metal acts, also known as "head bangers" or "hair bands" such as Van Halen, Kiss, and Mötley Crüe, were just as popular as new wave groups such as Duran Duran, Frankie Goes to Hollywood, and Adam and the Ants. Country artists experienced mainstream popularity with crossover hits, such as Kenny Rogers' "Lady" and "The Gambler." The looks varied as much as the sounds. Metal bands and fans were identified by tight Lycra pants, T-shirts, and big hair. New wave fans were identified by bleached spiked hair, lace and ruffles (for men and women), and makeup (also for men and women).

Individual artists, such as Prince, Cyndi Lauper, Madonna, Tiffany, and Debbie Gibson, also made strong marks on the music industry and fashion. Whereas young performers such as Tiffany and Debbie Gibson took their music straight to where their young audience lived, the mall, Prince took his to the big screen with *Purple Rain*. Two of the most influential female solo artists of the 1980s, Cyndi Lauper and Madonna, erupted into the American consciousness with thundering dance rhythms and "flea-market" fashion looks. It was Madonna, however, who reigned as the biggest female performer of the decade, imitated by millions of teenage girls, known as "wannabes." The fluorescent clothes, excessive amounts of jewelry, and thrift-store look, including the off-the-shoulder shirt revealing bra straps, torn fishnet stockings, and lace gloves, was *the* look of the early 1980s. Her participation in the movie *Desperately Seeking Susan* (1985) gave even more exposure to her music, style, and persona.

One of the most influential African-American artists of the period was Michael Jackson, unanimously proclaimed as the King of Pop. In 1982, his album *Thriller* sold more than 40 million copies. Jackson introduced a particular style of dancing called "moonwalking" and was a leader in the fledgling music video industry. His single sequined glove on his right hand and leather jackets with zippers and chains were immediate fashion trends.

In 1979, Sugar Hill Gang released the first bona fide rap hit record, *Rappers Delight*. Rap music incorporated repeated lyrics that were often unintelligible and deemed obscene or violent by many and sampled previously recorded songs and record scratching. Acrobatic and break-dancing routines were also part of many early rap acts. Artists such as Kurtis Blow, M.C. Hammer, and 2 Live Crew showcased both ground-breaking music and fashions. The look cultivated by rap musicians was widely imitated by their fans, such as the case of M.C. Hammer's baggy silver parachute pants. The group Run DMC, however, brought rap fashion to the American mainstream when their crossover hit covering Aerosmith's *Walk this Way* caught the attention of pop, heavy metal, and rap fans. Soon, American youths were wearing versions of their black baggy clothes, large chain necklaces, and untied Adidas shoes. Also widely imitated by many young Americans were the clothing styles of urban break dancers, both male ("B-boys") and female ("fly girls").

Despite the self-indulgence of the 1980s, some musicians lent their name and time to support special causes, just as they did in the 1960s and 1970s. This time, instead of protesting war and discrimination, hunger was the cause. Irish singer Bob Geldolf organized *Band Aid* in 1984, an ensemble composed of prominent pop musicians, and released the song "Do They Know It's Christmas?" with proceeds benefiting famine relief in Ethiopia. In that same year, a group of American musicians recorded "We Are the World" as a fundraiser to fight worldwide hunger. The album sold more than 4 million copies. Geldolf followed up with another pioneering effort in 1985 with *Live Aid*, a concert event that continued to provide financial support for famine relief in Ethiopia. John Cougar Mellencamp launched a similar effort in Champaign, Illinois, in 1985. His concert, *Farm Aid*, was similar to Geldolf's event, but with proceeds benefiting American farmers.

LITERATURE

Literature in the last decades of the twentieth century was eclectic and targeted to specific markets. Some fiction works focused on social issues, such as William Kennedy's *Ironweed* (1984), Alice Walker's *The Color Purple* (1983), Larry McMurtry's *Lonesome Dove* (1986), and Toni Morrison's *Beloved* (1988). Other fiction works illustrated 1980s American consumerism and egocentricity, such as Tom Wolfe's 1988 tribute to the culture of money and luxury, *The Bonfire of the Vanities*.

Many works of popular literature in the 1980s drew inspiration from the Cold War with Russia, including Tom Clancy's *The Hunt for Red October* (1984) and *Red Storm Rising* (1986). Whereas works by suspense author Stephen King, such as *Christine* (1983), *Cujo* (1981), and *Pet*

Cemetery (1983) kept readers on edge, the romance novels of Danielle Steel swept America off its collective feet. Americans also embraced books by authors aiming to bring astronomy, physics, and other hard sciences to the general public, such as Stephen Hawkins's *A Brief History of Time* (1988). *Cosmos* (1985) by Carl Sagan was successful enough to even prompt a television series.

The importance of success in the business world also launched a number of books on business management up the bestseller chart, such as 1984's *In Search of Excellence* by Thomas J. Peters. Inspirational and self-help literature also became particularly popular in the period with publications such as Bill Cosby's *Fatherhood* (1986) and Stephen R. Coney's *The 7 Habits of Highly Effective People* (1990). The American obsession with fitness and dieting made bestsellers of manuals and cookbooks for several dieting programs. The first "Dress for Success" books appeared in the late 1970s, but the 1980s witnessed the appearance of many manuals coaching both men and women on wardrobe and grooming practices.

THEATER

Englishman Andrew Lloyd Webber dominated the new musical scene in the 1980s with Broadway and international hits such as *Evita* (1980), *Cats* (1986), *Starlight Express* (1987), and *The Phantom of the Opera* (1988). Stephen Sondheim became the most prolific American musical author of the period with shows including *Sunday in the Park with George* (1984) and *Into the Woods* (1988). Also successful was the French team of Claude-Michel Schönberg and Alain Boublil, responsible for the creation of *Les Miserables* (1987) and *Miss Saigon* (1991).

Distinguished American playwrights of the period included Lanford Wilson with *Fifth of July* (1980) and *Burn This* (1987), Lee Blessing with *A Walk in the Woods* (1988), and David Henry Hwang with *M. Butterfly* (1988). August Wilson was the most prolific playwright of the period with a series that encompassed the African American, including *Master Harold and the Boys* (1982), *Fences* (1987), and *Joe Turner's Come & Gone* (1988). Many Broadway plays also went on to become successful movies, including *Children of a Lesser God* (1980) by Mark Medoff, *Biloxi Blues* (1985) by Neil Simon, and *Six Degrees of Separation* (1991) by John Guare.

MOVIES

Movie genres in the 1980s were as diverse as the musical and literary offerings. Films offerings ranged in themes from Cold War tensions (the James Bond series) to culture (*Amadeus*, *The Last Emperor*, and *Dangerous Liaisons*) to exploration, of both space (*E.T.* and *The Empire Strikes Back*) and continents (*Raiders of the Lost Ark*). As a result, glamorous gowns, tuxedos, corsets, and fedoras filtered back into American fashions.

One of the most popular movies of 1980 was *American Gigolo*. *American Gigolo* epitomized the conspicuous consumption of the decade, with silk bed sheets, Mercedes Benz cars, and Armani suits. The movie made Giorgio Armani a household name in the United States because the film featured approximately thirty suits designed by him for Richard Gere's character. The movie emphasized the erotic appeal of Armani's creations (Steele 1997, 133) and turned him into the designer of choice for many stars.

Another movie synonymous with the 1980s' conspicuous consumption culture was *Wall Street* (1987), featuring Daryl Hannah, Charlie Sheen, and Michael Douglas. The movie centered on New York's yuppie stockbroker crowd and dressed perfectly groomed characters in elegant Italian double-breasted suits. Michael Douglas, as the main character Gordon Gekko, delivered the famous speech: "Greed, for lack of a better word, is good. Greed is right. Greed works," now considered the perfect manifesto of the self-centered culture of the 1980s. Another movie that portrayed the American business world was *Working Girl* (1988), in which Melanie Griffith played a secretary with an excellent sense for business. The actresses in the film were dressed in quintessential 1980s power suits, complete with tennis shoes for walking from the subway to the office.

With the popularity of "hanging out at the mall," movie producers had a captive teenage audience with money to spend and time to kill. Several movies in the 1980s focused on teenage life and coming of age. *Footloose* (1984), *Sixteen Candles* (1984), *Pretty in Pink* (1986), *The Breakfast Club* (1985), and *Fast Times at Ridgemont High* (1982) made Kevin Bacon, Sean Penn, and members of the "Brat Pack" (Molly Ringwald, Rob Lowe, Emilio Estevez, Ally Sheedy, and Andrew McCarthy) teen icons to be emulated. The most successful young actor, however, was Tom Cruise. He became a screen legend for dancing in his underwear in *Risky Business* (1983), but it was his performance in *Top Gun* (1986) that turned his military cropped haircut and bomber jackets into the trendiest look of the season.

Movies that focused on music and dance were particularly popular in the 1980s. Alan Parker's 1980 movie *Fame* was the first to make legwarmers popular among American teenagers, but the 1983 movie *Flashdance*

Michael Douglas as Gordon Gekko in the 1987 film *Wall Street*. [Courtesy of Photofest]

Yuppies. The December issue of *Newsweek* magazine declared 1984 the "Year of the Yuppie." As the American economy recovered in 1983 and the communications and electronics industries experienced a boom, a new breed of professionals appeared. Well-paid young urban professionals, known as yuppies, believed that social worth and status were primarily defined by income. The 1987 film *Wall Street* is often considered a defining example of American lifestyle in the 1980s. The poignant depiction of yuppie materialism and greed also provided a perfect illustration of excess in fashion and appearance among the powerful corporate set. During the 1980s, yuppies, such as those portrayed in the movie, enjoyed well-paid high-level positions and a disposable income that allowed them to become fashion innovators for several trends that were later adopted by the general population. Yuppies were the first market to embrace expensive gourmet coffee drinks, specialized branded running shoes, as well as the use of personal assistants, stylists, and buyers. The American media, and Hollywood in particular, exported this image to the rest of the world, often prompting criticism toward a nation already perceived abroad as too centered on individuality and capitalism.

was destined to make gym wear the next fashion craze in America. The movie made off-the-shoulder sweatshirts, tank tops, tight-fitting pants, torn jeans, and leg warmers ubiquitous in the country. Other films such as *Breakin'* (1984) and *Beat Street* (1984) helped to expand rap music to a broader audience.

The Motion Picture Association of America introduced a new movie rating, PG-13, in 1984. The new rating, placed between PG and R, was created to inform parents about violence and other inappropriate content. Movie rentals in the 1980s had become affordable and provided families with at-home entertainment, especially because most families immediately purchased the latest tech gadget, the VCR.

RADIO

Radio faced ever-increasing competition from television but remained a vital form of communication for many Americans, particularly during commuter rush hours. A number of radio stations provided specific formats of music catering to diverse audiences who were usually listening to FM stations as opposed to those in the AM band. The rise in popularity of MTV and availability of music (with video) over cable channels drove listeners at home to their televisions instead of radio on their "hi-fi" systems.

Important changes in radio regulations changed the business of American radio. In 1987, the Federal Communications Commission abolished the fairness doctrine requiring radio and television stations to show different sides for any controversial issue (Marty 1997, 282), allowing the rise of partial news casting. Loosening of ownership limits created dominance of large national chains in local markets, eliminating many small stations and providing stronger censorship over content, particularly after the rise of "shock radio" in the 1980s.

TELEVISION

No one show better typifies the 1980s than the CBS soap opera *Dallas*. Airing from 1978 to 1991, the show embodied the affluence of the decade. Centered on the financial and extramarital exploitations of Texan J. R. Ewing (Larry Hagman), each episode was a tribute to the trappings of wealth and power. The male characters drove luxury cars, and the female characters, constantly busy with charity fundraisers, were always dressed in extravagant gowns created by designers such as Ungaro and Valentino.

ABC's response to the success of *Dallas* was *Dynasty* (1981–1989), with costumes designed by Nolan Miller. The show's emphasis on fashion was so strong that many critics considered it a one-hour-long excuse to showcase glamorous apparel. The story's villain was Alexis Carrington, played by Joan Collins. She was dressed in bright vibrant-colored outfits made of silk and polyester with oversized shoulders, deep cleavage, tight skirts, tailored jackets, and elegant jewelry. The heroine of the story, Krystle, was played by Linda Evans in trouser sets, silk blouses, and simpler gowns, usually in subtle pastel colors to create a contrast with Alexis' striking appearance.

The television show "Dynasty," which ran between 1981 and 1989, illustrates the exaggerated shoulder look of women's fashions in the 1980s. [Courtesy of Photofest]

Another extremely popular drama was the NBC series *Miami Vice* (1984–1989). Focused on high-profile drug dealers from Latin America, the show was a glamorous and gritty departure from previous police shows such as *T.J. Hooker* and *Hill Street Blues*. Each week, the lead characters, Crockett, played by Don Johnson, and Tubbs, played by Philip Michael Thomas, pursued drug traffickers through undercover sting operations that required them to dress and live like celebrities. As such, Crockett donned pastel jackets with white pants and T-shirts instead of collared shirts. The character's unshaven look was complemented by his custom of wearing loafers without socks. Tubbs wore perfectly cut smooth dark suits as a clear contrast with Crockett's style. Both styles were evolved into crucial looks for men's wear of the period.

Other popular television shows that launched fashion trends included *The A Team* (1983–1987), which turned actor Mr. T, his gold chains, and his Mohawk into popular fashions. *The Dukes of Hazard* (1979–1985) was responsible for the widespread use of cut-out jean shorts known as "daisy dukes," named after the character Daisy Duke in the program. Additionally, Malcolm-Jamal Warner's crown hair style and Bill Cosby's bold, bright-patterned sweaters became popular as a result of *The Cosby Show* (1984–1992).

Interest in glamorous lifestyle was furthered by the reality show *Lifestyles of the Rich and Famous*, which ran from 1984 to 1995. This show emphasized the "good life," offering viewers a window into the lives of successful entertainers and other wealthy individuals. The tag line, "Champaign wishes and caviar dreams," became synonymous with success. Cable networks also began dedicating airtime to fashion-centric programming, including CNN's *Style with Elsa Klensch* in 1980 and MTV's *House of Style*, which debuted in 1989 with supermodel Cindy Crawford as host.

THE
1990s AND 2000s

ART MOVEMENTS

Postmodernism continued as the prevailing art form through the 1990s and beyond. Experimentation with materials and images expanded into non-Western imagery in the creations by many Western artists. In fashion, this was evident in the symbols used in body jewelry and tattoos, which came from a variety of cultures, including Japanese, Celtic, and Egyptian. The postmodern anti-design ideology was expressed through anti-functionalism trends in architecture and fashion. Although the ideas and experimentation behind the anti-design movement had little impact on industrial design, it was often featured in museum exhibits and academic discussions. Some of the anti-design trends, however, had a strong presence in wearable art pieces incorporating recycling, deconstructionism, and anachronistic historicism.

In the 1990s, artists began to increasingly experiment with video art installations. Video art, which may be either projected on a video screen or executed as a three-dimensional installation, used both video and audio elements to engage the viewer. As the end of the twentieth century drew to a close, video art leveraged new computer technologies to mount full-scale multimedia art installations. These three-dimensional installations encouraged viewers to interact with the installation by moving through architectural spaces. One of the leading video artists of the decade was American Bill Viola.

Other artists, such as James Turrell, experimented with controlling and projecting light to create the perception of form and shape, whereas work of other artists, such as Robert Mapplethorpe and Andres Serrano, stirred controversy at the national level. The Cincinnati Contemporary Arts Center was prosecuted under charges of obscenity in 1990 after exhibiting the work of Robert Mapplethorpe, which included erotic homosexual portraits and sadomasochist images. Andres Serrano's photography of corpses and his controversial "Piss Christ," a picture of a crucifix submerged in the artist's urine, also added to the debate regarding what constitutes art. Although some rushed to defend each artist's right to "artistic freedom," others considered the work offensive and devoid of social discourse.

MUSIC

Arena concerts, touring festivals, promotional materials, CDs, and music downloads all translated to big profits for musicians and music promoters in the 1990s. In the 1990s, concert venues and bands increasingly contracted the services of ticket brokers to manage the sale of concert tickets. Ticket prices for large arena shows skyrocketed during the decade, in part because of the additional fees charged by brokers such as Ticketmaster, increasing the price of concerts tickets to $100 or more. The day of the $20 ticket was over; music was big business with big profits.

In 1991, the inaugural Lollapalooza concert was held, featuring Jane's Addiction, Violent Femmes, Butthole Surfers, Nine Inch Nails, and others. The concert, reminiscent of Woodstock but geared to Generation X, traveled across the United States annually from 1991 to 1997 and was resurrected again in 2003. In 1997, the first Lilith Fair concert, featuring only female performers, was launched. Organized by Sarah McLachlan, the traveling concert was held annually through 1999, with some proceeds from ticket sales going to women's charities. The 1990s also saw a revival of Woodstock, with concerts in 1994 and 1999. However, the 1990s version of Woodstock failed to live up to the "peace and love" theme associated with the original 1969 concert, with ticket prices at $150 and Pay Per View cable television coverage.

When CDs were introduced by Sony in 1982, most people assumed that this format of digital music would dominate the market for several decades. Concerns also grew in the industry about the ease of creating high-quality copies when CD-burning technology became available to the public. In 1991, however, the MPEG-1 Audio Layer digital music format, better known as MP3, was developed quickly, replacing the popularity of CDs. Internet sites such as Napster, Audiogalaxy, and Kazaa developed in the 1990s, allowing individuals the opportunity to download and share music for free. The music industry reacted strongly to this new trend and fought to criminalize the practice. By 2006, downloading for a fee had become a common practice and an additional source of income for recording artists. In 2001, Apple released the first version of the iPod, an extremely small portable media player, along with the website iTunes, for downloading music. The device became an immediate favorite and somewhat of a fashion accessory as specialty covers or "skins" were designed to protect and transport the device.

In the years following the debut of MTV, other cable channels such as VH1, BET, and CMT appeared on the scene to serve specific populations. Fashion continued to be strongly influenced by the image portrayed by musicians in their videos. Dance crazes such as slam dancing, line dancing, the lambada, and the macarena often started and ended on music television. Musicians also chose to bring street trends to their videos, as was the case when Madonna popularized pose dancing in her video for

"Vogue." Pose dancing originated in Harlem with gay black and Latino males who imitated poses, struts, and stances of high-fashion models in *Vogue* magazine and on the catwalk.

Madonna, ever the music and fashion chameleon, continued to dominate the music scene in the 1990s, reinventing her sound and herself several times throughout the decade. For her *Blond Ambition* tour in 1990, she collaborated with fashion designer Jean-Paul Gaultier to create the "underwear as outerwear" look with corsets and bustiers reflecting fetish and dominatrix details. By the late 1990s, she also explored Goth looks and wore a Goth-inspired black satin gown designed by Olivier Theyskend for the 1998 Academy Awards. As Madonna moved into the new millennium, she continued to experiment with her sound and look, incorporating elements of Western, ghetto-fabulous, and 1970s disco fashions.

The pop music scene in the 1990s was dominated by "boy bands," vocal harmony groups composed of young men with dancing skills and fashion sense that would appeal to young women. The New Kids on the Block was the first successful boy band, releasing their first CD in 1988.

Does Sex Sell Children's Clothes? In the last two decades of the twentieth century and continuing to the present, American advertisers, as well as the entertainment media, have been under attack for the increased content of sexual material in products portraying children or marketed to them. The popularity of the Internet further increased the potential exposure of American children to graphic violence and sex. Children were also exposed to oversexualized imagery through popular music in which artists often wore revealing apparel and explicitly portrayed themselves as sexual objects. Girls began wearing makeup and fitted, revealing clothing at earlier ages inspired by such artists as Madonna in the 1980s and then Britney Spears and Christina Aguilera, as well as by dolls like Barbie and Bratz. (Ironically, Madonna appeared in the news media in the late 2000s declaring herself a strict mother who did not let her children watch television.) In the early 1980s, Calvin Klein was heavily criticized for a campaign featuring a very young Brooke Shields in an overt sexual pose and claiming, "Nothing comes between me and my Calvins." The company faced a stronger reaction in 1999 when it introduced an advertising campaign for boys and girls underwear featuring children as models in what many considered provocative poses. Billboards placed in New York were removed only a day after they appeared, and the ads prompted an investigation by the Federal Bureau of Investigation.

New Kids was followed by acts such as Take That in 1990, Backstreet Boys in 1996, and 'N Sync in 1997. The oversized jeans, T-shirts, and leather jackets with fade or flattop haircuts became *the* look for teenage and college youths across America.

The British group Spice Girls appeared in 1996 as a female version of the boy band. The fashion-aware members were distinguished stylistically by their "spice" names: Sporty, Baby, Scary, Posh, and Ginger. The 1990s also saw the rise of young female solo artists such as Britney Spears, Christina Aguilera, and Jessica Simpson, whose fashion styles were imitated by many young girls in the late 1990s the same way that Madonna was imitated in the 1980s.

Grunge was an underground music movement launched in Seattle that became popular across America in the early 1990s. Prominent bands that defined the look and sound of grunge music include Pearl Jam, Soundgarden, Hole, and Nirvana. Kurt Cobain and Courtney Love were the model icons for grunge fashion style. The grunge look consisted of homemade, shabby baby doll dresses for women and recycled jeans and flannel shirts

Grunge-rock band Hole, 1998. Shown from left: Melissa Auf der Maur, Courtney Love, Patty Schemel, and Eric Erlandson. Auf der Maur wears a corset-style bodice. [Courtesy of Photofest]

for men, with both sexes donning army boots. The grunge style influenced collections of some American designers, such as Anna Sui and Marc Jacobs, who sold "shabby chic" clothes at designer prices.

The mid-1990s also saw the explosion of Latin music in the United States. The first Latino artist to become widely known was Selena, a Tex-Mex singer murdered by a close friend in 1995. Other Hispanic artists that enjoyed popularity included Gloria Estefan, Ricky Martin, Jennifer Lopez, Marc Anthony, Enrique Iglesias, Shakira, and the Buena Vista Social Club. The preference for body-conscious fashions by Latino artists, such as Jennifer Lopez, and African-American artists, such as Destiny's Child, led Lopez and Destiny's Child lead singer Beyonce Knowles to launch their own apparel lines that emphasized women's voluptuous, "bootylicious" curves. The music scene of the early 2000s, although eclectic, was still dominated by young pop vocalists such as Britney Spears, Pink, and Christina Aguilera, or hip-hop acts such as Outkast, Kanye West, and Rhianna. The music market for children and teenagers was thriving in the 2000s with the popularity of Disney Channel programs *Hannah Montana* and *High School Musical*.

LITERATURE

Postmodern interpretations of love, small-town life, fear of death, family dynamics, and personal triumph were reflected in the literature of the 1990s. Pulitzer Prize winners of the period included *Rabbit at Rest* by John Updike (1991), *The Hours* by Michael Cunningham (1999), and *Empire Falls* by Richard Russo (2002). Other popular works of fictions included *Midnight in the Garden of Good and Evil* by John Berendt (1994), *Divine Secrets of the Ya Ya Sisterhood* by Rebecca Wells (1996), *Cold Mountain* by Charles Frazier (1997), and *Memoirs of a Geisha* by Arthur S. Golden (1997).

In popular literature, Americans particularly favored thrillers with detective, political, and medical plots. Popular authors in the genre were John Grisham and Michael Crichton. *The Firm* (1991) and *The Pelican Brief* (1992) by Grisham and *Jurassic Park* (1990) by Crichton both espoused themes warning of the lure of power and the danger of playing God. Another popular thriller of the period was Bret Easton Ellis's fictional portrayal of serial killer and fashionista Patrick Bateman in *American Psycho* (1991) in which Bateman's personal grooming and fashion sense are described in as much detail as his killings.

The downsizing, "right sizing," and globalization of American business resulted in numerous publications on business management. One of the most popular of the decade, *Who Moved my Cheese* by Spencer Johnson, used humor and two mice to discuss strategies for anticipating and coping with change in the work place. The volume of publications in the inspirational and self-help category of literature continued to increase. As the decade of "me" (the 1980s) closed, individuals were left searching for self-esteem and direction. People turned to *Chicken Soup for the Soul* (1990) for transformation and hope. *Chicken Soup for the Soul* was first in a series of highly successful publications by Jack Canfield and Mark Victor Hansen, which expanded to target niche audiences such as *Chicken Soup for Every Mom's Soul*, *Chicken Soup for Sisters*, *Chicken Soup for the African American Women's Soul*, and *Chicken Soup for the Scrapbooker's Soul*.

The audio books or books on tape of the 1980s were replaced first, in the 1990s, by books on compact discs and then at the turn of the millennium by downloads to PDAs (for personal digital assistants) and MP3 players. Digital libraries were established, allowing millions of people around the world to download and read books online. Project Gutenberg is the oldest of those initiatives and has made available several books that are currently in the public domain. Online bookstores such as Amazon and websites for popular booksellers such as Borders and Barnes & Noble provide readers with a search platform for locating rare and unique editions as well as purchasing current works.

THEATER

Broadway theater was framed by the experimentation and innovation of new plays and musicals. Successful musical revivals included *The King and I* (1996), *Chicago* (1997), *Cabaret* (1998), and *A Chorus Line* (2007). The long-standing practice of Broadway musicals becoming movies was reversed in the 1990s when several new musicals were inspired by previously released musical films. *Meet Me in Saint Louis* (1990), *The Producers* (2001), *Hairspray* (2003), *Legally Blonde* (2007), and *Spamalot* (2005), based on the 1974 film *Monty Python and the Holy Grail*, were all films before they were Broadway productions. Disney was particularly successful at bringing animated features to the stage with *Beauty and the Beast* (1994) and *The Lion King* (1998). Another trend was the creation of musicals based on the works of famous rock acts. The storyline for one such production, *Mamma Mia* (2002), was told by the strategic arrangement of the hit songs by 1970s Swedish pop group ABBA. Other productions that followed the *Mamma Mia* format included *Taboo* (2002), written by Boy George and based on his life and music, and *Movin' Out* (2003), inspired by Billy Joel's songs. Other important musicals of the period included *Crazy for You* (1992), *Rent* (1996), *Titanic* (1997), *Hairspray* (2003), and *Spring Awakening* (2007).

Theatrical plays continued to expound on a diverse array of themes. Distinguished American playwrights, such as Tony Kushner, presented *Angels in America* (1993 and 1994), which portrayed the ideological conflict between homosexuality and religion faced by many individuals. In 2003, Kushner's work was presented as a miniseries for cable on HBO. The series was the most widely watched miniseries on cable, winning both the Emmy and Golden Globe for Best Mini-Series in 2003. Many Broadway plays from previous decades, such as *Six Degrees of Separation* (1991) by John Guare and *Proof* (2001) by David Auburn, also went on to become successful movies during this period.

MOVIES

One of the biggest themes to dominate motion pictures of the 1990s was historic fiction. Successful historic movies of the decade included *Braveheart* (1995), *The English Patient* (1996), *Titanic* (1997), and *Shakespeare in Love* (1998). In the late 1990s, cable and big screen productions of three Jane Austen novels were completed: *Emma* (1996), *Sense and Sensibility* (1995), and *Pride and Prejudice* (1995 and 2005). Not surprisingly, with so much attention being paid to Austen's work, women's fashions of the late 1990s also witnessed a preference for Empire waists in both tops and dresses. So popular were the themes of Austen's work that they were also retold in modern adaptations. Amy Heckerling's *Clueless* (1995) was based on Austen's novel *Emma* and featured a detailed look at the life and fashion style of Los Angeles upper-class teenagers. In 2001, Baz Luhrmann's anachronistically postmodern *Moulin Rouge* also added to the interest for corsets and tulle skirts as a result of those featured in the musical film.

Science fiction movies regained popularity at the turn of the twenty-first century and brought innovative fashion trends to avant-garde fashion groups in the country. Some young people imitated the long vinyl and leather coats and black outfits seen in *The Matrix* trilogy from 1999 to 2003. George Lucas brought back the *Star Wars* franchise, releasing *Episode I: The Phantom Menace* in 1999, sixteen years after the last installment, *Star Wars Episode VI: Return of the Jedi* (1983). Many fans attended the premiere dressed as characters in the movie and purchased books that described the production, including the costume design. *The Lord of the Rings* trilogy (2001, 2002, and 2003), directed by Peter Jackson and based on the beloved books by J. R. R. Tolkien, was also extremely popular.

The last installment, *The Return of the King*, went on to receive the Academy Award for best movie in 2003. Another hit with worldwide audiences was the series of movies based on J. K. Rowling's *Harry Potter* books, which generated large profits not only in the box office but also in product licensing, particularly in the children's apparel sector.

Two films were released in the 1990s focusing on the fashion industry: *Ready-to-Wear* (1994) and *Unzipped* (1995). *Ready-to-Wear*, or "prêt-à-porter," by Robert Altman centered around fashion week in Paris, whereas *Unzipped* presents a day in the life of American designer Isaac Mizrahi. In 2006, the release of *The Devil Wears Prada* (Lauren Weisberger's 2003 novel) narrates the ordeal of a young personal assistant working for a fashion magazine editor rumored to be inspired on *Vogue's* editor Anna Wintour.

In the 1990s, Disney also experienced a renaissance with the production of animated film hits such as *The Little Mermaid* (1989), *Beauty and the Beast* (1991), and *The Lion King* (1994). The success of the new movies also motivated Disney to re-release their classic works on a video home system (VHS) or digital video discs (DVDs). The success of both the new ventures and the resurgence in popularity of the classics spawned a highly successful and lucrative marketing campaign for Disney toys and apparel, prompting the expansion of the Disney Store in malls across America. The Academy of Motion Picture Arts and Sciences created a category for animated movies in 2001, awarding movies such as *The Incredibles* (2004) and *Ratatouille* (2007) with Oscars.

RADIO

In the 1990s, radio had to compete with both television and the Internet for the attention of the listening public. Internet radio allowed listeners to access radio broadcasts from all over the world right on their computer. Local radio channels also had to compete with the new "robo DJ." Unlike local radio stations, which continued to refine and narrow their market niche, "Jack" radio stations are pre-programmed with thousands of songs that rarely repeat themselves, from a variety of genres in hopes of attracting the widest possible audience. By comparison, local channels may play the same Top 40 Billboard hits every hour in an order either selected by the DJ or the corporate programmer.

The popularity of satellite radio providers XM and Sirius also changed the face of radio during this period. By the new millennium, millions of individuals were paying for radio subscriptions in the same manner in which they had been paying for cable television. Satellite radio channels provide subscribers with hundreds of specialty programming channels such as NFL (the National Football League) sports, NASCAR (National Association for Stock Car Auto Racing), Martha Stewart, Oprah, and Howard Stern, as well as music channels dedicated to specific music styles, such as 1980s, punk, heavy metal, and rap.

TELEVISION

The way Americans watched television changed drastically in the last decades of the twentieth century with the newfound ability to record programs and watch them at a later time. First on VHS tape in the 1980s then on higher-quality format DVDs in the 1990s, and then on TiVo, introduced in 1997, Americans no longer had to be home when television programs were aired to be able to see them. Cable programming, satellite dishes, and digital cable with "on-demand" programming further expanded viewers' options for program content. By 1998, approximately 66 percent of all American households subscribed to cable television (Arden 2003, 32), which featured up to 200 or more channels. The abundance of channels to select from also generated a new concept, "channel surfing" right from the couch with a remote control.

Cable and satellite television offered channels devoted exclusively to sports, music, reruns of classic television, history, crafts, cooking, and other specific interest. E! Entertainment network's sister channel, the Style network, offered shows that concentrated exclusively on fashion, design, and lifestyle choices. Whereas the depth and breadth of content on cable channels expanded, the American alphabet networks such as NBC, ABC, CBS, and FOX encountered increased pressure from the general public and government agencies regarding the prevalence of violence and sexual content in their programming. The industry responded with the creation of devices that increased parental control on both network and cable channels and with a television rating system from the Federal Communications Commission in 1996.

By the end of the decade, television shows such as *Roseanne* (1988–1997), *Married with Children* (1987–1997), and *The Simpsons* (1989–present) presented the American public with the trial and tribulations of working-class families. The moral values and parenting practices were clearly different from those pictured in previous television programs that had carried forward the classic ideal family originally introduced in the 1950s. Sitcoms in the 1990s often centered on odd characters or families and incorporated depictions of the lifestyle of Americans in several different areas of the country. Particularly popular during this period were *Home*

Improvement (1991–1999), *Seinfeld* (1989–1998), *Frasier* (1993–2004), *Dharma and Greg* (1997–2002), and *Will and Grace* (1998–2006), which introduced the first male gay characters as protagonists of a primetime show. Whereas programming such as *Beverly Hills 90210* (1990–2000) focused on the privileged lives of California teens, *ER* (1994–2009) and *Party of Five* (1994–2000) focused on true hardships of alcoholism, death, and domestic violence.

The changing demographics of America, particularly the delay in marriage, resulted in more programs targeting twenty- and thirty-year-olds. Shows such as *Melrose Place* (1992–1999) and *Friends* (1994–2004) featured single characters living exciting, independent lives, without spouses or children. *Friends*, in particular, was so popular that many American women copied Jennifer Aniston's layered hairstyle, dubbed "the Rachel" after the show's character. Cable television also entered sitcom programming, targeting independent, career-minded single women. HBO's *Sex and the City* (1998–2004), based on the book by Candace Bushnell, focused on the lives and fashions of four single women in New York City, making Manolo Blahnik, Prada, and Jimmy Choo household names.

The quantity of magazine format or "info-tainment" television programming continued to increase in the last decade of the twentieth century, especially related to fashion. As if torn from the pages of *Vogue* magazine, E!'s *Fashion Emergency*, CNN's *Style with Elsa Klensch*, AMC's *Hollywood Fashion Machines*, and TLC's *What Not to Wear* became daily and weekly guides for style makeovers and fashionable dress. Also relevant were Bravo's *Queer Eye for the Straight Guy*, in which a group of gay men provided fashion and other lifestyle tips to participants, and *Project Runway*, in which young designers competed for runway spots at New York's fashion week. Television programs focusing on the search for successful fashion models included *America's Next Top Model* (2003–2008) and *Make Me a Supermodel* (2008). Oprah Winfrey, whose daytime talk show originated in the 1980s, continued as strong as ever into the late 2000s, offering advice, self-help, political discussions, celebrity interviews, and many shows on fashion and style, especially emphasizing fashion for busy and middle-class women.

Reality television had gained some strength in the 1970s and 1980s but experienced a boom in the late 1990s and again in the late 2000s as a result of the relative inexpensiveness of such programming compared with scripted and acted shows and the three-month television writers' strike of late 2007 to early 2008. MTV was the forerunner of the craze with the series *The Real World*, which debuted in 1992. The popularity of *The Real World* inspired several shows with similar format debuting in the early

2000s, including *Survivor*, *The Amazing Race*, *The Apprentice*, and *Big Brother*. Reality shows also followed the daily lives of celebrities, including Anna Nicole Smith, Jessica Simpson and Nick Lachey, the Osbourne family, and wrestler Hulk Hogan. Other reality shows focused on makeover programming, often incorporating extreme transformation and plastic surgery, such as *The Swan*, *Ten Years Younger,* and *The Biggest Loser*, which tracked dramatic weight loss in obese people.

REFERENCES

Arden, J. B. (2003) *America's Meltdown: The Lowest-Common-Denominator Society.* Westport, CT: Praeger Publishers.

Karney, R., ed. (1995) *Chronicle of the Cinema.* New York: Dorling Kindersley.

MacDonald, J. F. (1990) *One Nation Under Television: The Rise and Decline of Network TV.* New York: Pantheon.

Marty, M. A. (1997) *Daily Life in the United States, 1960–1990: Decades of Discord.* The Greenwood Press "Daily Life through History" Series. Westport, CT: Greenwood Press.

Phillips, L. (1999) *The American Century: Art and Culture 1950–2000.* New York: Whitney Museum of American Art.

Rielly, E. J. (2003) *The 1960s.* Westport, CT: Greenwood Press.

Steele, V. (1997) *Fifty Years of Fashion: New Look to Now.* New Haven, CT: Yale University Press.

4

Daily Life

The last half of the twentieth century witnessed an increase in the amount of disposable income individuals and families had to engage in leisure activities but, ironically, also witnessed a decrease in the amount of free time they had to pursue them. As the decade progressed, the emphasis on family and family values was replaced with an emphasis on work and the individual. Over the five decades that comprised the last half of the twentieth century, society shifted from family cohesion and social conformity (the 1950s) to questioning authority (the 1960s and 1970s) to business and individual success (the 1980s) to challenging the definition of success and family (the 1990s).

The changes in personal and family values are immediately identifiable by examining changes in weddings and wedding attire. The 1950s witnessed a return to traditional "white" weddings: the bride clad in a big white dress, escorted down the church aisle by her father, waiting to be whisked away to Niagara Falls for her honeymoon by her adoring groom. In contrast, weddings in the 1960s and 1970s became more about making individual statements of commitment than public ceremony. In fact, the number of weddings declined during the period, and the average age of those exchanging nuptial vows slightly increased. When individuals did elect to marry, the service (not ceremony) was just as likely to be outdoors in casual dress as in a church with a formal reception. The 1980s saw a return of the formal church wedding but not because of a nostalgia for tradition. The wedding day, not to mention the engagement party, bridal shower, bachelor party, and bachelorette party, was the pinnacle event for the "me" generation, a lavish affair dedicated to just two individuals. Whereas the 1990s saw a continuation of this trend for some couples, for others, the 1990s provided the ultimate challenge to the institution of marriage, same-sex weddings, and commitment ceremonies.

Concerns over diet, physical fitness, and overall appearance are consistent themes across the past fifty years. Smoking and drinking might have been commonplace in the 1950s, even for pregnant women, but, as the period progressed, the health risks associated with both resulted in the addition of surgeon general warning labels on cigarettes and alcohol. The days of the "three-martini business lunch" were gone, and, smoking was not only banned in the workplace but also in front of the workplace, in restaurants, and in bars.

Although "sweating" was considered unsightly, especially for women in the 1950s, attitudes regarding exercise rapidly changed. Health clubs, home fitness equipment, "workout" tapes and DVDs, marathon races, and Iron Man competitions grew in prevalence throughout the era. Diet pills and diet plans were plentiful, each promising to "take the weight off and keep it off." In the last two decades of the century, what could not be sweated off was cut off or sucked out through plastic surgery. The increasing pressure for women to be thinner year after year was cause for concern and led many to cite the fact that one of the greatest sex symbols of the twentieth century, Marilyn Monroe, would be considered overweight by today's standard size; she was a size 12.

The final decades of the twentieth century also saw America and the world struggle with effects of disease. As if the ever-increasing cancer rates during this period were not tragic enough, in the 1980s the world faced a new disease, AIDS. Virtually unstoppable for decades, the disease devastated the homosexual population and third-world nations, until successful treatment options could be developed at the beginning of the twenty-first century.

THE

1950s

SOCIAL OCCASIONS

Formality returned to weddings in the 1950s. Weddings in the 1940s were often informal affairs initiated by a call to war. Wedding dresses were often simple, whether the result of wartime rationing or a rushed ceremony. Three weddings, two fictional and one fairy tale, set the tone for all weddings in the 1950s. *The Father of the Bride* (1950) and *A Place in the Sun* (1951), both starring Elizabeth Taylor, depicted traditional weddings in which daughters were escorted to the altar by their fathers and not rushing to the justice of the peace. Women were eager to mimic the dresses and traditions portrayed in these two movies. The hourglass shape with full crinoline skirts, rounded shoulders, and pointed bosom was sculpted in satin and French lace, available again from the factories that were closed during the war. The fairy-tale wedding of Grace Kelly to Prince Rainier III in 1956 also influenced the look of wedding gowns. Her poise and elegance romanticized the dozens of yards of silk taffeta, peau de soie, and Valenciennes lace of her wedding gown.

Social occasions were centered on school, family, neighborhood, church, volunteer charities, and company outings in the 1950s. Families were active in the church during the fifties because the church reinforced the belief of a moral world. Church fellowship provided an opportunity to socialize with those who shared the same moral values and shared the same views of the world. Women, and mothers in particular, had full social calendars booked with girl scouts, cub scouts, school events, parent-teacher association meetings, typing the Sunday church bulletins, and organizing rummage sales. Women also had their own neighborhood routines, which included coffee with the girls after the men left for work and perhaps an afternoon card game. Participation in these gatherings ensured that one was kept abreast of the neighborhood gossip, instead of being the subject of it.

The man around the house was expected to include company social events on his calendar. The successful company man had a wife who was the consummate hostess as well as gracious cocktail party companion. She was refined and dignified, always complimenting the right person at the right time and knowing when to stay out of a conversation that was "company talk" and above her head. Instead of appearing well read from an intellectual perspective, she was expected to be able to converse with the ladies about domestic activities such as shopping, dining, school activities, and charity efforts.

The corporate mindset was focused not just on business but in building a community of employees who shared family values and forthright citizenship. Many large corporations or plants had a committee whose function was to arrange family outings and activities. Typical activities ranged from bus trips to see Broadway musicals and noteworthy museums, to adventure outings for the kids to Frontier City, to company picnics and carnivals. Many companies sponsored visits by children to the office or plant on a special day to tour the facility and see where "Daddy" worked. One of the biggest corporations of the period, IBM, also believed in fitness for the family and built country clubs with golf courses and swimming pools for the employees and their families to enjoy.

The "patio culture" of the 1950s was all about entertaining. Progressive suppers, cocktail parties, backyard barbecues, and holiday get-togethers were all a part of the "see and be seen" philosophy. Each event, of course, had its own unwritten dress code. A woman doing her part to support her husband's corporate aspirations had to have the right outfit for every time of day and event. The trick was never being seen twice in the same outfit, so it was important to know the guest list of each occasion to avoid embarrassment.

Aside from corporate-sponsored activities and the obligatory cocktail and dinner parties, religious events and community outreach also dominated the social calendar. Baptism, first communion, confirmation, bar/bat mitzvah, children's birthdays, debutante balls, Sweet Sixteen, high-school graduation, and weddings were events shared with friends and families of all faiths. The life and accomplishments of children were celebrated by all.

Socializing was important as early as kindergarten. Every child's birthday was celebrated in the classroom. Classroom mothers would bring in cupcakes and juice, and special time was set aside to recognize the honored child. Saturdays, of course, were for full-blown birthday parties. Little girls wore their party dresses and little boys wore clip-on neckties. Organized games such as musical chairs and pin the tail on the donkey were safe for

Women's Fashions for 1950s Entertaining. The successful company man had a wife who was the consummate hostess as well as gracious cocktail party companion. As many businessmen were now raising their families in the suburbs, the "patio culture" emerged. Entertaining after work and on weekends became a necessary part of corporate and neighborhood life. Every event, of course, required a specific type of outfit, and keeping up proper appearances was crucial to the future success of every businessman. Capri pants and slim-fit slacks with tight sweaters were worn for casual neighborhood activities, tea-length cocktail dresses with either pencil skirts or full skirts were worn for early evening cocktails, and glamorous full-lengths gowns with tight bodices were mandatory at all formal evening events.

everyone to enjoy, along with dancing to rock 'n' roll on 45 rpm records. Every child received a party favor even if they did not win a game.

Teenagers had mixed dance parties that were, of course, chaperoned. Sock hops after school in the gym gave boys and girls a chance to socialize in a safe environment. Meeting at the malt shop was not so much an occasion as it was a right of passage. Girls had pajama parties where they listened to 45 rpm records, practiced new dance steps, gossiped about boys in class, and dreamed up love stories about their favorite rock 'n' roll heroes and movie stars.

HEALTH AND LEISURE

Greater prosperity in the 1950s led to more disposable income to be spent in pursuit of leisure activities. The new jet-set crowd found extravagant leisure more desirable than the family-friendly routine. Club Med was introduced in 1950, giving young adults a tropical paradise escape. This was the new playground for the not quite rich and famous but for those who wanted to live like they were. Las Vegas also became a popular destination during the 1950s. Having cocktails, gambling, and watching the "Rat Pack" (Frank Sinatra, Dean "Dino" Martin, and Sammy Davis Jr.) perform were popular attractions for hip singles and young couples. The opening of the first Playboy Club in 1953 further glamorized the cocktail crowd as acceptable adult leisure activity.

With more cars on the road and better highway systems, family fun provided more choices for entertainment than ever before. A newfound freedom emerged for families as they hit the road. Vacations to destinations to national parks, such as Yellowstone, and theme parks, such as Disneyland, were now possible with improved highway systems and the family car. Museums, historic sites, and even manufacturing plants provided opportunities for educational vacations. Popular novelty trips of the era included visiting Kellogg's in Battle Creek, Michigan, to meet Tony the Tiger. After a factory tour, each member of the family received a variety pack of Kellogg's cereals. Family vacations included trips to see raw materials extracted from the earth at coal mines in Pennsylvania, marble quarries in Vermont, and iron, nickel, silver, and gold being mined across the northern and midwestern states. Families also experienced American history by visiting Colonial Williamsburg in Virginia and Ellis Island in New York. Travel lodges and motels sprang up on roadsides across Route 66 (America's "mother road" crossing from Chicago to Los Angeles) to accommodate the vacationing families. The greatest perk was a motel with a swimming pool.

Whereas the family of the forties gathered around the radio for entertainment, the modern family of the fifties gathered round the game board, television, or backyard. Monopoly, Scrabble, and card games were popular indoor activities, whereas badminton, horseshoes, and croquet were popular outdoor activities. For families fortunate enough to have memberships to a country club, golf, tennis, swimming, golf, and sailing were standard Saturday afternoon fare. The country club, either private or corporate sponsored, made sunbathing a popular "sport" as well. Lounging by the pool getting a glorious and healthy glow was a sign of financial security. For who else had time to waste on self-indulgence? Golfing was no longer a sport for the rich and famous but an accepted, and sometimes expected, corporate activity. To succeed in business, men needed to play golf. Having time to play golf or tennis was an indication that you had "made it" in the business world.

Although dieting was not yet a way of life, the corporate wife was interested in a shapely look to fit into the hourglass fashions of the 1950s. Jack LaLanne would enter the living room each morning on TV, providing women with healthy tips on eating and exercise. The housewife who was really serious about her shape would invest in an electronic belt that would "jiggle" the excess pounds away. Because it was not fashionable to show signs of perspiration, true exercise was not yet an accepted part of the daily routine.

The segregation of professional sports that had existed before the 1950s was now over. Willie O'Ree (hockey), Jim Brown (football), and Jackie Robinson and Hank Aaron (baseball) were now playing in the big leagues. Sports were all about winning now, not color. Adding to sports cache during this period, the Olympics were broadcast on television. Americans were able to witness for themselves the results of the contests being held across the seas. Of particular interest during this Cold War era were any competitions between the United States and the Soviet Union.

THE
1960s

SOCIAL OCCASIONS

The presidency of JFK touched all facets of U.S. society, and its impact was felt in the area of social occasions as well. Almost from the outset, the glamour and charm of the Kennedys captured the imagination of the country. The inaugural ball featured many celebrities (movie star Peter

Lawford was a cousin of the Kennedy family and introduced the president to Frank Sinatra, among others). In addition, JFK's birthday celebration at Madison Square Garden in 1962 featured Marilyn Monroe singing a breathy version of "Happy Birthday" to the president, a performance that only added to the magic of the Camelot years. Pictures of JFK sailing in casual clothes or playing touch football with his relatives helped to usher in a more informal dress for leisure activities. After all, if the president could dress more casually, it must be all right.

Throughout the presidency, Jackie Kennedy was the epitome of glamour and style, resulting in large part from her embrace and dictation of the latest styles. She hosted numerous dinners at the White House for visiting dignitaries, and what had been boring affairs in previous administrations were transformed into newsworthy events by her mere presence and appear-

The always well-dressed first lady Jacqueline Kennedy in her Chanel suit. [AP / Wide World Photos]

ance. After her husband's assassination, the state funeral provided a number of indelible images. Perhaps the most famous was of a grieving Jackie Kennedy, dressed in black, telling John Kennedy Jr. to salute his father's casket as it passed.

As the Vietnam War escalated throughout the decade, many families across the country, from large, urban areas to small towns, had to deal with the loss of loved ones. The majority of the war's 55,000 deaths occurred during the 1960s. The pall of the war and the institution of the military draft dampened the celebratory mood of such rites of passage as high-school prom and graduation. What had once been simply an important milestone now also signaled the entry of millions of young men into the draft pool.

The youth culture still revolved around some of the staples of previous decades, including attending movies, dances, and other school functions. As the decade wore on, dating became less popular because teenagers preferred to "hang out" with larger groups of people in more informal settings. By the late 1960s, the proportion of boys dating by the time they turned 15 had fallen to 59 percent from 78 percent; just 65 percent of girls went on formal dates compared with 82 percent a decade earlier (Modell 1989, 292). Improved roadways now meant that young adults could travel farther distances for their entertainment, and the automobile, always at the top of the list, was now an even more effective tool for taking advantage of different forms of entertainment.

With the British Invasion and the explosion of Beatlemania, the rock concert also became a more frequent, if not parentally endorsed, social outing. As has been noted, music and rock shows, including the rise of music festivals such as Monterey Pop and Woodstock, became not only a force for spreading new ideas about society and politics but also by their very nature encouraged a more informal style of dress. When the Beatles appeared on *The Ed Sullivan Show* in 1964, they wore matching gray suits. Just three years later, with the release of the album *Sgt. Pepper's Lonely Hearts Club Band*, they were wearing brightly colored outfits that reflected the impact of the counterculture.

The increase in the number of young Americans going to college had many consequences. Holidays took on an added meaning, because times such as Thanksgiving and Christmas came to represent the few guaranteed times when families could be together again. While at colleges and universities, young Americans were being exposed to new ideas, courtesy of the counterculture. Favorite pastimes included hanging out at coffeehouses, where the folk music revival was in full swing, attending rallies and protests, and participating in counterculture events such as be-ins. Many of these activities encouraged people to express themselves through their appearance, so face and body painting and tie-dye shirts were natural offshoots. Bookstores also became places to meet socially, and the rise of beat poets such as Allen Ginsburg made gatherings at these venues opportunities to share ideas.

More and more adults were delaying marriage, a trend that continued into the following decade. Those that did embark on family life enjoyed a standard of living that would have been unimaginable just years earlier. The growing middle class also possessed more time and more money with which to pursue leisure activities. Dining out became a more frequent activity, with restaurants and supper clubs popular destinations. Spectator sports also grew in popularity, with sports such as football and basketball competing with Major League Baseball for an audience.

HEALTH AND LEISURE ACTIVITIES

In the 1960s, health and exercise became areas in which much progress was made. As part of LBJ's Great Society program, Medicare and Medicaid were created in 1966 and helped extend healthcare to segments of the population that had not previously enjoyed such access. Overall spending on medical care increased from $19.1 billion in 1960 to more than $42 billion by 1969 (Kurian 1994, 111). A heightened awareness of physical fitness and obesity also occurred during the decade. Jean Nidetch, a housewife in Queens, New York, formed Weight Watchers in 1963. The organization was so popular that it had to expand rapidly to keep up with the demand across the country of people who sought help with losing weight.

On the downside, the nation was filled with cigarette smokers. The popularity of cigarettes was unaffected by a report, "Smoking and Health," published in 1964 by the Surgeon General's Advisory Committee on Smoking and Health. The committee's research found a link between smoking and incidents of lung cancer in both men and women. More than 57.1 billion packs of cigarettes, an arresting average of 205 packs for each adult, were sold in 1968. In 1969, 49 percent of all respondents to a Gallup survey had smoked in the past week.

Another development was the rise of fast food. In general, dining out became much more popular, with the amount Americans spent on meals and beverages climbing from $16.2 billion in 1960 to $26.7 billion by decade's end (Kurian 1994, 111). The increase in the number of women in the workforce contributed to a need to feed the family cheaply and quickly. The fast-food industry rushed in to make sure Americans had enough hamburgers and fries. Ray Kroc acquired exclusive rights to the McDonald's name and increased the number of franchises from 230 in 1961 to more than 700 restaurants by mid-decade. Burger King also expanded throughout the 1960s, and Hardee's and Wendy's, founded in 1961 and 1969, respectively, also joined the fray. Other fast-food franchises included Domino's Pizza, Long John Silver's, and Taco Bell (Rielly 2003, 97). Diet Rite (1962) and Tab (1963) were the first two diet soft drinks, and empty calories in the form of Pop Tarts, Pringles, and Cool Whip also made their debut during the decade.

The public took advantage of the extra time and money captured from the economic boom to enjoy more leisure activities. Annual applications for U.S. passports rose from around 300,000 in 1950 to more than 2,200,000 in 1970 (Farber-Bailey 2001, 56). The expansion of the airline industry made international and domestic air travel more popular. Meanwhile, the Federal-Aid Highway Act of 1956, which had committed more than $25 billion to the upgrade of the nation's roadways, meant that cross-country vacations by automobile were made easier.

By 1966, the number of people who named television as their favorite leisure activity had risen to 46 percent (Jones 1980, 120). When people were not watching sports events in the comfort of their homes, they were increasingly attending them in person. Aided by television, all of the major sports franchises grew in popularity during the 1960s. Attendance for Major League Baseball alone rose by more than 10 million people by the end of the decade as people flocked to see stars such as Sandy Koufax, Bob Gibson, Mickey Mantle, and Willie Mays. Two football leagues, the National Football League and the American Football League, were able to thrive side by side (a merger would be crafted in 1970). The first Super Bowl was played in 1965, a contest between the Green Bay Packers and the Kansas City Chiefs. The Packers would win five championships over the course of the decade.

The popularity of spectator sports also translated to individual participation in competitive and leisure sports. Traditional activities such as bowling, hunting, fishing, and boating enjoyed widespread popularity. Growing numbers of athletes also took part in marathon running, bicycling, skiing, skateboarding, and surfing (aided by the music of the Beach Boys, no doubt). As an indication, the total number of bikes purchased more than doubled over the course of the decade. Furthermore, cities and towns, recognizing the growing segment of the population that was interested in exercising regularly, accommodated these activities by committing more money and resources for local recreational sports activities and facilities.

THE
1970s

SOCIAL OCCASIONS

The growing informality in everyday life that began to flower in the 1960s continued throughout the next decade. The trend was propelled by the rising number of people who were attending college and spending more time in a collegiate environment. Women, for instance, increasingly saw graduate school as an important stepping-stone in their careers. The percentage of female law school students more than quadrupled from 1960 to 1974 (Bailey 2004, 108), and women were more likely to attend college than were men by mid-decade (Lambert 1978, 159). The influence of movies also contributed to the rise of informality. Diane Keaton's character in *Annie Hall* wore clothes that were traditionally seen as masculine, but the popularity of the film and Keaton's sense of style paved the way for a wider variety of women's styles.

Big business had long realized the importance of catering to young adults, but they found new ways to raise the profile of their products among this important demographic. Anheuser-Busch, for example, began to give away T-shirts to college students on spring break in San Diego and Miami, and it soon became a status symbol to come back from vacation sporting these shirts. Indeed, young adults saw the T-shirt not only as comfortable clothing but also as a way to distinguish themselves from the crowd. Shirts with logos and other sayings became much more prevalent during the decade. Such apparel was perfect to attend popular events such as stadium rock shows (Bob Dylan and the Rolling Stones both mounted tours unprecedented in their scale and the number of fans that attended) and blockbuster movies such as *Star Wars* and *Jaws*.

Traditional social occasions were also affected by the trend of informality. The traditional wedding ceremony, although still popular, had to compete with a variety of new approaches. Informal ceremonies, such as civil services, and those influenced by new-age religions were much more frequent compared with previous decades. Outdoor weddings, especially in places such as California, gained popularity. The Reverend Sun Myung Moon, the leader of the Unification Church, married 777 couples at the same time on October 21, 1970. By the end of the decade, however, traditional weddings were again on the rise.

For young adults, high-school proms and graduations were benefiting from a rollback in the legal drinking age. Before the late 1960s, the drinking age had been twenty-one, but states across the nation began to set their own standards. In many states, high-school seniors were able to purchase alcohol legally on turning eighteen, making this birthday an important rite of passage. As new generations of Americans gained access to alcohol in their teens, alcohol again became the drug of choice.

More traditional dating, such as formal dates and dressing up and going out for dinner and dancing, resumed. However, the mid-1970s disco craze, with the emphasis on staying out late and partying, ushered in a more widespread use of cocaine and other drugs. The use of alcohol and illegal drugs among teens was on the rise throughout the decade (Hine 1999, 270) despite the deaths of many 1960s cultural icons. The deaths of Jimi Hendrix, Janis Joplin, and Jim Morrison within twelve months of one another served as a warning sign to a whole generation about the effects of experimentation and the rock 'n' roll lifestyle.

As the economy worsened and the U.S. population had to spend more money on gas and other necessities, families found themselves with less disposable income with which to enjoy leisure activities and to recognize birthdays, anniversaries, and other special occasions. The government did its part by rolling out huge celebrations to mark the country's bicentennial on July 4, 1976. New York City's festivities alone drew more than 6 million spectators, and cities across the nation marked the day with spectacular fireworks displays, parades, and other activities. Many products took on a red, white, and blue color scheme in solidarity with the holiday.

HEALTH AND LEISURE ACTIVITIES

Although Jim Fixx's *The Complete Book of Running* was not published until 1977, the decade as a whole saw the public experience a heightened awareness of the need to attend to physical and spiritual well-being. After spending so much time and effort addressing the major sociopolitical problems of the 1960s, many people turned inward in the 1970s in an attempt to feel better. The jogging craze was just one indication of this trend: during the 1970s, more than 40 million Americans ran on a regular basis. Even President Jimmy Carter participated in road races, famously passing out during a 6.2-mile event in 1979.

Another indication of the heightened awareness of health was the rise of bodybuilding as a sport. Although this sport had been around since the 1940s, it was seen mainly as a hobby in places such as Venice Beach in California. Bodybuilding came into its own during the 1970s, thanks in large part to Arnold Schwarzenegger. An Austrian immigrant, Schwarzenegger became the sport's most recognizable face and proved to be its most savvy promoter. The documentary *Pumping Iron*, released in 1977, provided a behind-the-scenes look at the sport and served to introduce bodybuilding to a whole new audience of Americans eager to look better and feel better.

One of the more significant developments to the overall health of the U.S. public was the rise of women's athletics in the 1970s. Title IX of the Education Act of 1972 prohibited sex discrimination in any education program receiving federal aid. It went into effect in 1978 and had an immediate impact on female participation in athletics: in 1971, women constituted just 7 percent of all high-school athletes; by 1978, that figure had risen to 32 percent (Schulman 2001, 161). Furthermore, a growing number of women athletes enjoyed increased visibility, none more so than Billie Jean King. When she defeated Bobby Riggs, a fifty-five-year-old former professional tennis player and Wimbledon champion, in a nationally televised tennis match watched by 45 million people in 1973, she announced the arrival of a new kind of female athlete. King also helped establish the Virginia Slims tennis circuit in the early 1970s, thus providing female tennis players with increased visibility.

For many people, attending to one's spirituality became the key to overall health. According to a 1976 Gallup poll, more than 19 million Americans participated in some kind of new-age religion with the aim of personal growth. Transcendental meditation is a form of meditation developed by the Maharishi Mahesh Yogi and involves chanting a mantra repeatedly for fifteen to twenty minutes. Some of the fringe new-age groups included the Erhard Seminar Training (also known as "est"), which was founded by Werner Erhard. The est training was designed to help individuals overcome personal obstacles and involved trainers yelling obscenities at practitioners until they overcame their "hang-ups."

A national poll conducted in 1974 indicated that the average American spent thirty-eight and a half hours each week on recreation, an increase of four hours from ten years earlier. Perhaps more telling, the preferred activity by 46 percent of those surveyed was watching television. Reading was a distant second, with 14 percent of the respondents (Lambert 1978, 217). The U.S. public collectively spent just over $40 billion on recreational activities in 1970, and this figure would grow to $117 billion by the end of the decade (Kurian 1994, 111). So, despite the preference for television viewing, Americans were still leaving home for their recreational activities.

The increasing popularity of spectator sports reflected both of these patterns. The broadcasts of all the major sports continued to enjoy steadily growing audiences. In baseball, Cincinnati's Big Red Machine won two championships in the middle of the decade, with the New York Yankees, led by Reggie Jackson, taking several titles in the late 1970s. In football, the Pittsburgh Steelers, featuring the Iron Curtain defense, won four Super Bowls. The Dallas Cowboys christened themselves "America's Team," recording two Super Bowl triumphs and bringing the Dallas Cowboy Cheerleaders into American living rooms each week. *Monday Night Football*, which debuted in September 1970, contributed to the sport's increased reach. The National Basketball Association (NBA) was still a decade away from achieving greater visibility, but players such as the dynamic Julius Erving attracted growing numbers of fans. Boxing also continued to command massive interest, particularly the two classic Muhammad Ali-Joe Frazier fights (in 1971 and 1975), as well as Ali's bout with George Forman, dubbed the "Rumble in the Jungle." (The documentary *When We Were Kings* chronicles the event.)

The Olympic Games produced a number of notable performances and elevated standout athletes to celebrity status. At the 1972 games in Munich, U.S. swimmer Mark Spitz won seven gold medals. The 1976 games in Montreal featured Nadia Comaneci, a Romanian gymnast, who received the first perfect score (a 10.0). She went on to become a darling of the media and spectators alike. On the men's side, U.S. runner Frank Shorter took gold in the marathon, and Bruce Jenner won the decathlon.

THE
1980s

SOCIAL OCCASIONS

The 1981 marriage of Diana Spencer to Prince Charles in England was considered by many *the* social event of the 1980s. After a reported 750 million people watched the wedding on television, every girl getting married in the 1980s demanded a wedding dress like Lady Diana's. Her wedding gown was designed by Elizabeth and David Emanuel and featured a full skirt gathered at the waist and a twenty-five-foot train. The most distinctive elements in the dress were the oversized bulky sleeves and the 10,000 pearls and sequins used to embellish the garment. The puffy sleeves and bodice embellishments such as flounces, bows, and lace from her dress became popular in the United States and around the world.

The royal wedding returned to popularity traditional wedding ceremonies, which waned in popularity in the 1970s. Classic wedding traditions were practiced by Americans during the period, including the money dance in which the newlyweds collected bills from guests wishing to dance with them during the reception, the tossing of the bride's bouquet and garter over a group of single women and men, respectively, and glass clinking to motivate the couple to engage in a kiss.

Debutant balls, the American version of rites of passage for young women, remained an important special occasion during the 1980s. Cotillions, a southern tradition involving the presentation of young ladies to society at the age of eighteen, remained alive with some wealthy families in the South. Debutants and escorts participating in these events were still elegantly dressed in ball gowns and tuxedos. Charity balls proliferated for healthcare, museum, and political fundraisers. Formality was back in style, and everyone was dressing up, even for cocktails. Glamorous gowns with gold and glitter prevailed in most special occasions in the 1980s. Men returned to tuxedos for the most formal affairs, with black tuxedo jackets, satin lapels, and pleated pants with a decorative satin braid.

New holidays as well as traditional holidays were celebrated in the United States in the 1980s. In 1982, legislation was approved for the creation of Dr. Martin Luther King Day to be celebrated on the third

Monday of January each year. Millions of signatures for the creation of the holiday were collected in 1982 by The M. L. King Center for Nonviolent Social Change, and President Ronald Reagan signed the bill in 1983 (Dennis 2002, 262). The Fourth of July remained a favorite holiday for Americans, providing an opportunity for picnics, outdoor concerts, and firework displays. Apparel bearing the American flag, eagles, and other patriotic symbols was widely worn during the days surrounding the festivities. In 1986, a special Fourth of July celebration took place in New York to commemorate the centennial of the Statue of Liberty. Many celebrities attended the event, which also saw the largest gathering of Navy boats in New York Harbor since WWII.

Other holidays continued providing retailers with opportunities to increase product sales during certain periods of the year. Merchandise for Valentine's Day, celebrated on February 14, usually included red items embellished with hearts, cupid figures, and other romantic, often Victorian-inspired, imagery. Easter merchandise was offered in pastel colors and incorporated bunnies, painted eggs, and similar images associated with the celebration. Easter Sunday remained one of the days of the year when more Americans attended church. Parishioners usually wore elegant outfits for the celebration. St. Patrick's Day, an Irish holiday celebrated on March 17, provided many Americans with an opportunity to wear green apparel, whereas Cinco de Mayo, commemorating a Mexican victory over the French army in 1862, provided retailers with another opportunity to capitalize with the sale of Mexican-inspired products.

HEALTH AND LEISURE ACTIVITIES

The 1980s obsession with status and economic success motivated Americans to spend more time at work and decreased the number of hours devoted to leisure. Americans faced increased expectations and demands from their bosses and dealt with higher stress levels and shrinking vacation time. More than 7 million Americans, many of them women, were moonlighting by the end of the 1980s (Schor 1991, 11). The increased pace of American daily life took a toll not only on the health of employees but also on family interactions and the care of children.

The 1980s fitness craze saw American's devoting long hours to working out at the gym after a long day in the office. Americans went crazy for aerobics, a new form of cardiovascular exercise based on dance moves set to popular music. Jane Fonda sold more than 17 million copies of her *Jane Fonda Workout* VHS tape in 1982, the first in what would become a series of over twenty workout videos hosted by Fonda. The popularity of her video routine not only got American women (and men) exercising in their living rooms but also brought leotards, tights, and legwarmers out of the living room and onto the street as casual wear.

Exercise, however, was not the only component of a healthy lifestyle. Americans experienced an obsession with weight loss, buying into fad or trendy diets aimed at achieving a slim figure. Following on the popularity of the 1970s Scarsdale Diet, the Pritikin Diet and the Atkins Diet were two of the most popular diet plans in the 1980s. However, other fad diets, such as the Beverly Hills Diet, which was based on eating only fruit, encouraged "yo-yo dieting" in which the faithful regained weight as quickly as they lost it. The approval of aspartame in 1983 by the Food and Drug Administration as an artificial sweetener for diet soft drinks increased the consumption of soft drinks by almost 20 percent (Marty 1997, 291). When diet and exercise failed to obtain the desired results, cosmetic, or plastic, surgery presented another method for achieving the "perfect bod" in the 1980s. Women increasingly went "under the knife" for eye lifts, chin lifts, face lifts, tummy tucks, and breast implants for the sake of beauty. The obsession with body perfection also made sun tanning largely popular in the period, but, by the mid-1980s, the American Academy of Dermatology was highly vocal regarding the risks, including skin cancer, associated with overexposure and sunburns.

Alcohol consumption continued to rise in the United States during this period. Alcohol addiction and abuse remained a leading cause for automobile accidents as well as a number of other diseases of the liver, pancreas, and kidney. The toll on public health and the financial burden that alcohol abuse produced motivated the creation of organizations such as Students Against Drunk Driving, founded in 1981, and Mothers Against Drunk Driving, active since 1980. Mothers Against Drunk Driving pressured Congress to enact a federal law returning the minimum drinking age back to twenty-one. This controversial law, which pressured states to either comply with the requirement or lose millions of dollars of federal highway funding, was challenged and upheld by the Supreme Court and signed by President Reagan in 1987.

The health risks of smoking continued to be a topic for debate in the 1980s. A 1982 report by the surgeon general clearly indicated that smoking was a cause of cancer. An affirmation of his report was followed in 1984 by another report detailing the dangers of second-hand smoke. Additionally, growing concerns regarding smoking during pregnancy, a common practice in the 1950s and 1960s, surfaced when data indicated that female smokers outnumbered male smokers in the 1980s. Drug-trafficking control remained a relevant issue and a budgetary demand for the American government. Substance abuse prevention campaigns were abundant, including Nancy Reagan's "Just Say No" program during the Reagan presidency. The National Organization for the Reform of Marijuana Laws continued fighting for the legalization of marijuana by contending that the problem with drugs was the criminalizing of their possession.

The first case of gay-related immunodeficiency, now known as AIDS, was reported in 1981. The name was changed when it was discovered that individuals outside the homosexual population were affected. The gay community, nonetheless, was the first to experience the effects of the disease in a widespread manner. News of the death of actor Rock Hudson in 1985 brought awareness of the disease to the general public. Also significant was the 1991 announcement made by basketball player Ervin "Magic" Johnson that he too was HIV positive. Two Broadway plays, *The Normal Heart* by Larry Kramer and *As Is* by William Hoffman, both debuting in 1985, presented early depictions of the consequences of the disease. In the following years, Americans learned the extent of the disease, and ultimately the AIDS crisis created awareness of the importance of "safe sex" practices, marking a turning point in the sexual life of the American people.

The Olympics of 1980, 1984, and 1988 gained broad media exposure for men's and women's sports, especially from the winter games hosted in Lake Placid in 1980 and the summer games hosted in Los Angeles in 1984. In 1980, for instance, millions of Americans watched the unthinkable Miracle on Ice when the American team defeated the more experienced Soviet team during the winter Olympic Games in Lake Placid, New York. The summer games of 1984 saw the United States dominate men's running, with Carl Lewis winning four gold medals, and make an impressive show in women's running with Florence Griffith-Joyner winning a silver medal. Flo Jo, as she would come to be known, won three gold medals and one silver medal in the 1988 games, as well as set a fashion trend with her long hair, long nails, and one-legged running pants. Mary Lou Retton was the all-around gymnastics champion. With five medals in 1984, one gold, two silver, and two bronze, her broad smile and sassy cropped hair cut made Retton a popular sports icon.

Tennis provided Americans with many idols, including John McEnroe, distinguished by a bright red headband on the court, and Andre Agassi, who captured attention not only for his excellence on the court but also for his marriage to actress Brooke Shields and later to tennis player Steffi Graf. Chris Evert, one of the top female tennis players of the 1980s, also launched a tennis and fashion revolution when, in 1987, she appeared on the tennis courts wearing an inline diamond bracelet. The bracelet might never have been noticed if it had not broken during play, bringing the match to a halt. Ever since Evert's bracelet incident, inline diamond bracelets have been known as "tennis bracelets."

The NBA was responsible for the creation of several popular culture icons in the 1980s, including Michael Jordan, Kareem Abdul-Jabbar, Larry Bird, Dennis Rodman, and Scottie Pippen. Although these and other NBA players regularly appeared on team, NBA, and other product advertisements, it was Michael Jordan who built an empire out of his talent and name. Jordan, often considered the greatest American basketball player ever, is also one of the savviest businessmen ever. His endorsement deals included companies such as Coca-Cola, Chevrolet, Gatorade, Hanes, McDonald's, and Ball Park Franks, to name a few. However, it is his association with Nike and its creation of an athletic shoe for him, the "Air Jordan," that has proven to be his most lucrative opportunity. When first commercially introduced in 1985, the demand for Air Jordans so exceeded the supply that "shoe jackings" (individuals being robbed for their shoes) were regularly reported throughout the mid- to late 1980s. Nike subsequently spun-off Air Jordans into their own line, expanding the footwear collection to include various types of athletic wear.

THE
1990s AND 2000s

SOCIAL OCCASIONS

The minimalist tendencies of the 1990s and the increased popularity of casual and comfortable clothing in the United States made formalwear less prevalent in many occasions. Women wore black and neutral-tone gowns with mostly simple lines and minimum decorations. Besides the ubiquitous tuxedo, men favored flat-front trousers and simply cut outfits in dark shades. Conspicuous consumption was out and with it went the elaborate balls and formal attire of the 1980s.

As the over-indulgent '80s came to an end, debutant balls and coming-out parties, so popular in that decade, became less important. However, Sweet Sixteen parties remained a staple in the United States and ranged from very formal occasions similar to cotillions to informal parties in which no formal apparel was required. In 2006, elaborate Sweet Sixteen parties increased in popularity as the MTV network launched a reality show that followed the plans for Sweet Sixteen celebrations for wealthy, elite teens. The Hispanic version, quinceañera, became more prevalent as the Latino populations increased in America. During the event, the young woman, who had just turned fifteen years old, is formally presented to society in a ceremony, often accompanied by fifteen elegantly dressed male and female friends. Some Hispanic families spent fortunes (on scale with a wedding) on the elaborate formal parties, which are often accompanied by a sit-down dinner.

Historicism and minimalism, two main trends in fashion during the 1990s, influenced wedding dress designs. Historicism brought back styles from the past such as corset-fitted tops and dropped waistlines. Minimalism popularized narrower skirts and reduced embellishments. Informal wedding ceremonies became more prevalent in the 1990s and 2000s, with many brides choosing to marry in garments ranging from cocktail dresses to casual outfits. White was no longer the only option because many brides donned colored or even patterned wedding dresses. The United States experienced a boom in commitment ceremonies among same-sex couples after Massachusetts legalized gay weddings. Other states attempted similar initiatives, resulting in heated debates regarding the legal definition of marriage. Same-sex weddings were often organized to mirror traditions seen in heterosexual ceremonies.

Mourning practices in America changed little after 1980. Black and other somber colors continued to be worn at funerals where either formal or semiformal attire was worn. Black ribbons or armbands were worn occasionally to indicate mourning, especially by athletes during games to honor the memory of a lost team member. State funerals followed traditional practices as in the case of former President Ronald Reagan in June 2004, with ceremonies starting in California and then moving to a public viewing in Washington, DC.

The most significant social change in the 1990s may have been perceptions of death and dying. Dr. Jack Kevorkian made the debate front page news with his "suicide machine," which he provided to terminally ill individuals whom he believed had a right to die. A heated debate ensued over euthanasia, an individual's right to end his/her life, and the role doctors should play in that act. Kevorkian was imprisoned for assisting approximately one hundred individuals with their planned deaths. The debate spurred many individuals to write living wills with "do not resuscitate" orders rather than risk being suspended in a vegetative state, indefinitely hooked up to life-support systems. Images of death were also used in the fashion industry, particularly by fashion photographers wanting to explore the public's limit on the acceptance of violent visuals. In the 1990s, *Spin* magazine actually included fashion photographs featuring models as if they were dead.

Giant retailer Macy's continued sponsoring the famous Thanksgiving Day Parade in New York City in the 1990s, and the day after Thanksgiving remained the busiest shopping day of the year, with retailers opening earlier and offering drastic discounts to customers. However, activist groups concerned with the consumerism associated with the Thanksgiving holiday promoted "Buy Nothing Day," encouraging citizens to avoid conspicuous consumption on the day after Thanksgiving. Toward the end of the millennium, Americans grew used to seeing Christmas merchandise share shelf space with Hanukkah and Kwanzaa products. Hanukkah, or the Festival of Lights, was celebrated by many traditional Jewish families. However, by the late 1990s, some Jewish-Christian families were celebrating a combined holiday dubbed "Chrismukkah." Kwanzaa, a series of ceremonies based on African traditions celebrating the harvest season, was created in 1966 by Ron Karenga. The holiday gained popularity with African Americans throughout the late 1980s and early 1990s and continues.

Historical influences were also seen in costumes created for the Mardi Gras celebration. The carnival-type parade, mostly know for the large celebration in New Orleans but also celebrated in other places, takes place during Fat Tuesday, the last day before the Catholic Lent season. Floats featured on Mardi Gras parades often incorporated masquerade outfits and ball gowns made in luxurious fabrics and embellished to great detail. Sadly, Hurricane Katrina, which devastated New Orleans in 2005, has diminished Mardi Gras celebrations in succeeding years, especially in 2006.

The 1990s also noted an increase in ethnic and social group parades celebrating the diversity of the population of the United States. Large urban centers, such as New York City and Chicago, but also smaller towns sponsored parades that often showcased ethnic music, dance, and apparel. These included the Puerto Rican Day Parade, Mexican Independence Day Parade, St. Patrick's Day Parade (Irish), Pulaski Day (Polish), and Columbus Day (Italian). Gay Pride celebrations and parades were also held annually to educate and promote understanding between the homosexual and heterosexual cultures. The parades and celebrations featured floats, music, and, most notably, clothing related to many subgroups of the gay community, ranging from drag queens to leather fetish enthusiasts.

HEALTH AND LEISURE ACTIVITIES

In the 1990s, more Americans were looking for options outside the corporate world. A boom on the communication and Internet sectors created a new class of worker in the technology sector in which "casual Friday" and other practices promoting relaxing office apparel originated and later spread to other sectors. The period also experienced the rise of the "creative class" engaged in activities related to design and aesthetics. They embraced different values, attitudes, and dress codes that often responded to their higher education background and lifestyle (Florida 2002, 77).

As air travel became less expensive, flying was no longer perceived as an elite activity. Americans enjoyed vacation travel to the mountains, the beach, and city destinations as well as international trips. At the inception of air travel, Americans dressed up to board a plane. Now, as Americans fully embraced casual clothing, they also relaxed their travel attire. Travelers often wore short pants or sweatpants, flip-flops, and T-shirts. Flight attendant uniforms also became more casual, especially at Southwest Airlines where the uniform consisted of khaki pants and polo shirts. Airlines often engaged in "airfare wars" trying to capture each other's market by lowering prices. Low-cost airlines such as AirTran and JetBlue took market share, and private and charter flights became more common. Traveling guides and magazines were widely available in print and also on the World Wide Web. They often targeted specific markets such as families, budget travelers, or gay and lesbian patrons. American designers and retailers offered travel gear and accessories for every kind of traveler. Fashionable tourists chose from a variety of designer luggage with names such as Tommy Hilfiger, Liz Claiborne, Calvin Klein, and Vera Bradley.

By the early 1990s, Americans had embraced a variety of exercise activities, including walking, jogging, swimming, and weight lifting. Stationary bikes and home exercise machines became prevalent in many American households, and many "empty nesters" converted bedrooms into home fitness rooms. Also popular were biking, in-line skating, skateboarding, surfing, and racquet sports. The clothing industry was steadfast to produce shoes and apparel specific to each activity.

The popularity of bodybuilding contests first seen in the 1970s increased in the 1990s and were regularly featured on television. Bodybuilding competitors now also counted women amongst their ranks. Health and fitness magazines, such as *Men's Fitness*, *Iron Man*, and *Women's Physique World*, included exercise and diet tips as well as success stories to inspire Americans in their search for a better physique and health.

Where sweat and determination left off, or when they failed, science picked up. The plastic surgery craze of the 1980s morphed into new body-sculpting techniques. Liposuction literally vacuumed fat out of the body, whereas collagen (fat) injections filled in lips and eyes. If the collagen treatments were not sufficient to target "fine lines and wrinkles," then Botox injections and chemical peels were sought out. The risk of skin cancer may have reduced sun tanning, but no one wanted to be without a tan. People now flocked to ultraviolet radiation tanning beds or turned to tanning sprays and creams, some of which, if not applied carefully, made the individual appear more orange than tan.

The 1990s diet craze sparked a number of diet plans based on low-fat, low-calorie, measured portions. Among the most successful diet plans were the Atkins and South Beach programs. The Atkins label was placed, for example, on a number of products in the early 2000s, including chain restaurant menus. TV dinners and frozen meals were also adapted to the requirements of these different diets and were retailed under the Atkins and South Beach names.

In general, the United States became more aware of healthier food choices. Concerns over cholesterol, fat, and carbohydrate contents grew, and a new law in 1990 forced manufacturers to provide detailed information on product labels (Marty 1997, 291). The public, however, was often confused by contradictory claims about the health benefits or risks of different types of meats, fruits, and vegetables. The confusion only grew when both red wine and chocolate were touted for their antioxidant properties. An interest in organically grown foods brought the "natural" or "whole" food trend from small, locally owned stores to national supermarket chains. Organic or green products were often more costly than regular products because of more elaborate harvesting and processing practices. In contrast, fast-food chains remained popular but faced increasing criticism for the contents of their food and the practice of "over-sizing" or "super-sizing" meals.

Mood disorders such as depression, anxiety, and bipolar disorder received more attention during the period as millions of Americans received medications for these conditions. Children were often diagnosed with attention deficit disorder and attention deficit hyperactivity disorder and were prescribed drugs such as methylphenidate, sold mostly under the Ritalin brand name. In 1988, Prozac was approved as appropriate medication to treat depression. Critics were concerned with the large numbers of Americans self-diagnosing for such disorders and the widespread prescription of mood-enhancing drugs. In the eyes of those opposing the trend, American physicians and researchers ignored the possibility that mood disorders were caused, at least in part, by the new fast pace of American society, the hyperactive nature of media and entertainment, and the ever-changing availability of images and activities offered to the public. American researchers continued working on cures for other diseases such as various types of cancer and Alzheimer's disease as the baby boom generation rapidly approached their retirement years.

In the 1990s, several states successfully sued the tobacco industry claiming it underplayed their own research outlining the harms of tobacco. The money from many of these tobacco settlements was used in a number of community projects and often funded aggressive anti-smoking campaigns. In the 2000s, there was a decrease in public smoking as many cities passed laws forbidding smoking in public spaces, including restaurants and bars. Hollywood and the fashion industry were under constant scrutiny for glamorizing smoking and ignoring the associated health hazards. The general public was also often outraged by the alluring portrayal of drugs and drug addictions in movies, advertising, and promotion for fashion designer's lines. The "junkie chic" or "heroin chic" fashion trend of the mid-1990s presented models sporting a stylish version of the heroin-addict look with extremely slim silhouettes, unkempt, pale faces, and torn clothes. Not only was this look thought to glamorize drug addiction, it was also believed to encourage dangerous eating disorders such as anorexia and bulimia for women and girls to maintain a thin look.

In general, the period was distinguished by the increased popularity of televised sports, with networks paying large amounts of money for broadcasting rights for exclusivity deals. Special events such as the Super Bowl (football), the World Series (baseball), the NBA playoffs (basketball), the Stanley Cup finals (hockey), and March Madness (college basketball) became television rating bonanzas. The advent of cable television provided twenty-four-hour-a-day, seven-day-a-week sports coverage on new networks such as ESPN. Television brought not only games but information about athletes' private lives closer to the American public. Audiences followed closely the NBA new players draft, franchise relocations, salary negotiations, and violent outbursts among athletes and spectators. One example of the increased coverage of athletes' personal lives was the Lance Armstrong story. Not only was Armstrong's dominance of race cycling, including his seven Tour de France victories, covered by sports networks, but his surgery and recovery from brain and testicular cancer was also chronicled.

The twenty-four-hour cable networks also helped fledgling sports gain broader appeal. Women's basketball, at both the professional (WNBA) and college levels, developed national followings. Cynthia Cooper became the first WNBA superstar to be widely recognized. Soccer also benefited from the increased availability of sports coverage. Both male players, such as Alexei Lalas, Tim Howard, and Claudio Reyna, and female players, such as Mia Hamm and Brandi Chastain, gained celebrity, especially when the U.S. Women's Soccer team won the World Cup in 1999. The attention even gained Hamm an endorsement deal with Nike and increased the popularity of sport bras, when Chastain revealed hers by removing her shirt to celebrate the World Cup win.

Golf, skateboarding, and cycling also caught the public's attention in the 1990s. Golf, previously dominated by Jack Nicklaus, now had a new, modern champion, Tiger Woods. His total domination of professional golf throughout the 1990s increased the popularity of the sport with minority groups and garnered him a contract with Nike for his own clothing line. The increased popularity of skateboarding amongst teenagers brought Tony Hawk to national prominence in the 1990s and 2000s. Coverage of his "trick" skating not only promoted skateboarding as a sport but also promoted the "skater" look.

REFERENCES

Bailey, B., Farber, D., eds. (2004) *America in the '70s*. Lawrence, KS: University Press of Kansas.

Dennis, M. (2002) *Red, White, and Blue Letter Days: An American Calendar*. Ithaca, NY: Cornell University Press.

Farber, D., Bailey, B. (2001) *The Columbia Guide to America in the 1960s*. New York: Columbia University Press.

Florida, R. L. (2002) *The Rise of the Creative Class: And How It's Transforming Work, Leisure, Community and Everyday Life*. New York: Basic Books.

Hine, T. (1999) *The Rise and Fall of the American Teen*. New York: Avon Books.

Jones, L. Y. (1980) *Great Expectations: America and the Baby Boom Generation*. New York: Coward, McCann, and Geoghegan.

Kurian, G. T. (1994) *Datapedia of the United States, 1790–2000*. Lanham, MD: Bernan Press.

Lambert, R., ed. (1978) *America in the Seventies: Some Social Indicators, The Annals of the American Academy of Political and Social Science*. Vol. 435, January.

Marty, M. A. (1997) *Daily Life in the United States, 1960–1990: Decades of Discord*. The Greenwood Press "Daily Life through History" Series. Westport, CT: Greenwood Press.

Modell, J. (1989) *Into One's Own: From Youth to Adulthood in the United States, 1920–1975*. Berkeley, CA: University of California Press.

Rielly, E. J. (2003) *The 1960s*. Westport, CT: Greenwood Press.

Schor, J. (1991) *The Overworked American: The Unexpected Decline of Leisure*. New York, NY: Basic Books.

Schulman, B. J. (2001) *The Seventies: The Great Shift in American Culture, Society, and Politics*. Cambridge, MA: Da Capo Press.

5

The Individual and Family

Marriage is one of the cornerstones of American society. Traditionally, marriage has helped individuals identify their role in society, provided stability to communities, and served as the basis for family structure. During the last half of the twentieth century, all of the basic tenets associated with marriage were challenged, including the institution of marriage itself.

In the 1950s, everyone expected to get married after high school or, at the latest, after college. Once married, most women stayed home to raise children and men went out into the world to provide financially for their families. Over the next two decades, the institution of marriage would be challenged by American youths, who, in an act of defiance against authority, turned to "living together" instead of making formal (and legal) commitments in a church. Over the course of the fifty-year period from 1950 to 2000, average ages for first marriage for men and women would shift almost five years, from 22.8 and 20.3 to 26.8 and 25.1, respectively. The new reality was that men and women were single for more of their adult lives than any previous generations had been before.

Another threat to traditional notions of stability was the increasing rate of divorce. In the 1950s, the stigma and risk of social ostracism was enough to keep couples together "for the sake of the children." However, over the next decade, as state laws changed, allowing for "no fault" divorce rulings, divorce rates escalated, from approximately 5 per 1,000 married women in 1950 to approximately 20 per 1,000 by 2000.

For those who chose to marry and for those marriages that did remain intact, the roles and responsibilities of marriage changed. Many women no longer stayed home tending the nest; they joined men in the work-force. In fact, by the 1990s, women had obtained nearly equal footing with men in most sectors of the labor market and sometimes even earned more than their male counterparts. By the time the Family and Medical Leave Act was passed by Congress in 1993, a new trend in marriages and families was perceptible: some men were leaving their jobs to stay home and raise children, and women remained in the workforce as the primary provider.

Whereas marriage rates were declining, or at least delayed, amongst heterosexual couples, another group of individuals was challenging the traditional definition of marriage and family: homosexuals. Although gay and lesbian individuals and couples were increasing accepted in American society during the last half of the twentieth century, they were not allowed the same legal status of "marriage" as heterosexual couples. Same-sex couples were also raising children at an increasing rate, at the same time traditional couples were postponing starting families. This challenge to the basic norms and mores of American society brought extreme reactions in the court of public opinion from both liberals and conservatives.

One concept undergoing great change during the last half of the twentieth century was that of childhood. The innocence of childhood vanished with the 1950s. Children coming of age in this period were sub-jected to fears of atomic weapons during the Cold War and sexual preda-tors via the Internet. Playtime decreased as expectations to excel increased homework from school. Along with decreased physical play came increases in childhood obesity and increases in stress levels and prescrip-tion medication to control "disorders" some viewed as a product of their environment.

First television and then video games and the Internet became the "babysitter" as increasing numbers of children became "latchkey kids," returning home after school to an empty house. Left on their own for two to three hours without adult or parental supervision, children were trusted to "be good" yet, with increasing peer pressure and gang influence, experimented with drinking, drugs, and sex. At the close of the century, increasing numbers of children lived below the poverty level, were without healthcare, and lived in single-parent homes, quite a different end to the period than the idyllic family suburban lifestyle from which it began.

THE
1950s

MARRIAGE AND FAMILY

A favorite jump-rope ditty of the fifties recited, "first comes love, then comes marriage, then comes Barbara with a baby carriage." This childhood rhyme best sums up expectations for women during the 1950s: girls were expected to finish school and get married, then raise a family, in that order. Marriage was a major life step, and weddings were public displays appropriate to one's position in society. Shortly after high-school graduation, girls could expect to be bridesmaids or brides themselves. Social etiquette included an engagement announcement in the newspaper, followed by a detailed wedding announcement. The wedding announcement in the newspaper included not only a picture of the bride but often included a list of significant guests; description of the gown, veil, and flowers; the reception menu; music; and gifts for the guests. This was an opportunity for the parents to show the world how important and stylish they were. Wedding ceremonies and receptions resembled fairy tales and gowns were fit for a princess. Protocol gave the bride and groom the first dance, and, of course, the bride always had a dance with her father.

Despite the lavish wedding, honeymoons were simple affairs. Young couples typically had limited savings for an expensive trip and would most likely drive to their destination. For those close enough, Niagara Falls became the quintessential honeymoon destination. For those out of driving range, it became the model to emulate finding the closest seaside cottage or cabin in the mountains.

More affluent girls had the opportunity to go to college, but marriage rather than a career tended to follow graduation. In fact, graduation was not the generally expected result from college. Many parents sent their daughters to college with the expectation that they would earn their "Mrs." degree, not their bachelor's degree. There was no stigma for girls who dropped out of college to get married.

Women were bombarded with marketing and media instructing them that their most important role was that of wife and mother, a message contrary to that received a few years earlier during WWII when their efforts were key to saving the country. For many women, it was a difficult transition to make, from independent worker to subservient housewife. Television programming and magazine articles were there to help guide women's return to the home with tips on how to make a husband happy.

Men had more options. They could get a job out of high school, join the military, or go to college. They were not rushed into marriage as girls were, but neither were they allowed to delay for too long. At most, a man could delay marriage until after college or military service without violating social norms. A man with a wife and children represented stability to the corporate world, and, without a family, a man would not be able to move up the corporate ladder.

Emphasis on the family unit representing a wholesome environment made it difficult for those who did not prescribe to the norm. Individualism was thought to be odd, even dangerous to society, and was not readily

A fashionable woman poses in a suit and furs and hat, ca. 1950s. [George Marks/Retrofile/Getty Images]

Nice Girls Wear Hats and Gloves. In the 1950s, no well-dressed, proper woman would consider leaving the house without the appropriate accessories. Hats were worn in every season and at every age. Little girls wore hats and frilly half hats to worship, and teenagers, wanting to look older, wore hats more similar to their mothers. Any visit to a store, church, synagogue, luncheon, office, or bank building required the appropriate hat, not to mention the matching handbags, gloves, and shoes. Gloves were a social necessity for the proper woman or young woman of the 1950s. Etiquette required gloves to be worn on all but the most informal occasions. Little girls followed their mothers' examples, donning gloves when accompanying their mothers on social calls, shopping downtown, or attending religious services. Toward the end of the fifties, hats began to lose favor as hairstyles went from simple ponytails and pageboys to complex beehives. As the 1960s progressed, the relaxed social norms and an increasing trend toward informality witnessed the slow decline in hats and gloves, except for more formal or proper social occasions.

accepted. The traditional two-parents-with-children nuclear family was the model to be emulated in all American households. Supported by industry, television, Hollywood, and advertising, the traditional family unit was the expected norm that represented safety, God, and country. Adherence to this norm, a strong father and nurturing mother, left no room for dissonance or communism. Women of marrying age who were single by choice were considered unusual and did not have a full role in society. They were pitied and referred to as "old maids." Men who remained bachelors for too long may have their masculinity questioned.

Some women, whether single or married, did pursue and succeed at careers such as school teacher, librarian, secretary, or nurse, but their social activities were limited by the stigma associated with the single or married working girl. Widows, especially the numerous younger women left widowed by WWII, were also pitied, especially if they had children. However, because they did not fit the traditional family model, they were often excluded from neighborhood or other social activities. Divorce was generally not accepted and often not legally possible in the 1950s. Divorcees posed a threat to married women with children because they could only be after one thing: someone else's husband. Gossip ran rampant in the suburbs, and the children of divorced parents suffered because they too were ostracized from social gatherings. The prevailing fear was that children from divorced parents would have a bad influence on children from "proper" families because their mothers were assumed to be loose.

SEXUALITY AND MORALITY

Conservative morals and Christian-Judeo values ruled sexuality and morality in the 1950s. "Good girls" were expected to dress and act properly and were not to be seen with "undesirables" who could tarnish their reputations. Although group activities such as school dances were permissible for younger teens with appropriate supervision, dating and courtship was governed by extensive rules. Good girls could be seen holding hands in public with a steady boyfriend and perhaps receive a peck on the cheek at the end of an evening. It was never appropriate for a girl to be seen "making out." Only loose girls with a bad reputation would dare to be caught in a compromising situation. Boys were taught to hold a door for their female companions and good manners, including keeping hands to one's self. Girls had curfews and the boys obliged, wanting to please the girl's parents. Good girls who got pregnant in high school went away to live with an aunt. One year later, they returned to normal life and the temporary disappearance was never discussed. Pregnant girls who had nowhere to go or who decided not to hide their condition were ostracized by the community.

Television did its part in promoting a unrealistic view of life through ultra-conservative eyes. Televisions programming was wholesome and family oriented. There was never a hint of impropriety or the slightest inference of sexuality. TV husbands and wives slept in twin beds, never in the same bed, and children appeared as if by magic, not through pregnancy. Pregnancy was banned on the airwaves, not even the words were spoken. Sexuality was a private matter and not a subject for public broadcast.

The 1950s trophy wife portrayed in movies did not exist outside of Hollywood. A corporate wife was expected to look sophisticated, not sexy. Proper foundation garments ensured that a shapely woman was confined to a tight hourglass package, revealing only enough to trigger imagination. Strapless and backless gowns were appropriate for formal occasions, but they never dipped below the small of the back or revealed cleavage. Form-fitting, yes, but revealing, no. Even swimsuits were conservative by today's standards. A skirt flap was drawn across the legs to hide the crotch, belly buttons were covered, and molded cups kept things discreetly in place. Slacks still had zippers on the side, and shorts were not very short.

Despite attempts to camouflage sexuality and sexual relationships in the 1950s, premarital sexual relationships were still occurring. In the 1950s, birth rates amongst teens between fifteen and nineteen years of age reached their highest point at the dawn of the last half of the twentieth century: 96 per 1,000 births were to teen mothers compared with only 49 per 1,000 births by 2000 (Boonstra 2002, 7). Although only 13 percent of these births were to nonmarried teens, many of the pregnancies occurred before marriage and resulted in the shotgun wedding in which the "happy couple" was rushed to the altar before the embarrassment of swelling abdomen would disgrace the families.

Growing Up in America

The idealistic life as portrayed by television in the 1950s did exist for some. The growing middle class experienced the "good life" with solid employment at solid wages and a new home in the suburbs. Growing up in the suburbs during the 1950s was a safe and peaceful time, isolated from some of the harsh realities of the rest of the world and those less fortunate on the other side of town.

Children were raised to respect their parents and never talk back. Children were taught to say "yes, ma'am" and "no, sir" to their elders and not speak unless spoken to. Children were also instilled with a sense of responsibility by being issued a $1 bill to carry to school each week for deposit in their school savings account. Schools focused on the importance of conformity and citizenship. All children proudly recited the Pledge of Allegiance to the American flag every morning at school.

A special summertime treat was finding a big tree to sit beneath after chasing down the ice cream truck. Children played outside until dark and listened for the whistle unique to their own dad calling them home for the evening. Christian families went to church and attended religious classes on Sunday, and their Jewish friends went to temple on Saturday. Summer vacation meant a road trip adventure. Everyone in the neighborhood would gather to watch the family station wagon back out of the driveway and gather again on the family's return from vacation to see souvenirs and Kodak pictures. This was the new middle class.

Families celebrated Thanksgiving by outlining their children's hands to draw a turkey and remembering the peace between the early settlers and Native Americans. Families marched in parades and hung American flags proudly. Children across the country all wanted a collie dog like Lassie. It was a very special treat to get a hamburger at a drive-in restaurant. Modern conveniences such as air conditioning were not widely available in homes, but there was a comfort in snuggling beneath the crisp clean sheets that brought the outside freshness inside from hanging out on the line.

In the idyllic suburbs of the 1950s, girls played with dolls and boys played with trucks. Moms taught table manners to children, the preparation of economical meals to daughters, and dancing lessons to sons. Mom magically removed grass stains, and dad mowed the lawn and tuned the car.

However, all was not equal or idyllic. Segregation and discrimination, although illegal, were still present. The "white flight" to the suburbs left minorities segregated to urban centers. Those African-American families that tried to pursue the suburban dream of the 1950s often found themselves subjected to racially discriminatory housing practices. They were simply informed that nothing was available on the block, although for sale signs might dot the lawns.

This segregation extended to education facilities, both primary and secondary. In 1954, Chief Justice Earl Warren and other members of the Supreme Court wrote in *Brown v. Board of Education* that separate facilities for blacks did not make those facilities equal according to the Constitution. Integration of whites and blacks in primary schools and institutions of higher learning began across the nation. In 1956, Autherine J. Lucy successfully enrolled in the University of Alabama at Tuscaloosa. In 1957, Elizabeth Eckford was the first black teenager to enter the then all-white Little Rock Central High School in Little Rock, Arkansas. These changes created confrontation at many locations and resulted in an increased presence by the National Guard throughout the country as a peacekeeping force.

For middle- and upper-class children, college became the new expectation. Families and children took pride in being the first to go to college. With more students than ever having the opportunity to attend college, it was expected that high-school students would select a college before the end of their senior year. Being away from home for the first time led to a new sense of independence for America's youths. Whereas many continued to observe dress codes and conduct codes, college pranks such as stuffing telephone booths and fraternity and sorority pledge hazing rituals became the rage.

Those who really tried to separate themselves from the conservative mainstream would either associate themselves with the beatniks or the greasers. The "beats," or beatniks, were antiestablishment and anti-everything. Beats would hang out in coffee shops, dressed from head to toe in black garb, including sunglasses, recited non-metered poetry and conversed in their own made-up language, which included phases such as "cool, man," "daddy-o," and "squaresville." The greasers were a group of hot-rodders and bikers. They wore black leather with chains, smoked cigarettes, hung around public spaces in large groups, and thrived on intimidating the clean-cut preppies. These two fringe groups did not generally infiltrate "your town, USA" but developed in pockets around larger cities and universities.

THE
1960s

MARRIAGE AND FAMILY

On the surface, the state of the American family at the beginning of the 1960s looked as if it was continuing the same trajectory of the previous decade. More than 70 percent of all households reflected the traditional nuclear family: the father was the breadwinner, and the wife tended to domestic chores and raised the children (Mintz and Kellogg 1988, 203). Median income, which had been rising steadily since 1947, stood at around $5,600 per family in 1960 (Kurian 1994, 111). Although this was the picture for the average family, blacks and other minorities faced a starkly different reality. The number of blacks living in poverty rose steeply during the decade, and illegitimate births and children raised in single-parent homes increased dramatically (Mintz and Kellogg 1988, 210).

Other developments were also beginning to have an impact on the American family, the most important of which was the entry of massive numbers of women into the workforce. During WWII, women worked in factories to take the place of men who were fighting overseas, a trend that did not necessarily end with the war. By 1960, around 23 million women, 36 percent of women over the age of 16, were working for wages. Although many women still played the role of full-time housewives (this image was reinforced on numerous television shows, such as *Leave It to Beaver* and *I Love Lucy*), the number of two-income households was on the rise. By 1969, women constituted more than 40 percent of the entire workforce. Furthermore, one-third of all women had husbands who were making less than $5,000 a year (Zinn 1995, 496). The median household income reflected this progression, increasing to nearly $9,500 by the end of the 1960s.

As more women were faced with the choice of staying at home to raise a family or taking a full-time job, the fledgling feminist movement began to gain momentum. Betty Friedan's book *The Feminine Mystique*, published in 1963, examined traditional gender roles and articulated the emptiness she felt as a housewife. The work found a sympathetic audience among women across the country who were reexamining their own lives and marriages. Friedan founded the National Organization for Women (NOW) in 1966 as a way to channel the groundswell of support for women's issues. NOW's initial focus, as spelled out in its charter, was to "confront with concrete action, the conditions which now prevent women from enjoying equal opportunity and freedom of choice which is their rights as individual Americans, and as human beings" (Carroll 1982, 34). Many of the women involved in the movement had taken part in civil-rights protests and had worked alongside black leaders, so they knew how to organize and apply pressure to accomplish their goals. The organization's primary objective was to remove barriers to opportunities in the workplace by working through traditional channels, namely the federal government.

Title VII of the 1964 Civil Rights Act included a clause that had outlawed discrimination on the basis of sex at businesses larger than twenty-five employees, but NOW applied pressure for legislation that went even further. In 1967, LBJ signed an executive order banning sex discrimination for all federally connected employment. These two important pieces of legislation during the Johnson administration were steps in the right direction, but much remained to be accomplished in this area. On average, women's wages were just a bit more than half of what men earned for similar work.

As women transitioned from the home to the workplace, the glaring need for daycare facilities was exposed. A 1964 study, commissioned by the Department of Labor, found that there were more than 1 million "latchkey" kids, children who spent at least a portion of the hours after school without parental supervision. The daycare industry was for all intents and purposes nonexistent: although 43 percent of women with school-aged children worked, nursery schools and care facilities could only accommodate 2 percent.

The array of choices that were available to women in the 1960s led to several interesting trends. First, more and more women were choosing to go to college; the end result was that many women postponed getting married and starting a family until after graduation. The 1970 census revealed that the number of unmarried women under the age of twenty-four had risen by one-third over the course of the decade (Carroll 1982, 33). Another indication of this pattern was that the marriage rate had dropped by the end of the 1960s to just 10 marriages per 1,000 people. A byproduct of waiting to get married was a precipitous decline in the population's birthrate. In 1960, total births for women aged sixteen to forty-four were 118 per 1,000; by 1969, that figure had dropped to 86.5 (Rielly 2003, 31).

In addition to waiting longer to get married, putting off child-rearing until later, and taking advantage of the benefits of higher education, women were also contemplating the idea of divorce more often. A general

Feminism and the Well-Dressed Woman of the 1960s. The role of women in society changed dramatically over the course of the decade, and the avenues that were opened to the average woman as a result of the feminist movement had a profound effect on their clothing. Once consigned to be housewives or work as secretaries, nurses, or teachers, the late 1960s saw the number of women entering the workforce significantly increase. Likewise, a growing segment of the female population began to pursue higher education as a means to more professional options, and the growth of the population attending universities and delaying marriage translated into a preference for more casual styles of clothing. The rise of feminism also led women to question conventional clothing styles and opt for choices that conveyed a reluctance to follow the paths previous generations had established.

awakening among American females, partly because of more exposure to the workplace and other opportunities and partly because of the influence of the feminist movement, empowered women and led to the realization that they no longer had to stay in unhappy marriages.

Divorce retained a social stigma at the beginning of the decade, but the combination of new laws making it easier to dissolve a marriage and the increasing frequency of divorce slowly changed the public perception. New York State, even as late as 1966, allowed for divorce only on the grounds of adultery. Many other states had laws governing divorce that were similarly flawed and in need of reform. The effect was sweeping: from the mid-1950s to 1970, the divorce rate jumped by more than two-thirds for women under forty-five. The group that experienced the highest increase was women between the ages of twenty and twenty-four, an indication of the impact of the strong changes sweeping through society (Carroll 1982, 33). These women no longer had to rely solely on men for financial support, and they had opportunities that had not been available to their counterparts in previous generations.

SEXUALITY AND MORALITY

The Kinsey Reports, released in 1948 (*Sexual Behavior in the Human Male*) and 1953 (*Sexual Behavior in the Human Female*), were arguably the first shots in the sexual revolution and helped lay the foundation for an open discussion of sexuality in American society. Alfred Kinsey's work also opened the door for other researchers to examine patterns of sexual behavior. William Masters, a gynecologist, and Virginia Johnson, a psychologist, began conducting experiments and observing and measuring patterns in more than 700 subjects in 1957. They published *Human Sexual Response* in 1966, and it quickly became a bestseller. Among the report's contributions were a detailed analysis and discussion of the female experience during sex. The book's success was partly the result of liberalized attitudes toward sex, the large segment of the population that was at an age of experimentation, and a general cultural awakening of the status of women in society.

At the same time that Masters and Johnson were conducting their groundbreaking research, magazines, literature, the women's movement, and other factors were helping to heighten the impact of their work. Although Hugh Hefner had begun publishing *Playboy* magazine in 1953, by the 1960s, he managed a publishing and entertainment empire. His magazine's circulation was in the millions (68 percent of the magazine's readers were between the ages of eighteen and thirty-four [Weiner and Stillman 1979,

172]), and this success allowed him to open the first Playboy Club in Chicago in 1960. By 1971, twenty-three clubs were in operation. Moreover, Hefner also expanded into television and hosted such shows as *Playboy's Penthouse* and *Playboy After Dark*. The availability of offerings under the Playboy brand helped bring sexuality into the mainstream.

Other magazines also shifted the tone and subject matter of their stories. Helen Gurley Brown, the author of *Sex and the Single Woman*, published in 1963, became the editor of *Cosmopolitan* magazine in 1965, and her influence was felt immediately. Whereas in 1964 the publication had featured articles such as "Catholics and Birth Control" and "Young Americans Facing Life with Dignity and Purpose," after her arrival, typical features included "The Ostentatious Orgasm" and "Pleasures of a Temporary Affair."

The feminist movement played a role not only in the transformation of how the media portrayed women but also in the rejection of previously accepted ideas of women's sexuality. Betty Friedan and other leading women had already begun to question the traditional idea of what women desired, and these groups had an impact on publications aimed toward the female segment of the population. Eva Moskovitz noted that "women's magazines misrepresented women as fulfilled, thereby keeping them in the private world of home and bedroom, in contrast to feminists who presented women with the truth about their condition, encouraging them to free themselves from the bondage of domesticity" (Moskowitz 1996, 66). Organizations such as NOW, in the process of fighting for women's equality in the workplace, also sparked a reexamination among women about what their place in society should be.

One indication of the movement's effect on the bastions of traditional society was the 1968 Miss America pageant. Two feminist groups, Women's International Terrorist Conspiracy from Hell and Radical Women, staged a protest of the pageant and its objectification of the female contestants. In addition to picketing the event, the groups crowned a sheep as Miss America and threw copies of *Cosmopolitan* and *Playboy* in the garbage to protest the "ludicrous beauty standards" that society held for women (Bailey and Farber 2004, 111).

Other factors contributed to a growing sense of empowerment of women over the course of the decade. The Pill, an oral contraceptive for women, was approved by the Food and Drug Administration in 1960. Although it was initially prescribed only to married women, more and more single women turned to it as their preferred contraception as the decade progressed. The impact of The Pill was that it allowed women to exercise more control over reproductive issues, choices that had heretofore required a man's participation. Still, as late as 1970, several states still prohibited the sale of any contraceptives to minors, and the high cost of birth control limited its use among the poorer segments of society.

All of these factors—a growing acknowledgement and more open discussion of sexuality, an increase in the emphasis on sex in the media and literature, the rise of the feminist movement, and the development and availability of female oral contraception—helped magnify the growing sexual revolution. More women waited longer to get married and instead pursued higher education and careers. Whereas the number of men enrolled in colleges, universities, and other institutions of higher education nearly doubled from 2.2 million in 1960 to 4.1 million in 1968, so too did women's enrollment, reaching 2.8 million in 1968 (Kurian 1994, 142).

Indications of this changing behavior abounded. In 1962, Illinois became the first state to decriminalize all forms of sexual conduct between consenting adults; many states followed suit soon after, although some, particularly in the South, were slow to remove all restrictions on such behavior. The practice of unmarried couples living together also became much more prevalent throughout the course of the decade: in 1960, only 17,000 couples in the entire country were sharing a residence; that number had increased by 900 percent as the decade drew to a close.

Although much progress was made in the area of sexual relations, there were still some areas that remained taboo. In the 1960s, interracial marriage was still a felony in many states. At the beginning of the decade, there were around 51,000 black-white couples in the country, but the number of interracial couples climbed 26 percent during the course of the sixties (Moran 2001, 221). Although the Supreme Court, in its *Loving v. The Commonwealth of Virginia* decision, invalidated all state laws against interracial marriage, tolerance and acceptance, especially in certain parts of the country, would come much later. Similarly, gays and lesbians were largely invisible in society during the decade. In June of 1969, a raid of gay nightclubs in New York sparked the Stonewall Riots. The event marked the beginning of the gay rights movement, one that would make significant process in the following decade.

GROWING UP IN AMERICA

The distribution of the U.S. population underwent a drastic change during the 1960s. In general, the country became less rural, with the agricultural population dropping by 5 million people over the course of the decade (Kurian 1994, 177). At the same time, several factors contributed to an explosion in the suburban population. The migration of southern blacks to the northern cities resulted in white flight from urban areas, as middle-class whites decamped to the suburbs. This exodus was facilitated by the cheaper land available in the suburbs and by the rise of the inter-state highway system. The latter factor made the automobile the main form of transportation for suburban families, allowing them the ability to get to the cities when necessary. As the decade opened, American house-holds were located primarily in the suburbs, although just 5 percent of black families lived in those communities. As a result, the cities and sub-urbs were both racially and socioeconomically segregated.

The youth culture of the 1960s was dominated by two characteristics. First, the post-WWII baby boom had created a demographic bulge that reached maturation by mid-decade. Indeed, more than 41 percent of the nation's nearly 200 million people were below the age of nineteen in 1965. Never before had the youth segment been so large, and conse-quently this group had a huge impact on all facets of society.

As a consumer bloc, teens helped fuel the rise of several different indus-tries. Because the average teen allowance was $6 a week for boys and $4 a week for girls, the collective buying power of the youth segment was about $12 billion a year. This consumer group purchased 55 percent of all soft drinks, 53 percent of all movie tickets, and 43 percent of all record albums. Furthermore, more than 20 percent of all high-school seniors drove their own car (Jones 1980, 73). It is no coincidence that the fast-food industry's meteoric rise occurred at the same time that so many teens were looking not just for food after school but also for jobs to support their spending habits. Other industries experienced a similar boost by serving and catering to teens: spending on radios, televisions, records, and musical instruments rose from just $3.4 billion in 1960 to more than $7.8 billion by 1969. Sales of toys and sports supplies enjoyed a similar jump (Kurian 1994, 152). Among the favorite items were super balls, slot cars, board games, Barbie dolls, and G.I. Joe dolls. Manufacturers even made black versions of the latter two products under pressure from minority groups (Rielly 2003, 108).

Throughout the decade, rock music provided an almost ever-present soundtrack for teens. Just four years after the Beatles' breakthrough per-formance on *The Ed Sullivan Show*, the group had sold more than $154 million in albums (Farber 1994, 212). Music sales actually eclipsed the total revenues of the motion picture and professional sports industries combined. Rock 'n' roll also produced some of the most enduring, charis-matic stars of any musical period: Bob Dylan, Jim Morrison, Janis Joplin, Jimi Hendrix, James Brown, and Otis Redding, to name just a few. Because music for teens was almost inseparable from rebellion, many of these artists were at the leading edge of cultural and social change.

One area that the Beatles' impact was felt almost immediately was on hairstyles. Although the initial issue surrounding those who emulated the "moptop" involved a blurring of the established gender roles—long hair was for girls, after all—it was only a few years later that the true significance of hairstyles would become apparent. The musicians, entertainers, and other teen role models that were pushing the envelope of what traditional society believed was acceptable often sported long hair. If a teen wanted to assert independence from authority and demonstrate a certain fearlessness in the face of inevitable derision and possible punishment, long hair was an easy first step. Although pictures of JFK playing touch football and relaxing without a coat and tie led Americans to feel that such dress was within the boundaries of good taste, the youth culture's approach to dress and personal grooming was an altogether different thing. A man in Kentucky made his son get a dog license because he would not cut his hair; in schools across the nation, long hair was treated as a disturbance, and students were regularly suspended as a result.

Colleges and universities across the country became places where young men and women came together to share ideas and mount protests against traditional American society. In the decade from 1963 to 1973, total enrollment at all institutions of higher learning doubled to 9.6 million, from 4.7 million (Jones 1980, 82), so there were many more students, with much more energy, to push the envelope of accepted activities. As student movements gained steam, driven by activities in places such as Berkeley, California (the home of the free-speech and dirty-speech movements), and San Francisco, a person's informality, in dress as well as personal grooming, came to identify the side of the fight with which an individual was affiliated. In 1965, more than 100,000 young people organized and participated in protests against the Vietnam War (Palladino 1996, 21). Indeed, the counterculture and war protests became intertwined and culminated in mass demonstrations in Chicago during the Democratic National Convention. Radical leaders such as Abbie Hoffman and Jerry Rubin exhorted young people to descend on the city and disrupt the proceedings.

It is also important to note the class aspect of the counterculture movement. Because not everyone could afford a college education, student protests, and by extension the hippie culture, were seen as being populated by the middle- and upper-class liberal elite. In addition, higher education became a way to avoid the draft for the Vietnam War, with those in college receiving student deferments. As a result, the lower classes and ethnic minorities served at disproportionately higher rates than their counterparts. The clashes in Chicago at the Democratic National Convention between blue-collar cops whose sons were serving in the military and students and hippies who had gotten out of the draft via higher education served to fuel the violent clashes.

Another aspect of the counterculture was the promotion and celebration of drug use and experimentation. From Timothy Leary at the beginning of the decade to Ken Kesey and his Merry Pranksters, to the Grateful Dead and Jimi Hendrix singing the praises of mind-expanding drugs, it is no wonder that drug use among the youth segment increased dramatically. By the mid-1960s, marijuana had become the drug of choice: from 1960 to 1970, people who had tried marijuana jumped to 8 million, from a few hundred thousand (Jones 1980, 112), and in one survey, just 17 percent of those surveyed admitted to not being part of the drug culture (Weiner and Stillman 1979, 112). The government outlawed amphetamines and barbiturates in 1965, and cocaine slowly filled the void. The release of *Easy Rider* in 1969, in which characters snorted the drug, did its part to popularize cocaine.

THE
1970s

MARRIAGE AND FAMILY

The institution of marriage in the 1970s was facing challenges on several fronts. The average American family was deeply affected by the country's economic woes: although the average household income more than doubled over the course of the decade, rising gas prices and inflation put pressure on families to do more with less. Indeed, by 1976, only 60 percent of the jobs paid enough to support a family with one wage earner. Overall, the percentage of women in the workforce increased to 51.2 percent by the close of the decade (Wandersee 1988, 127). Out of necessity, women achieved a sort of economic emancipation during the decade. In 1975, legislation ended financial practices that restricted the ability of a woman to obtain a credit card without her husband's written approval.

Still, many families were struggling, and, from 1970 to 1982, the percentage of American children living in poverty rose from 14.9 percent to 21.3 percent (Weitzman 1985, 357). Black households faced greater challenges: the median income of black families in 1976 was just 59 percent that of whites, meaning that these households had to get by on $4,000 less than the median income of $12,750 in 1975 (Zinn 1995, 31). Additionally, 35.3 percent of all black families were headed by single women, up from 20 percent in 1960, illustrating the erosion of the traditional family unit in the black community that occurred over the decade (Zinn 1995, 77).

More and more young adults were taking more time to experience life before plunging into marriage. The average age for a first marriage in 1980 was 22.1 years for women and 24.6 years for men, a full year higher than just five years earlier (Carroll 1982, 279). What's more, when people did get married, they were having fewer children. The birthrate in 1975, 15 per 1,000, was almost half the figure from 1957.

It was divorce, however, that had the most profound impact on marriage in the 1970s. California was the first state, in 1969, to pass no-fault divorce legislation, and the majority of states quickly followed suit. As a result, the divorce rate skyrocketed. Over the course of the decade, the number of divorces rose from 4.5 million in 1971 to more than 9 million by 1979, when the divorce rate stood at 5.3 per 1,000.

The economic effects of divorce cannot be minimized. In most cases, women were granted custody of the children, and the number of households headed by single mothers grew to 7.7 million by 1977 (Wandersee 1988, 133). As a result, one in three families headed by women were living below the poverty line. Because the median per capita income for divorced women who did not remarry was just over half that of divorced men who remained single, women faced an uphill struggle. An increasing number of women entered the workforce, particularly those with small children. The number of working mothers with children under the age of six grew from 30 percent in 1970 to 46 percent in 1976 (Bailey and Farber 2004, 109). With the prospect of lower incomes as well as the added burden of raising and providing for children, single and divorced mothers found it especially difficult to get back on solid footing.

It is no wonder then that the women's movement resonated so strongly during this period. One of the only social movements to survive the tumult of the late 1960s, it gained traction during the 1970s as women searched for solutions to the problems they faced. In addition to divorce, other pressing issues included the quest for economic equality and reproductive rights. Women became increasingly visible in a number of different social and political channels. Shirley Chisholm, a black congresswoman from New York, ran for president in 1972. At the political conventions, the involvement of female leaders and the number of female delegates increased markedly from past elections. At the 1968 Democratic National Convention, just 13 percent of the delegates were women. Four years later, that number had risen to 40 percent. Furthermore, politicians such as Bella Abzug, Pat Shroeder, and Jane Byrne gave voice to women's issues and ensured that the Democratic platform included a plank on reproductive rights.

The movement solidified around attempting to gain passage of the ERA (Equal Rights Amendment) to the U.S. Constitution. The ERA needed passage in thirty-eight of fifty states. It passed thirty-five and then stalled, in part because of its strong association with abortion (thirty states ratified it before *Roe v. Wade*) and because of a strong, well-organized opposition. Despite 60 percent approval rating among the American public, the ERA was three states short as the March 1979 deadline for ratification drew near. Supporters won a three-year extension, but anti-amendment groups mobilized. Phyllis Schlafly, a conservative activist and ERA opponent, testified in front of four state legislatures and helped to block the amendment's passage. Despite the ERA's defeat, the campaign had helped to raise the awareness for both women and men across the country to the plight of women in society.

To that end, the women's movement was quite successful. Not only did it advocate empowerment, but it also pushed the boundaries of what paths were deemed acceptable for women to pursue. The apex of the movement was the National Women's Conference in Houston, in 1977. Delegates from across the country attended in hopes of forging agreement on an agenda. No consensus was reached, however, and the movement ultimately would splinter into a number of factions.

The combination of economic necessity and the influence of the feminist movement helped women to pursue new career opportunities. Building on the growing numbers of women in the 1960s who attended college, the proportion of female students pursuing professional degrees climbed as well. The percentage of students receiving law degrees who were women rose from 5.4 percent at the beginning of the decade to 28.5 percent in 1979. Similarly, female students constituted 23 percent of the medical school enrollment, up from just 8.4 percent. Furthermore, more than 30 percent of all business degrees in 1979 were earned by women, foreshadowing an influence yet to come in the corporate world.

SEXUALITY AND MORALITY

The liberalization of attitudes toward sex that began in the 1960s truly started to be felt in the 1970s. Because more people were delaying the decision to get married, there were more single people and more couples living together outside of marriage. By 1980, there were more than 3 million households composed of unrelated people living together, and attitudes seemed to reflect this new reality. In 1972, a survey posed the question, "If a man and a woman have [non-marital] sex relations do you think it is always wrong, almost always wrong, wrong only sometimes, or not wrong at all?" Although 47 percent of respondents said it was wrong more often than "only sometimes," three years later, just 42 percent of the sample responded similarly (Model 1989, 306). A 1973 Gallup poll further demonstrated the shift from the 1969 statistic that 68 percent of all respondents thought premarital sex was wrong, to only 48 percent five years later. Another survey in 1976 found that only 33 percent held the view that unmarried people were "sick," "immoral," or "neurotic" compared with more than half in 1950. So, although opinions were changing slowly, a majority of the U.S. public was tolerant if not accepting of unmarried couples cohabitating and engaging in sexual activity.

At the same time, organized religion experienced a resurgence mid-decade as 60 percent of the U.S. population expressed confidence in religion. The return to traditional religion was coupled with a quest for spiritual enlightenment in the form of new-age religions. *Life* commented that "the wilting flower child has blossomed into the Jesus freak," and the influences of organized religion could be found throughout music and pop culture, for example, in the musical *Jesus Christ Superstar* (Edelstein and McDonhough 1990, 110). The line between some new-age religions and cults was often blurry, as evidenced by the People's Temple, led by the Reverend Jim Jones. In November of 1978, in Jonestown, Guyana, Jones instigated a mass suicide among his followers that resulted in the deaths of 913 people.

The publication of several books and magazines helped to break new ground sexually. Alex Comfort's *The Joy of Sex*, released in 1972, took an unadorned view of sexuality. A year later, Erica Jong's *The Fear of Flying* discussed such topics as female longing and sexual fulfillment. Pornography also gradually became more mainstream. The 1972 hardcore film *Deep Throat* grossed $30 million, just part of what had become a $4 billion industry for sexually explicit materials. *Playboy* and *Penthouse* magazines both began including full-frontal nudity in their publications. A backlash to these graphic and increasingly available depictions of nudity and sexuality led to the arrest of Larry Flynt, the publisher of *Hustler* magazine, on charges of indecency. Alternative lifestyles such as swinging and wife swapping also gained notoriety. Although it was estimated that only 1 percent, or 1 million people, engaged in such practices, the overwhelming majority of the population looked upon swinging with disapproval (Hunt 1974, 256).

In the 1970s, the role of gays in society experienced a transformation. The Stonewall Riot in 1969, which involved protests in New York City's

Greenwich Village, marked the beginning of the gay rights movement. The ensuing years saw gays mobilize on a mass scale: more than 600 gay groups and publications were formed in the 1970s and collectively constituted the foundation of the gay-liberation movement. Protests by gay groups had the result of challenging traditional ideas about sexuality and masculinity, because the gay subculture accepted more effeminate identities. Although the United States was becoming more tolerant in regard to changing heterosexual mores, the general public was not ready to embrace the homosexual lifestyle. A backlash against gays occurred, with several municipalities, including Miami, revoking anti-discrimination laws that had passed during the civil rights movement. Much of the anti-disco rhetoric had an undertone of homophobia as a result of the music's embrace of the gay subculture that frequented clubs such as Studio 54 in New York City. The assassination of Harvey Milk, an openly gay San Francisco city councilman, and Mayor George Moscone by a police officer indicated that discrimination and violence against gays was alive and well as the decade drew to a close.

As with other parts of society in the 1970s, feminism played an important role in the areas of sexuality and what was deemed morally acceptable by American society. Gloria Steinem launched *Ms.* magazine in 1971, and, two years later, the Boston Women's Health Book Collective published *Our Bodies, Ourselves*, one of the first books that was specifically geared to women's health issues. The feminist movement also raised awareness about issues such as domestic abuse and rape. Susan Brownmiller's *Against Our Will: Men, Women, and Rape*, published in 1975, was a landmark book on the topic. The first battered wives' shelter was established in St. Paul, Minnesota, in 1974; by 1979, there were 250 such shelters nationwide. In 1973, the Federal Bureau of Investigation reported 51,000 forcible rapes (believed to be just one-fifth of the actual total), an increase of 62 percent over five years.

The women's movement had a number of factions that included a lesbian contingent. As Winifred Wandersee noted, "The ideological rationale for a lesbian lifestyle seemed the logical extension of a woman-centered identity, and for that reason, some lesbian feminists began to perceive their position as politically more correct than one that allowed for heterosexuality" (Wandersee 1988, 66). Literature such as Rita Mae Brown's *The Rubyfruit Jungle* also brought attention to lesbian sexuality.

No issue demonstrated the rising influence of the feminist movement in U.S. society more than the battle for legalized abortion. A Harris poll in 1969 found that 64 percent of those surveyed believed the issue was a private matter (Zinn 1995, 500). Before 1970, about 1 million abortions were performed each year, although approximately only 10,000 were done legally. Clandestine abortion-referral services were set up in many cities. In Chicago, for instance, a group of feminists maintained a network called "Jane" that performed about one hundred abortions a week. Groups such as the National Association for the Repeal of Abortion Laws (formed in 1969) were instrumental in making the case for a more progressive approach to the issue of abortion. In 1970, the New York legislature agreed to reform the state's century-old abortion law, permitting termination of pregnancies resulting from rape or incest. By mid-1970, eleven other states had enacted similar reforms (Carroll 1982, 27). Challenges by opposition groups eventually led to the Supreme Court's landmark decision on *Roe v. Wade*, which effectively legalized abortion by acknowledging that an individual's right to privacy included decisions on abortion. Seven years later, the National Opinion Research Center found that from 82 and 91 percent of the sample approved of abortion in cases of rape, incest, or mother's health, whereas 50 percent endorsed it on grounds of poverty or unwanted children. Only 7 percent opposed abortion on any grounds (Carroll 1982, 270).

Growing Up in America

In 1970, the country and its youths had to contend with the aftermath of many policies and programs from the previous decade. In 1969 alone, the population had witnessed both the lunar landing and Woodstock within months of each other. The war in Vietnam was still raging, although President Nixon's pledge to bring the conflict to an end had lowered the troop levels there slightly. Various movements, from civil rights to free speech to feminism, had staged protests against traditional institutions and raised questions about society's foundations. It was in this environment that a whole generation of America's youths came of age.

As a country, the population had continued to shift to cities or the suburban areas surrounding them. The agricultural population continued to dwindle, dropping from 9.7 million people in 1970 to just 6 million by the end of the decade (Kurian 1994, 177). By 1974, more than 151 million people, or nearly three fourths of the U.S. population, lived in the 264 largest metropolitan areas, leaving less than one third of the population in rural settings. At the time, the impact of this redistribution was recognized as one of the most important developments in the way communities and the people in them interacted (Zinn 1995, 103).

Regardless of where young people lived or went to school, the specter of the Vietnam War and the draft was never far behind. Although the armed services required fewer inductees for military operations in Asia in the early 1970s than it had five years earlier, the draft was still in effect, resulting in a heightened awareness among college students about the government's policies toward Vietnam. Hundreds of thousands of students staged protests against the Nixon administration's policies, and, on May 4, 1970, National Guardsmen fired on a student gathering at Kent State University, killing four people. The fallout from this event as well as the failed policies caused a majority of the American public to turn against the war effort.

By the time the government discontinued the draft in 1973, nearly 500,000 young men had failed to register with their local Selective Service chapter, 172,000 had registered as conscientious objectors, and an additional 50,000 had left the country or gone underground. Overall, less than 10 percent of the 27 million young men who were eligible for the draft from 1964 to 1973 actually served, with those with a high-school education or no education accounting for 21 and 18 percent of inductees, respectively (Palladino 1996, 221).

With the war over, young people could focus their attention on more pressing matters, namely dating and mixing with the opposite sex. The behavior and attitudes of the previous generation had been passed on to those coming of age in the 1970s, and, for the majority, settling down and having a family were not the top priority. During the first half of the decade, the number of single men living by themselves more than doubled; women experienced similar gains (Modell 1989, 275). Singles constituted 23 percent of the population by 1980, and the impact of this new consumer group was evidenced in everything from housing shortages and single-serving food items to the growth of the pet-care industry (Carroll 1982, 280). Furthermore, the number of households established by unmarried couples tripled, to 1.6 million, over the course of the decade. The idea of going to school, getting married, and having kids as soon as possible had fallen from favor among America's youths.

High-school and college students were instead using this time to experience life with less of an emphasis on adhering to the mores of previous generations. Sexual experimentation among young people was increasing, and sexual relations were no longer considered the first step to courtship and marriage. Most realized the fleeting nature of high-school romances. These attitudes are reflected in statistics on sexual activity among young people: according to the Alan Guttmacher Institute, by age nineteen, four-fifths of males and two-thirds of females had had sexual intercourse, with an average initiation age of sixteen. Teen pregnancies rose to 1 million a year by 1978, and 400,000 abortions were performed in 1977 (Carroll 1982, 280). The element of sexual experimentation in dating was reflected in the 1977 movie *Looking for Mr. Goodbar* (based on a novel by Judith Rossner). The film followed one character's experiences during the sexual revolution, and its main themes were control of one's body, the impact of feminism on dating, and the search for fulfillment through sex.

The new opportunities available to women, thanks in part to feminism's influence, were reflected in the changing composition of student enrollment in college. No longer content with choosing between entry-level jobs or traditional female occupations such as nursing and teaching, an increasing number of women elected to pursue other areas of study as well as professional degrees. In fact, by mid-decade, women were more likely than men to attend colleges and universities. Once at school, a new spate of women's studies classes helped to expose a new generation of students to the tenets of feminism and the ongoing struggle for equal rights.

Among the youth culture, recreation in the form of sports, music, and other similar activities remained popular, with women gaining an equal footing with men. As mentioned previously, Title IX of the 1972 Education Act prohibited discrimination in any program receiving federal aid, thus guaranteeing the funding of women's athletics in high schools and colleges. As a direct result, women's participation in high-school athletics increased fivefold by the end of the decade. At the same time, skateboarding became a popular activity, in part because it combined a sport with a subculture lifestyle that prominently featured music. By

Punk Rock and Skateboard Fashion in the 1970s. A number of popular activities among the youth segment of the country contributed to the rise of new trends and clothing styles. Punk rock, a reaction to the corporate rock scene, boasted the lure of not only subversion and anarchy but also clothing styles that immediately set its fans apart from the rest of society. Black leather jackets, ripped T-shirts held together by safety pins, and Mohawk and spiked hairstyles became instantly recognizable symbols of the punk movement. The popularity of skateboarding amongst American's youths exploded in the 1970s and brought with it a distinctive style of clothing. Baggy jeans, T-shirts, and sweatshirts allowed for a greater range of movement while skateboarding and became the signature look for the skateboard subculture. Punk and "skater" styles reasserted themselves in the 1990s and 2000s.

1976, skateboarding had become a quarter-billion-dollar industry enjoyed by more than 10 million people (Hoffman and Bailey 1991, 330).

On the music front, punk rock emerged as an alternative to the corporate rock on most FM radio stations. Its appeal stemmed in part from the music's aggression, rebellion, and overt rejection of the mainstream. Punk rock quickly came to encompass a subculture that spawned tight-knit communities that included underground fanzines, clubs, and record stores. The Sex Pistols, the Dead Kennedys, the Germs, and the Clash were some of the more popular punk rock groups. Another component of the genre's appeal was that it did not require a high degree of proficiency on the part of musicians. In this way, punk's reach was very democratic and inclusive in that everyone felt like they had enough talent to be in a punk band.

As with previous generations, young people in the 1970s did their fair share of experimentation with drugs and alcohol. In general, the use of marijuana and other illicit drugs was on the rise throughout the decade. One survey found that one in four high-school students drank more than once a week, and 40 percent smoked pot on a weekly basis (Norman and Harris 1981, 87). According to the National Institute of Drug Abuse, in 1977 there were approximately 16 million people smoking pot in the United States. Likewise, a 1977 Gallup poll revealed that 35 percent of all Americans had tried marijuana at least once, evidence that, in many cases, the younger generation of apples were not falling too far from the parental tree.

THE
1980s

Marriage and Family

In 1986, the Reagan administration produced a report entitled *The Family: Preserving America's Future*. It was offered as a reaction to "two decades of liberal abrasive experiments with the family," and it expressed dissatisfaction with trends such as sex education, population control, and value clarification in schools. The report proposed to affirm "home truths" to keep families interacting and spending time together but also motivated parents to be more actively involved in raising their children (Carlson 2003, 162). The report was part of a rising concern with the rapidly changing panorama of the American family.

Despite the conservative climate and political rhetoric espousing a return to traditional families and marriage, the statistics for the decade a revealed a different picture. Approximately 16 million (7 million men and

9 million women) individuals were identified as divorced in the 1980 census report. Additionally, the U.S. Census revealed that, although 17.1 percent of American households were composed of an individual person in 1970, by 1989 that number had risen to 24.6 percent. Approximately 51 million individuals, almost equally distributed amongst men and women, registered under the "never married" category of the census. Changes in the structure of American families and society that began in the 1970s continued to escalate throughout the 1980s.

These changes in living arrangements influenced American society in several ways. Urban and suburban development, for instance, was impacted by the number of people searching for smaller living quarters. In urban settings, the demand for apartments steadily increased throughout the decade as post-high school and now post-college numbers of men and women lived alone instead of settling down in a house in the suburbs. Whereas single people and young married couples migrated to large cities, the suburbs remained the place of choice for more traditional families. Retailers followed these trends by targeting specific product lines to singles in the city with disposable income that were different in composition from those for their suburban, married counterparts. Many fashion and lifestyle magazines became more focused on the singles phenomenon. Publications such as *Vogue*, *Elle*, and *GQ* oriented article and advertisements to single male or female consumers or young couples.

The lauded view of the traditional family was also challenged by the rise in the number of unmarried persons living together. The relaxation of attitudes toward sex and the reticence toward marriage as a result of the large number of divorces were some of the reasons that motivated younger Americans to "play house" before making a formal and legal commitment. As such, the average age for marriage continued to rise. By the mid-1970s, the average age at marriage was 21.1 years for women and 23.6 for men (Carroll 1982, 279). A decade later, in 1987, the age for marriage increased almost two and a half years, to 23.6 for women and 25.8 for men.

The increased number of divorces in America motivated many religious groups, particularly the Catholic Church, to require premarital counseling for couples before the wedding. Religious organizations also sponsored marriage counseling and marriage encounter weekend retreats to help married couples build and strengthen their relationships. Secular organizations also provided counseling or couples therapy sessions for those who preferred to separate religion from marriage. The 1980s also witnessed an increase use of prenuptial agreements ("pre-nups") amongst the less optimistic that marriage was "forever." Pre-nups were designed to protect an individual's premarital estate in the event of a divorce, outlining the conditions and terms of the divorce in advance of the wedding.

Ethnic or religious practices and traditions added to the diversity of family structure and size in America. Hispanic families as a norm tended to be larger and often included non-nuclear members in the household. These extended families often consisted of grandparents, aunts, or uncles and other related individuals beyond the traditional mother-father-children nuclear structure. Mixed or interracial marriages, once taboo and even illegal, continued to increase and become more accepted as the decade progressed. By 1990, more than two thirds of the American population surveyed approved of interracial marriages, as opposed to the 10 percent approval rating from a similar 1960s survey (Farley and Haaga 2005, 191). American designers, manufacturers, and retailers understood the complexity of ethnic families in America and responded by expanding product lines to accommodate special needs or interests and hosting store events to celebrate special occasions such as Black History Month and Hispanic Heritage Month.

Women's roles and responsibilities continued to expand throughout the decade. Women had fought hard in the 1970s for their right to be on equal footing with men in the workplace. Many women climbed the corporate ladder and political ladder and then struggled to balance work, marriage, and children. Gender roles, still firmly entrenched from the 1950s image of *Leave it to Beaver*, were slowly shifting as men began to take more responsibility at home for household chores and childrearing. However, at the end of the day, the majority of the cooking, cleaning, laundry, and child-related matters still fell to women. Many women found themselves questioning if the price of "having it all" was worth it or not.

With the ever-increasing numbers of working mothers, there was an ever-increasing demand for daycare for both preschool-aged children and after-school care. Daycare centers rapidly increased throughout the cities and suburbs, and some progressive companies even added on-site daycare for their employees. Families who could afford to do so turned to live-in help with nannies or au pairs. For those who could not afford assistance or after-school programs, the number of latchkey children continued to increase if a family member (often a grandparent) was not available to substitute for the watchful eye of mom.

SEXUALITY AND MORALITY

The debate over sexuality and morality was intense in the United States during the 1980s. The division in values and points of view was evident in the discussions around issues such as abortion, sex in the media, and gay rights. Politicians, therapists, women's magazines, and religious groups all weighed in their opinions, hoping to guide the moral compass of the nation.

Subjects that were previously left to the realm of self-help books or *Playboy* were openly discussed on radio and television and became tolerated to a greater degree when endorsed by mature women such as Dr. Ruth Westheimer or Sue Johanson, CM, RN. Americans grew used to open discussions about the technical aspects of sexual relations as well as the playful side, when the person giving the advice resembled a grandmother's face. Westheimer ran a radio show *Sexually Speaking* beginning in 1980 and followed her efforts with several books and a television show. Johanson's *Sunday Night Sex Show* debuted on radio in 1984 and expanded to television in 1985. Both women spoke about sex and relationships frankly and without any vulgar undertones, putting the country at ease.

Turning from works on sexual techniques and self-gratification of the 1970s, discussions about sexual relationships in the 1980s again began to focus on the "relationship" part. The day of free love and "doing what feels good" was past. Self-help literature on sex, marriage, and relationships was expanded beyond the *Joy of Sex* to focus on self-esteem and personal growth in relationships, especially for the increasing population rebounding from divorce. Popular guides to life and love for the era included Robin Norwood's *Women Who Love Too Much* (1986), John Gray's *Men Are From Mars, Women Are From Venus* (1992), and Louise Hay's *You Can Heal Your Life* (1984). Through these and other avenues, individuals began to address the "emotional baggage" that kept them from finding happiness in a traditional relationship.

The country remained deeply divided in opinions related to acceptance of homosexuality. Most Americans, however accepting of the lifestyle choice, remained uncomfortable with the idea of fully incorporating homosexuality into American normality. In 1986, the Supreme Court affirmed the constitutionality of sodomy laws as mandated by some states that criminalized homosexual practices. Early attempts to recognize gay marriages in San Francisco and other urban centers also failed. As visibility of homosexual life increased in the American mainstream, the debate was posed to be one of the central issues on sexuality and morality to be reckoned with in the early part of the twenty-first century.

The strongest opposition to the gay plight came from conservative religious groups that gained strength during the 1980s with the rise of televangelism. Jerry Falwell and his Moral Majority group preached strongly against homosexuality and abortion and in favor of school prayer and traditional family values since the 1980s. A perceived support of conservative ideas during the George H. W. Bush administration (1989–1993), however, brought some of these issues back to the forefront of public discussion.

Adding to the conservative culture of the 1980s, Americans also were confronted with two non-curable sexually transmitted diseases in the 1980s. Both genital herpes and HIV/AIDs became prevalent enough in the 1980s that, despite the conservative climate, safe sex campaigns were launched. These educational campaigns targeted high-risk groups in inner cities, as well as colleges and high schools. The message was that no one, regardless of socioeconomic status, was immune from these diseases. The battle raged between promoting abstinence and recognizing the reality: many nonmarried individuals were engaging in sexual relations and must learn how to do so without increase the spread of disease.

Growing Up in America

The last decades of the twentieth century experienced a drastic change in the attitude toward childcare. Children born in the "new families" of the period were expected to be more independent and to have greater responsibilities than those born before them. Many children also stayed in school past normal childcare hours to allow parents to work additional jobs or take care of urgent matters.

Many children from minority families, however, faced other problems such as extreme poverty, lack of medical insurance, and even homelessness. The McKinney Act of 1987 aimed to assist homeless children by requiring states to provide free and appropriate education for them. However, because no significant efforts were made to solve transportation and housing problems for many of these children, the act failed to achieve its goal (Blair, Siegel, and Quiram 1997, 103).

Another alarming issue was the increase in the number of missing children. The American public was made aware of the crisis during the 1980s because of the strong attention the media gave to tragic child abductions and runaway cases. Parents who thought they left the dangers of the city behind when they moved to the suburbs were reminded that the dangers of child abduction and exploitation can exist anywhere.

At the end of the twentieth century, the science and education fields portrayed children as efficient learning machines. Developmental researchers T. G. R. Bower in *The Rational Infant* (1985) and Peggy Eastman in *Your Child is Smarter Than You Think* (1985) argued that children have a powerful learning system that should be tapped into while they are young. This new attitude, although commendable, also implied a reduction of the amount of playtime allotted to children and placed them under extreme pressure for success. From early ages, children were encouraged to put down finger paints and Legos and get involved in classical music programs not because of the aesthetic enjoyment they could derive from it but because of the assumption that it would help them develop skills applicable to other areas, particularly mathematics (Hymowitz 2000, 17).

Children were also increasingly considered capable of becoming independent adults and making their own decisions at early ages. The Emancipation of Minors Act passed by the California legislature in 1982 allowed children to petition to become legal adults, with some limitations, if they felt there were reasons to separate from their parents. Although this act was directly a result of constant children-parent conflicts in the California entertainment industry, it was also a measure of the country's new attitude toward children as independent, free-minded individuals.

This new-found independence of children influenced the way clothes were marketed. Whereas in the past children's clothes were promoted almost exclusively to their parents and grandparents, starting in the 1980s, more young children were allowed to choose their own garments. Retailers developed visual merchandising experiences in their stores aiming to appeal to children and teenagers. Accessories, jewelry, and cosmetic lines were developed just for young girls and were packaged to remind children of their favorite toys or candy.

Video game consoles, such as Nintendo and Atari, and other electronic toys came to prime in the 1980s and also captured a considerable amount of children's time. The popularity of video games after the 1980s contributed to the reduction in the amount of time children spent involved in outdoor and physical activities. They also compounded another concern with American children: the rise in obesity rates from 15 percent in the 1970s to 21 percent by 1990. The consumption of fast food and non-nutritional meals was blamed for the problem, but few Americans changed their eating habits or promoted healthier eating habits for their children. The rise of obesity among children also implied an increase of potential eating disorders such as anorexia and bulimia (Blair, Siegel, and Quiram 1997, 76).

Religious-based secondary education remained vital in the country and, although often seen as conservative by some, was respected for its quality and value-centered emphasis. Several religious and private institutions continued requiring students to wear uniforms, whereas others allowed students to wear casual "school" clothes. In the 1980s, private high schools were notorious for the "preppy" or preparatory school style when affluent young men and women would dress in elegant and formal clothes to showcase their wealth. *The Official Preppy Handbook* was published in 1980 by Lisa Birnbach. Part parody and part how-to manual, the book provided detailed information about the appropriate clothing choices and promoted the use of items such as chino pants, Fair Isle sweaters, polo shirts, and penny loafers.

THE
1990s AND 2000s

MARRIAGE AND FAMILY

In 1995, 57.1 percent of all American families were composed of only one or two people, whereas 32.5 percent of the families included three to four people living in a household (Blair, Siegel, and Quiram 1997, 4). The number of single-parent homes reached 26.6 percent by 2000, an increase of more than 10 percent from the previous decade and double the rate from 1970. Childcare became a financial burden for many American families, especially single-parent families. In 2000, the expense for childcare often ran as high as 25 percent of a family's income (Farley and Haaga 2005, 217). In 1990, the U.S. Congress passed the Child Care and Development Block Grant. This was the first comprehensive childcare legislation in the United States that authorized financial resources to states to assist families in need with daycare expenses.

Whereas historically children were cared for by relatives when both parents worked outside the home, now most childcare arrangements involved group facilities such as daycare centers and schools rather than one-on-one supervision. By 2000, 30 percent of preschool-aged children with working mothers were in daycare facilities (Hymowitz 2000, 70), and 60 percent of all children were cared for by someone not related to them (Blair, Siegel, and Quiram 1997, 28). Only one in six children were under the care of a parent during working hours, and, additionally, only one in six children were under the care of a single individual, either employed by the family or a member of the extended family.

The country experienced increased demand for affordable daycare and paid family leaves as a result of the increased number of households in which both parents were employed and the greater number of employed single mothers. An important victory for families was the passing of the Family and Medical Leave Act of 1993, which guaranteed parents time off work, albeit without pay, to attend to family needs. This act required employers to provide up to twelve weeks of unpaid leave per year to employees who needed to care for newborn or adopted children or to stay home while their children were sick. This act also allowed men to take time off from work after the birth or adoption of a child as well as women, shifting the role of primary caretaker in some families from the mother to the father.

What constituted family at home varied greatly amongst socioeconomic and ethnic groups during the period. Children from Asian-American families, for instance, were more likely to live in a traditional family (26 percent), followed by whites (24 percent), and Hispanics (22 percent). However, only 6 percent of African-American and 14 percent of American-Indian children lived under similar conditions (Farley and Haaga 2005, 187). Many children from minority families faced problems such as extreme poverty, lack of medical insurance, and even homelessness. The percentage of children living under the poverty level was larger than the number of adults. Statistics clearly indicated that poverty was sharper among minority children with rates of 33 percent among African-American children and 28 percent among those of Hispanic descent (Ingoldsby and Smith 1995, 358). As a result of the extremes of poverty and the strains of childcare, many minority and underprivileged children suffered from health problems, drug dependency, alcoholism, smoking, juvenile delinquency, and violence.

Another dramatic change in the structure of American society was the increase in the number of people living singly; the 2000 U.S. Census revealed that 25.5 percent of all American households were composed of one person, a significant increase from the 1970 rate of 17.1 percent. A new market segment emerged composed of almost 58 million "never married" individuals living alone and another 21 million divorced individuals living alone. Television programming, which was once dominated by programs focusing on traditional nuclear families, now reflected the popularity of single living in America. Whereas in the 1980s some of the most popular shows included family-centered entertainment such as *Family Ties*, *The Cosby Show*, and *Thirty Something*, in the 1990s, television was dominated by programs centered on single people such as *Seinfeld*, *Friends*, and *Will and Grace*.

The accepted view of traditional marriage and family was also challenged by the rise in the number of unmarried persons living together. By the year 2000, the number of opposite-sex couples cohabitating was estimated at 3.8 million, a sharp rise from 440,000 in the free-love era of the 1960s. The 2000 census also indicated that there were more than 500,000 same-sex couples in cohabitation (Farley and Haaga 2005, 174), another drastic change in family and relationship structures. Attitude surveys still revealed that most Americans expected to marry eventually; 72 percent of all people surveyed in 1998 expressed such intent (Farley and Haaga 2005, 171). However, large numbers of Americans were choosing to marry at a later age. The median age for marriage increased about one and a half years in the space of one decade, from 25.8 for men and 23.6 for women in 1987 to 27 for men and 25 for women in 1997.

The increase in singles and couples cohabitating (whether married or not, whether heterosexual or not) combined with the increased age of marriage did not go unnoticed by real estate developers. The market demand for not just apartments but also condominiums (condos) rapidly increased in the 1990s. Women, as well as men, had increased disposable income as a result of delaying marriage and children and rolled that income into real estate investments. Unlike their parents before them, singles were not interested in the responsibility of homeownership, only the financial benefits of real estate. Singles and young couples were too busy with work and play to mow lawns and repair roofs.

Another significant change in family and relationship in the 1990s was the increase in the number of people over sixty-five. The number grew from 16.5 million to 20.5 between 1990 and 1999 alone. By 2000, 25 percent of the total population of the United States was over the age of sixty-five. Many seniors required substantial medical care, which created serious demands on programs such as Medicare and Medicaid, as well as financial and emotional strain on adult children. Increased longevity also resulted in increased second marriages amongst older Americans who were widowed. New families were formed when senior individuals with adult children and grandchildren remarried. The purchasing power of retired patrons was also recognized. Condominium developments that were age-specific retirement communities or assisted-living centers developed across the country. Manufactures and retailers also took note of this new market segment and developed products and apparel specifically targeted to retirement-age individuals.

SEXUALITY AND MORALITY

Cable television and the entertainment industry continued exploring the limits of the American audience's tolerance toward sexuality with television shows such as HBO's *Real Sex, Taxi Cab Confessions,* and *Sex and the City,* and shows addressing the sexual lives of the gay community such as Cinemax's *Queer as Folk* and *The L Word.* Although sexuality was more prominent on cable television and movies, the display of nudity on network television still faced strong opposition from the public. The entertainment industry received an enormous backlash in 2004 after the controversy surrounding the halftime show for Super Bowl XXXVIII when singer Justin Timberlake removed a breast cup to expose Janet Jackson's breast covered only by a nipple shield. Even after the musicians and the network claimed that the brief nudity originated from a wardrobe malfunction, the Federal Communications Commission imposed heavy fines on the network.

The entertainment and fashion industries were often chastised during the period for presenting overly sexualized images, particularly of teenagers. Semi-nudity and insinuated nudity were staples in fashion advertisement by the late 1990s. Spreads in fashion magazines, like those by Calvin Klein, and fashion catalogs, like Abercrombie & Fitch, became more sexualized over the period, showing less clothing and more explicit sexual situations.

The World Wide Web was also teeming with sexual content potentially exposing children and teenagers to the commercialization of sex and sexual predators. By 1998, 40 percent of all American households owned computers that were available to children. Several software programs were developed to assist families with the task of controlling access to the Internet and selected websites. Bombarded with sex imagery, American teenagers were having sexual experiences earlier than previous generations. The age for sexual debut lowered for both boys and girls in the mid-1990s, with 56 percent of all boys and 51 percent of all girls in the age range of fifteen to seventeen reporting to be sexually active.

In 1995, the Centers for Disease Control reported that 53.1 percent of all youths in grades nine to twelve had not only already had sexual intercourse but clearly linked sexual activities to alcohol and drug experimentation (Blair, Siegel, and Quiram 1997, 118). Often the lack of experience or information about safe sex practices led to unwanted pregnancies and sexually transmitted diseases among teenagers. The rate of teenage pregnancy was 54.4 per 1,000 women aged fifteen to nineteen, with two-thirds of those pregnancies declared as unwanted and ending in abortions (Therborn 2004, 222). Although abortion numbers actually decreased in the 1990s, one in five women seeking abortion was a teenager (Blair, Siegel, and Quiram, 125).

The country also remained deeply divided regarding the source (nature versus nurture) and acceptability of homosexuality. A 1992 survey indicated that 4.5 percent of all men and 3.4 percent of all women said they had a homosexual experience at some point in their lives (Therborn 2004, 211). Other estimates claimed that the gay community in the United

States may be as high as 10 percent of the total population. Many states repealed such laws prohibiting homosexual activity in the last part of the twentieth century. Those that did not had their laws invalidated by the 2003 landmark U.S. Supreme Court case *Lawrence v. Texas*, which decriminalized such sexual practices in all states.

This shift in the legal climate gave gay rights activists hope for the legalization of gay marriage. In 1972, the Supreme Court had decided that the issue was an independent decision for each state. However, in 1996, Congress passed the Defense of Marriage Act establishing that states were not required to give effect to a law from any other state regarding same-sex marriage. Several states, including Texas and Louisiana, passed constitutional bans on all same-sex unions, whereas other states banned same-sex marriage. Some progress was made, however, by the end of the millennium in 1999, Vermont passed a law indicating that legal benefits could not be denied to same-sex couples and, by 2000, allowed civil unions for homosexual couples. In 2003, Massachusetts opened the door to same-sex marriage in the United States, but, when similar initiatives were attempted in other states, they were defeated by political efforts.

During the 1990s, gay and lesbian individuals became more prominent in public life through successful television shows such as *Spin City* and *Will and Grace* and with the notoriety of gay sports celebrities, including Olympic swimmer Greg Louganis and baseball player Billy Bean. Several magazines, including *Out*, *The Advocate*, and *Instinct*, catered to the gay and lesbian community. Designers, manufacturers, and retailers were

Rights for Gays and Lesbians. Gay and lesbian Americans fought strongly for equal rights during the 1980–2005 period, making some progress as civil unions among same-sex couples were recognized in some states and new legislation protected their rights at home and work. Increased visibility in the entertainment industry and public openness about their sexuality resulted in wider mainstream acceptance for the gay community. The coded messages embedded in apparel by homosexuals to identify each other in the early decades of the twentieth century were exchanged for more open expressions of sexual identification through clothing. Gay pride parades organized across North America included participants from a number of "subgroups" easily identifiable for their clothing choices. Rainbow flags and pink triangles, considered open symbols of homosexuality, were incorporated into clothing and accessories.

quick to tap into the gay market, composed largely by individuals with disposable income. By the end of the 2000s, gay men have been inducted as arbiters of good taste in fashion by television shows such as *Queer Eye for the Straight Guy* (which ended in 2007), *Project Runway*, and *Tim Gunn's Guide to Style*.

As if harkening back to the 1950s, the 1990s witnessed a full-scale assault on the acceptability of planned single motherhood. In opposition to unplanned pregnancy amongst single women (which garnered sympathy and concern from the American public), some women were purposely planning to become single mothers. With an increase in the number of women delaying marriage or never marrying, some women were opting for artificial insemination from a sperm bank donor rather than watch their biological clocks wind down. This trend was brought into the media limelight in 1992 and raged into a heated debate after the title character in the television series *Murphy Brown* proudly gave birth to a child as a single mother. Then Vice President Dan Quayle criticized the fictional plot as an assault on the family. The series producers responded the following season with an episode discussing the diversity of the family experience in the United States.

GROWING UP IN AMERICA

By 1997, children were spending at least two more daily hours in school and preschool than they did in the early 1980s (Hymowitz 2000, 17). As adults in the United States worked longer hours, so too did children; on average, American children lost about ten hours of playtime per week during the decade. School work became increasingly demanding even for kindergarten students, who were no longer expected to just have fun and pick up social skills while attending preschool facilities.

By the end of the millennium, virtually all American children between ages five and seventeen were attending primary school. Enrollment for school-aged children rose from 42 million of 45 million in 1990 to 51 million of 53 million in 2000 (Blair, Siegel, and Quiram 1997, 91) whereas dropout rates declined from 6.7 percent in 1973 to 5 percent in 1993 (Blair, Siegel, and Quiram 1997, 99). About 83 percent of all Americans graduated from high school in 1999, a drastic increase from 1960 when that number was only 41 percent.

However, the gap between public and private education remained disproportioned. A considerable difference was also evident amongst facilities and resources available in public suburban schools and those in rural and inner-city public schools. Even at the end of the twentieth century, many of America's public schools struggled with deteriorating facilities, lack of resources, and insufficient technology. Technology and the cultural revolution of the Internet reached affluent schools considerably sooner than public schools, thus widening the gap in the preparation of pupils for college or the job force. By the twenty-first century, most American students depended primarily on the World Wide Web for homework as well as online communication and social networks through websites such as Facebook, Hi-5, and MySpace.

Curriculum differences also remained substantial because private schools had more freedom over controversial issues such as prayer in school, the inclusion of evolution theory in the curriculum, and the relevance of cultural diversity and multiculturalism. The inclusion or exclusion of certain topics in the curriculum remained a controversial issue in American schools as the country remained polarized on matters such as school prayer, evolution, and homosexuality. In 1993, for instance, New York City schools were under pressure over the *Children of the Rainbow* curriculum, which discussed social injustice and biases, gender roles, tolerance, and respect for minorities, including homosexuals (Washburn 1996, 63).

Violence in schools remained a central issue. The country stared in disbelief in 1999 when two students killed thirteen people at Columbine High School in Littleton, Colorado. Even after other similar events occurred, attributable in part to the accessibility of weapons to teenagers, the country remained divided in views related to gun control. Juvenile delinquency and participation in gangs remained a challenge to American society, and more minors were tried as adults for their crimes. Gang colors, worn to show affiliation, became more prevalent in American schools, leading many schools to enact dress codes or uniforms in an attempt to thwart gang-related activities. Violence in American schools was often associated with alcohol and drug abuse. Marijuana and "date rape" substances actually became more widespread in American schools by the end of the period. Several drug prevention campaigns were in place, including DARE (for Drug Abuse Resistance Education), established in 1983.

For the most affluent sectors of American society, the spending allowance was increased so that children and teenagers could satisfy their taste for expensive and designer items. Children fully entered the consumer market at the end of the millennium, spending billions of dollars of allowance money on their favorite brands and styles. It was estimated that teenagers' spending was around $238 billion annually, mostly in nonessential goods (Blair, Siegel, and Quiram 1997, 61). These trends continued into the 2000s as teenagers, as well as adults, bought expensive designer handbags, shoes, and other accessories. A related trend is the designer "knock off," in which such items as high-fashion handbags, in addition to clothes, are sold in cheaper copies, made of inferior materials and less well-constructed. They sometimes look, to the untrained eye, very much like the real thing. These cheap copies are usually sold on the street in Manhattan and in other large cities. Police are now beginning to crack down on these sales.

Television also played a prominent role in shaping childhood in America. Throughout the country, television sets were placed in prime places in homes and often in each bedroom in the house for affluent families. By 2000, it was estimated that the average child watched more than twenty-seven hours of television each week, making television their dominant leisure activity (Bertman 1998, 72). Logos and characters from these and many other popular programs appeared in apparel products and toys.

The most controversial development in children's health was the rise of cases for personality disorders such as attention deficit hyperactivity disorder and attention deficit disorder. By the dawn of the twenty-first century, some researchers were criticizing what they considered twenty-five years (1980–2005) of overdiagnosed personality disorders. They also claimed that the diagnosis of personality disorders responded to popularity trends. The 1980s, for instance, saw an increase of schizophrenia cases, whereas the 1990s saw the rise of diagnosis for bipolar disorders. Ritalin and lithium were among the most commonly prescribed drugs for behavioral problems. Parents and physicians were also often accused of avoiding responsibility and sparing themselves the effort of working with children who had grown up in a fast-paced and technologically advanced world.

REFERENCES

Bailey, B., Farber, D., eds. (2004) *America in the '70s.* Lawrence, KS: University Press of Kansas.

Bertman, S. (1998) *Hyperculture: The Human Cost of Speed.* Westport, CT: Praeger Publishers.

Blair, C., Siegel, M. A., Quiram, J., eds. (1997) *Growing Up in America.* Wylie, TX: Information Plus.

Boonstra, H. (2002) "Teen Pregnancy: Trends and Lessons Learned." *The Guttermach Report on Public Policy* 5:7–10.

Carlson, A. (2003) *The "American Way:" Family and Community in the Shaping of the American Identity.* Wilmington, DE: ISI Books.

Carroll, N. (1982) *It Seemed Like Nothing Happened.* New York: Holt, Rinehart, and Winston.

Edelstein, A. J., McDonough, K. (1990) *The Seventies From Hot Pants to Hot Tubs.* New York: Dutton.

Farber, D. (1994) *The Sixties: From Memory to History.* Chapel Hill, NC: The University of North Carolina Press.

Farley, R., Haaga, J., eds. (2005) *The American People: Census 2000.* New York: Russell Sage.

Hoffmann, F. W., Bailey, W. G. (1991) *Sports & Recreation Fads.* Binghamton, NY: Harrington Park Press.

Hunt, M. M. (1974) *Sexual Behavior in the 1970s.* Chicago: Playboy Press.

Hymowitz, K. S. (2000) *Ready or Not: What Happens When We Treat Children as Small Adults.* San Francisco: Encounter Books.

Ingoldsby, B. B., Smith, S. D. (1995) *Families in Multicultural Perspective*, Perspectives on Marriage and the Family. New York: Guilford Press.

Jones, L. Y. (1980) *Great Expectations: America and the Baby Boom Generation.* New York: Coward, McCann, and Geoghegan.

Kurian, G. T. (1994) *Datapedia of the United States, 1790–2000.* Lanham, MD: Bernan Press.

Marty, M. A. (1997) *Daily Life in the United States, 1960–1990: Decades of Discord.* The Greenwood Press "Daily Life through History" Series. Westport, CT: Greenwood Press.

Mintz, S., Kellogg, S. (1988) *Domestic Revolutions.* New York: The Free Press.

Modell, J. (1989) *Into One's Own: From Youth to Adulthood in the United States, 1920–1975.* Berkeley, CA: University of California Press.

Moran, R. F. (2001) *Interracial Intimacy: The Regulation of Race and Romance.* Chicago: The University of Chicago Press.

Moskowitz, E. (1996) "It's Good to Blow Your Top," *Journal of Women's History* 8:66.

Norman, J., Harris, M. (1981) *The Private Life of the American Teenager.* New York: Rawson, Wade.

Palladino, G. (1996) *Teenagers: An American History.* New York: Basic Books.

Rielly, E. J. (2003) *The 1960s.* Westport, CT: Greenwood Press.

Therborn, G. (2004) *Between Sex and Power: Family in the World, 1900–2000.* International Library of Sociology. Milton Park, Abingdon, Oxon: Routledge.

Wandersee, W. D. (1988) *On the Move: American Women in the 1970s.* Boston: Twayne Publishers.

Washburn, K., Thornton, J. F., eds. (1996) *Dumbing Down: Essays on the Strip Mining of American Culture.* 1st edition. New York: W. W. Norton.

Weiner, R., Stillman, D. (1979) *Woodstock Census: A Nationwide Survey of the Sixties Generation.* New York: Viking Press.

Weitzman, L. J. (1985) *The Divorce Revolution: The Unexpected Social and Economic Consequences for Women and Children in America.* New York: The Free Press.

Zinn, H. (1995) *A People's History of the United States.* New York: Harpers Perennial.

PART II

Fashion and the Fashion Industry, 1950–2008

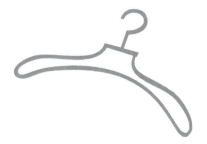

6

The Business of Fashion

Fashion is more than an artistic statement, it's a business. As the era begins, the fashion industry is ruled by the dictates of Paris couturiers. However, many couture houses in Paris found themselves in financial difficulties in the 1950s. With an ever-dwindling client base, haute couture must reinvent itself or parish. Couturiers must become businessmen, not just designers, and broaden their reach to a new middle-class audience to remain profitable. Couturiers expand into ready-to-wear garment and licensed products, such as hosiery, neckwear, jewelry, and cosmetics, exchanging their name for profits. Profits made from licensing agreements and mass-produced ready-to-wear garments help sustain haute couture, especially in the "Big '80s" when conspicuous consumption reigned.

The growth of the middle class during this period expanded the demand for ready-made clothing. The active American lifestyle demanded clothing that moved. American designers stepped up to the challenge, reinterpreting Paris fashions for the American woman and man. Although women might always turn to Paris for overall style, especially in formal-wear, over this fifty-year period, they increasingly turned to American designers for their "daywear," known now as sportswear.

American designers also discovered a new market in the 1950s: children. The post-WWII baby boom resulted in an unprecedented birth rate and a new demand for children's wear that was unique, not miniaturized versions of adult clothing. As the decades progress, the children's market was further segmented in preteen, teen, and college markets, each with its own look.

The expansion of retail operations, both high-end department stores and mass merchandisers, promoted the American vision of fashion. As manufacturing techniques improved and sizing became standardized, the quality of ready-to-wear clothing improved drastically over the course of the decade. The rapid production and distribution methods also meant that a new fashion trend, once only available to the elite, could now be instantly reproduced at all price points. The same fashion trends could be found at Chanel, Macy's, Banana Republic, Old Navy, and Wal-Mart simultaneously.

The fashion industry, like any good business, also learned the importance of targeting its audience. Whether it was the *Mickey Mouse Club* in 1955 or MTV's *House of Style* launched in 1989, fashion used the new medium of television to promote its message. The most forward promoters were also quick to adopt cable television (*The Home Shopping Network*) and the Internet to reach their audiences twenty-four hours a day, seven days a week. Fashion was ready whenever, wherever shoppers lived.

HAUTE COUTURE

1950s

After years of deprivation brought on by the Great Depression and WWII, polite society regrouped and gala balls once again filled the social calendars of the upper classes. Previously rationed materials were again available for use in fashion, and Paris responded with both increased volume and opulence in women's fashions for both day and evening. Haute couture was again the ticket to entry into upper-class society, a badge of membership within the social elite. Haute couture, or literally "high fashion," was and is the personification of the fashion industry: luxurious clothing, custom fit, made by hand.

The "New Look," first launched by Christian Dior in 1947, had women across the world cinching themselves into corseted dresses with voluminous swirling skirts and adorning themselves with accessories. During the 1950s, nearly 50 percent of all Paris couture exports were from the House of Dior. With a desire to remain as the top couturier, Dior diversified into an unprecedented number of fashion-related products bearing his label. He created an entirely new business by establishing licensing agreements with select manufacturers to distribute his products in boutiques around the world. Stockings, lipsticks, and other accessories provided a new class of consumer's access to the world of couture. Every woman could own a Dior, even if it was just a lipstick, regardless of income or class.

After the struggles during WWII and postwar reconstruction, most couturiers were concerned about the financial stability and ultimate longevity of their houses. Their customer base was beginning to decline, and American women, cutoff from Paris during WWII, were now frequenting the newly popular American fashion designers. Seeing the success of Dior's pioneering diversification, other Parisian couture houses expanded into licensed products to secure financial solvency and broadcast their name across the American market. A new era of Parisian couture was launched, one that began to combine mass-manufactured goods with high-end hand-tailored apparel, all under one roof.

1960s AND 1970s

Haute couture in Paris in the 1960s was subdivided into two distinct segments: conservative fashion for married women and "happening" fashions for youths. Couturiers who rose to prominence in the 1950s, such as Dior, Fath, and Balenciaga, continued to produce conservative fashions for proper women "of a certain age" in the upper classes. Simple yet elegant fashions, epitomized by Audrey Hepburn (Givenchy) or Jacqueline Kennedy (Oleg Cassini), that were less restrictive than the New Look, became the norm for the conservative, married woman of the 1960s.

However, a new breed of couturiers invaded the Paris haute couture scene in the 1960s who experimented with color, form, and materials to promote hip, innovative, and often antiestablishment fashions. Pucci worked with vivid, psychedelic prints, Courreges with "space-age" materials, and YSL with color blocking. However, regardless of color or material, most importantly, the form they all worked with was the miniskirt. The miniskirt, popularized by Mary Quant of Britain and Andre Courreges of France, became the hallmark of the youth explosion of the 1960s. Whereas old-guard couturiers such as Chanel resisted the miniskirt, this new breed embraced it.

This division between young and old in Paris couture also meant that, for the first time, Paris did not present a single, unified fashion statement (Baudot 1999, 186). A range of fashion choices were now presented by Paris each season, allowing women, young and old, to develop a personal style. Paris couturiers also began looking to street fashions, young actresses such as Brigitte Bardot, and models such as Twiggy and Jean Shrimpton, for inspiration for youthful fashions. Fashion trends were no longer exclusively dictated from Paris to the public, but, instead they came from the public to Paris.

Haute couture fashion trends were also no longer the exclusive purview of Paris. Italian designers, such as Pucci and Valentino, British designer Mary Quant, and American designers Oleg Cassini and Geoffrey Beene expanded the geographical boarders of haute couture. Paris couture now had competition.

As the 1970s began, the haute couture customer base rapidly dwindled. The number of affluent that had both the time and money for seasonal trips to Europe for custom fittings continued to decline. The increasing number of women who entered the workplace looking for careers, not husbands, also demanded clothing that conveyed a seriousness of purposes. The frivolity, or perceived frivolity, of French fashions would not work for the career woman, and, with increased frequency, women turned to American fashion designers for their wardrobes.

Couture houses became laboratories for "experimenting" with fashion trends and generating publicity for the ready-to-wear fashion industry. Fashion trends became increasingly splintered throughout the decade, with unique looks appealing to distinct groups: business women (Armani), ethnic looks (YSL), mods (Cardin and Courreges), pre-Raphaelite (Laura Ashley), and punk (Zandra Rhodes and Vivienne Westwood). Couture houses, however, rarely operated at a profit. To compensate, haute couture continued its expansion into product licensing. Lines of perfumes, cosmetics, hosiery, jewelry, belts, ties, handbags, and home linens could be purchased under the name of Dior, Chanel, Gucci, and others. Some couturiers, such as Pierre Cardin, became so adept at licensing his name, that he ultimately became better known for accessories and secondary lines than for his avante garde 1960s fashions.

Cardin, along with Givenchy, YSL, and others, realized that the key to profitability and success lay in launching prêt-à-porter (French ready-to-wear) lines. Parisian couture houses in the 1970s rapidly opened boutiques, featuring their prêt-à-porter lines, in Europe and the United States. The success of these upscale ready-to-wear lines allowed couturiers to fund their houses and produce the unprofitable haute couture collections.

1980s TO THE PRESENT

By the mid-1980s, a conspicuous consumption craze had swept across the United States. New wealth from Texas oil barons and the success of the stock market created a new upper class who demonstrated their arrival in society through a display of luxury goods. This demand for luxury goods did not escape the attention of Paris couturiers, who were ready to cater to nouveau riche Americans. Cocktail parties, charity balls, and coming-out parties were back in vogue, as were ball gowns and tuxedos. The ideals of the 1960s and 1970s youth revolution and antiestablishment attitudes disappeared with the end of the 1970s economic recession.

Haute couture responded to these social changes with formalwear that was big, bold, and dripping with ornamentation. Couturiers such as Christian Lacroix and Oscar de la Renta paved the way for opulent women's fashions, whereas Giorgio Armani and Ralph Lauren captured the sophisticated, elegant look of menswear. Everyone required Gucci or Fendi bags, Rolex watches, and designer blue jeans. Fashion was again presented as a homogenous trend that all would adopt. The splinter groups of the 1970s disappeared, at least for a decade. Haute couture capitalized on the conspicuous consumption trend and again prospered financially.

Supermodels also became celebrities and ambassadors in this internationalized world of fashion and moved beyond the haute couture runway into enterprises such as acting in films, hosting television shows, and even launching their own clothing line. Top American models such as Cindy Crawford, Christie Brinkley, and Christy Turlington were no longer seen only on the runway. Crawford became a Hollywood actress and hosted MTV's *House of Style*. Brinkley, the first model to appear on three consecutive *Sports Illustrated* swimsuit special edition covers (1979–1981), also used her voice to warn about the dangers of nuclear disasters as a member of Standing for Truth about Radiation. Turlington became an outspoken anti-smoking activist.

By the end of the twentieth century, the fashion business had become a complex engine propelled by an increase in consumerism, a search for comfort in American society, and a surge of influence amongst entertainment and pop culture icons. Every couturier and designer had an entertainment superstar attending their openings and donning their gowns on the red carpet. Parisian fashions remained influential, but American designer labels became just as important as a status symbol for the affluent. The wealthy elite continued to purchase luxurious fashions at seasonal fashion shows and exclusive stores in Paris, London, and Milan. However, American designers themselves paid tribute to the culture of success, achievement, and greed by producing and promoting their own luxury items, and both the social elite and celebrities vigorously embraced the new American designer fashions.

From the Garment District to the exclusive stores on Fifth Avenue and in SoHo, New York City remained the center of American haute couture (Murray 1989, 214). American fashion designers kept their workshops in New York City and held seasonal fashion shows in the heart of the garment district to promote their lines. Throughout the last decade of the twentieth century and into the 2000s, American fashion designers became pop culture celebrities themselves. Fashion show audiences began to draw a wide variety of prominent show business attendees, which brought more publicity to the designers and to the fashion industry. In 1995, Isaac Mizrahi was the star of *Unzipped*, a film directed by Douglas Keeve documenting one day in the life of the designer. The film went on to win the Audience Award at the Sundance Film Festival and increased interest in Mizrahi's persona. Other American designers such as Tom Ford, Tommy Hilfiger, Michael Kors, Vera Wang, and Betsey Johnson enjoyed similar popularity: Ford as an actor, Hilfiger hosting his own reality television show, and Kors, Johnson, and Wang as guest judges in several television programs. As American designer fashions became more accepted, often replacing European haute couture, American designers enjoyed increased worldwide popularity and influence, becoming household names not just in the United States but also in Europe, Latin America, and other regions.

READY–TO–WEAR

1950s

Before WWII, ready-made clothes often meant inferior workmanship and poor fit, especially for women's apparel. However, improved manufacturing techniques developed during wartime production (Fashions of an Era) combined with standardized women's sizes derived from the War Production Board's measurement of over 100,000 women (Milbank 1989, 175) resulted in better-fitting, higher-quality ready-to-wear garments. As such, the perception of ready-to-wear clothing for working-class individuals who could not afford better drastically changed.

America's isolation from the influence of Paris fashions during WWII gave American designers the opportunity to create high-end ready-to-wear for department stores. Their designs were trend setting and fit the new, active American lifestyle. American ready-to-wear, previously only for the working class, was now segmented into two tiers: mass-produced ready-to-wear, and "originals," ready-to-wear garments that were produced in limited quantities and sold in top department stores (Milbank 1989, 175). Originals elevated American designers such as Normal Norell, Claire McCardell, and Pauline Trigere to prominence in the fashion industry, so that, even when Paris returned as the center of the fashion world after WWII, American women continued to turn to American ready-to-wear fashion designers for their daily wear.

Sportswear became the mainstay of American ready-to-wear, and, whereas American designers turned to Paris for general directions in fashion trends, the world turned to America for sportswear trends. The popularity of leisure and sports activities in America, such as camping and weekends in the country, escalated the demand for sportswear throughout the 1950s. The American wardrobe became increasingly casual as the population shifted from the city to the suburbs. Sportswear became the dominant form of dress, and the new suburban mall became the destination for acquiring it.

1960s AND 1970s

As society became increasingly less formal in the 1960s, American designer sportswear became to epitomize fashion design. Ready-to-wear, no longer stigmatized as it was in the previous decades, allowed all Americans the opportunity to participate in fashion trends, just at varying price points. Sportswear, no longer just for athletic activities, became the catch-all phrase for the everyday unstructured, less embellished apparel worn by the modern woman. The demand for American designer originals continued to escalate throughout the 1960s, launching the careers of Bill Blass, James Galanos, Anne Klein, and others. Their fashions were interpreted by department stores, such as Macy's, and mass merchandisers, such as Sears, at a range of price points and distributed simultaneously from the east coast to the west coast.

By the 1970s, American designers were not just putting forth fashion trends, but they were selling entire lifestyles. American ready-to-wear designers became associated with lifestyles choices and developed lines targeted to specific customers. Anne Klein marketed coordinating, interchangeable separates for modern working women. Ralph Lauren portrayed an image of power and "old money" for the country club set. Calvin Klein offered the unisex, urban youth look with tight jeans, T-shirts, and a controversial ad featuring a fifteen-year-old Brooke Shields stating "nothing comes between me and my Calvins."

1980s TO THE PRESENT

The ready-to-wear business thrived in the last part of the twentieth century and continued its instrumental role in the "democratization" of fashion. New fashion trends were no longer the purview of the elite. Advances in manufacturing and distribution allowed ready-to-wear to replicate new fashion trends virtually simultaneously in a Paris salon, in a

New York boutique, and in a Small Town, USA, Wal-Mart. Regional apparel marts devoted to the wholesale of apparel products were created in large cities around the country, including Dallas, Atlanta, and Chicago, contributing to the decentralization of production, distribution, and sales (Guérin 2005, 225).

In the closing decades of the twentieth century and early twenty-first century, fashion was no longer exclusively dictated by Paris to the American ready-to-wear market. Although the American concern with comfort and good value turned sports items and daywear into successful ready-to-wear products (Lehnert 2000, 92), it was the obsession with brand and status that propelled ready-to-wear to the top of the market as a consumer product. The timing was perfect. The conspicuous consumption of the 1980s drove consumers on a quest for luxury goods. American designers such as Donna Karan, Perry Ellis, Tommy Hilfiger, and Ralph Lauren rapidly rose to the forefront of American designer fashions.

Designers discovered how to tap into the buying power of the ever-growing middle and working classes and to increase their financial profits through stores like Target and Kohl's. Target launched a line by Isaac Mizrahi, while Kohl's introduced a line by Vera Wang. While Target helped resurrect Mizrahi's failed career, the Wang line at Kohl's was met with mixed reviews, tarnishing Wang's image as a perfectionist who knows how to dress women. While Mizrahi's partnership with Target brought him enough recognition to be installed as the creative director at Liz Claiborne, the verdict is still out on the impact of a mediocre line launch on Wang's career.

Brand identification made the ready-to-wear business the perfect platform to display taste and status through choice labels. Every item of apparel or accessory became branded. Footwear, such as Adidas and Reebok in the 1980s and Diesel and Puma in the 1990s, not only provided Americans with functional sportswear but was also an indicator of the owner's status. Underwear, another product that became chic as a result of branding, was offered in a wide spectrum of choices, from popular brands such as Fruit of the Loom, Jockey, and Joe Boxer, to more exclusive ones such as Calvin Klein and Victoria's Secret. Maintaining a brand image to drive consumer demand became the focus of the ready-to-wear industry. Some labels, such as Esprit and Guess, were able to reinvent their image with each new fashion trend and remain popular across several decades, whereas others, such as Izod and Ocean Pacific, were so closely bound to a fashion movement that they virtually disappeared from the market—or at least went into hibernation—as a trend passed.

RETAIL OPERATIONS

1950s

In the 1950s, the race was on to "keep up with the Joneses," to have the newest and flashiest everything, from cars, to clothing, and even home appliances. This new consumer society was jumpstarted with the advent of the credit card system in 1950, and department stores were perfectly poised to take advantage of this trend. When the population began shifting from the cities to the suburbs in the 1950s, the department stores shifted with them. The shopping mall was born, and shopping became a new form of recreation for teens.

By the 1950s, women were beginning to abandon home sewing and small dressmaker shops in favor of department stores. The larger stores provided convenience, choices, and affordability, with one-stop shopping for the entire family. The busy corporate housewife could afford to buy several high-quality ready-to-wear stylish outfits for the price of one tailor-made outfit.

Department stores modified their approach to retail, adding designer shops and dedicating increasing levels of square footage to sportswear. Upscale department stores such as Marshall Field's and Hudson's installed "boutiques" such as the twenty-eight Shop and Oval Rooms, respectively, to cater to upper-class clients seeking designer originals. Although some of these shops imported couture, others, through agreements with the couture houses, purchased couture originals and made line-for-line copies to sell at greatly reduced prices.

1960s AND 1970s

The expansion of dedicated square footage for sportswear continued throughout the 1960s and 1970s and became increasingly segmented into subcategories of activewear, separates, and coordinates. As dresses continued to decline in favor, their presence, or lack of presence, on the selling floor became apparent. A new category, suits or "career separates," rapidly gained territory on the sales floor as the new American career woman demanded a professional wardrobe.

The 1970s also marked a turning point in the manufacturing of American sportswear. Favorable trade agreements with Mexico in the 1960s had already enticed some manufacturing facilities to leave America soil. The low wages combined with proximity to the United States made it a natural choice for the relocation of manufacturing positions. Spurred by the economic recession in 1973, apparel and textile manufacturers began to look for more cost-effective measures for producing apparel and textiles. Throughout the mid-1970s, approximately 30 percent of all apparel sales were derived from imported goods (Figueroa 1996, 34–40), a trend that would escalate in future decades, even after the slump from the recession ended. American sportswear would no longer be the exclusive purview of American manufacturers; instead, countries such as Taiwan, Hong Kong, and the Dominican Republic would dress Americans.

In addition to driving production offshore, the recession of 1973–1975 drove Americans from department stores to discount stores. Although people still went to the mall "to look" and gazed starry eyed at the quarterly "dream book" catalogs distributed by department stores, an increasing segment of the population shifted to discount shopping. Wal-Mart, Kmart, Target, Sears, Ward's, and J.C. Penney became the primary destinations for purchasing fashions.

1980s TO THE PRESENT

Suburban sprawl again increased in the 1980s, and, along with it, more shopping malls were opened. Unlike previous shopping centers, the new malls provided opportunities to socialize, as well as purchase clothing. Restaurants, bars, movie theaters, and video arcades were included in the mall, along with department stores and specialty retailers, transforming shopping malls into gathering spots, especially for teens and preteens. "Hanging out" at the mall became the favorite pastime for many teens and exposed a new target market under pressure to conform to the latest trends.

However, department stores and shopping malls faced strong competition from mega chain and discount retailers spreading around the United States. Wal-Mart, in particular, became a powerhouse on apparel and accessories with a competitive "roll back" price policy, assuring customers of bargains. Discount retailers, such as Loehmann's, Ross, Marshall's, and Filene's Basement, specialized in selling designer overstocks and discontinued lines at drastically discounted prices (Wolfe 2003, 226). Factory outlet shopping became widely popular, and several outlet malls were installed just outside large cities or in tourist areas, allowing consumers to buy directly from the designers or manufacturers at reduced prices. Despite the glamour and popularity of department stores and shopping malls, consumers had alternative venues for purchasing identical goods, often at reduced rates.

Many department stores merged to form bigger chains and leverage buying power. One of the most notable mergers of the period was between Marshall Field's, Hudson's, Dayton's, and Macy's. Additionally, department stores began to explore different ways to make the shopping experience more attractive to their customers, making the department store a destination. Department stores often incorporated additional facilities such as coffee shops, daycare, convenience groceries, valet parking, and video games in their premises to motivate consumers to spend more time at the store.

General merchandise department stores such as Sears and J.C. Penney continued to have some success, though they struggled, while other companies such as Montgomery Ward and Kmart Corp. faced financial difficulties in the 1990s. Kmart filed for bankruptcy in 2002; with total assets over $17 billion it became the biggest bankruptcy ever for an American retailer.

Many city centers and neighborhoods were reinvigorated by the resurgence of specialty shops and small boutiques during the last decades of the twentieth century. Specialty store chains such as Casual Corner and The Limited strategically placed their stores in geographic areas most densely populated by their specific targeted markets instead of at large malls in the suburbs. The Gap Inc. was among the most successful retailers to use this approach as well as apply a three-tiered marketing approach with their brands Banana Republic, The Gap, and Old Navy, ensuring market saturation at every price point. Specialty stores such as The Gap and J. Crew did not sell national "designer" brands. Instead, they staffed large product development departments to design private label goods sold exclusively in their stores. Retailers such as The Limited even created their own brand labels, Forenza and Outback Red, each with a unique brand image.

American retail at the end of the 20th century presented customers with numerous shopping options. A portion of the American public continued buying apparel and general merchandise the old-fashioned way, from mail-order catalogs such as J.C. Penney, Sears, and Spiegel. However, new forms of retail shopping were on the horizon. Home shopping through television developed in the late 1970s and achieved wide recognition in 1985 with the launch of HSN (Home Shopping Network) and in 1986 with the creation of QVC (Quality Value Convenience) by Joseph Segel. By the mid-1990s, direct marketing sales on television were responsible for launching fashion trends in just a few hours by reaching millions of customers/viewers worldwide.

The advent of the Internet and the World Wide Web changed the way both catalog and home shopping functioned. By the end of the century, full store catalogs for major department stores and specialty boutiques were available online. Virtually every fashion item, whether current or vintage, could be located with the use of an Internet search engine, regardless of size, material, or price. Online apparel sales were not restricted to retailers; in 2005, eBay, an online person-to-person trading community, was one of the top vendors on the World Wide Web, and its fashion section was amongst its most popular.

FASHION COMMUNICATION

1950s

Television had the single greatest impact on all facets of life in the 1950s, and fashion was no exception. As TV became available in almost every home in America, the culture of the middle-class suburbs was flashed across the screen for eager consumers in a constant stream of programming and advertisements. Women were perky and well refined, always dressed to please husbands, and children were polite and respected their parents. Donna Reed of *The Donna Reed Show*, Harriet Nelson of *Ozzie and Harriet*, and June Cleaver from *Leave It to Beaver* were never seen at home without a full-skirted, pinched-waist dress, heels, and a single strand of pearls.

TV also simultaneously communicated directly or indirectly other major fashion trends for men, women, and children across the country. When Elvis Presley appeared on *The Ed Sullivan Show* in 1956, young men across the country adopted his pompadour hairstyle. The televised pregnancy of Lucille Ball on the *I Love Lucy* show was not only controversial for its time but also raised new interest in maternity fashions. *The Mickey Mouse Club* in 1955 brought children across the country together for an hour, influencing how children should dress as well as act.

An Attractive Wife Is Key to Success. Fashion magazines outlined and demonstrated the how-to's for the well-dressed woman, whereas television brought fashion and glamour into every living room. Television brought an endless stream of programming and advertising into every household, teaching people how to dress and act in a variety of social situations. The pressure from every media source was overwhelming, and the message was universal: women's role was in the home, attending to domestic duties while maintaining the perfect curvaceous figure. From Donna Reed to the Lucky Strike girl, the same hair, makeup, tight bodice, and cinched waist appeared over and over again in both print media and television. The rationale was, if a man had a beautiful wife to greet him at the door each night, he would be happy, and a happy man was a high performer at work.

Fashion magazines, such as *Vogue*, *Harper's Bazaar*, and *Ladies Home Journal*, continued to play a prominent role in promoting fashionable dress. The advent of jet planes made press coverage of Parisian, American, and European designers increasingly easier. In addition to covering the new lines each season, the magazines offered their interpretations of how to combine all of the appropriate pieces into the proper look. In *Vogue's* 1952 feature "What to Wear with What," the magazine provided twenty-five color schemes to link with a chart of coordinating shoes, handbags, gloves, hats, belts, jewelry, and other accessories.

1960S AND 1970S

One of the most important sources of fashion information in the 1960s was Jacqueline Kennedy. America had never had royalty to dictate fashionable dress like Europe. However, when Jacqueline Kennedy entered the White House in 1961, her fashion sense entered every woman's wardrobe. Her simple sense of style, pastel colors, unadorned A-line dresses with matching jackets, and dyed-to-match hats, shoes, and bags were easily and immediately imitated. American designer Oleg Cassini, primarily known for his costume designs for Hollywood films, was selected by Mrs. Kennedy as her personal designer and stylist. Together, they dictated women's fashions for at least the next five years, a dictation women were happy to take because it completely released them from the restrictive New Look of Christian Dior.

Fashion magazines in the 1960s began to expand their coverage of American designers. Virtually ignored by *Vogue* and *Harper's Bazaar* for decades, an increasing number of pages were dedicated each season to the coverage of American fashion designers. Fashion advice columns also expanded beyond proper dress for ladies' luncheons to offer wardrobe advice for the new career woman. Whereas women before the 1970s primarily wore one-piece dresses, now women needed to learn strategies for mixing-and-matching sportswear separates.

New editors, such as Helen Gurley Brown, were also brought in to give traditional women's magazines a face lift. Brown, appointed editor of *Cosmopolitan* magazine in 1965, added content of personal and professional interest to liberated women of the 1960s and 1970s. The youth movement of the 1960s and 1970s also increased the interest and circulation of teen magazines such as *Young Miss* and *Seventeen*, which were similar in content to women's magazines, with age-appropriate content. The increased interest in niche marketing also gave birth to magazines such as *Right On!*, first published in 1971 targeting African-American teens.

Although fashion magazines continued to have an important role in promoting fashion, fashion models for the first time took on a celebrity status of their own. Models such as Twiggy, Jean Shrimpton, and Peggy Moffat in the 1960s became synonymous with the fashionable images they represented, sometimes becoming more widely known than the designers themselves. Although the "supermodel" concept would not dominate the fashion industry until the 1980s, fashion was given its face by 1970s fashion models Janice Dickerson, Cheryl Tiegs, Iman, and Christie Brinkley, whose personal style was emulated beyond the designs they wore on the runway.

The ever-increasing reach of television and movies across the United States and internationally was perhaps the fastest and most thorough means of fashion communication. Even when unintended, no medium distributed its message more effectively than television and movies. For example, the wardrobe selections made for the movie *Annie Hall* immediately changed the way women all across the United States dressed, and *Saturday Night Fever* sent every man to the department store in search of a three-piece white suit and black shirt. The intention of neither movie was to move the general direction of fashion, and, yet, with each movie premiere, in a single day new ideals of fashion and beauty were simultaneously launched across the country.

1980s TO THE PRESENT

Lifestyle marketing and brand-name promotion dominated advertising and publicity for fashion. Designers and manufacturers placed brand names and logos prominently on fashion items, particularly T-shirts and pants. Companies such as Lacoste and Polo successfully turned their logos into world-wide recognized brands. Media product placement and celebrity endorsements became a highly effective means of launching new fashion trends.

Athletes, television personalities, and film and music stars remained faithful to specific designers or manufacturers and often appeared in their print and television ads. Advertising campaigns, such as John McEnroe for Adidas, Adrien Brody for Ermenegildo Zegna, Halle Berry for Revlon, and Sarah Jessica Parker and Madonna for Gap, leveraged high-profile celebrities who are emulated by thousands to increased brand awareness and adoption. Nike even went beyond mere endorsement to actually name a style of athletic shoe, the Air Jordan, after basketball player Michael Jordan, who was featured prominently in its advertising.

Product placement in movies and on television became another effective vehicle for promoting fashions. By association with commercially successful movies, books, music, and videos, Ray Ban (*Men in Black*), Adidas (Run DMC songs and videos), Manolo Blahnik (*Sex and the City*), Lacoste and Chloe (*Bergdorf Blondes*), and Reebok (Electronic Arts video games) all became highly sought after by the general public. Reality television, one of the biggest media trends of the early twenty-first century, provided another unique opportunity for product placement, particularly in makeover shows such as *What Not to Wear*, *Fashion Emergency*, and *The Swan*, in which America was able to witness firsthand how the selection of certain fashionable items could transforms one's life.

Target markets for fashion magazines became narrower in demographics through niche marketing. The fashion-conscious female consumer was subdivided into publication niches, such as *Seventeen* and *Teen People* for teenagers, *Glamour* and *Lucky* for college-aged women, and *Vogue* and *Cosmopolitan* for upscale thirty-somethings. High-end magazines covering fashion for men included *GQ* and *Esquire*, with *Details* and *Cargo* serving the college-aged population. Other magazines served even more specific markets, including *Latina* for Hispanic women, *Ebony* for African Americans, *Gothic Beauty* for the goth subculture, and *Genre* and *Out* for gay men. Fashion designers and retailers leveraged the segmented market by developing ad campaigns targeting the lifestyles of each demographic.

Other sources for fashion information included newspapers such as *The Wall Street Journal* and *USA Today*, which offered fashion sections to their readership. *The New York Times* also produced *Fashion of the Times*, a magazine devoted to discussing the latest trends. Fairchild's *Women's Wear Daily*, the self-proclaimed "bible of fashion," provided the industry as well as the general public with daily information on manufacturing, design, and retailing, whereas *DNR* (*Daily News Record*) covered information for the male fashion industry.

A novelty in fashion advertising was the overt use of nudity and sensual imagery to promote fashion styles. This practice first developed in the 1980s with the new-found popularity of underwear advertising, particularly with the often controversial Calvin Klein ads and the sexy campaigns for Victoria's Secret. The trend escalated with some retailers and designers, who let the models' physical appearance became more important than the clothing being advertised. Retailer Abercrombie & Fitch, for instance, was widely criticized for including numerous images of nude models in their fashion catalogs instead of models clothed in the latest fashions. Fashion photography frequently used images of models engaged in active and thrilling activities set in exotic locals, appealing to the consumer's sense of adventure, pleasure, sensual enjoyment, and luxury living.

Calvin Klein and other designers were also widely criticized for popularizing the ultra-thin "heroin chic" look, most notably exemplified by model Kate Moss. The anorexic, waif look stirred concern over social responsibility in the fashion industry, suggesting that the fashion industry was promoting, more so than in past decades, an unattainable ideal of beauty that puts young women at risk for physical and mental health. In response to the social outcry, Italy, followed by Spain, banned "skinny" models, establishing minimum body weights and imposing sanctions for noncompliance. The death in 2002 of Brazilian model Ana Carolina Reston, who weighed only 88 pounds, also prompted the Council of Fashion Designers in America to issue recommendations for helping women with eating disorders and to urge the New York City Council to discuss bans similar to those in Italy.

Fashion communication was also drastically changed with the emergence of the Internet, where apparel items were ever-present, being advertised through the use of pop-up windows and banners. The American public enjoyed online access to entire fashion magazines, store catalogs, and fashion shows, gaining information that could transform anyone into an expert stylist, buyer, or fashion promoter. Fashion and advice on what was fashionable was now available twenty-four hours a day, seven days a week across the entire globe. The message was no longer isolated to magazine subscribers.

FASHION TECHNOLOGY

1950s

The biggest technological fashion innovation of the 1950s was the creation of synthetic fabrics from petrochemicals. Nylon, which was introduced before WWII but not widely used until after the war, followed by acrylic in 1950 and polyester in 1953, revolutionized fashion design from the inside out. The fabrics made from these new synthetic fibers were promoted as "drip dry" or "wash-and-wear" and required minimum laundering and very little ironing. Expensive at first, garments made from these fibers were highly coveted for their performance characteristics and easy-care properties and, with escalating demand, soon became affordable for the mass market.

This new fiber technology was timed perfectly for the sportswear revolution taking place in America. The sports and leisure lifestyle in America demanded clothing that was both easy to care for and easy to move in. Camping, swimming, skiing, and golfing all benefited from the wrinkle-reducing, waterproof, drip-dry nature of synthetic fabrics.

Synthetic fibers provided the firm support and shaping in foundation garments, such as brassieres and girdles, required to sculpt the New Look, and stockings and socks could now be garter free for both men and women thanks to the stretch properties of nylon and polyester. Although intimate apparel and sportswear felt the most immediate impact of the artificial fibers, couturiers such as Dior, Fath, and Balmain could not resist the lure of these new fibers and also integrated them into their designs, especially as structural supports for the silhouettes.

1960s AND 1970s

Synthetic fibers continued to gain popularity in the 1960s space age; by 1965, more than 40 percent of all fibers used in apparel were manufactured, not natural (American Fiber Manufacturer's Association). The fascination with space and technology is the 1960s gave fashion designers the perfect opportunity to experiment with new manmade fibers. The fact that Neil Armstrong's spacesuit incorporated nylon fibers was not lost on the American public when they watched him walk on the moon in 1969.

Acrylic, first produced in the 1950s, became widely used to make faux fur fabrics that were adapted into coats, boots, and other garments. Whether dyed to resemble "natural pelts" or dyed pink, silver, or blue, faux fur garments provided every socioeconomic group with the opportunity to own a fur. Spandex, first produced in the United States in 1959, was also perfect for the 1960s space-age fashions. Spandex, also commonly known by its brand name, Lycra, provided stretch and support to tights and the new pantyhose that were an absolute necessity under miniskirts. Spandex was also incorporated into the leotards and body stockings that were worn in the 1970s. The wide use of the girdle and garter belt disappeared in the late 1960s.

Alternative materials were also incorporated into 1960s fashion, such as polyvinyl chloride (also known as vinyl or PVC), plastic, and paper. Paco Rabanne, Andre Courreges, Pierre Cardin, and others experimented with incorporating premolded, dye-cut plastics into garments to create futuristic looks. Vinyl or PVC provided the ultimate in futuristic fabrics, and it was completely waterproof and required no laundering, it was simply wiped clean. Originally used for rain coats and boots as protective wear, the fiber could be dyed any color and extruded into slick, shiny fabrics for go-go boots and dresses. A natural extension of the "disposable consumer society" that was developing in the 1960s was disposable clothing. The late 1960s witnessed a brief fad for dresses made out of paper, printed with bright pop art designs. Shown on Paris runways in 1967 and quickly adopted by America's youths, the dresses were too impractical to have a lasting impact on fashion but provided a fun novelty item in an era of experimentation.

As the youthful fads of the 1960s faded, Americans realized that paper dresses, plastic disks, and PVC, although fun, ultimately were not comfortable, did not move with the body, and did not breathe. Americans and fashion designers turned to polyester, better known in the 1970s under the brand name Dacron. Although polyester had been produced in the 1950s, it was not until the 1970s that it came to dominate the fashion world. First, polyester was wrinkle free and could be manufactured as "permanent press." For women who no longer had time to stay home and iron, polyester fabrics with creases and pleats permanently heat-set into a garment were indispensable. Second, polyester fibers and fabrics were inexpensive to produce, reducing the overall cost of a garment, another necessity during the economic recession of the 1970s. Finally, and perhaps most importantly, polyester provided stretch and drapability when knitted into double knit and jersey fabrics, ideal for the body-conscious, fitted fashions of the era, especially those worn for disco dancing.

Another important change in fashion technology in the 1970s was the introduction of federal standards for flammability for children's sleepwear. During the late 1960s, there was a growing concern over the increased injury rate, and even death, amongst children whose sleepwear came in contact with heat sources (matches, cigarettes, stove burners, etc.) and burst into flames. This concern led the Consumer Product Safety Commission to introduce the Flammable Fabrics Act in 1971 requiring that all children's sleepwear be flame retardant. The natural flame-retardant properties of many synthetic fabrics lead to their increased use in children's sleepwear during this period to satisfy consumer protection demands.

1980s TO THE PRESENT

Developments in computer and machine technology transformed the fashion business at the end of the twentieth century. Computer programs were used for activities ranging from the creation of designs for knitted garments to the body-scanning method introduced in 1994 by Levi's to improve the fit of jeans. Computer-aided designs became the method of choice for many design and product-development experts. Digital technology allowed for the precise printing of textiles. Retail merchandising also benefited from technological improvements, including the further development and widespread use of barcode labeling and the introduction of quick response, which allowed for faster merchandise replenishment when stocks ran low

(Wolfe 2003, 87). Software programs were also used to design the layout of stores and determine the ideal location for fixtures and products.

Synthetic textiles continued enjoying popularity and were improved by new technological developments. Textile finishes could make a fabric resistant to mildew, flames, ultraviolet exposure, wrinkles, and even bacteria. Improved technology in the textile testing field allowed scientists to accurately examine the thermal, laundry, and waterproofing properties of fabrics. Novelties such as microfiber, polar fleece, Tencel, and heat-molded seaming had a strong influence on sports performance apparel, whereas improved textiles were developed for the benefit of the medical and scientific communities.

At the turn of the twenty-first century, with a renewed interest in natural fibers, cotton became the most prevalent textile fiber in the United States. Cotton Incorporated, the research and marketing firm of American cotton growers and importers, proudly advertised this in the early 2000s with a series of advertisements calling cotton "the fabric of our lives." This popularity of natural fibers can also be attributed to growing environmental concerns. The textile industry, responding to constant accusations of poor handling of waste and dangerous materials, became more concerned with the creation of environmentally responsible

Sustainable Style. Environmental concerns grew during the last decades of the twentieth century and into the twenty-first. The American government was heavily criticized for its slow response to the challenges presented and particularly for delaying the enforcement of federal guidelines to reduce global warming, pollution, and proper management of toxic waste. The textile and apparel manufacturing industries came under close scrutiny and were forced to revise standards and procedures. Cotton farming, for instance, was deemed as highly destructive to soil, water, and air. The clothing industry responded with several initiatives aimed at producing sustainable and environmentally responsible products. Several manufacturers embraced the use of recycled materials obtained without the use of harmful pesticides and chemicals. The Sustainable Cotton Project promoted the use of organic cotton produced under fair labor conditions. The Sustainable Style Foundation was created to supply information and educate consumers about resources and products that allow them to embrace a sustainable personal lifestyle. The term "eco-fashion" was used in reference to apparel designed around consumer health, fair working conditions, and the use of organically grown or recycled materials.

manufacturing conditions and with the development of biodegradable synthetic fabrics. The Biological Agriculture Systems in Cotton program created in 1995 was an example of the industry's response to these challenges. It aimed to research and promote methods of weed and insect management that reduced the use of dangerous pesticides. Companies such as Nike and Patagonia devoted themselves to the development of environmental products using sustainable fibers and contents. Naturally colored cottons and natural dyes, although expensive, were used by small green manufacturers. Several publications and specialty stores promoted sustainable and environmentally responsible apparel products.

The global popularity that American fashion enjoyed in the 1980s was soon challenged by the globalization of apparel, with other European and Asian markets presenting strong competition. China and Korea, among other countries, provided highly competitive prices on apparel and textile manufacturing, motivating American companies to increase the level of outsourcing to other areas of the world. Some companies faced criticism for contributing to the reduction of the domestic production of apparel products, endangering the environment in third-world countries and offering low wages and poor working conditions in manufacturing centers often referred to as "sweat shops."

REFERENCES

Agins, T. (1999) *The End of Fashion: How Marketing Changed the Clothing Business Forever.* New York: William Morrow.

American Fiber Manufacturers Association. *A Short History of Manufactured Fibers,* http://www.fibersource.com/f-tutor/history.htm.

Baudot, F. (1999) *Fashion: The Twentieth Century.* New York: Universe Publishing.

Fashions of an Era. *1950s Glamour,* http://www.fashion-era.com/1950s_glamour.htm.

Figueroa, H. (1996) "In the Name of Fashion: Exploitation in the Garment Industry." *NACLA Report on the Americas* 29:34–40.

Guérin, P. (2005) *Creative Fashion Presentations.* 2nd edition. New York: Fairchild Publications.

Lehnert, G. (2000) *A History of Fashion in the 20th Century.* Cologne, Germany: Könemann.

Milbank, C. R. (1989) *New York Fashion: The Evolution of American Style.* New York: Abrams.

Murray, M. (1989) *Changing Styles in Fashion: Who, What, Why.* New York: Fairchild Publications.

Wolfe, M. G. (2003) *The World of Fashion Merchandising.* Tinley Park, IL: Goodheart-Willcox Co.

7

Women's Fashions

Women's fashions in the last half of the twentieth century witnessed vast transformations, mirroring the transformation in women's lives. At the beginning of the 1950s, women's expected role was that of wife and mother. The hourglass silhouette, created through padding and shaping, presented a womanly silhouette clearly announcing as well as limiting women's place in society. The equal rights movement that began in the 1960s rejected that narrow role for women and, although camouflaging curves, ironically opted for preteen, child-like fashions. Realizing that they would never be taken seriously when dressed like school girls, women's fashions in the 1970s responded by adopting aspects of men's wear, including pants, to create a more serious image that better aligned with the goal of independence and equal opportunity in the workplace. By the 1980s, women had made vast inroads in the workplace and continued climbing the corporate ladder in broad-shouldered, tailored power suits. Having "made it" by the 1990s, women were able to drop the unisex suit and incorporate softer feminine touches into their wardrobes, celebrating having it all: being an executive, wife, and mother.

The last half of the twentieth century also witnessed the birth and death of fashion standards. The miniskirt was born in the 1960s and, with it, the revolutionary pantyhose. The rise in informality also brought death to headwear as hats virtually disappeared after the 1960s. As women pursued careers instead of families, the singles population increased and so

179

too did singles social activities. From the 1970s on, discos, clubbing, and happy hours replaced formal balls and receptions, blurring the line between casual wear and formalwear and requiring "transitional dressing": pieces that could go from the office to a night on the town.

Sources for fashion trends and the quantity of fashion trends also changed over the course of the past fifty years. In the 1950s, Paris couturiers dictated fashion trends, and all women followed. Whatever the direction, all categories and price points of apparel followed the same overall silhouette and color palette. Beginning with the 1960s, fashion split between avante styles for youths and more conservative styles for women. Various subcultures also began to impact the overall direction of fashion, as fashions "trickled-up" to Paris from the streets. The mods and hippies paved the way for trickle-up influences in the 1960s, whereas rap, hip-hop, and new wave subcultures influenced fashions in the 1980s and 1990s. By the 1970s, fashion trends varied not only amongst age groups but also across apparel categories. Whereas formalwear and casual wear in the 1970s was feminine and body conscious, business wear was man tailored. In the last decades of the twentieth century and early twenty-first century, there was no longer one single vision for fashion; instead, there were multiple concurrent trends, providing a diverse array of fashions for every segment and niche of the population. Women had choices for dressing.

THE
1950s

FORMALWEAR

Silhouette

Marilyn Monroe was the sex goddess of the decade. The glamour of her eveningwear accented the relationship between waist and hips and between neck and shoulders. The New Look, launched by Christian Dior in 1947, continued to dominate the 1950s with its figure-eight, or hourglass, silhouette, whether the garments were haute couture or bargain basement. The hourglass figure featured a pinched waist, rounded shoulders, pointed bosom, and spike high-heeled shoes. Crinolines and hoop skirts were added under many dresses to make the waist look even tinier.

Ball gowns were opulent, physically revealing, and aesthetically charged, and elegance abounded with tight waist, full skirt, and low necklines where fine jewelry could be displayed. The favorite look for eveningwear during most of the fifties was the strapless gown with sweetheart bodice. Many designers would add a sheer mesh layer over the bodice or removable filmy jacket to provide covered shoulders for a more modest appearance.

Skirts

Hem length was one of the deciding factors in determining what was appropriate for an early evening cocktail party, an 8:00 P.M. show, or evening ball. For evening formalwear, floor-length skirts were either straight as a pencil, hugging every curve of the waist and hips, or tremendously full skirted, supported by petticoats, hoops, and crinolines. Slim-line or pencil skirts were tight, tight, tight, with a sexy slit up the side or back to allow the wearer to walk. The after-five dress code required a cocktail or party dress. Cocktail dresses were also worn with a tight waist and either a full skirt supported by crinolines or a pencil skirt. The only difference was that cocktail dresses fell between mid-calf and ankle length.

Pat Nixon poses in the evening gown she selected for her husband's vice presidential inauguration ball, 1957. The blue satin bouffant gown features a bell-shaped skirt, topped by a bodice embroidered with pearls and crystals. A matching handbag and elbow-length gloves complete the ensemble. [AP / Wide World Photos]

Bodice

Strapless or off-the-shoulder bodices dominated women's formalwear, whether ball gown or cocktail length, full or fitted. Bodices were tightly fitted, ended at the natural waistline, and most frequently completed with a sweetheart neckline to reveal a small glimpse of décolletage. Straight necklines were seen in strapless dresses and deep scoop necklines seen in sleeveless dresses. Another popular alternative to the strapless dress was the one-shoulder dress created by draping the dress fabric diagonally across the bustline over one shoulder to form a strap or sleeve. Many designers would add a sheer overlay to the bodice or a removable filmy jacket to eveningwear to provide covered shoulders for a more modest appearance.

Sleeves

The predominant dress style in eveningwear was strapless. Occasionally, small cap sleeves or short fitted sleeves were seen in formalwear.

Decorative Details

The rules of appropriate dress dictated that only certain fabrics could be worn for specific activities, time of day, or season. Certain fabrics, such as brocade, could not be worn before 6:00 P.M. Heavy luxurious fabrics were key to obtaining the full skirts of the 1950s. Brocades, taffetas, satins, and French laces were draped, ruched, smocked, pleated, ruffled, and gathered to form voluminous skirts. Skirts and bodices were further embellished with the glitter of rhinestones and sequins and elegance of pearls.

BUSINESS WEAR

Silhouette

A well-tailored suit was a necessity in the fifties. The practicality of suits appealed to women because suits were considered appropriate for many different occasions. Any activity in town, whether it be a meeting, luncheon, or shopping, called for a trim, closely fitting tailored suit emphasizing sloping shoulder line, curve of the bust and hips, mid-calf to ankle length, topped with a little hat, gloves, and matching handbag. The sheath silhouette for business wear closely mimicked that of eveningwear but was more straight and tubular than hourglass.

Dresses

Business dresses were simple straight and tubular sheaths, paired with a tailored jacket with narrow lapels or a bolero jacket. Simple chenille wool knit dresses or skirt and sweater set provided an alternative to more tailored office wear. Dresses might have pointed collars opening to a V-neck, but the most popular neckline was round and collarless.

Suits

Suits were more common than dresses for office wear. Typically, short jackets with fitted waists were paired with flared or pencil skirts. The silhouette was not as extreme in business wear as it was in daywear, and popular alternatives to Dior's New Look were introduced. One alternative was the belted chemise suit, with straight jacket falling mid-hip, slim just-below-the-knee skirt, large round collar, large decorative buttons, and decorative belt embellished with a bow at the closure, which provided a less rigid option for office attire.

Coco Chanel wasted no time in the fifties resurrecting her classic boxy suit jackets with slim skirts. Her suits also provided a less restrictive alternative to the hourglass silhouette. Her simple yet elegant suits, accessorized by a strand of pearls, were easy to copy and thus flooded department stores and chain stores. Dior's version of the suit included a tightly fitted jacket accenting the waist and shoulders, with a straight mid-calf-length skirt (Fashions of an Era).

Separates

Separates were not worn by women for business in the 1950s.

Decorative Detail

Tailored suits and dresses had little surface embellishment. Occasionally, buttons, bows, or faux fur might serve as decorative elements. The visual interest in business wear was created through structural seams, darts, godets, pleats, and princess seams. Dark solid-colored wool gabardines and tweeds were the primary fabrications.

CASUAL WEAR

Silhouette

The decade of the 1950s may have opened with the New Look, but, for casual daytime dress, the fifties became a time of experi-

Models in pencil skirts and short fitted jackets stand with Christian Dior in this 1957 photo. [AP / Wide World Photos]

mentation with silhouette. Dior launched H-, A-, and Y-lines, named for the silhouette shape each invoked. The H-line was a slender tunic with slim waist and raised hemline that pushed the bust up and waistline down to the hips. By 1955, this shape evolved into the A-line with narrow shoulders, undefined waist, and slightly flared skirt. This silhouette finally gave way to the Y-line, which inverted the A-line, placing the emphasis on broader shoulders tapering to a narrow hemline. Other couturiers, such as Givenchy and YSL, also experimented with silhouette, promoting the "sack" and "trapeze" forms. Givenchy's sack was a straighter waistless shift, which was later modified to create the full, swinging triangular-shaped trapeze. In 1950, Paris decreed that hemlines should be exactly sixteen inches from the ground, but, by 1958, Paris had a new decree: hemlines should be above the knee.

Dresses

Casual cotton shirtwaist dresses or dresses for backyard barbecues or "household management" typically had short sleeves with high, round collarless necklines. The snug-fitting waist usually had a belt or large decorative buttons that flared to a mid-calf-length skirt. Oversized odd-shaped patch pockets on the skirt with contrasting piping or fabric gave the dress a "modern" look. Alternative forms included dresses with convertible collars, square or V necklines, or wrap fronts. Very popular in the fifties was the sweater dress with a crew or cowl neck made from Orlon. This was a form-fitting dress that required the right undergarments to accentuate curves and hide bulges. The trapeze dress with flared hemline, round collar, and three-quarter-length sleeves allowed the quintessential strand of pearls to be visible, whereas the shorter-length sleeve allowed a matching bracelet to be displayed.

Separates

Just as shopping, business meetings, and cocktail parties required their own specialized wardrobes, so did backyard barbeques, trips to the beach, and camping. However, despite the casual nature of the activities, women never went anywhere looking sloppy. The idea of separates gave new life to styling in blouses, sweaters, slacks, and skirts. Blouses moved away from the man-tailored look and gained more feminine touches. The use of smocking, embroidery, and pleats made the blouse exciting rather than just functional. Sweaters went with everything and over everything. Whether short or long sleeved, high on the waist or low on the hips, sweaters were worn with both skirts and pants. Sweater sets, or twin sets, could be dressed up with pearls or dressed down with a colorful scarf. Tight sweaters were often finished with a rounded Peter Pan collar to preserve the look of innocence. Capri pants with fitted legs and waists came in solids as well as paisleys, stripes, plaids, and houndstooth. Zippers were either at the center back or the side to preserve the appearance of a smooth, tight fit. Skirts, either pencil or flared, paired nicely with a blouse or sweater for a neighborhood gathering.

Jacqueline Bouvier with her then-fiancé, John F. Kennedy, wearing Bermuda shorts, 1953. [Hy Peskin/Time Life Pictures/Getty Images]

Play clothes, such as shorts and halter tops, necessities for summer-time leisure activities, were generally of Sanforized cotton with a firm weave to prevent shrinkage. Although a bare midriff may appear with a halter or cropped top, never did a bellybutton appear; instead, the waistband of the shorts was designed to ride higher than the natural waist to conceal the risqué bellybutton. Shorts, with an elastic waist, center back zipper, or side zipper, were less fitted than pants and ended at mid-thigh. Bermuda shorts, ending at mid-thigh with a cuff, became particularly popular when paired with tropical print Hawaiian shirts.

Decorative Details

For casual wear, the decorative detailing was provided by the fabric itself. Brightly colored novelty prints, tropical prints, plaids, tweeds, stripes, and checks required no further enhancements to create visual interest. Simple collars, bows, buttons, and pockets were the only detailing necessary on an already busy fabric.

OUTERWEAR

Coats

A coat completed almost every ensemble in the 1950s. Big, loose coats were worn with dresses or suits, often with three-quarter-length sleeves. Full-length coats fell just below the skirt hemline, whereas car coats fell midway down the thigh. Full-length coats were worn for formal occasions, business, and church, whereas shorter coats and jackets were found during more casual outings. Since long coats could not easily fit over the voluminous layers of the crinoline skirt of the era, many jackets were either semi-fitted hip length or full swing-back styles. Whereas swing jackets could be found in both solids and plaids, the full-length swing coat was considered more sophisticated in solid dark colors for fall and winter or winter white and pastels for spring. The swing coat also provided a practical and stylish solution for the many pregnant women during the postwar baby boom of the fifties.

Coats and jackets for casual wear did not follow the swing silhouette. Short leather jackets belted to emphasis a trim waist were usually worn with a pencil skirt or tight pants. Ladies "play" jackets in corduroy, cotton poplin, or wool fleece were boxy across the shoulders with a front button or zip closure and gathered at the waist with elastic or a belt. Cuffs and collars were finished in knit, fur, fleece, or leather. Rain gear followed the same lines as daily wear coats with either a belted or swing style, ending at above mid-calf. Shorter rubberized versions for more active wear usually had bend-over frog fasteners rather than buttons or zippers.

Other garments

Fur coats were fashionable for daytime as well as eveningwear. Fur stoles or mink scarves were regularly draped over suit jackets. Marmot, squirrel, mink, silver fox, and red fox jackets were a requirement in any corporate wife or society lady's wardrobe. Fur jackets carried the fullness of a swing coat, just shorter. Inexpensive Orlon and Dynel were used in both short and full length to mimic real fur for the budget-conscious consumer.

SWIMWEAR AND SPORTSWEAR

Swimwear

One-piece stretch bathing suits, either strapless or halter top, were more popular than bikinis in the 1950s. Designers, such as Claire McCardell, introduced soft draped stretch jersey for swimsuits, producing suits that were both functional and stylish. Swimwear took advantage of new man-made fibers in creating figure-controlling suits with preformed or padded bra cups to complete the hourglass figure normally achieved by wearing a girdle. Swimsuits came in every color combination, pattern, and print imaginable. Although formfitting, they were not provocative; the hourglass figure was molded, but sexuality was hidden. Cleavage was modestly covered, and a skirt or fabric drape crossed the bottom section to discreetly cover the crotch of the suit. Matching beach jackets or sarongs completed the look and provided the appropriate cover-up for poolside activities.

Whatever the bathing suit style, bathing caps could be found at every swimming pool, lake, and ocean side. These caps were both functional, keeping the hair dry, and colorful. Bathing caps could be found in bright colors with synthetic streamers, flowers, birds, feathers, fur, and other contraptions. The wilder and more colorful the bathing cap, the better.

A halter-top one-piece swimsuit, 1954. [AP / Wide World Photos]

Golf

Women were not frequently found on the golf course because it was seen as a haven for businessmen or the rich and famous. Movie stars such as Katharine Hepburn made golf more acceptable for women. For women who did venture to the golf course or at least the golf club, appropriate ladylike attire was always required on the golf course. Golf ensembles consisted of a button-front blouse paired with a colorful pull-over or cardigan sweater (either crew or V-neck) and a slightly tapered mid-calf-length skirt or culottes in plaid. Shorts were not acceptable.

Tennis

Tennis was still considered a gentile sport in the fifties, and proper attire was required on the tennis court. Ladies returning carefully lobbed balls did so in mid-calf-length white pleated tennis skirts paired with short-sleeve button-front blouses. Short cropped cotton cardigan or pullover cotton tennis sweaters with colored stripes at the cuff, waist band, or neckline were added in cool weather.

Skiwear

Glamour followed the ladies to the ski slopes. New fabric technology provided an opportunity for material that would stretch with a skier's bends and turns going downhill. Although the ski bunnies mostly stayed in the lodge, their outfits were still as functional as their athletic counterparts. Side-zip stretch pants tapered down to the ankle, where a strap under the foot kept them in place. Turtleneck sweaters over fitted knit long-sleeved shirts fell just at the hips, keeping to the prevailing curvy silhouette. Ski jackets often had faux fur at the cuffs and collar. Ski suits with matching coats and pants were de rigueur.

UNDERWEAR AND INTIMATE APPAREL

Underwear

Curves were all important for catching a man, or so women were told by Hollywood, magazines, and television. Close-fitting hourglass outfits required squeezing the body into the tiniest possible configuration. To obtain the requisite tight waists, flat tummy, and firm bust, long line bras with stiff bones and girdles that covered the thighs were essential undergarments. The "sweater look," promoted by starlets like Jane Russell, required a preformed conically stitched bra to sculpt the bust into two separate cone-shaped mounds.

A new American undergarment industry thrived under the demand for support garments that sculpted women's bodies into the prevailing silhouette. Corsets were often custom made through personal fittings. The confining garments were given appealing names such as the "Merry Widow," "Pink Champagne," and "Romance" to entice prospective wearers. Likewise, brassieres that were stitched and padded to provide uplift and cleavage were daintily named "Lovable" and "Sweet and Low."

To provide support for more revealing eveningwear with plunging necklines and bare backs, bras had to stand up on their own. As in the turn of the century, whale bones were still used early in the decade as well as steel for stiffeners. These materials were gradually replaced with celluloid bones and zippers for faster fastening. Nylon or cotton poplin petticoats with lots of frills were necessary to give volume to full skirts, both casual and formal. Crinolines and hoop skirts emphasized the tiny waist of the hourglass figure. Found in both half slips and full slips, crinoline was an essential component to complete the look.

Sleepwear

Traditional forms of nightwear in cotton or satin were worn for comfort with a matching satin belted bathrobe or cotton terrycloth bathrobe and fuzzy slippers. Quilted full-length robes and dusters were presentable enough to answer the door, if necessary, because they were fitted and styled in the same manner as a day dress. Satin was more elegant, and it came in a range of solid colors with dark or light piping for contrast. Cotton pajamas generally came in prints and plaids with button-front top and elastic-waist pants.

Lingerie

After the smash hit *Baby Doll* in 1956 starring Carroll Baker, baby-doll nightwear made from nylon with fluffy slippers changed the look of the bedroom. Frilly bloomer panties were topped by a shortie swing-style dress in sheer nylon or tricot with hand smocking at the bodice and puffed sleeves. Charm and elegance in the bedroom followed Hollywood's trend of layered sheer nylon with plenty of scallops and lace. Full robes falling just below the knee tied with ribbon at the neck made a charming illusion of floating gracefully across the room. Or, for a more dramatic effect, a floor-length pleated nightgown with full sweeping skirt in ruby red, sapphire blue, or onyx black would make any housewife look like a budding starlet draped in luxurious layers of sheer nylon and lace. Fuzzy slippers or sandals with high plastic heels completed the ensemble.

HEADWEAR, HAIRSTYLES, AND COSMETICS

Headwear

No well-dressed woman would consider leaving the house without the appropriate head covering. Any visit to a store, church, or office building required the appropriate hat. Petite and demure, big and demanding attention, or adorned with accessories such as feathers and netting, a hat completed the ensemble. Hats were worn in every season. Millinery was big business, and upscale department stores had in-house designers who created elaborate confections for their customers. Styles varied widely, including tie-on scarf hats, close-fitting jerseys, chemise cloches, pleated turbans, and berets all with brims from small to large. Hats were sculpted out of wool, fur, or straw dramatically emphasized with netting, feathers, flowers, ribbons, pearls, glitter, or fur. As travel abroad became convenient and affordable, thanks to Pan American Airlines in 1958, sequins and beads from Hong Kong and Japan could be found adorning caps, bags, and gowns. Balenciaga introduced the pillbox form early in the decade, and it became the hat of the fifties as well as the sixties.

Hairstyles

Short hair was very fashionable in the 1950s, cut tight to the head and pin curled. The fashionable face-framing curls in the early 1950s were achieved by pinning the hair before drying or with a permanent wave. Women with long hair pulled their locks back in a French twist or chignon for a classical polished look. Toward the end of the decade, women spent increasingly more time at hair salons having their hair combed back, teased, and sprayed into a high mound, the bigger the better.

Cosmetics

Color films had an enormous impact on cosmetics as the huge screen illuminated the unblemished appearance of the stars. Glamour was what it was all about in the fifties. Cosmetics were advertised as the essential element for luring a man into marriage. After all, the most promising career role for a woman of the fifties was as wife and mother. Following Hollywood's lead, cheeks were lightly rouged, and the eyes were emphasized with eyeliner and mascara and only a hint of shadow. Pan-sticks developed from theatre makeup soon replaced the older loose powder for creating flawless foundations. The lips were advertised as the irresistible element to catch a man, and red was the color of choice. As the decade came to a close, color choices moved to the softer baby-doll pale shimmering lipsticks and pastel pearly pinks.

FOOTWEAR AND LEGWEAR

Footwear

With a demanding fashion protocol, women in the 1950s needed specific shoes for every occasion. The quintessential 1950s shoe, the pointy-toed stiletto, could attain towering heel heights of five inches. This engineering marvel was achieved by combining steel with wood in the heel shaft for strength and stability. The stiletto heel drew attention to the calf and ankle and the movement of the hips. One could not help but swing the hips from side to side as a matter of maintaining balance! The downside was the destruction of flooring materials due to the pings of the stiletto heel. The pump, similar to the stiletto but with a more modest heel height, was the basic shoe. Pumps came in a wide range of styles, including pointed toes, spectator (open)-toed curved vamps, and V-shaped vamps. Pumps also came in every color imaginable to ensure a precise match between the shoe and the garment. The pump also came in a flat heel for casual day dresses and capri pants.

Snow boots were getting some attention as fashionable rather than purely practical footwear. A spike-heeled boot just over the ankle was stylish for church or shopping, providing a bit of protection against the elements but, most importantly, sparing a good pair of shoes from the slush and snow of city streets in winter. More practical boots were flat but had a splash of panache with faux fur or fleece lining the top. In leather or synthetics, these boots had a bit more style than their pull-on rubberized predecessors.

Legwear

Nylon stockings were once again available and more affordable in the 1950s. Nylons held their shape better than the original versions, and, by the middle of the decade, seamless nylon stockings were available for the bare-leg look of a shorter skirt above the knee. Socks, of course, were the staple for casual wear. Knee socks were worn with Bermuda shorts, and bobby socks were worn with casual pants.

NECKWEAR AND OTHER ACCESSORIES

Jewelry

June Cleaver, the TV mother in the television show *Leave It to Beaver*, was never without her single strand of pearls. Pearls were worn to complete a business suit, cocktail dress, and, in TV land, the house dress. Pearls would dress up any outfit for almost any occasion. Mamie Eisenhower wore a single strand of costume pearls for the inauguration of her husband, President Dwight D. Eisenhower. Ladies everywhere emulated her simple elegance and good taste. Thanks to artificial and simulated pearls, most women could now afford this exclusive and conservative necklace. Pearls were the accessory of choice for just about everything. During a time when housewives were expected to always look stylish, pearls were the natural choice.

Handbags

Taking the lead from actress and Princess Grace Kelly, handbags continued to be both a necessity and fashion accessory. Held by the hand or over the forearm, they generally had an outside pocket to conveniently stow one's gloves and possibly car keys. With a clasp at the top, the interior had two or three compartments to keep cosmetics and a mirror handy for touchups, an address or appointment book, and sunglasses. The well-dressed woman not only changed from black to white seasonally, but she had a handbag that matched the color, fabric, and texture of each pair of shoes.

Eyeglasses

Eyeglass frames exaggerated the application of eyeliner by including outrageous wings that curved up from the corner, often studded with rhinestones for an extra glitzy effect. Spectacles became a fashion accessory in the 1950s. The exaggerated wings flaring out at the corners were scattered with glitter dust in frames of metallic, bold black, or brightly colored plastic.

Gloves

A well-dressed woman always wore her gloves. Without gloves, she was not properly accessorized. Wrist-length "shorties" were worn with tea-length gowns, whereas opera-length gloves were worn at weddings, balls, and other formal occasions. Gloves were worn to church, to tea, to lunch, and shopping downtown as well as to the theater, restaurants, and other entertainment venues. Women always had several pair, and they were not necessarily all white. Gloves came in many colors to match various outfits and occasions, but white and cream were the favored choice. As difficult as they were to keep clean, however, multiple pairs were often a convenience rather than a fashion statement. Cotton gloves were easier to launder and affordable.

Scarves

The most versatile accessory of the fifties was the scarf. Scarves were both functional and decorative. Draped over the head and tied under the chin, a scarf could protect a carefully coiffed hairdo from the elements. It could be tied around the neck as a colorful accent, draped around the waist as a fashionable belt, or wrapped about as a halter top. More popular for the younger crowds was a colorful chiffon scarf to tie back a ponytail. The jacket of the New Look suit was too formfitting for a blouse but could be freshened up with a dash of color by a carefully draped scarf peeking above the neckline.

Actress Audrey Hepburn wears dark beatnik-style clothing in the 1957 film *Funny Face,* as Fred Astaire watches her dance. [Courtesy of Photofest]

ALTERNATIVE FASHION MOVEMENTS

Beatniks

The countermovement group of the fifties was, of course, the beatniks. Considered one of the first subcultures, they questioned traditional values of mainstream America during the highly conformist post-WWII era. A favorite choice for the beatniks was wearing all black. Oversized chunky black sweaters were worn with pencil-thin long black skirts and black tights or tight black stretch pants with stirrups. Black ballet slippers completed the look. During a time when good girls wore sweater sets, the beat ladies shocked onlookers by wearing slinky, formfitting bodysuits in public. Previously seen only under the big top on trapeze artists or on stage on ballet dancers, beatniks made a rebellious statement by adding the leotard to their basic wardrobe.

THE 1960s

FORMALWEAR

Silhouette

The fashionable silhouette for eveningwear consisted of a long, straight sheath or shift, slightly A-line, with no defined waist. Compared with the hourglass silhouette of the 1950s, women were again able to move and breathe without the weight of restrictive garments. For America's youths, the silhouette was adapted into the baby-doll silhouette, with an empire waist that concealed any trace of womanly curves, and puffed sleeves. Ensemble dressing dominated both daywear and eveningwear. Because many dresses were sleeveless, a coat in matching fabric was a crucial component of the evening ensemble. In fact, shoes, purses, and hats were often all made out of the same fabric as the coat and dress, creating a monochromatic color scheme.

Skirts

Dresses for formal eveningwear called for long, straight skirts that were often tubular in appearance, skimming the outline of the body rather than accentuating the curves. By the middle of the decade, the popularity of the miniskirt had crept into eveningwear, and short skirts, especially for younger women, were also acceptable for formal occasions. The 1960s also witnessed an increased popularity in pants as an alternative for formalwear. Designers such as Givenchy and Norman Norell presented silk and velvet pants, both tapered and flared, paired with long tunics as an alternative to the formal gown.

Bodices

The majority of dresses had unstructured bodices with no defined waistline. Some bodices did use simple darts or princess seams to create soft shaping in shift or A-line silhouettes. If a waistline was defined, it was either empire (under the bustline) for baby-doll dresses or blouson (banded at the hip line), creating the illusion of a two-piece ensemble. A simple jewel neckline prevailed for all eveningwear.

Sleeves

Evening dresses were predominantly sleeveless throughout the decade. Some youthful fashions used short puff or melon sleeves. Evening jackets had straight set-in sleeves typically three-quarter length, without cuffs.

Decorative Details

Decorative details for eveningwear in the 1960s were either staid and conservative or young and funky. For older women, in the first half of the decade, the color palette for either eveningwear was dominated by pastel colors and neutrals: peach, pink, yellow, beige, and cream. Surface ornamentation was limited to the area around the jewel neckline and could be quite elaborate, forming a faux collar through beading. Self-covered buttons and structural seaming were other means of creating visual interest without that addition of surface embellishment. Luxurious fabrics such as raw silk, silk shantung, and metallic brocades provided texture and sheen in dresses and coats. Black and white or vivid colors were used in op art and pop art patterns in youthful ensembles. Stripes, chevrons, checkerboards, swirls, color blocks, and trompe l'oeil effects created attention-grabbing effects on simple silhouettes. As the decade progressed, fashions for all women used strong colors and increased surface embellishment with sequins, palliettes, beads, and glitter.

BUSINESS WEAR

Silhouette

Women were on the verge of independence in the 1960s, and their wardrobes were beginning to respond. Single-breasted, boxy jackets paired with matching dresses, skirts, or even pants were the mainstay of the working woman's wardrobe. The general shift or sheath silhouette seen in eveningwear carried over into other forms of dress. Unlike suits of the 1950s, which were so tailored as to not allow room for a shirt underneath, suits in the 1960s became more relaxed and functional.

Dresses

Simple A-line sheath dresses with jewel necklines were the most common form for women's business wear. Dresses were typically sleeveless and ended around the knee, becoming increasingly shorter with the popularity of the miniskirt.

Suits

In the early part of the decade, women's suits were primarily jacket and skirt or jacket and dress combinations. Jackets were boxy and typically single breasted. When paired with skirts, jackets ended at the waistline and had long, straight sleeves. When paired with dresses, jackets ended about five inches above the dress hemline and had straight three-quarter-length sleeves. Skirts were simple A-line silhouettes. By the end of the decade, pants with full flared legs were becoming more common in women's suiting.

Separates

Mix-and-match coordination did not yet exist for women's business wear. However, a wide range of softly tailored shirts were available to pair with suits. Blouses were softly fitted, with long straight sleeves. Round Peter Pan collars often had a small bow at the neck. Some shirts were blouson (gathered into a fitted band at the hip), worn on the outside of the skirt rather than tucked in.

Decorative Details

Surface embellishment was minimal for business wear. Visual interest was created through structural seaming, darts, pleats, and gathering. Pastel colors and neutrals were most typically seen. Some jackets were trimmed with Chanel-style braid on the lapels, cuffs, and pockets.

CASUAL WEAR

Silhouette

For the first time in fashion history, there was no one single fashion trend or silhouette; instead, both Paris and America concurrently debuted several different trends on the catwalk each season. Fashion split between young and old, conservative and antiestablishment, mainstream and subculture. The overriding silhouette of the period was the sheath or A-line. However, this basic shape was modified into several different adaptations depending on which segment of fashion trend one opted to follow: the Jacqueline Kennedy look, the baby doll, the romantic, the mod, or the hippie. Depending on the trend followed, garments for casual wear ranged from dresses to pants, miniskirts to maxi skirts, stretch pants to bell-bottoms. Garments could skim the body, concealing the overall form, or have extensive cutouts, revealing more skin than in any previous period. In the era of "anything goes" and "do what feels good," fashion certainly took heed of the message.

Dresses

More conservative women wore the standard A-line sleeveless sheath dress with a jewel neckline for daywear. Those following mod fashions wore brightly colored, A-line sheaths often with cutouts on the side panels or center front to reveal the body. Whereas some cutouts were left completely open, others were filled with clear or transparent vinyl to create a space-age feel. Mod looks also experimented with inserting large plastic zippers and Velcro for closures. Baby-doll dresses had high empire waists with short skirts gathered under the bust line. A modification of the baby-doll look resulted in the adoption of jumpers with turtlenecks for a "little girl" appearance. Romantic looks also adopted the baby-doll empire waist but with longer, softer skirts. Long "granny dresses" with flounced hemlines and high necklines were popular amongst the hippie set who frequented antique stores, ethnic shops, and army-navy outlets to assemble their outfits.

Separates

Basic straight skirts and A-line skirts were worn by more conservative women at approximately knee length for casual day functions. Those pursuing youthful mod and baby-doll fashions wore miniskirts that inched upward over the course of the decade. Absent from both skirt categories were waistbands; skirts were designed with unfinished, unstructured waists so they could ride lower onto the hip. By the late 1960s, fashion designers, tired of making variations on miniskirts, attempted to introduce the new maxi skirt. This new floor-length style was universally rejected by women of all ages. After several failed attempts by designers to sway women to the maxi, a compromise was reach around 1968, the midi. The midi adjusted hem lengths back to just below the knee. The midi was typically made in dirndl form, with the skirt gathered into the waistband, a style that paired well with the ethnic peasant blouses that were becoming popular in the later part of the decade. Although the midi was adopted by more fashion-forward women at the close of the decade, it was not universally adopted by women until the 1970s.

Blouses came in styles to meet every fashion category of the 1960s. Peasant blouses with full sleeves and deep necklines were available for hippie fashions, as were fringed vests. Mod looks were fitted turtleneck sweaters and dyed faux fur vests. Lacy high-neck blouses with velvet jackets helped create romantic looks. An array of knit shirts and T-shirts in solids, patterns, and logo prints were available to pair with jeans. More conservative women wore cotton blouses with Peter Pan collars or knit tops with bateau or boat necklines.

Pants became increasingly accepted for woman for all occasions in the 1960s. Whereas women in the 1950s typically wore dresses or skirts and tops for daily activities, the modern woman of the 1960s wore pants. Knit stretch pants with long narrow legs inspired by futuristic space-suit designs were popular in the early part of the decade. As the decade progressed, hip-hugger styles, with a waistline below the natural waist and without a waistband, and full-cut legs prevailed for all women. Variations on hip-huggers included knickers, knee-length pants with the fullness gathered into a band at the knees, and gaucho pants, knee-length pants with the fullness flared out at the knees, in the last years of the decade. Bell-bottoms, synonymous with late 1960s and early 1970s fashions, originated with the leg fitted to the knee and then flared over the calf, a style that progressed into overall flare and fullness by the end of the decade.

Decorative Details

Conservative casual wear incorporated little to no decoration. Surface interest was created through fabric texture, structural seams, and self-covered buttons. Hippie fashions incorporated a range of patchwork, embroidery, tie-dye, block prints, macramé, and fringe to create an eclectic look. Mods added novelty to their garments by incorporating plastic, metal, Mylar, battery-operated lights, and other eccentric novelty items. Romantic and baby-doll looks both used lace, ruffles, and flounces to accent their attire.

OUTERWEAR

Coats

Coats in the 1960s mirrored the silhouette dominated in apparel: straight, slightly A-line, loosefit skimming the body, rounded shoulders, no waistline. Because many dresses were sleeveless during the 1960s, the coat became an important part of a woman's ensemble, often made of the same fabric as the dress. Coats were both single and double breasted, were often made with three-quarter-length sleeves, and had simple, wide rolled collars. Some coats had dropped shoulders or kimono sleeves.

Fur coats were still popular in the 1960s, but, with an increased awareness on endangered species, many women turned to fake furs as an alternative. Acrylic fibers could be manufactured to mimic the appearance of real fur, with an added bonus: instead of being limited to traditional animal prints, fur coats could now be dyed any color and pattern desired. Vinyl raincoats also appeared in bright colors as a new form of protective raingear. In addition to keeping the wearer dry, slick, shiny vinyl raincoats fed the public's penchant for space-age apparel. Vinyl coats were produced in either knee lengths or waist lengths, often with big plastic zippers in matching or contrasting color.

Shawls/Wraps

Toward the end of the decade, ethnic-inspired shawls increased in popularity. Fringed, patterned shawls, typically donned by those following the hippie movement, worked their way into mainstream fashion as the "peasant look" or "gypsy look" gained favor. Variations of wraps, such as capes and ponchos, were also worn in the 1960s. Long capes, with or without hoods, made the perfect dramatic complement to eveningwear, whereas crocheted waist-length ponchos were the perfect topper for casual miniskirts.

Other Garments

Advances in waterproofing fabric improved the quality of outerwear worn for sports in the 1960s. Anorak coats, with thermo-insulated polyester-filled jacket and a nylon shell, now provided a much warmer and waterproof alternative for outerwear. These jackets were often quilted for added warmth and were produced in bright colors, such as electric blue, or geometric patterns, such as polka dots, with big, plastic zippers (Lee-Potter 1984, 71).

SWIMWEAR AND SPORTSWEAR

Swimwear

Nothing more clearly revealed the change in ideals of beauty and the fashionable figure as much as swimwear. At the beginning of the 1960s, swimwear continued along the same silhouette as it had in the 1950s, emphasizing the hourglass figure. However, by the time fashion models such as Twiggy entered the fashion scene in the late 1960s, women's fashions moved from shapely curves to a preteen flat-chested, no-hips silhouette. Swimsuits, with their minimal coverage of the body, made the silhouette change immediately apparent. The padding and underwires were removed from swimsuit tops, leaving a soft, natural shape on the chest instead of the previous cones. Instead, swimwear was made from nylon and spandex for shaping and support that moved with the body.

One-piece maillot swimsuits worn more at the beginning of the decade were more body conscious and less body sculpting. Styles were similar to apparel designs, featuring cutouts on the side, front, and/or back of the torso, or color blocking to create the appearance of cutouts. Some one-piece suits were made with high, jewel necklines or collars. One interesting variation on the one-piece swimsuit was the monokini design by Rudi Gernreich in 1964. The monokini was a topless suit with suspenders that came up over the shoulders instead of a top. Although Gernreich sold 3,000 monokinis, they were rarely seen on the beaches, especially in America (Millbank 1989, 223).

Two-piece bikinis dominated swimwear in the 1960s. The most popular style was composed of a boy-shorts brief with a bra-style or tank-style tops. Bikini bottoms rode low on the hips, for the first time revealing a women's bellybutton. Whereas most bikinis were made from traditional nylon and spandex materials, other bikinis, more for sunbathing than swimming, experimented with less traditional materials and decoration. Appliqués, beading, ruffles, fringe, plastic, vinyl, metal, and crochet were incorporated into swimwear designs.

Swimwear, regardless of form, was typically brightly colored in apple green, lemon yellow, turquoise, blue, or hot pink. Swimwear patterns followed the same op art and pop art trends noted in apparel designs. Although some swimwear was a solid color, the majority was boldly patterned with contrasting colors of stripes or chevrons or in wild Pucci-style prints. Black and white op art patterns were also available.

Golf

Golf fashions stayed as sedate as previous periods. Basic skirts and knit tops were worn on the golf course or for the more "lady-like" game of croquet. Occasionally, women did wear knee-length skirts or plaid shorts with knee socks for golf paired with knit polo tops or boat-neck tops.

Tennis

The short, sleeveless A-line dresses that were popular for daywear were also brought to the tennis court. Unlike the fitted, restrictive tennis costumes of previous periods, the unfitted silhouette popular in the 1960s actually allowed women to play tennis. Tennis ensembles continued to be all-white for serious players, but many included small splashes of color on neckbands, collars, or other edges.

Skiwear

Skiing or après skiing was extremely popular in the 1960s. Ski resorts continued to grow in number throughout the United States, and, with increased access to air travel, Americans also visited ski resorts abroad. The development of molded, one-piece clip-on ski boots in the late 1960s advanced both the technical abilities of skiers and their fashion sense (Lee-Potter 1984, 70). In the early part of the decade, skiwear typically consisted of a jacket and pants combination, often brightly colored and quilted. However, when Susie Chaffee appeared in a one-piece silver jumpsuit in the 1968 Olympics, a shift to the more space-age ensemble was immediately noted. The slick, stretch fabric, paired with molded white plastic ski boots, was the ski resorts' equivalent of Neil Armstrong's space suit. The new lightweight unitard, typically made from nylon, also served to decrease wind resistance for serious skiers swooshing down the mountain.

UNDERWEAR AND INTIMATE APPAREL

Undergarments

To complement the revolution being seen in women's apparel, women's undergarments also had to complete their own revolution. The new A-line silhouette no longer required the body to be molded and shaped in the manner of the 1950s New Look. Pointed bra cups distorted the silhouette, and benefits of waist cinchers could not be seen under garments that hung straight from the shoulders. Bras, which were previous feats of engineering, now provided simple support that stretched and moved with the body, thanks to spandex fibers. Girdles and corsets disappeared and were replaced by bodysuits. Bodysuits were one-piece garments knitted from spandex without any seams that provided natural shaping and support without restricting movement. Most bodysuits resembled the modern-day leotard, but some were full-body stockings, covering the wearer from head to toe.

The popularity of the miniskirt also served as a death sentence to garters and stockings. Tights, followed by the new pantyhose, became absolute necessities as skirts grew shorter and shorter throughout the decade. Panty styles evolved into the smaller brief or hipster styles still worn in the twenty-first century. Bras and panties were frequently sold in matching sets in bright or pastel colors and prints.

Sleepwear

Women's sleepwear came in a wide range of styles in the 1960s. Pajama tops with pants or shorts, night shirts, and baby-doll or shortie gowns with matching panties were all popular styles. Colors varied from pastels to brights and were available in a range of solids and patterns, including the popular op art and pop art motifs.

HEADWEAR, HAIRSTYLES, AND COSMETICS

Headwear

The 1960s ushered in the beginning of the end for hats and headwear. The shift to a more casual society, the emphasis on youth, and anti-establishment undercurrents all combined to undermine the prevalence of headwear in American society. Before the 1960s, a proper woman would never leave her house without an appropriate head covering. Now, as millions of Americans watched first lady Jacqueline Kennedy attend many public functions hatless, they took note and followed her lead. Furthermore, the large bouffant hairstyles popular in the early part of the 1960s made donning a hat nearly impossible. When hats were worn, the dominant form was the large, brimless pillbox style designed by Halston and popularized by Jacqueline Kennedy. The pillbox form sat on the top of the hair rather than being pulled down onto the head. Other hat forms occasionally seem included space-inspired helmets or hoods worn by younger women. Women would pull these designs completely over their head, and there would be a cutout for their face. The effect was very dramatic but not too practical for daily wear. Some hoods were made in fur, velvet, or silk with giant bows tied under the chin for eveningwear. Some women added jeweled brooches or small bows to their hair to compensate for the loss of the hat.

Hairstyles

The bouffant was the hairstyle of the early 1960s. Bouffant styles were created through elaborate rituals of backcombing and teasing the hair at the roots into a voluminous mass, then smoothing the top back. Many women went to bed at night with hair set in jumbo curlers ready for a fresh teasing in the morning. Those without enough hair or lacking the talent for backcombing would purchase artificial hair pieces to help create the bouffant look. Women adopting the baby-doll look sculpted mounds of small ringlets or curls out of their hair. In contrast to hairstyles in the early part of the 1960s, hairstyles moved in a drastically different direction by the end of the decade. Instead of backcombing and rollers to achieve volume, women now awoke every morning to iron or press their hair flat and straight for a more natural appearance. Long, straight, flat hair became vogue around 1967, making the old-fashioned bouffant immediately passé.

Cosmetics

Much like hairstyles in the 1960s, cosmetics witnessed a distinct transition as well. In the early 1960s, pale lipsticks were paired with eyeliner, mascara, and pastel eye shadow. By the mid-1960s, the "cookie-cutter" or "doll-face" look became popular. Key features of this look included thick, heavily lined eye lids, mascara or false eyelashes that clumped eyelashes together to resemble the painted on eyelash lines on baby dolls, and eye shadows became pronounced color blocks in lavender, blue, green, and yellow. In response to this extreme cosmetic style, by the late 1960s, women shifted to a more natural appearance with minimal makeup to complement their natural straight hair.

FOOTWEAR AND LEGWEAR

Footwear

Footwear in the 1960s can be summed up in a single word: boots. Whether ankle high or thigh high, boots were worn with stretch pants, miniskirts, and dresses in the 1960s. The most popular form was the low-heeled, squared-toe, ankle-high boots with zippers or elastic gussets on the sides, referred to as Chelsea boots because of their association with the Beatles look and mod fashions trends launched in London. As skirts inched up the leg, so too did boots. The newly exposed leg was covered with either knee-high or thigh-high boots, always with low heels and squared toes. Tall boots, sometimes referred to as go-go boots, were made in leather, suede, and crocodile, as well as space-age vinyl. Tall boots, both knee high and thigh high, were laced up, zipped up, or simply pulled on.

For basic daywear or formal occasions, some women would wear boots, whereas others opted for simple pumps, t-bar pumps, or sling backs. In keeping with the simple straight lines seen in apparel styles, the womanly curves seen in 1950s footwear disappeared. Shoes became straight. Heels were low, often stacked, and in a square, block cut. Toes were either squared or blunt. Shoes typically had little surface decoration, at most a buckle, either metallic or self-fabric, would be added to the toe, or the leather would be punched or perforated to create a pattern. Often shoes were made in the same fabric, or at least dyed the same color, as the ensemble. Rounded-toe Mary Jane shoes were the perfect complement to the baby-doll look worn by younger women.

Legwear

Pantyhose revolutionized women's legwear in the 1960s. Without the invention of pantyhose, miniskirts would have never been able to climb above the knee without showing the garters. Tights were also an important component of women's legwear in the 1960s. Tights came in bright colors, animal prints, geometric patterns, and Pucci-style patterns, as well as a range of textures, such as fishnet or crochet. Some pantyhose and tights also added embellishments such as rhinestones or embroidery at the ankle or up the entire center front of the leg. Knee-high stockings were sometimes worn instead of tights or pantyhose by women wanting to complete the little girl look popular in the early to mid-1960s. Knee-high socks came in the same colors, patterns, and textures as tights and stockings.

OTHER ACCESSORIES

Jewelry

For formalwear in the early part of the decade, jewelry was simple: a basic strand of pearls worn to edge the jewel neckline with simple earrings. As the decade progressed, large jeweled or enameled brooches were added to evening ensembles. Young women wore brightly colored plastic or Lucite jewelry in bold geometric shapes with their mod ensembles, whereas a small ribbon tie around the neck was the only accessory required for the baby-doll look.

Handbags

Small clutch purses resembling envelopes were carried for eveningwear, typically of the same fabric as the dress. For day, a wide range of leather and alligator clutches and handbags in envelope and pouch shapes were carried. Clear and colored Lucite bags shaped like boxes were a novelty item for younger women.

Other

The predominance of sleeveless dresses in the 1960s increased the frequency of gloves. Long or opera-length gloves were worn for evening, and three-quarter-length or wrist-length gloves were worn for day. Some women adopted "granny glasses," with small round frames to complete the hippie look.

ALTERNATIVE FASHION MOVEMENTS

The Mods

London in the 1960s gave birth to the youth revolution knows as the mods. The mods were an extension of the 1950s "Teddy Boys." The mod movement was originated by men who dressed impeccably in Italian shirts and tailored three-button Nehru jackets, with crisp pressed narrow trousers and cropped haircuts. However, the rise in popularity of the Beatles expanded the mod style to an international audience, including women. The mod movement, originally focused on wearing finery and maintaining a clean-cut image, also expanded to become synonymous with "Swinging London's" free-love, self-expression drug scene. The center of mod activities was Carnaby Street, and, for women, the fashion leader of the mod movement was Mary Quant and her *Bazaar* shop. The apparel and accessories Quant designed and carried in her store became the foundation for the mod look. Flamboyant miniskirts, mini-

Designer Mary Quant, wearing one of her typical mini-length designs, and with a "mod" hairstyle. [Courtesy of Photofest]

dresses, and tights in psychedelic color- and pattern-clashing ensembles were the hallmark of the mod look. Completing the look was straight cropped or bobbed hair, and baby-doll makeup, eye shadow and mascara applied in thick coats, painted on to resemble the eyes of a baby doll.

The Hippies

The late 1960s witnessed the appearance of hippies in the United States. Hippie gatherings first began around 1967 and culminated in the ultimate hippie event, Woodstock, in 1969. The hallmarks of the hippie lifestyle, communal living, arts and crafts, religion, and revolution, were reflected in their wardrobe choices. The media coverage of sit-ins, be-ins, protests, and Woodstock made the hippie appearance popular with youths, even if they did not adopt the hippie lifestyle. Women who followed the hippie lifestyle, or just the fashions, had a gypsy-like appearance with long hair, long skirts, and sandals. Much of the attire was inspired by ethnic dress, particularly that of India, and was created from

Dou Doumba, left, and Camara, both with the African National Dance Company from Guinea, wear African-print dashikis and caftans, 1967. [AP / Wide World Photos]

thrift-store finds. Love beads, feathers, embroidery, and hand-painted motifs provided decorative elements for the colorful ensembles. Denim, whether in jeans or jean jackets, was frequently worn to show solidarity with the working class and was often embroidered with antiwar messages.

Black Power
The civil rights movement of the 1960s led to the popularity of traditional African attire amongst African Americans. The promotion of "black pride" and "black is beautiful" led many to adopt dashikis, a collarless, wide shirt with kimono-type sleeves, and caftans, a similar floor-length garment for business and casual dress. Many of the garments were made from tie-dyed fabrics or traditional kente cloth from Ghana in traditional patterns and colors. Afros and corn row braided hairstyles were also adopted by those supporting African culture and heritage. Jewelry made from ebony, amber, and ivory imported from Africa was worn by individuals affiliating themselves with this movement, and it also became popular with mainstream society.

THE
1970s

FORMALWEAR

Silhouette
As American society became increasingly informal, so too did formalwear. Informality combined with the economic recession decreased the quantity of formal social occasions in the United States and decreased the need for formalwear. The growth in singles living alone also changed the shape of social activities and with it the style of eveningwear. Balls were out, discothèques were in. The stiff A-line of the 1960s receded into a soft, natural silhouette that gently followed a woman's curves. Bias cuts and jersey

knits created flowing garments that skimmed the body, returning the waistline to its natural position. Designer jeans were just as acceptable for evenings out, even at upscale clubs, as were dresses. The increase of working women meant that fashions had to be able to transition from day to night, with the simple removal of a blazer.

Skirts

Miniskirts continued to be worn until 1975. For eveningwear, minis as well as floor-length maxis were both popular lengths for skirts and dresses until the mid-1970s. Skirts for maxi dresses were either bias cut to drape across the hip or bloused at the waist with either a string tie wrapped in Grecian style or a wide inset elastic band. The just-below-the-knee-length midi replaced both minis and maxis for eveningwear in the last years of the decade. In addition to full-cut, knee-length styles, midi skirts and dresses were also made with asymmetrical and handkerchief hemlines. The interest in dance and dance fashion also led to the adoption of wrap skirts and dresses.

Donna Summer, as Nicole Sims, wears a "disco dress" in the 1978 film *Thank God It's Friday*. [Courtesy of Photofest]

Bodices

Halter tops, creating bare shoulders and bare backs, dominated eveningwear in the 1970s. An alternative to the halter was the jewel neckline modified with deep keyholes or Vs in the front or back to create flashes of tanned skin. Strapless bodices for tops and dresses were popular thanks to spandex and nylon jersey knits that would stay in place without the addition of the uncomfortable stays or boning that would prohibit dancing.

Sleeves

The majority of eveningwear looks were sleeveless in the 1970s. When sleeves were present, they were long and fitted, without cuffs. Some designers developed eveningwear designs featuring only one sleeve to complement asymmetrical hemlines and necklines.

Decorative Details

The 1970s are sometimes referred to as the "beige decade" because of the preference for ranges of beige tones, such as khaki, sand, taupe, linen, ecru, and fawn (Milbank 1989, 242). It was as if the extreme use of color and pattern in the 1960s had overstimulated fashion, and it responded by unleashing an almost exclusively neutral color palette devoid of pattern, even for eveningwear. Surface ornamentation and pattern were virtually nonexistent in the 1970s. Simple unembellished matte jerseys, chiffons, and crepe de Chines were bias cut to drape and cling to the body.

BUSINESS WEAR

Silhouette

The fiftieth anniversary of the Nineteenth Amendment to the Constitution, giving women the right to vote, was in 1970, a cause for celebration amongst feminists. The 1970s also witnessed an increase in the use of birth control, an increase in the age of marriage, and a delay in childbearing for women, providing women with more choices. The choice was clear: women were choosing careers, not jobs, and not marriage or family. The youthful look of the 1960s was out, and women needed a more serious wardrobe to be taken seriously in the workplace. Masculine tailored shirts, blazers, and trousers were lifted from men's wardrobes and adopted by women; dresses were out and suits were in, especially pantsuits. Serving as yet another fashion first, for the first time styles varied between evening and business wear. Eveningwear was soft, draping, and feminine. Business wear was crisply tailored in tweeds and gabardine. Before the 1970s there was no distinct variation between looks for day, evening and business.

An androgynous suit by Scott Barrie, 1972. Women were beginning to wear much less conventionally feminine clothes. [AP / Wide World Photos]

Dresses

Shirtdresses provided an alternative to suits for business dress. The shirtdress, not seen since the hourglass, crinolined 1950s, resembled a lengthened tailored men's shirt and was worn with a thin belt about the waist and topped with a blazer. Some long-sleeved, midi wrap dresses were worn under blazers, but ultimately the wrap dress provided too impractical for the office.

Suits

Women were ready to demonstrate "who wears the pants" in the office. Trouser suits or pantsuits based on tailored men's suits were adopted by

women working their way up the corporate ladder. Tailored trousers with full-cut legs and
matching single-breasted jacket became the new
uniform for working women. Underneath, women
wore button-down oxford shirts, tunics with band
collars, or wing-tipped shirts. Some women even
wore men's ties. In 1977, John Molly published
his *Dress for Success* book, providing advice on
appropriate office attire for women. Molly cau-
tioned against wearing pantsuits to the office,
advice most women did not heed.

Separates

Coordinating separates were the new working
woman's best friend to "dress for success." Separates
provided the greatest range of flexibility for career
dressing, as well as provided transitional day-to-
evening options. Coordinating separates were a
new concept for women in the 1970s, and women
required training and advice in how to mix and
match components to make appropriate ensembles.
Magazines such as *Vogue* and *Cosmopolitan* served
as a tour guides through this uncharted territory of
colors, patterns, and textures.

A black pantsuit with satin trim by Calvin
Klein, 1978. [AP / Wide World Photos]

The blazer became the most important building block of the separates
wardrobe. Single-breasted, one-button blazers with notched lapels were
worn with every office ensemble. Underneath the blazer, man-tailored
oxford, banded collar, pleated front, wing collar shirts were worn in solids,
chambray, and stripes. Tailored pants were the preferred coordinate, but
straight fly-front and dirndl skirts were also available. Vests were worn in
addition to or as an alternative to the blazer. Fedoras and neckties were
worn by women adopting the most extreme masculine attire.

Decorative Details

Shades of beige dominated women's business wear because it was easy to
mix and match. Earth tones such as brick, olive, rust, and gold were interspersed with beige neutral to add color to separates. A new interest in
ecology spurred an increased use of natural fibers such as wool, cotton,
linen, and silk rather than polyesters and acrylics in business wear. Men's
wear fabrics such as tweed, herringbone, and pinstripe were the most
common fabrications for women's business attire.

CASUAL WEAR

Silhouette

Casual wear was dominated by shirt and pant combinations. Blue jeans became the most common item of casual wear, transcending both class and age groups. Casual pants began the decade, riding low on the hip with tapered legs, and gradually returned to the natural waistline while flaring the leg to form bell-bottoms. Although miniskirts and hot pants made a brief impact on the early part of the decade, by the middle of the decade, skirts were worn at midi length, in either dirndl or bias drape cuts. By the mid 1970s, the prevailing silhouette in women's fashions emphasized the natural body; bust, waist, and hips were all back to their natural positions with gentle support rather than rigid shaping.

Dresses

Dresses became less common for casual wear in the 1970s. By the mid 1970s, after the end of the miniskirt craze, the most popular casual dress styles were the wrap dress and the halter dress. Other one-piece dresses that pulled over the head had elastic waists or drawstring waists or were worn with a skinny belt or cord tie to blouse the top of the dress, creating emphasis on the waist. Pullover dresses often had scoop or jewel necklines and cap sleeves, similar to T-shirts.

Separates

Skirts declined in popularity as did dresses during the 1970s, being replaced in the casual wardrobe with pants. The popularity of the ethnic peasant look resulted in the miniskirt being replaced by dirndl and wrap skirts by the mid-1970s. Dirndl skirts had slight fullness gathered into the waistband and often came in ethnic-inspired prints. Wrap skirts that flared slightly at the hem were inspired by the increased popularity in dance and the adaptation of dance apparel for casual wear.

Pants continued to increase in popularity throughout the decade. Hot pants, or extremely short shorts, were a brief novelty in women's casual wear in 1971. Hot pants provided an alternative to miniskirts but were a short-lived fad too extreme for most women. Jeans were the most common form of casual pant in the 1970s. A preference for faded jeans in the late 1960s and early 1970s gave birth to second-hand stores such as The Gap (founded in 1969), which specialized in the resale of Levi's and other jeans. Jeans were straight legged with button flys in the beginning of the 1970s but shifted to the notorious bell-bottom, or flared leg, form in the middle of the decade. By 1978, the designer jean craze had begun, and jeans by Calvin Klein and Gloria Vanderbilt were worn straight legged, tapered to the ankle, and so tight that many women had to lie down to zip their jeans. In additional to jeans, painter's pants, the forerunner of the cargo pant, sailor pants, with double placket front-button closure, and army fatigues were also worn.

The blazer was an integral component of the casual wardrobe. Worn with pants, jeans, and skirts, blazers came in denim, corduroy, and other fabrics for casual wear. Blazers were worn over T-shirts, lacy Edwardian-inspired blouses, leotards, and camisoles, ending at just below the waist-line and closing with a single button. Daring women would wear the blazer as a top, without a bra.

A wide range of tops and blouses were available for casual wear. Tops, whether woven or knit, had high, tight armholes and narrow, fitted sleeves. An interest in dance and exercise brought the leotard into vogue for casual wear, especially when paired with wrap skirts. Halter tops, "tube" tops (strap-less knit tops), and T-shirts were the most casual options for daytime. T-shirts came printed with a wide array of logos, messages, and concert venues to announce the wearer's affiliation and participation with various groups and causes. Rib-knit sweaters, cardigans, and cardigan sets (twin sets) were another option for casual wear. Sweaters and sweater vests were worn alone or over tailored shirts and turtlenecks. Cardigans were worn long, around mid-thigh. Sweaters and cardigans were typically belted at the natural waist with either a matching sash or a thin leather belt. Edwardian lace blouses and lace camisoles were worn to dress up jeans. Tailored button-down shirts were left unbuttoned to breast point to display the firm body achieved through exercise.

Decorative Details

Casual wear was made from natural fibers such as cottons, wool, and silk, as well as the synthetic polyester and spandex. The ethnic peasant look at the beginning of the decade used tie-dye, patterns, fringe, and embroidery for decorations. However, by the middle of the decade, solid colors in neutral shades of beige dominated the color palette. Small patterns or prints were found in some casual wear, as were broad horizontal stripes, but, in general, solid colors gained favor. Garments were softly structured throughout the decade as opposed to the more tailored feeling in casual wear in the 1960s. Jersey knits, double knits, chiffons, lace, and charmeuse draped the body, revealing natural curves.

OUTERWEAR

Coats

Women's coats in the 1970s were knee length to match the new midi skirt length. Coats were both single and double breasted, fitted at the natural waist and flared to the hem. Many coats had self-fabric (or matching fabric) tie belts. Collars and lapels were wide, and many coat styles featured oversized patch pockets. For winter, collars, lapels, cuffs, and pockets were often made from or trimmed in fur or faux fur. Down or fiber-filled quilted jackets and vests were worn for casual winter wear. Nylon windbreakers with small stand collars were worn for casual summer wear. Jean jackets were worn in both long and waist lengths for casual wear. The denim was often embellished with patchwork, appliqués, embroidery, and metal studs.

Shawls/Wraps

Shawls were a popular alternative to traditional coats in the 1970s. Ethnic print and embroidered shawls with fringe complemented the peasant or hippie gypsy look that carried over from the late 1960s into design by YSL and other fashion designers.

SWIMWEAR AND SPORTSWEAR

Swimwear

A healthy, tanned glow was the most important "suit" for swimwear in the 1970s, and swimwear was designed to provide maximum exposure of the skin's surface. In fact, cosmetic and skincare manufacturers worked diligently to develop creams and oils that would help to accelerate the tanning process, unaware of the dangers of skin cancer. Over the course of the decade, the low-rise, boy-leg bikini with bra or tank-style top of the 1960s evolved into the modern bikini swimsuit. Halter and bandeaux tops replaced the bra or tank style and were fabricated with detachable straps to avoid tan lines. The 1970s also gave birth to the string bikini, literally an assemblage of triangular fabric sections held together by two ties on the top and a tie on each side of the hip.

The popularity of leotards and dancing in the late 1970s brought a return to vogue for one-piece swimsuits. Unlike their predecessors, these suits had deep plunging necklines, low or no back, and high-cut legs. Some styles were made with complex criss-crossing of strings or bands across the bare back or with shirring down the center front. These elaborate one-piece designs were occasionally worn with jeans or skirts to discothèques.

Regardless of style, swimwear continued to be made from spandex. However, unlike the 1960s, swimwear was no longer embellished with surface decorations or appliqués. Instead, the visual interest for 1970s swimwear came in the form of shine. Although swimwear in past decades was bright, it was always matte, never glossy. Now swimwear glistened as if wet in bright colors as well as metallic bronze, gold, or silver.

Golf

Although founded in 1950, the Ladies Professional Golf Association (LPGA) did not experience significant growth until the leadership of JoAnne Carner in the 1970s. The timing was perfect for expansion: the Women's Liberation Movement and publicity for the EPA gave women the perfect impetus for joining men on the golf course. Adding to the publicity was the popularity of Australian golf player Jan Stephenson. Stephenson, voted the 1974 Rookie of the Year and dubbed the "glamour girl" of the LPGA tour, brought sex appeal to women's golf. The unisex, tomboy look adopted by women in the 1970s easily translated to the golf course in the form of oxford bags (oversized knickers or bloomers), unstructured jackets with wide lapels, short, wide kipper ties, and Baker boy caps. The smart sassy look was perfect for the bold new woman who wanted to compete on the "men's turf."

Tennis

Traditional white tennis skirts and tops were never the same after the sexual revolution of the 1970s. Tennis courts now featured halter tops, bare midriffs, and bright splashes of color, bringing new excitement to the game of tennis. Rosie Casals' tennis ensemble at the 1972 Wimbledon tournament feature bold purple scrolls (Tortora and Eubank 2005, 453). Colored headbands were also a novelty item for tennis wear in the 1970s.

Skiwear

The sleek, fitted one-piece ski suits of the late 1960s continued to be worn into the early 1970s. However, by the mid-1970s, one-piece suits were replaced by jacket and pant ensembles. Much like the bell-bottom trousers of the decade, ski pants also developed flared cuffs to splay over ski boots. But, unlike bellbottom pants, ski pants were constructed with an inner fitted leg with a knit or elastic cuff that was tucked into the boot to keep the skier warm and dry. The 1960s fascination with zippers continued into the 1970s. Jackets were engineered to transform into vests by zip-off hoods and sleeves. By the end of the decade, tapered stirrup pants were replacing flared pants on the slopes.

Other Activewear

Roller skating and jogging were all new athletic trends in the 1970s, and the apparel worn for these sports extended to daily-wear fashions. Track suits or jogging suits in fleece and terry cloth might also double for day-wear when fabricated in colorful stretch velour or satin. Shiny spandex leotards paired with jogging shorts or wrap skirts were equally acceptable at the roller rink as the discothèque.

Underwear and Intimate Apparel

Undergarments

Despite the much publicized bra-burning demonstrations that took place during the women's liberation movement, going braless was not something that the majority of American women would even consider. In fact, at no point in history were women's brassieres more comfortable than during the 1970s. The modeled, padded, and wired cups of the 1950s were gone. In their place, nylon and spandex provided soft fabric with support with light underwires that did not bind or pinch. A variety in bra and cup styles became available to complement fashion styles and body types. Demi-bras and bandeau bras, worn under tube tops and strapless dresses, were new options for women. The most exciting bra design of the 1970s was the seamless bra. Seamless bras were molded from thermoplastic fibers (fibers that melt on contact with heat) in one continuous piece. No seams meant no bumps or pulls under the popular sheer clingy jersey knits of the era.

Sleepwear

Sleepwear and pajamas changed little from the 1960s. Long and short gowns and pajama sets with tops and either shorts or pants were all available in cotton or tricot knit. During the economic recession and energy restrictions of the 1970s, flannel pajamas and brushed tricot pajamas increased in popularity out of necessity for warmth. Some women even opted for adult versions of children's all-in-one footie pajamas.

Other Garments

The sexual revolution of the late 1960s and early 1970s was readily apparent in the availability of sexy lingerie from retailers such as Frederick's of Hollywood. Long negligees with slits from the ankle to the hip in lace or satin in either red or black were worn by the new liberated woman. Matching panties and satin robes completed the sets.

Headwear, Hairstyles, and Cosmetics

Headwear

The hatless trend begun in the 1960s continued in the 1970s. Hats were no longer an important component of women's ensembles. Some women wore scarves as a component of the peasant look. For a brief period, some women sported fedoras after the style worn by Diane Keaton in *Annie Hall* in 1977. Berets, knit caps, and fur-trimmed hats were worn in winter more for necessity than fashion.

Hairstyles

Without hats to interfere, women experimented with styling their hair and changed hairstyles more frequently. In the early part of the 1970s, long, straight hair was a must. By the middle of the decade, hairstyles were becoming shorter, around shoulder length, with soft natural waves. The short and sporty "wedge" rose in popularity after Dorothy Hamill's medal winner appearance in the 1976 Olympics. Simultaneous to the wedge, Barbra Streisand's frizzy curls in the 1976 film *A Star is Born* launched the next hair craze for frizzy or kinky hair with a thick fringe of bang. A third alternative for hairstyles was also presented in 1976 by the new show *Charlie's Angels*. Star Farrah Fawcett-Majors sported a mane of "feathered" hair with blond highlights. In addition to wedges, frizzy, and feathers, women worked their hair into side ponytails instead of the traditional center back ponytail, as well as side chignon or buns. Both options complemented the asymmetrical necklines seen in many dresses of the late 1970s.

Cosmetics

One outcome of the women's liberation movement was the notion that women were too busy and intelligent to be forced to spend time on their appearance and that makeup was frivolous and unnecessary. The reality was that the natural look took just as much time and makeup to create as any other cosmetic style. Foundations, blushes, mascaras, and lip glosses were formulated in lighter, natural shades to provide sun-kissed tanned skin. Bold, dramatic looks were created for disco nights. High-gloss lipsticks, cheek bones accented with blush, smudged eyeliner, and electric blue eye shadow were favorites under the disco ball.

FOOTWEAR AND LEGWEAR

Footwear

Platform shoes and boots, popular at the close of the 1960s, continued to dominate footwear in the early 1970s. Wedge soles were popular alternatives to platforms. Both platforms and wedges featured stacked heels, a technique of layering materials, often in alternating colors, to create the heel of a shoe. By 1975, the craze for platform and wedge heels had faded. Lower versions of platform and wedge heels were seen throughout the decade in casual footwear such as leather vamped, wooden-heeled clogs, cork-heeled sandals, and canvas espadrilles. The new interest in athletics and sports also brought increased interest in "gym" shoes, such as those by Nike and Adidas, for daily wear.

The new working woman of the 1970s demanded a more sensible low-heeled shoe for daily wear. Business women adopted mules, ankle boots, and heeled brogues (similar to men's wingtips) to pair with their suits and separates in the office. Knee-high boots, both pull-on and lace-up styles, were worn for work or play.

In the middle of the decade, sandals typically had thick single straps across the vamp and thick buckle straps or ties around the ankle. However, by the end of the decade, sandals had taken on a lighter, strappier, more elegant form in gold and silver metallic for evening and leather for day.

Suede, leather, and canvas were popular materials for 1970s footwear. Leather was often perforated or punched to create surface interest, executed in patchwork or silvered. Colors were often solid and plain earth tones.

Legwear

Pantyhose continued to dominate women's legwear in the 1970s. Pantyhose or tights were typically found in a range of browns and beiges to complement the neutral color palette of the decade. Pantyhose with control tops became another important component of underwear (along with the seamless bra), for holding in protruding tummies to create a smooth appearance under bias cut and clingy jersey knits. Socks, tights, and pantyhose continued to be produced in textures and patterns, although the patterns were much more subdued (argyles, chevrons, and checks) compared with their 1960s counterparts.

OTHER ACCESSORIES

Jewelry

The body-conscious fashions of the 1970s limited the amount of jewelry that could be worn without interrupting the fluid lines of dresses and separates. Even for formal occasions, accessories were minimal. Simple gold wire hoops or diamond stud earrings and multistrand gold chain necklaces were the most typical jewelry forms. Cuff and bangle bracelets in gold or snakeskin were the largest pieces of jewelry worn.

Handbags

Shoulder bags replaced the previous decade's clutch and pouch style purses. Tan, brown, and burgundy leather or suede were popular for day bags. Soft satchels with long shoulder straps in ethnic patterns or patchwork were alternatives to leather. Saddle bags and briefcases in tan, brown, or burgundy leather were carried by the new working woman to the office each day.

Other

Large tortoise-shell sunglasses and aviator-style sunglasses, both with dark lenses, were fashion must-haves in the 1970s. Watches with gold-rimmed faces and leather bands, or the new digital watches, first introduced in 1976, were a must on every wrist.

THE
1980s

FORMALWEAR

Silhouette

The description of women's apparel in the 1980s was usually preceded by the word "big": big shoulders, big hair, and big makeup. Although female fashion was certainly dominated by the broad and somewhat excessive styles popularized by the entertainment industry, the 1980s were also a time of varied and eclectic styles. Formalwear choices were driven by the enthusiasm and momentum of the dynamic, active, and empowered woman wanting to showcase not only her independence but also her sense of glamour. American trendsetters saw eveningwear and formalwear as the perfect vehicle to openly display status and success. With the American woman celebrating her achievements in the business world, it is no surprise that the power suit influenced the look of formalwear. Two-piece tailored ensembles borrowed lines and textures from traditionally male business wear but added a feminine touch with the incorporation of skirts, seaming, and narrow-fitted waists (Milbank 1989, 267). Wide padded shoulders, darts, slits, long sleeves, and a narrow waist were essential to the creation of a fitted look that showcased the sensual curves that many women achieved by spending hours at the fitness center (Clancy 1996, 176).

Skirts

Skirts varied in length but were typically wide and voluminous. Puffed skirts, also dubbed the bouffant or bubble, were popular for eveningwear and were created by complex draping effects and finished with bows, ruffles, and other decorative fastenings. The skirt circumference was supported by substructures similar to Victorian bustles and hoops (Tortora and Eubank 2005, 526). Other popular styles included slim-fitting pencil skirts in knee or just-below-the-knee lengths, A-lines, and skirt alternatives such as harem pants and jumpsuits.

Bodices

Shoulder pads were used to sculpt the upper torso's natural curves, increasing the feminine look of bodices. The emphasis on shoulders was at times exaggerated, with extremely large shoulder pads and designs that triangulated the upper body. Puffy sleeves matched the fullness seen in skirts and contributed to the enlargement of the torso. Blouses in soft fabrics showcased draping effects created by gathers, ruffles, and bows and were reminiscent of the Romantic and Victorian styles of the late nineteenth century. Shawls were a common accessory for formalwear, and some tops were designed with draping effects emulating the folds and fringes of shawls. Fitted blouses with princess seams were also standard as well as tailored styles with high necklines and peplums extending below the waistline. A variety of necklines were used for eveningwear. The most popular designs included single-shoulder asymmetrical, strapless, off-the-shoulder, backless, and deep plunging styles (both front and back). When collars were applied to eveningwear designs, they were simple and soft finished bows, soft ties, or ruffles.

Sleeves

Sleeve styles were also quite eclectic, varying in length and volume. Puffed and leg-of-mutton sleeves were used to complement the voluminous style of typical evening gowns, but long fitted sleeves with simple cuffs were equally popular. Some designers experimented with creating visual interest and drama through the use of a single sleeve.

Decorative Details

The popularity of natural fibers that resurfaced in the 1970s continued in the 1980s. Elegant eveningwear was created with luxurious fabrics, including suede, cashmere, silk, satin, or velvet and often complemented by fur or faux fur scarves, coats, and stoles. Shiny fabrics in bold colors ranging from emerald green and candy-apple red to royal blue and deep purple made a statement about the wearer's strong personality and reflected the influence of bold television characters such as *Dynasty*'s Alexis Carrington (Lehnert 2000, 87). On the same show, and often in real life, pastel colors and pale shades of pink, green, and blue were associated with a subdued and conservative style favored by elegant retirees and young debutants. Toward the end of the decade, black was used to mix and match with either pastel or bright shades. Striped and polka-dotted fabrics were also fashionable for chic cocktail dresses, and beading and sequins sparkled on elegant evening gowns. Other evening styles showed historic influences by the use of complex draping and pleating techniques reminiscent of classic Greek apparel and Fortuny pleats.

Business Wear

Silhouette

In the 1980s, women active in the business and political arena created a clothing style that combined authority, confidence, and feminine touches (Carnegy 1990, 20). Power dressing or "dressing for success" was an integral part of everyday fashion for most American women. The conservative silhouette featured variations and adaptations of masculine business fashion with broad cuts and large padded shoulders. Wide jackets were often matched with slim pants, fitted dresses, pencil skirts reaching just below the knee, and occasionally with fuller skirts.

Dresses

The most common styles for business wear included basic sleeveless, fitted sheaths, with some styles ending above the knee. In most cases, these were made in soft, draping fabrics that might be pleated, draped, or seamed with darts to shape the figure and emphasize round hips. Necklines were usually conservative, round jewel necklines to accommodate the heavy necklaces worn during this period. Dresses were typically sleeveless and topped by a tailored jacket or blazer with heavily padded shoulders to produce the broad-shouldered look prevalent at this time.

Suits

Suits were the uniform of power dressing for the 1980s business woman, and the skirted suit was the dominant pairing. Jackets were suspended off the shoulder with large shoulder pads from which they tapered drastically to narrow at the hips (Carnegy 1990, 32). Slim-line knee-length shirts with slits or inverted center back pleats or knife pleat or box-pleated skirts with hip yokes matched the suit coat. Some suits were paired pants that were pleated at the waist to create a full hip but tapered to narrow openings at the ankles. For a short period, some fashion innovators wore Bermuda shorts as a substitute for suit bottoms (Lehnert 2000, 87). Most suit jackets were double breasted, and some designers experimented with extremely large and asymmetric suit coats.

Separates

A crucial part of the 1980s dress for success practice was the flexibility that separates allowed women. Wide blazers with shoulder pads cut in a broad style were worn with pencil, pleated, peg-top (cowl draped), or slim-line knee-length skirts, or with pleated pants. White embroidered silk blouses were commonly worn under suits, but soft pastel colors were also seen. One of the most popular blouse styles for women was the draped neck blouse popularized by Susan Dey on *L.A. Law.* Fitted knit cardigans, sweaters, or shells provided additional choices for wardrobe variations. Necklines and collar styles were simple and conservative. Scarves, bows, and neckties were often used to add a feminine touch to the otherwise masculine lines of the outfit.

Decorative Details

High-quality natural fabrics such as wool tweed, wool crepe, cashmere, and silk were dominant in business wear, but polyester and other synthetic materials remained in use for blouses. Earth tones in the suits and jackets contrasted with white and pastels on blouses. Pinstripes, checks, and houndstooth typically seen in men's business suits were adopted for women's business attire. Patch pockets and buttons were large and included gold metallic detailing. Small appliqué and embroidery figures softened the straight lines of some jackets, typically on the breast pocket.

CASUAL WEAR

Silhouette

There was no prevalent silhouette for casual wear in the 1980s; as a matter of fact, American women explored a wealth of possibilities during the period (Milbank 1989, 279). Casual wear combined equally the oversized look of business wear, seen in sweaters and tops, with the body-enhancing styles of eveningwear present in the fitted synthetic dresses worn widely in the 1980s. The American obsession with a fit and athletic physique brought influences from sports and swimwear to daily wear. Aerobics and gym garments such as Lycra leggings, legwarmers, fitted leotards, headbands, and special shoes were seen in street fashion, often combined with elements of business attire (Lehnert 2000, 86).

Dresses

Dresses varied from loose, wide skirted styles made with cotton or polyester blends to fitted ones made out of synthetic fiber blends. Rounded shoulders were common, but other styles featured drop shoulders and leg-of-mutton sleeves. Sleeve styles, whether short or long, were usually straight and simple for casual wear. Summer dresses were usually sleeveless and featured halter tops and narrow straps. Deep V and round revealing scoop necklines might be decorated with ribbons and flounces. Waistlines were truly diverse, with extremes ranging from high empire to dropped waists inspired by 1920s fashion to inset peplums. Some dresses featured princess seams, and loose shirtwaist styles were tied with large belts. Other featured styles included denim or khaki jumpsuits, sacks or sheaths, rib-knit sweater dresses, and Lycra stretch mini-dresses.

Separates

Casual wear was largely defined by the popularity of denim products, particularly pants and jackets. Denim was acid washed, stone washed, dyed, frayed, slashed, and patchworked. Semiformal, loose, button-down silk blouses with padded shoulders and plunging necklines were worn with jeans and high heels. Blouses were often detailed with ruffles, streamers, rhinestones, and metal studs. Round neck, turtleneck, and standing collar sweaters in bright-colored stripes or bold jacquard novelty patterns were worn over skirts and pants. Oversized sweaters and sweatshirts, inspired by the movie *Flashdance*, were worn off the shoulder with cuts or slashes to reveal tank tops underneath. Leotards, sweatshirts, and other athletic wear items were used as tops. Cotton T-shirts with messages and logos were worn with feminine touches such as embroidered figures, appliqué, and sequins. Pants and skirts varied in length and featured a variety of novelties, including zippered ankles and decorative patch pockets. Mini-skirt styles also reappeared during the period. Designer jeans and nylon parachute pants with zipper details popularized by break dancing and Michael Jackson's *Thriller* music video were worn by most young American women.

Decorative Details

The color palette ranged from pastel shades often seen in sportswear to neon fluorescent colors introduced for the adolescent and college market. Animal prints and bold geometric patterns were seen in blouses, shirts, and sweaters. Rayon, polyester, and other synthetic fabrics were finished to closely resemble natural textiles. Knits and fleece were widely used in casual wear. Denim was chemically treated to produce "worn" effects or embroidered for decoration.

OUTERWEAR

Coats

Large, often dramatic coats complemented the oversized looks and shapes of formalwear and casual wear. Coats had exaggerated padded shoulders, just as other garments did, high collars, and wide lapels, and the waistline was cinched with wide leather or self-fabric belts. Shorter coats were also fairly popular and kept the same broad lines of longer ones. Common materials included wool tweed and synthetic blends. Coats shared the same color range as other garments, including earth tones, soft pastels, and patterns such as pinstripe or houndstooth. Black or colored leather bomber (aviator) jackets, suede jackets, and parkas trimmed with fur were seen in casual outerwear. Trench and polo coats were still popular around the United States as well as jean jackets.

Shawls/Wraps

Oversized silk scarves with bold nature prints were often used as decorative outerwear or to accessorize a coat. Rectangular and triangular wool shawls were used in a variety of ways, including over both shoulders, one shoulder or even as headscarves. Some shawls imitated ethnic looks such as the South American poncho and the Moroccan burnoose. Ruffles, ribbons, and other details were used as embellishments in some wraps for evening. The finest shawls were made of silk, cashmere, mohair, and angora. Large capes or caplets in bold and pastel colors of satin or taffeta were used for elegant occasions to top the array of strapless dresses.

Other Garments

Embroidered cardigans and other types of sweaters were popular alternatives to coats and shawls. Many of these outwear sweaters were knitted with metallic threads to add sparkle for the evening. Knitted sweater coats, reaching below the knee, were another option occasionally adopted by younger American women.

SWIMWEAR AND SPORTSWEAR

Swimwear

The 1970s revolution in swimwear extended into the 1980s when the emphasis on fitness brought a variety of body-revealing and body-enhancing styles. Bikinis, one-piece suits, and even string bikinis and thongs shared the American swimwear market. In general, the silhouette called for higher leg lines with revealing thighs and derriere. The prevailing cut in one-piece suits was a high inverted V shape at the hip paired with a matching elongated V on the front and/or back of the top (Tortora and Eubank 2005, 520). Bikini tops were structured from string, halter straps, and bandeaus, and bottoms remained minimalist. Swimwear followed trends from casual wear in fabrics and colors. Bold prints, bright neon shades, geometric shapes, and neoprene accents decorated Lycra and nylon swimsuits. Padding devices were used to shape the body, particularly the breasts as well as control panels to hold in the tummy. Scarves were also used as sarong coverups.

Popular musician and designer Gwen Stefani. [Courtesy of Photofest]

This late 1990s photo of the Season 2 cast of *That '70s Show* shows an array of popular 1970s fashion. [Courtesy of Photofest]

John Travolta and Karen Lynn Gorney are shown in the 1977 film *Saturday Night Fever*. [Courtesy of Photofest]

HBO television series *Sex and the City*, season 4, 2001. Shown: standing, Kristin Davis (as Charlotte York McDougal), seated, Cynthia Nixon (as Miranda Hobbes), Sarah Jessica Parker (as Carrie Bradshaw), and Kim Cattrall (as Samantha Jones). [Courtesy of Photofest]

This late-1970s photo of Emmylou Harris illustrates the "peasant style." [Photofest, Inc.]

A break-dancing outfit from the 1984 film *Beat Street*. [Courtesy of Photofest]

The cast of Wes Anderson's 2001 film *The Royal Tenenbaums*, with examples of 1970s-style jogging suits. [Courtesy of Photofest]

An image from the very popular *Jane Fonda's Workout* videotape, illustrating the typical workout wear of the 1980s, with leggings and leotard. [Courtesy of Photofest]

Singer Cyndi Lauper wears a neon-flourescent outfit in this 1985 photo. [Courtesy of Photofest]

The women's fashion of bare-midriff shirts and low-rider pants is shown here on NBC's *Jennifer Lopez in Concert*, November 20, 2001. [Courtesy of Photofest]

The Nehru jacket suit, with beads and fitted trousers, is shown here in the Beatles' 1967 movie, *Magical Mystery Tour*. [Courtesy of Photofest]

Don Johnson (as Det. James "Sonny" Crockett) and Philip Michael Thomas (as Det. Ricardo "Rico" Tubbs) on the NBC television show *Miami Vice*. [Courtesy of Photofest]

Tom Cruise wears a crop cut as Maverick in the 1986 film *Top Gun*. [Courtesy of Photofest]

San Francisco Mayor Willie Brown models Urban Flava cranberry wool charging rhino sweater and olive zip off cargo pant by Ecko Unlimited, 1997. [AP Photo/Robin Weiner]

A model sporting a Viking helmet walks down the runway wearing Betsey Johnson's sequined silver foil tube top and skins, 1997. [AP Photo/Todd Plitt]

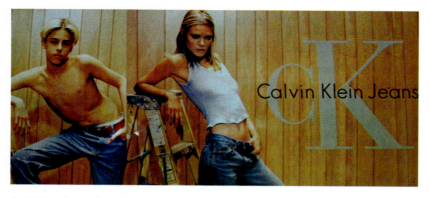

A 1995 Calvin Klein advertisment for grunge fashion. [AP Photo/L.M. Otero]

A model wears an Asian-print silk bikini top with red patent leather quilted hotpants, and a pink faux-fur stole at the Baby Phat Fall 2002 fashion show. [AP Photo/Mark Lennihan]

Model Ines de la Fressange presents a light glencheck suit worn with a white guipure sailor's collar blouse, as part of the 1988 Spring Summer haute couture collection by designer Karl Lagerfeld for Chanel. [AP Photo/Lionel Cironneau]

Golf

Most women continued wearing loose pants, either ankle or capri length, often matched with tube socks and their polo shirts. Experimentation in textile science created fabrics capable of adapting to climate changes.

Tennis

After the 1970s color revolutions in tennis uniforms, all white once again dominated the tennis courts. Women still wore tops and skirts or dresses, but shorts or skorts also became accepted forms for women's tennis garb.

Skiwear

Tapered pants and wool sweaters were still used by many women, but ski suits were becoming increasingly popular. Bright colors and bold geometric patterns were commonly seen in skiwear. The introduction of new textiles such as polar fleece and microfiber enhanced thermal and waterproof qualities of professional skiwear (Bryant 2004, 185). Other high-tech fabrics were developed to minimize wind resistance (Tortora and Eubank 2005, 521). Technological advancements also improved ultraviolet filtering in goggles and created more resistant helmets and shin guards.

Other Activewear

With the increased popularity of fitness training and competitive sports at all levels of American society, sportswear took center stage, influencing and defining other areas of apparel. Fitted leotards and leggings in shiny fabrics came in a range of colors from black to neon or fluorescent. The tendency was for sportswear to become more relaxed and comfortable, perhaps the very reason why so many sportswear items and looks were adopted into casual wear. Color-blocked workout garments, headbands, and the quintessential legwarmers were among the items brought from the gym into the street.

UNDERWEAR AND INTIMATE APPAREL

Undergarments

During the last two decades of the twentieth century, underwear served many purposes beyond the protective and functional aspects usually associated with it. A woman's undergarments translated as sex appeal and became an intrinsic part of her fashionable wardrobe. Advertising for those previous "unmentionables" was bold and direct, with images of women in their underwear appearing on billboards and magazine spreads. With an expanding market to serve, traditionally male brands introduced women's lines, including "Jockey for Her" in 1982. Cleavage-revealing wired bras with molded cups accentuated natural lines, and briefs became smaller than in previous periods (Clancy 1996, 166). Many new strapless, convertible, and wireless bras were introduced to keep underwear from interfering with the prevailing strapless, backless, sleeveless, and plunging necklines. Femininity was also expressed through breast enhancements with push-up bras becoming widespread and breast implants providing a more drastic option.

Sleepwear

Sleeping robes, negligees, pajamas, and other traditional nightwear were still used in the 1980s, but oversized T-shirts began gaining popularity as an option for sleepwear.

Other Garments

Novelty underwear in nylon lace and satin was originally introduced in red and black for special occasions such as Valentine's Day and later influenced casual lingerie. Victoria's Secret, and the racier Frederick's of Hollywood, became the most successful purveyors of fancy underwear and often introduced styles that trickled down to the general market. Housecoats, bed jackets, and robes used as loungewear came in a variety of styles and in colors ranging from soft pastels to shiny metallic and neon.

HEADWEAR, HAIRSTYLES, AND COSMETICS

Headwear

Boater, fishing, and fedora hats were still worn on special occasions by elegant American women. Small caps with veils would occasionally appear with formal eveningwear. Visors, scarves, kerchiefs, and some ethnic-inspired head wraps were also used as headgear, but, in general, the hatless trend begun in the 1960s continued. Popular hair accessories for the younger crowd in the 1980s included banana and butterfly clips, headbands, lace bands (popularized by Madonna's *Like a Virgin* music video), and scrunchies.

Hairstyles

Long, wavy hairstyles of the late 1970s turned into full large manes of the early 1980s. The Farrah Fawcett-Majors feather hairstyles gave way to high, puffy hairstyles with bangs teased straight up and held in place with gel and hairspray. Dubbed "mall hair," the most extreme puffy, frizzy versions of these styles were adopted by adolescent girls who hung out at retail malls after school and on Saturdays. Perms were obtained in salons (or at home) to provide volume and to allow the hair to remain curly for a longer period.

By the middle of the 1980s, softer, more natural looks and short unisex cuts were also in style. Some celebrities such as Annie Lenox and Grace Jones wore extreme versions of these short cuts that were smooth and tight to the head, with large amounts of hair gel. By the end of the decade, the trend of hair coloring initiated in the punk movement was adopted by many young American women. Colored wigs in deep solid shades such as red and blue were used along pastel colors and metallic tints. Colored hair gels and mousses could be purchased at drugstores for temporary color accents.

Cosmetics

Bold makeup accompanied the 1980s big fashions and large hairstyles. Natural shades were used for foundation and lips were outlined with a shade darker than the already dark lipstick (Tortora and Eubank 2005, 523). Fingernail polish ranged from classic colors of red and burgundy to glitter and neon variations. Eye shadow was equally bright, electric blue and purple being the two most popular colors. Innovations in beauty care included anti-aging products and rejuvenators featuring alpha-hydroxy acids (Seeling 2000, 515). A more extreme alternative was embraced by some women choosing to have eyeliner, lip liner, and eyebrows permanently tattooed (Seeling 2000, 515).

FOOTWEAR AND LEGWEAR

Footwear

High or mid-range stiletto or spike-heeled pumps and mules, sophisticated strapped sandals, and other classic styles in leather, suede, and fabrics were worn for formalwear. Dyed-to-match shoes, not popular since the 1960s, returned again. Flower corsages, ribbons, glass beads, rhinestones, and embroidery were used as decorative elements on elegant shoes. The fitness craze made brand sneakers and aerobic shoes acceptable items for casual wear. Nike, Adidas, and other labels experimented with color in sport shoes by adding neon and fluorescent detailing, implemented high-tech fabrications, and displayed their logos as decoration in prominent places including the shoe's tongue. Doc Martens manufactured some of the most popular styles among young women (and men). See-through materials, particularly in plastic jelly shoes, were common in casual footwear. Wedge-heel shoes and sandals with ethnic prints and shapes were also trendy with younger Americans.

Legwear

Pantyhose continued being worn by women for business wear and formal-wear. Flesh tones were dominant, but black, pale, and opaque shades were also seen (Payne 1992, 633). Legwear decoration included appliquéd or beaded motives adhered to the nylon at the ankle. Patterned pantyhose and tights reminiscent of the 1960s appeared with decorations, including exotic rainbow compositions, tie-dye motifs, leaves, flowers, tartan prints, and animal prints (Farrell 1992, 83). Legwarmers were the quintessential item of legwear for the decade, appearing in gym wear, street styles, and even haute couture.

NECKWEAR AND OTHER ACCESSORIES

Jewelry

Large earrings, necklaces, brooches, and bracelets accessorized the oversized garments and hairstyles of the period. Gold was more prevalent than silver. Necklaces were large, almost collar-like to complete the basic round necklines that abounded in apparel. Earrings were equally large and often heavy, causing many women to suffer from tears in their pierced ear lobes. Glamorous items with precious and semiprecious stones were favored by the American elite. Pearls also enjoyed a return to popularity in the 1980s when they became a symbol of success (MacDonell Smith 2003, 137). In contrast, younger women wore striking plastic and rubber jewelry, including large round or hoop earrings and religious crosses popularized by pop music sensation Madonna. Many trendy women had their ears pierced two or three times to be able to wear multiple earrings simultaneously. Swatch watches created a craze in the early 1980s when they became collectible items.

Handbags

Classic, elegant styles of handbags returned to eveningwear and formalwear in the 1980s (Johnson 2002, 8). They were often oversized and prominently displayed designer logos. Patchwork, embroidery, real or faux crocodile skin, and bold color combinations were seen in day styles, often with gold chain-linked handles. Purses in the shape of backpacks and fanny packs were worn by teenagers and college students. Gym bags manufactured in a number of styles, colors, and shapes became a fashion accessory for active women (Dubbs and Hehl Torem 1993, 190).

Other

Worn at the natural waist or low on the hips, wide belts with large buckles, jewels, metal studs, embroidery, or gold chain links accessorized women's wear. Eyeglass and sunglass frames were equally large and round with tinted glass and curved stems. Diamond tiaras, inspired by Princess

Diana, were another status symbol worn by some women in the United States for formal occasions. Long lace gloves, often without fingers, completed the look for strapless or sleeveless evening gowns.

ALTERNATIVE FASHION MOVEMENTS

Preppies

The Official Preppy Handbook by Lisa Birnback, first published in 1980, was a humorous reference guide to fitting in or at least looking like upper-class WASP (white Anglo-Saxon Protestant) society. "Preps" or "preppies" were individuals from wealthy families who were sent to college preparatory schools (prep schools) by their parents. During the wealthy "me" decade of the 1980s, the nouveau riche, as well as the working class, aspired to preppy status by adopting the conservative boarding school or prep school uniform. Navy blue blazers, button-down oxford shirts, polo shirts, khaki pants, monogrammed crewneck sweaters, and loafers were key elements for cultivating the preppy look. Building on those elements, literally, the preppy look was a series of clothing layers. It was not enough to wear one polo shirt under an oxford shirt; the proper look required wearing two, three, or four shirts simultaneously with a sweater tied over the shoulders, with all collars starched stiffly erect. Preps worked with a color palette of pink and Kelly green, as well as madras and tartan plaids. Turtles and whales appeared as individual motifs on shirts, skirts, pants, and belts or as all-over patterns. The most famous motif and logo of the preppy look was the Izod alligator by Lacoste. Other sources for preppy fashions included L.L. Bean, Polo Ralph Lauren, and J. Crew.

Valley Girls

For a brief period in the 1980s, regardless of where you lived in the United States, every young teen-aged or college-aged female aspired to be a valley girl. This short-lived fad, originally mocked by the 1982 Frank Zappa song *Valley Girl*, became a serious national, albeit brief, phenomenon after the release of the 1983 movie *Valley Girl*, starring Nicolas Cage. Born from the San Fernando Valley of Los Angeles, California, in the early 1980s, the valley girl, or "val," was the stereotypical, spoiled mall brat, more interested in how she looked and who she knew than what she knew. Vals not only had their own look but also their own language, peppered with phrases such as "like," "as if," "totally," and "gag me with a spoon." The val look included blond or bleach-blond hair, neon colors, leggings, skirts with lace, netting and ruffled flounces, shirts with stand collar, and cap sleeves, also with ruffled edges. Completing the look included slouch boots and plastic jelly shoes worn with bobby socks with lace or ruffled edges.

Punk

American female fashion in the 1980s was influenced by a variety of subculture movements. American punk had grown out of the rebellious British punk bands of the late 1970s. From punk's inception, fashion became an important manifestation of the anarchist attitude of its followers. In the United States, female punk fashion was influenced by the popularity of Vivienne Westwood's designs. By the early 1980s, elements of punk fashion were widespread in America, in both street styles and haute couture.

Black torn clothes covered with graffiti surface designs and outrageous messages on T-shirts were adopted by American punk women. Vinyl, rubber, and leather were used for garments ranging from fitted dresses to loose overcoats. Mohawks, colored or bleached hair, body piercing, chains, and tattoos appeared alongside studded and spiked jewelry elements. Combat boots and fishnet stockings accessorized the legs.

Rap and Hip-Hop

Rap and hip-hop fans and performers adopted some of the same items seen in male urban clothing of the time, including Kangol hats, loose baggy pants, excessive jewelry, and large sunglasses. Also seen were fitted garments showcasing sensual curves and often displayed strong neon colors and West African kente prints. African-inspired jewelry and accessories were also incorporated into the apparel of some African-American women. Hairstyles included cropped looks with flat tops and loose rolling curls often known as Jheri curls. Girl break dancers, known as "B-girls," wore hip-slung trousers and fitted tops including "wife-beaters," similar to the styles worn by male break dancers (Chandler and Chandler-Smith 2005, 241).

Rastafarians

Dreadlocks were worn by followers of the Rasta movement who often wore clothes made out of the three colors used to identify the group: red, yellow, and green. Rasta clothing was in itself built on the grounds of moderation, simplicity, and the use of natural fibers, but it was soon to be commercialized by American manufacturers. Belts, bags, shoes, jackets, and other accessories were decorated with Rasta colors and often included maps of Africa and other Rasta symbols.

THE
1990s

FORMALWEAR

Silhouette

As the 1990s approached, the excess of the previous decade slowly disappeared. Formalwear followed the minimalist trend with figure-hugging garments, including the very popular narrow blazers of the decade. The tendency to neutral tones and a restrained classic figure has been described by some historians as "purism" because of its tendency to return to a basic elegant shape without major sculpting (Buxbaum 1999, 152). Designers, however, also looked to history for inspiration in eveningwear. It was not uncommon to see austere 1940s-inspired gowns, 1800s empire waist styles with slight trains, 1920s flapper looks, 1950s full-skirt silhouettes, and figure-revealing outfits in soft and semitransparent fabrics modeled after the 1930s bias-cut look.

Skirts

Skirt styles varied greatly for eveningwear. Skirts were shorter and narrower than previous periods, often reaching just below knee, full and wide, or long and fitted. However, the bouffant treatments prevalent in the 1980s had disappeared, and volume diminished along with decorative trims. There was no one dominant skirt shape or length for this decade. Women could select from a variety a silhouettes and lengths what would best complement their figures.

Bodices

Bodices were often strapless, sleeveless, backless, or halter. Some had minimal shoulder straps or "spaghetti" straps. Fitted bodices were decorated with sequins, lace, slashes, and cutouts. Some formalwear still included tailored blouses (Tortora and Eubank 2005, 528).

Sleeves

The simplicity of the decade was expressed through the widespread acceptance of sleeveless gowns. If an evening gown had sleeves, they might be either short or long and fitted with very little decoration.

Decorative Details

Black, the color of the decade, was accessorized with shades of other basic colors or with finishes such as sequins and lace. Animal prints and tartans appeared in formalwear, accessories, and even some household furnishings.

Striped gowns, particularly in black and white, were often seen, usually with conical skirts that were somewhat reminiscent of Christian Dior's 1950s New Look. Discrete floral motifs appeared on evening gowns delicately placed around hemlines, edges, or adorning the bust and back areas. Such decorations were often embroidered, beaded, or trimmed with lace. Slits, mesh insets, and piping added both structural and decorative details to gowns.

BUSINESS WEAR

Silhouette

The excess width and shoulder pads of the previous decade had disappeared by the mid-1990s, giving room to more fitted and feminine silhouettes usually achieved with knit fabrics and stretch blends. The variety of new silhouettes allowed American women to continue projecting an image of strength in the workplace but opened the door for more feminine, sexy, and glamorous options (Steele 1997, 146). Women, now more established in the workplace, were able to abandon their dress-for-success power suit in favor of softer business fashions. Loose and fitted pantsuits became as fashionable as classic skirted suits. Vintage styles paid homage to the Chanel suits of the 1950s, and classic styles with knee-length or shorter fitted skirts regained popularity.

Dresses

Most dresses were fitted and simple, reaching just below the knee. Necklines were modest and collars conservative. Sleeveless outfits were fashionable alongside dresses with spaghetti and decorative wider straps. Fabrics were usually sheer and soft, and some were cut following inspiration from classic 1930s bias-cut gowns. Jewel, bateau, and V necklines appeared on dresses and were often complemented with silk scarves.

Suits

Most blazers were narrow, but some styles were also large and loose. Shoulders looked relaxed, and fabrics were soft and elegant. Pantsuits were widely worn, but tailored day-to-evening cocktail suits with short and fitted skirts remained trendy during the period. Basic tailored shirts, shells, and cardigans were worn under jackets.

Separates

Classic men's wear-inspired navy blue blazers with feminine fitted lines, cropped jackets, fitted coats with princess seams, and peplums added variety to jackets in business wear. Jackets were either single or double breasted with narrow lapels. Soft blouses, man-tailored shirts, and turtlenecks were all worn under jackets. The popularity of corset or bustier-style bodices also translated to more fitted styles for business blouses in which darts and princess seams were used to create a fit across the torso. Skirts came in many different lengths, but they were much simpler and straight with minimal structural details than most of the styles seen in the 1980s. Tailored flat-front pants were worn more frequently than skirts, with either tapered or full-cut legs.

Decorative Details
Drab and neutral colors, such as gray, black, and blue, were favored, but tweed fabrics in pastel colors were also fashionable. Herringbone, checks, and pinstripes were all regularly used in suits. Natural fabrics continued in popularity, and luxury materials such as cashmere, alpaca, and suede were often used in business wear.

CASUAL WEAR

Silhouette
As the decade progressed, the silhouette lost the broad-shouldered excess seen in 1980s styles. Simplicity brought feminine touches through a more relaxed, natural silhouette that was softly fitted and sometimes revealing. The ever-increasing popularity of casual and comfortable clothing in the United States allowed women to freely mix and match casual wear with elements of formal and business attire. Dresses and skirts were often shorter than before, with fitted miniskirts and short flounced skirts becoming very popular. Pants and simple T-shirts or button-down shirts dominated casual day wear. From a few simple styles, the possibilities for mix and match were seemingly endless in the postmodern 1990s.

Dresses
Historic influences were clearly seen, including high-waist baby-doll and tank top dresses inspired by the nineteenth-century empire style, bias cut fitted looks imitating 1930s techniques, and dropped waistlines adopted from 1920s fashions. The trend of underwear as outerwear resulted in dresses that were reminiscent of nightgowns and intimate apparel. Known as slip dresses, these lightweight, sheer dresses were often made of polyester or silk charmeuse with spaghetti straps and lace finishes or from multiple layers of chiffon. Bodices ranged from loose to fitted and even corseted variations, whereas sleeves remained simple and mostly fitted. Necklines were round and low, and collars were rare.

Separates

Cotton T-shirts with political logos, advertising, or trendy sayings remained popular. Chain stores and designers prominently displayed their names and logos on T-shirts, blouses, and sweatshirts. Crop tops, bare midriffs (or belly shirts), and bra tops were widely worn, as well as sheer light blouses, nylon fitted shirts, and camisoles inspired by undergarments. More modest alternatives included hooded sweatshirts, embroidered or appliquéd vests, and peasant-style blouses with long flared bell sleeves or ruffled cuffs. Short flounced skirts or long "broomstick" skirts were trendy, but many young American women opted for shorts and just-below-the-knee skirts in daywear. A variety of pants styles were available, including straight, baggy, cargo, stirrup, and capri.

Decorative Details

Stretch and sheer fabrics were widely used in casual wear. Denim, especially chemically treated denim, continued being popular for pants, jackets, and skirts. Decorative details used in the period included frills, ruffles, fringes, lace, and beads. The color palette for the 1990s was more subdued than the previous decade, but color blocking brought new options to fashion in the period (Feldman 1992, 14). Flower and animal prints, tartan patterns, and ethnic motifs were also widely used.

OUTERWEAR

Coats

Coats in the 1990s were plainer and smaller than those of the 1980s, with single-breasted coats becoming more widely worn than double breasted. Most overcoats were roomy and prominently featured patch pockets. Wool winter coats were made mostly in dark shades, principally black, blue, and gray, but novelty coats came in vivid colors and often had quilted or patchwork embellishments or brightly colored linings. Trench and rain coats followed the same lines of the previous decade, with beige and black being the most common colors for trench coats and rain coats appearing in a variety of colorful waterproof materials. Anti-fur protesters continued voicing their concerns but received a major defeat when designers began incorporating fur again in their collections. Fake fur, once a popular alternative to real fur, was criticized for its non-biodegradable and flammable qualities (Mendes and de la Haye 1999, 256).

Shawls/Wraps

Pashmina, silk, and blend shawls were largely popular in the period. Neckscarves and stole wraps were also in style. Drab colors dominated the

1990s, but, as the decade progressed, vibrant bright colors and shawls with surface embellishment became trendier.

Other Garments

Novelty sweaters were seen in patterns that included tartans and gingham as well as patchwork and embroidery detailing. Parkas, hooded sweatshirts, and knitted wraps also enjoyed popularity in America during the 1990s.

SWIMWEAR AND SPORTSWEAR

Swimwear

A variety of styles were popular in the postmodern 1990s, including thongs, G-strings, maillots, and slingshots. More daring Americans even wore topless suits, and the less daring layered revealing items over more conservative ones. Synthetic fabrics such as spandex, as well as other high-stretch blends, were widely used in the period (Tortora and Eubank 2005, 521). Other innovations included see-through sheer and tan fabrics, as well as shaping push-up devices. Toward the end of the decade, more conservative, often historically inspired styles entered the market. Bikinis were seen with skirted bottoms and shorts. The tankini also evolved as an answer to the revealing bikini, allowing women to have a two-piece swimsuit with a tank-top style top instead of the standard bra top. In some cases, waistlines were placed above the navel and tops were matched with trunk or loose shorts. Bikini tops paired with casual shorts or Lycra bike shorts were also used for sun tanning, inline skating, and other types of activities.

Golf

Short loose pants and polo shirts were still regular attire for women in golf. In some instances, they also wore long-sleeved knit tops and turtlenecks. Gloves, visors, and leather shoes with soft or metal cleats were common accessories.

Tennis

The preferred style remained knit tops and white skirts, shorts, or skorts, usually in white, although other colors were used. More tennis players wore one-piece skirted bodysuits and sleeveless tops, following trends set by younger professional players. A comfortable fit was enhanced by the use of sport bras and elastic waistbands.

Skiwear

Styles from the 1960s and 1970s, including tight knit tops, quilted parkas, and stretch pants, were revived during the period. The general public also wore suits made out of materials with finishes similar to those worn by professionals. Innovative new fabrics improved air penetration and temperature control. Polypropylene materials with quick-drying capabilities that eliminated body moisture were used in ski and other winter sports clothing (Tortora and Eubank 2005, 521).

Other Activewear

Stretch fibers, including spandex and Lycra, were used in body-hugging gym clothes and biking shorts and were also incorporated in casual street wear. Other recurrent styles in activewear of the 1990s included divided skirts for biking, gym unitards, cropped tops for jogging, wet suits for aquatic sports, and protective garments for skateboarding.

UNDERWEAR AND INTIMATE APPAREL

Undergarments

Underwear as outerwear was a major trend in the late 1980s and early 1990s. Parts of bras and camisoles could be seen under regular garments, making the visible parts of intimate apparel more elaborate and decorative. Casual wear was often modeled after undergarment styles, and camisole tops were fully accepted as street wear by the end of the 1990s. Sex appeal and comfort were equally important for American women. General underwear styles in this period indicated a more natural look with easier lines enhanced by control pantyhose or briefs and wireless bras. Form-enhancing underwear was also used often to achieve a better figure. Some examples include the Wonderbra by Sara Lee, the Miracle Bra by Intimate Brands, and the glass-reinforced Biofor Bra (Farrell and Gau 2002, 167). The continued popularity of sportswear as casual wear, especially with tank tops, led to widespread popularity of racer-back bras for daily wear. Briefs continued decreasing in size, and more exotic and revealing styles, such as thongs and Y-strings, were introduced. In postmodern style, old-fashioned high-rise panties could be matched with a Wonderbra, a sports bra, or any other type of tank top or bra (Clancy 1996, 198).

Sleepwear

Oversized T-shirts gave way to actual nightshirts in light pastel colors and were decorated with popular cartoon characters, logos, or nature motifs. Robes were made in colorful fleece, knits, and high piles and were often decorated with appliqué or quilting techniques (Tortora and Eubank 2005, 521). Women also began pairing men's boxers with T-shirts for sleepwear or lounging.

Other Garments

Baby dolls and other loungewear in soft satin and silk fabrics were used as essentials to increase sex appeal. Images of bondage and fetishism were explored in some forms of sexy lingerie. Corsets, leather, beads, black lace, and fur were common materials used for effect.

HEADWEAR, HAIRSTYLES, AND COSMETICS

Headwear

Formal hats were still used by American women in special occasions. Among the African-American community, for example, the tradition of wearing colorful hats for church has continued through the many decades. Younger women adopted the use of hats and headscarves as a novelty in the 1990s, particularly after vintage styles became trendy. Other types of hats worn during the period included male fedora shapes, berets, turbans, and hats with narrow brims (Feldman 1992, 57). Baseball caps also became standard wear among young college women.

Hairstyles

Postmodern variety was also apparent in female hairstyles of the 1990s, with hairdos inspired by nearly every period of the century. For elegant and formal occasions, some American women were seen with 1920s marcel waves, 1960s beehives, 1970s afros, and 1980s perms. Long hair, straight, frizzy, or with or without bangs, was just as common as short hair parted on the side or the middle. Hair dying allowed women to try different shades of color and to add highlights for contrast. The layered "Rachel," named after the character played by Jennifer Aniston in the television series *Friends*, was the most copied hairdo of the period (Seeling 2000, 572).

Cosmetics

The return to a natural silhouette in fashion also saw a return to a more natural look in makeup in the 1990s. The science of makeup continued to advance, and there were improvements with long-lasting lipstick, ultra-deep cleansing products, makeup removers that also acted as moisturizers, and chemical tanning products. Organic, botanic, or earth-friendly green products were also popular as the industry responded to environmental challenges and an increasing preference toward natural products in some segments of the American market. Aromatherapy was introduced in day spas as a healing and relaxation technique with some medicinal claims.

FOOTWEAR AND LEGWEAR

Footwear

Lower-heel shoes gained popularity during the period as women searched for comfort in footwear. Professional women often walked down the streets dressed in business suits and sneakers, changing into formal heeled shoes on arriving to their offices. High-heel stilettos, classic pumps, penny loafers, and platform shoes reappeared during the last decade of the century attributable, in part, to the interest in vintage styles. New styles inspired by the past were created. In 1994, for instance, Peter Fox created the "Toddler" shoe, a cross between a Mary Jane and a baby slipper. The shoe was controversial because some groups considered the style to be condescending toward women (O'Keeffe 1996, 236). Mules, strapped sandals, two-tone shoes, knee-high laced boots, and half boots were also among the styles popular in the United States and around the world (Clancy 1996, 194). Some designers experimented with high-heel shapes, metal heels, and decorations with metallic finishes, chains, fringes, encrusted jewelry, and mesh. Moccasins, court shoes with low heels, Chinese canvas shoes, jewel and metallic trims, and several styles of athletic shoes added to the variety of postmodern footwear. Fitness shoes were technologically enhanced for different activities such as cross training, walking, indoor court sports, and running.

Legwear

The naturalization of women's fashions in the 1990s meant a return to standard pantyhose in the usual range of beige, brown, and black. The increased popularity of pants and pantsuits translated to an increase in the adoption of trouser socks and knee highs. For the physically fit, thigh-high stockings that stayed in place without garters were a sexy alternative to pantyhose. Low-cut socks with reinforced heels were used for athletic activities along with decorated tube and crew socks in pastel colors.

NECKWEAR AND OTHER ACCESSORIES

Jewelry

Oversized glamorous accessories, often with faux and replica materials, were worn by women across the United States (Feldman 1992, 57). Silver became preferred over gold. Smaller jewelry influenced by classic styles was also popular. Collecting costume jewelry was actually a popular pastime, and it made beaded pieces, floral brooches, ethnic, and vintage styles a hot commodity. Animals, insects, and celestial imagery were recurrent motifs in costume jewelry. Novelty pins were also designed in the shape of hats, shoes, gloves, and other clothing accessories (Dubbs and Hehl

Torem 1993, 213). Piercing was a widely spread practice in the United States, with younger women decorating their navels, lips, noses, and several other body parts. Tattoos, whether permanent or temporary, were another popular form of body ornamentation.

Handbags

More American designers, including Kate Spade and Judith Lieber, ventured into the handbag design business working with exotic materials and animal skins (Mendes and de la Haye 1999, 269). Quilted, patterned, and beaded bags were widely popular around the country. Classic European bags, such as those designed by Hermes, Gucci, and Louis Vuitton, were embraced as a symbol of elegance and status.

Other

Scarves worn in many different styles continued being a staple of the feminine look and came in fabrics ranging from wool to silk to metallic, and patterns including plaids and paisley. In addition to being head or shoulder coverings, scarves were also often used as belts as part the popular peasant look. Gloves were seen in casual wear and eveningwear. Fur- or faux-fur-trimmed accessories were also popular.

ALTERNATIVE FASHION MOVEMENTS

Goth

Punk subculture influenced goth fashion, which became widely known in the United States during the 1990s. Goth women wore mostly black items inspired by Victorian and Medieval gothic styles. Corsets and full skirts were part of the silhouette, although fitted and miniskirts or pants were also seen. Black lace, netting, leather, and floral brocade were common forms of decoration. Hair extensions included dreads, braids, fringes, and tubes and were often colored or highlighted with metallic hues. High platform shoes and boots were also part of the style, along with monster fur accessories such as legwarmers and coats. A striking contrasting effect was often achieved by the use of white makeup and black eyeliner. Asian influences in goth fashion included kimono sleeves and Cheongsam dresses.

Toward the end of the decade, goth females began incorporating other colors in their wardrobe, particularly red. Japanese and other Asian influences were predominant, above all in a style known as Gothic Lolita that aimed to create a look that mixed the innocence of high-school girls with a touch of sensuality and rebellion. The popularity of techno music among goths also brought the adoption of synthetic and shiny fibers and bleached hair, creating a trend usually referred to as cyber-goth.

Grunge

In the early 1990s, grunge, a new music and dance phenomenon that originated in Seattle, became popular around the country. Grunge was characterized by a strong beat, heavy electric guitar presence, and mosh-pit dancing among fans. Female followers dressed taking inspiration from grunge musicians, particularly Courtney Love. Baby-doll dresses with high empire waists made in light fabrics were accessorized with fishnet stockings and hair scrunchies. The disheveled look was also often accomplished by the use of vintage dresses. Oversized sweaters, old flannel shirts, and worn-out silk blouses were also among the elements adopted by grunge women to create a relaxed, untidy appearance.

THE
2000s

FORMALWEAR

Silhouette

Evening gowns in the early 2000s were glamorous and elegant but playfully quoted many styles from the past. This was evident in the popularity of vintage formalwear. Silhouettes ranged from fitted to elegantly draped full skirts. Body-revealing cuts remained popular with backless gowns, plunging necklines, sleeveless dresses, and see-through fabrics.

Skirts

For formal eveningwear, most skirts were long, whether full or fitted, with some displaying short trains and decorative hemlines. As social occasions continued to be less formal, full ball gowns were replaced with cocktail or after-five dresses with skirts just above the knee.

Bodices

Fitted, boned, and corset-like bustiers again sculpted a woman's curves, producing décolletage necklines. The décolletage was further highlighted with ruffles, pleats, laces, beads, and cowls. In opposition to these sexy treatments, a popular alternative in eveningwear was the turtleneck.

Sleeves

Sleeveless gowns or spaghetti-strapped gowns continued to dominate eveningwear. Simple fitted sleeves, long, short, or single arm, were also seen.

Decorative Details

Colorful, metallic, sequined, and beaded materials were as popular as black, white, red, and other classic colors. Scarves and lace trimmings were often used to complement elegant looks.

BUSINESS WEAR

Silhouette

The silhouette for the first part of the twenty-first century did not present substantial changes from the 1990s. Classic, conservative styles continued in popularity. Pantsuits continued to be more popular than skirted suits, but the presence of suits in the workplace continued to diminish. Casual Fridays, a day to dress down at work, evolved into the daily dress code and pushed the importance of separates forward in business dressing. Classic tailored shirts in discreet color schemes and with little embellishments were seen, and classic Chanel tweed suits remained in style.

Dresses

Dresses were worn on a limited basis for work. Those available were softly fitted, skimming the body, but comfortable. Round and V necklines accompanied either short-sleeved or sleeveless dresses or wrap dresses and were typically paired with a cardigan or jacket, whereas conservative and relaxed collar lines accompanied long-sleeved dresses.

Suits

Double- and single-breasted pantsuits or skirt suits were worn. Lines and styles were similar to the 1990s, but American women experimented more with color, separates, and texture during the early 2000s. Jackets lengths were typically high on the hip, reminiscent of Jackie Kennedy's 1960s Chanel suits, with three-quarter-length sleeves, rounded necklines without lapels, and cropped styles. Some with inverted center back pleats to create flare became increasingly popular forms of tailored jackets for business women. Pants were flat front with full-cut legs with cuffs. Skirts were often below the knee and paired with tall boots. Mix and match separates were often more popular than matching pieces, providing more opportunities to experiment with color and texture combinations.

Separates

Relaxed short skirts remained largely popular whether they were full, pencil, or pleated. Long-line skirts, straight short skirts, and pleated or flat-front pants were also used to match a variety of coats and blouses. Blazers, fine sweaters, and cardigans continued being worn as tops, and vests regained some popularity. Short-sleeve rib tops and soft short- or long-sleeve button-down styles with princess seams were regular separates in business wear. Lower round and open necklines and traditional tailored style collars were among the most popular trends in the period.

Decorative Details

Natural material garments were abundant, as evidenced by the popularity of silk satin and crêpe de Chine blouses, suede skirts, and wool flannel or camel tweed suits. Synthetics, however, were also widely used, particularly rayon and polyester blends. Polyester-cotton blends that provided wrinkle-free, easy-care fabrics were marketed to women who were now traveling extensively for work and needed a wardrobe that could withstand packing. Textured and patterned fabrics regained popularity in the early 2000s as an alternative to the light tones of most blouses and the dark shades usually seen on business suits.

CASUAL WEAR

Silhouette

No single silhouette ushered in the new millennium. Unlike the unisex space suits that were predicated in the 1960s to be fashionable by the twenty-first century, fashions proved to be quite the opposite. Casual wear continued becoming more varied and relaxed. American women practiced garment layering, adding variety to the tradition of mixing separates. Comfortable knit wear, especially novelty T-shirts, continued for daily wear.

Dresses

Dresses for daywear remained simple and relaxed, some resembling the cut of loose shirts. Day dresses and cocktail dresses might be off-the-shoulder, halter tops, strapless, or backless depending on the individual wearer's preferences. Day shift and full-cut A-line dresses with V necklines or scoop necklines in colorful prints were also widely worn.

Separates

Cotton polo shirts, T-shirts, and button-down blouses remained an important component of the casual wardrobe. Corset tops became a novelty in casual wear and could be made out of elegant fabrics, leather, or any other materials. Fitted jackets, sweaters, hooded pullovers (or "hoodies), and denim and leather jackets were among the preferred fashions in the early 2000s. Pant styles from the 1990s carried over into the new century. A new trend was the use of low-rise pants, which sat just below the waist, creeping ever lower as the new millennium progressed. Pinstriped long pants, resembling the style worn in business wear, were also popular for casual wear as well as cargo pants with topstitching and patch pockets on the thighs and calves.

Decorative Details

Black and white dominated the palette, but brown became the new dominate neutral to combine with other basic colors. Color blocking and floral prints remained in use. Other embellishments included cutouts, ruching or stitched gathers, hems finished with lace, embroidered and jeweled denim, ribbons, and beading. Rayon, polyester, and silk blends were extensively used, and luxurious fabrics included velveteen, moleskin, and cashmere.

OUTERWEAR

Coats

By the early twenty-first century, the silhouette for overcoats was fairly standard, fitting closely along body lines with a slight flare down from the waistline and reaching just below the knees. As the close of the first decade approached, the flare became more pronounced, resembling styles from the 1950s and 1960s, including three-quarter-length sleeves. Winter coats were almost exclusively seen in dark colors such as black, gray, and blue. Casual outdoor jackets followed the lines of overcoats. Fur and faux fur coats and trimmings maintained popularity and were often dyed in bright colors. Bold colorful prints were use on leather coats and jackets.

Shawls/Wraps

Cashmere was used in pashmina and other type of shawls (Tortora and Eubank 2005, 537). Knit, crochet, and lace wraps and shrugs were also worn. These were frequently beaded, fringed, pleated, or embroidered. A variety of colors were available, and some wraps were inspired by patterns coming from Africa, India, and Asia. Silk bandanas, mufflers, and stoles were also common items.

Other Garments

Open or closed sweaters and vests were used by American women as part of the popular layered look of the early 2000s. Fleece or polar fleece jackets with hoods or high collars were worn by younger women for casual outerwear. Historically influenced coats, wraps, and shawls were also commonly seen as a result of the popularity of vintage clothing.

Swimwear and Sportswear

Swimwear

A variety of styles remained popular in the first years of the new century. Retro-fashion looks included the traditional bikini, as well as one-piece suits and bandeau tops. Sarong wraps and tied scarves were often used to cover the bottom part of the suit. Experimentation in design brought a number of curiosity items usually associated with fantasy and fetish wear to swimwear. Some tops were designed to look like camisoles, called tankinis, and more fitted styles resembled corsets. Haute couture and street styles for more adventurous Americans included embellishments such as jewelry, zippers, and fringes as well as pasties and body painting instead of actual fabricated garments.

Golf

The period enjoyed a return to more traditionally feminine patterns, including floral and nature prints. American golf players wore loose-fitting capri pants, short pants, and skirts in a variety of lengths and waist styles. Knit polo shirts and sleeveless blouses were common tops. Accessories included golf gloves, baseball hats, and visors.

Tennis

Tennis wear for women also experienced a return to classics at the end of the 1990s and in the early 2000s, with argyle, plaid, and tartan prints reappearing in sweaters and vests. Fitted tops were worn alongside polo shirts, sleeveless blouses, and spaghetti straps. Capri pants, loose or fitted, were just as popular as long trousers, depending on the season. Some tennis pants were designed with low rises as in popular casual wear.

Skiwear

More feminine looks reappeared in female skiwear with pastel colors and floral prints in waterproof jackets and vests. Designers such as Prada and Versace created ski outfits that could also be used as casual wear. Technological improvements increased performance of professional athletes with thin suits made of foam and lined in synthetic fabrics as well as active insulation products that could transport heat from one part of the body to another.

Other Activewear

The line between casual wear and athletic wear continued to blur as fitness apparel incorporated the same cutout designs, midriff-revealing shirts, and tank tops as street wear. Fleece fabrics and jersey knits continued enjoying popularity. Sport shorts had raised hemlines and low-rise waistlines and often display letters and logos across the entire derriere.

UNDERWEAR AND INTIMATE APPAREL

Undergarments

At the turn of the twenty-first century, a variety of classic-cut and revealing bras and panties were worn by American women. In addition to widespread adoption of the thong, new forms for bottoms included tap panties, boy briefs, and hip briefs. Briefs of all styles also came in low rise to complement the popularity of low-rise pants. Feats of engineering continued to be applied by Victoria's Secret and others to develop bras that would support and shape while concealing closures and straps. Molded, one-piece seamless cups, demi cups, and self-adhesive cups were available to provide support under the most revealing garments.

Sleepwear

Pajamas, lingerie, and nightgowns followed trends similar to those seen in the last decades of the twentieth century.

HEADWEAR, HAIRSTYLES, AND COSMETICS

Headwear

Baseball hats, beanies, bandanas, and headbands were favored by younger American women. Hair jewelry and accessories such as tiaras and diadems were also used for special events. Metallic barrettes with rhinestones and gems, barrettes with novelty prints, and small butterfly clips were worn as hair adornment by young women for neo-bohemian looks. Some other styles previously worn, such as fedoras and turbans, appeared on occasion.

Hairstyles

Shoulder-length or longer hair prevailed in the early years of the 2000s. Vintage-inspired looks resulted in both flat-iron straightened hair or romantic natural loose waves. Other popular hairdos of the period included French braids, corn rows, ponytails, dreadlocks, and buzz cuts. Jeweled hairsticks, hairpins, and other accessories were used to hold hairstyles in place and to add decorative elements. For those would did not want long hair on a daily basis, hair extensions and hair weaves became popular alternatives.

Cosmetics

Cosmetic surgery, silicone injections, and liposuction were adopted by Americans as an alternative for rapid beauty enhancement. By the early

2000s, Botox injections promised wrinkle reduction and fuller skin. Shining products could add sparkle to a woman's face. Younger women and members of some subculture movements wore beauty marks, fake moles, face paints, facial tattoos, and facial piercing in the nose and eyebrows.

FOOTWEAR AND LEGWEAR

Footwear

A variety of formal shoe styles remained popular. The new century saw experimentation with free-flowing undulating lines in design, straps, fringes, and different types of animal skins. Decorated flat and low-heel slippers, canvas shoes, colored hush puppies, new versions of Mary Janes, and bowling shoes, as well as comfortable shoes in stretch fabrics also abounded in the American market. Tall boots with metal accents became popular with knee-length skirts and dresses for business and casual wear. Novelty sneakers came in a variety of styles. Classic vintage designs were recreated with newer materials and decorative touches that ranged from cartoon character figures to graffiti and distressed canvas. Flip-flop sandals, no longer limited to beach apparel, were introduced in casual wear and also in designer collections in which small heels or wedges were added (Tortora and Eubank 2005, 535).

Legwear

Fishnet stockings and pantyhose with visible seams or woven designs, in bright or neutral colors, were popular novelties in 2000s legwear. The patterns and textures were perfect to peek out at the gap between knee-length skirts and tall boots. Toe socks, a novelty item from the 1970s, returned in calf- or thigh-high lengths in stripes, polka dots, or herringbone patterns and were briefly adopted by younger women. Many women went without any stockings at all, with a bare-leg look very popular.

NECKWEAR AND OTHER ACCESSORIES

Jewelry

Chokers, necklaces, and other pieces continued showing a variety of influences from the previous century. Chandelier and drop earrings were as popular as smaller stud and hoop earrings. Silver still remained more popular than gold in the early years of the century.

Handbags

With the popularity of cellular telephones, personal digital assistant devices, and iPods, handbags and purses included special compartments to carry these devices. Some designers even began producing special lines of covers and pouches just for the devices. Coach, Gucci, Chanel, and Fendi all made designer versions of cell-phone pouches. Equally popular were the giant leather purses with large belt-buckle style cinched tops and single- or double-handled straps. These satchel style bags came in gold, lime green, and silver, in addition to the standard black and brown. The trend for these oversized bags was propelled by Hermès' "Birkin" bag featured in the storyline of *Sex and the City*, in 2001. Clutch purses, novelty bags, and messenger-style bags were among the popular trends in the early part of the twenty-first century. Quilted bags were also widely adopted by American women, particularly those created by Vera Bradley.

Other

Most accessories, including glasses, belts, and sunglasses, became larger in dimension again in the twenty-first century. Novelties such as jeweled cuffs and rings, pearl and colored leather watchbands, and acrylic accessories were widely worn. Classic leather belts with metal-work buckles, studs, and other ornamentation were worn to further emphasize the low-rise waist in women's pants and skirts. Technical innovations in the production of eyewear allowed eyeglasses to be made without frames. Eyeglasses and sunglasses were both embellished with decorative elements such as fake diamonds, designer logos, and colored lenses. Soft plastic bracelets with mottos in support of a variety of causes became an important trend by 2004 inspired by American bicyclist and seven-time Tour de France winner Lance Armstrong's battle with cancer.

ALTERNATIVE FASHION MOVEMENTS

Hip-Hop

Hip-hop fashion continued developing in the twenty-first century with new creations such as long fitted Lycra or jersey dresses modeled after popular sports teams' uniforms. Sports-inspired jumpsuits, denim items, sneaker shoes, and sport jackets continued being worn by hip-hop fans as casual wear, whereas eveningwear and formalwear remained body fitting with bold prints and brightly colored tube dresses, jumpsuits, and minidresses. American firms such as Baby Phat, FUBU, and Rocca Wear were world leaders in the marketing of hip-hop fashion. The playful styles of "pimp and ho" were taken to extremes with the popularity of ghetto-fabulous looks that showcased voluptuous female bodies with an overload of "bling-bling" or striking jewelry, luxurious furs, and expensive accessories (Chandler and Chandler-Smith 2005, 243).

Hip-hop and rap stars and fans often borrowed some elements from male urban wear, including oversized shirts, baggy pants, baseball hats, and track suits; however, many of them also opted for revealing and fitted garments in Lycra, terrycloth, and jersey knits. As a matter of fact, hip-hop stars frequently challenged the status quo by wearing extremely short bottoms, fitted tops, wife-beater T-shirts, revealing tops with wide necklines, and pasties.

Neo-Bohemian and Retro-Chic

Neo-bohemian and retro-chic styles of the early 2000s relied heavily on a variety of influences, including Indian bindi marks and henna tattoo or mehndi. Kabala bracelets were popular after celebrities such as Madonna and Britney Spears donned them. Ethnic blouses, long flowing skirts reminiscent of hippie looks of the 1960s and early 1970s, and flat boots or sandals completed the look.

Cyber-goth

The cyber-goth trend included huge platform shoes paired with garments made out of glowing metallic and glow-in-the-dark materials. Hot pink, lime green, and neon violet were among the most popular colors. Camouflage, parachute fabrics, and military uniforms were also used by goth women. Cyber-goth fashions continued to be closely influenced by Japanese Lolita fashion and incorporated ruffled dresses, bonnets, knee-high socks, aprons, and capes. All of these items aimed to create a tension between the innocence and the sexual appeal of the wearer.

REFERENCES

Baker, P. (1991) *Fashions of a Decade: The 1950s.* New York: Facts on File.

Bryant, M. W. (2004) *WWD Illustrated: 1960s–1990s.* New York: Fairchild Publications, Inc.

Buxbaum, G., ed. (1999) *Icons of Fashion: The 20th Century.* New York: Prestel.

Carnegy, V. (1990) *Fashions of a Decade. The 1980s.* New York: Facts on File.

Chandler, R. M., Chandler-Smith, N. (2005) *Flava in Ya Gear: Transgressive Politics and the Influence of Hip-Hop on Contemporary Fashion.* Twentieth-Century American Fashion. New York: Berg.

Clancy, D. (1996) *Costume since 1945: Couture, Street Style, and Anti-Fashion.* New York: Drama Publishers.

Dubbs Ball, J., Torem, D. H. (1993) *The Art of Fashion Accessories.* Atglen, PA: Schiffer Publishing.

Farrell, J. (1992) *Socks & Stockings.* Costume Accessories Series. London: B. T. Batsford.

Farrell-Beck, J., Gau, C. (2002) *Uplift: The Bra in America*. Philadelphia: University of Pennsylvania Press.

Fashions of an Era. *1950s Glamour*, http://www.fashion-era.com/1950s_glamour.htm.

Feldman, E., Cumming, V., eds. (1992) *Fashions of a Decade. The 1990s*. New York: Facts on File.

Johnson, A. (2002) *Handbags: The Power of the Purse*. New York: Workman Publishing.

Lee-Potter, C. (1984) *Sportswear in Vogue since 1910*. New York: Abbeville Press.

Lehnert, G. (2000) *A History of Fashion in the 20th Century*. Cologne, Germany: Könemann.

MacDonell Smith, N. (2003) *The Classic Ten: The True Story of the Little Black Dress and Nine Other Fashion Favorites*. New York: Penguin Books.

Mendes, V., de la Haye, A. (1999) *20th Century Fashion*. London: Thames and Hudson.

Milbank, C. R. (1989) *New York Fashion: The Evolution of American Style*. New York: Abrams.

O'Keeffe, L. (1996) *Shoes: A Celebration of Pumps, Sandals, Slippers & More*. New York: Workman Publishing.

Payne, B., Winakor, G., Farrell-Beck, J. (1992) *The History of Costume: From Ancient Mesopotamia through the Twentieth Century*. 2nd edition. New York: HarperCollins.

Seeling, C. (2000) *Fashion: The Century of the Designer 1900–1999*. English edition. Cologne, Germany: Könemann.

Steele, V. (1997) *Fifty Years of Fashion: New Look to Now*. New Haven, CT: Yale University Press.

Tortora, P. G., Eubank, K. (2005) *Survey of Historic Costume: A History of Western Dress*. 4th edition. New York: Fairchild Publications.

8

Men's Fashions

Whereas women marked the beginning of the last half of the twentieth century with the New Look a la Christian Dior, men continued down the pre-WWII path in the same conservative look. After the war, men resumed their traditional roles as husband, father, and provider and donned the same suit, tie, and shirt they had been wearing for decades. However, just as the equal rights movement sparked a significant shift in women's lives, so too were men's lives affected. During the last decades of the twentieth century, men now had to compete with women for positions at work and assume responsibilities for housework and childcare at home. The 1950s cookie-cutter "man in the gray flannel suit" was transformed through evolving social norms and a "peacock revolution" that expanded the definition of men's formal, business, and casual wardrobe to include color, pattern, and texture.

The dominance of suits as the only acceptable form of men's business wear continued to decline, being replaced by Nehru jackets in the 1960s, leisure suits in the 1970s, and ultimately business casual separates in the 1990s. Giorgio Armani suits may have defined "power dressing" for men in the opulent, egocentric 1980s, but he and other designers, such as Calvin Klein and Ralph Lauren, also expanded men's wardrobes beyond suits to include a wide range of separates for the office and casual wear. As the last half of the century progressed, men also enjoyed greater freedom in hairstyles, hair styling products, and cosmetics; the universal crew cut was out, and so too were men's hats.

The typical well-dressed businessman's suit is shown in this scene from the 1957 film *Sweet Smell of Success*. Shown from left: Burt Lancaster (as J.J. Hunsecker), Tony Curtis (as Sidney Falco), Marty Milner (as Steve Dallas), and Sam Levene (as Frank D'Angelo). [Courtesy of Photofest]

The increasing informality in society, combined with a delay in marriage, also transformed America from the baby-boom, family-focused suburbs to "single and fabulous" urban chic. Social calendars changed from formal cocktail parties with fiancées and wives to singles night at the disco. After-work happy hours, hanging out in sports bars and clubbing brought the same need for a new category of "going-out" clothing to men as it had for women. Suit jackets were worn over T-shirts with khakis, jeans were paired with button-down tailored European-cut shirts, and baggy hip-hop jams topped with oversized sports logo T-shirts and baseball caps became the new staples of men's wardrobes by the end of the century.

Men's fashions, although slower to change than women's, were influenced by sources similar to those that launched fashion trends for women. England and Italy, known for superb tailoring, were more influential in overall fashion trends for men than was Paris. Movie stars and celebrities, once the fashion leaders, were replaced by musicians and sports figures. Men's fashions also splintered into the same subcultures as women's. Whether mod, hippie, disco, hip-hop, punk, or prep, men could find their niche amongst the various fashion trends that crossed age, ethnic, and economic boundaries. As the century concluded, no one single fashion trend dominated men's wear, and men's fashions began responding to changes in overall styling at a more rapid pace. The peacock revolution begun in the 1960s was now complete. Men too had choices for dressing.

THE
1950s

FORMALWEAR

Silhouette

President Eisenhower refused to bow to tradition at his inauguration in 1953, and, rather than wearing a top hat and cutaway jacket, he chose to wear a suit jacket, striped trousers, and a homburg. This was the beginning of a less formal look for formal occasions. Full evening dress with white tie and cutaway tailcoat for formalwear lost favor to the increasingly popular tuxedo. Morning dress, featuring a cutaway coat, vest, trousers with suspenders, double-cuffed shirt, stiff white collar, and cravat, however, could still be found at weddings early in the decade. Black-tie events called for the now-popular tuxedo.

Jackets and Vests

Morning suits featured single-breasted cutaway tailcoats and single-breasted decorative vests. Vests were typically decorated with topstitching or embroidery. In contrast to the formal morning suit, the tuxedo was worn with a single-breasted straight jacket, without vents. The collar was either a rounded shawl style or had peaked lapels and was edged with black silk or satin. Although typically black, a white tuxedo jacket could be worn in the summer. Cummerbunds, made from the same fabric as the jacket lapels, were becoming more popular than vests for tuxedo suits.

Shirts

Whether morning suit or tuxedo, the shirt underneath was the same. A crisp white shirt with stiff turned-down collar and French cuffs was the standard. Some morning suits were also paired with stiff wing-tipped collars.

Pants

For morning suits, pants were fabricated from the same fabric as the jacket. The trouser legs were straight, without cuffs, and worn with suspenders. For tuxedo suits, the trousers had a slightly fuller-cut leg, were always black, even if the jacket was white, and had a silk ribbon or braid running the full length of the outseam (outer side seam).

Decorative Details

Men's formalwear had few decorative elements during the 1950s. Morning suits were either gray or black and were typically pinstriped. Tuxedos were solid black or solid black pants with a solid white jacket. The primary decorative elements in both ensembles consisted of cufflinks, shirt studs, and pocket squares.

BUSINESS WEAR

Silhouette

Conservatism is the defining word for men's wear in the 1950s. The trim, quiet look was in vogue, allowing men to blend in by wearing dark colors and shades of blues, browns, and grays. The clean-cut image of the company man was complete with dark suit, white shirt, and narrow and conservative necktie. Wives dressed husbands in the image of the successful, clean-cut, sophisticated businessman portrayed by Hollywood actors Cary Grant, Rock Hudson, and Jimmy Stewart and by the television stars of *Dragnet*, *Perry Mason*, *Father Knows Best*, and *Make Room for Daddy*.

Jackets and Vests

Jackets for business suits were single breasted, slim cut, and had either two or three buttons. The shoulders were narrow, and jackets had either a single center back vent or no vent. By the middle of the decade, the jacket was becoming longer, as was the lapel line.

Shirts

Tailored button-down white shirts with turned-down spread collars completed the business uniform for men. Shirt were stiffly starched, and collars were reinforced with stays to keep the points sharp and crisp.

The Man in the Grey Flannel Suit. The movie *The Man in the Grey Flannel Suit* epitomized men's business wear in the fifties. The fear of communism that permeated the United States translated to conservative, clean-cut fashions for men. A man who conformed to the corporate uniform could be trusted and promoted. Television and Hollywood helped women learn what to buy for their husbands' business wardrobes as they watched stylish and handsome actors such as Cary Grant and Rock Hudson portray successful businessmen. Even the sitcoms *I Love Lucy*, *Father Knows Best*, and *Make Room for Daddy* always showed the leading man coming home from work in the standard dark suit, narrow dark necktie, and white shirt. Anything else would be suspect.

Pants

Pants were always fabricated from the same materials as the jacket. Pants may be either flat front or pleated, with tapered trouser legs. By the middle of the decade, pant cuffs disappeared, and the majority of pants were cuffless.

Decorative Details

Decorative details were nonexistent in men's business wear of the 1950s. Men attempted to blend into the background, not differentiate themselves through decorative details. Colors were dark, and the gray flannel suit became ubiquitous with success in the business world by 1953. Although there was no radical change in suit styling over the decade, the availability of new manmade fabrics reduced the weight of fabric and provided an opportunity for restrained experimentation with texture and color.

CASUAL WEAR

Silhouette

With a majority of households having a television, casual wear in the 1950s was greatly influenced by the costumes worn on western programs such as *Gunsmoke*, *Maverick*, and *Rawhide*. The western-style shirt and string tie gave men that rugged "I'm in charge but still in style" look. The rugged and often romantic heroes of the 1950s westerns provided a welcome escape from the office grind and the gray flannel suit. In opposition to the rugged western look, the continental look provided a sophisticated alternative. Celebrities such as Bing Crosby, Frank Sinatra, and Fred Astaire promoted a "hip" alternative with polo shirts, blue blazers, and chinos for the various outings and activities of the family man who was also a company man.

Jackets

Navy blue blazers with gold buttons dominated the men's continental look. Dressier than a plaid shirt but not as stuffy as a business suit, a blazer could be worn over a polo shirt, button-down shirt (without necktie), pull-over sweater, or a sweater vest. Plaid or tweed sport coats added flair to the wardrobe through their pairing with colored trousers or corduroys. The fringed buckskin jacket was the epitome of weekend casual wear for men.

Shirts

Plaid shirts were the most popular casual shirt of the 1950s. Plaid shirts came in an array of colors and styles. Plaids were large or small. Shirts had either button or snap closures, shirt tails or banded waists, and slash or flap pockets (some with western detailing). For the continental look, shirts were often worn open at the neck with an ascot and, if not already paired with a blue blazer, may be accompanied by a cardigan, pullover sweater, or sweater vest. Roll-neck, shawl, boat-neck, turtleneck, and crewneck sweaters were also popular casual wear sweater styles. Complex jacquard patterns, not just argyle diamonds, appeared in brushed "hairy" wool sweaters, some of which came with matching socks.

Pants

Cuffed wash-and-wear trousers or chinos were perfect to pair with blazers, sweaters, or plaid shirts. Trousers had either belt loops or adjustable waist tabs. White, tan, or gray trousers completed the continental look, whereas trousers in blue, brown, and rainbow pastels completed plaid shirt and sport coat ensembles. The new Dacron polyester fiber provided a shrink-free, quick-drying, wash-and-wear fabric that was fade resistant and could be permanently pressed.

Decorative Details

Decorative details for casual wear were primarily limited to men's shirts. The popular western look used fringe, embroidery, top-stitching with contrasting thread, pearlized silver-rimmed buttons, and satin piping on pockets for surface embellishment on shirts and jackets, whereas other button-down shirts obtained their interest through bold color combinations in plaid weaves. Pants and jackets could also be colorful but had few structural or decorative elements.

OUTERWEAR

Coats

Three-buttoned overcoats complemented the well-dressed businessman. Topcoats of wool tweed or cashmere bore either slash pockets with finished edge or two straight flap pockets. Colors were conservative in solids, tweeds, or occasionally a window pane plaid in black or gray. Overcoats had a straight silhouette with either a dolman sleeve or fitted shoulder that ended at the wrist with a button placket. Collars and lapels were narrower than in the previous decade and generally had a single buttonhole in the left lapel. Raincoats could double as an overcoat and with a zip-in plush Orlon pile lining for colder weather. Raincoats came in black, gray, navy blue, or khaki. Raincoats were either in the same silhouette as overcoats or double breasted with belted waist.

Other Garments

Bomber and flight jackets were popularized by the Hollywood mystique of WWII pilots and by Dwight D. Eisenhower. The "Eisenhower jacket," in leather or canvas, ended at the waist in a knit or fabric band, had notched lapels, square shoulders, and a center front zipper or button closure. The flight jacket style was made of horsehide or cowhide with a rayon knit waistband and cuffs and a rayon and wool lining for warmth. The zippered front had a leather overlay for extra protection. Both the Eisenhower and flight jackets displayed two prominent breast flap pockets and two lower front slash pockets. Bomber jackets did not sport flap pockets but instead had roomy slash pockets incorporated into broad angular seams that ran from the waistband to the shoulder yoke. Bomber jackets also had tall turned-up collars. Those who preferred the rebel look of James Dean, Marlon Brando, and Elvis Presley sported a straighter black leather jacket without the knit waistband. Embellishments of extra zippers or buckles made the jacket ever more daring.

SWIMWEAR AND SPORTSWEAR

Swimwear

Matching plaid beach suits let men show off their individuality. Bright colors and wild patterns of madras plaid, tropical flowers, or large geometric patterns were the norm. Made of cotton twill, rayon, or nylon, men's swim shorts came with matching short-sleeved shirts with finished straight hem and one breast pocket. Both elastic and drawstring waists helped to keep the shorts in place, and an extra front panel support added comfort. The cover-up shirt allowed men to be seen in beachwear but maintain a conservative appearance.

Golf

After WWII, America looked to President Eisenhower for leadership. Eisenhower, a golf fanatic, led the country from the boardroom to the golf course. As he made the greens an extension of the Oval Office, so too did American business men. Country clubs sprung up all across the country, and golf became one of the favorite pastimes for the new suburban family man. Traditional suits composed of pants, shirts, jackets, and even ties were worn by the most conservative men. However, a slightly relaxed look pairing polo shirts with cardigans or V-neck sweaters and khakis began to replace the more traditional suit. Although the traditional suit decreased in popularity, the new mix-and-match separates were produced in subdued solid colors. Straw or canvas trilbies or tams completed the look.

Skiwear

Sun Valley Ski Resort in Idaho paved the way for a great American ski tradition. When the resort opened in 1936, it attracted film makers and movie stars such as Clark Gable, Claudette Colbert, Ingrid Bergman, and Gary Cooper. By the 1950s, the focus on family vacations, especially to sites on the new highway systems, increased the popularity of ski resorts and the demand for functional yet attractive skiwear. The traditional woolen pants, knickers, or riding breeches provided warmth but restricted movement. The first true ski pant, woolen with baggy voluminous legs tucked into socks, provided mobility but did not meet the chic standards of the Hollywood ski crowd. This style was replaced by a slim-fitting, tapered ski pant produced by American companies such as Sun Valley Ski Clothing Company, Slalom Skiwear, and White Stag. The pants were still made from wool, but some companies experimented with adding Latex and elastic to create a material with increased stretch. These new slim pants were topped with woolen sweaters and hooded quilted parkas that were often belted at the waist. Compared with the multiple layers of clothing worn previously, the new parka provided warmth without weight and increased mobility. Another new addition to the fashionable ski ensemble of the 1950s was the Henke boot, the first boot that buckled rather than laced up. As the decade closed, experimentation with plastic and fiberglass for boots provided a sleek look, with a close fit and increased performance.

Other Activewear

The classic activewear look for camping, picnicking, and beach holidays in the fifties included penny loafers or saddle shoes with argyle socks, chinos, and a tennis sweater tied around the shoulders. American tourists to Bermuda during the tourism explosion of the fifties brought Bermuda shorts back to the states, launching a new trend in activewear. Because showing off legs was not yet acceptable, the knee-length Bermuda shorts were always worn with knee socks. Bermudas shorts were made from colorful madras plaids and bright solid colors and paired with equally colorful short-sleeve shirts.

UNDERWEAR AND INTIMATE APPAREL

Underwear

Boxers and briefs were still the dominant forms of men's underwear. Whereas briefs and boxers did not change much in form, a new multitude of colors and new fabrics was now possible. Lycra, spandex, rayon, Dacron polyester, and DuPont nylon were incorporated into men's underwear to enhance performance and comfort. Besides white, briefs and boxers now also came in pastels, stripes, plaids, wild prints, geometric patterns, and themed scenes, including girls and tropical beaches. The length of boxer shorts crept up from above the knee to mid-thigh or shorter by the end of the decade. Sleeveless or short-sleeve T-shirts in both V necks and crew-necks regained popularity again but, unlike boxers and briefs, only came in white. T-shirts were necessary under dress shirts for businessmen because office space was not yet regularly air-conditioned, and perspiration stains were not dignified.

Sleepwear

Unlike men's suits, men's broadcloth and flannel pajamas came in a wide array of colors and patterns. Button-down shirts and elasticized-waist straight-legged bottoms could be found in solid colors, solid colors with contrasting lapels and cuffs (both pant and sleeve), geometric patterns, themed pictures such as fishing, golfing, and surfing, or traditional stripes and plaids. Cotton knit pajamas with banded-waist pullover shirts and elasticized-waist bottoms were a new option in men's sleepwear and were available in the same range of colors and patterns as broadcloth and flannel pajamas. Pajamas were topped with knee-length bathrobes of cotton broadcloth, seersucker, or flannel with rounded collars, patch pockets, and tie waist belts. An upscale version was made in quilted satin or velvet, in long or shorter "smoking jacket" lengths.

HEADWEAR, HAIRSTYLES, AND COSMETICS

Headwear

The fedora was still the classic choice of headgear for men throughout the 1950s. A center-creased crown and tapered-brim hat in various dark colors from black to gray and brown to tan was seen everywhere, not just for business but at all times. Worn straight on the head, it was a symbol of the well-dressed gentleman. A slight tilt off-center gave it a jauntier appearance for celebrities such as Frank Sinatra and other popular stars of the day. For extremely formal occasions, a black or gray silk top hat was worn with morning suits.

Hairstyles

Hair was either parted neatly on the side and slicked back with Brylcreem or cut into a flat top or crew cut. Rebellious younger men went for the DA, or ducktail haircut. To achieve the DA, hair was grown slightly longer, slicked into a fuller pompadour style (combed back on the sides but rounded over on the crown) and combed into a peak at the nape of the neck like a duck's tail.

Cosmetics

Although men in the 1950s had not yet discovered the benefits of spa treatments as today's male metrosexual has, some men still spent time and money on personal grooming. Brylcreem, pomade, and hair tonic were important components of a man's morning toiletries for sculpting hair into either a sleek appearance or a pompadour. The popularity of clean-shaven faces combined with the decline of being shaved each morning by a barber also meant that men learned to apply aftershave or shaving balms as part of their morning grooming ritual.

FOOTWEAR AND LEGWEAR

Footwear

For formalwear, men wore highly polished, black or black patent leather oxfords. Lace-up leather oxfords in either black or cordovan were also worn for business wear. More daring businessmen wore the flashier wing tips with topstitching between the lace holes and the toe. A variation of the oxford, the "buck," with soft rubberized soles, uppers in sueded leather, in white, tan, gray, or brown, was available for casual wear. Saddle shoes, penny loafers, and other slip-on styles were worn with slacks and sweaters for casual wear. Cowboy boots were very popular alternatives to slip-on styles with "dungarees" and other casual trousers. The continental crowd preferred brown leather slip-on deck shoes with decorative white laces and soft white rubberized soles to match their chinos and blue blazers. Inclement winter weather required overshoes or galoshes to protect leather dress shoes. Overshoes came in two styles: slip on "rubbers" that were flexible and conformed to the shape of the shoe, and rubberized boots that came up above the ankle and fastened up the front with a series of adjustable buckles.

Legwear

The white cotton sock, although appropriate for athletic activities and mowing lawns, was never appropriate with business attire. The traditional dark suit and conservative necktie could show a hint of panache by incorporating a subtle design in the otherwise dark nylon dress sock. Swirls and twirls of color above the ankle added a bit of style, if known only to the wearer. Dress socks had to be long enough that, when legs were crossed, no skin would be visible. As color range in slacks increased, so did the color range for socks. Socks of wool, nylon, and cotton were made to match both trousers and sweaters. A gray fuzzy sweater called for gray fuzzy socks, argyle socks were worn with matching argyle sweaters, and a patterned jacquard sweater made matching socks of the same garish pattern perfectly acceptable.

NECKWEAR AND OTHER ACCESSORIES

Neckwear

Colorful hand-painted ties of the early fifties did not make it to the board-room. Wool-lined rayon or rayon-nylon crepe neckties were bold, wide, and colorful. Scenes of wildlife, cityscapes, tropical trees and flowers, and even pinup girls adorned neckties for a time after the war. As men moved back into industry, however, the conformity of a basic, narrow, geometric patterned necktie without too much color became the acceptable accompaniment for a dark business suit. For formal occasions, neckties or ascots in gray or black with contrasting diagonal stripes were worn with morning suits. Black silk or satin bowties were worn with tuxedos.

Jewelry

Jewelry was limited to wrist watches for businesswear and casual wear in the 1950s. However, tuxedos and morning suits were accessorized with silver, gold, or platinum cufflinks and shirt studs.

Other Accessories

A handkerchief was a requirement, and, if not displayed in the breast pocket, it was at least carried in an inside pocket. A white silk handkerchief always completed the breast pocked of a tuxedo, which might also sport a white silk neckscarf. The defining article of the businessman was the briefcase. Businessmen always carried briefcases, whether or not they actually carried paperwork home at night. Early in the decade, the familiar stand-up style briefcase in black, brown, or cordovan with a hinged opening at the top and a strap with buckle to keep it pulled closed could be found beside every manager's desk. Sunglasses became a necessity for driving because cars did not have tinted windows and men were spending more time behind the wheel commuting to work and driving the family to vacation destinations. Unlike the beatniks who wore dark shades both inside and outside, the company man removed his glasses after they were no longer needed.

ALTERNATIVE FASHION MOVEMENTS

Beatniks

The nonconformists of the fifties were the beatniks. Their unusual poetry and cool jazz music made coffeehouses the favorite hangout for this group. Oddly, their rejection of the "establishment" and the conservative conformity of the day created a subculture of conformity in itself. Men belonging to the beat crowd wore all black, all the time. Straight-legged black chinos with black socks and black ankle-high boots, black turtleneck long-sleeved shirt, and black sunglasses (both indoors and out). Although the hairstyle was still slicked back, it was a bit longer down the nap of the neck. Every true male beatnik completed the look with a black beret and a neat mustache and goatee. The winter look included an oversized chunky black sweater.

Rebels

Another emerging subculture included biker gangs and rock 'n' rollers. Marlon Brando in the film *The Wild One* made black leather jackets and motorcycles the symbol of rebellious youth. Boppers and greasers sprang up in urban ghettos and the suburbs. Black biker boots, straight-legged Levi's with hems rolled up into a big cuff, T-shirts, and black leather jackets with lots of snaps, zippers, and buckles appealed to the roughneck crowd. Chain belts completed the look.

THE
1960s

FORMALWEAR

Silhouette

Slim, narrow cuts dominated men's formalwear in the 1960s. Suits were tapered and streamlined in keeping with the space-age ideals of the period and, as in women's clothing, possessed little surface embellishment. The definition of formalwear continued to expand as the 1950s tuxedo and bowtie was replaced by single-breasted, collarless jackets under which no tie was worn. Formalwear also expanded beyond black and white to include more colors and patterns in the era known for psychedelic patterns and bold colors, with navy, burgundy, and green being three of the more popular color options now available.

Jackets and Vests

Jackets were typically single breasted with long slim-cut sleeves and two back vents. Short narrow lapels rolled into either a high single-button or three-button closure. For variety in evening attire, some jackets were collarless, had small spread collars without lapels, or had small band or Nehru collars. Jackets were either pocketless or possessed a single flat patch pocket on the breast and two on the body, and pocket flaps were virtually eliminated to streamline the silhouette. Some double-breasted jackets were worn amongst the mod set. Single-breasted waistcoats were worn by men who followed the earlier Teddy Boys fashions of dressing with Edwardian flair.

The Nehru Jacket. The Nehru jacket or Nehru shirt derived its name from the Prime Minister of India, Jawaharlal Nehru. The prime minister wore jackets that buttoned up the center front to the base of the neck, with the neckline crowned with a small band collar. The style was co-opted in the mid-1960s by Pierre Cardin, whose designs were greatly influenced by his travels abroad to India. The fascination with India and Eastern mysticism during the 1960s, led by the Beatles and other prominent individuals, led to the widespread popularity and mainstreaming of the Nehru jacket and shirt.

Toward the end of the decade, collars and lapels began to widen to complement the equally wide neckties, and pocket flaps were reinstated.

Shirts

Shirts were slim cut to fit under the narrow-cut jackets. Although plain white shirts were worn by conservative men, other men began experimenting with pairing solid colors under their black, cream, or blue jackets. The more adventurous wore shirts with bold patterns or ruffled fronts. Shirts had small, narrow collars, or band collars. Some men who adopted the Nehru jacket for formalwear did not require shirts for formal occasions and could instead wear a turtleneck under their Nehru jacket. Toward the end of the decade, shirt collars became taller and wider to accommodate the new wide ties.

Pants

Pants were flat front and slim cut, with straight or tapered legs and no cuffs. For eveningwear, the outseam may still be embellished with satin ribbon, in either black to match the trouser or a contrasting color such as blue or even possibly pink. Toward the end of the decade, pant legs began to flare slightly from the knee to the cuff and ride low on the hip.

Decorative Details

Men's suits for formalwear were made from wool, silk, and velvet. Although the majority of men still wore black, cream, or dark blue, others began experimenting with colors, such as pink, green, and red, or prints, such as paisleys and polka dots. Surface embellishment was limited in keeping with the space-age aesthetic. Buttons were often covered in the same fabric as the jacket so as to blend in, not stand out. Piping on lapels and collars was the most common surface embellishment in men's formalwear, especially on Nehru jackets.

BUSINESS WEAR

Silhouette

Suits for business attire followed the same narrow shoulder, trim silhouette as did formalwear. Men also began to deviate from the standard-issue gray flannel three-piece suit in favor of blazers and Nehru jackets. With men ready to expand beyond the basic suit for work, fashion designers that had typically catered to female audiences began offering men's lines. Designers such as YSL and Pierre Cardin led the charge in bringing designer style, and a little color, to men's business attire, ushering in the peacock revolution. By the mid-1960s, this revolution in men's wear meant that men were finally allowed to admit to having an interest in fashion and that fashion design, once limited to women's wardrobes, was expanding into the men's wear market.

Jackets and Vests

Single-breasted jackets with either a high single-button or three-button closure dominated men's business attire. Lapels and collars were short and narrow in the early part of the decade but lengthened and widened in the latter part. Unlike formalwear, men's business jackets typically incorporated pocket flaps into either patch pockets or welt pockets. Initially, small flaps covered pocket openings, but, just as collars, lapels, and ties increased in dimension, so too did pocket flaps. Jackets ended at approximately hip length for the majority of the decade but became fitted at the waist and extended in a flare to mid-thigh by the end of the decade. Vest or waistcoats disappeared from men's business attire for all but the older generation.

Shirts

Plain white shirts continued to dominate the business world, but men also attempted to incorporate color into their business wardrobe by infusing soft shades of pink, green, yellow, and blue. Pinstripe and pattern shirts were worn by those who could be more fashion forward at the office, laying the foundations for the peacock revolution of the mid-1960s and the leisure suits of the 1970s. Shirts were slim cut, with small collars in the early part of the decade, which expanded to accommodate wider ties at the end of the decade.

Pants

Pants that accompanied suits were flat front and slim cut, with either straight or tapered legs and no cuffs. As the decade drew to a close, pant legs began to flare slightly from the knee to the cuff, foreshadowing the bell-bottoms yet to come. Although pinstripes continued to be a popular and accepted alternative to solid colors, the stripes were becoming increasingly wider and more colorful as the decade progressed.

Decorative Details

Vivid, patterned ties and pocket squares were the main source of decoration for men's business wear in the 1960s. For those who were able to move beyond the gray flannel suit, the colors and patterns in suits and shirts provided all the decorative elements required by male peacocks.

CASUAL WEAR

Silhouette

Casual wear was greatly influenced by fashions from the swinging London social scene. The British youth movement, known as the mods, frequented shops on Carnaby street where they purchased European-cut suits and shirts that fit tight on the body, even for casual wear. The influence of the peacock revolution in the middle of the decade brought a new emphasis on casual dress to men's wear. No longer relegated to chinos and Hawaiian print shirts, men's casual wear expanded into new dress forms and new fabrications, including body-skimming tunics and velvet. As the decade progressed, the influence of the hippie movement brought a relaxed fit to men's fashions as individuals began frequenting second-hand shops rather than tailors to acquire fashionable clothing.

Jackets

For casual wear, jackets came in three silhouettes: fitted, Nehru, and sack. Fitted jackets were predominantly single breasted, although double-breasted styles were also worn, with narrow shoulders, high button placement, short, narrow collars, and high, narrow lapels. Nehru jackets were either fitted or slightly flared from waist to hem resembling a tunic, with straight sleeves and small band collars. Sack jackets were unstructured jackets without collars or lapels that had a single button for the closure at the center front baseline of the neck. By the end of the decade, the hippie movement increased the popularity of military influence in jacket styles as many individuals purchased old military uniforms from thrift stores for casual wear. As a result, jackets became longer and fuller cut. Some styles flared from the waist to the mid-thigh-length hem. Frogs, toggles, and other similar closures became popular alternatives to standard buttons, especially after the release of the 1967 *Sgt. Pepper's Lonely Hearts Club Band* album by the Beatles.

Shirts

Shirts allowed men to truly embrace their inner peacock, with bright colors and patterns influenced by Italian fashions and the Far East. Italian-influenced shirts were fitted and had small collars, some in the rounded Peter Pan style, and came in vivid geometric patterns. The popular Nehru jacket was adapted into Turkish or Greek tunic-style shirts in bright colors that often featured embroidery on the banded collar or down the center front placket. Indian motifs, such as paisleys, ogees, and elephants, were common design elements for prints, patterns, and embroidery. Other more effeminate-style shirts were full cut, featuring full sleeves gathered into flounced cuffs, necklines with ruffled collars instead of spread collars, and, for the more flamboyant, either pleated or ruffled fronts. Turtlenecks, originally worn under Nehru jackets, were worn independently with pants.

Pants

Casual pants and jeans were slim cut with tapered legs and high-waisted flat fronts in the first half of the decade. Although denim was a very popular choice for casual wear, the influence of the mods and the peacock revolution could be seen in the popularity of wool, cotton, and velvet trousers in bright colors, bold stripes, and floral prints. White or cream trousers and jeans were also extremely popular. As the decade drew to a close, waistlines dropped, moving to the hip-hugger silhouette that would dominate the next decade, and pant legs began to flare from the knee to the hem, harkening the coming age of wide-legged bell-bottoms.

Decorative Details

The peacock revolution gave men creative freedom in their casual apparel, even if they were still somewhat restricted in their business attire. The influence of Italian tailoring could be seen in the inclusion of yokes, topstitching, piping, welt pockets, and pocket flaps in shirts, jackets, and pants. Casual jackets, especially those without collars or lapels, were frequently edged with contrasting piping to give definition to the silhouette that would have been provided previously by collars and lapels. Textured fabrics, such as velvet, corduroy, crepe, satin, and brushed cotton, replaced regular broadcloth and twill, and embroidery provided additional surface interest and a tactile quality to men's fashions. Men's color palette expanded to include pink, mustard, mint green, cinnamon, and midnight blue to complement the feminine Peter Pan collars, flounced cuffs, and pleated fronts found on shirts.

OUTERWEAR

Coats

Single-breasted as well as double-breasted overcoats continued to be worn for business or formal occasions. These coats were knee length, with narrow lapels and small collars in the early part of the decade. Collars and lapels began to widen and elongate as the decade progressed. The peacock revolution also spurred men to wear fur and fur-trimmed coats in short (mini), knee (midi), or long (maxi) lengths that paralleled women's skirt lengths.

Other Garments

For casual wear, men turned to short, hip-length jackets with knitted waistbands and cuffs. These coats were made from wool in the winter and cotton twills, canvas, or denim in the spring. Casual coats had center front zippers, shoulder yokes, patch pockets, and, occasionally, fur or faux fur trim on the knitted cuffs and collars.

SWIMWEAR AND SPORTSWEAR

Swimwear

The average man continued to wear basic short-style swim trunks in the 1960s, just in brighter colors and bolder patterns than had previously been available. Some more fashion-forward men adopted the "men's bikini," known today as the Speedo. Swimwear in the 1960s was not just about swim trunks. Men embraced beach wardrobes the same as women. Short-sleeve cotton "cabana" shirts in prints and checks were worn with matching shorts and espadrille canvas shoes with rope soles. Also popular were one-piece pull-on knee-length terrycloth jumpers with center front zippers, elastic waists, or self-fabric ties.

Golf

The popularity of golf amongst businessmen and the upper class continued in the 1960s. Men continued to wear unique and colorful outfits on the golf course, even if they still wore the same brown suits in the boardroom. Knickers or knee breeches were still the most common form of pants for golf, but straight-legged slim-fit trousers were gaining popularity. Whatever the pant form, the patterns were big, bold checks and stripes or sometimes solid velvets. Wool V-neck sweaters or cardigans in colors that coordinated with the pants topped button-down shirts. Although headwear fell out of fashion for men in the 1960s, caps or tams were still worn on the golf course.

Tennis

Tennis attire remained true to tradition and continued to be dominated by all white. Men wore short-sleeved polo shirts and other knitted collarless shirts, with tailored cotton shorts. White canvas shoes, white socks, and white caps or visors completed the look on the court.

Skiwear

Ski resorts continued to develop across America and became increasingly popular with movie stars and the jet set. Ski ensembles in the 1960s, whether on the slopes or après, were greatly influenced by the interest in space travel. Quilted jackets with large center front or diagonal zippers trimmed with faux fur collars and cuffs were popular for men as well as women. Ski pants were slim and straight legged, following the fashionable silhouette for pants of the period. Warm sweaters and turtlenecks were worn underneath. Ski goggles with chrome frames and tinted lenses and shiny plastic boots with metal clip fasteners completed the space-aged ski look.

UNDERWEAR AND INTIMATE APPAREL

Underwear

Boxer shorts also fell under the influence of 1960s op art and pop art designs. The once staid garment received an infusion of color and pattern the same as women's wear and men's ties. Solid white was gone, and paisleys, geometric patterns, and wide stripes in bold, bright colors were now in vogue. Undershirts also became an important component of underwear again as men adopted Nehru jackets and other styles of collarless jackets. The banded collar structure of the Nehru jacket precluded the wearing of a standard dress shirt so that an undershirt became a mandatory layer between the skin and the jacket.

Sleepwear

Ensembles with pajama tops, bottoms, dressing gowns, and leather slippers were standard for men's sleepwear in the 1960s. Cotton pajama sets with button-down shirts, straight-legged trousers, and knee-length wrap dressing gowns or robes were also popular. For the more sophisticated man, pajama ensembles were available in satin or velvet with quilted collars and cuffs on the dressing gown. Narrow stripes, bold prints, or solid bright colors in hues of blue, red, green, and gold were popular. Some men's pajamas imitated the popular Nehru jacket by offering a collarless shirt with the trouser. Patch pockets with contrasting piping were standard surface decorations, and occasionally, fringe or tasseles were added to belts of dressing gowns.

HEADWEAR, HAIRSTYLES, AND COSMETICS

Headwear

JFK's bare head at his presidential inauguration set the tone for headwear for men in the 1960s: none. Hats virtually disappeared from the top of the American male head. The small gray or brown trilby, with narrow curled brim and tall crown, was all that remained. Small caps, tams, and "Dutch boy" caps in suede or velvet with soft floppy crowns and small brims were worn by some men for casual wear or sporting activities.

Hairstyles

The pompadour and crew cuts of the 1950s were deflated and lengthened in the 1960s into the new "Perry Como" or "French crew" cuts. Men's hair was straight and worn around ear length on the sides and slightly longer in the back. Considered long when measured against the previous decade's crew cut, hair was either parted on the side with deep bangs combed across the forehead or "mop top" with no part at all, hanging straight down from the center of the head. Side burns were kept short, narrow, and trim. Older men continued to wear close-cropped hair or crew cuts. Hair length and style was an immediate visual cue to indicate whether you embraced the youth revolution of the 1960s or continued to support the establishment. The rise of the hippie movement toward the end of the decade spawned an increase in popularity for even longer hair as well as facial hair.

Cosmetics

The concept of skin care and grooming was still minimal for men in the 1960s, although the peacock revolution that would take place at the end of the decade combined with 1970s glam rock would initiate a change in men's toilet in the next decade. Basic hair tonics were used to keep hair smooth, straight, and shiny, and aftershaves were used to calm and soothe skin after using the modern disposable razor for a morning shave.

FOOTWEAR AND LEGWEAR

Footwear

Men's footwear broke from tradition in the 1960s. Traditional shoe forms were out, and boots with stacked heels were in. Dubbed the "Beatle boot" because of their association with the quintessential 1960s band, these ankle-high boots came in black or brown leather with either a square or pointed toe. The boots either zipped up the side or had elastic gussets to allow them to be pulled on. Some more avant-garde youths donned colored snake skin versions to complement their psychedelic wardrobes. When shoes were worn, wide straps and buckles replaced the more traditional lace-up form, and the uppers were embellished with perforated or punched designs.

Legwear

Legwear changed little from the previous decade. Basic socks were worn but rarely seen thanks to the popularity of ankle boots.

NECKWEAR AND OTHER ACCESSORIES

Neckwear

Men's ties provided the perfect canvas for 1960s op art, pop art, and psychedelic prints. Bright colors and bold geometric patterns, including stripes, polka dots, paisleys, and flowers, adorned men's ties in the 1960s. Ties were initially narrow but continued to widen throughout the decade, reaching, at their most extreme, five inches in width. Although ties provided a means to pattern and color for men's wear, the popularity of Nehru or banded-collar jackets and shirts meant that, in many formal and informal settings, men no longer wore any tie.

Jewelry

The popularity of collarless or banded-collar shirts and jackets and turtlenecks meant that men's previous accessory, the tie, could no longer universally adorn men's necks. The replacement was necklaces. For the first time in fashion history, men co-opted an item of adornment that had been the exclusive purview of women. Gold and silver chains terminating in medallions or pendants were the perfect solution to the void left by ties.

Other Accessories

Sunglasses, especially those popularized by John Lennon, became a standard component of the modern man's wardrobe. Men who completely embraced the peacock revolution also wore earrings and bracelets, and some even carried purses or "man bags."

ALTERNATIVE FASHION MOVEMENTS

Mods

The modernists, or mods, took their name from a youth movement begun in London's Carnaby Street fashion district. Although music by the Beatles gave sound to the mod movement, at heart, mods were all about fashion. Unlike the Teddy Boys of the 1950s who preferred fancy, fussy attire, the mods opted for simplistic yet impeccable fashions. Good taste, immaculate grooming, and high-quality apparel were the tenets of the mod movement. The mod uniform consisted of a Nehru jacket or other collarless single-breasted jacket, crisp pressed trousers without cuffs, crisp white French or Italian shirt with small rounded collar, and pointed-toed, stacked-heel Chelsea boots. The mod haircut was a simple, straight, side-parted shag, quite the opposite of the Teddy Boys' greased pompadour. As the Beatles increased in popularity and British music came to dominate the airwaves, the mod movement was co-opted by swinging London and reinterpreted to include a wider range of psychedelic colors and patterns and longer, shaggier hairstyles evolving into the stereotyped image many now associate with the 1960s mod movement.

Hippies

Like the mod movement of the 1960s, the hippie movement of the late 1960s was synonymous with music and was reflected in apparel choices. Unlike the mods' penchant for high-end fashions, hippies favored an unkempt anti-establishment appearance. The hippie lifestyle was strongly influenced by communal living, religion, and anti-

Two male models in mod fashions from the Fox Brothers Consort collection in London, England, on Feb. 1, 1967. [AP / Wide World Photos]

establishment protests. The ultimate hippie gathering, the Woodstock music festival, occurred in 1969, about two years after hippies were first noted in the United States. Between Woodstock and televised sit-ins and protests, the hippie movement gained prominence with America's youths, influencing the way mainstream America thought and presented itself. Blue jeans, ethnic dress, long hair, and sandals were the hallmarks of the hippie wardrobe. Denim was particularly key for men's attire and was often embroidered or painted with emblems of peace or antiwar messages. T-shirts were a staple of the hippie wardrobe, as were tunics and vests that were embroidered or embellished with fringe. Men wore their hair long hair, sometimes pulled back in a ponytail or braid, or wore bandanas as head bands. Thrift stores provided the main source of apparel for true hippies, whereas those adopting the appearance but not the lifestyle could purchase ethnic-inspired pants and shirts in major department stores.

Black Power

Many African-American males were empowered by the black pride and civil rights movements of the 1960s. A resurgence of traditional African

A hippie is shown at a "happening" in Golden Gate Park in San Francisco in the 1968 documentary *Revolution*. [Courtesy of Photofest]

dress was seen not only on women but also on men during this period. Men adopted traditional dashikis, a collarless tunic with kimono-style sleeves paired with jeans or trousers for casual dress. Devoted followers of the "black is beautiful" philosophy even adopted caftans, a garment similar to dashikis, but floor length, for casual or even business attire. Caftans and dashikis were brightly colored, featuring traditional African motifs, in either tie-dye or kente cloth. Men also wore their hair in afros or corn-row braids.

<h1 style="text-align:center">THE
1970s</h1>

FORMALWEAR

Silhouette

Fewer truly formal events were held in the 1970s than in any previous decade. Just as women abandoned ball gowns in the 1970s, men were often able to wear regular suits or pants with blazers to events that twenty years previously would have required a tuxedo. However, when black tie was called for, men answered in luxurious black, red, or navy silk or velvet tuxedos or pastel rainbow shades of gabardine.

Jackets and Vests

Both single- and double-breasted tuxedo jackets with side vents were popular throughout the decade. Single-breasted styles had one-, two-, or three-button closures. Both styles were fitted and narrow through the shoulders with long slim sleeves. Collars and lapels were wide and could be edged in a contrasting fabric or color to the main body of the jacket. Most jackets had two front patch pockets with flaps and were often piped in contrasting fabric or color the same as the lapel edges. When waistcoats or vests were worn, they were typically single breasted and collarless and made of the same fabric as the jacket.

Shirts

White starched shirts were the norm under tuxedos. Shirts were fitted, with long narrow sleeves and deep cuffs. Wide pointed spread collars were complemented by large black velvet bow ties. Fashion-forward men opted for ruffled front shirts, some with the ruffles edged to match the fabric of the tuxedo. Toward the end of the decade, collars began to decrease in depth, and shirts with pleated fronts became popular.

Pants

Tuxedo trousers were flat front and fitted with a slightly flared hemline. Styles with and without cuffs were equally popular. In keeping with tradition, satin ribbon or braid trimmed the outseam of the pant legs.

Decorative Details

Black continued to be the primary color for formal tuxedos, although some velvet and crushed velvet tuxedos were seen in red and navy. Some men opted for tuxedos in pastel blue, salmon, or green. Lapels, collars, and pockets were edged in satin or velvet to provide decorative interest. Black velvet bow ties adorned most necks, but men selecting pastel tuxedos typically opted for coordinating pastel bow ties.

BUSINESS WEAR

Silhouette

The double-breasted suits of the 1960s were gradually replaced with single-breasted suits in the 1970s. Business attire generally became less restrictive and less conservative, mirroring the trend toward casual lifestyles in society. Leisure suits were even offered as an alternative to the standard business suit, promising both comfort and professional appearance that could transcend to after-five or weekend attire. Businessmen struggled to

Richard Pryor wears a leisure suit in this 1977 photo. [Courtesy of Photofest]

define their appearance in suits. Some opted for trendy stripes and plaids in bold colors, while others tried to incorporate subtle aspects of fashion trends, such as flared pants, into otherwise conservative looks. It would not be until the emergence of Giorgio Armani in the 1980s that men's suits would have a true master at incorporating fashion and business.

Jackets and Vests

Single-breasted jackets with side vents were the dominant form for men's suits. Jackets had straight narrow sleeves and were cut narrow through the shoulders and fitted at the waist. Collars and lapels widened throughout the first part of the decade and then began to recede in the closing years. Breast pockets for silk handkerchiefs and patch pockets with flaps were standard for most jackets. Leisure suit jackets were unstructured with little tailoring when compared with standard suit jackets. Leisure suit jackets had straight center front closures without lapels. Some had shoulder yokes and inverted pleats at the center back. Some men in executive positions still wore vests or waistcoats under their suit jackets. When worn, the waist coat was typically in the same fabrication as the suit jacket and pants. Waistcoats were fitted, collarless, and single breasted.

Shirts

Standard button-down shirts were worn under suits. The shirts were tailored, narrow through the shoulder, and fitted at the waist, with slim sleeves and wide spread collars. In addition to the standard white shirt, men donned dark blues, reds, oranges, yellows, and even pink shirts under their suits. Shirts worn under leisure suits typically had bold patterns and were worn without ties.

Pants

Suit pants were fitted through the hip with a slightly full-cut and flared leg. Pants were typically in the same fabrication as the suit jacket. Most styles were flat front with cuffs. Pants worn with leisure suits had fuller-cut legs with wider flared hems. Some styles opted for tab closures, eliminating the need for a belt, and sported large pockets with flaps on both the front and back of the pant.

Decorative Details

Wool tweed and gabardine were the primary fabrications for men's business suits. Although many continued to be produced in navy, green, and brown, some pinstripe, chalk stripe, and wide stripe styles experimented with fashionable colors such as rust and orange. Surface decoration for suits was minimal, typically topstitching or patch pockets. Instead, brightly colored ties with large-scale prints, stripes, and plaids served as the visual interest in men's suits. Leisure suits were made from double-knit polyester in a wide range of colors and patterns, typically with topstitching throughout the garments.

CASUAL WEAR

Silhouette

The influence of the hippie movement in the late 1960s continued to influence men's casual wear in the early 1970s. Although no longer purchased from second-hand stores, men continued to mix and match patterns for an eclectic, antiestablishment look. As the decade progressed, the influence of *Saturday Night Fever* and the disco movement could be seen in men's casual wear. Clothing became more fitted through the shoulders and hips. The overall silhouette was elongated through full-cut flared pants and platform shoes. By the end of the decade, men adopted a more manicured appearance compared with the hippie fashions that launched the 1970s.

Jackets

As society was becoming increasingly more casual, jackets began to disappear as a staple of the casual wardrobe. When worn, casual jackets, also known as blazers, were typically single breasted in suede, denim, or tweed. Many jackets featured shoulder yokes and large patch pockets with flaps and topstitching. The lapels were wide and long, the sleeves were narrow and straight, and many jackets had side vents. The safari jacket with short sleeves, epaulets, and patch pockets provided an alternative to the blazer.

Shirts

Casual shirts grew in breadth and depth in the 1970s as new levels of "casual" were established. For the most casual occasions, a wide variety of T-shirts with novelty prints, logos, and rock bands were paired with jeans. T-shirts came in a wide variety of color combinations, including brown, teal, yellow, orange, and rust. A step up from T-shirts were polo shirts. Whether Izod or an imitation, solid and striped polo shirts were staples in men's casual wardrobes. Button-down shirts with wide, pointed collars were the "dressy" side of a man's casual wardrobe. However, unlike past decades, button-down shirts in the 1970s were worn with the top two or three buttons unbuttoned and without an undershirt. For the first time, men were showing bare chests. Button-down shirts were fitted, with long slim sleeves, and came in a wide variety of solids, prints, plaids, and, of course, denim. Sweaters and sweater vests were worn over polo shirts and button-down shirts. Some fashion-forward men also adopted wrap cardigan sweaters with large patch pockets and self-fabric tie belts, or velour pullover sweaters and vests.

Pants

Denim, whether blue or colored, was the dominant pant form for men's casual dress in the 1970s. Jeans had full-cut legs with flared hems, fit tight through the hips, with the waistband falling just below the natural waist-line. Many jeans were detailed with topstitching, large cargo or patch pockets on the front and back, patch work, embroidery, or metal studs. Khakis and cords (corduroy pants) provided dressy alternatives to jeans, but the overall styling was the same, full-cut, flared legs, with flat fronts and fitted through the hips. In place of belts, many khakis or cords came with tab closures. Although solid browns, blacks, and denims were the predominate colors, some wide stripes and plaids were also popular, particularly in tight-fitting double-knit polyester pants.

Decorative Details

The primary decorative details for men's casual wear were topstitching and metal studs. Both elements embellished pants, shirts, and jackets, especially those made from denim. Other decorative details were structural formations such as oversized patch pockets, shoulder yokes, and large zippers. Color and pattern combinations provided the most visual interest in men's casual wear. Paisley was worn with plaid and stripes with novelty prints. Browns, oranges, teals, greens, yellows, and rusts might all appear in the same ensemble or even in the same garment.

OUTERWEAR

Coats

Denim, corduroy, and leather dominated men's outerwear in the 1970s. Blazers, bombers, and Norfolk-style belted jackets in denim, leather, suede, and corduroy were executed in patchwork, decorated with embroidery or fringe, and lined with shearling. Tan, brown, burgundy, and hunter green were the most popular color choices. Jackets were predominately single breasted, hip length, and had wide collars and lapels. Shoulder yokes, zippers, belts, and patch pockets gave visual interest to men's outerwear. Ski jackets also began appearing off the slopes for casual winter wear. Parkas and other nylon-shell quilted jackets replaced pea coats and Chesterfields for casual wear. Some ski jackets were even made with detachable hoods and sleeves so that the coat could be converted to a vest.

Other Garments

Vests became popular alternatives to jackets as society continued to become less formal in the 1970s. Denim, leather, and corduroy were popular fabrications for vests as well as jackets. Vests were single breasted, without collars or lapels, and waist length. Vests received the same decorative treatments as jackets; fringe, patchwork, and topstitching or embroidery provided visual interest on the slim-fitting garments.

SWIMWEAR AND SPORTSWEAR

Swimwear

Swim trunks continued to dominate men's swimwear in the 1970s. The trunks were short and fitted, with the waist dropped down to the hip. Many trunks had narrow belts and large tab belt loops. Solids and brightly colored prints were equally popular. Speedos provided a daring alternative to trunks for men bold enough. The increasing informality of society meant that men were less concerned about wearing beachwear or cover-ups away from the pool; more often a simple novelty print T-shirt served as the sole cover-up to swim trunks.

Golf

Bright colors and wild plaids dominated men's golf apparel in the 1970s. Oranges, blues, reds, and rusts popped against the lush green golf course. Plaids and stripes were not restricted to just horizontal and vertical but also appeared in diagonal weaves in pants that sat slightly lower on the waist and had an athletic fit that hugged the body. Polo shirts, turtlenecks, V-neck sweaters, and cardigans were worn in equally bright colors and patterns. Collars and lapels increased in width for golf shirts the same as in men's regular apparel. Baseball caps replaced tams and fedoras.

Tennis

Knit polo shirts or Izods, shorts, and sweater vests continued as the standard tennis ensemble. Ribbed knit waistbands, cuffs, armscyes, and necklines were trimmed with narrow bands of red and blue to accent the otherwise solid white ensembles. White canvas Converse or Adidas were the most popular brand of tennis shoes. Sweatbands for head and wrists and visors were the new fashion accessory for every male tennis player.

Skiwear

The space-age influence in ski wear of the 1960s continued into the sleek high-tech look of the 1970s. Fabrics, such as spandex, and fibers, such as nylon, polyester, and Lycra, continued to offer increased performance while keeping skiers dry and warm. Those who preferred the "racer look" donned long-sleeved unitards that were sleek and tight, whereas others paired sleek pants with hip-length turtleneck sweaters and quilted parkas. Regardless of the apparel form, bright colors and wild patterns dominated the slopes. Knitted caps, dark goggles, and multicolored gloves completed the look.

Other Activewear

An increased interest in health and fitness in the 1970s led to a jogging craze that gripped the United States and, with it, the launch of a new item of apparel, the jogging suit. Two-piece jogging suits in jersey knit with racing stripes down the outseam of the pants were worn by joggers and non-joggers alike. The jacket typically had a small stand collar or knitted band around the jewel neckline. Collars and cuffs were often added in a contrasting color that matched the racing stripe on the outseam of the pants. Sweatbands for the head and wrists and gym shoes completed the look. True fashionista joggers matched their Nike gym shoes with their jogging suits to create coordinated jogging ensembles.

UNDERWEAR AND INTIMATE APPAREL

Underwear

The popularity of color and pattern in men's underwear that began in the 1960s continued in the 1970s. The peacock revolution expanded beyond shirts and pants to include fashionable offerings in underwear. Although Y-front briefs were still the most popular form of underwear, bold colors and patterns that matched or coordinated with undershirts replaced plain white. Briefs became smaller to correspond with the slim-fitting hip-hugger pant style popular during this era.

Sleepwear

Throughout the 1970s, the distinction between sleepwear and casual sportswear virtually disappeared. The popularity of athletic attire, particularly jogging suits, greatly influenced the look of men's sleepwear. Sleepwear coordinates that offered mix-and-match pants, shorts, tops, and robes replaced the standard pajama set for men. The influence of ethnic-inspired apparel was also seen the in variety of kaftan- and kimono-style robes that were popular during this period.

HEADWEAR, HAIRSTYLES, AND COSMETICS

Headwear

Headwear continued to decline in popularity. Although a few conservative, older men still donned fedoras or trilbies, the only headwear seen on America's youths was the baseball cap or an occasional knitted tam or skull hat. Visors were worn for tennis or other sports.

Hairstyles

For the first time in decades, men's hairstyles became as elaborately coiffed and varied as women's. Whether side or center parted, men experimented with feathers or layered looks and shaggy, tousled styles. The infamous mullet, with hair longer in the back than on the sides, was also a product of 1970s experimentation in men's hairstyles. Ethnic influence and the black pride movement lead to a wide range of afro styles that were dubbed names such as "the Duke," "the executive," and "the sportsman" to distinguish the different lengths, amount of fullness, and degree of curvature of the afro. The look was so popular that Caucasian men visited hair salons to have their hair permed, or permanent waved, to replicate the afro style. Men were also seen in hair salons having their feathers or layers highlighted or "frosted" with blond streaks for a natural sun-kissed look.

Facial hair experienced a resurgence in popularity in the 1970s as well. Sideburns, especially the full mutton chop, were grown wide and long down the side of the face. Thick full mustaches were also in vogue. The Fu Manchu mustache, so named after the character in the late 1960s film *The Many Lives of Dr. Fu Manchu*, was characterized by a full mustache that extended down around each side of the lips to the jaw line. Many men also grew full beards.

Cosmetics

The androgyny of the 1970s increased the popularity of men's fragrances. Aramis, which had been sold in department stores since the 1960s, now had competition from Paco Rabanne pour Homme and Geoffrey Beene's Grey Flannel. In the late 1970s, Fabergé's Brut toiletry line gained popularity with the average middle-class male after a television commercial depicted the sex symbol of the late 1970s, Farah Fawcett-Majors, shaving football superstar Joe Namath.

FOOTWEAR AND LEGWEAR

Footwear

Low stacked-heel ankle boots were popular in the early part of the 1970s. However, just like women, men soon adopted the thick platform soles for their footwear too. The peacock revolution meant that men were no longer restricted to black and brown footwear. Shoes and boots were available in red, green, blue, and patchwork. Embellishments such as punch work or tassels provided surface decoration. White leather became the new dress shoe to complement the white disco suit. Cowboy boots and boots with exposed zippers and buckles were also popular. Nike, Adidas, and Converse tennis shoes and running shoes in leather or canvas with leather or suede accents provided a casual alternative to shoes and boots with jeans.

Legwear

Basic dress socks changed little in the 1970s. The same standard dark styles were available for business wear or formalwear. However, with a decrease in formal dressing, tube socks were regularly seen on men. Tube socks were white, pulled up to the knee, and featured two or three bands of color on the ribbed knit top. Tall tube socks were the perfect complement to the short shorts of the 1970s. The 1970s also witnessed a short-lived fad for toe socks. Toe socks provided a pocket for each individual toe and were worn in wild patterns and colors with sandals or thongs.

NECKWEAR AND OTHER ACCESSORIES

Neckwear

Ties became increasingly wider during the beginning of the decade to complement ever-increasing collars and lapels. The width of the ties, up to five inches at their most extreme, provided an ample canvas for bold stripes, design motifs, and novelty prints similar to those seen in the 1940s. Orange, teal, brown, rust, and blue were the dominant color choices, sometimes appearing together all in the same tie. By the end of the decade, ties had returned to their standard two-and-a-half-inch width. The influence of the peacock revolution and England's Carnaby Street could be seen in the substitution of lace cravats for ties in some men's fashions.

Jewelry

Whereas conservative men wore only watches, trend seekers and setters adopted rings and medallions in the early part of the decade and gold chains, heavy chain-link gold bracelets, and puka shell necklaces in the closing years of the decade. Sunglasses, particularly in the aviator style with gold frames, long silk scarves with fringe, and large leather shoulder bags were donned by the most fashionable men.

ALTERNATIVE FASHION MOVEMENTS

Punk

The British response to the mod movement of the 1960s was the punk movement of the 1970s. Punks were anti-establishment, anti-government, and antisocial. Born from the frustrated working class of Great Britain, the punks gave voice to their beliefs through the preeminent punk band the Sex Pistols in 1975. Sid Vicious, the lead singer of the Sex Pistols, was unlike anything the world had ever seen. Dressed in black leather pants, combat boots, and a dog collar, Vicious was infamous for promoting heroin use and violence through his lyrics. The image he projected was adopted by punks and middle-class kids alike. The punk look was menacing and would come to influence mainstream fashions for the next decade. The signature punk appearance included tall black leather boots, tattered and ripped shirts that were held together with safety pins, distressed leather jackets, shaved heads, Liberty spikes or mohawks dyed DayGlo colors, spiked dog collars, and body piercing.

THE
1980s

FORMALWEAR

Silhouette

Most formalwear in the last years of the twentieth century provided variations and interpretations of traditional styles. Classic-cut tuxedos in black wool with silk-faced peaked lapels and black bow ties remained the staple for eveningwear. American men's wear design houses competed with and were inspired by *the* master suit designer of the 1980s, Giorgio Armani. His influence was seen in the work of Ralph Lauren, Calvin Klein, and Donna Karan.

Jackets and Vests

Black tuxedo jackets with satin lapels were either double or single breasted. Some men experimented with pastel-colored cummerbunds or vests and, occasionally, an entire pastel-colored tuxedo suit. White dinner jackets were seen in formal day occasions (Payne, Winakor, and Farrell-Beck 1992, 624). Other formalwear jackets of the 1980s were mostly single breasted, fitted with slightly padded shoulders, and typically in dark colors, although double-breasted jackets with wide collars were also seen.

Shirts

White fitted shirts with narrow collars and straight fitted sleeves and cuffs remained the norm for formalwear. Tuxedo shirts were often pleated, tucked, piqued, and occasionally ruffled. The pastel hues seen in tuxedos were also seen in formal shirts. Shirt collar styles varied in size and shape, including the classic wing collars and the larger spread collar.

Pants

Formal pants, including tuxedo styles, were mostly fitted and without cuffs. The traditional satin braid was still used on tuxedo pants. Front-pleated pants were more popular than flat-front pants.

Decorative Details

Pleated black cummerbunds usually accompanied tuxedos, but some men experimented with colored and patterned cummerbunds. Other suits styles worn for formalwear were usually solid black or included very small pin-stripes, checks, or plaids.

BUSINESS WEAR

Silhouette

Broad shoulders and longer jackets, similar to styles seen in female power dressing, were popular in male business attire. As the decade progressed, however, suits inspired by the designs of Giorgio Armani became the quintessential look for the 1980s. Armani's easy-fitting style was inspired by late 1930s and featured softer shoulders and wider lapels. Suits dominated men's business wear, although men in noncorporate positions may wear blazers with pants.

Jackets and Vests

The unfitted jackets of the late 1970s and early 1980s gave way to more fitted styles in materials inspired by Italian men's wear. Double-breasted jackets with narrow lapels, deep armholes, and padded shoulders dominated men's business wear. Buttons and lapels were placed lower in some jacket styles. Vests matching the suit jacket were worn by some executives, although entertainers and younger men occasionally experimented with pastel- and bright-colored vests. As an alternative to the suit jacket, blazers sometimes fabricated in corduroy or with leather elbow patches were worn when a less executive look was appropriate.

Shirts

Slim-cut shirts with narrow collars and single pockets were dominant. Patterns remained simple, with most business shirts featuring solid colors.

Colored or printed shirts with white collars and cuffs were popular alternatives to traditional shirts (Tortora and Eubank 2005, 541). Pointed collars,
button-down collars, French cuffs, double-button cuffs, and topstitching
were used in some business-wear shirts.

Pants

Cuffs and front pleats were seen in most business-wear trousers during
the early part of the decade but slowly began to disappear toward the end
of the decade. Pleated high-waist pants worn with suspenders were also
common in business wear (Payne, Winakor, and Farrell-Beck 1992, 623).
In general, pants showed narrower waistbands, creating a more fitted
look. Legs ranged from straight to modestly full.

Decorative Details

Black was only used in suits for extremely formal occasions, whereas classic dark earth tones, browns, tans, and grays, were used for most business
suits. Patterns were simple with pinstripes remaining the most widely
used. Some American men experimented with vivid colors and nontraditional patterns, but, in most cases, such attempts were considered eccentric. Suits were made from heavy wool gabardine or flannel for winter and
in lightweight wool crepe or other fabrics for the summer.

Military Uniforms

American military uniforms further improved as a result of technological
developments in bullet proofing, lightweight webbing, and fabric finishing.
The M81 Woodland camouflage pattern was introduced in combat gear in
the 1980s (McNab 2000, 24), and a nighttime pattern was developed to
confuse night-vision equipment (Newark 1998, 106). The PASGT (Personal Armor System, Ground Troops) vest used the new Woodland pattern
and had increased bullet resistance. Formal military uniforms did not show
great changes in silhouette or style, but the traditional army tan and khaki
colors were mostly replaced by dark green and blue shades.

CASUAL WEAR

Silhouette

The 1980s casual silhouette ranged from fitted garments showcasing an
athletic male physique to the broad-shouldered looser outfits influenced
by business styles of corporate America and the entertainment industry.
The television series *Miami Vice*, for example, promoted the use of white
casual suits with pastel T-shirts and dark double-breasted jackets with
white pants. Other factors affecting general casual trends were the

importance of brand labels as a symbol of status and the widespread use of gym and sports clothes on the street, often matched with more formal garments such as blazers and loafer shoes worn without socks.

Jackets

Broad-shouldered double- and single-breasted blazers were matched with anything from jeans to chinos and tailored pants. Lightweight suit jackets or blazers came in white and a variety of pastel colors as well as basic black, navy, and brown. Denim jackets, often with acid-wash treatments, were worn by younger men. Loose oversized knitted sweaters with broad shoulders and striking geometric patterns were very trendy. Sweatshirts with printed sports team logos were common and often found tied around the waist by the sleeves.

Shirts

Button-down and spread-collared shirts, whether long or short sleeved, were manufactured in pastel colors, bright solids, stripes, and feminine decorative patterns. Some shirt styles were long and loose, featuring two breast pockets. Polo shirts also came in a variety of colors and patterns but always with a prominently displayed designer label, Lacoste and Members Only among the most popular. Polo shirts were short sleeved or long sleeved and in either cotton pique or polyester jersey knit. Many polo shirts had a single horizontal stripe across the chest to visually broaden the chest and shoulders. Some men even wore two or three polo shirts at the same time or a polo shirt under a button-down oxford shirt, with the polo collar turned up. Cotton and bright synthetic shirts continued carrying political messages, product and service advertisements, or brand logos. T-shirts and polo shirts were regularly worn under suit jackets or blazers for casual wear.

Pants

Tailored pleated pants were more popular than flat fronts; cuffs were often upturned and visible. Chino cotton trousers featuring military influences also enjoyed popularity. Z'Cavaricci was the most popular brand, showcasing wide tight waistbands and several front pleats. The importance of branding was evident in the popularity of designer jeans, which prominently displayed the label or included embroidered details and buttons, indicating the manufacturer's or designer's name. Some jeans featured low crotches and snap cuffs. Acid-washed and torn denim jeans were worn by younger Americans who also sported warm-up suits, sweat pants, and gym shorts as casual apparel.

Decorative Details

Colors ranged from pastel and bright to subdued earth tones and patterned fabrics, including Hawaiian prints. Acid wash and other denim treatments including embroidered emblems and sport patches decorated casual wear. Brand labels were a common form of decoration for men's apparel.

OUTERWEAR

Coats

Trench coats, although longer than before, were embellished with epaulets, storm flaps, adjustable cuffs, belts, and often double rows of buttons. Single- and double-breasted wool Melton overcoats, however, were the symbol of American yuppie elegant business wear. They were mostly seen in dark shades, elegantly lined in silk, and often accompanied by a scarf. The Mackintosh, and other waterproof coats, sported the bright colors and patterns that were denied to trench coats and overcoats. The velvet-collared, historically inspired Chesterfield coat was also common (Payne, Winakor, and Farrell-Beck 1992, 624).

Other Garments

Besides the ubiquitous oversized, acid-washed jean jackets of the 1980s, bombers and other types of leather jackets were also common. In all cases, shoulders pads were present and collars were smaller. Parkas, partly influenced by the winter garments of the Alaskan Inuit, also enjoyed popularity in the 1980s because they provided protection from the cold and icy winter in several areas of the United States. Windbreaker jackets with small stand collars constructed in light fabrics, mostly cotton and nylon, were also seen along with gym sweatshirts and warm-up suits (Payne, Winakor, and Farrell-Beck 1992, 622).

SWIMWEAR AND SPORTSWEAR

Swimwear

The love affair with Lycra in other sportswear barely reached men's swimsuits. American men continued wearing conservative long swim trunks that, in many cases, extended to the knees. Swim trunks were available in a wide range of colors and patterns, typically the brighter the better, and often had contrasting piping or trims. Speedo swimsuits, popular elsewhere in the 1980s, were rarely seen in the United States but continued being worn by professional swimmers. Even rarer for men were other daring styles such as thongs and fitted trunk shorts.

Golf

Solid or striped polo shirts came in a variety of colors, including bright shades for younger players and classic white jersey knits for the older crowd. Sweatshirts and jackets were similar to the prevalent outerwear styles and occasionally featured broad shoulders and colorful patterns. Pants and shorts were typically loose with pleated fronts.

Tennis

Uniforms for tennis players remained fitted and predominantly white. Neon colors, however, appeared in modest amounts as decoration on shorts and sweater or shirt cuffs, collars, and waistbands and particularly in headbands. Some tennis players wore fitted Lycra shorts under their regular uniform.

Skiwear

Professional athletes wore tight-fitting bodysuits made from innovative fabrics, such as Gore-Tex and Thinsulate, that offered better wind resistance and waterproof capabilities compared with past garments. Amateur skiers wore mostly corduroy knickers, insulated pants, patterned Nordic sweaters, colorful jackets, and a variety of patterned wool stockings (Tortora and Eubank 2005, 543).

Other Activewear

Baggy shorts, jeans, and nylon or Lycra shorts were mixed and matched with T-shirts and hooded sweaters for skateboarding and mountain bike racing. Protective accessories included helmets, as well as knee and elbow pads. Warm-up suits, sweatpants, and gym shorts were used for jogging and running (Tortora and Eubank 2005, 542). Designer, sports teams, and college logos, among others, were placed on accessories such as baseball hats, shoes, and socks.

UNDERWEAR AND INTIMATE APPAREL

Undergarments

The 1980s are famous for creating a revolution in the world of male (and female) underwear by turning underclothes into a fashion statement. Designers, such as Calvin Klein, placed their brand prominently on waistbands and advertised by showing celebrities wearing their garments, as in the well-known Calvin Klein campaign with rap star Marky Mark (Mark Wahlberg). Briefs remained popular and were sold not only in white but also in a variety of colors. Bikini briefs, string bikinis, and mesh briefs were also popular novelty items. Boldly patterned and colored loose boxer shorts dominated the men's underwear business, outselling briefs in the American market by the mid-1980s. Cotton and polyester remained the most common fabrics used in undergarments. T-shirts and muscle shirts were openly used as outerwear and became an important element in a series of layered garments, because they were worn with open jackets or just paired with jeans or shorts.

Sleepwear

Traditional pajamas were still sold in the American market, but younger men were wearing loose fleece pants matched with T-shirts and other pullovers for sleepwear. Terrycloth bath robes and some styles of elegant morning loungewear were worn in the United States. Some robes were constructed in kimono styles and incorporated shawl collars (Tortora and Eubank 2005, 543).

HEADWEAR, HAIRSTYLES, AND COSMETICS

Headwear

Most American men in urban areas did not wear any type of formal hat in the last decades of the millennium. Cowboy and fedora hats remained popular in western and southwest areas of the country and were heavily influenced by the styles of country music stars, television shows such as *Dallas*, and the *Indiana Jones* franchise. Baseball hats enjoyed widespread popularity and were at first embroidered with team logos but later became a perfect tool for advertisement and promotion of a variety of products. Winter knit hats and other styles of ski caps were also seen in casual wear, and cotton and spandex headbands were occasionally worn out of the gym. African-inspired crown hats were worn by African-American men.

Hairstyles

Shorter neat hair, often parted on the sides, and well-groomed sideburns were the chosen look for 1980s American yuppies. Hair gel and products were essential to those men aiming for a classic professional appearance. Clean-shaven looks dominated, but facial hair remained popular among older American men, with many of them sporting full beards. College students and younger men wore short spiked hair. Some entertainers and music stars carried long manes, often curled or feathered, in styles similar to the predominant female cuts. Athletes, particularly football players, helped popularize the mullet, hair cut short in front and long in back, as well as long thin ponytails also known as rat tails. Styles popular in some subcultures included the African-American flat tops, punk Mohawks, and Rasta dreadlocks.

Cosmetics

In the 1980s, male beauty products appeared on the American market as men abandoned the rugged image of the 1970s for a smoother and more refined look (Carnegy 1990, 19). Designer fragrances became popular in the 1980s, and designers began expanding into a number of other male grooming products and tools, including shaving creams and aftershave lotions. Facial care products were specifically created for men, including peel-off mask treatments, anti-aging creams, facial scrubs, and acne treatments.

FOOTWEAR AND LEGWEAR

Footwear

Formal shoes returned to classic styles, with black oxfords and brown or two-tone shoes enjoying popularity (Payne, Winakor, and Farrell-Beck 1992, 626). Western boots remained popular in large areas of the United States because of the popularity of the television show *Dallas*. Sneakers or tennis shoes, in a wide range of colors and patterns, were worn by men not only for sports activities but also as daily wear, matched with casual and semiformal looks. A variety of specialty athletic shoes were available, including footwear for skating, basketball, running, soccer, and other sports. Brands were important in sports footwear, with the Adidas stripe and the Nike swoosh among the most recognized logo brands of the 1980s.

Legwear

Men's socks in the 1980s included the introduction of more color and pattern choices, such as argyle and stripes. Sport socks remained white and often featured colored stripes or logos on the top. American men favored high-quality, hard-wearing socks that were resistant to laundry cycles; thus, socks with reinforced toes and heels were very common. Sport socks were made with breathable fibers and occasionally featured cushioned soles for improved performance. Many American men adopted a "no sock" look, wearing anything from sneakers to loafer shoes without any sort of legwear.

NECKWEAR AND OTHER ACCESSORIES

Neckwear

Neckties and bow ties were narrower than they had been in the 1970s, with skinny knit ties becoming popular in casual wear. Designer neckwear was an important element in the dress for success movement and was associated with the power and upwardly mobile culture of corporate America. The four-in-hand, half Windsor, and full Windsor knots were still used in ties with a variety of patterns, including floral, bold abstract prints, and paisley designs. Solid, polka dots, and striped ties were also available. Western bolo or bola ties were used in country wear but also as a novelty item among young American men.

Jewelry

By the 1980s, many men were piercing one of their ears, occasionally both of them, and wearing solitaire diamonds and loop earrings. Piercing other body parts, some visible, some not, was also becoming popular. Elegant cufflinks and tiepins were worn to complement fashionable formalwear or business wear. Thin silver and gold chains with small pendants and simple rings or bracelets were worn by some American men. African-American rap artists often wore layers of large chains with big medallions. Digital watches were the new rage in technology, and colorful plastic and rubber bands were a novelty item in the period.

Other

Suspenders and pocket squares regained popularity in formal and business wear to complete the polished professional look. Sunglasses and umbrellas became a designer item and were often purchased based on brand name. Sunglass frames were seen in a variety of colors, and lenses ranged from black to mirrored tints.

ALTERNATIVE FASHION MOVEMENTS

Preppy

Men as well as women adopted the identical preppy uniform described in Lisa Birnback's *The Official Preppy Handbook* (1980). The reference guide, a satirical look at upper-class boarding school life, provided the 1980s "me" decade of conspicuous consumption with the perfect bible of how to look like old-moneyed WASP society. Preps or preppies were individuals sent to college preparatory school or boarding school by their parents instead of public high schools. The preppy look was inspired from the conservative uniforms: navy blue blazers, button-down oxford shirts, polo shirts, khaki pants, monogrammed crewneck sweaters, and loafers. Preppies layered those elements, polo under oxford, both under a monogrammed crewneck sweater, or perhaps two under an oxford; whatever the combination, a must was always a starched collar standing straight up. Male and female preps both wore the same color palette of pink and Kelly green, as well as madras and tartan plaids. Turtle and whale motifs appeared on men's shirts, pants, and belts, as well as women's clothing. Popular purveyors of preppy fashions included L.L. Bean, Polo Ralph Lauren, and J. Crew. However, the pinnacle of preppy style was the Lacoste Izod alligator logo.

Punk

Male punk anti-fashion had the same nihilistic attitude as the female style and became as widespread in America as abroad. Slashed and torn clothes

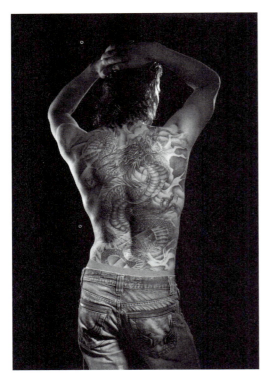

Tatoos started becoming commonplace for young people in the 1980s and into the 1990s, as shown by this tatooed man. [© Domenico Gelermo/ Dreamstime.com]

and T-shirts with graffiti designs or rebellious messages were worn along with items made out of vinyl, rubber, and leather. Thrift stores provided the basis for clothing that was altered to fit the punk motif. Punk music stars had a penchant for exposure and nudity and often displayed their body piercing and tattoos in public. Makeup was often worn by males whose hairstyles were usually colored or bleached, spiked, shaped into Mohawks, or shaved bald.

New Wave

Gender-bending fashion was imported from England, following on the steps of the 1970s glam rockers. Fashions were inspired by bright and lavishly decorated shirts, pants, and jackets, usually finished with velvet and lace decorations. Pop stars, such as Prince and Boy George, and bands, such as Duran Duran, heavily promoted and influenced new wave fashions for men. Men adopting the new wave look wore eyeliner, mascara, and lipstick and colored, highlighted, or bleached their long manes.

Rap and Hip-Hop

Urban fashion associated with rap and hip-hop music fans included Kangol hats, oversized T-shirts, loose baggy and drawstring pants, and track suits. The look was often accessorized with excessive gold chains and rings, leather medallions, large sunglasses, sweatbands, and crown hats. In some instances, men shaved words into their closely cropped hair or sported the fade haircut, high on top but cropped on the sides. High running shoes with untied shoelaces were worn, with a fondness for Adidas black and white striped sneakers. Break dancing experts, or B-boys, used some of the same elements but wore padded track suits in bright colors with protective pads.

Rastafarians

Followers of Rastafarian traditions and reggae music wore modest clothes, mostly made out of natural fibers, accessorized with objects such as African map medallions and beaded necklaces made out of the three colors used to identify the group: red, yellow, and green. T-shirts were usually bright and included complex designs, often featuring Bob Marley, the celebrated icon of reggae music. Dreadlocks were accompanied by Rasta-colored caps, also known as tams or kufis.

THE
1990s

FORMALWEAR

Silhouette

The silhouette for evening and formalwear moved to a more fitted, or European, cut in the 1990s. Jackets were narrower across the shoulders compared with the preceding decade. Double-breasted styles disappeared as the decade progressed. Tuxedos had fewer decorative elements and remained mostly black with basic white shirts.

Jackets and Vests

Long and wide plunging lapels were seen in both double- and single-breasted evening and tuxedo jackets. Most jackets had moderated side vents. In general, single-breasted one- or two-button suits were more popular than three-button suits, but three-button suits increased in popularity as the decade progressed. Vests enjoyed a return in popularity but remained simple for formalwear.

Shirts

Shirts for formalwear continued to be fitted, with long straight sleeves and deep cuffs. French cuffs with cufflinks became increasingly popular. Collars were either button style, wing-tipped, or spread. Shirts lost the pleats, ruffles, and pintucks of the previous decade and returned to simple flat fronts. Rarely were formal shirts anything but white.

Pants

Pleated pants were popular in the early part of the 1990s but were replaced by flat fronts as the decade progressed. Most pant legs were straight or tapered and without cuffs. Pant pockets were discreet slits, and satin braid trimmed the outseam of the pant leg.

Decorative Details

Following minimalist styles, formalwear showcased simple, classic lines without any embellishment. Tuxedos and suits were black, shirts were white, and cummerbunds and vests were rarely embellished or seen in colors other than black.

BUSINESS WEAR

Silhouette

The wide shoulder pads and wide lapels of the 1980s turned into the minimalist trend of the 1990s. Straight trousers with pleats paired with fitted jackets, typically in dark colors, were the norm for most of the 1990s. Contrasting fabrics and textures were also seen in the last part of the decade. Casual Fridays were a clear indication that the American business world was opening up to a more relaxed style in the office. Accordingly, suit pieces were often matched with elements of casual clothing, including jeans and polo shirts.

Jackets and Vests

Broad-shouldered jackets disappeared into a new soft, sloped shoulder line as part of the new slim, lean fit (Mendes and de la Haye 1999, 256). Single-breasted jackets were more common than double-breasted styles. Jackets typically had one or two buttons; however, the ultra trendy English and European cuts had three buttons. Blue blazers with slightly structured shoulders and traditional gold buttons were seen along with unconstructed sports jackets in light colors. Restrained patterns such as herringbone, houndstooth, tweeds, and plaids dominated suit and sport coats. Vests were occasionally worn to work.

Shirts

Corporate dress codes still called for white and light-colored shirts for top executives, but striped and checked shirts were widely worn by those on the lower rungs of the business ladder. Classic blue-striped shirts were popular and often offered contrasting collars and cuffs in white or other solid colors. Dress shirt collars came in a variety of shapes including button-down, banded, and spread. Straight collars, button cuffs, and simple pockets were the norm. Collarless shirts with small banded necklines were worn by some American men in the early 1990s, imitating a trend seen mostly in casual wear.

Pants

By the end of the 1990s, business wear was favoring pants with a slim look and no pleats or cuffs. Khakis and corduroy trousers were also widely worn for Casual Fridays paired with blazers and tailored shirts without ties. Wrinkle-free trousers were well-received by American businessmen.

Decorative Details

Most suits came in traditional solid and pinstripe patterns, but checks and plaids were also seen. Many American businesses accepted less-formal ties, including some displaying cartoon and comic images, unusual textures, and bright colors. Ties provided an element of self-expression and humor in the typical male wardrobe. In some less-formal business offices, men completely eliminated ties.

Military Uniforms

Additional developments in body armor, such as the use of ceramic plates and a resistant synthetic material known as Kevlar, increased protection for combat soldiers and provided them with lightweight materials for ease of movement (Newark 1998, 112). Cream-colored camouflage, popularly known as "chocolate chips," was incorporated during the Gulf War to increase protection for desert combat. Intercommunication devices were incorporated into several combat uniforms.

CASUAL WEAR

Silhouette

Casual wear was more openly accepted in the business world during the 1990s, and ideas such as Casual Friday were seen by many as an opportunity to showcase elegant sportswear. The silhouette was slimmer than in the early 1980s, with fitted jackets and sweaters and flat-front pants gaining an advantage over pleats. The most important change in the 1990s silhouette was the practice of garment layering adopted by American men. The new style allowed not only the layering of T-shirts, dress shirts, and jackets but endless variations such as long-sleeved knit shirts under polo shirts or a thin sweater below a short-sleeved woven shirt.

Jackets

Long lapels were incorporated into unstructured casual jackets with sloped shoulders. Blue blazers and light-colored sports jackets were matched equally with tailored trousers and jeans. Fabric vests were often worn as casual outerwear, and sweaters and cardigans kept classic lines and were available in stripes or color-blocked patterns.

Shirts

Turtleneck and polo shirts continued enjoying popularity for casual men's wear as did plaid flannel shirts. Retro bowling shirts and other cabana-style short-sleeve button-down shirts without tails were fashionable alternatives to standard button-down shirts. Color blocking and bold stripes were used in long- or short-sleeved knit shirts and popularized by brands such as Tommy Hilfiger. T-shirts and tank tops were worn under jackets or as outerwear, and some were manufactured in bright colors. Muscle shirts reached the fashionable status in the 1990s when several designers and stores created lines taking advantage of new stretch fabrics available for sportswear.

Pants

Flat-front, narrow-legged pants dominated men's casual wear, and pleats were completely out of fashion by the end of the 1990s. The versatility and appeal of cargo pants, either long or short, made them a staple item for young men, along with camouflage pants, corduroys, and khakis. Torn and distressed jeans remained popular in the period, with wide boot-cut legs becoming prevalent.

Decorative Details

Black was often referred to as "the color of the 1990s," and it came in and out of fashion in fast cycles. Comfortable and easy-care fabrics were favored in casual wear. Overall styles might have been simple, but often fabrics were luxurious, including cashmere, mohair, and silk. The newly available microfibers were used in bomber jackets and hoodies, and micro-suede was used in shirts. Sports team logos were embroidered or printed on items such as jerseys, track suits, and baseball hats.

"Sportswear." Fans spent millions of dollars in the 1990s on officially licensed apparel, identifying their favorite teams from the major professional sports leagues including the National Football League, Major League Baseball, the National Hockey League, the National Basketball Association, and the National Association for Stock Car Auto Racing. Sports apparel with identifying logos included a wide range of products such as T-shirts, baseball hats, shorts, headbands, socks, and shoes. World Wrestling Entertainment (WWE), previously known as the World Wrestling Federation, was one of the most successful sport licensing enterprises of the late twentieth century. The company, primarily own by Vince McMahon, organized live wrestling events and promoted them on television and the internet. The popularity of WWE during the 1990s created a bonanza for brand promotion, product sales, and licensing of products featuring the company's logos as well as images of famous wrestlers such as The Rock, Chyna, and "Stone Cold" Steve Austin.

OUTERWEAR

Coats

Trench, Mackintosh, and other kinds of overcoats worn in the 1990s were essentially similar to those of the previous decade with one marked difference: the structure of the upper chest after the shoulder pads were removed. In general, overcoats followed the same softening of the shoulder line as other men's wear. Overall, colors and patterns were more subdued than those of the 1980s.

Other garments

Sweaters, as well as denim and windbreaker jackets, returned to fitted styles with less patterning and more restraint in coloring. Hooded Adirondack or barn coats with water-repellent finishes and plaid flannel linings were popular during the period, especially those from J. Crew and Eddie Bauer. Lightweight spring jackets, inspired by golf wear, were a popular form of casual outerwear. Leather blazers and shearling jackets also enjoyed some popularity.

SWIMWEAR AND SPORTSWEAR

Swimwear

By the 1990s, board shorts with bold prints and floral motifs were widely seen on American beaches and in swimming pools. This style of swim trunks was longer and wider than most male bathing items seen in the twentieth century, reaching at times below the knee and often having a baggy appearance. Shorter and more fitted swimwear styles, more popular in other parts of the world, were less prevalent in America. Trunk-style swim shorts, similar to the Brazilian sunga, were successfully promoted in the gay market.

Golf

Casual polo shirts and pleated shorts and pants remained the standard for male golfers. Colors in the 1990s were subdued, with tan and earth tones used for bottoms and solid primary colors in tops. Argyle, checks, and stripes were seen on sweaters and vests. Baseball caps and visors with apparel and sporting gear manufacturer logos were worn typically worn by amateurs and professionals alike.

Tennis

Just like women's tennis apparel, white continued to dominate male tennis clothes. The 1990s, however, saw the further popularization of subtle color coordination, with black, red, and blue accents incorporated into shorts, shirts, and wristbands. Amateur players wore a variety of casual styles, including polo knit shirts, sweaters, and pullovers with simple patterns matched with shorts and long pants.

Skiwear

Professional athletes continued to benefit from new technologically enhanced fabrics, including Activent, Durepel, Entrant, Sympatex, and Ultrex. Professional skiers wore fitted one-piece ski suits. Amateur skiers wore coordinating separates, not matching ensembles as in previous decades. Ski pants and jackets were lined and padded for warmth but were not as bulky as in previous decades, thanks to the new hollow-core fibers. Polar fleece jackets were also popular alternatives to sweaters or for warmth under jacket shells. The sport of snowboarding was also gaining popularity, and ski apparel was being adapted to suit the needs of the new sport.

Other Activewear

In-line skating and skateboarding enjoyed popularity among young American men who wore long shorts, jeans, and cargo pants matched with T-shirts, hooded jackets, or other types of tops, along with protective pads and helmets. Lycra bike shorts were worn by themselves or under loose and longer types of shorts, especially for basketball. Diving suits or wet suits became more affordable and were used also for wind surfing and triathlons.

UNDERWEAR AND INTIMATE APPAREL

Undergarments

In the 1990s, men's fashion magazines continued polling their readers about their preferred type of undergarments, returning results that showed that American men were divided equally among the use of briefs, boxers, and boxer briefs. Boxer briefs were a new form of fitted brief with legs being extended over the upper thighs that were introduced in the 1990s. Bold colors and patterns were less popular. Black, navy and heather gray were the most common colors. However, some undergarments did have color-blocked sections, colored seams, and colored front pouches. Thongs, string briefs, and bikinis were considerably less popular. Patterned shiny boxers made out of silk or silk-like synthetics were very common during the period and became a novelty item often offered as a gift on special occasions such as Christmas and Valentine's Day.

Sleepwear

Cotton pajama bottoms matched with T-shirts or Henley tops remained the main choice in the American male market. Sets of cotton and flannel crew sweatshirts and pants were also worn for sleepwear. Silk pajama sets enjoyed some popularity in this period. Long-sleeved nightshirts, bath robes, and lounge robes were seen less frequently. Those that were available were in solid colors, simple patterns, or color blocks, occasionally in satin fabrics or velvet.

HEADWEAR, HAIRSTYLES, AND COSMETICS

Headwear

Baseball hats remained an important element in casual wear for young Americans, whether they were worn with the flap to the side, the back, or the front. Do-rags, bandanas, and other types of head wraps were seen in the African-American community, whereas western hats remained a staple of country music stars and fans.

Hairstyles

Trendy hairstyles for young American men in the 1990s resembled the 1980s well-groomed looks but often experimented with designer cuts and hair products to increase volume and create spiked peaks. More men began to highlight or color their hair. The popularity of surfer-inspired haircuts, with long bangs and shaggy cuts, allowed men to sport fashionable looks that were also accepted in the office environment. Men frequently sported the "right-out-of-bed" hairstyle, with short hair simply arranged by hand with the minimal amounts of product to purposely create a "messy" or tousled look.

In the early 1990s, young men and college students grew goatees. A number of variations were possible, ranging from neatly trimmed goatees to soul patches to goatees with a long strand of hair at the chin. The "five-o'clock shadow" look was popular, a look in which men kept a trim nascent beard. Long sideburns were popular among young Americans. Alternative hairstyles such as Mohawks, dreadlocks, and military cuts were still seen in the United States.

Cosmetics

By the 1990s, men could choose from a variety of shaving tools that incorporated two, three, and even four layers of blades plus lubricating strips and pivoting capabilities. Fake tanning products and skincare creams were also abundant and often incorporated chemical and physical sun blockers to protect against UVA and UVB rays. Men's skincare lines continued to expand, and day spas, specializing in skincare for men, were found in major metropolitan areas such as New York, Chicago, and Los Angeles.

FOOTWEAR AND LEGWEAR

Footwear

Classic styles remained the norm in formal shoes during the 1990s. Most shoes were broad and square. Top stitching was often used as a decorative element, particularly on the front cap-toe section of the shoe. Penny loafers and tasseled loafers were used as an alternative for less formal occasions. Cushioning insoles were widely used for comfort or therapeutic purposes. Vintage sneakers appeared in the American market and competed with a variety of new styles that displayed technological improvements or elaborated detailing such as air pumps and lighted soles. Shoes for snowboarding and skateboarding were worn with casual wear along with stylish hiking boots. Open-toe sandals such as Birkenstocks, with adjustable leather straps, and Tevas, with adjustable Velcro bands, were also popular during the period.

Legwear

Most legwear for the period was simple. Dark ribbed and discreetly patterned socks were used for formal, business, and casual dress, whereas white remained the dominant color in sport socks. Ankle-high sport socks were used by younger generations, particularly while wearing shorts. Reinforced, cushioned, and thermal socks remained available in the market for specialty sports activities such as running, skiing, or tennis.

NECKWEAR AND OTHER ACCESSORIES

Neckwear

In general, ties were wider and came in matte finishes as opposed to the shiny looks from the previous decade. Although most ties were available in subdued patterns, it was also possible to obtain neckties with cartoon characters, art and architecture samplings, carpet patterns, and even science-inspired designs. Neckties continued to provide men with a creative outlet for their wardrobe. Clip-on ties were available in the American market, and many men opted to go tieless for casual and semiformal occasions.

Jewelry

Moderate and conservative styles of watches, bracelets, and chains prevailed. Retro or vintage watches were worn with metal, leather, or rubber straps. Earrings, studs, and other body piercings continued enjoying popularity. Bead necklaces and pendants on fabric or leather cords were worn by younger men. Hip-hop artists displayed large amounts of gold and diamond (or rhinestone) jewelry, usually referred to as bling-bling.

Other

Designer sunglasses remained popular and offered protection for UVA rays. Vintage and reversible belts were worn, and narrower trendy shoulder bags were accepted as appropriately masculine. Tattoos continued growing in popularity.

ALTERNATIVE FASHION MOVEMENTS

Goth

Goth male fashions, dominated by the color black and inspired by historic styles, were less elaborate but just as striking as their female counterparts' garb. Black pants and shirts were accompanied by high shoes, spiked dog collars, and wallet chains. Hair was usually dyed black and built up or totally shaven. Some goth men wore skirts and kilts and used white makeup and black eyeliner. Other influences seen in goth subculture included vampire capes or shirts and cyber-goth looks created with synthetic metallic fibers and bleached hair. Although leather and fetish elements were incorporated occasionally by goths, these were usually associated more closely with a segment of the gay subculture, which adopted leather, rubber, and vinyl attire, complemented by straps, chains, caps, black boots, chaps, and even corset-like fitted tops.

Grunge

Grunge music's male fans danced frantically in the mosh pit sporting a disheveled look with worn-out or homemade clothing. Flannel button-down long-sleeve shirts, layered with a T-shirt or a denim vest, were common, as were oversized sweaters and hooded jackets. Baggy jeans, corduroy pants, or cargo pants in camouflage patterns were often ripped and torn and worn below the natural waistline, making boxer shorts visible. Doc Martens and vintage tennis shoes such as Converse and Vans were the preferred footwear.

Hip-Hop

Hip-hop stars and fans continued wearing oversized shirts, baggy pants, baseball hats, and track suits. Extreme styles that carried over from the late 1980s included the reversed pants worn by musical duo Kriss-Kross

Rock band Nirvana pioneered the "grunge look." From left: Krist Novoselic, Kurt Cobain, and Dave Grohl. [Courtesy of Photofest]

and the low-crotch baggy trousers popularized by MC Hammer. Rappers proudly displayed oversized garments with the menacing XXL label and excessive amounts of gold chains and other oversized gold jewelry. As the decade progressed, baggy pants continued to be worn lower and lower on the hips, displaying the tops of boxer briefs, which typically sported a designer's name on the waistband. Designing clothes for the hip-hop market became big business, and soon labels such as FUBU and Karl Kani, along with those developed by entertainers such as Sean Puffy Combs (Sean John) and Russell Simmons (Phat Farm), were being carried in mainstream department stores across the United States.

Ravers

Electronic music continued enjoying popularity, and house music fans often wore 1970s-inspired items such as colorfully printed bright shirts, logo T-shirts, and tight short pants. Ravers, young adults who danced to strong beats at large private parties while often experimenting with the drug ecstasy, wore T-shirts with mottos, psychedelic prints, and other hippie-inspired elements. Bright or glow-in-the-dark clothes and fluorescent jewelry were also an important component, particularly for those interested in creating dance effects with fluorescent lights.

THE
2000s

FORMALWEAR

Silhouette

Formalwear for men continued the slim-cut trend begun in the 1990s. Overall pant and jacket silhouettes became even more fitted. Single-breasted tuxedos became dominant for black-tie events. Tailcoats and classic cutaway styles were used only in very formal occasions, particularly weddings. The casual culture of the 1990s exerted its influence on formal events in the new millennium, resulting in the acceptance of suits and dinner jackets for formal activities rather than tuxedos.

Hip-hop star and fashion designer P. Diddy wears his signature style at the MTV Video Music Awards, 2003. [AP / Wide World Photos]

Jackets and Vests

Classic tuxedo and dinner jackets remained the choice for formalwear, with single-breasted, three-button styles becoming predominant. Jackets still showed long lapels faced with satin. Vests retained the classic shape but were manufactured in a wider variety of colors.

Shirts

Tuxedo shirts with fine pleats continued being worn for formalwear, as did plain-front shirts. Shirt collars were typically wing-tipped or spread, with fitted sleeves and either deep cuffs or French cuffs. White was still the dominant color choice.

Pants

Tuxedo pants retained the flat-front, tapered leg of previous decades with satin trim or braid on the outseam.

Decorative Details

Pinstriped, paisley, and colored vests and cummerbunds were worn to add flair to traditional tuxedos. Black bow ties were the preferred match for tuxedos, but four-in-hand ties were also donned occasionally. Neckwear often matched the pattern and color of the vest and/or the cummerbund.

BUSINESS WEAR

Silhouette

Business retained the fitted silhouette of the 1990s with more moderate shoulder pads. Trousers were slim, straight legs, with or without cuffs. The overall appearance was long and lean.

Jackets and Vest

Single- and double-breasted suit jackets with two or three buttons came mostly in dark colors, although khaki, light gray, and lighter blue shades were also seen. Single-breasted styles dominated the business wear trends, and three-button European-cut jackets were preferred by trendy businessmen. However, American men who adopted the European cut often kept the lower button of the suit jacket undone. Navy jackets, wool sport coats, and blazers were also worn for more casual office wear. As an alternative to jackets, some men wore fine wool or cashmere sweaters over a dress shirt and tie.

Shirts

Solid button-down shirts with straight collars remained popular, with white and blue dominating the palette, but several other color combinations were available, ranging from subdued tones to vivid bold colors. Upscale businessmen preferred to mix bold vertically striped shirts with pinstripe suits. Spread and point collars were also common, with widespread collars considered more fashion forward. Several American manufactures eliminated front pockets from dress shirts.

Pants

Pants were primarily flat front, but some styles included pleats. Pockets were invisible side slits on the front or welts on the back. Some designers experimented with included tabs or other decorative elements on the waistbands of pants. Slim-cut pants with tapered legs were worn without cuffs, whereas fuller-cut legs typically ended in cuffs.

Decorative Details

A variety of fabric textures and patterns were used in men's suits, including plaids, checks, pinstripes, and herringbone. Bold color and pattern combinations in ties were combined with striped and checked shirts. Gold, red, turquoise, and orange ties were mixed with multicolored striped or checked shirts to create striking combinations. Wide tone-on-tone striped pants added further visual interest to the fashion-forward ensembles.

Military Uniforms

Military uniforms witnessed minor changes at the beginning of the new millennium. Basic forms from the 1990s were retained and upgraded with improved waterproof and flame-retardant finishes and digital camouflage.

CASUAL WEAR

Silhouette

The layered look remained popular in the early twenty-first century, with an emphasis on a long, narrow silhouette. American men showcased a sense of postmodern freedom by using garments in nontraditional ways. Tuxedo shirts, for example, were paired with jeans or corduroy pants, whereas tuxedo pants could be matched with turtlenecks or designer T-shirts.

Jackets

Corduroy sport coats, velvet blazers, and cotton twill jackets were popular in casual wear. Motocross-style jackets with narrow band collars, tweed sports coats, and pinstripe suit jackets were also regularly paired with casual trousers. In most cases, all of these jackets were single breasted and fitted. Sweaters and cardigans were available in a variety of patterns and colors, with argyle patterns making a return to fashion.

Shirts

Solid, striped, checked, and patterned button-down shirts in a variety of muted and bright colors were typically worn with jeans or khakis at the turn of the century. Typically, the shirt tails were not tucked in, and often the top two buttons were left open displaying the neckline of the undershirt. Polo shirts, turtlenecks, and striped Henley knit tops were also seen for casual wear. Fitted distressed T-shirts and colorfully bold printed tank tops and muscle shirts became a fashionable item among younger American men. Vintage prints on T-shirts were successfully marketed by several American manufacturers, including American Eagle and Old Navy.

Pants

Tailored flat-front pants with narrow pockets with or without cuffs were worn slightly shorter than in past eras to reveal colorful and patterned socks. Cargo pants and distressed jeans remained popular. Denim was occasionally embellished or embroidered on the pockets. Reversible jeans were introduced in the market in 2005.

Decorative Details

Argyle, houndstooth, herringbone, stripes, and madras patterns were seen throughout casual men's wear. Pattern mixing became a fashionable practice where, for instance, striped pants could be matched with a paisley shirt and a solid scarf. Colors ranged from bright to muted shades, paired with either brown or black.

OUTERWEAR

Coats

Topcoats retained basic lines from the 1980s and 1990s, extending below the knees and mostly worn in shades of black and navy blue. Double-breasted pea coats were offered with a variety of collars, pockets, finishes, and lining choices. Finer fabrics, particularly cashmere, were the choice of American businessmen for outerwear.

Other Garments

Zippered Barbour coats, inspired by barn and hunting jackets, featured heavy-duty zippers, sturdy pockets, and drain holes for water and were used as outdoor activewear. Cardigan and cable-knit sweaters were also worn in the new millennium, along with hooded sweaters, suede shearling coats, and corduroy coats. Leather coats, in biker or blazer styles, were regularly worn for casual wear. Denim and canvas jackets also returned to fashion.

SWIMWEAR AND SPORTSWEAR

Swimwear

Board shorts remained the most popular type of swimsuit, sometimes featuring multiple pockets such as those seen on cargo pants. Fitted and shorter styles of swimsuits included trunk shorts, bikini suits, and Speedo briefs. Some trendy American men wore sarongs and other types of wraps as cover-ups. Nylon and spandex bodysuits, known as "jammers," were worn by casual and competitive athletes for speed advantage.

Golf

Pleated pants and shorts in earth tones continued being worn with long- or short-sleeved polo knit shirts. Colorful floral prints and stripes also appeared in shirts and outerwear. Fleece pullovers, solid or patterned vests, and windbreaker jackets were donned along with specialized thermal-control gloves, if weather required.

Tennis

White shirts and pants were accented with a variety of other colors for tennis wear. Polo-collared shirts, crewneck shirts, and sleeveless muscle shirts were all seen on the tennis courts. Long nylon pants and fleece jackets were worn in winter months.

Skiwear

Layering for protection and fashion became highly important in skiwear. The outer layer was often composed of windproof and waterproof jackets or parkas that were quilted, insulated, or trimmed in synthetic fur. Shirts varied from thermal crew tops to fashionable turtlenecks and were worn over thermal underwear. New high-performance fabrics included Supplex, Tactel, and Taslan. As snowboarding became more prominent, wild graffiti patterns and bold geometric patterns appeared in ski jackets and pants. Whether for skiing or boarding, pants and jackets were rarely worn in matching patterns.

UNDERWEAR AND INTIMATE APPAREL

Undergarments

Forms of men's underwear witnessed little change at the start of the new millennium. Classic briefs, knit boxer briefs, as well as woven or knit boxers were all equally popular. Retailers and designers continued turning boxers and boxer briefs into fashion trends through the use of pattern. Trendy low-rise pants, particularly those worn by urban youths, exposed portions of the briefs, providing designers with a new canvas for designer logos, tartan plaids, cartoons, and graffiti. Although some men welcomed the display of their undergarments, other men opted to select low-rise briefs to prevent the unwanted exhibition. Microfiber and stretch fibers were used for briefs, T-shirts, and muscle shirts.

Sleepwear

Although traditional pajamas are still available, many men opted for playfully patterned cotton or fleece pajama bottoms paired with sweatshirts or T-shirts for nightwear. Others wore the same T-shirts, sweatshirts, and pants they would wear for athletic activity. Luxurious white Turkish cotton terrycloth robes, silk robes, and cotton flannel robes in all-over patterns or plaids were also available.

HEADWEAR, HAIRSTYLES, AND COSMETICS

Headwear

Baseball hats remained the headwear of choice during the period. Kangol and beanie knit caps were worn in winter months, whereas do-rags, bandanas, and other types of head wraps were widespread among urban youth groups.

Hairstyles

Well-groomed hair usually short on the sides and built up on top was prevalent among American men. Other styles, including sharp military buzz cuts, short faux Mohawks, mullets, pompadours, and long bangs were also seen. Sideburns amongst younger men were usually long, but short sideburn clips were also seen. Facial hair was rare, but some young men wore a patch of hair under their lips, usually referred to as a "soul patch."

Cosmetics

The market for hair products remained strong in the last decades of the twentieth century and into the twentieth-first century. Hair gel was offered in a variety of strengths and consistencies. Hair coloring products designed for men were available for full coverage and highlights. The market was also flooded with a variety of products to strengthen hair and prevent hair loss. In the 2000s, the term metrosexual was assigned to men who openly focused on personal grooming, including trips to the hair salon, day spa, and nail technician. Haircare and facial protection products remained popular, and new kinds of post-shaving toners, balsams, and soothers were introduced. Some designers developed makeup products for men wanting to cover blemishes and other imperfections and improve their overall look.

FOOTWEAR AND LEGWEAR

Footwear

By the 2000s, fashionable men were matching designer leather sandals with casual and semiformal apparel. Colorful and patterned Teva sandals were worn in informal occasions. Oxford lace-ups and loafers remained the style of choice for business wear. Many dress shoes had blunt square toes with decorative topstitching. The popularity of military looks made combat boots and shoes with camouflage fabric trendy. Shoes inspired by bowling styles with colored laces, decorative stripes, and complex designs, such as those created by Diesel and Skechers, were popular particularly with college students. Suede lace-up shoes and lace-less pull-on boots were also trendy in the new millennium.

Legwear

Casual and dress socks remained virtually unchanged from the previous decade and were offered in a broad range of colors and patterns. Colored and patterned socks provided men, who no longer wore neckties to the office each day, with the opportunity to make a fashion statement. Some technological developments in socks included antimicrobial finishes to stop odor and redistributed cushioning to avoid blisters.

NECKWEAR AND OTHER ACCESSORIES

Neckwear

Ties continued to narrow in width. Silk ties were popular, but blends of silk, wool, and synthetics were also available. Shiny solid ties were very popular in the early 2000s but trended toward patterns and textures in matte finishes as the millennium progressed.

Jewelry

More designers emerged to produce lines of male jewelry in the new millennium. Leather bands or bracelets, tags, small pendants, and cufflinks were typical men's accessories. Expensive watches, frequently with square faces, such as Rolex, or aeronautical watches were the most common male accessory. Charity plastic wristbands, such as Lance Armstrong's Live Strong band, were worn by many men to show affiliation with a cause.

Other

Solid or striped scarves in fine fabrics such as cashmere regained popularity. Other vintage-inspired accessories popular in the period included leather and brass key chains, horn frames in glasses, and military-inspired striped canvas belts. The biggest impact, however, was created by the adoption of technological devices as a new generation of accessories related to iPods, BlackBerries, global positioning system devices, and cellular phones was integrated into apparel and accessories by trendy American men.

ALTERNATIVE FASHION MOVEMENTS

Hip-Hop

Hip-hop fashion in the twenty-first century evolved into a variety of styles, including the pimp look of the ghetto-fabulous style. Luxurious oversized designer coats trimmed in fur, striking jewelry, alligator- or snake-skin shoes, and custom-made hats created a fantastic look for stars and fans alike (Chandler and Chandler-Smith 2005, 243). Gold and diamonds (or rhinestone) provided the bling-bling necessary to properly accessorize the ghetto-fabulous look.

Neo-bohemian and Retro-chic

Neo-bohemian and retro-chic styles, dominant in female fashion, were also seen in male apparel in which sarongs, kilts, and other forms of skirts became popular among some groups. Eastern and new age influences were observed in jewelry, piercings, tattoos, and T-shirts. Vintage hats, capes, and shirts were adopted along with tie-dyed or embroidered garments. Other styles appropriated by the bohemian chic trend included denim or leather biker jackets and vests, Latin-American ponchos and textiles, and beaded or embroidered materials inspired by Middle Eastern and Far East cultures.

REFERENCES

Baker, (1991) *Fashions of a Decade: The 1950s*. New York: Facts on File.

Carnegy, V. (1990) *Fashions of a Decade: The 1980s*. New York: Facts on File.

Chandler, R. M., Chandler-Smith, N. (2005) *Flava in Ya Gear: Transgressive Politics and the Influence of Hip-Hop on Contemporary Fashion*. Twentieth-Century American Fashion. New York: Berg.

McNab, C. (2000) *Modern Military Uniforms*. London: Chartwell Books.

Mendes, V., de la Haye, A. (1999) *20th Century Fashion*. London: Thames and Hudson.

Newark, T. (1998) *Brassey's Book of Uniforms*. 1st English edition. London: Brassey's.

Payne, B., Winakor, G., Farrell-Beck, J. (1992) *The History of Costume: From Ancient Mesopotamia through the Twentieth Century*. 2nd edition. New York: HarperCollins.

Steele, V. (1997) *Fifty Years of Fashion: New Look to Now*. New Haven, CT: Yale University Press.

Tortora, G., Eubank, K. (2005) *Survey of Historic Costume: A History of Western Dress*. 4th edition. New York: Fairchild Publications.

9

Children's Fashions

Two major factors distinguished children's fashions in the last half of the twentieth century from those in the first half: the suburbs and television. The shift to the suburbs not only signified a change in living styles in the United States, it also signified a change in family structure. Men worked, women stayed home, and children, for the first time, were children. Whereas children in the last half of the twentieth century had chores and homework, for most middle-class families, children were no longer required to contribute to the household income, complete cross-stitch samplers, practice singing and piano (unless they wanted to), or generally behave as miniature adults. Children were now seen and heard and, as the decade progressed, began to keep their own very full social calendar.

Television was a major change agent for the role of children and communicated how children should act and dress. In the 1950s, *The Mickey Mouse Club* and *Leave It to Beaver* provided the model for ideal children, whereas families in the 1960s and 1970s turned to *The Brady Bunch* and *The Partridge Family*. The 1980s and 1990s had their role models, too. *Family Ties*, *The Cosby Show*, and others reflected how America thought families should be, even if at times they were far from accurate depictions.

With children's new role came new wardrobes and a new category of clothing: play clothes. As society was slowly becoming less formal, children's clothing reflected that transformation. In the 1950s, children still dressed "appropriately" for school, dresses for girls and chinos for boys, and then came home and changed into play clothes, jeans and T-shirts or special costumes. By the 1960s, restrictions began to ease, especially for girls who began wearing pants to school for the first time, but play clothes were still a separate class of after-school attire worn for running around in the yard. By the 1970s, perhaps because of the economic recession or the increase in working mothers, the line between school clothing and play clothing became blurred. Children rarely wore anything except jeans and knit tops to schools; even girls had abandoned dresses and skirts for school clothes. From this point forward, children simply had clothing, not two wardrobes, one for school and one for play. This trend continued through the end of the century, even when the economic upturn in the 1980s meant that parents were increasingly purchasing designer clothing for their children.

THE
1950s

FORMALWEAR: CHILDREN TO PRETEEN

Silhouette

Little girls always dressed up for church and for birthday parties. The prevailing dress form for young girls consisted of short, full skirts supported by nylon petticoats, fitted waists with a sash tied in a bow at the center back, and short puffy sleeves. Little boys were dressed like miniature men in suits but donned short pants rather than full-length trousers until school aged.

Girls' Ensembles

For formal occasions, girls primarily wore dresses, not skirt and blouse ensembles. The skirt of the dress was a full circle, gathered into a narrow waist. The skirt was supported by nylon netting or tulle petticoat or multiple layers of ruffles and typically ended at mid-thigh for young girls and above the knee for preteens. Gathered waistlines were concealed with large satin sashes that were tied in large full bows at the center back. Fitted bodices buttoned down the center back and had full puffed sleeves, finished with narrow bands and round necklines. Necklines were often finished with small, rounded Peter Pan collars in the same fabric as the dress, in lace, or trimmed with lace or ruffles.

Boys' Ensembles

Young boys typically wore navy blue suits with white cotton button-front shirts and silk or rayon clip-on bow ties for formal occasions. Young boys paired navy blue blazers with short pants, whereas older school-aged boys donned full-length cuffed trousers. Folded pocket squares or handkerchiefs and suspenders completed the look. Some children's wear manufacturers sold clip-on bow ties with dress shirts.

Decorative Details

Ruffles, lace, and ribbon provided the decorative details in little girls' dresses. Dresses were fabricated in satin and taffeta from rayon or silk in solid pastel colors. Pastel pinks, blues, yellows, and greens, as well as white, dominated the color palette. In addition to ruffles, small embroidered floral motifs also provided surface decoration. Boys' suits were primarily fashioned from wool gabardine; however, the new trend for wash-and-wear resulted in some suits being fabricated from a rayon/nylon gabardine. Dark colors dominated suits and were typically paired with a white shirt. Pocket squares, bow ties, and suspenders provided an outlet for checked and striped patterns in blue, red, or green.

FORMALWEAR: TEEN TO COLLEGE

Silhouette

Young women tried to appear as glamorous as movie stars, such as Elizabeth Taylor. Prom and debutante dresses were soft, feminine, and romantic with tea-length (below mid-calf) or full-length skirts. Strapless gowns with sweetheart bodice in either the bouffant or princess style dominated young women's formalwear. Bouffant skirt silhouettes had a full, balloon-like skirt gathered into a waist seam. The princess silhouette was created with princess seams that allowed for a fitted silhouette throughout the torso, without a waist seam. Young men's suits mirrored the "continental" suit style of adult males, with slim-fit single-button jackets and pleated trousers. A young man's first tuxedo, purchased for prom, maintained the same single-breasted styling, with either rounded shawl or traditional lapels and pleated trousers, as adult males.

Girls' Ensembles

Although nice girls would never dream of wearing anything sexy, the most popular formalwear in the fifties was strapless. Strapless bodices, with either a straight or sweetheart neckline, were often covered with sheer chiffon or organza overlays or topped with a removable sheer bolero jacket to provide a more modest appearance. Spaghetti straps or tank-style bodices were also popular. Strapless bodices either cut across the back just below the shoulder blades or dipped low, tapering down to the small of the back.

Full skirts, either gathered into a waist seam or created with princess seams and gores, were either tea length or full length, depending on the social occasion. Full, voluminous skirts were created by layering nylon netting or tulle under satin, taffeta, or lace. Fitted bodices were shaped through structural seams, such as darts, and sculpted on the interior with boning or stays, to create an hourglass figure.

Boys' Ensembles

Black tuxedos and dark navy suits were the standard issue for young men's formalwear. The conservative styles that dominated men's formalwear were also apparent in their younger counterparts. Jackets, whether suit or tuxedo, were single-breasted jackets, with either no vent or a single center back vent, and flap pockets. Lapels were narrow and pointed for suit jackets and slim and rounded for tuxedo jackets. Pants were slim fitting, with front pleats and cuffs. Tuxedo pants had the addition of a satin band or braid on the outseam of the trouser leg. Basic white shirts, with or without pleated fronts, completed the formalwear look for both suits and tuxedos.

Decorative Details

Surface decoration was minimal in young women's formalwear. Small waist sashes with bows or rosettes adorned narrow waistlines or small ruffles or rosettes trimmed skirt hems. Strapless bodices were adorned with rhinestone brooches or clips. Visual interest was provided through the fabrics themselves; taffeta, satin, organza, and tulle were woven with metallic threads, warp-dyed floral patterns, palliates, sequins, and glitter. Dark gabardine suits and tuxedos for young men were complemented by cummerbunds, cufflinks, shirt studs, suspenders, pocket squares, and bowties for decorative interest.

CASUAL WEAR: CHILDREN TO PRETEEN

Preteen Silhouette

The clean-cut all-American image prevailed in children's casual wear during the 1950s. Children's casual clothing became less restrictive than in past periods but still seemed somewhat formal by today's standards. Girls still predominantly wore dresses for casual wear, and boys wore chinos and button-down shirts. Play clothes, worn after school or on the weekends, provided a much more relaxed wardrobe for children, including jeans, shorts, and knit shirts for both young boys and young girls.

Girls' Ensembles

Dresses and Skirts: New designs in the 1950s took into consideration the growing needs of a child, and, although dress clothes were still restrictive, play clothes and school clothes now allowed for movement and overall comfort of the child. Girls' skirts were full circles fitted at the waist. Self-tie sashes, patch pockets, and appliqués, including the ubiquitous felt poodle appliqué, were typical adornments. Ric-rac, braid, and ribbons trimmed hemlines and pockets. Skirts were made from stiff fabrics such as corduroy, quilting, wool, cotton, and felt and were supported by petticoats or crinolines and came in every color imaginable. When paired with saddle shoes and white ankle socks with cuffs, known as bobby socks, preteen girls were dubbed "bobby-soxers" (Sills 2005, 37).

Pants: Slacks and shorts were strictly for playtime for girls in the 1950s; it was simply not acceptable for a young girl to wear pants to school (Sills 2005, 36). Shorts were usually part of a matched set, paired with a coordinating blouse. Shorts and tops may be of the same fabric or sold in complementary colors and patterns, sharing common piping or trims. Shorts were slim fit with a banded waist, with either zippers or buttons. Young girls, like adults, wore Bermuda shorts with knee socks. A popular alternative to shorts were pedal pushers or clam diggers, pants that fell several inches below the knee with large patch pockets with flaps. Slacks and jeans were not worn to school, birthday parties, or other occasions, only for after-school playtime. Slacks came in a variety of colors and fabrics, including cotton twill and corduroy. Both slacks and jeans had long straight legs, but jeans typically had rolled-up cuffs.

Tops: An assortment of shirts and sweaters were paired with skirts and slacks for young girls. Simple cotton blouses were embellished with ruffles, smocking, embroidery, and lace. The rounded Peter Pan collar was the standard for young girls. Although straight long and short sleeves were common, short puffy sleeves were very popular, especially under jumpers or bibbed pants. Two-toned cotton western-style shirts with multicolored embroidered yokes were popular for after school with jean and cotton twill chinos. Sleeveless cotton blouses without collars were popular for summertime play outfits to coordinate with shorts and pedal pushers. Cotton blouses came in a wide range of colors and patterns, including plaid and madras. For fall, wool button-down cardigan sweaters and crewneck pullover sweaters topped blouses. Sweaters were often decorated with embroidery and appliqués.

Boys' Ensembles

Pants: School clothes looked like a miniature of Dad's weekend clothes with slacks and a cotton plaid button-down shirt. For school, cotton twill chinos and corduroys had banded waistbands, side inseam pockets, and straight legs with cuffs. Dungarees or jeans were not typically worn to school by young boys; they were reserved for playtime. The complement to any playtime cowboy outfit was a pair of chaps worn over jeans. For extra warmth during winter play, dungarees were lined with plaid cotton flannel, which was displayed on rolled-up cuffs. Young boys wore shorts for summer play. Just like young girls, shorts for young boys were often sold in sets with matching or coordinating tops.

Tops: Button-down cotton shirts in solid colors, novelty patterns, or plaids were worn for school, as were two-toned western-style shirts with multicolored embroidered yokes. For winter, cotton was replaced with flannel for classic school looks. Wide arrays of knit shirts were commonly worn for after-school playtime. Long- and short-sleeve knit shirts, either T-shirts or polo style, were knitted with wide horizontal stripes or screen printed with western scenes or Walt Disney characters. Knit shirts were colorful and covered with either geometric patterns or other novelty motifs such as fish, horses, baseballs, and skis. Some screen print knit shirts had elaborate western scenes that resembled popular shows such as *The Lone Ranger* or *Gunsmoke*. Cable-knit sweaters and cardigans were worn over woven and knit shirts for warmth during the winter for both school and play. Geometric patterns, snowflakes, argyles, and other novelty motifs were knit into wool and nylon sweaters for young boys.

Scouting in America was very popular in the 1950s. Cubs wore blue uniforms (slacks and long-sleeved button shirt) with yellow trim and neckerchief. A matching cap with a bill was always worn outdoors. Boy Scouts wore olive drab uniforms with campaign caps. In warmer climates, Bermuda shorts with matching olive knee socks could be worn. Both Cub Scouts and Boy Scouts proudly donned their uniforms to wear to school on troop meeting days.

CASUAL WEAR: TEEN TO COLLEGE

Silhouette

Clothing for teens became an important market during the fifties. The college prep, or preppy, look dominated the teen and college market during the decade, and retailers capitalized on the trend by developing their own labels and brand images based on the college prep look. The Bobbie Brooks label became the dominant brand for college prep fashions for young women, and Sears promoted the Fraternity Prep label for young men. Whether male or female, mainstream American youths aspired to appear clean-cut, proper, and well mannered at all times. Trim bodices, very full knee-length skirts, and boxy jackets or blouses with pencil-straight skirts were the hallmark of the women's college prep silhouette of the 1950s. Chinos, sweater vests, sport coats, button-down shirts, and penny loafers formed the foundation of the sophisticated preppy look for young men.

Girls' Ensembles

Dresses and Skirts: Young women wore dresses or skirt and sweater sets to high school and college. The basic shirtwaist dress, popularized by Christian Dior's New Look, with a tight bodice, nipped-in waist, and full skirt personified the 1950s ideal of conformity and uniformity. The shirtwaist dress was the standard "uniform" for young women and was available at every price point and was seen in every women's magazine. The shirtwaist dress was either a one-piece dress or two-piece ensemble consisting of a fitted button-front bodice with either a rounded Peter Pan collar or standard pointed collar, slim-fitting sleeves, either just above or just below the elbow, and a full circle either gathered into the waist band or pleated that fell just below the knees. Variations on the standard form included sleeveless bodices for summer without collars, full-circle skirts with trim and appliqués, and shirred, pleated, or pintucked front shirt yokes. Teenagers also wore full felt, corduroy, and quilted circle skirts appliquéd with the ubiquitous felt poodle. The skirts were supported by petticoats, paired with saddle shoes and bobby socks (ankle high socks with cuffs), earning teenage girls the moniker bobby-soxer.

Pants: As an alternative to the full crinoline shirtwaist skirt, girls donned fitted pencil skirts that also fell just below the knee. Slacks were not worn to high school or college by young women, only for the most casual occasions. Tapered, slim-fit cotton chinos in solids, plaids, or houndstooth checks were worn for casual activities. Pedal pushers and capri pants were worn for backyard parties and the beach. Pedal pushers fell just below the knee and were cut fuller than capri pants, which fell around the mid-calf. The explosion of tourism in the 1950s fueled the fad for Bermuda shorts, which were tailored with a structured waistband and belt loops and fabricated in colorful madras plaids and bright colors. Jeans or dungarees were worn only for camping or outdoor activities.

Tops: In addition to the shirtwaist blouse, woven blouses were worn with pencil shirts, chinos, and capri pants. Woven button-down blouses were fitted with darts or princess seams to emphasis an hourglass silhouette, even with pants. Peter Pan collars were the most popular neckline finish; however, point collars, shawl collars, scoop necks, and V necks were also worn. "Good girls" wore sweater sets or cardigans over woven shirts, both of which looked particularly proper when accessorized by a single strand of pearls. Button-front cardigans, sweater sets, and pullover sweaters with simple round necklines accented with pearls, scarves, or detachable Peter Pan collars were paired with skirts and slacks.

Boys' Ensembles

Pants: Young men in high school and college adopted the sophisticated preppy look. The classic look of the fifties included penny loafers or saddle shoes with argyle socks, chinos, a button-down shirt, and a tennis sweater tied around the shoulders. A blue blazer topped the ensemble, unless the young man was an athlete, in which case the letter sweater and letter jacket trumped all.

The college prep or Ivy League style required a slim-cut, flat-front trouser. Cotton twill, combed cotton, and wool gabardine were the most common fabrications. Jeans or dungarees were not part of the daily college prep look but were worn for casual outdoor activities after class or on the weekends. The popularity of camping and traveling led to the adoption of shorts, particularly Bermuda shorts, for casual beach outings and summertime cookouts. Although solid neutral colors dominated men's pants, shorts were bright, colorful garments, often in plaids or madras.

Tops: Blazers and sport coats were a major component of the Ivy League look. A navy blue blazer with gold buttons could be worn with a collared polo shirt, a button-down shirt, or over a pullover sweater or vest. Blazers and sport coats were versatile and "smart" looking for young men. Besides the standard navy, jackets were available in subtle plaids and tweeds that were combined with white, tan, navy, black, and gray slacks or plaid trousers. Jacket lapels continued to narrow during the decade. Neckties were optional for the Ivy League look and may either be omitted all together or replaced with an ascot.

Woven button-down shirts were the staple for young men's casual wear. Tailored shirts with button-down collars or spread collars and front breast pockets came in a wide array of fabrics, colors, and patterns. Cotton broadcloth, chambray, and poplin were worn for summer, while flannel, corduroy, and gabardine were worn for winter. Colors, geometric prints, and plaids were popular patterns. Short-sleeve shirts were a common option over the standard long sleeves for summer. Knit polo shirts and T-shirts in solids or horizontal stripes were fashionable substitutes for the woven shirt.

Sweaters and sweater vests were also components of the casual wardrobe for young men. Turtlenecks, crewnecks, and V-neck sweaters and sweater vests were worn alone or over woven and knit shirts. Sweaters were either plain or cable knits in solid colors or all-over jacquard patterns. Cardigans were worn in place of blazers and sport coats, especially for athletes who lettered in high school or college sports. Varsity letter sweaters were a badge of pride that signified athletic ability and school spirit.

OUTERWEAR: CHILDREN TO PRETEEN

Coats

Children had two types of coats; those for play (everyday) and those for dress up (formal occasions). Play jackets for little girls fell between the waist and hips and had either a zipper or button-front closure. Button fronts had elongated tubular wooden buttons, also known as frogs or toggles, rather than traditional round flat buttons. Zippered jacket were usually of water-repellant nylon, and button coats were often of cotton sateen or wool/wool blends. Most play jackets came with hoods that could be fastened tightly beneath the chin and two side pockets. Dress coats for little girls were long, single or double breasted, and fashioned "just like Mom's," with a small round Peter Pan collar possibly in velvet or trimmed in velvet. Coats were cut full to fit over full-skirted dresses. Winter coats were typically in dark colors or gray, and spring coats were either navy or pastel.

Little boys had the same two categories of coats as little girls. Casual or play jackets were hip length, had either regular collars or rib-knit collars, either two breast pockets with flaps or side welt pockets, and long straight sleeves that frequently ended in rib-knit cuffs. Dress-up gray or navy wool coats, "just like Dad's," in either single- or double-breasted styles landed at the knees and had narrow collars and side pockets.

OUTERWEAR: TEEN TO COLLEGE

Coats

The car coat was the perfect pairing for a full crinoline skirt for young women. Although a full-length coat was impossible to wear over the top of formal gowns, the hip-length semi-fitted jacket with a swing-back yoke was the ideal topper for formal dress. Car coats had small round collars and either a single row of buttons or a single button (or jeweled clasp) at the neck. Made from wool, fur, faux fur, velvet, and satin, car coats could be just as luxurious as the dresses they topped. Stoles and wraps in fur, velvet, satin, and lace provided alternatives to car coats. For daily wear, full-length coats fell just below skirt length (around mid-calf). Coats were also full for daywear, with round collar, deep armholes, and tapered cuffed sleeves to accommodate the New Look silhouette worn by young women. To provide shaping, many coats were made with either princess seams or with a half-belt across the back to control the fullness and still provide an hourglass silhouette.

Young men generally wore simple hip-level jackets with front zipper closures, breast pockets with flaps or side welt pockets, and ribbed knit or fold-down collars. The letter jacket was similar in style to other casual jackets but was fabricated with the school colors and names and typically snapped close up the center front. Letter jackets became an important component of the teenage wardrobe, and a girl wearing her boyfriend's letter jacket was a sign of a serious relationship. Young men also adopted the rebellious black leather jackets popularized by Elvis Presley and Marlon Brando. Similar in style to the traditional jacket, the black leather jacket would include extra flaps, zippers, buckles, and chains for a "tough" appearance. For formalwear, young men wore the same full-length wool or Mackintosh jackets as adult men, in either single- or double-breasted styles, occasionally with velvet collars.

SWIMWEAR AND SPORTSWEAR: CHILDREN TO PRETEEN

Swimwear

Children's swimwear was quite modest and loose fitting. Girls wore halter-style tank tops embellished with layered rows of ruffles or shirred and smocked. Bottoms ballooned with elastic waist and leg openings and rows of ruffles or shirred panels, both on the front and back. Little boys wore swim sets of shorts with elastic waist and a matching top shirt that buttoned down the front. Even little boys were expected to cover up once they got out of the water! Swimwear and cover-ups for both boys and girls were brightly colored tropical prints, checks, and madras plaids, often incorporating nautical themes.

SWIMWEAR AND SPORTSWEAR: TEEN TO COLLEGE

Swimwear

One-piece bathing suits, either strapless or halter style, were more popular than bikinis for young women. When worn, two-piece swim suits were modest, covering the navel and, despite the preformed padded bra cups, were careful not to reveal any cleavage. The hourglass figure, so desired in this period, was carefully sculpted in swimwear, even for young women, but carefully constructed tops and skirt panels ensured that swimwear was not provocative. Shirred side and center front panels, ruffles, lace, and bows were all standard embellishments for swimwear. Whether one-piece or bikini, most swim bottoms incorporated either a skirt or draped panel across the hips to conceal the "private area." Suits came in every color combination, pattern, and print imaginable. Matching beach jackets or sarongs completed the look and provided the appropriate cover-up for poolside activities. The majority of young women wore decorative swim caps to protect their coiffures and hair dye.

Matching plaid beach suits let young men show off their individuality. Bright colors and wild patterns of madras plaid, tropical flowers, or large geometric patterns were the norm. Made of cotton twill, rayon, or nylon, men's swim shorts came with matching short-sleeved shirts with a straight hem and one breast pocket. Both elastic and drawstring waists helped to keep the shorts in place, and an extra front panel provided support and comfort. The cover-up shirt allowed men to be seen in beachwear but maintain a conservative appearance.

HEADWEAR, HAIRSTYLES, AND COSMETICS: CHILDREN TO PRETEEN

Headwear

Hats were still an important fashion accessory for little girls, complementing an ensemble and providing a proper appearance. Little girls primarily wore hats to church or other formal occasions. Hats were designed to match Sunday coats in winter, usually of wool felt and trimmed in black velvet, whereas spring or Easter hats typically had either a turned-up brim with a satin ribbon and cluster of silk flowers or were half hats trimmed with frills and pearls. Young boys rarely wore hats for formal occasions but regularly wore beanies or small caps for casual wear. Both young boys and girls wore knit wool stocking caps in winter for casual dress. Knit caps came in a range of solids and patterns, and girls often had matching or contrasting pom-poms or tassels at the center top.

Hairstyles

Both short and long styles were very neat and manicured. Ponytails, pigtails, and braids were staples for young girls with long hair, all with the bangs combed forward. Scarves and ribbons were tied around the elastic bands that held hair into position. Very short curly hair was called the poodle cut, and straight short hair cuts were dubbed the bubble cut. Later in the decade, the flip became a popular daytime style for preteens. Parted on one side, the hair was teased slightly for volume on top and then combed down to flip up on the ends. Ribbons, headbands, and velvet bows were worn with all hairstyles, sometimes as a clip on one side only. Young boys all had the same look, very short hair usually parted on one side and combed back like Dad's. Very few variations in the infamous flat top or crew cut were seen, the shorter the better, saving Mom trips to the barber.

HEADWEAR, HAIRSTYLES, AND COSMETICS: TEEN TO COLLEGE

Headwear

Older teens wanted to look more mature and less little-girlish and selected headwear similar to adult women. Young women adopted new hat shapes designed to be worn straight on top of the head, like a bandeau to pair with smart suits and "going into town" looks. Wide-brim hats were still popular for summer months and were selected to match suits and dresses with jackets. The small pill-box style became more popular at the end of the decade and was considered "high fashion." Young men did not typically wear hats for formal occasions; some donned beanies or small caps for casual wear, but young men, in general, did not wear hats until they entered the workforce.

Hairstyles

Young women wore more sophisticated versions of ponytails: poodles and bubble hairstyles. Short cropped curly styles with pin curls (so dubbed because they were created by letting hair dry while bobby pinned in place) were very popular in the early part of the decade, but hair became increasingly teased and sprayed into ever larger bouffants, with or without flipped ends, and beehive styles as the decade progressed. To support these styles, young women learned early how to sleep in rollers and head scarves to protect their teased and sculpted styles.

Teenage boys had a choice of two looks: the preppy or Ivy League look and the greaser look. The Ivy League look was neat, short, parted on one side, and combed back smooth with a little dab of Brylcreem. The alternative was the greaser look. Taking their cue from Hollywood and rock 'n' roll idols such as Elvis Presley, Jerry Lee Lewis, James Dean, and Marlon Brando, the greasers were considered rebels. The signature greaser look incorporated the famous ducktail, or DA, created by slicking hair back from the sides to the center back of the head into a point or "ducktail," and the pompadour, created by slicking bangs back over the top of the head. In addition to the Ivy League and greaser styles, crew cuts were worn by young men who respected authority. A blunt cut across the back of the neck and sideburns guaranteed conformity. The older boys who were more style conscious would leave a good one-quarter inch on top for the flat-top look.

Cosmetics

Young women wore the same makeup as adult women. In the 1950s, the focus was on creating soft, round "doe eyes." Heavy makeup outlined the eyes and eyebrows. Natural eyebrows were widened with pencil, eyelids were shaded, and the corners of the eyes were penciled to slope slightly upward. As eye makeup intensified, powder and foundation were lighter and lips became paler, with a chalky pink becoming the craze with teenage girls.

FOOTWEAR AND LEGWEAR: CHILDREN TO PRETEEN

Footwear

Two comic strip characters, Buster Brown and his sister Mary Jane, dominated children's footwear in the 1950s. The simple round-toe, instep strap, black or white patent leather shoes worn by Mary Jane in the comic strip was the quintessential shoe for little girls for all dress-up and special occasions. Boys wore leather tie Buster Brown shoes, usually in brown, because black was considered too severe for young boys for daily wear and special occasions. For casual playwear, both boys and girls donned "sneakers." Made with canvas uppers and rubber soles, little girls wore pointed-toed Keds, and boys wore high-top Converse All-Stars with Chuck Taylor's signature in the logo circle.

Legwear

Ankle socks for the girls and argyle socks for the boys helped to define the look of the fifties. Girls' socks folded over into a cuff that was either plain for casual wear or edged with lace for dress. Boys' argyle patterned socks in a wide array of color combinations were worn with dress pants as well as chinos and blue jeans.

FOOTWEAR AND LEGWEAR: TEEN TO COLLEGE

Footwear

Penny loafers and saddle shoes were popular for girls and boys of all ages. They were an instant status symbol for sophisticated leisure. The saddle shoe was a white leather tie shoe with a "saddle" of brown or black across the center portion of the shoe. A versatile shoe, it could be worn with a skirt or dungarees. The penny loafer in black, brown, cordovan, or mulberry, worn with argyle socks, a tennis sweater tied around the shoulders, and a pair of chinos, completed the Ivy League look for young men. Young women also wore various pumps, ballet slippers, and sandals in a variety of flat, wedged, and low heels with pointed or peep toes, and straight, curved, or V-shaped vamps. Stiletto heels were reserved for adult women, a style to aspire to but not wear. Practical yet stylish boots with faux fur or fleece lining the top and low heels with treads provided women with a more stylish alternative to bad weather than the traditional pull-on, buckled, or zipped rubberized boots and galoshes worn by young men.

Legwear

Starting out as a rebellious fad, bobby socks became a teen fashion staple for young women in the 1950s. Bobby socks were either ankle socks with a folded over cuff or calf-high socks folded down to form cuffs and had to be thick to survive "sock hops," after-school gym dances where teenagers would remove their shoes and dance in their stocking feet. Bobby socks were worn with every ensemble, whether skirt, capri pant, or jean. When worn with full-length jeans or chinos, pant legs were rolled up or cuffed to prominently display the bobby socks underneath. Boys' socks were as decorative as their neckties in the 1950s. Argyles, stripes, and geometric patterns in a wide assortment of color combinations were worn for casual and dress wear. The vivid colors and patterns were also prominently displayed during after-school sock hops.

ACCESSORIES

Jewelry

Little girls and teenagers alike loved jangly jewelry. The charm bracelet was a way to collect and display representations of all the things loved, as well as the places traveled. Common charms included megaphones for cheerleaders, a key to success for graduation, and a 45 rpm record. These bracelets were such a key fashion accessory that blouses were designed with three-quarter-length sleeves or "bracelet sleeves" to prominently feature the charms. Young women were given a string of pearls as a gift for their Sweet Sixteen birthday or perhaps high-school graduation. Wearing a single strand of pearls became popular, at all age levels, after Mamie Eisenhower wore a strand for her husband's inauguration. Often a strand of pearls was the only accessory worn, with both casual and dressy ensembles, especially with cashmere sweaters or sweetheart necklines.

Gloves and Handbags

Handbags were understated but an essential accessory in the 1950s. Small rectangular bags with thin straps were carried over the wrist for most daily activities. All young women had a least one summer bag (white or a light color) and one winter bag (black or a dark color), as well as small clutch bags dyed to match shoes, jackets, and dresses for special occasions.

Females of all ages wore gloves in the 1950s. Short white gloves were most commonly worn and were often decorated with embroidery or crocheted lace. Colored gloves were dyed to match shoes and purses. Gloves were worn in a variety of lengths depending on the sleeve style, including wrist, forearm, and opera (upper arm) lengths. Gloves were an absolute requirement for church and other special social functions.

Neckwear

Clip-on bow ties made a little boy look like a little man. Small and square, bow ties were very neat in appearance and came in a wide variety of colors and patterns. Neckties for men went through a transition in the fifties, from wide and colorful early in the decade to thin and understated at the close of the decade. Colorful prints in novelty prints, wide stripes, and geometric patterns could be found through the middle of the decade. As the decade drew to a close, ties became substantially thinner and plainer in either solid darker colors or narrow diagonal strips.

Decorative detachable collars were another important accessory for young women. Round Peter Pan collars with lace trim and collars with pearls, beads, sequins, rhinestones, and gold lamé were worn to dress up the neckline of a plain sweater, dress, or shirt.

Other Accessories

Young women wore wide elasticized cinch belts with skirt or capri pants to emphasize a narrow waist and hourglass silhouette. Scarves were a versatile and popular accessory because they could be draped as a belt, wrapped as a halter top, or tied around the head, ponytail, or neck. Scarves were also souvenirs from vacation destinations. Decorated with scenes from the Eiffel Tower to totem poles, these colorful scarves advertised where a girl had been. Handkerchiefs, whether carried by a young lady or young man, expanded beyond plain white. Handkerchiefs came in bold colors and prints, often with vacation destinations or maybe embroidered with the owner's initials.

THE
1960s

FORMALWEAR: CHILDREN TO PRETEEN

Silhouette

The early 1960s witnessed a continuation of 1950s influence on children's formalwear. Girls wore dresses with fitted bodices and full-circle skirts, and boys wore short pants with jackets and bow ties. As the decade progressed, the trend toward simple A-line dresses and empire waist for women's eveningwear was also adopted for young girls' formalwear. Young boys also participated in the changing world of fashion by discarding their suit jackets in favor of the Nehru jackets worn by men.

Girls' Ensembles

Young girls predominately wore dresses for formal occasions. Depending on the occasion, dresses were short, around mid-thigh, or full length. The basic A-line sheath dress was the dominant silhouette for the majority of the decade. Simple sheath dresses were either sleeveless or short sleeved. Short-sleeved styles featured either straight sleeves or puffed sleeves gathered into elastic bands. Square and jewel necklines or small band collars were typical for most dresses. Sheath dresses also featured empire waistlines, which were trimmed with appliqués, ribbons, and bows.

Boys' Ensembles

Young boys' formalwear incorporated many of the same features as men's formalwear. Suit jackets were single breasted and slim fitting and paired with slim-fit tapered pants. Basic button-down shirts were worn with bow ties or regular ties. Young boys also donned the new Nehru jackets rather than traditional jackets for formal occasions. Nehru jackets featured a center front closure and small stand or banded collar. Unlike traditional jackets, Nehru jackets were worn without shirts and ties.

Decorative Details

Young girls wore dresses in soft pastel colors, such as pink, green, blue, and yellow, and white. Fabrics ranged from satins and taffetas for the most formal occasions to cotton piques for less formal settings. Eyelet and lace were also popular formalwear fabrics. Sheath dresses featured minimal surface decorations; typically, only a single ribbon, bow, or appliqué was featured. Young boys' formalwear was often more adventurous than young girls' fashions. Bold plaids and stripes in brown, orange, and blue were seen in pants that were paired with solid-color suit or Nehru jackets in cream, navy, or burgundy. In addition to the traditional wool gabardines, young boys' suits were also made out of velvet.

FORMALWEAR: TEEN TO COLLEGE

Silhouette

The fashionable silhouette for young women was based on the simple sheath A-line form. The silhouette appeared narrow at the shoulders and flared slightly at the hemline, a noticeable departure from the 1950s hourglass silhouette. Additionally, young women wore empire waist baby-doll dresses for formalwear. The baby-doll silhouette featured the same, simple bodice as sheath dresses, but the skirt was gathered into an empire waist that fell just below the bustline. Young men's formalwear was greatly influence by the mod movement and the Beatles. Traditional suits were still worn in the new slim fit, but, the new Nehru suits became more prevalent for young men who wanted to be considered hip and modern.

Girls' Ensembles

A classic, refined elegance dominated eveningwear for young women. Dresses were simple sheaths made from luxurious fabrics. Dresses were predominately sleeveless, featuring jewel, bateau, and scoop necklines. Sheath dresses either hung straight or were cinched in at the waist with a wide ribbon belt. Baby-doll-style dresses featured fitted bodices, with scoop and jewel necklines and full skirts gathered or pleated into an empire waistline. Unlike sheath dresses, baby-doll dresses typically featured full long or short sleeves gathered into the armscye at the top and into an elastic band at the bottom. Dresses in either style may be either full length or knee length, depending on the formality of the occasion.

Boys' Ensembles

Young men's suits were slim cut. Jackets were hip length, fitted, and featured a center back vent. Single-breasted styles were most prevalent, in both two- and three-button closures. Jacket collars and lapels were short and narrow. Nehru jackets, popularized by the mod movement, were substituted for traditional suit jackets. Nehru jackets were also hip length and fitted, but, instead of a traditional collar and lapel, Nehru jackets featured a small stand or band collar, as well as a multi-buttoned center front closure. As the decade progressed, some Nehru jackets also extended beyond hip length, reaching as far as the mid-thigh, and were fitted at the waist to create a flared hemline. With both jackets and Nehru jackets, young men wore slim-fitting pants with flat fronts and tapered legs. Tuxedos were rarely worn by young men.

Decorative Details

Inspired by the soft colors preferred by Jackie Kennedy, young women's formalwear was dominated by pastel shades of pink, green, yellow, and blue. In keeping with the modern aesthetic, the streamlined, modern fashions of the 1960s featured minimal surface decoration. Luxurious fabrics, such as satin, taffeta, chiffon, lace, and eyelet, incorporated only simple ribbons, bows, and sashes. Structural princess seams, darts, ruffles, gathers, and pleats were used instead of surface ornamentation to create visual interest. The color palette for young men expanded beyond black, navy, brown, and white, embracing the new colors of the psychedelic era. Both jackets and pants were fabricated in bold colors, including blue, burgundy, and green, and strong patterns, including wide stripes and plaids. In addition to wool gabardine, young men's suits were also available in velvets.

CASUAL WEAR: CHILDREN TO PRETEEN

Silhouette

Children, a rich consumer market, were able to participate in all the adult trends, and magazines such as *Vogue* and *Harper's Bazaar* published back-to-school issues covering the latest trends in children's fashions (Olian 1999, v). Participation in women's fashion trends was particularly easy for young girls because the prevailing silhouette de-emphasized womanly curves and focused on youthful and girlish colors and trims. Young girls wore the same sheath or A-line mini-dresses as their adult counterparts. Young boys' casual wear also followed the prevailing men's wear trend for slim-fit pants, turtlenecks, and ruffled shirts.

Girls' Ensembles

Dresses and Skirts: Simple tank and sheath mini-dresses and jumpers were extremely popular in the 1960s. These A-line forms were constructed with princess seams or made softly shaped into shifts. Waistlines were either empire (just below the bustline) or dropped to the hip. Jewel, square, and scoop necklines or small band or Peter Pan collars topped bodices. Sleeveless and short-sleeve styles were typical of the period. Many hip-waisted dresses were made to resemble separates, with the top and skirt in different fabrics, but the two components were joined into a common seam that was camouflaged by a belt or sash in self-fabric or in a contrasting color or material. Polo-style knit mini-dresses and ribbed-knit sweater dresses were also popular for casual dress. A-line miniskirts, box-pleated skirts, and wrap skirts provided alternatives to dresses.

Pants: The restrictions against girls wearing pants for casual wear and school were no longer observed in the 1960s (Sills 2005, 38). Pants, whether long or capri, began to replace dresses and skirts as a key component of dress during the 1960s. Young girls regularly wore slim-fitting capri pants, knit stirrup pants, and twill sailor pants for daily wear. Fitted shorts, pedal pushers, and culottes were also widely worn for summertime.

Tops: Woven tops with Peter Pan collars, smocks, tunics, and boxy tops with small convertible collars were paired with skirts and pants or worn under jumpers. However, knit wear dominated girls' tops in the 1960s. Turtlenecks, polo shirts, T-shirts, and other pullovers in plain, rib, and cable knits were the preferred casual tops to pair with pants, skirts, and jumpers. Knit tops, as with wovens, followed the preference for sleeveless styles and featured contrasting knit bands on necklines, arm-holes, and, when present, sleeve cuffs and hems.

Boys' Ensembles

Pants: Boys wore slim-fitting chinos and jeans for casual wear. All pants featured flat fronts and slim tapered legs, with or without cuffs. Tailored, fitted shorts were worn during the summer.

Tops: Fitted button shirts paired with cardigan sweaters were popular for young boys in the 1960s. However, just like girls, knit wear dominated young boys' tops during this decade. T-shirts, turtlenecks, polo shirts, and other pullover styles in plain, cable, and rib knits were paired with slim-fitting pants and jeans throughout the decade.

Decorative Details

Pastel blues, pinks, yellows, and greens were popular for young girls' colors. However, bright red, navy, lime green, turquoise, avocado, and gold were also common components of the color palette. Large- and small-scale floral prints, gingham checks, plaids, and stripes were popular patterns in dresses, skirts, and pants. Many dresses, skirts, and tops were edged with white collars, cuffs, and plackets, and topstitching decorated pockets, waistbands, hems, and collars.

The peacock revolution of the 1960s did not pass by fashions for young boys. Just like their adult counterparts, although silhouettes remained simple, colors and patterns became increasingly complex. Basic cardigans were enlivened with stripes and Nordic motifs in icy blues, golds, and avocados. Knit tops came in bold horizontal and vertical stripes with blues, browns, golds, and oranges. Pants were even more colorful when acid green, gold, brown, white, and blue combined into bold wide stripes, small paisley or ethnic-inspired motifs, and plaids. Topstitching in matching or contrasting colors also became a regular decorative element in all pants and tops.

CASUAL WEAR: TEEN TO COLLEGE

Silhouette

The youth movement, swinging London and the Beatles strongly influenced fashion for mainstream America's teen- and college-aged youths. Young men and women closely emulated their fashionable counterparts on London's Carnaby Street, adopting slim-fitting stovepipe pants, tunics, and Mary Quant's new miniskirt. Young women wore simple A-line sheath dresses and baby-doll empire-waist dresses, and young men adopted European-cut jackets, shirts, and pants. Fashions for both genders were either modern, with bold colors and patterns, or soft and romantic, in velvet, lace, and ruffles. However, a new influence would be felt on fashions for youths by the close of the decade: the hippies, whose anti-establishment counterculture movement changed both the clean-cut look and image of America's youths.

Girls' Ensembles

Dresses and Skirts: Miniskirts and dresses were the quintessential garments of 1960s young women's apparel. Simple A-line sheath or shift minidresses, sleeveless with jewel necklines, were the cornerstone of a young woman's wardrobe. Numerous variations upon this body-skimming shape were seen throughout the decade, including baby-doll dresses, T-shirt dresses, polo shirt dresses, and princess seam jumpers. Each variation completely concealed the waist by eliminating the waist seam or shifted the waist up to the bustline, as in baby-doll dresses, or dropped the waistline down to the hips. In the case of the latter, wide belt loops and wide belts were positioned along the hipline, further emphasizing the dropped position of the waist. Hip-waisted dresses were also designed to resemble separate tops and skirts, with each component being fabricated from a different material, often a knit for the top and a woven for the skirt and then joined together into a hipline waist seam to be concealed by a sash or belt. Miniskirts were also available in A-line silhouettes, or wrap, pleated, and full circle styles.

Pants: Slim-fitting capri and stirrup pants were popular for casual wear throughout the 1960s. Over the course of the decade, the pant waistline slowly shifted lower, dropping well below the natural waistline into the hip-hugger silhouette. Waistbands also disappeared from the new hip-hugger or hip-rider styles. The drop waist was further emphasized by the addition of wide belt loops and a wide belt or sash in either self-fabric or in a contrasting color or material. Jeans and corduroys were also popular fabrications for stovepipe pants (fitted pants with slim, tapering legs). During the 1960s, pants rarely featured pockets, inset, welt, or patch, and typically used side zippers instead of fly zippers to keep a neat, streamlined appearance. Toward the end of the decade, fitted pant legs displayed large, flounced cuffs or began to flare slightly from the knee, a telltale sign of the wide bell-bottoms that would become synonymous with 1970s pants.

Tops: Knit tops and sweaters dominated young women's casual wear in the 1960s. Cowl necks, bateau or boat necks, and turtlenecks and necks in plain, rib, and cable knits were worn with skirts, pants, and jumpers. Knit shirts were fitted and often featured zippers down the center fronts or center backs. T-shirts, tank tops, and polo shirts were other popular shirt forms. Tunics, both knit and woven, became extremely popular during the last years of the 1960s. Tunics were hip length to mid-thigh, fitted at the waist, and were either worn instead of a shirt or as a vest over a shirt. Tunics worn as shirts were both long and short sleeved and often featured center front plackets and either banded or convertible collars. Woven shirts with small collars and ruffled fronts were worn under jumpers or long tunic vests. Fitted, woven camisole tops and halter tops were cropped below the bustline, exposing bare midriff.

Boys' Ensembles

Pants: Young men wore slim-fitting, flat-front chinos known as stovepipes during the 1960s. Stovepipe pants featured narrow, tapered legs that ended at the ankle with or without a cuff. These mod pants sat high on the waist in the early part of the decade but slowly progressed lower and lower, moving toward the hip-hugger form that would conclude the decade. The slim stovepipe pant legs also slowly transitioned throughout the decade, moving from narrow columns to a more relaxed form that slightly flared from the knee to the hem by the end of the period. Dark denim blue jeans were also an important component of young men's casual wear and followed the same overall silhouette as chinos.

Tops: The mod influence was also seen in young men's shirts and tops. Although woven, European (fitted)-cut button-down shirts with small collars were worn for casual wear, and turtlenecks and mock turtlenecks became a staple in the mod young man's wardrobe. Turtlenecks and mock turtlenecks came in both thin plain knits and heavier rib knits and fit tightly to the body, ending with a rib-knit waistband on the hips. Knit polo shirts and T-shirts were also fundamental components of a casual wardrobe. Both long and short sleeves were seen on all types of knit shirts. Other woven shirts included the romantic full-cut shirts with full sleeves, flounced cuffs, and ruffled collars and jabots.

Body-skimming tunics and Nehru jackets were also key to capturing the mod look. Nehru jackets were either fitted or slightly flared from waist to hem with a center front button closure and a small band collar. Over the course of the decade, the Nehru jacket grew in length, up to mid-thigh, and increased in flare. The Nehru jacket was also adapted into vests, with or without collars, and tunic shirts with open plackets and band collars. In addition to buttons, frogs, toggles, and chains were used as closures on Nehru and Nehru-inspired garments reminiscent of closures seen in the uniforms worn by the Beatles on the 1967 *Sgt. Pepper's Lonely Hearts Club Band* album.

Decorative Details

Young men's and women's casual wear reflected the prevailing trend toward bold colors and psychedelic patterns preferred by the mod movement. Bright yellow, purple, turquoise, and lime green as well as deep golds, oranges, and avocados were popular colors, along with black and white. Acrylic knits and wool blend jersey knits and gabardines provided fit and stretch for the body-conscious fashions of both sexes. Wide stripes and large-scale paisley, floral, polka dot, plaid, and check patterns were seen on pants, skirts, shirts, and dresses, with some ensembles combining more than one pattern at a time. Casual wear for both genders featured little surface embellishment, relying more on color and pattern than ornamentation. Large buttons, embroidered motifs, frog closures, and fringe provided the extent of the surface decorations for most garments. Additional interest was created through the use of contrasting colors on collars, plackets, cuffs, waistbands, and edging.

OUTERWEAR: CHILDREN TO PRETEEN

Coats

For more formal occasions, children wore coats similar to adults. Tailored wool Melton coats topped dresses for girls and suits for boys. For casual wear, a wide range of jackets in cotton, leather, wool, nylon, and polyester were available. For spring, short waist-length coats with knit collars, cuffs, and waistbands were standard. Young girls also wore vinyl rain slickers in a wide range of bright colors. For fall and winter, car coats, coats that were mid-thigh length with hoods and large patch pockets, were fashionable. These coats had large button, frog, or toggle closures. Parkas, with or without hoods, with nylon shells and polyester filling, were popular for both boys and girls. Parkas came in a wide array of colors and patterns, and girls' styles frequently featured dyed faux fur-trimmed hoods, collars, and cuffs.

OUTERWEAR: TEEN TO COLLEGE

Coats

Young adult outwear mirrored the sophistication of adult styles in the 1960s. Pea coats, Chesterfields, and other tailored wool coats and trench coats were standard for formal and semiformal occasions. Young men wore denim jackets, leather jackets, and plaid C.P.O. jackets (for chief petty officer in the navy) for casual wear with jeans and chinos. Young women had a wide array of vinyl jackets in bold colors, geometric patterns, and even see-through, to wear over miniskirts and mini-dresses. These coats were particularly popular, especially when worn with matching vinyl or leather go-go boots. Fur and faux fur were the most popular options for young women's winter coats. Faux fur, created from acrylic fibers, could be fabricated in a wide range of piles to represent rich minks, leopard, or curly lamb and dyed pink, green, red, or white. These coats were typically double breasted, with large buttons, a waist belt that fastened at the center back or a sash. Capes and ponchos in faux fur, wool, crochet, or vinyl also became very popular in the last years of the decade.

SWIMWEAR AND SPORTSWEAR: CHILDREN TO PRETEEN

Swimwear

Young girls wore both tank-style swimsuits and bikinis in the 1960s. The tank style had a modest scooped neckline and low-cut legs. Bikini styles had bra or tank-style tops paired with bottoms that sat high on the hip. Young boys wore basic trunks with elastic waists. Both boys' and girls' styles came in bright solids as well as tropical prints. Swim caps in a wide array of patterns and colors continued to be a staple for young girls.

SWIMWEAR AND SPORTSWEAR: TEEN TO COLLEGE

Swimwear

Swimwear for young women in the early part of the 1960s continued to follow the trends of the 1950s, emphasizing a woman's curves through the use of padding and underwire. However, as the fashionable silhouette shifted to idealize the preteen form (flat chest and no hips), swimwear quickly lost its padding and wires and became more natural. One-piece maillots with cutouts on the side, front, and/or back of the torso were popular; however, the bikini dominated swimwear in the 1960s. Young girls wore bottoms similar to briefs that rode low on the hip, revealing the belly–button. The corresponding bikini top was either a bra or tank style. Young men continued to wear standard swim trunks with elastic waists in the 1960s. Those bold enough donned the men's bikini, known today as the Speedo. Appliqués, ruffles, fringe, vinyl, and crochet were incorporated into many swimwear designs. Bright colors, such as apple green, lemon yellow, turquoise, or hot pink, and bold, geometric patterns, such as stripes, chevrons, or Pucci-style prints, were seen in both young men's and young women's swimwear.

HEADWEAR, HAIRSTYLES, AND COSMETICS: CHILDREN TO PRETEEN

Headwear

Hats virtually disappeared for young children during this period, with the exception of sun hats and baseball caps for playtime. Young girls did wear an assortment of headbands, scarves, ribbons, and bows, some of which came in fabrics to match their dresses or skirts.

Hairstyles

Young girls wore their hair shoulder length or slightly longer during most of the decade. Hair was either worn straight or set in soft waves and either parted down the middle or on the side. Ponytails and pigtails were common styles, both adorned with ribbons and bows. Although bangs were prevalent in the early part of the decade, they disappeared by the end of the period. Young boys continued to wear close-cropped and military-style crew cuts for most of the period. However, longer bowl-cut styles, inspired by the Beatles, were seen in the closing years of the decade.

HEADWEAR, HAIRSTYLES, AND COSMETICS: TEEN TO COLLEGE

Headwear

Although hats were rarely worn by young women in the 1960s, small, brimless pillbox styles popularized by Jacqueline Kennedy were the perfect complement to bouffant hairstyles on formal occasions. For less formal occasions, young women might opt to don hoods, berets, and newsboy caps in faux fur, vinyl, or wool plaids and tweeds. Jeweled brooches, headbands, barrettes, and ribbons were alternative hair adornments that replaced hats. Young men were also hatless during the 1960s. Some young men wore a small gray or brown trilby, with narrow curled brim and tall crown. Small camps, tams, newsboy, or Dutch boy caps in velvet, leather, and wool tweeds or plaids were also worn.

Hairstyles

Young women predominantly wore their hair shoulder length and straight. Hair was teased across the crown of the head to add volume and height and then either flipped up or flipped under on the end. Hairstyles either featured long bangs combed sideways across the forehead or were bangless. The preference for a youthful appearance led many young women to continue wearing ponytails and pigtails. Some young women wore short hairstyles inspired by fashion model Twiggy and *Laugh-In's* Goldie Hawn. These styles were typically parted on the side and either combed smooth, resembling a helmet, or teased at the crown into a bouffant puff. Young men following the college prep trend wore the new Perry Como or French crew cuts, a close-cropped style worn straight, clipped over the ears. The new mod look, inspired by the Beatles and swinging London fashions, provided an alternative to the cookie-cutter crew cut: the mop top. The mop top was either parted on the side with deep bangs combed across the forehead or had no part at all, hanging straight down from the center of the head. Considered long, the mop top would soon seem short compared with the long hippie-influenced hairstyles that would come to dominate the 1970s.

Cosmetics

Young women wore pale lipsticks, paired with eyeliner mascara and pastel eye shadow in the early 1960s. However, by the mid-1960s, the cookie-cutter or doll-face became the distinct fashion trend for cosmetics. Eyelids were heavily lined, and thick coats of mascara or false eyelashes were worn, clumping the eyelashes together to resemble the painted-on eyelash lines on baby dolls. Eye shadows were no longer soft and subtle but formed distinct blocks of lavender, blue, green, and yellow on the eyelid and upper eye area. Young men turned to hair tonics to keep their mop tops smooth, straight, and shiny.

FOOTWEAR AND LEGWEAR: CHILDREN TO PRETEEN

Footwear

Young girls wore patent vinyl flats with rounded toes in bright colors, white, and black. Both ballerina flats and flats with buckle straps were popular. Toward the end of the decade, buckle straps with a T across the vamp forming cutouts were more popular than plain ballerina flats. White Keds tennis shoes with rounded toes were paired with jeans and shorts as an alternative to flats. Short ankle boots were worn for winter with center back zippers or side buckle closures. Young boys wore lace-up oxfords for dress, in white, black, or brown leather. Short lace-up or buckle boots were also worn for dress and casual wear, although canvas tennis shoes were becoming increasingly popular for casual wear.

Legwear

Ankle and knee stocks continued to be standard for young girls, although by the end of the decade patterned and textured tights were more common than knee socks with skirts. White was the dominant color for socks, but other bright colors were available in both socks and tights. Young boys wore dark-colored socks with argyle or checked patterns for dress and white socks for casual wear.

FOOTWEAR AND LEGWEAR: TEEN TO COLLEGE

Footwear

Because the overall ideal of beauty in the 1960s was based on the preteen image, young women and adult women both wore the same footwear as their younger peers. Patent vinyl in white and bold colors dominated young women's footwear. Flats with round, square, and pointed toes with low square heels were the basic form for all footwear. Vamps were formed from T-straps, shaped into geometric cutouts and, of course, flower petals. Large buckles or thick ribbons were used for the closures. Short leather or vinyl ankle boots were popular with fitted, hip-hugger pants, and tall vinyl "go-go" boots often replaced flats with mini-dresses and miniskirts. Short boots incorporated details such as side vents or cutouts, gold chains, buckles, and snaps. Whether ankle high or tall, boots also had low, square heels and could have round, pointed, or square toes.

Young men's footwear, greatly influence by the Beatles, consisted of short ankle boots. Chelsea or Beatle boots featured stacked heels and either square or pointed toes. Gussets, cutouts, or vents were incorporated into the sides' construction, and decorative buckles, snaps, and chains were added. Black and brown leather were the most common colors, but white was a truly hip alternative. In addition to basic leather, leather embossed to resemble snake skin or crocodile was also popular. Lace-up oxfords and loafers with tassels or buckles were alternatives to the more popular mod boots.

Legwear

Young women wore both knee-high socks and tights with their miniskirts and mini-dresses. Both socks and tights came in a wide range of neon colors, bold patterns, and textures. Legwear was typically worn in contrasting colors to the skirt. Bright blues, pinks, and yellows were worn as solid colors or combined into Pucci prints. Socks and tights also came fabricated from knit lace, fishnet, ribbed knit, and cable knit. Young men's legwear changed little from the 1950s and, with the popularity of ankle boots, was rarely visible. Basic dark color socks with argyle, checks, and other patterns were still worn.

ACCESSORIES

Jewelry

For formalwear, young women took note of the simple strand of pearls, simple drop earrings, and jeweled or enameled brooches that adult women selected to complement their formal looks. However, for daily wear, young women adopted brightly colored plastic or Lucite jewelry in bold geometric shapes. Large hoop earrings, round or square bracelets, and beaded necklaces were thick, chunky, and prominently displayed. As an alternative to heavy plastic jewelry, a simple thin ribbon tied around the neck or wrists was the only accessory required for the baby-doll look. Silver and enamel medallions and pendants on long chains were also key elements of the young mod look for both young men and young women.

Gloves and Handbags

For formal occasions, long or opera-length gloves were paired with sleeveless dresses by young women. Some young women continued to wear wrist-length gloves for day wear in the early to mid-1960s, but the practice was less common. Although formal occasions called for small, envelope clutch purses fabricated to match the dress, hat, and shoes, the increasing informality of the youth movement brought alternate shapes and materials to handbags for young women. Clear, brightly colored, and faux tortoiseshell Lucite bags shaped like boxes, pails, and baskets were a novelty item for younger women. These bags often had patterns etched into the Lucite or had paste jewels inset. The closures were also unique, resembling latches and padlocks. Vinyl provided another alternative material for young women's handbags. Purses shaped like pouches, envelopes, and satchels of brightly colored vinyl came as part of a matching set with ponchos, go-go boots, newsboy caps, and rain slickers.

Neckwear

Young men's ties co-opted the op art, pop art, and psychedelic prints seen in young women's fashions. Stripes, polka dots, flowers, and Pucci prints in bright colors and geometric patterns covered ties that were initially very narrow at the beginning of the decade but expanded to up to five inches wide by the end of the period. Young women also adopted neckscarves with the same colors and motifs as young men's ties to substitute for necklaces.

Other Accessories

Sunglasses became a staple in the young adult wardrobe in the 1960s. Two distinct types of sunglasses were worn throughout the decade: oversized plastic and small metal granny glasses. The oversized sunglasses were a perfect complement to the mod look; large white or brightly colored square, circular, or oval plastic frames with dark lenses. The granny glasses, popularized by John Lennon, also originated with the mod look but later became synonymous with the hippie movement.

THE
1970s

FORMALWEAR: CHILDREN TO PRETEEN

Silhouette

As society continued to become less formal, so too did children's formal-wear. Fancy dresses and suits that were required in past decades were only seen at the most formal gatherings. Simple A-line dresses continued to be popular for young girls in the early part of the decade, whereas peasant-inspired floral print dresses with full gathered bodices and skirts dominated the last part of the decade. The definition of formalwear for young boys continued to expand throughout the decade. Suits were replaced by the new leisure suit or by pant and vest combinations. Silhouettes relaxed, and jacket collars, lapels, and pockets all increased in dimension.

Girls' Ensembles

In the early part of the decade, young girls continued to wear simple A-line sheaths. The sheaths featured simple jewel or band necklines and either empire waists or waistbands positioned at the hip line. The dresses were typically very short, even above mid-thigh. As women began to abandon A-line and baby-doll dresses in the 1960s in favor of more natural, relaxed silhouettes, young girls' dresses followed suit. The waistline returned to its natural position from which gathered and dirndl skirts sprung. Hemlines were often trimmed with large ruffle flounces. Bodices also relaxed and were either gathered or softly shaped into the waistband. Large flounces and ruffles adorned necklines and sleeves. Dress lengths continued to be short but at the new maxi lengths.

Boys' Ensembles

Boys rarely wore suits during the 1970s. Instead, leisure suits and vest and pant combinations were more typical in this era of casual dress. Boys' leisure suits featured hip-length, single-breasted jackets with large patch pockets. Collars became increasingly wider throughout the decade, and any trace of a lapel virtually disappeared. Some leisure suits featured wide self-fabric belts with large metal buckles. The suit pants had wide-cut, flared legs and flat fronts. The new Perma Prest fabrics meant that even the most restless boy could keep a neat crisp crease down the center front of his pant leg. Vests made an acceptable substitute for suits at most formal gatherings. Vests were single breasted, hip length, and collarless. Some vests also featured wide self-fabric belts with metal buckles. In place of buttons and belts, chains and frogs were also used for vest closures. Underneath leisure suit coats and vests, young boys wore full-cut button-down shirts with wide collars, full sleeves, and deep cuffs.

Decorative Details

In the early part of the 1970s, girls' formal dresses were typically fabricated from satin, lace, eyelet, velvet, and taffeta. However, as the decade progressed and formalwear became more casual, cotton poplins, double knits, and jersey knits became more common fabrications. The color palette for young girls shifted from soft pastels of the 1960s to bright vibrant reds, greens, blues, and yellows. Floral prints and stripes were popular patterns for dresses or provided contrast to solids for trims, ruffles, sashes, and bows. Although boys' suits continued to be available in traditional colors and pinstripes fabricated from wool and wool blends, the new polyester double knits and Perma Prest became more common treatments. Bold, wide stripes for pants and vests in bright orange, green, brown, rust, and blue were paired with solid-color jackets. Large-scale stripe and floral patterns were also seen in boy's shirts.

FORMALWEAR: TEEN TO COLLEGE

Silhouette

Young women's formalwear dresses continued the youthful baby-doll and sheath styles begun in the late 1960s during the opening years of the 1970s, with hemlines remaining extremely short. However, the growing hippie movement and a preference for ethnic or peasant styles rapidly shifted young women's dresses away from short, girlish mini-dresses to more adult styles, featuring soft bias draping and romantic ruffles. Hemlines also lengthened, bringing skirts down below the knee and even to the floor, for the first time in a decade. Young men's formalwear continued to become more informal as men adopted clingy double knits for suiting. Leisure suits, vests, and blazers all replaced the traditional suit in men's formalwear.

Girls' Ensembles

With a marked decrease in truly formal events, young women were able to wear a greater range of dresses for special occasions. In the early part of the 1970s, dresses remained extremely short, well above mid-thigh. The straight sheath and baby-doll styles became slightly more fitted, with princess seams and darts beginning to suggest the shape of womanly curves for the first time since the late 1950s. The previously simple necklines also began to display increasingly wider collars. Formerly bare arms were now covered with long bell, flare, and Juliet sleeves or straight sleeves with deep cuffs. As the decade progressed, these girlish styles were quickly replaced by soft, bias-cut draped dresses. Dirndl, gored, and full-circle skirts were gathered and pleated into waistlines that returned to their natural position. Simple bodices were replaced by halter tops, full gathered bodices with deep scooped necklines, and shirtwaist bodices with wide, pointed collars. Hem lengths dropped below the knees and often reached the floor. For young women old enough to attend discothèques, a range of asymmetrical and handkerchief hemlines were also popular.

Boys' Ensembles

Young men were provided with an ever-increasing range of wardrobe choices in the 1970s. Jackets and blazers increased in portion and fit during the decade. Single-breasted styles with two buttons were preferred. Jackets and blazers became slightly longer, ending well below the hip, and featured deep center back vents, shoulder yokes, and half-belts across the back. Collars and lapels became wider, as did pocket welts, patch pockets, and pocket flaps. Pants had full, flared legs but fit snuggly across the hips and thighs. Tab waistbands and exposed button-front flys replaced traditional waistbands and hidden flys. The new Perma Prest fabrics allowed for center front creases to be permanently set into pant legs. Fitted, single-breasted vests were a new alternative to jackets and blazers for special occasions. Vests, either worn alone or as part of a three-piece set, were fabricated to match either the pant or the blazer. The ultimate, and yet short-lived, trend of the 1970s, the leisure suit, was a popular choice with young men, especially for evenings at discothèques. Leisure suit jackets, unlike blazers, rarely had lapels and featured center front button closures. Completing the look for young men, shiny, "wet-look" nylon or polyester knit shirts in bold colors and patterns provided a fitted silhouette with plenty of stretch for disco dancing. These shirts had wide, pointed collars and fitted sleeves with deep cuffs.

Decorative Details

The innocent pastel colors and small florals and polka dots of the young women's late 1960s and early 1970s dresses gave way to bold colors and large-scale patterns that became synonymous with the decade. Delicate chiffons, laces, satins, and voiles were universally replaced with jersey and double knits. Surface decoration remained minimal, but patterns and textures increased in scale. High-sheen nylons, large-scale floral, paisley, and animal prints, quilting, smocking, shirring, and flounces provided visual interest instead of the architectural seaming seen in the 1960s. Belts, either self-fabric or in contrasting colors and materials, helped to emphasize the return of the natural position of the waistline. Cream, brown, navy, red, rust, and orange colors replaced the soft pastels. Young men's fashions also witnessed an increased application of high-sheen nylons and large-scale floral, abstract, and animal prints. Topstitching and stitched pleats were incorporated into young men's jackets, pants, and vest, and the double-knit Perma Prest fabrics allowed for creases and pleats to be permanently pressed into jackets and pants. Men's color palette continued to expand throughout the decade to include a wide range of earth tones, as well as pastels and neutrals.

CASUAL WEAR: CHILDREN TO PRETEEN

Silhouette

Minimal generational or gender variances were seen in casual wear in the 1960s. Young girls and boys both wore T-shirts, polos, sweater vests, and jeans or corduroys for daily wear. Children's clothing followed the same general trend as adults: pants rode low, below the natural waistline, pant legs were wide and flared, and shirts were fitted. Neither color nor pattern nor garment form (aside from dresses and skirts) clearly announced a child's gender. For the first time, children's fashions were truly unisex.

Girls' Ensembles

Dresses and Skirts: Miniskirts and mini-dresses disappeared in the early 1970s, and, when they did, young girls rarely wore dresses for daily wear. A-line dresses and jumpers continued through the first years of the 1970s but were slowly replaced by a preference for jeans and corduroy pants. When required, young girls donned dirndl skirts, pleated skirts, wrap skirts, bib-front jumpers, and T-shirt dresses when dressy looks, like on school picture day, were required.

Pants: Young girls wore less fashion-forward versions of the jeans and corduroys worn by teenagers and adult women. Pants rode low on the waist but did not achieve the same snug hip-hugger silhouette as in adult fashions. Pant legs also reflected scaled-down versions of the fullness and flare legs or bell-bottoms seen in adult styles. Bib overalls were an important new trend for young girls' casual wear and featured flared legs, decorated and embroidered bibs, and straps with ruffled trim. Pockets and pant legs were other highly decorated features on jeans, pants, and overalls. Whether patch, welt, or slash, pockets were added in contrasting colors and fabrics to the front and back of all pants. Pockets were also embroidered and appliquéd with small animals, flowers, and rainbows.

Tops: Knit shirts, whether pullover or button down, were the dominant material for casual shirts for girls. Plain and rib knits were used for T-shirts, polo shirts, and other pullovers, whereas jersey and double knits were used for button-down shirts. Polo and button-down shirts both featured the wide, pointed collars. Button-down shirts also featured full sleeves with deep cuffs, whereas polo shirts, T-shirts, and other pullovers had long or short fitted sleeves. V necks and jewel necklines were popular for pullover knit shirts, which typically featured rib-knit waistbands and sleeve cuffs. Young girls also wore hip-length woven and double-knit tunics similar to their adult counterparts, with or without sleeves and collars. Peasant tops with ruffled collars and sleeves were another fashionable option for young girls. By the mid-1970s, sweater vests were a key element of young girls' wardrobes. Sweater vests were waist length, with V or scoop necklines, and were either pullovers or buttoned up the center front.

Boys' Ensembles

Pants: Full-cut, flared-bottom jeans and corduroys were proportionally sized with less exaggerated flare for young boys. Topstitching in a range of colors was executed down side seams, across waistbands, and around pockets. Patch, welt, and slash pockets were applied to the fronts and backs of pants and jeans and embellished with topstitching, embroidery, and appliqués. Unique to the 1970s, young boys' pants were the new Toughskins from Sears. During the economic recession of the 1970s, Toughskins, fabricated from heavy denim and featuring reinforced knees, were a mother's answer to keeping her rambunctious boy from wearing holes in his jeans too quickly.

Tops: Pullover and button-down shirts were worn with jeans and pants for daily wear. Popular pullover styles included T-shirts, rugby shirts, turtlenecks, and polo shirts. Rugby and polo shirts, like button-down shirts, featured wide pointed collars. Short- and long-sleeve styles were popular for pullover shirts, but button-down shirts typically featured full sleeves and deep cuffs. In addition to button plackets, pullover shirts also sported center front zippers. Young boys wore sweaters and sweater vests over pullovers and button-down shirts. In the early part of the decade, sweater vests were hip length and often belted. By the middle of the decade, hip-length sweaters and sweater vests had receded in length to the natural waistline.

Decorative Details

Children's jeans were fabricated in dark denim the same as adults and featured topstitching, embroidery, and appliqués on the pockets and down the legs. Twill, brushed twill, and small-wale corduroy were also used for pants. Distinct reds, oranges, golds, and greens provided alternatives to dark blue denim, although wide stripe and plaid patterns were as popular as solids.

Denim, twill, and corduroy were also used in skirts for girls, as were plaids, poplin, and broadcloth. Multicolor patchwork, diagonal stripes, and horizontal stripes were seen in rib, plain, and jersey knits tops, and plaids and checks were popular choices for button-down shirts. Geometric, argyle, Nordic, and stripe patterns were seen in sweater vests. Colors for children's wear included bright primary colors, such as reds, blues, yellow, and greens, as well as the more "adult" fashion colors of gold, avocado, cranberry, and rust. Smocking and gathers were used to create the peasant look in girls' woven tops.

CASUAL WEAR: TEEN TO COLLEGE

Silhouette

The classic teenage uniform, jeans and T-shirts, firmly took root in the 1970s, displacing all other forms of dress for most casual activities. Casual wear fashions were also virtually unisex and could not necessarily be distinguished by color or pattern. For both young men and young women, jeans and other pants rode low on the hip during the early part of the decade, slowly rising back to the natural waistline by the end of the decade. During the first half of the decade, pant legs were fitted on the thigh and then flared out at the knee in ever-increasing dimensions, forming bellbottoms. By the middle of the decade, pant legs had an all-over fullness that slowly returned to a natural, relaxed straight-leg form by the close of the decade. Unisex T-shirts, fitted and sporting logos and slogans, and other knit shirts became the norm for casual dressing.

Girls' Ensembles

Dresses and Skirts: Miniskirts and mini-dresses were still a standard component of casual dressing at the beginning of the 1970s. Simple A-line dresses, sheaths, and jumpers that were worn in the late 1960s continued through the first years of the 1970s, with hemlines slowly inching downward. By the middle of the decade, the mini length was replaced by the midi length, with hemlines hovering around the mid-calf. Dirndl skirts, pleated skirts and kilts, wrap skirts, and circle skirts provided young women with skirt separates to mix and match with blouses and knit tops for a variety of looks. The peasant look, popularized by YSL and romanticized by Laura Ashley, also produced a wide range of floral print skirts and dresses with ruffles and deep flounces and even white eyelet petticoats. Dresses also featured peasant drawstring or elastic necklines that were worn off one or both shoulders and trimmed with flounces. Waistbands also returned to skirts as the waistline returned once again to its natural position. T-shirt dresses and shirtwaist dresses, dresses resembling a men's button-down shirt, were also popular alternatives for casual dressing.

Pants: Pants, particularly jeans and corduroys, were preferred by young women for most casual activities. Now universally socially acceptable, young women no longer hesitated to wear jeans and pants to school, shopping, or social gatherings. Hip-hugger styles remained popular for the first few years of the 1970s but were not nearly as popular as when they originated in the 1960s. Slim-fitting pant legs also relaxed, gaining fullness and flare over the course of the decade before slimming down again. In the early 1970s, the flare was limited to below the knee, but, by the mid-1970s, pant legs in general had widened, still retaining flared legs or bell-bottoms, a form that remained until the last two years of the decade, when pant legs began shifting to a full but straight line. Pants and jeans had flat fronts, center front zipper or exposed button flys, and, as waistlines re-emerged, waistbands. Pockets, in all shapes and sizes, were an important decorative element on 1970s pants and jeans. Welt, slash, and patch pockets in self-fabric or contrasting fabric were displayed on the fronts and backs of all pants. Pant cuffs also returned to popularity by the middle of the decade.

Tops: The majority of casual wear tops in the 1970s were made from plain, jersey and rib knits. T-shirts, turtlenecks, polo shirts, and other pullover knit shirts were paired with jeans, corduroys, and skirts. Knit shirts were body conscious and clingy, featuring V, scoop, and jewel necklines or wide, pointed convertible collars. Straight long and short sleeves were popular for most of the decade, but alternative sleeve forms, such as raglan, kimono, and drop shoulder, became popular at the end of the decade. Most knit shirts also ended with rib-knit waistbands, fitted across the high hip. Woven shirts with wide pointed collars and full sleeves with deep cuffs were also worn. Woven and knit halter tops, tube tops, and tank tops were also worn during the summer.

The early 1970s also witnessed a continued popularity for late 1960s woven and double-knit tunics. Long-sleeve, short-sleeve, and sleeveless tunics, with jewel necklines or convertible collars, around mid-thigh in length were worn over the top of pants and skirts. Vests also enjoyed popularity throughout the decade. Long crocheted, suede, or leather vests were popular for casual wear over knit and woven tops in the early part of the 1970s. Waist-length sweater vests with V or jewel necks and tailored, single-breasted vests replaced long vests in the last half of the decade.

Boys' Ensembles

Pants: Jeans and corduroys also dominated young men's casual wear in the 1970s. Once the domain of rebellious youth, the ubiquitous jeans were no longer just for hippies. Young men, just like their female counterparts, wore hip-hugger styles in the first few years of the 1970s. Although waistlines slowly returned to their natural position, young men's pants continued to fit snug across the hips and thighs, to reveal narrow hips and muscular thighs. Pant legs flared out from the knee in the early part of the decade, growing in overall fullness with flared legs or bell-bottoms that did not decrease until the closing years of the decade. Young men's pants were predominantly flat front with center front fly zippers. Pockets were also a key style element in young men's pants and jeans. Welt, slash, and patch pockets were incorporated on the fronts and backs of all pants.

Tops: T-shirts, rugby shirts, polo shirts, turtlenecks, and other pullover-style knit wear formed the foundation of young men's casual shirts. Plain, jersey, and rib knits were worn tight, revealing athletic physiques earned through the new fitness craze. Pullover knit shirts featured V and jewel necklines, wide, pointed collars, and short or long fitted sleeves. Jewel and collared shirts also featured plackets with either buttons or zippers. Woven and knit button-down shirts with wide pointed collars and full sleeves with deep cuffs, preferably in shiny nylon with graphic prints, were also worn, especially at discothèques. Sweaters and sweater vests were also key components of a young man's wardrobe. Sweaters and sweater vests featured V or deep round necklines and were worn over knit and woven shirts. In the early part of the decade, sweaters and sweater vests were longer, down to the hip, and often belted. By the middle of the decade, sweater and sweater vest lengths had returned to just below the natural waistline. Suede and leather vests with fringe were also briefly popular in the early part of the 1970s.

Decorative Details

Dark denim was the preferred treatment for blue jeans by both sexes. Topstitching and saddle stitching (double rows of curved topstitching across the pant seat) in orange, white, gold, and red decorated blue jeans. Jean pockets were also covered with embroidery and appliqués. Twill, brushed twill, and small-wale corduroy were also popular fabrics for pants for both genders, as was polyester double knits. Pants were still as colorful as in the 1960s, in red, orange, gold, and avocado, but patterns were reduced to wide stripes and plaids only; ethnic and other graphic prints were no longer seen in pants. Skirts for young women were also made from denim, twill, and corduroy as well as tweeds, tartan plaids, poplin, and broadcloth. Romantic floral prints and small paisleys were seen in peasant-style skirts and tops, trimmed with lace and eyelet.

Rib, plain, and jersey knits were popular for shirt fabrications and were often knit or sewn together in patchwork multicolor patterns or in diagonal or horizontal stripes. Velour and terrycloth also became popular new fabrics for pullover shirts. Any and all colors were seen in shirts in the 1970s. Muted earth tones, such as loden, cranberry, pumpkin, and plum, and bright primary colors, such as red, blue, and yellow, were both equally popular for young men and young women. Plaids, checks, and diagonal stripes were seen in both woven and knit versions of button-down shirts. Geometric, argyle, Nordic, and stripe patterns were seen in sweater vests.

OUTERWEAR: CHILDREN TO PRETEEN

Coats

Young children wore brightly colored stadium jackets for winter wear. These jackets were typically fabricated with a nylon shell and filled with either down or polyester batting for warmth. Decorative topstitching formed quilted patterns across the jacket. Most jackets were hip length, but some were slightly longer and featured self-fabric belts with either buckle or toggle closures. In addition to nylon stadium jackets, suede or wool Melton jackets were also popular. These jackets featured large patch pockets, with center front closures of either buttons, frogs, or toggles. Girls' jackets regularly featured hoods that were often trimmed in fur or faux fur. For spring, both young boys and young girls wore jean jackets and cotton poplin jackets. Young girls also wore knitted or crocheted ponchos with tassels.

OUTERWEAR: TEEN TO COLLEGE

Coats

In the early 1970s, outerwear for young women came in two distinct styles, mini and maxi, designed to complement the two available skirt lengths, but settled into either hip length or mid-calf length by the close of the decade. Both double-breasted and single-breasted styles of trench coats with wide collars and lapels were popular, and many displayed a military influence with wide epaulets. Most coats also displayed wide sashes and belts or wide inset waistbands. Faux fur and faux fur trims in natural colors and fashion colors remained popular. Faux fur trims appeared on both long and short coat collars, cuffs, and around hemlines. Winter and spring coats also featured ethnic-inspired details such as embroidery or paisley fabrics, reflective of the new peasant look shown by YSL and others.

Unisex suede jackets and vests with long fringe and Western-style yokes and pockets became a symbol of affiliation with anti-establishment movements for youths. In addition to the unisex suede fringe jackets, young men also wore leather blazers and leather bomber jackets. Leather jackets were typically single breasted and featured deep shoulder yokes and large patch pockets. Trench coats for spring and pea coats for winter continued to be popular, but the collars and lapels continued to widen throughout the decade. Both young men and young women also wore unisex parkas and stadium coats in suede backed with shearling or nylon filled with down or polyester batting. For both sexes, these jackets featured hoods and deep cuffs that were lined with fur, faux fur, or shearling and large toggle or frog closures. Another unisex trend that dominated the decade and became synonymous with the hippie movement was denim or jean jackets. Jean jackets were hip length, typically dark denim, and featured either gold or orange topstitching.

SWIMWEAR AND SPORTSWEAR: CHILDREN TO PRETEEN

Swimwear

Young boys continued to wear swim trunks in bright colors and bold geometric patterns. Trunks had either elastic waistbands or zip flys with snap closures and large patch pockets with snap or zip closures or large flaps. Swim wear in red, white, and blue color schemes became especially popular during the United States bicentennial celebration of 1976. Young girls wore bikinis with brief bottoms and bra-style and halter-style tops. Floral prints, plaids, and diagonal stripes in bright colors and Easter egg pastels were popular.

SWIMWEAR AND SPORTSWEAR: TEEN TO COLLEGE

Swimwear

Young men's trunks were short and fitted. Trunks featured wide waistbands with tabs, belt loops, and top stitching and large patch pockets. The popularity of athletic wear influenced the design of young men's swim trunks. In addition to solids and prints, athletic racing stripes in white provided contrasting trim on the outseam and around the hem of trunks.

Young women wore slightly less conservative versions of the bikinis and one-piece maillots worn by adult women. Over the course of the decade, halter- and bra-style tops continued to decrease in size, forming increasingly smaller triangles with simple string tie closures. Bikini bottoms were shaped like briefs, which could be adjusted based on personal preference via drawstrings on the side. Those daring enough could draw up the string, bringing the waist of the brief down to the hip. Bandeaux tops with or without keyholes, either as a bikini top or on maillots, became popular because the straps could be detached to avoid tan lines. Maillot styles featured simple scoop necklines or plunging necklines with fabric loops or chain clasps at the center front to link the top together from side to side. Bikinis and maillots for young girls were also influenced by athletic wear, featuring racing stripes around the outer edges of bikini and bandeaux tops and down the side seams. Young women's swimwear came in a wide range of colors and patterns, with bright colors and floral prints popular in the early 1970s, trending toward solid, muted colors by the end of the decade.

HEADWEAR, HAIRSTYLES, AND COSMETICS: CHILDREN TO PRETEEN

Headwear

Headwear was only seen on young children for very formal occasions or as part of rain or winter weather gear.

Hairstyles

Young girls wore their hair long and straight, typically in ponytails, pigtails, or braids throughout the 1970s. Even when young and adult women began adopting shorter hairstyles, long straight or naturally wavy hair was considered most appropriate for young girls. Some young girls also folded their braids into looped pigtails, wore French braids, or wore their hair straight with small single braided strands on each side. Headbands, barrettes, and ribbons were used to fasten, tie back, and hold hair in place for young girls. Young boys wore their hair trimmed neatly, collar length in back and over the ears on the sides. Hair was either parted deep to one side, with bangs sweeping across the forehead, or not parted at all, brushed straight down, forming the bowl haircut.

HEADWEAR, HAIRSTYLES, AND COSMETICS: TEEN TO COLLEGE

Headwear

Young men and women rarely wore headwear on a daily basis in the 1970s. Some young women wore large-brimmed canvas, straw, or denim hats, crocheted berets, or long headscarves to complement peasant-inspired or hippie-style ensembles. Instead of hats, some young women and young men wore leather, suede, or fabric headbands across their foreheads. These headbands were similar to those worn by individuals following the hippie movement and were often beaded, embroidered, or studded with ethnic-inspired motifs. Baseball caps and visors were popular with both genders for athletic wear.

Hairstyles

Young women wore their hair long and straight and typically parted in the middle in the early 1970s. Hair length typically fell to the center back and was combed smooth and straight or pulled into ponytails and pigtails. As the decade progressed, hair length rose to the shoulders and displayed natural (or manmade) wave, and bangs returned to popularity. By the end of the decade, the popularity of Dorothy Hamill, the gold medalist in skating in the 1976 Olympics, inspired young women to adopt sassy short haircuts, dubbed the wedge. The 1976 hit television show *Charlie's Angels* also inspired the new layered feathered hairstyle, in long and short lengths, which were popularized by the show's star Farrah Fawcett-Majors.

Young men also experimented with hairstyles and facial hair during the 1970s. The mop cuts of the 1960s gave way to shags, afros (obtained by Caucasian men through permanents), feathers, and mullets. Hair was typically parted deep on the side, rather than in the middle, grown to the collar line at the back, and to or just below the ears on the sides. The small trim sideburns of the 1960s also exploded into full, thick mutton-chop sideburns. Both thick sideburns and mustaches were grown by young men as soon as they were able.

Cosmetics

The heavy cookie-cutter makeup worn by young women in the 1960s was replaced by a more natural look in the 1970s. Eye shadow, eyeliner, blush, lipstick, and mascara were still worn but in warm subtle tones that produced a healthy, suntanned glow. The only exception to this look came in the late 1970s when disco dancing surged in popularity. For those young women old enough to attend disco clubs, the preferred disco look was dramatic and shiny. Electric blue eye shadow was paired with smoky eyeliners and glossy lipsticks.

FOOTWEAR AND LEGWEAR: CHILDREN TO PRETEEN

Footwear

Children's footwear followed the overall style elements of adult footwear, except for the platform soles. Overall proportions were thick and chunky, with stacked heels and soles, but never crossed into the extreme platforms and wedges of adult shoes. Mary Janes and oxfords for young girls and oxfords and loafers for young boys were fabricated with the same pieced and perforated vamps and tongues as adult shoes. The multipart construction of the vamp allowed children's shoes to appear in patchwork multi-color combinations of reds, blues, greens, and yellows. Mary Janes also had the wider straps and large buckles seen on women's shoes. Tennis or gym shoes were popular choices in footwear for young children's casual wear and contained scale models of adult Adidas stripes and Nike swooshes. Tennis shoes were available in canvas or with nylon uppers and suede and leather accents.

Legwear

Young girls wore tights in heavy cable and rib knits with their dresses, skirts, and jumpers. For more formal occasions, lighter-weight tights in opaque colors were worn. Solid and patterned knit socks in colors designed to match casual pants were worn by young girls for casual wear. Young boys and young girls both wore tube or gym socks for casual wear. These white knit socks came to mid-calf and had rib-knit bands on the top, typically with horizontal bands of color. Young boys wore dark socks with argyle, check, and paisley patterns for dress.

FOOTWEAR AND LEGWEAR: TEEN TO COLLEGE

Footwear

Wedge and platform shoes were popular with young women in the early 1970s. However, wedge and platform heels were replaced by thick, chunky, square heels by the middle of the decade. Whether platform, wedge, or chunk, on top of the heels were sculpted vamps with round toes. Thick straps, either horizontal or crisscrossed, formed the vamp for sandals, whereas heavy, performed vamps were seen on spectators, wing-tips, ghillies, Mary Janes, and clogs. Spectators, wing-tips, and ghillies fastened closed across the vamp with thick grosgrain ribbons, but Mary Janes featured wide straps with large buckles. Spectators, wing-tips, and ghillies were often pieced from several different colors of leather, suede, vinyl, or canvas, forming two-tone and three-tone designs in red, blue, yellow, white, and brown. Tall boots continued in popularity throughout the entire decade. Tall boots were available in stretch vinyl, leather, and suede and embellished with either decorative or functional laces and buckles.

Young men also wore platform shoes in the early 1970s. Slip-on loafers, spectators, and oxfords featured the same platform and thick, chunky squared heels and round toes as young women's shoes. Spectators and oxfords also came in two-tone and three-tone designs, with colorful, perforated vamps and contrasting color shoestring ties. Slip-on loafers featured large metals buckles or clips and tongues in contrasting colors or with reptile embossing.

Particularly popular amongst young men and women were tennis or gym shoes. Companies such as Converse, Nike, and Adidas manufactured gym shoes in canvas or in leather with nylon mesh inserts in a wide range of colors. Originally intended as athletic wear, gym shoes moved beyond the gym, dominating youth casual footwear.

Legwear

Young women wore pantyhose and tights with their skirts and dresses, typically in a range of nude or suntan colors. Both pantyhose and tights were also seen in patterns, such as chevrons or argyles, and textures, such as cable knit or lace. Metallic yarn or high-sheen Lycra was added to tights and pantyhose that were paired with disco ensembles. Thick wool patterned and striped stocks and leg warmers were also briefly popular in the late 1970s. These thick socks and leg warmers were worn with skirts and over the legs of pants and then folded down over the top of the boot (Skinner 1998, 83). In keeping with the preference for gym shoes, knee-high tube socks with two or three color bands on the ribbed knit top were popular for both young men and young women. In addition to tube socks, both genders wore an assortment of solid color, striped, and argyle patterned sock in muted earth tones. Colorful, wildly patterned toe socks were also briefly popular in the 1970s amongst the young of both genders.

ACCESSORIES

Jewelry

Young women wore simple hoop earring and chains or serpentine necklaces and bracelets, typically in gold. Gold charm bracelets were also popular with young women. Although jewelry for young women became more minimalist, jewelry for young men actually increased in size and quantity. Large gold chains, medallions, rings, and bracelets were worn by trendy young men. Simple strands of pearls, chokers with pendants, or medallions on long chains were worn by young women with casual ensembles.

Gloves and Handbags

Soft satchels or envelope-style purses on long straps were worn cross-wise across the body by young women. Leather bags featured embossed floral motifs or multicolored patchwork construction. Canvas, crochet, and corduroy were also popular alternatives to leather and suede for purses. Topstitching, embroidery, and bead work provided simple embellishments for canvas, crochet, and corduroy purses, whereas zippers, toggles, and buckles provided decorative and functional elements for leather and suede bags.

Neckwear

As an alternative to necklaces, young women and young men often tied colorful bandanas or scarves around their necks. The knot was typically placed on either the left or right side of the neck with the scarf tails hanging down over each side of the shoulder. Long silk scarves with fringe were also worn by both genders, draped around the neck or crossed over one shoulder. Over the course of the decade, neckties for young men became increasingly wider, up to five inches at their most extreme, before returning to the standard two-and-a-half inches by the close of the decade. Neckties displayed bold stripes, paisleys, and other ethnic-inspired prints in oranges, teals, browns, rusts, and blues.

Other Accessories

Sunglasses were a key and unisex fashion accessory in the 1970s. Young men and women wore gold-rimmed aviator-style sunglasses with dark lenses. Young women also wore large circular, oval, and square sunglasses in tortoiseshell and fashion colors. Suspenders were also a short-lived fashion accessory for both young men and young women in the mid- to late 1970s. Suspenders in solid colors and stripes were worn with khakis, jeans, and dress pants by both genders.

Belts were another important fashion accessory for young women in the 1970s. With a decreased emphasis on jewelry, belts became a primary source for adorning and distinguishing an outfit. Belts were worn low on the hip and came in leather, chain link, canvas, and silk cord. Leather belts for young women came in a range of dimensions, forming wide waist cinchers to small circlets and were perforated and embossed in a manner similar to footwear. Chain-link and silk cord belts were multi-stranded, with the strands either braided together or swagged. Canvas belts, worn by both young men and young women, were approximately one inch wide and featured metal "seat belt" style buckles. Young men also wore wide leather belts with large buckles and embossed or perforated detailing. Particularly popular were leather belts with double and triple rows of eyelets perforated around the entire belt.

THE
1980s

FORMALWEAR: CHILDREN TO PRETEEN

Silhouette

The 1980s brought a new trend for designer baby apparel with the appearance of elegant bodysuits, leggings, tops, hats, and other items. Tommy Hilfiger and Ralph Lauren were among the first American designers to explore the market for formalwear for infants and toddlers. Silhouette changes in children's formalwear followed trends similar to those seen in adults during this period. For girls, this included an emphasis on broad shoulders with princess seams that incorporated box and side pleats to create the fuller silhouettes. Boys' suits were also more fitted with broad shoulders.

Girls' Ensembles

Gowns for first communion, weddings, and other religious ceremonies were usually fitted on top and full from the waist down. However, the trend toward a more casual society meant that skirts and pants may be worn by young girls for formal occasions such as weddings and religious ceremonies rather than dresses. Full dirndl or circle skirts, whether as part of a dress or two-piece ensemble, dominated young girls' formalwear. However, some young girls also wore the 1980s bubble skirts, just like their adult counterparts. Most girls' tops were fitted with princess seams and often incorporated peplum and basque additions at the waist. Necklines were conservative and decorated with lace or satin finishes. Dresses featured classic Peter Pan collars including variations such as the bertha and puritan. Baby-doll or puffed sleeves completed the bodice of dresses and tops. Some dresses were topped with brocade vests in paisley and floral weaves.

Boys' Ensembles

Young boys wore either long pants or shorts for formal occasions. In keeping with the 1980s trends, both shorts and pants had pleated fronts, high waistbands, and were often paired with suspenders. To top off basic woven dress shirts, young boys either wore suit jackets or blazers, with or without vests, or vests alone. Double-breasted jackets, blazers, and vests were more popular than single breasted and displayed the same wide-peaked, notched lapels as adult male suits. For extremely formal occasions, young boys wore tuxedos, with pants or shorts or even knickerbocker suits. For less-formal occasions, boys paired cardigan sweaters with embroidered crests over woven tops and pants.

Decorative Details

Christening gowns and formal layettes for infants were often handmade, usually in white with lace trimmings, small pastel ribbons, and smocking. Keepsake-quality baby clothes often included decorative detailing such as smocking, hand topstitching, embroidery, and lace. Other decorative techniques commonly used were crochet edgings, binding, piping, and ruffles. Formalwear for girls was predominantly black and white but was also seen in bright reds and purples or soft pastel pinks, blues, greens, and yellows. Velvet was the top fabric choice for girls, but velveteen, organza, taffeta, corduroy, and other wool and cotton blends were also seen. Decorative trimmings included eyelet, ruffles, taffeta bows, and lace with metallic finishes. Velvet, velveteen, and other fine fabrics were commonly used for formalwear for young boys. For slightly less formal occasions, herringbone, broken or chalk stripes, polka dots, and other classic patterns were seen in wool and linen suits. Decorative nontraditional buttons were often used along with crested pockets in boys' suits. Fine cottons and linens were used for woven dress shirts, which may incorporate the same pleated and pin-tucked shirt bibs as adult male shirts. Colorful bow ties or four-in-hand ties, pocket squares, and suspenders completed the ensembles.

FORMALWEAR: TEEN TO COLLEGE

Silhouette

Teenagers and college students usually wore variations of adult styles; thus, the 1980s saw a plethora of bright wide-shouldered prom dresses with puffed skirts and bows. Equally popular were feminine dresses showcasing fitted silhouettes with princess lines. Young American men usually wore classic-cut tuxedos for formal events, also emphasizing broad shoulders. Black remained the color of choice for most formalwear for both young men and young women, although other shades were used, particularly in the 1980s when pastels were often seen at high-school proms.

Girls' Ensembles

Full and puffed skirts appeared in 1980s formalwear worn by younger American women, typically embellished with bows and ruffles. For proms and other special events, dresses were either tea length (mid-calf) or floor length. Shorter, knee-length styles were worn for cocktail parties and semiformal dances. Dress bodices were fitted with princess seams and incorporated large shoulder pads and puffed sleeves. Strapless and off-the-shoulder styles were seen in some gowns, but the emphasis on broad shoulders meant that the majority of dresses had at least cap sleeves.

Bodice designs also incorporated yokes with inset ruffles, gathers, or shirring, inspired by the wedding dress of Princess Diana. Natural waistlines were emphasized with either ruffled peplums or sashes tied in large bows at the center back.

Boys' Ensembles

For the most formal occasion, young men donned black tuxedos. The tuxedos consisted of formal straight-leg pants without cuffs that had pleated fronts and double-breasted jackets. Pastel vests, suspenders, pocket squares, bow ties, and cummerbunds were worn under some tuxedos, especially to high-school proms, when the goal was to match the color of the man's accessories to his date's dress. For less formal occasions, suits were frequently worn. Suit jackets were either one or two button and double breasted with moderate side vents. As an alternative to the standard suit jacket, some young men's suits came with waist-length jackets finished with a waistband, a look popularized by bands such as Duran Duran. Suit pants had straight legs, typically no cuff, and front pleats. Shirts, under both tuxedos and suits, were fitted, with narrow collars and slim sleeves. Tuxedo shirts may have pleated, tucked, or even ruffled front yokes. Bow ties were typically worn with tuxedos, but suits were accompanied by increasingly skinnier ties in a wide array of bold colors and graphic prints.

Decorative Details

Luxurious materials such as cashmere, satin, lace, and velvet were used extensively in young women's formalwear in the 1980s. Crisp taffetas and organzas were also preferred to create full, voluminous shapes and stiff ruffles. Dresses were embellished with metallic yarns, sequins, beads, and palliates and accessorized with lots of gold jewelry. Pastels and black dominated the color palette, especially for prom dresses. Young men's tuxedos applied the standard satin ribbon or braid on the outseam and satin edging on the lapels. Tuxedos were typically black, and suits favored ranges of blacks and grays. Dress shirts for young men were most frequently white, but some men did experiment with pastel colors, particularly pink.

CASUAL WEAR: CHILDREN TO PRETEEN

Silhouette

Most infants and toddlers were dressed in simply shaped clothes aimed to promote ease of movement, to provide warmth and safety, and for ease of care. The silhouette for young children remained simple and similar to those first seen in the 1920s but became slightly exaggerated in portion, just as all fashions did in the 1980s. Children's wear also participated in the conspicuous consumption of the "me" generation. It was never too early to participate in fashion trends. Casual clothing for children was emblazoned with designer names and logos the same as adult clothing. Osh Kosh was no longer the only recognized name brand in children's apparel. Designers such as Ralph Lauren and Donna Karan entered the children's market, as did private-label retailers such as The Gap, The Limited, and The Chess King.

Girls' Ensembles

Dresses and Skirts: Young girls wore A-line and shift dresses and jumpers with lowered waistlines and princess seams for school and other casual activities. Sleeveless sundresses, with matching decorated diaper covers for toddlers, were popular for summer play wear. Dresses were typically knee length, sleeveless or short sleeved, and had simple round or square necklines. Sailor dresses with big collars were also popular. A popular alternative to dresses was overalls, in either denim or colorful cotton twills, with buckled straps and large pockets.

Pants: Jeans continued to gain acceptance as the preferred form of clothing for girls for school and after-school activities. In the 1980s, jeans and denim shorts were often acid washed, with pleated fronts and tapered legs. Girls' denim often incorporated appliqué and embroidered decorative details. Chinos and corduroys were also worn by young girls for casual wear and were produced with the same silhouette and style features as jeans. Slim-fitting capri pants, leggings, and stirrup pants provided an alternative to jeans and chinos for young girls. A-line and wrap skirts, in cotton twill, tweed, and denim, also included decorative appliqué, metal studs, and other forms of embellishment.

Tops: A wide range of knit and woven tops were available for young girls. Basic T-shirts with novelty prints and cartoon characters, such as the Smurfs, My Little Pony, Strawberry Shortcake, turtlenecks, mock turtlenecks, polo shirts, and tank tops came in a wide range of solids and stripes. Basic woven tops with Peter Pan, sailor, and mandarin collars had short puffed sleeves to keep the emphasis on broad shoulders in the 1980s. Tapestry vests, sweater vests, cardigans, V-neck sweaters, and crewneck sweaters were layered over both knit and woven shirts. Sweaters typically were long sleeved with ribbed-knit necklines, waistbands, and cuffs. Bright solid colors were prevalent, and, frequently, sweaters and woven shirts were emblazoned with monograms. Oversized sweaters with novelty patterns were worn with leggings and stirrup pants. Both knit and woven shirts were worn with jeans, chinos, and shorts as well as under overalls and jumpers.

Boys' Ensembles

Pants: As with girls, young boys' trousers were dominated by blue jeans. Stone-washed, acid-washed, and distressed finishes were applied to denim jeans, shorts, and jackets. Flat-front jeans were standard, but some young boys also wore pleated-front jeans. Black jeans also became a dressy alternative to trousers for young boys, although cotton twill chinos were crucial for young boys emulating the *Miami Vice* and preppy looks.

Tops: Young boys wore a range of knit and woven shirts for school and casual wear. T-shirts, polo shirts, rugby shirts, and turtlenecks in solids and wide horizontal stripes were popular choices for everyday wear. Polo and rugby shirts typically had white or contrasting color collars, plackets, and cuffs. T-shirts came with a wide range of logos, slogans, cartoon characters, sports teams, and musicians silk screened or transfer printed across the chest or back. Woven shirts with button-down collars were worn in solid colors, pink, green, and yellow being the trendiest, and patterns, with stripes and small ethnic motifs being the most popular. Woven shirts were often layered over polo shirts and T-shirts.

Decorative Details

Young girls' dresses, skirts, and woven tops were decorated with appliqué work, lace, eyelet, ricrac, and piping, especially on pockets, collars, cuffs, and necklines. Most apparel was available in a range of bright solid colors; however, nautical motifs, safari animal prints, and large floral prints were also popular alternatives. Young boys' clothing had minimal decoration, with patterns limited to stars, planets, aeronautical symbols, and licensed cartoon motifs such as the Superfriends and the Transformers. Topstitching, especially in contrasting colors or in white or gold for denim, was common throughout both boys' and girls' clothing. Girls wore bright colors, but boys often wore the new trendy pastels, including pink, yellow, and green, although red and navy remained staple colors. Most fabrics used for children's apparel were natural wools and cottons to prevent the allergic reactions caused by some synthetic fabrics.

CASUAL WEAR: TEEN TO COLLEGE

Silhouette

American teen- and college-aged individuals mixed trendy sports and active wear with formalwear and street wear to create unique casual wear looks. Drawing inspiration from new wave, rap, and metal music, sports, *Miami Vice*, and the Valley, a multitude of fashion trends converged in the 1980s, providing youths with a wide range of fashion choices.

However, every niche fashion segment still had one thing in common: bigger, bolder, and brighter was always better. For both young men and women, broad shoulders, narrow waists, and narrow hips dominated the fashionable silhouette of the 1980s. The growth of suburban shopping malls also meant that America's youths had an after-school and weekend hangout for browsing and purchasing all the latest fashion trends.

Girls' Ensembles

Dresses and Skirts: The 1980s witnessed the return of the mini-dress and miniskirt, a drastic change from the maxis and long peasant skirts of the 1970s. Dresses in the 1980s featured rounded or drop shoulders supported by large shoulder pads. Necklines were simple scoop or jewel styles. Dresses also typically featured a dropped waist, around the hip line or upper thigh. Below the dropped waist, skirts were either straight or gathered into ruffled flounces and ended around mid-thigh. Sweater, T-shirt, and polo shirt dresses were casual alternatives for preppy or Valley Girl-inspired looks. For those interested in cultivating a new wave Cyndi Lauper or Madonna image, neon, pink, and black lace were used for flounced skirts, and drop-waist tubular bodices were replaced by fitted tanks and bustiers with sweetheart necklines. Miniskirts, which ended around mid-thigh, came in a range of styles and fabrics. A-line jean skirts with gold or white topstitching were very popular, especially when displaying the Calvin Klein, Guess, or Jordache labels. Other miniskirts made from cotton twills, rib knits, and corduroy incorporated hip yokes, flounces, tiers of ruffles, and gathering to create volume.

Pants: Miniskirts and jeans were two staples of a young woman's wardrobe. Jeans came in a range of finishes, including stone, acid, and distressed, as well as colors such as pink, green, and black. Jeans were either worn extremely tight, with legs so tapered that ankle slits or zippers had to be incorporated to allow the foot to pass through, or baggy with a pleated front and tapered legs. Jean pockets were embroidered in gold or white and, most importantly, displayed the name of the designer. Capri pants, leggings, stirrup pants, and nylon parachute pants were popular alternatives to jeans and miniskirts.

Tops: Knit and woven tops provided even more opportunities for young women to create their own unique looks. Drop-shouldered T-shirts and sweatshirts were either cut up or came with bateau necklines, worn asymmetrically to expose one shoulder, and layered over rib-knit tank tops to emulate the styles seen in *Flashdance.* Lace and mesh tops, popularized by Madonna, were also worn over tank tops and camisoles and exposed the midriff, much to the concern of parents (Harris and Brown 2002, 52).

Valley Girls and preps wore polo shirts, button-down oxfords, and crew-neck sweaters in a range of colors and patterns. Oversized sweatshirts, embellished with metal studs and rhinestones, and oversized sweaters in black and bright colors were worn with slim-fit capri pants, leggings, and stirrup pants. Bold, bright sweaters, typically with black backgrounds and neon-colored geometric patterns by Esprit and Benetton, were a must-have for every young women's wardrobe.

Boys' Ensembles

Pants: Young men had just as many fashion trends to select from as young women in the 1980s. Blue jeans became the staple pant for young men in the 1980s, even replacing traditional trousers in semiformal occasions. The new black jeans and pleated fronts gave denim a dressy look and became widely accepted at most semiformal occasions. Stone, acid, and distressed treatments were applied to denim for jeans and shorts. Jeans also incorporated a number of novelty features such as large patch pockets and decorative zippers, as well as designer names. Despite the widespread popularity of jeans, some young men opted to wear chinos or khakis with straight legs and pleated fronts as an alternative to jeans for a more sophisticated preppy or *Miami Vice* look.

The popularity of rap music and break dancing in the 1980s also provided two other fashion alternatives for young men: warm-up suits and parachute pants. Many rap artists wore fleece and velour warm-up suits by Nike and Adidas in solid colors with racing stripes down the outer leg and outer arm, a look immediately adopted by aficionados of this new musical form. Similarly, the popularity of Michael Jackson's *Thriller* album and break dancing brought parachute pants, made from nylon and worn by break dancers to facilitate their sliding and spinning movements, into mainstream popularity. Parachute pants came typically in red, black, or camouflage and had large patch pockets and decorative zippers.

Tops: Young men who opted for the preppy look wore polo shirts, rugby shirts, button-down oxfords, and crewneck sweaters in pastel colors, navy, red, and white or bold horizontal stripes. Typically, the trend involved layering two or more of the preceding garments into one ensemble. Those opting to imitate Don Johnson on *Miami Vice* wore pastel-colored T-shirts and three- or five-button Henley shirts under sports jackets. Other popular shirt styles included T-shirts featuring product logos, slogans, band names, and sports emblems, dropped shoulder sweatshirts, woven shirts with band or mandarin collars, turtlenecks, tank tops, and muscle shirts. Blazers, jean jackets, and leather coats were no longer relegated only to outerwear but became common additions to daywear ensembles.

Decorative Details

Young men's and women's casual wear in the 1980s was more about color, pattern, and texture than embellishment. Fabrics such as fleece, lace, mesh, nylon, and denim provided texture, whereas neon and pastel geometric shapes and animal prints provided visual interest. Zippers, oversized buttons, topstitching, and, most importantly, designer labels and logos provided the limited surface embellishment for casual wear in this era.

OUTERWEAR: CHILDREN TO PRETEEN

Coats

Denim jackets were extremely popular in the adult market in the 1980s and therefore were customized for the children's market with embroidered and appliquéd decorations. The fascination with the Cold War also rippled from the adult market into children's outerwear in the form of sailor- and army-inspired jackets with broad shoulders for both boys and girls. Colored leather and vinyl jackets enjoyed wide popularity in the late 1980s thanks to Michael Jackson. These jackets often had asymmetrical closures, stand collars, shiny or neon finishes, and decorative piping or zippers. Reversible jackets were also common in the children's market.

OUTER WEAR: TEEN TO COLLEGE

Coats

Young women wore oversized coats with large shoulder pads and high collars in the 1980s. Most formal and semiformal coats were made in earth tones and soft pastels, but casual coats came in a range of hues, including the popular pastel and neon colors seen in other apparel. Faux fur trimmings appeared in many girls' coats. Denim jackets, however, dominated casual wear for young Americans during the 1980s. Denim jackets for both young men and young women were stone washed, acid washed, and piece dyed. Although embroidery, metal studs, and rhinestones embellished girls' jackets, pins and patches were popular additions to young men's denim jackets. Bomber and other types of leather jackets, parkas, and windbreaker jackets were widely worn.

SWIMWEAR AND SPORTSWEAR: CHILDREN TO PRETEEN

Swimwear

One-piece Lycra spandex swimsuits were the top choice in girls' swimwear, although two-piece bathing suits were also popular. Colors remained bright and displayed geometric and floral motifs. Bottoms were often covered with skirted portions or ruffles. Boys wore mostly draw-string nylon shorts with neon colors and bold patterns in the 1980s.

SWIMWEAR AND SPORTSWEAR: TEEN TO COLLEGE

Swimwear

The emphasis on fitness seen in adult clothing during the 1980s reached the teenage market in which body-enhancing styles were created with nylon spandex. Bikinis and one-piece suits for teenagers and college-aged women usually came in bright colors and elaborate prints, often with abstract and floral motifs. Higher leg lines, also known as French cuts in 1980s swimwear, were often covered with ruffled skirts and other types of coverups. New one-piece designs with cutouts across the sides, stomach, and back rivaled bikinis for popularity. Although Lycra and similar mate-rials were used to create a close fit in girls' swimwear, young men's swim-ming trunks remained conservatively long and loose, often reaching below the knees. Young men's swim trunks were also brightly colored, using either color blocking or tropical motif.

Other Activewear

The conspicuous consumption of the 1980s did not escape the teen mar-ket, and a perfect place to display wealth and status was the high-school ski club. Teenagers and college students embraced a variety of skiwear outfits such as tapered pants and wool sweaters in vivid colors during the 1980s. Fashionable teens, both male and female, donned matching ski jackets and ski pants as they hit the slopes with their classmates. The 1980s fitness craze, spurred on by Jane Fonda, movies such as *Flashdance*, and musicians such as Madonna, popularized gym wear in the teen mar-ket, including leotards, unitards, and leggings in Lycra spandex. The black or neon spandex workout clothes moved beyond the gym to be incorpo-rated into daily casual wear for teens.

HEADWEAR, HAIRSTYLE, AND COSMETICS: CHILDREN TO PRETEEN

Headwear

As headwear use among adults declined during the period, children con-tinued wearing classic old-fashioned styles for formal occasions such as sailor hats and straw hats decorated with ribbons and flowers. American young girls also wore colorful ponytail holders, hair bows, flower head-bands, barrettes, scrunchies, and multi-ribbon bows. Infants wore decorated wool or synthetic caps, usually in pastel colors, with gender-appropriate decorations. Baseball caps became ubiquitous in boys' wear during the

1980s and incorporated sports and product logos, as well as favorite children's characters from video games and television.

Hairstyles

Most American girls wore variations of short and long hairstyles seen in adult women, but long hair worn in ponytails, braids, or French braids remained a favorite style for girls. Boys also imitated the styles worn by adult men, including close-cropped spiked styles, flat tops, mullets, and rat tails. Hairstyling products such as gels and mousse were also adopted by young girls and boys to create the same coiffures as their older counterparts.

HEADWEAR, HAIRSTYLE, AND COSMETICS: TEEN TO COLLEGE

Headwear

During the 1980s, some teenagers and college-aged women wore classic boater and fedora hats for special occasions or with trendy outfits to mimic looks by Madonna and Debbie Gibson. Hair accessories for casual wear included banana and butterfly clips, bangles, headbands, and scrunchies. Cowboy and fedora hats were worn by young men in some regions of the United States, but, despite the popularity of musicians such as Boy George of Culture Club, the majority of young men rarely donned more than a baseball hat.

Hairstyles

Teenagers and college-aged women fully adopted the variety of hairstyle choices of the 1980s, which included large manes, puffed-up hairdos, perms, and softer cuts. Colored wigs were also used as a novelty item, and permanent or temporary hair dyes came in a wide range of colors, including neon and metallic tones to create streaks or stripes of color, emulating Cyndi Lauper. The 1980s also witnessed the birth of the "mall bangs," so dubbed because of the practice amongst teenage girls (who frequented malls) to rat their bangs into tall peaks or mounds, plastered in place with hairspray. American preppy boys wore their hair short and well groomed during the 1980s, incorporating hair gel to create a look that emulated dominant trends among adults. American boys also imitated styles seen in athletes or musicians, including Mohawks, long manes, rat tails, dreadlocks, mullets, and flat tops.

Cosmetics

In the 1980s, female teenagers adopted bold makeup trends such as dark shades in lipstick, neon nail polish, and glitter eye shadow. Bright green, orange, and yellow became popular alternatives to the standard purples and blues for eye shadow, lipstick, nail polish, and mascara. A well-groomed look was important for many American boys in the 1980s, too. The popularity of new wave bands such as Duran Duran, whose male musicians wore makeup, spurred young men across America to apply eye shadow, eye liner and even rouge. Teens and college-aged youths, both male and female, also widely adopted designer perfumes and colognes, now readily available in suburban shopping malls.

FOOTWEAR AND LEGWEAR: CHILDREN TO PRETEEN

Footwear

Infants continued wearing footed pajamas and novelty bootee shoes with cartoon and animal figures popular in children's television shows and books, such as Sesame Street and Winnie the Pooh. Athletic shoes were at the top of the market for children during the 1980s, and major brands, such as Nike, developed miniaturized versions of their adult gear for children. Toddler girls wore pastel and candy-colored canvas shoes with bows and flowers, and toddler boys wore athletic shoes with dinosaurs, sport equipment, and car motifs. Jellies, or plastic sandals, in pastel colors, moccasins, and Mary Jane shoes remained staples in American girls' footwear and were often embellished with decorative perforations, pinking, and fringed tongues. Boys' standards continued to be penny loafers and Docksiders.

Legwear

Girls' socks were colorful and often incorporated lace, appliqué, or embroidered decorative figures. Colorfully printed socks in pastels and bright hues were as popular as patterns such as stripes, flowers, and dolls. Classic white ankle socks with lace trim and small pink bows were still the staple for dressy occasions for young girls. Colorful nylons or tights were worn by older girls for special occasions. Some young girls even dressed in legwarmers to keep up with a big sister. Most boys wore white tube socks decorated with colored bands or motifs such as planes, animals, and cartoon characters for daily wear. Dark-colored socks, either solid or argyles, were standard for dressy occasions.

FOOTWEAR AND LEGWEAR: TEEN TO COLLEGE

Footwear

With the popularity of brand labels and a variety of styles available, the teen market emerged as a strong segment for footwear in the 1980s. Sneakers and aerobic shoes were worn not only at the gym and sports activities but also became the dominant form of casual footwear. Manu-facturers added lines with feminine colors and detailing aimed at young American women who often opted for colorful canvas or leather shoes, fluorescent shoelaces, and prominently displayed logos such as Adidas or Nike. Teenage and college-age girls wore a variety of jellies, pointed-toe granny or lace-up boots, soft suede ankle boots, and Candies leather strap wedge- or spike-heeled sandals. Dyed-to-match satin pumps and sandals dominated proms and formals in the 1980s because young women required shoes that perfectly matched their formal dresses.

Brand athletic shoes were equally important for teenage boys during the 1980s, with names such as Vans, Reebok, Nike, Adidas, and Converse dominating the market. Sneakers were enhanced for a number of athletic activities such as skating, jogging, basketball, and soccer. Vans offered a slip-on canvas shoe that could be customized by the owner with a range of colors and geometric patterns. Nike, Adidas, and Reebok all offered the new black leather athletic shoe, providing young men with a dressy gym shoe as an alternative to regular leather hard-soled shoes. Fashion-conscious teen boys wore solid or two-tone oxford lace-ups and tasseled penny loafers, both preferably Italian, as well as Sperry Docksiders or boat shoes, boots, and half boots.

Legwear

Legwarmers were a favorite novelty item among teenagers and college-aged girls during the 1980s. Girls' socks were usually colorful, with pastels and neons both being very popular during the 1980s. Wild animal prints and other patterns regularly adorned socks. Fashion-forward young women wore fishnets, neon or pastel tights, and lace-patterned nylons rather than standard flesh-toned pantyhose. Even those who wore regular flesh-tone or off-black pantyhose often purchased those with small rhine-stones or embroidered flowers at the ankle. Young American men also adopted colorful and patterned socks in the 1980s. Pin-striped, argyle, and herringbone patterns were broadly worn by young men with their chinos. Sport socks, however, remained mostly white with stripes or logo accents. When wearing Vans or Docksiders, young men regularly omitted wearing any socks.

ACCESSORIES

Jewelry

The age at which young girls had their ears pierced continued to decrease during the decade. Some mothers even took their young daughters to have their ears pierced as early as six months. Other young girls, teens, and young women were having one or both ears double and tripled pierced to allow multiple pairs of earrings to be simultaneously worn. Some young women even had pierces around the entire edge of their ear. Earrings were typically big and bold in the 1980s and were either gold or brightly colored plastic. Hoops and crosses were the two most prevalent earring forms during the decade. Earrings were also no longer always worn as matching sets; instead, young women wore different earrings in their right ear from their left. Young men also began to pierce their ears, but typically only the right or left ear was pierced, not both. Single diamond (or cubic zirconia) solitaires, gold lightning bolts, or gold hoops were preferred earrings for young men.

Big, bright hard plastic and rubber bracelets or bangles were also extremely popular during this period. Several bangles in varying size and color would be worn concurrently on both arms. Vintage brooches, chokers, and earrings also became popular during the 1980s, and many young women frequented thrift shops looking for unique pieces to add to their wardrobes. Watches were also an important fashion accessory for all ages of youths in the 1980s. From young children to college aged, colorful plastic Swiss Swatch watches became a fashion staple, including changeable Swatch bands and Swatch face guards.

Gloves and Handbags

Young men and women both wore gloves as popular accessories during the 1980s for both casual wear and dressy occasions. For young women, the gloves were lace, were either wrist length or elbow length, and were either fingerless or covered only the back of the hand. Black, white, and pink were the dominant colors for lace gloves, which were often sold with matching lace headbands that sported large lace bows. Young men donned either fingerless black leather gloves, popularized by Billy Idol's *Rebel Yell* music video, or a single stretch sequined or metallic glove, as popularized by Michael Jackson.

Young women primarily carried clutch or envelope purses in the 1980s. Black, brown, and wine-colored leather bags by Coach, Gucci, and Fendi were popular status symbols during the period. Equally popular were Chanel or Chanel-inspired quilted leather bags with gold chain handles, in black or red. Backpacks were also popular amongst all youths from preschool to college. Young children carried backpacks in bright colors either adorned with or shaped to resemble their favorite cartoon or video game characters (Harris and Brown 2002, 58), whereas teens carried backpacks in denim or leather emblazoned with brand names such as Guess or Levi's.

Neckwear

Young men and women both also wore neckties in the 1980s. It was not uncommon to see young women wear neckties or lace neckscarves with casual outfits as well as formal dresses, a look inspired by pop singer Debbie Gibson. Young men wore narrow neckties in a range of patterns and pastel colors during the 1980s for both casual Don Johnson looks as well as formal occasions. In addition to the standard woven necktie, knitted neckties were also popular, typically in solid pastel colors. Interest in wealth or appearing wealthy motivated some young men to adopt ascots or the western bolo ties seen on the television show *Dallas*, instead of regular neckties.

Other Accessories

Perhaps the epitome of the wealthy "me" decade was the adoption of designer receiving blankets, diaper bags, and toys that were must-have status symbols. Designer baby clothing and accessories became big business for Polo, Guess, and private-label companies such as The Gap, which launched Baby Gap.

Belts were also important accessories in the 1980s. Young women and men both donned black leather belts with metal studs and metal rings. Young men also wore canvas striped belts with their Dockers and jeans. Young women wore a range of leather and chain belts, slung low on the hips in the early part of the decade. Wide leather belts, often in pastel or neon colors, typically had large buckles and other decorative embellishments, such as studs and rhinestones, whereas slim leather belts or double belts were wound twice around the wearer's hips and closed with small metal buckles or clasps. Chain-link belts may have been single strands fastened around the waist or hips or have swagged loops suspended from the main chain. Additionally, during the 1980s, some teenagers, primarily boys but also girls, wore bandanas in a variety of colors tied around their legs.

THE
1990s and 2000s

FORMALWEAR: CHILDREN TO PRETEEN

Silhouette

The voluminous silhouettes of the 1980s deflated in the 1990s. Perhaps inspired by some popular Jane Austen movies, dresses for young girls featured empire waists and straight skirts rather than the full, gathered skirts of the 1980s. Young boys' suit silhouettes also became more reserved and slim fitting.

Girls' Ensembles

Dresses for young girls featured empire waists, small cap sleeves, and straight skirts. Skirts were set into the empire waist with soft gathers, pleats, box pleats, or inverted pleats. Bodices featured simple scoop and square necklines and may have incorporated smocking, gathers, or embroidery. A wide sash was often worn around the empire waistline and tied in a large bow at the center back.

Boys' Ensembles

Young boys wore tuxedos or suits for formal occasions, with either shorts or pants. Shorts and pants had straight legs and were flat front or elastic waist, depending on age. The accompanying jacket was single breasted with narrow lapels and shoulders. Jacket lapels were either notched or shawl and may be edged in satin for the most formal occasions. For less-formal occasions, young boys wore shorts or pants, with button-down shirts and a sport coat, cardigan, sweater, or sweater vest.

Decorative Details

Soft pastel colors were popular for young girls' formalwear. Small floral patterns or embroidery and smocking or gathers provided visual interest on otherwise simple silhouettes. Young boys wore basic black or white tuxedos and suits, accompanied by bow ties, cummerbunds, and suspenders in every possible color. Argyle patterns were preferred for sweaters, sweater vests, and cardigans.

FORMALWEAR: TEEN TO COLLEGE

Silhouette

Teenagers and college students usually wore variations of adult styles, causing continued concern that America's youths were growing up too fast. In the 1990s and 2000s, minimalist figure-hugging gowns in neutral tones and dresses inspired by classic vintage styles were dominant in formal events at American high schools and colleges. Young American men usually wore classic-cut tuxedos. Black remained the color of choice, although other shades were seen at high-school proms. More relaxed codes for formalwear at the end of the twentieth century made dark suits and dinner jackets an accepted alternative for certain events.

Girls' Ensembles

The influence of several historical periods was seen in formalwear for young women. Jane Austen-inspired gowns with empire waists and slight trains, 1930s bias-cut gowns, and 1920s beaded flapper styles were equally popular throughout the first part of the 1990s. As the decade progressed and launched into the new millennium, the influence of the Iraq war brought 1940s pin-up girl inspiration to fashion as well as classic 1950s full skirts with sweetheart bodices. Regardless of historical influence, formalwear bodices could be either strapless, off the shoulder, or halter and were typically sleeveless. Deep plunging necklines, both front and back, continued to plunge lower and lower as the decade progressed, influenced by the ghetto fabulous trend and hip-hop music. Skirts were typically straight and fitted, or clingy from bias draping, with a trend toward fuller circle skirts by the early 2000s. Long and short lengths were both considered equally appropriate for most formal occasions. Long skirts typically featured high-cut slits placed at the center front or over one thigh.

Boys' Ensembles

The European influence seen in men's formalwear was also felt in young men's formalwear. Jackets were typically slim fitting with narrow lapels, with short side vents. Pants were also slim fitting with flat fronts and without cuffs. Tuxedo pants continued to incorporate the classic satin braid but thinner than in past decades. Tuxedo jackets also continued to feature satin lapels. Shirts fit close to the body and usually had narrow collars and slim sleeves. Tuxedo shirts, just like the adult version, were often pleated, tucked, piqued, and occasionally ruffled. French cuffs and cuff links became the new standard for impeccably dressed young men.

Decorative Details

Young women's formalwear was dominated by neutral colors, black, white, gray, and brown, as well as deep rich purples, brick reds, and other earth tones. The classic little black dress was just as important to young women as it was to adult women and served as the basic canvas for embellishment with jewelry and accessories. Sequins, beads, and lace were applied to many designs, but strong structural seams, such as princess seams, architectural shapes, such as corsets, and geometric cutouts were more popular in the first half of the decade. Cutouts were often filled with mesh or other sheer fabrics to add visual interest. Young men's formalwear was dominated by black suits and tuxedos and white shirts. Ties, socks, and pocket squares were often in subdued, muted earth tones. Watches and cufflinks in silver with precious and semiprecious stones at first provided sophistication to young men's formalwear but, as the decade progressed, became more elaborate and flashy, a source of ghetto fabulous bling for young men.

CASUAL WEAR: CHILDREN TO PRETEEN

Silhouette

Casual wear silhouettes shifted from the emphasis on fullness and broad shoulders in the 1980s to become extremely oversized and baggy. Although less pronounced in apparel for young children, oversized jeans and T-shirts dominated casual wear for both genders. As in the 1980s, designer labels were just as important for children's wear as adult clothing, and an increasing number of men's and women's designers launched children's labels, including Tommy Hilfiger, an influential designer in the urban hip-hop scene.

Girls' Ensembles

Dresses and Skirts: Young girls wore dresses less frequently in the 1990s than in past decades. Simple shifts and A-line dresses and jumpers were worn for church, birthday parties, and other social gatherings. Dresses typically had empire waists with short sleeves. Skirt length ranged from mid-thigh for younger girls to mid-calf for older girls. Sailor dresses and baby-doll dresses were worn by young girls, typically with matching bloomers or ruffled panties. Separate skirts and blouses were also worn for casual social gatherings. Dirndl and handkerchief skirts were popular, especially in peasant and ethnic print patterns. Many straight skirts had two tuck pleats on each side of the front fly with either a small center front or center back slit. Wrap skirts and flared skirts in cotton twill, corduroy, and denim were also worn.

Pants: Khakis, cargo pants, and jeans dominated girls' casual wear. Girls' denim pants often incorporated appliquéd and embroidered decorative details on the pockets. Jeans again had flat fronts, and jean legs became increasingly wider; many young girls "pegged" their jeans by rolling the hem into a tight cuff at the ankle. Khaki pants and cargo pants (cotton pants with numerous oversized patch pockets) were popular alternatives to jeans, as were cotton and denim overalls. By the end of the decade, jeans, khakis and cargo pants, capri lengths, and lightweight fabrications were as popular as shorts for summer wear.

Tops: Young girls wore a wide selection of woven and knit shirts. For more formal social gatherings, young girls wore woven shirts with small Peter Pan collars or convertible spread collars in the 1990s. Sleeves were typically long and straight; however, long flared sleeves or fitted sleeves with deep flounced cuffs were also trendy. Knit tops continued to dominate casual wear for children. T-shirts, tank tops, polo shirts, and turtlenecks continued to be fashion staples, but the proportions, influenced by the growing popularity of hip-hop music, continued to grow into oversized, baggy silhouettes. Bright colors and color blocking were popular treatments for knit tops, and logos and cartoon characters appeared on T-shirts. Sweaters, cardigans, sweatshirts, and hoodies (knitted or fleece jackets and pullovers with hoods) topped both woven and knit shirts for warmth.

Boys' Ensembles

Pants: Young boys wore basic jeans, khakis, and cargo pants for casual wear. Flat fronts and wide legs dominated all three types of pants. Pants were oversized, and pocket dimensions were exaggerated in proportion to the pant leg and seat. Cargo pants featured numerous pouch or cargo pockets with box pleats. Pocket flaps were secured by large buttons, stripes of Velcro, or industrial zippers. Double rows of topstitching, in either matching or contrasting colors, helped to emphasize the oversized proportions of the pants. Although denim shorts remained a key wardrobe item for summer, cargo shorts and board shorts became popular alternatives. Cargo shorts were longer, even below knee length, featuring the same details as cargo pants. Board shorts were popularized by surfers and skateboarders and were made from either nylon or cotton twill. Board shorts ranged in length from mid-thigh to just below the knee and came in either neon or muted colors and wild abstract patterns.

Tops: Young boys wore slightly less exaggerated versions of the urban trend of wearing oversized T-shirts, sweatshirts, and polo shirts. Color blocking and wide horizontal stripes were standard for T-shirts, rugby shirts, and polo shirts. Young boys' knit shirts also featured logos, cartoon characters, and especially college and professional sports team insignias. Interest in skateboarding, snowboarding, and surfing at the end of the decade also influenced the patterns and logos seen on young boys' knit shirts. For church, parties, and other casual social gatherings, simple button-down oxfords in solids and plaids were worn alone or over T-shirts and turtlenecks.

Decorative Details

Color blocking in bold, bright colors dominated children's wear patterns in the 1990s. Ethnic patterns, including Indian, Asian, and Caribbean, were also incorporated in children's wear. T-shirt graphics featured Barney, the Teletubbies, Dora the Explorer, and SpongeBob SquarePants, as well as sports team logos. In general, girls' apparel was less embellished than in previous periods, but ricrac, ruffles, and ribbon was still seen on hemlines, cuffs, and collars. Jean pockets were decorated with appliqués and embroidery but also, more important, designer names and logos. Clothing for both young girls and boy made extensive use of topstitching on inseams, outseams, plackets, pockets, and hems.

CASUAL WEAR: TEEN TO COLLEGE

Silhouette

In the 1990s, fashions for teens and college-aged students became simpler and more minimalist. Silhouettes for young women moved into two distinctly different directions: oversized and underwear as outwear. Whereas hip-hop music influences brought oversized baggy proportions to young women's fashions, the influence of Madonna and other pop stars brought lingerie, camisoles, corsets, and bra tops into vogue. Overall fashion direction was not as diversified in the male silhouette during the period, but young men were also subjected to the same oversized hip-hop influence as young women's clothing. Another popular trend of the last part of the twentieth century was the transition to casual comfort wear or athletic wear. American juniors often mixed trendy sportswear and activewear with formalwear or street wear to create looks inspired by hip-hop, surf, skate, and other social or music trends.

Girls' Ensembles

Dresses and Skirts: Eclecticism reached casual dress for American teenagers in the 1990s and 2000s with a variety of options, including high-waist baby-doll, tank top, and bias-cut dresses. Baby-doll dresses featured square or scoop necklines and empire waists with gather skirts that ended around mid-thigh. Baby-doll dresses came in a wide range of colors and both large and small prints and were typically paired with tights or thigh-high stockings and Mary Jane shoes. Tank dresses were fabricated from both knits and wovens, with scoop or V necks. These one-piece dresses clung to every curve, ending anywhere between mid-thigh and mid-calf, with longer styles featuring side slits. Some woven tank dresses featured self-fabric ties at the center back to help shape the dress at the waist. Bias-cut dresses softly draped the figure in satins or jersey knits. As with tank dresses, bias-cut dresses also had scoop or V necklines, were typically sleeveless, and could range in length from just above the knee to mid-calf. However, unlike tank dresses, bias dresses incorporated godets, gores, and other inset panels into the bodice and skirt to create structural interest in the dress. Fitted knit skirts in short and long lengths, with elastic waist-band and slits, and bias-cut skirts were also available for those who wanted to mix and match separates. Straight miniskirts and jean skirts provided alternatives to pants and also featured the same increasingly lower rise, patch or cargo pockets, and embroidered detailing. Box-pleated cheerleader skirts and mini versions of Catholic schoolgirl skirts also became popular after the release of the music video *Baby One More Time* by Britney Spears in 1998.

Pants: Flat-front jeans with wide legs were worn by young women in the early 1990s, often with pegged bottoms (a method of making the hem narrower by pleating and rolling the edge into a cuff). By the mid-1990s, jeans were worn full and straight or with flared legs or bell-bottoms and began to ride lower, below the natural waistline, often finished without a waistband. By the end of the decade, jeans were available in a continuum of full to skinny cuts, with either straight legs or boot cuts. In addition to a range of pant leg cuts, jeans also came in a wide range of low-rise styles, from just below the natural waistline to just above the hip line. Cordu-roys, or cords, and cargo pants were also available in the same range of leg styles and rises as jeans. Jeans, cords, and cargo pants all featured a range of novelty embellishments throughout the decade, including patch pock-ets, pocket flaps, large buttons, industrial zippers, embroidered pockets and hems, and topstitching.

Tops: Woven shirts, either shaped or fitted with princess seams, came in both cotton and rayon in the 1990s. Woven shirts featured long straight sleeves, flared sleeves, and ruffled or flounced cuffs and were ei-ther collarless or had small collars. Ethnic- or peasant-style blouses with drawstring necklines and either short puffed sleeves or long full sleeves were also popular. The lingerie trend brought camisoles, corsets, and bra tops out into the daylight, paired with shoulder shrugs (short- or long-sleeved, bolero-style jacket ending below the bustline), cropped jackets, and crocheted sweaters. Large oversized T-shirts, sweatshirts, and turtle-necks were also fashion staples in the early part of the decade. However, by the end of the 1990s, midriff tops or "belly shirts" replaced the exag-gerated knitwear as navel rings and tattoos became more popular with young American women. Tube tops, cropped T-shirts, and hoodies with novelty logos, such as Hello Kitty and Sesame Street characters, became popular with teen- and college-aged females.

Boys' Ensembles

Pants: Two majors fashion trends influenced young men's apparel in the 1990s: hip-hop and college prep. Both movements featured flat-front jeans, khakis, and cargo pants with proportion providing the defining difference. Hip-hop-inspired pants were extremely oversized, with wide legs, and worn low on the hip to reveal colorful boxer shorts. The college prep look was a less exaggerated proportion, with only the slightest hint, if any, of the colorful boxer shorts worn beneath. Both trends featured novelty patch pockets, cargo pockets, pocket flaps down the legs, large buttons, Velcro closures, and large zippers. As the decade came to a close, the influence of surfing, skateboarding, and snowboarding could be seen in the adoption of nylon and cotton twill board shorts in solid colors and large-scale patterns. Cargo pants also emerged in short mid-calf lengths.

Tops: T-shirts, hoodies, polo shirts and rugby shirts with color blocking or bold horizontal stripes were also key components of both young men's trends. The distinguishing difference was again proportion: hip-hop featured exaggerated, oversized apparel, but the college prep look was only slightly oversized. Hip-hop fashions prominently featured designer labels from Tommy Hilfiger, FUBU, and Karl Kani, whereas the college prep look was defined by J. Crew, Eddie Bauer, and The Gap. The hip-hop looks paired knit tops with oversized sports logo zip-front fleece jackets, stadium jackets, and sweatshirts, but the college prep look incorporated mock turtlenecks, turtlenecks, woven button-down plaid shirts, and canvas barn jackets lined with plaid flannel.

Decorative Details

Casual wear in the 1990s subscribed to minimalism, preferring structural seams to surface embellishment to create visual interest. Flat-felled seams, godets, inset panels, and flares were prominently featured in sleeves, skirts, and pants. Zippers, cargo pockets, topstitching, and embroidered pocket details provided decorative elements for jeans, cargo pants, and khakis. Retro graphics, tie-dye, and graffiti-style fonts were applied to both young men's and young women's apparel. Logos from college and professional sports teams as well as sportswear manufacturers such as Nike and Reebok featured prominently in casual wear for both genders. Colors for both tops and bottoms ranged from soft pastels to bold primary colors to muted earth tones, depending on the season and fashion trend.

OUTERWEAR: CHILDREN TO PRETEEN

Coats

Leather jackets were popular, especially with boys, in the 1990s and through the 2000s. However, the biggest trend in children's outwear was in polar fleece and hooded jackets. Polar fleece jackets or nylon jackets lined with polar fleece that were water repellant typically had center front pouches on pullover jackets or oversized pouch pockets on zip-front jackets. Hoods were incorporated into the majority of these jackets and often had novelty details such animal ear shapes, faces, or feet to make the hood appear to be the body of an animal.

OUTERWEAR: TEEN TO COLLEGE

Coats

By the 1990s and 2000s, trench and rain coats lost their oversized, "big '80s" silhouette and appeared in a variety of colorful, waterproof materials that featured playful all-over patterns or embellishments for young women. Young men wore classic styles of trench, Chesterfield, and pea coats similar to those seen on young women but in a more limited range of colors, with double-breasted pea coats being one of the most popular styles. Also popular among teenagers and college students were a variety of sports-inspired jackets and hoodies, as well as sweatshirts with colorful motifs and collegiate letterman jackets. Hoodies particularly came to dominate the outerwear market and came in a range of fabrications, including polar fleece, jersey knits, waffle weaves, and Mexican blanket. In the 1990s and 2000s, hooded jackets and zip-front jackets featured a number of vintage logos and manufacturer advertisements, especially those for athletic wear by sportswear companies such as Nike, Puma, and Reebok. Shearling, suede, and corduroy coats were popular among younger men by the 2000s, when they became an important component of garment layering and the retro 1970s vintage fashion trends.

SWIMWEAR AND SPORTSWEAR: CHILDREN TO PRETEEN

Swimwear

Girls continued to wear one-piece Lycra spandex swimsuits in the 1990s. Bright colors with novelty prints were typical for young girls. Young boys' swim trunks typically displayed color blocking or Hawaiian-inspired floral prints. Swim trunks for young boys followed the same general trend toward longer, baggier styles as men's swimwear.

Other Activewear

The increasing affluence in American families, as well as the never-ending desire to keep up with the Joneses, meant that young children participated in organized sports at earlier ages and required appropriate attire just like their adult counterparts. Skiwear, skate boarding, snowboarding, and soccer became important after-school and weekend sporting activities for both young girls and boys, and top designers and activewear manufacturers expanded their offerings to include active apparel lines for young children. Nike, Northface, Reebok, Columbia, and others now marketed performance gear to these young up-and-coming athletes in the same colors, patterns, and silhouettes as their adult lines.

SWIMWEAR AND SPORTSWEAR: TEEN TO COLLEGE

Swimwear

The 1990s brought a larger variety of swimwear styles to young women's beach attire. Vintage or retro bikini and one-piece styles drew from 1960s and 1970s swimwear, with hipster brief bottoms and boy-leg shorts paired with bra-style tops, bandeaus, halters, and tanks (dubbed the tankini). Lycra spandex remained the dominant swimwear materials, but some vintage style were made from cotton jersey or macramé. Colors and prints ranged from traditional bright and tropical patterns to retro browns, oranges, and teals. Young men's swim trunks remained conservatively long and loose, often reaching below the knees. Floral board shorts became the item of choice for swimwear during the 1990s and were usually long and loose with a baggy appearance, often featuring cargo pockets.

Other Activewear

Teen and college students increasingly embraced sports such as snowboarding, skateboarding, and mountain biking. Each sports genre had its own fashion trend based on both performance and the need to distinguish itself from mainstream skiing, biking, and rollerblading. For both young men and young women, the look was similar: baggy long shorts or pants with cargo pockets, flared pant legs, retro T-shirts, often worn in layers, pullover hoodies with center front pouches, and knit caps. These overall silhouettes and garment details were incorporated into the apparel worn for each sport, although the garment performance characteristics for each sporting activity were uniquely different.

HEADWEAR, HAIRSTYLES, AND COSMETICS: CHILDREN TO PRETEEN

Headwear

Headwear continued to be reserved for formal occasions in the 1990s but continued to disappear from daily wear. Sailor hats and other large-brimmed hats were worn by young girls for formal occasions. Headbands, ponytail holders, hair bows, and ribbons decorated ponytails, pigtails, and braids for young girls. Headwear for young boys was rarely seen, even in the most formal occasions, unless it was a baseball cap.

Hairstyles

Shoulder-length or longer hair continued to be norm for young girls and was typically pulled back in braids, ponytails, or pigtails. Shorter hair and military cuts were more prevalent among boys after the 1990s, but the retro trends in the late 1990s and early 2000s brought a return to shaggy hair cuts.

Cosmetics

The 1990s brought products that incorporated aromatherapy essential oils and natural ingredients used in infant products such as lotions and diaper rash creams. Lavender, aloe, and other natural ingredients became popular additions to traditional products or offered organic alternatives to modern, socially aware parents. Increasing numbers of health and beauty aid product lines featuring nail polish, cosmetics, and perfumes were marketed to young girls. Glitter eye shadows, lip gloss, nail polish, soap, and shampoo sported popular cartoon characters, such as Hello Kitty and Bratz, to attract the attention of young consumers and came in novelty bottles and containers, shaped like their namesakes.

HEADWEAR, HAIRSTYLES, AND COSMETICS: TEEN TO COLLEGE

Headwear

The consistent popularity of baseball caps amongst young men led designers and manufacturers to develop more feminine alternatives for young women. In the 1990s, baseball caps began being offered in pastel colors such as pink and baby blue, with redesigned logos, such as the Nike swoosh in floral patterns or plaids. The baseball cap was now as ubiquitous amongst college-aged women as it was amongst college-aged men. The increasing popularity of snowboarding brought with it a rage for knit caps with pom-poms, tassels, and ear flaps for both young men and young women. Rap and hip-hop music inspired young male listeners to don bandanas and do-rags.

Hairstyles

Daily hairstyles in the 1990s were quite conservative compared with the extreme styles of the 1980s with big hair and mall bangs. Hairstyles for young women became more natural, whether long or short, with soft waves and curls. Hair products, although growing in number and type, were also formulated to keep hair looking natural, not greased, gelled, or sprayed into position. In the 1990s, boys wore their hair fashionably groomed with spiked ends, long bangs, and pompadours. Toward the end of the decade and into the early 2000s, the retro look brought back the popularity of shaggy, longer hairstyles for young men. Blond hair became increasingly popular among young men, and many young men began bleaching and highlighting their hair to obtain the desired coif. The majority of young men were clean shaven in the 1990s, but goatees and long sideburns were popular among trendy young urban males. Also fashionable was growing a small patch of hair under the lower lip, known as a "soul patch."

Cosmetics

Just as hairstyles became more natural in the 1990s, so too did makeup. Makeup for young women was dominated by soft earth tones and neutral colors compared with the electric and neon color palette of the 1980s. The emphasis was on healthy skin and a natural glow achieved through lighter-weight foundations and soft blushes. New specialized skin care and cosmetic products became available, such as long-lasting lipstick and artificial tanning products. The increasing concern over sun exposure and skin cancer led many cosmetic companies to include sunscreen into foundations, moisturizers, and lipsticks. Green or environmentally responsible cosmetics, shampoos, and soaps were popular among many young Americans. At the turn of the twenty-first century, many young American men embraced the idea of the metrosexual look and adopted the use of specialized hair care and facial protection products and occasionally makeup products to cover blemishes and acne marks. However, the use of mascara, eyeliner, and lipstick seen in the 1980s disappeared amongst the majority of young men.

FOOTWEAR AND LEGWEAR: CHILDREN TO PRETEEN

Footwear

Young children's shoes were embellished with cartoon, television, and video game characters as well as small animals, dinosaurs, and cars. Increasingly popular were child-sized versions of adults' Nikes, Reeboks, and Puma shoes, as parents' opted to dress their small tots as miniature adults. High-top sneakers with bright colors, stripes, or color blocking enjoyed popularity during the 1990s as well as toe-cap black rubber canvas shoes and soft leather sandals with crisscrossed thin straps. Lightweight suede, vintage shoes and go-go boots were other novelty footwear worn by girls by the end of the twentieth century. Boys' sneakers also featured mesh detailing, Velcro straps, colorful shoelaces, and even small pockets to store money or trinkets. Wrestling-inspired lace-up boots were also popular. The classic shoe style for formalwear for girls remained the Mary Jane, whereas boys wore loafers, lace-up oxfords, and wing-tip shoes.

Legwear

Young girls wore tights in a wide array of colors and patterns with both formal and casual dresses. Ankle-high socks, just as colorful as tights, with embroidery, appliqués, or all-over novelty patterns were worn with pants, jeans, and skirts. Young boys wore dark socks for dress and basic white athletic socks, sometimes with colored bands, for casual wear.

FOOTWEAR AND LEGWEAR: TEEN TO COLLEGE

Footwear

In the 1990s, strapped sandals, mules, Chinese canvas flats, and playful plastic sandals or jellies were produced by several American designers and manufacturers for the teen and college market. In the 2000s, flip-flops or thongs came to dominate young women's casual footwear during warm weather, whereas mules or clogs and ballet flats were worn during cooler weather.

Sandals and shoes in the 1990s and 2000s were heavily embellished with metallic finishes, charms, chains, wood or glass beads, rhinestones, buckles, and other jewelry pieces. As the decade progressed, soles became thicker, and platform sandals, boots, and shoes were resurrected. Footwear for formal occasions included high-heel pumps, strappy sandals with Cuban heels, and mules. Young men's dress shoes were square toed and incorporated topstitching and perforations for decoration. For casual wear, as an alternative to tennis shoes, young men wore Birkenstocks and Teva sandals in the 1990s and adopted flip-flops in the 2000s; some also wore hiking boots. In the 2000s, young American men embraced bowling-inspired shoes with colorful decorative stripes and shoelaces. The snow-boarding and skateboarding trends also influenced young men's and young women's footwear, making vintage-style athletic shoes as popular among both male and female teenagers as athletic shoes with innovative features such as lighted soles and air pumps. Other athletic shoes of the 1990s, by manufacturers such as Skechers, resembled gym shoes on the surface but had thick platform soles, making them appropriate only for casual wear, not athletic wear. Tall, fur-lined boots were another popular alternative for young women. UGGs, worn by celebrities like Cameron Diaz and Paris Hilton, were widely adopted and paired with skinny jeans and casual skirts in winter and summer.

Legwear

Open-toe hose, low-ankle footies, and thigh-high stockings were widely worn by young women in the 1990s, whereas the 2000s brought trends such as visible seams, embroidery motifs, and fishnets into stockings. The colorful hosiery of the 1980s was replaced by sheer blacks and nudes. The bare leg look is also popular in the 2000s, no matter how cold the weather. Flip-flops, including more expensive and high-fashion designs, are worn extensively. Casual socks were also toned down and became abbreviated to ankle length for both young men and young women, but some teenagers wore shoes without socks in the 1990s. For more formal occasions, young men wore subdued navy, black, and brown color socks with discreet tone-on-tone patterns.

ACCESSORIES

Jewelry

Smaller, vintage jewelry became trendy in the 1990s, with the emphasis shifting to precious and semiprecious stones from the costume jewelry of the 1980s for formalwear accessories. For casual wear, ethnic-inspired silver, stone, beaded, and enamel earrings, necklaces, and bracelets were popular amongst young women. Long dangling earrings, wide cuff bracelets, and medallion necklaces all had intricate ethnic patterns etched into silver. During this period, some young men also wore bead necklaces and pendants on fabric, leather, and hemp cords.

New forms of jewelry, piercing and tattooing, were also increasing in popularity amongst teenagers and college students. Eyebrows, lips, noses, nipples, navels, and other parts of the body were pierced and ornamented with silver, gemstones, and enamel rings that sported subculture and ethnic motifs. Tattooing, another form of body decoration, was adopted by teenagers during the 1990s and 2000s, and popular motifs were inspired by various subcultures and ethnic groups, especially Asian and Indian cultures.

Gloves and Handbags

In the 1990s and 2000s bags worn by teenagers offered a variety of options, including patchwork, quilted detailing, animal prints, beads, and embroidery, reflecting the same ethnic inspiration as seen in jewelry designs. Purses and bags were often small pouches worn sideways across the body rather than over the shoulder. Young men carried leather bags and distressed military-style canvas bags for carrying school supplies. For more formal occasions, young women carried small rectangular purses with shoulder straps or hand straps. Silver or brass buckles and hardware replaced the previous decade's preference for gold jewelry and accessories.

Neckwear

Young women donned beaded and embroidered scarves and shawls to complement their ethnic or neo-bohemian fashions. Young men's ties began to widen again and included traditional floral, paisley, polka dot, and stripe motifs, although novelty ties featuring cartoon characters, sports imagery, and logos were popular alternatives.

Other Accessories

The newest accessories in the 1990s and 2000s were geared toward teenagers' and college students' adoption of technology such as cell phones and iPods. Purses were redesigned to include small slots to hold these devices. Special holders that could hang or clip on bags and belts were also designed to hold cell phones and iPods. Sunglasses were designed that incorporated "hands-free" ear pieces for cell phones. Clothing manufacturers even created iPod-ready garments that allowed the wearer to control the buttons on the iPod by touching keys on the shirt or jacket sleeve.

REFERENCES

Harris, C., Brown, M. (2002) *Twentieth-Century Developments in Fashion and Costume: Children's Costume.* Broomall, PA: Mason Crest Publishers.

Olian, J., ed. (1999) *Everyday Fashions of the Sixties: As Pictured in Sears Catalogs.* New York: Dover Publications.

Sills, L. (2005) *From Rags to Riches: A History of Girls' Clothing in America.* New York: Holiday House.

Skinner, T. (1998) *Fashionable Clothing from the Sears Catalog, Late 1970s.* Atglen, PA: Schiffer Publishing.

Glossary, 1950 to the Present

A-line: A garment silhouette whereby a garment gradually flares out from the narrowest part of the body, either the shoulders or waist, to the hem.

ascot (also known as a stock neckline): A high neckline with a scarf or ties that wrap around the neck and tie in a loop at the center front neck with the ends left hanging loose.

balloon sleeve (also known as a bouffant sleeve): A sleeve that is gathered at the armscye (armhole) and wrist with voluminous fullness in between.

band collar: A narrow collar attached to the neckline and standing straight on the neck.

Barbour coat (also known as a barn coat): A coat made of cotton that has been weatherproofed with oil, typically worn for outdoor work.

barn coat: See **Barbour coat**.

basque: A tight-fitting bodice.

bateau neckline (also known as a boat or Sabrina neckline): A neckline with a shallow curve from shoulder to shoulder.

bell-bottoms: A style of men's and women's pants, fitted across the hips and thighs, and flaring outward from the knees to the ankles, forming a flare or bell shape.

Bermuda shorts: A style of men's and women's shorts, either cuffed or uncuffed, with the hem approximately one inch above the knee. Bermuda shorts were first developed for the British Army for tropical and desert uniforms.

boat neckline: See **bateau neckline**.

bouffant sleeve: See **balloon sleeve**.

buckram: A cotton or linen fabric that has been stiffened to provide support and shaping under other fabrics.

bustier (also known as a merry widow): A corset-style garment, typically strapless, that combines the support of a waist cincher and brassiere ending at the waist or hips.

capri pants: A pant with a finished length at or below the mid-calf but above the ankles, typically slim cut.

chambray: A lightweight fabric with colored warp and white filling yarns.

chevron (also known as herringbone): A broken twill weave structure whose interlacing pattern results in a fabric that appears to have a series of interlocking Vs for a zigzag effect, or any pattern derived from interlocking Vs.

Chinese collar (also known as a mandarin or Mao collar): A stand collar approximately one inch tall with a slight gap between the right and left edges at the center front. The Chinese collar is similar to the Nehru collar, but the Chinese collar has square corners, whereas the Nehru collar typically has rounded corners.

chino: A plain or twill weave cotton fabric often used to make men's pants.

clam diggers (also known as pedal pushers or jams): A style of pant typically fuller cut than a capri pant with a finished length anywhere below the knee but above the ankles.

cowl neckline: A neckline, either in the front or back of a bodice, with fullness draped from shoulder to shoulder.

crinoline: A stiffened underskirt of either buckram or tulle worn to support full skirts.

Cuban heel: A medium high heel with a slight curve.

culottes: See **skort**.

cut-away shoe: See **open-toe shoe**.

décolleté: A neckline cut very low to reveal the shoulders, neck, and bustline cleavage. Décolleté may also be cut very low across the back, revealing the lower back or derrière.

dirndl: A slightly full skirt with a gathered waistline set into a waistband.

do-rags: A piece of cloth, often a handkerchief, bandana, or stocking, worn to cover the head. Originally worn by African-American men while sleeping to retain solutions used in chemically treating hair, also used now to support hair weaves.

dolman sleeve: A sleeve with a wide armscye (armhole) that may span from the shoulder to the waist with a sleeve that tapers to a tight fit at the wrist.

dreadlocks: A hairstyle characterized by ropes of hair that form by not combing hair for an extended period time.

empire waist: A waistline that is positioned just under the bustline. The name is derived from the fashions popular during the reign of Napoleon Bonaparte, Emperor of France 1804–1815.

epaulet: A tab or stripe of fabric that lies across the collarbone from the nape of the neck to the shoulder cap. Epaulets may also be used on sleeves or pant legs to position a rolled-up hem.

espadrille: A shoe with a rope sole and canvas upper.

godet (also known as a gore): A triangular piece of fabric inserted into a skirt hem to add fullness.

gore: See **godet**.

herringbone: See **chevron**.

inseam: The interior seam on the leg of a pant.

jams: See **clam diggers**.

jewel neckline: A round, shallow neckline that curves close to the nape of the neck.

Jheri curls: A hairstyle worn by African Americans named for Jheri Redding created by applying creams and chemical solutions to create tight, wet-look curls.

kameeze or kameez: Long tunic with side vents.

kente cloth: A narrow woven and printed fabric originating from Ghana.

layette: A complete ensemble for a newborn infant consisting of garments, toiletries, and bedding.

leg-o-mutton sleeve: An extremely full, puffy sleeve that is created by gathering fullness into the armscye (armhole) that tapers down the length of the upper arm into a fitted, narrow cylinder covering the forearm ending at the wrist.

loafer: A simple slip-on low-heeled shoe finished with a strap across the vamp that may have a slit to hold a coin (**penny loafer**) or tassels.

madras: A plaid or checked patterned lightweight cotton fabric originating from Chennai, India.

maillot: A one-piece tank-style swimsuit with a variety of necklines and high-cut or French-cut legs.

mandarin collar: See **Chinese collar**.

Mao collar: See **Chinese collar**.

Mary Janes: A rounded-toe, medium-heeled shoe with strap across the vamp, often in black or white patent leather.

merry widow: See **bustier**.

microfiber: The finest, thinnest manmade fibers available, one hundred times finer than human hair.

microsuede: A knit microfiber that feels like suede but is highly stretchy.

mule: A slip-on shoe with either a high or low heel with either an open or closed vamp but no back.

Nehru collar: A stand collar approximately one inch tall with a slight gap between the right and left edges at the center front. The Nehru collar is similar to the Chinese collar, but the Chinese collar has square corners, whereas the Nehru collar typically has rounded corners.

open-toe shoe (also known as a cutaway or peep toe): A shoe form that encloses the foot but leaves a small opening at the tip of the toe.

organza: A transparent, high-sheen fabric of silk, polyester, or nylon often used in bridal wear and formalwear.

outseam: The seam that forms the outer edge of the pant leg.

oxford shoe: A basic shoe form with either a lace, buckle, zip, or button closing.

patch pocket: A pocket sewn to the outside of any garment with or without a flap cover.

pea coat: A double-breasted coat of heavy felted wool or fulled Melton with a notched two-way collar that could be worn with the lapels flat or folded closed.

peau de soie: A medium-weight to heavyweight drapable fabric with a satin weave and delustered finish.

pedal pushers: See **clam diggers**.

peep-toe shoe: See **open-toe shoe**.

penny loafer: See **loafer**.

peplum: A short flounce or ruffle attached to the waistline of a blouse, jacket, or dress.

Peter Pan collar: A narrow, flat collar with rounded edges.

pinafore: A sleeveless garment, similar to an apron, that fastens in the back and is worn over a dress.

platform shoe: Any shoe, boot, or sandal with cork, plastic, rubber, or wood with extremely thick and high soles that run the full length of the shoe.

polar fleece: A soft, napped synthetic fabric used in winter outerwear made from recycled plastic.

polo: A knit shirt with a two- or three-button placket, rib-knit collar, and rib-knit-edged long or short sleeves.

pompadour: A men's or women's hairstyle whereby the hair is brushed into loose rolls or waves around the face.

princess line: A structural seam that runs from the shoulder or armscye (armhole) down the bottom edge of a shirt or dress or from the waist down to the skirt hem that allows a garment to be form fitted to the body.

raglan sleeve: A sleeve created in one piece with the bodice shoulder rather than through an inset armscye (armhole).

Sabrina neckline: See **bateau neckline**.

sanforize: A technique used to preshrink fabric before cutting the fabric for assembly into a garment.

sari: A long piece of fabric originating from India worn wrapped and draped around the body.

sarong: A rectangular piece of fabric wrapped around the body to form a skirt.

scoop neck: A deep, rounded neckline.

shalwar or salwars: Trousers that have full, loose legs at the top and taper to become narrow and fitted on the calf.

shearling: A tanned sheep hide with the wool left on.

sheath: A basic dress form, slightly fitted with darts or princess seams to create shape.

shift: A basic dress form with skims but does not fit close to the body.

shirtwaist: In the late nineteenth century until the 1920s, it meant, for women or girls, a blouse with buttons down the front, tailored like men's shirts. Later, in the 1930s, shirtwaist began to refer to a kind of dress that had a shirt opening to the waist and a skirt below.

skort (also known as culottes): Shorts that have been fabricated to resemble a skirt from the front.

sling-backs: A shoe with no cover across the heel, just a thin strap fastening around it to hold the shoe on.

stock neckline: See **ascot**.

T-bar shoes: Any shoe formed with a T-shaped fastening across the vamp of the shoe.

taffeta: A stiff, shiny fabric made from silk or synthetic fibers typically used in bridal wear and formalwear.

tulle: A net fabric typically used to stiffen and support garments.

turtleneck: A shirt, typically knit, with a high, close-fitting collar that covers the neck. True turtlenecks have a single fold or roll, while mock turtlenecks are only a single layer of fabric.

tweed: A twill weave fabric with slub or nubby yarns interspersed to create a textured surface. English, Harris, Scotch, and Donegal tweeds are popular tweed variations.

U neckline: A variation on the scoop neckline that plunges deeply across the chest in the shape of a horseshoe.

vamp: The forward section of any shoe.

vent: One or more slits cut into the back or sides of men's and women's suit jackets and blazers, or occasionally men's and women's shirts, from the bottom edge of the hem up into the body of the garment approximately six inches long.

wedge shoe: Any boot, shoe, or sandal with the sole and heel formed from one continuous piece of material and is typically thick at the heel and tapers to a thin layer under the ball of the foot.

yoke: A structural element used on either the neck and shoulder or hip to provide style lines and fit control.

zazous: A French anti-Nazi cultural youth movement influenced by jazz and swing that preferred an exaggerated clothing style similar to the American zoot suit.

zoot suit: An exaggerated look composed of an oversized jacket that fell almost at the knee, sporting wide lapels, exaggerated shoulders, and a contrasting lining. The trousers had a three inch waistband, had a baggy low crotch, was full at the knees, had suspender buttons, and tapered at the ankle.

Resource Guide, 1950 to the Present

PRINT AND ONLINE PUBLICATIONS

Agins, T. (1999) *The End of Fashion: How Marketing Changed the Clothing Business Forever*. New York: William Morrow.

American Fiber Manufacturers Association. *A Short History of Manufactured Fibers*, http://www.fibersource.com/f-tutor/history.htm.

Anastos, E. (with Levin, J.) (1983) *'Twixt: Teens Yesterday and Today*. New York: Franklin Watts.

Arden, J. B. (2003) *America's Meltdown: The Lowest-Common-Denominator Society*. Westport, CT: Praeger Publishers.

Arnold, E. (1978) *Flashback! The '50s*. New York: Knopf.

Bailey, B., Farber, D., eds. (2004) *America in the '70s*. Lawrence, KS: University Press of Kansas.

Baker, P. (1991) *Fashions of a Decade: The 1950s*. New York: Facts on File.

Ball, J. D., Torem, D. H. (1993) *The Art of Fashion Accessories: A Twentieth Century Retrospective*. Atglen, PA: Schiffer Publishing.

Barlow, A. L. (2003) *Between Fear and Hope: Globalization and Race in the United States*. Lanham, MD: Rowman & Littlefield.

Bankston III, C. L., ed. (1999) *Encyclopedia of Family Life*. Pasadena, CA: Salem Press.

Baudot, F. (1999) *Fashion: The Twentieth Century*. New York: Universe Publishing.

Bayor, R. H., ed. (2003) *Race and Ethnicity in America: A Concise History*. New York: Columbia University Press.

Beckerman, B., Siegman, H., eds. (1973) *On Stage*. New York: Arno Press.

Berkin, C., Miller, C. L., Cherny, R. W., Gormly, J. L. (1995) *Making America: A History of the United States*. Boston: Houghton Mifflin.

Berman, B., Evans, J. R. (2001) *Retail Management: A Strategic Approach*. 8th edition. Upper Saddle River, NJ: Prentice Hall.

Berry, K. A., Henderson, M. L. (2002) *Geographical Identities of Ethnic America: Race, Space, and Place*. Reno, NV: University of Nevada Press.

Bertman, S. (1998) *Hyperculture: The Human Cost of Speed.* Westport, CT: Praeger Publishers.

Biskind, P. (1998) *Easy Riders, Raging Bulls.* New York: Touchstone.

Blair, C., Siegel , M. A., Quiram, J., eds. (1997) *Growing Up in America.* Wylie, TX: Information Plus.

Boonstra, H. (2002) "Teen Pregnancy: Trends and Lessons Learned." *The Guttermach Report on Public Policy* 5:7–10.

Braunstein, P., Doyle, W. M., eds. (2002) *Imagine Nation: The American Counterculture of the 1960s and '70s.* London: Routledge.

Broussard, A. (2000) *African-American Holiday Traditions: Celebrating with Passion, Style, and Grace.* New York: Citadel Press/Kensington Publishing.

Bryant, M. W. (2004) *WWD Illustrated: 1960s–1990s.* New York: Fairchild Publications, Inc.

Buchanan, P. D. (2005) *Race Relations in the United States: A Chronology, 1896–2005.* Jefferson, NC: McFarland & Co.

Busch, A., ed. (1998) *Design for Sports: The Cult of Performance.* 1st edition. New York: Cooper-Hewitt National Design Museum, Smithsonian Institution, and Princeton Architectural Press.

Buxbaum, G., ed. (1999) *Icons of Fashion: The 20th Century.* New York: Prestel.

Carlson, A. (2003) *The "American Way:" Family and Community in the Shaping of the American Identity.* Wilmington, DE: ISI Books.

Carnegy, V. (1990) *Fashions of a Decade: The 1980s.* New York: Facts on File.

Carroll, P. N. (1982) *It Seemed Like Nothing Happened.* New York: Holt, Rinehart, and Winston.

Chace, R. (2003) *The Complete Book of Oscar Fashion: Variety's 75 Years of Glamour on the Red Carpet.* New York: Reed Press.

Chandler, R. M., Chandler-Smith, N. (2005) *Flava in Ya Gear: Transgressive Politics and the Influence of Hip-Hop on Contemporary Fashion.* Twentieth-Century American Fashion. New York: Berg.

Clancy, D. (1996) *Costume since 1945: Couture, Street Style, and Anti-Fashion.* New York: Drama Publishers.

Clothesline Journal. *Icon: Tracing the Path of the 1950s Shirtwaist Dress,* http://www.clotheslinejournal.com/shirtwaist.htm.

Cosgrave, B. (2000) *The Complete History of Costume & Fashion: From Ancient Egypt to the Present Day.* London: Octopus Publishing.

Damhorst, M. L., Miller, K. A., Michelman, S. O. (1999) *The Meanings of Dress.* New York: Fairchild Publications.

Dennis, M. (2002) *Red, White, and Blue Letter Days: An American Calendar.* Ithaca, NY: Cornell University Press.

Denton, N. A., Tolnay, S. E., eds. (2002) *American Diversity: A Demographic Challenge for the Twenty-First Century.* Albany, NY: State University of New York Press.

Dolfman, M. L., McSweeney, D. M. (2006) *100 Years of U.S. Consumer Spending: Data for the Nation, New York City, and Boston*. BLS Report 991. Bureau of Labor Statistics.

Dubbs Ball, J., Torem, D. H. (1993) *The Art of Fashion Accessories*. Atglen, PA: Schiffer Publishing.

Edelstein, A. J., McDonough, K. (1990) *The Seventies From Hot Pants to Hot Tubs*. New York: Dutton.

Ettinger, R. (1995) *'50s Popular Fashion for Men, Women, Boys, & Girls*. Atglen, PA: Schiffer Publishing.

Ewing, E. (1977) *History of Children's Costume*. New York: Charles Scribner's Sons.

Ewing, E. (1978) *Dress and Undress*. New York: Drama Book Specialists.

Farber, D. (1994) *The Sixties: From Memory to History*. Chapel Hill, NC: The University of North Carolina Press.

Farber, D., Bailey, B. (2001) *The Columbia Guide to America in the 1960s*. New York: Columbia University Press.

Farley, R., Haaga, J., eds. (2005) *The American People: Census 2000*. New York: Russell Sage.

Farrell, J. (1992) *Socks & Stockings*. Costume Accessories Series. London: B. T. Batsford.

Farrell-Beck, J., Gau, C. (2002) *Uplift: The Bra in America*. Philadelphia: University of Pennsylvania Press.

Fashions of an Era. *1950s Glamour*, http://www.fashion-era.com/1950s_glamour.htm.

Feldman, E., Cumming, V., eds. (1992) *Fashions of a Decade: The 1990s*. New York: Facts on File.

Figueroa, H. (1996) "In the Name of Fashion: Exploitation in the Garment Industry." *NACLA Report on the Americas* 29:34–40.

Florida, R. L. (2002) *The Rise of the Creative Class: And How It's Transforming Work, Leisure, Community and Everyday Life*. New York: Basic Books.

Galbraith, J. K. (1958) *The Affluent Society*. Boston: Little, Brown.

Garber, M., Walkowitz, R. L., eds. (1995) *Secret Agents: The Rosenberg Case, McCarthyism and Fifties America*. New York: Routledge.

Greif, M. (1978) *The Holiday Book: America's Festivals and Celebrations*. 1st edition. Clinton, NJ: Main Street Press.

Guérin, P. (2005) *Creative Fashion Presentations*. 2nd edition. New York: Fairchild Publications.

Guttmann, A. (1992) *The Olympics*. Urbana, IL: University of Illinois Press.

Harris, C., Brown, M. (2002) *Twentieth-Century Developments in Fashion and Costume: Children's Costume*. Broomall, PA: Mason Crest Publishers.

High Heels Newsletter. http://www.highheelsnewsletter.com.

Hine, T. (1999) *The Rise and Fall of the American Teen*. New York: Avon Books.

Hobbs, F., Stoops, N. (2002) *Demographic Trends in the 20th Century*. U.S. Department of Commerce.

Hoffmann, F. W., Bailey, W. G. (1991) *Sports & Recreation Fads*. Binghamton, NY: Harrington Park Press.

Holland, G. (1999) *The 1960s*. San Diego: Lucent Books.

Hunt, M. M. (1974) *Sexual Behavior in the 1970s*. Chicago: Playboy Press.

Hymowitz, K. S. (2000) *Ready or Not: What Happens When We Treat Children as Small Adults*. San Francisco: Encounter Books.

Ingoldsby, B. B., Smith, S. D. (1995) *Families in Multicultural Perspective, Perspectives on Marriage and the Family*. New York: Guilford Press.

Jackson, J. A. (1998) *American Bandstand: Dick Clark and the Making of a Rock 'n' Roll Empire*. New York: Oxford University Press.

Jarnow, J. A., Guerreiro, M., Judelle, B. (1987) *Inside the Fashion Business: Text and Readings*. 4th edition. New York: Macmillan.

Johnson, A. (2002) *Handbags: The Power of the Purse*. New York: Workman Publishing.

Jones, L. Y. (1980) *Great Expectations: America and the Baby Boom Generation*. New York: Coward, McCann, and Geoghegan.

Julier, G. (1993) *The Thames and Hudson Encyclopedia of 20th Century Design and Designers*. World of Art. London: Thames and Hudson.

Kain, E. L. (1990) *The Myth of Family Decline: Understanding Families in a World of Rapid Social Change*. Lexington, MA: Lexington Books.

Karney, R., ed. (1995) *Chronicle of the Cinema*. New York: Dorling Kindersley.

Kinder, C. *Changing Attitudes in America*, http://www.yale.edu/ynhti/curriculum/units/1994/4/94.04.04.x.html.

Kurian, G. T. (1994) *Datapedia of the United States, 1790–2000*. Lanham, MD: Bernan Press.

Lambert, R., ed. (1978) *America in the Seventies: Some Social Indicators, The Annals of the American Academy of Political and Social Science*. Vol. 435, January.

Lee-Potter, C. (1984) *Sportswear in Vogue since 1910*. New York: Abbeville Press.

Lehnert, G. (2000) *A History of Fashion in the 20th Century*. Cologne, Germany: Könemann.

Leonard, T., Crippen, C., Aronson, M. (1988) *Day By Day: The Seventies, Volume II*. New York: Facts on File Publications.

Levittown, New York. http://www.blue-dragons.com/preserve.dahs1997/levittown.htm.

Lomas, C. (2000) *The '80s & '90s: Power Dressing to Sportswear*. Milwaukee, WI: Gareth Stevens Publishing.

Lone Star College–Kingwood Library. *American Cultural History*, http://kclibrary.nhmccd.edu/decade50.html.

MacDonald, J. F. (1990) *One Nation Under Television: The Rise and Decline of Network TV*. New York: Pantheon.

MacDonell Smith, N. (2003) *The Classic Ten: The True Story of the Little Black Dress and Nine Other Fashion Favorites*. New York: Penguin Books.

Mackrell, A. (2005) *Art and Fashion*. London: Batsford.

Maga, T. (2003) *The 1960s*. New York: Facts on File.

Man's Touch. *History of Men's Underwear*, http://manstouch.com/mensunderwear/historyofmensunderwear.html.

Marty, M. A. (1997) *Daily Life in the United States, 1960–1990: Decades of Discord*. The Greenwood Press "Daily Life through History" Series. Westport, CT: Greenwood Press.

McNab, C. (2000) *Modern Military Uniforms*. London: Chartwell Books.

Melanson, R. A. (2000) *American Foreign Policy Since the Vietnam War*. New York: M. E. Sharp.

Mendes, V., de la Haye, A. (1999) *20th-Century Fashion*. London: Thames and Hudson.

Milbank, C. R. (1989) *New York Fashion: The Evolution of American Style*. New York: Abrams.

Mintz, S., Kellogg, S. (1988) *Domestic Revolutions*. New York: The Free Press.

Modell, J. (1989) *Into One's Own: From Youth to Adulthood in the United States, 1920–1975*. Berkeley, CA: University of California Press.

Moran, R. F. (2001) *Interracial Intimacy: The Regulation of Race and Romance*. Chicago: The University of Chicago Press.

Moskowitz, E. (1996) "It's Good to Blow Your Top," *Journal of Women's History* 8:66.

Mulvey, K., Richards, M. (1998) *Decades of Beauty: The Changing Image of Women, 1890s–1990s*. New York: Checkmark.

Murray, M. P. (1989) *Changing Styles in Fashion: Who, What, Why*. New York: Fairchild Publications.

Myron, R., Sundell, A. (1971) *Modern Art in America*. New York: Crowell-Collier Press.

NASA. *History of Sputnik*, http://www.hq.nasa.gov/office/pao/History/sputnik/.

Nathan, G. (1975) *Affirmative Discrimination: Ethnic Inequality and Public Policy*. New York: Basic Books.

Newark, T. (1998) *Brassey's Book of Uniforms*. 1st English edition. London: Brassey's.

Norman, J., Harris, M. (1981) *The Private Life of the American Teenager*. New York: Rawson, Wade.

O'Keeffe, L. (1996) *Shoes: A Celebration of Pumps, Sandals, Slippers & More*. New York: Workman Publishing.

Oldenburg, R. (1989) *The Great Good Place: Cafes, Coffee Shops, Community Centers, Beauty Parlors, General Stores, Bars, Hangouts, and How They Get You through the Day*. New York: Paragon House.

Olian, J., ed. (1999) *Everyday Fashions of the Sixties: As Pictured in Sears Catalogs*. New York: Dover Publications.

Olian, J., ed. (2002) *Everyday Fashions of the Fifties: As Pictured in Sears Catalogs.*
New York: Dover Publications.

Packard, V. (1959) *The Status Seekers: An Exploration of Class Behavior in America.*
Baltimore: Penguin.

Palladino, G. (1996) *Teenagers: An American History.* New York: Basic Books.

Patinkin, S. (2000) *The Second City.* Naperville, IL: Sourcebooks.

Payne, B., Winakor, G., Farrell-Beck, J. (1992) *The History of Costume: From Ancient Mesopotamia through the Twentieth Century.* 2nd edition. New York:
HarperCollins.

Peacock, J. (1996) *Men's Fashion: The Complete Source Book.* New York: Thames
and Hudson.

Phillips, L. (1999) *The American Century: Art and Culture 1950–2000.* New York:
Whitney Museum of American Art.

Polhemus, T. (1994) *Street Style.* New York: Thames and Hudson.

Poli, D. D. (1995) *Beachwear and Bathing-Costumes.* Modena, Italy: Zanfi
Editori.

Powers, S., Rothman, D. J., Rothman, S. (1996) *Hollywood's America: Social and
Political Themes in Motion Pictures.* Boulder, CO: Westview Press.

Rielly, E. J. (2003) *The 1960s.* Westport, CT: Greenwood Press.

Roche, J. (1963) *The Quest for the Dream: The Development of Civil Rights and
Human Relations in Modern America.* New York: Macmillan.

Rubin, J. S. (1992) *The Making of Middlebrow Culture.* Chapel Hill, NC: University of North Carolina Press.

Sayre, N. (1995) *Previous Convictions: A Journey Through the 1950s.* New Bruns-
wick, NJ: Rutgers University Press.

Schor, J. (1991) *The Overworked American: The Unexpected Decline of Leisure.* New
York, NY: Basic Books.

Schulman, B. J. (2001) *The Seventies: The Great Shift in American Culture, Society,
and Politics.* Cambridge, MA: Da Capo Press.

Seeling, C. (2000) *Fashion: The Century of the Designer 1900–1999.* English edition. Cologne, Germany: Könemann.

Sills, L. (2005) *From Rags to Riches: A History of Girls' Clothing in America.* New
York: Holiday House.

Silverman, D. (1986) *Selling Culture: Bloomingdale's, Diana Vreeland, and the New
Aristocracy of Taste in Reagan's America.* 1st edition. New York: Pantheon Books.

Simon, R. J., Altstein, H. (2003) *Global Perspectives on Social Issues: Marriage and
Divorce.* Lanham, MD: Lexington Books.

Skinner, T. (1998) *Fashionable Clothing from the Sears Catalog, Late 1970s.* Atglen,
PA: Schiffer Publishing.

Steele, V. (1997) *Fifty Years of Fashion: New Look to Now.* New Haven, CT: Yale
University Press.

Steigerwald, D. (1995) *The Sixties and the End of Modern America.* New York: St.
Martin's Press.

Stevenson, I., Somlyo, R. A. (2001) *The Tony Award*, Portsmouth, NH: Heinemann.

Stewart, G. B. (1999) *A Cultural History of the United States through the Decades: The 1970s*. San Diego: Lucent Books.

Streatfield, D. (2001) *Cocaine: An Unauthorized Biography*. New York: Picador.

Taylor, N. (2000) *America Bizarro: A Guide to Freaky Festivals, Groovy Gatherings, Kooky Contests, and Other Strange Happenings across the U.S.A.* 1st edition. New York: St. Martin's Griffin.

Therborn, G. (2004) *Between Sex and Power: Family in the World, 1900–2000*. International Library of Sociology. Milton Park, Abingdon, Oxon: Routledge.

Tortora, P. G., Eubank, K. (2005) *Survey of Historic Costume: A History of Western Dress*. 4th edition. New York: Fairchild Publications.

Tucker, A. (1998) *The London Fashion Book*. New York: Rizzoli.

Tucker, A., Kingswell, T. (2000) *Fashion: A Crash Course*. New York: Watson-Guptill.

Vanderbilt, T. (1998) *The Sneaker Book: Anatomy of an Industry and an Icon*. A Bazaar Book. New York: New Press.

Wandersee, W. D. (1988) *On the Move: American Women in the 1970s*. Boston: Twayne Publishers.

Warren, G. (1987) *Fashion Accessories Since 1500*. New York: Drama Book Publishers.

Washburn, K., Thornton, J. F., eds. (1996) *Dumbing Down: Essays on the Strip Mining of American Culture*. 1st edition. New York: W. W. Norton.

Watson, L. (2004) *20th-Century Fashion*: *100 Years of Style by Decade and Designer, in Association with Vogue*. Buffalo, NY: Firefly Books.

Weiner, R., Stillman, D. (1979) *Woodstock Census: A Nationwide Survey of the Sixties Generation*. New York: Viking Press.

Weiss, M. J. (1994) *Latitudes & Attitudes: An Atlas of American Tastes, Trends, Politics, and Passions: From Abilene, Texas, to Zanesville, Ohio*. 1st edition. Boston: Little, Brown.

Weitzman, L. J. (1985) *The Divorce Revolution: The Unexpected Social and Economic Consequences for Women and Children in America*. New York: The Free Press.

Welters, L., Cunningham, P. A., eds. (2005) *Twentieth-Century American Fashion*. English edition. New York: Berg.

Wheeler, D. (1991) *Art Since the Mid-Century: 1945 to the Present*. New York: The Vendome Press.

Wolfe, M. G. (2003) *The World of Fashion Merchandising*. Tinley Park, IL: Goodheart-Willcox Co.

Worringham, R., Buxton, R. *Censorship*, http://www.museum.tv/archives/etv/c/htm/C/censorship/censorship.htm.

Zinn, H. (1995) *A People's History of the United States*. New York: Harpers Perennial.

FILMS AND VIDEO MEDIA

These films and videos of television shows offer good representations of typical styles of the era, or idealizations of styles, such as the nice dresses and pearls that the mother wore in the television sitcom *Leave It to Beaver*, even while cooking. Some may illustrate fashions that inspire and become adopted by the public, such as in *A Hard Day's Night* or *Sex and the City*, and some are from earlier historic eras, such as *Dr. Zhivago*, which also influenced fashion after its release.

1950s

Father Knows Best. Television show. American Broadcasting Company. ABC, October 3, 1954, to May 23, 1960.

I Love Lucy. Television show. CBS Television. CBS, October 15, 1951, to May 6, 1957.

Leave It to Beaver. Television show. American Broadcasting Company. ABC, October 4, 1957, to September 12, 1963.

The Mickey Mouse Club. Television show. Walt Disney Productions. ABC, October 3, 1955, to December 30, 1959.

Rebel Without a Cause. Film. Directed by Nicholas Ray. Warner Bros. Pictures, 1955.

The Seven Year Itch. Film. Directed by Billy Wilder. Charles K. Feldman Group, 1955.

To Catch a Thief. Film. Directed by Alfred Hitchcock. Paramount Pictures, 1955.

1960s

Alfie. Film. Directed by Lewis Gilbert. Lewis Gilbert, 1966.

The Avengers. Television show. ABC Weekend Television. ABC, March 28, 1966, to September 15, 1969.

The Brady Bunch. Television show. American Broadcasting Company. ABC, September 26, 1969, to August 30, 1974.

The Dick Van Dyke Show. Television show. CBS Television. CBS, October 1961 to September 1966.

Dr. Zhivago. Film. Directed by David Lean. Metro-Goldwyn-Mayer (MGM), 1965.

Easy Rider. Film. Directed by Dennis Hopper. Columbia Pictures Corporation, 1969.

The Graduate. Film. Directed by Mike Nichols. Embassy Pictures Corporation, 1967.

A Hard Day's Night. Film. Directed by Richard Lester. Proscenium, 1964.

Monkees. Television show. National Broadcasting Company. NBC, September 12, 1966, to September 9, 1968.

My Three Sons. Television show. American Broadcasting Company. ABC, September 29, 1960, to August 24, 1972.

Rowan and Martin's Laugh-In. Television show. George Schlatter-Ed Friendly Productions. NBC, January 22, 1968, to May 14, 1973.

1970s

Annie Hall. Film. Directed by Woody Allen. Rollins-Joffe Productions, 1977.

Charlie's Angels. Television show. Spelling-Goldberg Productions. ABC, September 22, 1976, to June 24, 1981.

Good Times. Television show. Bud Yorkin Productions. CBS, February 8, 1974, to August 1, 1979.

Shaft. Film. Directed by Gordon Parks. Metro-Goldwyn-Mayer (MGM), 1971.

Shampoo. Film. Directed by Hal Ashby. Columbia Pictures Corporation, 1975.

Saturday Night Fever. Film. Directed by John Badham. Robert Stigwood Organization (RSO), 1977.

A Star is Born. Film. Directed by Frank Pierson. Barwood Films, 1976.

Welcome Back Kotter. Television show. The Komack Company. ABC, September 9, 1975, to August 10, 1979.

Woodstock. Film. Directed by Michael Wadleigh. Wadleigh-Maurice, 1970.

1980s

The Breakfast Club. Film. Directed by John Hughes. Universal Pictures, 1985.

Dallas. Television show. Lorimar Television. CBS, 1978–1991.

Dynasty. Television show. Aaron Spelling Productions. ABC, 1981–1989.

Fast Times at Ridgemont High. Film. Directed by Amy Heckerling. Universal Pictures, 1982.

Miami Vice. Television show. Michael Mann Productions. NBC, 1984–1989.

Pretty in Pink. Film. Directed by Howard Deutch. Paramount Pictures, 1986.

Top Gun. Film. Directed by Tony Scott. Paramount Pictures, 1986.

Wall Street. Film. Directed by Oliver Stone. 20th Century Fox, 1987.

1990s

Friends. Television show. Bright/Kauffman/Crane Productions. NBC, 1994–2004.

Sex and the City. Television show. Darren Star Productions. HBO, 1998–2004.

Unzipped. Film. Directed by Douglass Keeve. Miramax, 1995.

The Wedding Singer. Film. Directed by Frank Coraci. New Line Cinema, 1998.

2000s

The Devil Wore Prada. Film. Directed by David Frankel. Fox 2000 Pictures, 2006.

Project Runway. Television Show. Bravo Cable. 2005– .

Sex and the City. Film. Directed by Michael Patrick King. Darren Star Productions. New Line Cinema. 2008.

Ugly Betty. Television show. Touchstone Television, 2006– .

What Not to Wear. Television Show. BBC Production USA (Also runs in the original British version on the BBC), 2003– .

MUSEUMS, ORGANIZATIONS, SPECIAL COLLECTIONS, AND USEFUL WEBSITES

MUSEUMS AND SPECIAL COLLECTIONS

The Art Institute of Chicago
111 S. Michigan Avenue
Chicago, IL 60603
312-443-3600
http://www.artic.edu
An extensive collection of art, architecture, painting, photography, and textiles. The contemporary paintings and photography are excellent resources for depictions of individuals and dress.

Bata Shoe Museum
327 Bloor Street West
Toronto, Ontario, Canada M5S 1W7
416-979-7799
http://www.batashoemuseum.com
A unique collection of more than 12,500 artifacts of footwear and related items, both Western and non-Western. Highlights include shoes worn by Marilyn Monroe and Elton John, as well as John Lennon's early "Beatles Boots."

Chicago Historical Society
Hope B. McCormick Costume Collection
1601 N. Clark Street
Chicago, IL 60614
312-642-5035
http://www.chicagohs.org
An extensive collection of more than 50,000 costume and textile artifacts, designed by and worn by Chicagoans from the famous (Abraham Lincoln and Michael Jordan) to everyday people.

Cincinnati Art Museum
953 Eden Park Drive
Cincinnati, OH 45202
513-721-2787
http://www.cincinnatiartmuseum.org
Has an extensive costume and textile collection, searchable online.

Cleveland Museum of Art
11150 East Boulevard
Cleveland, OH 44106
216-421-7340
http://www.clevelandart.org
Art collection consisting of Western and non-Western paintings, prints, photographs, textiles, and more. Searchable online database with images is an excellent resource to see depictions of individuals portrayed in paintings, prints,
   and photographs in period fashions.

Costume Museum of Canada
109 Pacific Avenue
Winnipeg, Manitoba, Canada R3B 0M1
204-989-0072
http://www.costumemuseum.com
Contains more than 35,000 artifacts from more than 400 years, including designers such as Chanel.

Elizabeth Sage Historic Costume Collection
Indiana University—Bloomington
1021 East Third Street
Bloomington, IN 47405
812-855-5497
http://www.indiana.edu/~sagecoll/exhibit.html
Includes "military, occupational, and sports uniforms; hand-crafted haute couture
   ensembles; ready-to-wear apparel; garments designed by Hoosier natives Bill
   Blass and Norman Norell; and home sewing patterns." (From the website.)

Fashion Institute of Design and Merchandising
Museum & Galleries
919 South Grand Avenue
Los Angeles, CA 90015–1421
213-623-5821
http://www.fidm.edu/resources/museum+galleries/index.html
Includes more than 10,000 costumes, accessories, and textiles, from the eighteenth
   century to the present, including a collection of Academy Award-nominated
   designs.

Fashion Institute of Technology
The Museum
Seventh Avenue at 27 Street
New York, NY 10001–5992.
212-217-5800
http://www.fitnyc.edu/aspx/Content.aspx?menu=FutureGlobal:Museum

One of the few museums in the world devoted entirely to fashion design, spanning more than 250 years of fashion and textiles.

Goldstein Museum of Design
University of Minnesota
240 McNeal Hall
1985 Buford Avenue
St. Paul, MN 55108
612-624-7434
http://goldstein.che.umn.edu
Selections from the Costume Collection are searchable online. It "features works from designers Elsa Schiaparelli and Issey Miyake to a Chinese Imperial Robe; from an assortment of beaded handbags to children's shoes." (From the website.)

Henry Ford Museum
PO Box 1970
Dearborn, MI 48121
313-982-6001
http://www.hfmgv.org/
The Clothing and Personal Effects Collection contains more than 10,000 items from 1750 to the present.

Indiana State Museum
202 N. Alabama Street
Indianapolis, IN 46204
317-232-1637
http://www.in.gov/ism
Features an online catalog of clothes donated to the museum, with items from the nineteenth century through the twentieth century.

Kent State University Museum
P.O. Box 5190
Rockwell Hall
Kent, OH 44242–0001
330-672-3450
http://www.kent.edu/museum
The museum provides an online dictionary of fashion, "Bisonnette on Costume" by Anne Bissonnette, curator of the Fashion Museum at Kent State, featuring photos of costumes from the eighteenth century to the present, mainly of American fashion and clothing but including designs from Asia, Greece, and Turkey. The museum also has a collection of ethnic dress. Its fashion collection was started by a donation of "fashion, historic costume, paintings, and decorative arts from

Shannon Rodgers and Jerry Silverman, partners in Jerry Silverman, Inc., a manufacturer of better dresses" in New York City. (From the website.)

Los Angeles County Museum of Art
5905 Wilshire Boulevard
Los Angeles, CA 90036
323-857-6000
http://www.lacma.org
LACMA's Department of Costume and Textiles contains more than 25,000 objects, from 100 BCE to the present, much of which is searchable online. "A Century of Fashion" presents significant fashion designs by decade, from 1900 to 2000.

Metropolitan Museum of Art
1000 Fifth Avenue at 82nd Street
New York, NY 10028–0198
212-535-7710
http://www.metmuseum.org
http://www.metmuseum.org/Works_of_Art/the_costume_institute
The museum's Costume Institute contains 30,000 costumes and accessories, from all over the world and from the last five centuries. The Met also provides a fashion blog on its website.

Royal Ontario Museum
100 Queens Park
Toronto, Ontario, Canada M5S 2C6
416-586-8000
http://www.rom.on.ca
The Patricia Harris Gallery of Textiles and Costumes, open in 2008, presents highlights of the museum's more than 50,000 artifacts that date from 1000 BCE to the present day.

Smithsonian Institute
4202 AHB/MRC-610
Washington, DC 20560
202-633-1000
http://americanhistory.si.edu/collections/subject_detail.cfm?key=32&colkey=8
http://www.si.edu
The National Museum of American History contains more than 30,000 artifacts of clothing, from the 1700s to the present day, ranging from ball gowns to T-shirts.

Tassenmuseum Hendrikje (Museum of Bags and Purses)
Herengracht 573
1017 CD Amsterdam, The Netherlands

+31 (0) 20-524 64 52

http://www.museumofbagsandpurses.com

A unique museum with a collection of bags and purses from the 16th century to present day. Select objects from the collection can be viewed online.

Victoria and Albert Museum

Cromwell Road, South Kensington

London SW7 2RL, UK

+44 (0) 20 7942 2000

http://www.vam.ac.uk

Among the V&A's holdings is a section devoted to fashion, jewelry, and accessories. The fashion collection covers "fashionable dress from the 17th century to the present, emphasizing progressive and influential designs." (From the website.)

Victoria and Albert Museum of Childhood

Cambridge Heath Road

London E2 9PA, UK

+44 (0) 20 8983 5200

http://www.vam.ac.uk/moc

Among its collections is the children's costumes section, with more than 6,000 items of children's clothing, from the sixteenth century to the present.

Western Reserve Historical Society

10825 East Boulevard

Cleveland, OH 44106

216-721-5722

http://www.wrhs.org

Includes costumes from the history of the northeastern part of Ohio, from the nineteenth century to the present.

Whitney Museum of American Art

945 Madison Avenue

New York, NY 10021

800-WHITNEY

http://www.whitney.org

Premiere collection of 20th-century American art. Paintings, drawings, and prints are excellent resources depicting individuals in period dress.

WEBSITES

About.com

http://fashion.about.com/od/historycostumes/Fashion_History.htm

Costume Gallery

http://www.costumegallery.com

Costumer's Manifesto
http://www.costumes.org/history/100pages/costhistpage.htm

Exec Style Fashion Dictionary
http://www.execstyle.com/Fashion_Dictionary.asp

Fashion-Era
http://www.fashion-era.com

Haute History
http://www.hautehistory.com/fashhist/index.html

Stylopedia Fashion Dictionary
http://www.snapfashun.com/stylopedia/00_a.html

Women's Wear Daily Fashion Dictionary
http://www.wwd.com/dictionary/fashion

PROFESSIONAL ORGANIZATIONS

Costume Society of America (CSA)
http://www.costumesocietyamerica.com

Council of Fashion Designers of America (CFDA)
http://www.cfda.com

International Textile and Apparel Association (ITAA)
http://www.itaaonline.org

Cumulative Index

Note: **Boldface** numbers refer to volume numbers; numbers followed by *f* refer to illustrations.

The A Team (TV show), **2**:82

Abstract Expressionism, **1**:55, **1**:78, **2**:49, **2**:51–52

Abzug, Bella, **2**:135

Academy Awards, 1929, **1**:69

Acetate, **1**:166

Acrylic, 1960s and 1970s, **2**:175

Addams, Jane, Progressive movement, **1**:4

Adolescence, new concept in the 1920s, **1**:136

Adolfo, **2**:35–36

Adrian, **1**:76, **1**:153, **1**:157

Advertising: 1900–1910, **1**:92; 1920s, **1**:35; 1980s to present, **2**:172–73; during WWII, **1**:47; to young adults, 1970s, **2**:105

Afghanistan invasion, 2001, **2**:43

African Americans: baseball, **1**:109–11; Black Power, 1960s, **2**:204, **2**:204*f*; Cadet Nurse Corps during WWII, **1**:50; early 1900s, **1**:26, **1**:33; education for children in the 1900s, **1**:125; female writers, 1970s, **2**:70; Great Depression and, **1**:44; Harlem, New York City, **1**:39; music in the 1910s, **1**:62–63; music in the

1920s, **1**:67–68; New Deal and, **1**:44; rap, urban, and hip hop music, **2**:7, **2**:76–77; rhythm & blues, **1**:80–81; 1960s, **2**:28–30; 1970s, **2**:34–35, **2**:134; 1980s, **2**:40; 1990s and 2000s, **2**:45–46; 1970s music, **2**:69; 1950s rock 'n' roll, **2**:53–54; segregation, **1**:20; during WWI, **1**:7; during WWII, **1**:50

Air travel: first flight, Kitty Hawk, NC, 1903, **1**:23; 1990s and 2000s, **2**:114–15

Albee, Edward, **2**:63

Alcohol consumption, 1980s, **2**:110

Alger, Horatio, **1**:53, **1**:57–58

Alien Registration Act of 1940, **1**:51

Allen, Woody, **2**:63

Alternative fashion movements: beatniks, **2**:54–55, **2**:125–26, **2**:192, **2**:192*f*, **2**:257–58; Black Power, **2**:204, **2**:204*f*, **2**:267–68; Cyber-Goth, **2**:244; Goth, **2**:235, **2**:244, **2**:295; Grunge, **2**:236, **2**:295, **2**:296*f*; Hippies, **2**:203–4, **2**:267, **2**:267*f*; Mods, **2**:203, **2**:266–67, **2**:267; Neo-Bohemian and Retro-Chic, **2**:244, **2**:304; New Wave,

Alternative fashion movements
  (*Continued*)
  2:286; Preppies, 2:225, 2:285; Punk,
  2:226, 2:277, 2:285–86f; Rap and
  Hip-Hop, 2:226, 2:243, 2:286,
  2:295, 2:297f, 2:303–4; Rastafarian,
  2:226, 2:286–87; Ravers, 2:296–97;
  Rebels, 2:258; Valley girls, 2:225–26
American Bandstand, 1950s, 2:58
American designers: building morale
  during WWII, 1:154; challenging
  Paris, 1920s and 1930s, 1:153;
  costume, 1:165; knockoffs of French
  designer fashions, 1:155; ready-to-
  wear manufacturers, 1:155; 1950s to
  present, 2:14
American dream, 1:48
American Federation of Labor, 1930s,
  1:40
American Fiber Manufacturer
  Association, 2:175
American Indian Movement (AIM),
  1970s, 2:35
American Viscose Corporation, 1:166
Anderson, Sherwood, 1:68
Andrews Sisters, 1:80
Animated movies, 1990s and 2000s,
  2:90
Anti-design ideology, 2:83
Anti-form, 1960s, 2:59
Anti-functionalism trends, 2:83
Aquino, Corazón, 2:39
Architecture, 1:57
Arlen, Michael, 1:68
Armani, Giorgio, 2:79, 2:163
Armed Forces Radio Services (AFRS),
  1:84
Armstrong, Louis, 1:39, 1:68
Arrangement in Grey and Black
  (Whistler), 1:61–62
Art deco, 1:54, 1:66–67, 1:71;
  orientalism and surrealism, 1:72
Art movements, 1:54; 1900s, 1:55–57;
  1910s, 1:61–62; 1920s, 1:66–67;

1930s, 1:71–73; 1940s, 1:78–79;
  1950s, 2:51–52; 1960s, 2:58–60;
  1970s, 2:67–68; 1980s, 2:74–75;
  1990s and 2000s, 2:83
Artificial fabrics, 1940s, 1:167
Arts and entertainment: 1900–1949,
  1:7–9, 1:53–83; 1950 to present, 2:7,
  2:49–93
Arts Decoratifs et Industriels Moderns,
  Paris, 1925, 1:67
Ash can art, 1:53, 1:56
Ashley, Laura, 2:162
Asian Americans, 1990s and 2000s, 2:46
Asian immigrants: after World War I,
  1:7; discrimination in the early
  1900s, 1:26
Astaire, Fred and Adele, 1:69
Auburn, David, 2:89
Automobiles: daily life, 1:9; dating
  in the 1920s, 1:134; driving in the
  1920s, 1:104–5; in early 1900s, 1:23

Baby boom, 2:11, 2:132
Bakke v. California, 2:35
Bakker, Jim and Tammy Faye, 2:36
Balenciaga, Cristóbal, 1:154
Banton, Travis, 1:76, 1:77, 1:153
Bara, Theda, 1:63, 1:65
The Barbarous Hun, WWI, 1:64
Barrie, Scott, 2:206, 2:206f
Barrymore, John, 1:68
Barrymore family, 1:60
Basie, Count, 1:79
Basquiat, Jean Michel, 2:75
Bateman, Patrick, 2:87
Bathing suit "policeman," 1:204f
Bauhaus, 1:54; modernist art school,
  1:67
Beatles: arrive in U. S. 1964, 2:60,
  2:102; effect on hairstyles, 1960s,
  2:133
Beatniks, alternative fashion, 1950s,
  2:54–55, 2:125–26, 2:192, 2:192f,
  2:257–58

Beaton, Cecil, **1**:67

Beauty contests, **1**:163, **1**:163*f*

Bebob, **1**:55, **1**:81

Beene, Geoffrey, 1960s fashion, **2**:162

Berard, Christian, **1**:73

Berendt, John, **2**:87

Berlin, Irving, **1**:59

Berlin Wall, fall in 1989, **2**:39

Bernhardt, Sarah, **1**:60, **1**:63

Bernstein, Carl, **2**:70

BET (Black Entertainment Television), **2**:75–76, **2**:84

Betty Crocker, **1**:103

Bhutto, Benazir, **2**:39

Big band era, **1**:54–55, **1**:73, **1**:79

Big business, early 1900s, **1**:4–5, **1**:29

Biker look, James Dean, **2**:56*f*

Biological Agriculture Systems in Cotton program, 1995, **2**:178

Birth control pill, 1960, **2**:130–31

Black Monday, 1987, **2**:38

Black Power, alternative fashion, **2**:204, **2**:204*f,* **2**:267–68

Blass, Bill, **2**:35–36, **2**:165

Blessing, Lee, **2**:78

Blouses/shirts, women's casual wear: 1900–1908, **1**:175; 1909–1914, **1**:184; 1914–1919, **1**:191–92; 1940–1946, **1**:227; 1947–1949, **1**:239

Bobbysoxers, **1**:335

Bodices, formalwear: 1900–1908, **1**:172; 1909–1914, **1**:181–82; 1914–1919, **1**:189; 1920–1930, **1**:198; 1930–1940, **1**:212; 1940–1946, **1**:224; 1947–1949, **1**:238; 1950s, **2**:181; 1960s, **2**:193; 1970s, **2**:205; 1980s, **2**:216; 1990s, **2**:227; 2000s, **2**:236

Bodybuilding, 1970s, **2**:106

Bonwit Teller, **1**:159

Boston Women's Collective, **2**:70

Boutique clothing shops, early twentieth century, **1**:158

Bouton, Jim, **2**:70

Bow, Clara, **1**:65, **1**:65*f,* **1**:69

Boy band fashions, 1990s, **2**:85–86

Boy's ensembles (children to preteen): casual wear: 1950s, **2**:310; 1960s, **2**:323; 1970s, **2**:336–37; 1980s, **2**:351; 1990s and 2000s, **2**:364; formalwear: 1950s, **2**:306–7; 1960s, **2**:320; 1970s, **2**:332–33; 1980s, **2**:347; 1990s and 2000s, **2**:361

Boy's ensembles (teen to college): casual wear: 1950s, **2**:312–13; 1960s, **2**:325–26; 1970s, **2**:339–40; 1980s, **2**:353; 1990s and 2000s, **2**:366–67; formalwear: 1950s, **2**:308; 1960s, **2**:321; 1970s, **2**:334; 1990s and 2000s, **2**:362; formalwear, 1980s, **2**:349

Brancusi, Constantin, **1**:71

Branding, 1980s, **2**:37, **2**:166, **2**:172

Braque, Georges, **1**:61

Breton, Andre, **1**:71

Brice, Fannie, **1**:69

Brinkley, Christie, **2**:163, **2**:172

Broadway, New York City: Great White Way, **1**:68; *Hair,* end of 1960s, **2**:61*f;* light comedy, **1**:61; operettas, **1**:61; 1900s, **1**:60; 1930s, **1**:74; 1960s, **2**:63; 1970s, **2**:70; 1980s, **2**:78; 1990s and 2000s, **2**:88; 1950s musicals, **2**:55; vaudeville, **1**:61

Brooks, Louise, **1**:69; 1920s hairstyle, **1**:208*f*

Brown, Helen Gurley, **2**:130, **2**:171

Brown v. Board of Education, **2**:20, **2**:23, **2**:125–26

Brownell, Frank, Brownie camera, **1**:57

Bryan, William Jennings, Scopes trial, **1**:38, **1**:137

Buckley, William F., **2**:19

Bugliosi, Vincent, **2**:70

Burgee, John, **2**:75

Burke, Billie, **1**:68

Burroughs', Edgar Rice, **1**:58

Bush, George, **2**:5, **2**:40

Bush, George W., **2**:5, **2**:43, **2**:45

Business management, 1920s, **1**:35

Business wear (men): 1900s, **1**:249–50; 1910s, **1**:257–58; 1920s, **1**:264–66; 1930s, **1**:273–74; 1940s, **1**:280–81; 1950s, **2**: 248*f*, **2**:250–51; 1960s, **2**:260–61; 1970s, **2**:269–71; 1980s, **2**:278–79; 1990s, **2**:288–89; 2000s, **2**:298–99

Business wear (women): 1900–1908, **1**:173–74; 1909–1914, **1**:182–83; 1914–1919, **1**:190–91; 1920–1930, **1**:199–200; 1930–1940, **1**:213–15; 1940–1946, **1**:225–27; 1947–1949, **1**:238–39; 1950s, **2**:182–83; 1960s, **2**:194; 1970s, **2**:206; 1980s, **2**:217–18; 1990s, **2**:228–29; 2000s, **2**:237–38

Buy now, pay later, 1920s, **1**:35

Byrne, Jane, **2**:135

Cabell, James Branch, **1**:68

Callot Souers, **1**:150–51; founded by Gerber sisters, **1**:150–52

Calloway, Cab, **1**:68

Calvin Klein, **2**:165, **2**:174, **2**:207*f*

Camille (Ibsen), **1**:60

Camp David Accords, **2**:33

Canfield, Jack, **2**:88

Capote, Truman, **2**:63

Cardin, Pierre, **2**:162, **2**:175

Carnegie, Dale, **1**:74

Carter, Jimmy, **2**:18, **2**:31, **2**:33

Cassini, Oleg, **2**:24, **2**:161; 1960s fashion, **2**:162, **2**:171 Castle, Irene and Vernon, **1**:98, **1**:98*f*

Casual Friday, **2**:114–15

Casual wear (children): 1900s, **1**:291–94; 1910s, **1**:298–302,

1:299–300*f*; 1920s, **1**:308–11, **1**:309*f*; 1930s, **1**:318–21, **1**:318*f*; 1940s, **1**:328–30

Casual wear (children to preteen): 1950s, **2**:308–10; 1960s, **2**:322–23; 1970s, **2**:335–37; 1980s, **2**:349–50; 1990s and 2000s, **2**:363–65

Casual wear (men): 1900s, **1**:250–51; 1910s, **1**:258–59; 1920s, **1**:266–67; 1930s, **1**:274–76; 1940s, **1**:282; 1950s, **2**:251–52; 1960s, **2**:261–62; 1970s, **2**:271–72; 1980s, **2**:279–81; 1990s, **2**:289–90; 2000s, **2**:299–300

Casual wear (teen to college): 1950s, 310–13; 1960s, **2**:323–26; 1970s, **2**:337–40; 1980s, **2**:351–54; 1990s and 2000s, **2**:365–67

Casual wear (women): 1900–1908, **1**:174–75; 1909–1914, **1**:183–85; 1914–1919, **1**:191–92; 1920–1930, **1**:200–201; 1930–1940, **1**:215–16; 1940–1946, **1**:227–28; 1947–1949, **1**:239–40; 1950s, **2**:183; 1960s, **2**:194–96; 1970s, **2**:208–9; 1980s, **2**:218–19; 1990s, **2**:229–30; 2000s, **2**:238–39

Cather, Willa, **1**:62, **1**:68

Catholic Legion of Decency (Hayes Department), **1**:75

Celanese, production of viscose, **1**:166

Censorship, 1910s, **1**:62

Centers for Disease Control, teenagers and sexual intercourse, **2**:151

Chanel, Gabrielle "Coco," **1**:152; perception of, after WWII, **1**:154; suit worn by First Lady Jackie Kennedy, **2**:101, **2**:101*f*

Chaplin, Charlie, **1**:63, **1**:69

Chenier, Clifton, **1**:81

Chernobyl disaster, **2**:39

Chesebrough, Robert Augustus, **1**:195

Chicago, Judy, **2**:67

Chicago Imagists, **2**:67

Child labor, **1**:124–25, **1**:130

Childbirth, 1900s, **1:**123

Children: as consumers, 1990s, **2:**154; growing up in America, 1900–1949, **1:**12–14; growing up in America, 1950s, **2:**124–25; health, 1990s, **2:**155; missing, 1980s, **2:**146

Children's fashions, **1:**289–339, **1:**293*f*, **2:**305–84; sexual material in, **2:**85

Children's health, 1900s, **1:**123–24

China: manufacturing business, 1980s, **2:**39; relations with America, 1970s, **2:**33

Chisholm, Shirley, **2:**135

Chrysler Building, 1930s, **1:**72

Churchill, Winston: meeting with FDR and Stalin in 1945, **1:**49; meetings with FDR, **1:**43

Civil Rights Act, 1964, **2:**6, **2:**29; Title VII, **2:**127–28

Civil Rights Movement: beginning after WWII, **1:**50; 1960s, **2:**25–26

Civilian Conservation Corps, **1:**42

Claiborne, Liz, **2:**166

Clancy, Tom, **2:**77

Clayton Antitrust Act of 1914, **1:**20, **1:**29–30

Clinton, Hilary, **2:**12, **2:**40–41

Clinton, William J., **2:**5, **2:**40, **2:**43, **2:**45

Club Med, 1950s, **2:**99

CMT (Country Music Television), **2:**75–76, **2:**84

Coats (children): children to preteen: 1950s, **2:**313; 1960s, **2:**326; 1970s, **2:**340; 1980s, **2:**354; 1990s and 2000s, **2:**367–68; 1900s, **1:**294; 1910s, **1:**302–3; 1920s, **1:**311–12; 1930s, **1:**321–22; 1940s, **1:**330–32; teen to college: 1950s, **2:**313–14; 1960s, **2:**326–27; 1970s, **2:**340–41; 1980s, **2:**354; 1990s and 2000s, **2:**368

Coats (men's outerwear): 1900s, **1:**251–52; 1910s, **1:**251–52; 1920s, **1:**267–68; 1930s, **1:**276; 1940s, **1:**283; 1950s, **2:**252; 1960s, **2:**263; 1970s, **2:**272–73; 1980s, **2:**281; 1990s, **2:**291; 2000s, **2:**300

Coats (women's outerwear): 1900–1908, **1:**176; 1909–1914, **1:**185; 1914–1919, **1:**192–93; 1920–1930, **1:**201–2, **1:**202*f*; 1930–1940, **1:**216–17; 1940–1946, **1:**228, **1:**230; 1947–1949, **1:**240; 1950s, **2:**185; 1960s, **2:**196–97; 1970s, **2:**209–10; 1980s, **2:**219–20; 1990s, **2:**230; 2000s, **2:**239

Cocteau, Jean, **1:**68, **1:**73

Cohan, George M., **1:**60

Cold war: post WWII America, **2:**17; 1960s, **2:**27–28

Cold War, stage set at end of WWII, **1:**49

College attendance, 1960s, **2:**102, **2:**104

Communism, **2:**19, **2:**22

Compact discs, **2:**84

Computer-aided designs, **2:**176

Computers, part of American life, **2:**10–11

Conceptual Art, 1960s, **2:**59

Coney, Stephen R., **2:**78

Congress of Industrial Organizations, 1930s, **1:**40

Conservatism (isolationism), **2:**19

Conspicuous consumption culture: haute couture and, **2:**162–63; movies of 1980s, **2:**79

Consumer goods, after WWII, **1:**48

Consumer Products Safety Commission, **2:**176

Cool jazz, **1:**55, **1:**81

Coolidge, Calvin, **1:**20, **1:**34; big business policies, **1:**34–35

Copeland, Aaron, **1:**73

Cork, use in shoes, **1:**167

Cornell, Katharine, **1:**69

Corolle collection, Christian Dior, 1947, **1:**154

Corporate culture, 1950s, **2**:97–98

Corsets, S-bend, 1900s, **1**:90, **1**:93*f*

Cosby, Bill, **2**:78

The Cosby Show (TV show), **2**:82

Cosmetics (children): 1910s, **1**:304–5; 1920s, **1**:314; 1930s, **1**:323–24; 1940s, **1**:332–33

Cosmetics (children to preteen), 1990s and 2000s, **2**:370

Cosmetics (men): 1900s, **1**:255; 1910s, **1**:262; 1920s, **1**:270; 1930s, **1**:278; 1940s, **1**:285; 1950s, **2**:256; 1960s, **2**:265; 1970s, **2**:275; 1980s, **2**:283–84; 1990s, **2**:293–94; 2000s, **2**:302

Cosmetics (teen to college): 1950s, **2**:317; 1960s, **2**:329; 1970s, **2**:343; 1980s, **2**:356–57; 1990s and 2000s, **2**:371 Cosmetics (women): 1900–1908, **1**:179; 1909–1914, **1**:187; 1914–1919, **1**:195–96; 1920–1930, **1**:208; 1930–1940, **1**:221; 1940–1946, **1**:234; 1947–1949, **1**:242; 1950s, **2**:189; 1960s, **2**:201; 1970s, **2**:213; 1980s, **2**:223; 1990s, **2**:233; 2000s, **2**:241–42

Cosmopolitan (magazine): 1960s and 1970s, **2**:171; 1980s to present, **2**:173

Costume design: 1930s, **1**:76–77; 1940s, **1**:165

Cotton Incorporated, **2**:177

Coughlin, Father Charles, anti-Semitic views, **1**:40

Counterculture movement, 1960s, **2**:7, **2**:133

Courreges, Andrew, **2**:161, **2**:175

Crawford, Cindy, **2**:163

Crawford, Joan, **1**:74*f*

Credit cards, 1970s, **2**:32

Credit installment plans: early twentieth century department stores, **1**:158; 1940s department stores, **1**:160

Cremplene fashions for men, **2**:62*f*

Crichton, Michael, **2**:87

Crosby, Bing, **1**:73, **1**:80

Cubism, **1**:54; 1910s, **1**:54, **1**:61; 1920s, **1**:66–67

Cullen, Countee, **1**:74

Cultural events, America, 1950s to present, **2**:17–47

Cunningham, Michael, **2**:87

Cyber-Goth, alternative fashion, **2**:244

Dacron, 1970s, **2**:176

Dadaism, **1**:54

Daily life: 1900–1949, **1**:9–10, **1**:87–113; 1950s to present, **2**:9–11

Dali, Salvador, **1**:71, **1**:73

Dallas (TV show), **2**:81

Dance: ballroom, **1**:98; Charleston, **1**:68; Jitterbug, **1**:110; pose, **2**:84–85; 1920s, **1**:69, **1**:104; in the 1930s and 1940s, **1**:8

Dancehalls, early 1900s, **1**:53–54, **1**:60

Darrow, Clarence, Scopes trial, **1**:38, **1**:137

Darwin, Charles, Theory of Evolution, **1**:38

Davis, Miles, **1**:81

Day suit, President Taft, 1900s, **1**:250*f*

Daycare: 1960s, **2**:128; 1980s, **2**:144, **2**:146; 1990s and 2000s, **2**:148

de Kooning, Willem, **1**:78

de la Renta, Oscar, **2**:35–36, **2**:163

de Meyer, Baron, **1**:67

de Mille, Cecil B., **1**:70

Death and dying, perceptions in 1990s, **2**:113

Debs, Eugene, **1**:21

Debussy, Claude, **1**:67

Debutante Assembly and New Year's Ball, **1**:106

Debutante Cotillion and Christmas Ball, **1**:106

Decorative details (children to preteen): casual wear: 1960s, **2:**323; 1970s, **2:**337; 1980s, **2:**351; 1990s and 2000s, **2:**364–65; formalwear: 1950s, **2:**307; 1960s, **2:**320; 1970s, **2:**333; 1980s, **2:**348; 1990s and 2000s, **2:**361

Decorative details (men's business wear): 1900s, **1:**250; 1910s, **1:**257; 1920s, **1:**265–66; 1930s, **1:**274; 1940s, **1:**280; 1950s, **2:**251; 1960s, **2:**261; 1970s, **2:**271; 1980s, **2:**279; 1990s, **2:**288–89; 2000s, **2:**298–99

Decorative details (men's casual wear): 1900s, **1:**251; 1910s, **1:**258–59; 1920s, **1:**267; 1930s, **1:**275–76; 1940s, **1:**282; 1950s, **2:**252; 1960s, **2:**259; 1970s, **2:**272; 1980s, **2:**280–81; 1990s, **2:**290; 2000s, **2:**300

Decorative details (men's formalwear): 1900s, **1:**249; 1910s, **1:**256; 1920s, **1:**264; 1930s, **1:**273; 1940s, **1:**280; 1950s, **2:**250; 1970s, **2:**269; 1980s, **2:**278; 1990s, **2:**287; 2000s, **2:**298

Decorative details (teen to college): casual wear: 1960s, **2:**326; 1970s, **2:**339–40; 1980s, **2:**354; 1990s and 2000s, **2:**367; formalwear: 1950s, **2:**308; 1960s, **2:**321–22; 1970s, **2:**334–35; 1980s, **2:**349; 1990s and 2000s, **2:**362–63

Decorative details (women's business wear): 1909–1914, **1:**183; 1914–1919, **1:**190–91; 1940–1946, **1:**225; 1947–1949, **1:**239; 1950s, **2:**183; 1960s, **2:**194; 1970s, **2:**207; 1980s, **2:**218; 1990s, **2:**229; 2000s, **2:**238

Decorative details (women's casual wear): 1900–1908, **1:**175; 1909–1914, **1:**184–85; 1920–1930, **1:**201; 1930–1930, **1:**216; 1947–1949, **1:**240; 1950s, **2:**185; 1960s, **2:**196; 1970s, **2:**209; 1980s, **2:**219; 1990s, **2:**230; 2000s, **2:**239

Decorative details (women's formalwear): 1900–1908, **1:**173; 1909–1914, **1:**182; 1914–1919, **1:**189; 1920–1930, **1:**198–99; 1930–1930, **1:**213; 1940–1946, **1:**224; 1947–1949, **1:**238; 1950s, **2:**182; 1960s, **2:**193; 1970s, **2:**205–6; 1980s, **2:**216; 1990s, **2:**227–28

Defense of Marriage Act. 1996, **2:**152

Delaunay, Sonia, **1:**67

Delphos gown, Mariano Fortuny, **1:**151, **1:**151*f*

Denishawn dance schools, **1:**69

Department stores: beauty salons, **1:**159; copies of designer garments, **1:**160; cosmetic counters, **1:**159; credit in early twentieth century, **1:**158; credit in 1940s, **1:**160; early twentieth century, **1:**158; fashion after 1920s, **1:**16; New York and Paris fashions, 1920s, **1:**159; Parisian imports, 1920s, **1:**159; 1940s, **1:**160; shifting to suburban shopping centers, **1:**160

DeStijl, **1:**66

Dickerson, Janice, **2:**172

Diet craze, 1990s, **2:**116

Dior, Christian, **1:**154, **2:**160; pencil skirts and short fitted jackets, **2:**183*f*

Disco, **2:**71

Discount stores, fashion and, 1920s and 1930s, **1:**159–60

Disney, Walt, **1:**82

Divorce: the 1920s, **1:**133; the 1960s, **2:**129; the 1970s, **2:**135; the 1980s, **2:**143

Doll House (Ibsen), **1:**60

Domestic Relations Act, 1910, **1:**127

Donna Karan, **2:**37–38

Dorsey, Tommy and Jimmy, **1:**73, **1:**79

Dos Passos, John, **1:**68

Downs, Rackstraw, **2:**68

Dr. Zhivago, 1965 film, **2:**64*f*

Drecoll, **1:**150

Dreiser, Theodore, **1:**68

Dresses (business wear), **1**:199; 1914–1919, **1**:190; 1920–1930, **1**:199; 1930–1940, **1**:214; 1940–1946, **1**:225; 1947–1949, **1**:238; 1950s, **2**:182; 1960s, **2**:194; 1970s, **2**:206; 1980s, **2**:217; 1990s, **2**:228; 2000s, **2**:237

Dresses (casual wear): 1900–1908, **1**:174–75; 1909–1914, **1**:183–84; 1914–1919, **1**:191; 1920–1930, **1**:200–201; 1930–1940, **1**:215; 1940–1946, **1**:227; 1947–1949, **1**:239; 1950s, **2**:183–84; 1960s, **2**:195; 1970s, **2**:208; 1980s, **2**:218–19; 1990s, **2**:229; 2000s, **2**:238

Dresses (children to preteen), casual wear: 1950s, **2**:309; 1960s, **2**:322; 1970s, **2**:335; 1980s, **2**:350; 1900s and 2000s, **2**:363

Dresses (teen to college), casual wear: 1950s, **2**:311; 1960s, **2**:324; 1970s, **2**:337–38; 1980s, **2**:352; 1900s and 2000s, **2**:365–66

Dressing sacques (1909–1914), **1**:187

Drip-dry, fashion innovation of 1950s, **2**:174

Drug Abuse Resistance Education (DARE), **2**:154

DuBois, W. E. B., **1**:7

Duke and Duchess of Windsor, wedding fashion, 1930s, **1**:213

The Dukes of Hazard (TV show), **2**:82

Duncan, Isadora, **1**:69

DuPont, production of viscose, **1**:166

DVDs, **2**:91

Dynasty (TV show), **2**:81, 82*f*

Earhart, Amelia, 1930s, **1**:41

Earthworks movement, **2**:59

Eastern European countries, 1990s and 2000s, **2**:44

Eastman, George, **1**:57

Easy Rider: new era in film, **2**:9, **2**:64; 1960s counterculture, **2**:134

Eccentric Abstraction, 1960s, **2**:59

Eco-fashion, 2000s, **2**:177

Economic trends: America, 1900–1949, **1**:4; America, 1950s to present, **2**:17; family disposable income in the 1970s, **2**:105–6; 1950s, **2**:20–21; 1960s, **2**:26–27; 1970s, **2**:31–32; 1980s, **2**:37–38; the 1900s, **1**:22–23; the 1910s, **1**:29–30; the 1920s, **1**:34–36; the 1930s, **1**:41–42; the 1940s, **1**:45–48; 1990s and 2000s, **2**:41–43

Edison, Thomas, movie cameras, **1**:64

Education: children in the 1980s, **2**:146–47; curriculum differences, 1990s, **2**:154; focal point for children, 1920a and 1930s, **1**:13, **1**:136

Education Act of 1972, Title IX, **2**:106, **2**:141

Edwardian (La Belle Epoque) era, **1**:171–80

Eggleston, William, **2**:68

Eighteenth Amendment, **1**:6

Eisenhower, Dwight D., **2**:4

Eliot, T. S., **1**:62, **1**:81

Ellington, Duke, **1**:39, **1**:68, **1**:79–80

Ellis, Bret Easton, **2**:87

Ellis, Perry, **2**:166

Emanuel, Elizabeth and David, Lady Diana's wedding gown, **2**:108

Empire revival, 1909–1914, **1**:180–88

Empire silhouette, formalwear (1909–1914), **1**:180

Empire State Building, 1930s, **1**:72

Environmental concerns, 1980s, **2**:39–40

Equal Rights Amendment (ERA), **2**:11, **2**:**136**

Erhard Seminar Training (EST), **2**:107

Erskine, John, **1**:68

Ethnicity: 1900–1949, **1**:6–7; 1900s, **1**:26–27; 1910s, **1**:31–33; 1920s, **1**:37–39; 1930s, **1**:43–44; 1940s, **1**:50–51; 1950s, **2**:23; 1960s, **2**:28–30; 1970s, **2**:33–35; 1980s, **2**:40; 1990s and 2000s, **2**:45–46

European Union, 1993, **2**:43

Evangelical Christian groups, 1980s, **2**:36

Evening gown: 1905, **1**:172*f*; Pat Nixon, **2**:181*f*; WWII-era, **1**:223*f*

Eyeglasses (women), 1950s, **2**:191

Factory Investigating Committee, New York State, **1**:32

Factory work: New York, **1**:32; young people in cities, 1920s, **1**:35

Fair Labor Standards Act, 1938, **1**:13, **1**:29

Fairbanks, Douglas, **1**:69

Fallingwater, Pittsburgh, **1**:72

The Family: Preserving America's Future, Reagan administration report, 1980s, **2**:142

Family and Medical Leave Act, 1993, **2**:148–49

Family life: growing up in America, 1900–1949, **1**:12–14; men's role in the 1950s, **2**:122; vacations and leisure, **2**:99; what constitutes a family. 1990s, **2**:149

Family values, 1950s, **2**:96–97

Farming, during the 1920s, **1**:35

Fashion communication, **1**:150, **1**:161–65, **2**:170–74; 1900–1920, **1**:161–62; 1920–1940, **1**:162–64; 1940–1949, **1**:164–65; magazines, **1**:161–62, **1**:163; mail-order catalogs and pattern catalogs, **1**:162, **1**:164; movies, **1**:162–63; newsreels, **1**:163; photography, **1**:162; 1950s, **2**:170–71; 1960s and 1970s, **2**:171–72; 1980s to present, **2**:172–74

Fashion designers: new type of couturier, 1930s, **1**:156; 1950s to present, **2**:14

Fashion industry: beauty ideals in different periods, **1**:17; business of, **1**:149–68, **2**:159–78; department stores, **1**:16; diversification by end of 1960s, **2**:61; Hollywood films and, **1**:16–17; magazines, **1**:16, **1**:164; mail-order catalogs, **1**:1:1:165, **1**:16; mass production techniques and, **1**:15; niche publications, **2**:15; 1900s, **1**:90; 1910s, **1**:96; 1920s, **1**:102, **1**:103*f,* **1**:135; 1990s movies, **2**:90; sexualized images, 1990s, **2**:151; TV programming about, 1990s and 2000s, **2**:92–93; U. S., 14–17; during WWII, **1**:153

Fashion technology, **1**:150, **2**:174–78; 1940s, **1**:167; 1950s, **2**:174–75; 1900s and 1910s, **1**:165–66; 1920s and 1930s, **1**:166–67; 1960s and 1970s, **2**:175–76; 1980s to present, **2**:176–78

Fast food, 1960s, **2**:103

Fath, Jacques, **1**:154

Faulkner, William, **1**:73, **1**:81

Federal Communications Commission (FCC), **1**:70, **1**:76; AM *versus* FM, 1965, **2**:65; regulation changes, 1987, **2**:81

Federal Emergency Relief Administration, **1**:42

Federal income tax, **1**:30

Federal Nurses Training Bill, banned racial discrimination, **1**:50

Federal Radio Commission, **1**:70, **1**:76

Federal Works Projects: Federal Theater Projects, **1**:74; murals supported by, **1**:72

Felt, use in shoes, **1**:167

Feminism: in the 1910s, **1**:126; in the 1960s, **2**:130; in the 1970s, **2**:138–39

Ferdinand, Franz, Archduke, assassination, **1**:30

Ferragamo, Salvatore, **1**:167

Ferraro, Geraldine, **2**:37

Field, Barbara, debutante in 1936, **1**:106

Field Painting, **2**:52

Fields, Shep, His Rippling Rhythm, **1**:80

Fish, Janet, **2**:68

Fitness and exercise: 1980s, **2**:109–10; 1990s, **2**:115

Fitzgerald, F. Scott, **1**:62, **1**:68

Fixx, Jim, **2**:106

Flammable Fabrics Act, 1971, **2**:176

Flappers, women in the 1920s, **1**:11, **1**:102, **1**:134–35

Follies Girls, **1**:64

Fonda, Jane, workout videos, **2**:109–10

Fontanne, Lynn, **1**:68–69

Footwear (children): 1900s, **1**:296–97; 1910s, **1**:306; 1920s, **1**:314–15; 1930s, **1**:324–25; 1940s, **1**:334–35

Footwear (children to preteen): 1950s, **2**:317; 1960s, **2**:329; 1970s, **2**:343–44; 1980s, **2**:357; 1990s and 2000s, **2**:371–72

Footwear (men): 1900s, **1**:255; 1910s, **1**:262; 1920s, **1**:271; 1930s, **1**:278–79; 1940s, **1**:285; 1950s, **2**:256; 1960s, **2**:265–66; 1970s, **2**:275–76; 1980s, **2**:284; 1990s, **2**:294; 2000s, **2**:302

Footwear (teen to college): 1950s, **2**:317–18; 1960s, **2**:330; 1970s, **2**:344–45; 1980s, **2**:357–58; 1990s and 2000s, **2**:372

Footwear (women): 1900–1908, **1**:179; 1909–1914, **1**:188; 1914–1919, **1**:196; 1940–1946, **1**:234–35; 1947–1949, **1**:243; 1920s, **1**:209–10; 1930s, **1**:221–22; 1950s, **2**:189–90; 1960s, **2**:201–2; 1970s, **2**:213–14; 1980s, **2**:223; 1990s, **2**:224; 2000s, **2**:242

Ford, Gerald, **2**:5,**2**:31

Ford, Henry, **1**:100

Ford, Tom, **2**:164

Form follows function, American architecture, **1**:57

Formalwear (children): 1900s, **1**:291; 1910s, **1**:297–98; 1920s, **1**:307–8; 1930s, **1**:316–18; 1940s, **1**:326–28

Formalwear (children to preteen): 1950s, **2**:306–7; 1960s, **2**:319–20; 1970s, **2**:332–33; 1980s, **2**:347–48; 1990s and 2000s, **2**:360–61

Formalwear (men): 1900s, **1**:248–49; 1910s, **1**:256; 1920s, **1**:263–64; 1930s, **1**:272–73; 1940s, **1**:280; 1950s, **2**:249–50; 1960s, **2**:258–59; 1970s, **2**:268–69; 1980s, **2**:277–78; 1990s, **2**:287; 2000s, **2**:297–98

Formalwear (teen to college): 1950s, **2**:307–8; 1960s, **2**:320–21; 1970s, **2**:333–35; 1980s, **2**:348–49

Formalwear (women): 1900–1908, **1**:171–73; 1909–1914, **1**:180–82; 1914–1919, **1**:189; 1940–1946, **1**:223–24; 1947–1949, **1**:237–38; 1920s, **1**:197–99; 1930s, **1**:211–13; 1950s, **2**:180–82; 1960s, **2**:192–93; 1970s, **2**:204–6; 1980s, **2**:215–16; 1990s, **2**:227–28; 2000s, **2**:236–37

Fortuny, Mariano, **1**:151

Frazier, Charles, **2**:87

Freed, Alan, **2**:52

Freidan, Betty, **2**:11

Frissell, Toni, **1**:73

Frost, Robert, **1**:62

Fundamentalist beliefs, 1920s, **1**:38

Galanos, James, **2**:35–36, **2**:165

Gaming devices, entertainment for teens and preteens, **2**:10

Garbo, Greta, **1**:70; 1920s hairstyle, **1**:209*f*

Garment production: large-scale, 1:157; mass production, 1:157; for soldiers, 1:157

Gaultier, Jean Paul, underwear as outerwear, 2:85

Gay Rights movement, 2:12–13, 2:138, 2:152–53

George, Grace, 1:68

Germany: invasion of other countries, 1930s, 1:43; WWI, 1:19, 1:28, 1:31, 1:36–37

Gershwin, George, 1:73, 1:74

Gesture, 2:52

GI Bill (Serviceman's Readjustment Act of 1944), 1:21, 1:46, 1:51, 2:23

Gibson, Charles Dana, 1:55, 1:121

Gibson Girl, 1:55–56, 1:56f, 1:121

Gimbels, 1:160

Ginsburg, Allen, 2:102

Girl's ensembles (children to preteen): casual wear: 1950s, 2:309, 2:311–12; 1960s, 2:322–23; 1970s, 2:335–36; 1980s, 2:350; 1990s and 2000s, 2:363–64; formalwear: 1950s, 2:306; 1960s, 2:320; 1970s, 2:332; 1980s, 2:347; 1990s and 2000s, 2:361

Girl's ensembles (teen to college): casual wear: 1960s, 2:324–25; 1970s, 2:337–38; 1980s, 2:352–53; 1990s and 2000s, 2:365–66; formalwear: 1950s, 2:307–8; 1960s, 2:321; 1970s, 2:333–34; 1980s, 2:348–49; 1990s and 2000s, 2:362

Givenchy, Hubert de, film-fashion, 1960s, 2:65, 2:65f, 2:161–62

Glamour (magazine), 1980s to present, 2:173

Glasnost, 2:38

Glenn Miller's Orchestra, 1:8

Glossary: 1900–1949, 1:341–46; 1950 to present, 2:375–79

Gloves (children): 1950s, 2:318–19; 1960s, 2:331; 1970s, 2:345–46;

1980s, 2:359; 1990s and 2000s, 2:373–74

Gloves (women), 1950s, 2:191

Godfrey, Arthur, 1:83–84

Gold Standard Act of 1900, 1:23

Golden, Arthur S., 2:87

Golden Age of Hollywood: films of 1930s, 1:75; films of 1940s, 1:82

Goldman, James, 2:63

Golf: men's sportswear: 1900s, 1:252; 1910s, 1:260; 1920s, 1:268–69; 1930s, 1:277; 1940s, 1:283; 1950s, 2:253; 1960s, 2:263; 1970s, 2:273; 1980s, 2:281–82; 1990s, 2:291; 2000s, 2:300–301; women's sportswear: 1900–1908, 1:176; 1909–1914, 1:185; 1914–1919, 1:193; 1940–1946, 1:231; 1947–1949, 1:241; 1920s, 1:205; 1930s, 1:219; 1950s, 2:186–87; 1960s, 2:198; 1970s, 2:211; 1980s, 2:221; 1990s, 2:231; 2000s, 2:240

Goodman, Benny (King of Swing), 1:79

Gorbachev, Mikhail, 2:38

Gordon, Gary, Tick Tock Rhythm, 1:80

Gordy, Barry, Motown Records, 1957, 2:54, 2:60

Goth, alternative fashion, 2:235, 2:244, 2:295

Gotham Ball, 1:106

Government and political movements: 1950s, 2:19–20; 1960s, 2:24–26; 1970s, 2:30–31; 1980s, 2:35–37; the 1900s, 1:21–22; the 1910s, 1:28; the 1920s, 1:33–34; the 1930s, 1:39–41; the 1940s, 1:44–45; 1990s and 2000s, 2:40–41

Graham, Martha, 1:75

Grand Ole Opry, radio broadcast, 1925, 1:71

Great Depression, 1:6; American art, 1:72; children's fashion, 1:316–26; discrimination against ethnicity,

Great Depression (*Continued*)
  1:39, 1:44; eating habits, 1:106–7;
  effects on haute couture, 1:152–53;
  effects on minorities, 1:43–44; five
  & dime stores, 1:160; men's fashion,
  1:272–79; shape of the 1930s, 1:41;
  strain on families, 1:13, 1:138;
  women in the workforce and, 1:11;
  women's fashion, 1:211–23
Greer, Howard, 1:77
Grey, Zane, 1:62
Griffith, D. W., 1:70
Gris, Juan, 1:61
Grisham, John, 2:87
Growing up in America, 1:136–38,
  2:139–42, 2:146–48; 1900s,
  1:123–26; 1950s, 2:124–26; 1960s,
  2:131–34; the 1910s, 1:129–30; the
  1930s, 1:140; the 1940s, 1:142–44;
  1990s and 2000s, 2:153–55; 1950s to
  present, 2:13–14
Grunge, alternative fashion, 2:86–87,
  2:86f, 2:236, 2:295, 2:296f
Guare, John, 2:78, 2:89
Guest Worker Plan, 2004, 2:45
Gulf of Tonkin Resolution, 2:25, 2:28
Guthrie, Woody, 1:81

Hairstyles (children): 1900s, 1:296;
  1910s, 1:304–5; 1920s, 1:314; 1930s,
  1:323–24; 1940s, 1:332–33
Hairstyles (children to preteen): 1950s,
  2:315–16; 1960s, 2:328; 1970s,
  2:342; 1980s, 2:356; 1990s and
  2000s, 2:370
Hairstyles (men): 1900s, 1:254; 1910s,
  1:262; 1920s, 1:270; 1930s, 1:278;
  1940s, 1:284–85; 1950s, 2:255;
  1960s, 2:265; 1970s, 2:275; 1980s,
  2:283; 1990s, 2:293; 2000s, 2:302
Hairstyles (teen to college): 1950s,
  2:316; 1960s, 2:328–29; 1970s,
  2:343; 1980s, 2:356; 1990s and
  2000s, 2:370–71

Hairstyles (women): 1900–1908, 1:179;
  1909–1914, 1:187; 1914–1919,
  1:195; 1940–1946, 1:234;
  1947–1949, 1:242; 1920s, 1:207–8,
  1:208f, 1930s, 1:221; 1950s, 2:189;
  1960s, 2:200–201; 1970s, 2:213;
  1980s, 2:222–23; 1990s, 2:233;
  2000s, 2:241
Haley, Alex
Halston, 2:24, 2:24f
Handbags: 1900–1908, 1:179–80;
  1909–19148, 1:188; 1914–1919,
  1:196–97; 1940–1946, 1:236;
  1947–1949, 1:243; 1920s, 1:211;
  1930s, 1:222; children, 1:325–26;
  1950s, 2:191; 1960s, 2:202; 1970s,
  2:214; 1980s, 2:224; 1990s, 2:235;
  2000s, 2:242
Handbags (children): 1950s, 2:318–19;
  1960s, 2:331; 1970s, 2:345–46;
  1980s, 2:359; 1990s and 2000s,
  2:373–74
Handy, William Christopher,
  1:62–63
Hansberry, Lorraine, 2:55
Hansen, Mark Victor, 2:88
Hanson, Duane, 2:68
Harding, Warren G.: return to
  normalcy, 1920, 1:6; scandals, 1:20,
  1:33
Haring, Keith, 2:68
Harlem Renaissance: 1920s, 1:39;
  1930s, 1:73–74
Harlow, Jean, 1:69
Harper's Bazaar (magazine): early
  1900s, 1:16; Hollywood stylists
  featured in 1920s and 1930s,
  1:153; photography, 1:162;
  1920s, 1:67; 1950s, 2:171; 1960s,
  2:171
Harris, Roy, 1:73
Harrison Narcotics Act, 1914, 1:100
Hats: blocking, 1:167; during WWII,
  1:153–54. *See also* Headwear

Haute couture, **1**:149; collapse during German occupation, **1**:152; effects of Great Depression, **1**:152–53; effort to reestablish Paris after WWII, **1**:154; perception of, after WWII, **1**:154; 1940s, **1**:153–55; 1950s, **2**:160–61; 1980s, **2**:37–38; 1960s and 1970s, **2**:161–62; the 1900s and 1910s, **1**:150–52; the 1920s and 1930s, **1**:152–53; 1980s to present, **2**:162–64

Hawkins, Stephen, **2**:78

Hayes, Helen, **1**:60

Head, Edith, **1**:76, **1**:77, **1**:153

Headwear (children): 1900s, **1**:295–96; 1910s, **1**:304–5; 1920s, **1**:314; 1930s, **1**:323–24; 1940s, **1**:332–33

Headwear (children to preteen): 1950s, **2**:315; 1960s, **2**:328; 1970s, **2**:342; 1980s, **2**:355–56; 1990s and 2000s, **2**:369

Headwear (men): 1900s, **1**:254; 1910s, **1**:261; 1920s, **1**:270; 1930s, **1**:278; 1940s, **1**:284; 1950s, **2**:255; 1960s, **2**:265; 1970s, **2**:275; 1980s, **2**:283; 1990s, **2**:293; 2000s, **2**:302

Headwear (teen to college): 1950s, **2**:316; 1960s, **2**:328; 1970s, **2**:342–43; 1980s, **2**:356; 1990s and 2000s, **2**:370

Headwear (women): 1900–1908, **1**:178–79; 1909–1914, **1**:187; 1914–1919, **1**:195; 1940–1946, **1**:233–34; 1947–1949, **1**:242; 1920s, **1**:207–9, **1**:207*f*; 1930s, **1**:220–21; 1950s, **2**:188–89; 1960s, **2**:200; 1970s, **2**:212; 1980s, **2**:212; 1990s, **2**:233; 2000s, **2**:241

Health and leisure: 1900s, **1**:93–95; 1910s, **1**:99–100; 1920s, **1**:103–5; 1930s, **1**:106–7; 1940s, **1**:109–12; 1950s, **2**:99–100; 1960s, **2**:102–4; 1970s, **2**:106–8; 1980s, **2**:109–12; 1990s and 2000s, **2**:114–18

Heat-molded seaming, 1980s to present, **2**:177

Hefner, Hugh, **2**:12, **2**:129–30

Held, Al, **2**:59

Held, John, Jr., **1**:101

Hemingway, Ernest, **1**:68, **1**:81

Hemp, use in shoes, **1**:167

Henri Bendel, **1**:159

Hepburn, Audrey, Hubert de Givenchy collaboration, 1960s, **2**:65, **2**:65*f*

Herbert, Victor, **1**:61

Heroin chic, mid-1990s, **2**:117, **2**:174

Hilfiger, Tommy, **2**:166

Hip-Hop. *see* Rap and Hip-Hop

Hippies, alternative fashion, **2**:203–4, **2**:266, **2**:267*f*

Hiroshima and Nagasaki, 1945, **1**:49

Hispanic Americans: 1960s, **2**:30; 1990s and 200s, **2**:46

Historic movies, 1990s, **2**:89

Historicism, 1990s, **2**:113

Hitler, Adolf, **1**:37, **1**:49, **1**:72

Hoff, Carl, **1**:80

Hoffmann, Josef, **1**:66

Holliday, Billie, **1**:39

Hollywood: films of 1950s, **2**:55–57; influence during WWII, **1**:164–65; McCarthyism and, **2**:9, **2**:19; new era in film, 1969, **2**:9; worldwide market, 1980s, **2**:9

Hollywood stylists, challenging Paris, 1920s and 1930s, **1**:1534

Home Shopping Network (HSN), **2**:169

Homelessness, 1980s, **2**:146

Homeowners Loan Corporation, **1**:42

Homosexuality, **2**:12–13, **2**:138; acceptance, 1980s, **2**:145–46; division regarding, 1990s, **2**:151–53

Hoover, Herbert: attitude toward Japan, **1**:43; Great Depression, **1**:6; limited government policies, **1**:34, **1**:36, **1**:41

Horst, Horst P., **1**:73

House of Dior, **2:**160

House of Style (TV show), **2:**82

House of Worth, **1:**150–51

Household innovations, in the
1900–1949 period, **1:**10

Housing, after WWII, **1:**48

Howard, Leslie, **1:**68

Hoyningen-Huene, **1:**73

Hughes, Langston, **1:**39, **1:**74

Human immunodeficiency virus
(HIV), **2:**13, **2:**37; first case, 1981,
2:111; 1980s, **2:**146

Humphrey, Hubert, **2:**25

Hurston, Zora Neale, **1:**74

Hutton, Barbara, debutante in 1930,
1:106

Huxley, Aldous Leonard, **1:**68

Hwang, David Henry, **2:**78

Ibsen, Henrik, **1:**60

Iman, **2:**172

Immigration: into America,
1901–1910, **1:**6–7, **1:**20, **1:**23,
1:26–27, **1:**31–33; debates in the
1990s, **2:**45; from Eastern Europe,
1920s, **1:**38; marriage for immigrant
families, 1900s, **1:**118–19; from
Mexico, 1920s, **1:**38

Immigration and Naturalization Act of
1952, **2:**20, **2:**34

Immigration Reform and Control Act,
1986, **2:**40

Indian Arts and Crafts Board, 1935, **1:**44

Indian Reorganization Act, 1934, **1:**44

Info-tainment television, **2:**92

International Council of Scientific
Unions, **2:**22

International developments: 1950s,
2:21–23; 1960s, **2:**27–28; 1970s,
2:32–33; 1980s, **2:**38–40; the 1900s,
1:23–26; the 1910s, **1:**30–31; the
1920s, **1:**36–37; the 1930s, **1:**42–43;
the 1940s, **1:**48–50; 1990s and
2000s, **2:**43–44

International Geophysical Year (IGY),
1955, **2:**22

International Ladies' Garment
Workers Union, **1:**32

International Money Fund (IMF), **1:**49

Iranian hostage crisis, **2:**33, **2:**36

Iraq war, 2003, **2:**43

Iribe, Paul, **1:**161

Irving, John, **2:**70

Isolationism, **1:**37

Italy: after WWI, **1:**36–37; invasion of
other countries, 1930s, **1:**43

J. C. Penney, Golden Rule Stores,
1913, **1:**158

Jackets and vests: men's business wear:
19303, **1:**272; 1900s, **1:**249; 1910s,
1:257; 1920s, **1:**265; 1940s,
1:280–81; 1950s, **2:**250; 1960s,
2:260; 1970s, **2:**270; 1980s, **2:**278;
1990s, **2:**288; men's casual wear:
1900s, **1:**250–51; 1910s, **1:**258;
1920s, **1:**266; 1930s, **1:**274; 1940s,
1:282; 1950s, **2:**251; 1960s, **2:**261;
1970s, **2:**271; 1980s, **2:**280; 1990s,
2:289; 2000s, **2:**299; men's
formalwear: 1900s, **1:**248–49; 1910s,
1:256; 1920s, **1:**263–64; 1930s,
1:272; 1940s, **1:**280; 1950s, **2:**249;
1960s, **2:**258–59; 1970s, **2:**269;
1980s, **2:**277; 1990s, **2:**287; 2000s,
2:297

Jackson, Michael, **2:**75–76, **2:**76*f*

Jahn, Helmuth, **2:**75

James, Charles, **1:**154

Japan: becoming a world power, 1931,
1:42–43; emergence as a world
superpower, **2:**39; in WWII, **1:**48–49

Japanese Americans, treatment during
WWII, **1:**45

Jazz Age, 1920s, **1:**8, **1:**54, **1:**67–68;
children's fashions, **1:**307–16; men's
fashions, **1:**263–72; women's
fashions, **1:**197–211

The Jazz Singer, first talkie, **1**:69

Jeaneret-Gris, Charles Edouard (Le Corbusier), **1**:72

Jewelry (children): 1930s, **1**:325; 1950s, **2**:318; 1960s, **2**:330–31; 1970s, **2**:345; 1980s, **2**:358–59; 1990s and 2000s, **2**:373

Jewelry (men): 1900s, **1**:256; 1910s, **1**:263; 1920s, **1**:271; 1930s, **1**:279; 1940s, **1**:286; 1950s, **2**:257; 1960s, **2**:266; 1970s, **2**:276; 1980s, **2**:285; 1990s, **2**:294–95; 2000s, **2**:303

Jewelry (women): 1900–1908, **1**:179–80; 1909–1914, **1**:188; 1914–1919, **1**:196; 1940–1946, **1**:236; 1947–1949, **1**:243; 1920s, **1**:210–11; 1930s, **1**:222; 1950s, **2**:190; 1960s, **2**:202; 1970s, **2**:214; 1980s, **2**:224; 1990s, **2**:234–35; 2000s, **2**:242

Jewish immigrants, Eastern Europe, **1**:26–27

Jim Crow laws, **1**:7, **1**:26, **1**:50, **2**:29

Jitterbug, **1**:110

Jogging, 1970s, **2**:106

Johnson, Betsey, **2**:164

Johnson, Lyndon Baines (LBJ): Great Society Program, **2**:3, **2**:18, **2**:25, **2**:102–3; tax cuts, 1964, **2**:26

Johnson, Philip, **2**:75

Johnson, Spencer, **2**:88

Johnson-Reed Act, 1924, **1**:37

Jolson, Al, **1**:69

Joyce, James, **1**:68

Juilliard School, **1**:81

Junkie chic, mid-1990s, **2**:117

Kandinsky, Wassily, **1**:67

Kaprow, Allen, **2**:59

Karan, Donna, **2**:166

KDKA, first commercial radio station, Pittsburgh, **1**:70

Keaton, Buster, **1**:69

Kellerman, Annette, **1**:177

Kennedy, Jacqueline Bouvier, **2**:24, **2**:24*f,* **2**:184*f;* social occasions, **2**:101, **2**:101*f;* source of fashion, 1960s, **2**:171

Kennedy, John Fitzgerald (JFK), **2**:4, **2**:17, **2**:24–25, **2**:24*f,* **2**:27–28, **2**:60, **2**:184*f;* impact on social occasions, **2**:100–101

Kennedy, William, **2**:77

Kent State University, 1970, **2**:140

Kenzo, **2**:39

Kern, Jerome, **1**:60

Kesey, Ken, **2**:63, **2**:134

Kiminos (1909–1914), **1**:187

King, Billie Jean, **2**:106

King, Stephen, **2**:70, **2**:77–78

King Tut, fashion inspiration, 1922, **1**:203

Kinsey Reports, sexual revolution, **2**:129

Klee, Paul, **1**:67

Klein, Anne, **2**:165

Klimt, Gustav, **1**:66

Korean Conflict, **2**:22–23

Kors, Michael, **2**:164

Krushchev, Nikita, **2**:27–28

Ku Klux Klan: after WWI, **1**:37; during WWI, **1**:33

Kushner, Robert, **2**:67

Kushner, Tony, **2**:89

Kyser, Kay, **1**:80

La Belle Epoque (Edwardian) era, **1**:171–80

Labor unions, **1**:20, **1**:40

Lacroix, Christian, **2**:38, **2**:163

Ladies Home Journal (magazine): early 1900s, **1**:16; 1950s, **2**:171

Lampshade tunic, **1**:181*f,* **1**:182

Landscapes, **1**:53

Lange, Dorothea, **1**:72

Lauren, Ralph, **2**:163, **2**:165, **2**:166

Lawrence v. Texas, **2:**152

Le Gallienne, Eve, **1:**69

League of Nations, **1:**31, **1:**36, **1:**42–43

League of Women Voters, **1:**6

Leary, Timothy, **2:**134

Lee, Harper, **2:**63

Legal drinking age, 1970s, **2:**105

Legwear (children), **1:**314–15; 1900s, **1:**296–97; 1910s, **1:**306; 1930s, **1:**324–25; 1940s, **1:**334–35

Legwear (children to preteen): 1950s, **2:**317; 1960s, **2:**329; 1970s, **2:**344; 1980s, **2:**357; 1990s and 2000s, **2:**372

Legwear (men): 1900s, **1:**255; 1910s, **1:**262; 1920s, **1:**271; 1930s, **1:**279; 1940s, **1:**285; 1950s, **2:**256; 1960s, **2:**266; 1970s, **2:**275–76; 1980s, **2:**284; 1990s, **2:**294; 2000s, **2:**303

Legwear (teen to college): 1950s, **2:**318; 1960s, **2:**330; 1970s, **2:**345; 1980s, **2:**358; 1990s and 2000s, **2:**373

Legwear (women): 1900–1908, **1:**179; 1909–1914, **1:**188; 1914–1919, **1:**196; 1940–1946, **1:**235; 1947–1949, **1:**243; 1920s, **1:**210; 1930s, **1:**222; 1950s, **2:**190; 1960s, **2:**202; 1970s, **2:**214; 1980s, **2:**223–24; 1990s, **2:**224; 2000s, **2:**242

Leisure activities, 1950s to present, **2:**10

Les Robes de Paul Poiret, **1:**161

Les Stix, **1:**67

L'Esposition Universalle, Paris, 1900, **1:**150

Lewis, Sinclair, **1:**68

Lifar, Serge, **1:**75

Life expectancy, 1910s, **1:**99

Lifestyle marketing, 1980s to present, **2:**172

Lifestyles of the Rich and Famous (TV show), **2:**82

Light bulb, 1910s, **1:**97

Lilith Fair concert, 1997, **2:**84

Lindbergh, Charles, 1930s, **1:**40–41

Lindsey, Hal, **2:**70

Lingerie, 1950s, **2:**188

Literature: 1950s, **2:**54–55; 1960s, **2:**63; 1970s, **2:**70; 1980s, **2:**77–78; 1990s and 2000s, **2:**87–88

Literature and music: 1900s, **1:**57–60; 1910s, **1:**62–63; 1920s, **1:**67–68; 1930s, **1:**73–74; 1940s, **1:**79–82

Living single in America: 1980s, **2:**143; 1990s and 2000s, **2:**149

Living together without marriage, **2:**149–50

Lloyd, Harold, **1:**69

Lollapalooza concert, 1991, **2:**84

Lombardo, Guy, **1:**73

London, Jack, **1:**62

Lost Generation, American writers, **1:**68

Loving v. The Commonwealth of Virginia, **2:**131

Lucky (magazine), 1980s to present, **2:**173

Lunt, Alfred, **1:**68–69

Lusitania, sunk by U-boat, 1915, **1:**31

Lycra, 1960s and 1970s, **2:**175

Maastricht meeting, 1992, **2:**43

MacConnel, Kim, **2:**67

Machine aesthetic, **1:**71–72

Machine Age Exhibition, 1934, **1:**71–72

Macy's, **1:**159

Madame Gres, couturiere, **1:**152

Mademoiselle (magazine), during WWII, **1:**164

Madonna, **2:**84–85

Mail-order catalogs: photography in, **1:**162; use in early twentieth century, **1:**16; during WWII, **1:**165

Mailer, Norman, **1**:81, **2**:63

The Man in the Grey Flannel Suit
(film), **2**:250

Mangold, Robert, **2**:59

Mankasci, Martin, **1**:73

Mann, Thomas, **1**:68

Mann Act (White Slave Traffic Act),
1:128

Mapplethorpe, Robert, **2**:68, **2**:83

Marcel wave, **1**:159*f*

Marcos, Ferdinand, **2**:39

Margueritte, Victor, **1**:102

Marijuana, 1910s, **1**:100

Marriage and family: 1950s, **2**:121–23;
1960s, **2**:126–29; 1970s, **2**:134–36;
1980s, **2**:142–44; the 1900s, **1**:58,
1:117–21; the 1910s, **1**:126–27; the
1920s, **1**:130–34; the 1930s,
1:138–39; the 1940s, **1**:140–41;
1990s and 2000s, **2**:148–50; 1950s to
present, **2**:10

Marshall Fields, **1**:159

Marshall Plan (European Recovery
Program), **1**:45

Mascara, origin in Vaseline, **1**:195

Massine, Leonie, **1**:69

Masters & Johnson, sexuality in the
1960s, **2**:129

Matisse, Henri, **1**:66

Maugham, W. Somerset, **1**:74

Max Factor, **1**:159

Maybelline mascara, **1**:195

Mayer, Edith and Irene, fur coats,
1:202*f*

McCardell, Claire, **1**:157, **2**:164; the
American look, **1**:15

McCarran Act (Control of
Communism Act), **2**:20

McCarran-Walter Act, **2**:23

McCarthy, Joseph, **1**:45; effect on
entertainment industry, **2**:9; political
landscape in the 1950s, **2**:19–20

McFadden, Bernard, *Evening Graphic*
periodical, **1**:136

McKay, Claude, **1**:74

McKinley, William, assassination,
1:22–23

McKinney Act of 1987, **2**:146

McMurtry, Larry, **2**:77

Medicare and Medicaid: 1966,
2:102–3; 1990s and 2000s, **2**:150

Medoff, Mark, **2**:78

Melting pot of American culture, **2**:6

Men's fashion, **1**:247–87, **2**:247–304

Mercer, Johnny, **1**:80

Mergers and acquisitions, 1990s, **2**:42

Metropolis (film), **1**:72

Mexican Americans: Great Depression
and, **1**:6, **1**:44; role in WWII, **1**:51

Meyerowitz, Joel, **2**:68

Miami Vice (TV show), **2**:82

Microfiber, 1980s to present, **2**:177

Microsoft, 1975, **2**:38

Middle East, 1990s and 2000s, **2**:44

Miller, Arthur, **1**:81

Miller, Glenn, **1**:79

Mills Brothers, **1**:73

Minimalism, **2**:49, **2**:52; 1960s, **2**:59;
1990s, **2**:113

Miniskirt, 1960s, **2**:161

Minuteman Project, 2005, **2**:45

Miss America, 1920s, **1**:163–64, **1**:163*f*

Miss America Pageant, 1968, **2**:130

Mix, Tom, **1**:69

Miyake, Issey, **2**:39

Mizrahi, Isaac, **2**:166

Modernism, **1**:55; in art, **1**:71, **1**:78;
in music, **1**:67

Mods, alternative fashion, **2**:203,
2:266–67, **2**:267

Moffat, Peggy, **2**:172

Mondale, Walter, **2**:37

Monk, Thelonious, **1**:81

Monroe Doctrine, **1**:23–25

Monterey Pop festival, **2**:102

Montgomery Ward: catalog sales,
1:158; first retail store, 1925, **1**:160;
mass production, **1**:157–58

Mood disorders, 1990s, **2**:116

Moore, Charles, **2**:75

Moore, Colleen, **1**:69

Moral Majority, **2**:36, **2**:145–46

Morning gown (1903), **1**:171*f*

Morrison, Toni, **2**:77

Morton, Jelly Roll, **1**:68

Morton, Ree, **2**:67

Mother Jones, child labor in the 1900s,
    1:125

Motion Picture Association of
    American: new ratings, 1984,
    2:80–81; ratings code, **2**:64

Motion Picture Story (magazine), **1**:65

Motion pictures: blockbusters, **2**:72; epic
    tales, **2**:56; fashion communication
    through, **1**:162–63; feature-length,
    1:63; Golden Age, **1**:55; Golden Age
    ends 1950s, **2**:55; independently
    produced, 1960s, **2**:64; influence of
    film, 1925, **1**:8; influence on fashion,
    1:16–17; introduction of "going out"
    ensembles, **2**:72; memorable films of
    1930s, **1**:75; music and dance,
    2:79–80; Office of War, 1940s, **1**:9,
    1:82; penny arcades in the 1890s, **1**:8;
    production code (self-censorship),
    1:1:1:139, **1**:2:1:64, **1**:75; 1960s,
    2:64–65; 1970s, **2**:71–72; 1980s,
    2:78–81; 1990s and 2000s, **2**:89–90;
    1950s to present, **2**:50–51; selling
    Liberty Bonds, **1**:64; silent screen
    stars, **1**:65; sound films, **1**:9, **1**:54;
    teenage focus, **2**:79. *See also* Theater
    and movies

Motoring costume, 1903, **1**:253*f*

Motown Records, 1957, **2**:54, **2**:60

Movies. *see* Motion pictures

MP3 player, **2**:84, **2**:88

MTV (Music Television), 1981, **2**:7,
    2:75–76, **2**:84

Murals, 1930s, **1**:72

Music: Beatles, 1964, **2**:7, **2**:60; bebop,
    1:55, **1**:81; big band, **1**:54–55, **1**:73,

1:79; black funk, **2**:7, **2**:49; blues,
    1:62–63; Bob Dylan, **2**:7; British
    Invasion, **2**:60–61, **2**:102; California
    surf sounds, **2**:54; cool jazz, **1**:55,
    1:81, **1**:104; Doo-Wop, **2**:54; ethnic,
    1:54; ethnic influences, 1970s, **2**:7;
    glam, costuming, **2**:69; Grunge
    movement, **2**:8, **2**:86–87, **2**:86*f,*
    internet downloads, 2000s, **2**:84;
    Latin, 1990s, **2**:87; Motown, 1957,
    2:54, **2**:60; musicians support special
    causes, 1980s, **2**:76–77; new wave
    and punk, **2**:7–8, **2**:49, **2**:69, **2**:142;
    psychedelic sound, mid-1960s, **2**:62;
    radio programming, 1920s, **1**:71;
    ragtime, **1**:53–54, **1**:104; rap, urban,
    and hip hop, **2**:7, **2**:49, **2**:76–77;
    rhythm & blues, **1**:80–81; rock 'n'
    roll, 1950s, **2**:7, **2**:49, **2**:52–53;
    1920's, **1**:67–68, **1**:104; 1950s, **2**:52–
    54; 1960s,
    2:60–62; 1970s, **2**:68–69; 1980s,
    2:75–77; 1990s and 2000s, **2**:83–87;
    seen as evil in 1900s, **1**:59; swing or
    swing jazz, **1**:79–80; varied genres
    and images, 1980s, **2**:76; videos, **2**:7,
    2:75–76; zydeco, **1**:81. *See also*
    Literature and music

Musical theater, 1910s, **1**:64

Mussolini, Benito, **1**:37

Nast, Condé, Mrs., Fortuny pleated tea
    gown, 1910, **1**:151*f*

National Aeronautical and Space Act,
    1958, **2**:22

National Aeronautical and Space
    Administration (NASA), **2**:22,
    2:28

National Association for the Repeal of
    Abortion Laws, 1969, **2**:139

National Endowment for the Arts,
    1960s, **2**:60

National Endowment for the
    Humanities, 1960s, **2**:60

National Environmental Policy Act, 1969, **2**:30

National Institute of Drug Abuse, 1977, **2**:142

National Organization for the Reform of Marijuana Laws, **2**:111

National Organization for Women (NOW), 1966, **2**:127

Native Americans: FDR's attempts to help, 1930s, **1**:6, **1**:44; role during WWII, **1**:50–51; 1960s, **2**:29–30; 1970s, **2**:35

Natural fibers, renewed interest in 2000s, **2**:177

Navajo language, use in WWII, **1**:50–51

Naval Research Laboratory's Vanguard proposal, **2**:22

Necklines, women's formalwear: 1900–1908, **1**:172–73; 1909–1914, **1**:182; 1914–1919, **1**:189; 1940–1946, **1**:224; 1947–1949, **1**:238; 1920s, **1**:198; 1930s, **1**:212

Neckwear (children): 1950s, **2**:319; 1960s, **2**:331; 1970s, **2**:346; 1980s, **2**:360; 1990s and 2000s, **2**:374

Neckwear (men): 1900s, **1**:255; 1910s, **1**:262–63; 1920s, **1**:271; 1930s, **1**:279; 1940s, **1**:285; 1950s, **2**:257; 1960s, **2**:266; 1970s, **2**:276; 1980s, **2**:284; 1990s, **2**:294; 2000s, **2**:303

Negri, Pola, **1**:69

Nehru jacket suit, **2**:259

Neo-Bohemian and Retro-Chic, alternative fashion, **2**:244, **2**:304

Neo-Classicism, 1930s, **1**:72

Neo-Expressionism, **2**:75

Neo-Plasticism, **1**:66

Neo-Pop art, **2**:75

Never married census category, 1980s, **2**:143

New age religion, 1970s, **2**:107

New Look: Dior's collection, 1947, **1**:154, **2**:160; fashion 1947–1949, **1**:237–43

New Wave, alternative fashion, **2**:286

Newspapers, elite population features, 1940s, **1**:162

Newsreels, fashion communication, **1**:163

Nickelodeons, 1900s, **1**:61

Nidetch, Jean, Weight Watchers, 1963, **2**:103

Nijinska, Bronislava, **1**:69

Nineteenth (Suffrage) Amendment, **1**:6, **1**:131

Nixon, Pat, evening gown, **2**:181*f*

Nixon, Richard, **1**:45, **2**:5, **2**:18, **2**:25, **2**:28, **2**:30, **2**:34, **2**:140

Nordstrom, **1**:159

Norell, Norman, **1**:157, **2**:164

North America Free Trade Agreement (NAFTA), **2**:18, **2**:41

North Atlantic Treaty Organization (NATO), **1**:50

Nuremberg Trials, **1**:49

Nylon, marketed in 1938, **1**:167

Odet, Clifford, **1**:74

Office of Racial Equality, **2**:34

Office of War Information, **1**:9, **1**:47, **1**:82

O'Keefe, Georgia, **1**:66, **1**:72

Oldenburg, Claus, **2**:59

Olympics: first televised, 1968, **1**:2:**1**:66; 1980s, **2**:111; Summer, 1924, **1**:104; Summer 1972, **2**:107; Summer 1976, **2**:107; Winter, 1932, **1**:107; Women's Swimming Team, 1936, **1**:218*f*

O'Neil, Eugene, **1**:74, **1**:81

Op Art, **2**:49, **2**:52; black and white beachshift, 1966, **2**:49, **2**:50*f*

Organization of Petroleum Exporting Countries (OPEC), 1970s, **2**:31–33

Orozco, Jose Clemente, muralist, **1**:72

Orry-Kelly, **1**:77

Outerwear (children): 1900s, **1**:294; 1910s, **1**:302–3; 1920s, **1**:311–12; 1930s, **1**:321–22; 1940s, **1**:330–32

Outerwear (children to preteen): 1950s, **2**:313; 1960s, **2**:326; 1970s, **2**:340; 1980s, **2**:354; 1990s and 2000s, **2**:367–68

Outerwear (men): 1900s, **1**:251–52; 1910s, **1**:259; 1920s, **1**:267–68; 1930s, **1**:276; 1940s, **1**:283; 1950s, **2**:252–53; 1960s, **2**:263; 1970s, **2**:272–73; 1980s, **2**:281; 1990s, **2**:291; 2000s, **2**:300

Outerwear (teen to college): 1950s, **2**:313; 1960s, **2**:326–27; 1970s, **2**:340–41; 1980s, **2**:354; 1990s and 2000s, **2**:368

Outerwear (women): 1900–1908, **1**:176; 1909–1914, **1**:185; 1914–1919, **1**:192–93; 1940–1946, **1**:228–30; 1947–1949, **1**:240; 1920s, **1**:201–3; 1930s, **1**:216–17; 1950s, **2**:185–86; 1960s, **2**:196–97; 1970s, **2**:209–10; 1980s, **2**:219–20; 1990s, **2**:230–31; 2000s, **2**:239

Palestine Liberation Organization, 1988, **2**:44

Palestinian National Authority, 1994, **2**:44

Panama Canal, **1**:24, **1**:29, **2**:33

Pants (children to preteen boys): casual wear: 1950s, **2**:310; 1960s, **2**:323; 1970s, **2**:336; 1980s, **2**:351; 1900s and 2000s, **2**:364

Pants (children to preteen girls): casual wear: 1950s, **2**:309; 1960s, **2**:322; 1970s, **2**:335–36; 1980s, **2**:350; 1900s and 2000s, **2**:363

Pants (men): business wear: 1930, **1**:274; 1900s, **1**:250; 1910s, **1**:257; 1920s, **1**:265; 1930s, **1**:274; 1940s, **1**:280; 1950s, **2**:251; 1960s,

2:260–61; 1970s, **2**:270; 1980s, **2**:279; 1990s, **2**:288; 2000s, **2**:298; casual wear: 1900s, **1**:251; 1910s, **1**:259; 1920s, **1**:267; 1930s, **1**:275; 1940s, **1**:282; 1950s, **2**:252; 1960s, **2**:262; 1970s, **2**:272; 1980s, **2**:280; 1990s, **2**:290; 2000s, **2**:299–300; formalwear: 1900s, **1**:249; 1910s, **1**:256; 1920s, **1**:264; 1930s, **1**:273; 1940s, **1**:280; 1950s, **2**:249; 1960s, **2**:259; 1970s, **2**:269; 1980s, **2**:278; 1990s, **2**:287; 2000s, **2**:297

Pants (teen to college boys): casual wear: 1950s, **2**:312; 1960s, **2**:325; 1970s, **2**:339; 1980s, **2**:353; 1900s and 2000s, **2**:366–67

Pants (teen to college girls): casual wear: 1950s, **2**:311; 1960s, **2**:324; 1970s, **2**:338; 1980s, **2**:352; 1900s and 2000s, **2**:366

Pants (women): casual wear: 1914–1919, **1**:192; 1940–946, **1**:227; 1947–1949, **1**:239–40

Paquin, **1**:150

Paris Peace Accord, 1973, **2**:32–33

Parker, Charlie, **1**:81

Parks, Rosa, **2**:20, **2**:23

Patio culture, 1950s, **2**:98

Patou, Jean, **1**:154

Pattern and Design movement, 1970s, **2**:67

PDAs (personal digital assistants), **2**:88

Pearl Harbor, **1**:20, **1**:44–45, **1**:48

Peche, Dagobert, **1**:66

Pencil-thin silhouette, fashion in 1920s, **1**:17

Pentagon Papers, 1995, **2**:31

People for the Ethical Treatment of Animals (PETA), **2**:39

Perceptualism, **2**:68

Perestroika, **2**:38

Performance Art, 1970s, **2**:67

The Perils of Pauline, **1**:63

Permanent press, 1970s, **2**:176

Perry Ellis, **2**:37–38

Peters, Thomas J., **2**:78

Phonograph, **1**:62, **1**:97

Photography, **1**:53–54, **1**:57; documentary-style realism, 1930s, **1**:72; fashion, **1**:67; fashion magazines, **1**:162; Kodachrome, **1**:62; Kodak camera, **1**:57; mail-order catalogs, **1**:162; modernist fashion photographers, **1**:73; surrealist, **1**:73

Photoplay (magazine), **1**:65

Photorealism, **2**:68

Picasso, Pablo, **1**:61, **1**:66, **1**:71

Pickford, Mary, **1**:63, **1**:69

Pinup and sweater girls, **1**:229*f*

Plastic surgery, 1990s, **2**:115

Playsuits (women): 1940–1946, **1**:228

Plessy v. Ferguson, **1**:26

Plunkett, Walter, **1**:77

Pocket Books, **1**:82

Poiret, Paul, **1**:102, **1**:151; fashion communication, **1**:161; minaret or lampshade tunic, **1**:181*f,* **1**:182

Polar fleece, 1980s to present, **2**:177

Politics: America, 1900–1949, **1**:5–6; America, 1950s to present, **2**:4, **2**:17–47

Pollack, Jackson, **1**:55, **1**:78

Polo shirt, **1**:275*f*

Polyester, 1970s, **2**:176

Pop Art, **2**:49, **2**:52; 1960s, **2**:58–59

Population, U. S., 1900–1949, **1**:3

Porter, Cole, **1**:74

Portman, John, **2**:75

Pose dancing, **2**:84–85

Postmodernism, **2**:49, **2**:74–75, **2**:83

Pound, Ezra, **1**:68, **1**:81

Poverty: families in the 1970s, **2**:134; U. S., 1900–1949, **1**:4

Preppies, alternative fashion movement, **2**:225, **2**:285

Presidential elections, 2000 through 2008, **2**:41

Prêt-á-porter, French term for ready-to-wear, **1**:157, **2**:162

Processed foods, 1920s, **1**:103

Progressive movement, **1**:4, **1**:19, **1**:28

Progressive Party, **1**:21

Prohibition, 1920s, **1**:101, **1**:105, **1**:134

Project Gutenberg, **2**:88

Proposition 187, California, 1994, **2**:46

Pucci, 1960s, **2**:161

Punk, **2**:7–8, **2**:49, **2**:69; alternative fashion, **2**:141, **2**:226, **2**:277, **2**:285–86*f*

Pure Food and Drugs Act, **1**:92

Quant, Mary: "Mod" designs, **2**:51*f,* **2**:203*f;* 1960s, **2**:161

Queen Elizabeth, first feature-length movie, **1**:63

QVC, **2**:169

Rabanne, Paco, **2**:175

Rachmaninoff, Sergei, **1**:73

Racial issues, after World War I, **1**:7

Radical Women, 1968, **2**:130

Radio: families in the 1920s, **1**:134; FDRs fireside chat, **1**:54, **1**:76; lifeline, 1940s, **1**:8; 1920s, **1**:54, **1**:70–71; 1930s, **1**:76, **1**:78; 1940s, **1**:83; 1950s, **2**:57; 1960s, **2**:65; 1970s, **2**:72–73; 1980s, **2**:81; 1990s and 2000s, **2**:90–91; transatlantic broadcasts, 1920, **1**:8

Radio Act of 1927, **1**:70

Radio City Music Hall, opens 1932, **1**:74

Raffia, use in shoes, **1**:167

Ragtime music, **1**:53–54

Rainey, Ma, **1**:68

Ralph Lauren, **2**:41

Rap and Hip-Hop: alternative fashion, **2**:226, **2**:243, **2**:286, **2**:295–96, **2**:303–4; music, **2**:7, **2**:49, **2**:76–77

Rastafarian, alternative fashion, **2**:226, **2**:286–87

Rationing, during WWII, **1**:45, **1**:157

Ravers, alternative fashion, **2**:296–97

Ray, Man, **1**:67, **1**:73

Rayon (viscose), **1**:166

Ready-to-wear (women), **1**:149; 1940s, **1**:157–58; 1950s, **2**:164–65; 1900s and 1910s, **1**:155; 1920s and 1930s, **1**:155–57; 1960s and 1970s, **2**:165; 1980s to present, **2**:165–66

Reagan, Nancy, fashion, **2**:35–36

Reagan, Ronald, **2**:4–5, **2**:18, **2**:35–36, **2**:142

Realism, 1910s, **1**:54

Reality television, **2**:92–93

Rebels, alternative fashion, 1950s, **2**:258

Remington, Frederick, **1**:56

Resins, use in shoes, **1**:167

Resource guide: 1900–1949, **1**:347–59; 1950 to present, **2**:381–95

Retail operations, **1**:150; 1940s, **1**:160–61; 1950s, **2**:167; 1900s and 1910s, **1**:158; 1920s and 1930s, **1**:158–60; 1960s and 1970s, **2**:167–68; 1980s to present, **2**:168–70

Revlon, **1**:159

Rhea, Mlle., 1920s fashion, **1**:207*f*

Rhodes, Zandra, **2**:162

Rhodoid (from Bakelite), use in shoes, **1**:167

Rhythm & Blues, **1**:80–81

Ricci, Robert, **1**:154

Right On! (magazine), 1970s, **2**:171

Rivera, Diego, muralist, **1**:72

Roaring twenties, **1**:100–101

Rock 'n' roll, **2**:7, **2**:49, **2**:52–53, **2**:68; FM radio, 1970s, **2**:72–73; 1960s, **2**:132

Rockefeller Center, 1930s, **1**:72

Rockers: early, **2**:52–53; polite, **2**:53; 1970s, **2**:68

Rockwell, Norman, **1**:61

Rodgers and Hart, **1**:74

Roe v. Wade, **2**:139

Rogers, Will, radio in the 1920s, **1**:71

Roosevelt, Eleanor, **1**:39–40

Roosevelt, Franklin Delano (FDR): alphabet programs, **1**:42; beginning of Cold War, **1**:49; entering WWII, **1**:20; fireside chats on radio, **1**:55, **1**:76, **1**:83; help for Native Americans, **1**:44; meetings with Winston Churchill, **1**:43; New Deal, **1**:6, **1**:44; popularity and policies, **1**:39–40, **1**:42; restoring American livelihoods, **1**:20

Roosevelt, Theodore: daughter Alice and the cause of the "new woman," **1**:121; democracy in newly acquired territory, **1**:24; Monroe Doctrine, **1**:23–25; new laws, **1**:5; Nobel Peace Prize, **1**:25; Panama Canal and, **1**:24; Progressive movement, **1**:4–5, **1**:19, **1**:22

Rosie the Riveter posters, **1**:46, **1**:47*f*

Rosine, perfume by a couturier, **1**:151

Rothko, Mark, **1**:78

Russell, Lillian, **1**:63–64

Russia, democratic elections, 1996, **2**:44

Russian Revolution, 1917, **1**:25

Russo, Richard, **2**:87

Russo-Japanese War (1904–1905), **1**:25

Sagan, Carl, **2**:78

Samaras, Lucas, **2**:59

Sandburg, Carl, **1**:62

Sanger, Margaret, **1**:97, **1**:127

Satellite radio, **2**:90–91

Satie, Erik, **1**:67

The Saturday Evening Post (magazine), **1**:61

Saturday Night Live, **2**:74

Scarves (women), 1950s, **2**:191

Schiaparelli, Elsa, **1**:73, **1**:152–54

Schönberg and Boublil, **2**:78

Schroeder, Pat, **2**:135

Schwarzenegger, Arnold, bodybuilding in the 1970s, **2**:106

Science fiction movies, 2000s, **2**:89

Scopes, John, teaching of Theory of Evolution, **1**:38, **1**:137

Seamstresses, early twentieth century, **1**:158

Sears and Roebuck: catalog sales, **1**:158; first retail store, 1925, **1**:160; mass production, **1**:157

Second City, Chicago, 1970s, **2**:70–71

Segal, Erich, **2**:70

Segregation: America in the 1940s, **1**:7, **1**:50; America in the 1950s, **2**:20, **2**:23, **2**:125; professional sports, 1950s, **2**:100

Selective Service Act, 1940, banning discrimination, **1**:50

Sennett, Mack, **1**:69

Separates: introduced by American designers, **1**:157–58; women's business wear: 1900–1908, **1**:174; 1947–1949, **1**:239; 1950s, **2**:183; 1960s, **2**:194; 1970s, **2**:207; 1980s, **2**:217–18; 1990s, **2**:228–29; 2000s, **2**:237–38; women's casual wear: 1900–1908, **1**:175; 1909–1914, **1**:184; 1914–1919, **1**:191–92; 1940–1946, **1**:227; 1947–1949, **1**:239; 1920s, **1**:201; 1930s, **1**:215–16; 1950s, **2**:184–85; 1960s, **2**:195–96; 1970s, **2**:208–9; 1980s, **2**:219; 1990s, **2**:230; 2000s, **2**:238–39

September 11, 2001, commemorative clothing, **2**:42

Serrano, Andres, **2**:83

Serviceman's Readjustment Act of 1944 (G. I. Bill), **1**:21, **1**:46, **1**:51, **2**:23

Seventeen (magazine): adolescent consumers after 1940s, **1**:16; 1960s and 1970s, **2**:171; 1980s to present, **2**:173

Seventeenth Amendment, **1**:5

Sex education, the 1910s, **1**:128

Sexual discrimination, role of women and, **2**:11

Sexuality and morality: America, 1900–1949, **1**:11–12; America, 1950s to present, **2**:12–13; 1900s, **1**:121–23; 1950s, **2**:123–24; 1960s, **2**:129–31; 1970s, **2**:136–39; 1980s, **2**:144–46; the 1910s, **1**:127–29; the 1920s, **1**:134–36; the 1930s, **1**:139; 1990s and 2000s, **2**:150–53

Shapiro, Miriam, **2**:67

Shaw, Artie, **1**:79

Shaw, George Bernard, **1**:60, **1**:68, **1**:74

Shaw, Irwin, **1**:81

Shawls/wraps, women's outerwear: 1900–1908, **1**:176; 1909–1914, **1**:185; 1920s, **1**:202–3; 1930s, **1**:217; 1960s, **2**:197; 1970s, **2**:210; 1980s, **2**:220; 1990s, **2**:230–31; 2000s, **2**:239

Shawn, Ted, **1**:69

Sheitl, **1**:27

Shirts: men's business wear: 1930, **1**:274; 1900s, **1**:249; 1910s, **1**:257; 1920s, **1**:265; 1940s, **1**:280; 1950s, **2**:250; 1960s, **2**:260; 1970s, **2**:270; 1980s, **2**:278–79; 1990s, **2**:288; men's casual, 2000s, **2**:299; men's casual wear: 1950, **2**:251–52; 1900s, **1**:251; 1910s, **1**:258–59; 1920s, **1**:266–67; 1930s, **1**:274–75, **1**:275*f*; 1940s, **1**:282; 1960s, **2**:262; 1970s, **2**:271–72; 1980s, **2**:280; 1990s, **2**:289–90; men's formalwear: 1900s, **1**:249; 1910s, **1**:256; 1920s, **1**:264; 1930s, **1**:272–73; 1940s, **1**:280; 1950s, **2**:249; 1960s, **2**:259; 1970s, **2**:269; 1980s, **2**:278; 1990s, **2**:287; 2000s, **2**:297

Shopping malls: department stores shifting to, **1:**160; suburban, 1950s, **2:**21

Shore, Stephen, **2:**68

Shrimpton, Jean, **2:**172

Silhouette (children to preteen): casual wear: 1950s, **2:**308; 1960s, **2:**322; 1970s, **2:**334; 1980s, **2:**349–50; 1990s and 2000s, **2:**363; formalwear: 1950s, **2:**306; 1960s, **2:**319–20; 1970s, **2:**332; 1980s, **2:**347; 1990s and 2000s, **2:**360–61

Silhouette (men's fashion): business wear: 1900s, **1:**249; 1910s, **1:**257; 1920s, **1:**264–65; 1930s, **1:**273; 1940s, **1:**280; 1950s, **2:**250; 1970s, **2:**269–70; 1980s, **2:**278; 1990s, **2:**288; 2000s, **2:**298; casual wear: 1900s, **1:**250; 1910s, **1:**258; 1920s, **1:**266; 1930s, **1:**274; 1940s, **1:**282; 1950s, **2:**251; 1960s, **2:**260, **2:**261; 1970s, **2:**271; 1980s, **2:**279–80; 1990s, **2:**289; 2000s, **2:**299; formalwear: 1900s, **1:**248; 1910s, **1:**256; 1920s, **1:**263; 1930s, **1:**272; 1940s, **1:**280; 1950s, **2:**249; 1960s, **2:**258; 1970s, **2:**268–69; 1980s, **2:**277; 1990s, **2:**287; 2000s, **2:**297

Silhouette (teen to college): casual wear: 1950s, **2:**310–11; 1960s, **2:**323–24; 1970s, **2:**337; 1980s, **2:**351–52; 1990s and 2000s, **2:**365; formalwear: 1950s, **2:**307; 1960s, **2:**320–21; 1970s, **2:**333; 1980s, **2:**348; 1990s and 2000s, **2:**361

Silhouette (women's fashion): empire (1909–1914), **1:**151; business wear, **1:**182–83; casual wear, **1:**183; formalwear, **1:**180; Great Depression (1930s), **1:**156; business wear, **1:**213–14; casual wear, **1:**215; formalwear, **1:**211–12; jazz age (1920s): business wear, **1:**199; casual wear, **1:**200; formalwear, **1:**197–98;

new look (1947–1949): business wear, **1:**238; casual wear, **1:**239–40; formal wear, **1:**237; pencil-thin, 1920s, **1:**17; 1950s: business wear, **2:**182; casual wear, **2:**183; formalwear, **2:**180–81; 1960s: business wear, **2:**194; casual wear, **2:**194–95; formalwear, **2:**192–93; 1970s: business wear, **2:**206; casual wear, **2:**208; formalwear, **2:**204–5; 1980s: business wear, **2:**217; casual wear, **2:**218; formalwear, **2:**215; 1990s: business wear, **2:**228; casual wear, **2:**229; formalwear, **2:**227; 2000s: business wear, **2:**237; casual wear, **2:**238; formalwear, **2:**236; S-curve (1900–1908), **1:**17, **1:**171, **1:**173, **1:**174; WWI (1914–1919): business wear, **1:**190; casual wear, **1:**191; formalwear, **1:**189; WWII (1940–1946): business wear, **1:**225; casual wear, **1:**227; formalwear, **1:**223

Simon, Neil, **2:**63, **2:**78

Simpson, Adele, **1:**157

Sinatra, Frank, **1:**80

Single motherhood, 1990s, **2:**153

Sitcoms (situation comedies), 1970s, **2:**73

Sixteenth Amendment, **1:**30

Skateboard fashion, 1970s, **2:**141

Skirts: casual wear: 1900–1908, **1:**175; 1909–1914, **1:**184; 1940–946, **1:**228; formalwear: 1900–1908, **1:**172; 1909–1914, **1:**181; 1914–1919, **1:**189; 1940–1946, **1:**223–24; 1947–1949, **1:**237; 1920s, **1:**198; 1930s, **1:**212; 1950s, **2:**181; 1960s, **2:**193; 1970s, **2:**205; 1980s, **2:**215; 1990s, **2:**227; 2000s, **2:**236

Skirts (children to preteen), casual wear: 1950s, **2:**309; 1960s, **2:**322; 1970s, **2:**335; 1980s, **2:**350; 1900s and 2000s, **2:**363

Skirts (teen to college), casual wear: 1950s, **2**:311; 1960s, **2**:324; 1970s, **2**:337–38; 1980s, **2**:352; 1900s and 2000s, **2**:365–66

Skiwear: men's sportswear: 1920s, **1**:269; 1930s, **1**:277; 1940s, **1**:283–84; 1950s, **2**:254; 1960s, **2**:264; 1970s, **2**:274; 1980s, **2**:282; 1990s, **2**:292; 2000s, **2**:301; women's sportswear: 1914–1919, **1**:194; 1940–1946, **1**:231; 1947–1949, **1**:241; 1920s, **1**:205; 1930s, **1**:218

Sleepwear (children), federal standards for flammability, 1970s, **2**:176

Sleepwear (men): 1900s, **1**:253–54; 1910s, **1**:261; 1920s, **1**:270; 1930s, **1**:278; 1940s, **1**:284; 1950s, **2**:255; 1960s, **2**:264; 1970s, **2**:274; 1980s, **2**:283; 1990s, **2**:293; 2000s, **2**:301

Sleepwear (women): 1900–1908, **1**:178; 1909–1914, **1**:186–87; 1914–1919, **1**:194–95; 1940–1946, **1**:232, **1**:232*f*; 1947–1949, **1**:242; 1920s, **1**:207; 1930s, **1**:220; 1950s, **2**:188; 1960s, **2**:200; 1970s, **2**:212; 1980s, **2**:222; 1990s, **2**:232

Sleeves, women's formalwear: 1900–1908, **1**:173; 1909–1914, **1**:182; 1914–1919, **1**:189; 1940–1946, **1**:224; 1947–1949, **1**:238; 1920s, **1**:198; 1930s, **1**:212; 1950s, **2**:181–82; 1960s, **2**:193; 1970s, **2**:205; 1980s, **2**:216; 1990s, **2**:227; 2000s, **2**:236–37

Smith, Bessie, **1**:68

Smith, Kate, **1**:80, **1**:83–84

Smithson, Robert, **2**:59

Smoking: debates in the 1980s, **2**:110; suits against the tobacco industry, 1990s, **2**:117; Surgeon General's Advisory Committee on Smoking and Health, 1964, **2**:103

Snow, Carmel, **1**:154

Social occasions: 1910s, **1**:98–99; 1920s, **1**:101–2; 1930s, **1**:105–6; 1940s, **1**:109; 1950s, **2**:96–99; 1960s, **2**:100–102; 1970s, **2**:104–6; 1980s, **2**:108–9; the 1900s, **1**:91–93; 1990s and 2000s, **2**:112–14

Socialist Party, **1**:21

Soft collar shirt for men, 1910s, **1**:258*f*

Solzenitzyn, Alexander, **2**:70

Sondheim, Stephen, **2**:78

Southern Christian Leadership Council, **2**:25

Soviet Union, dissolution, **2**:38–39

Spandex, 1960s and 1970s, **2**:175

Spanish-American War, **1**:23–24

Spice Girls fashion, **2**:86

Spiegel, mass production, **1**:157

Sports (athletics): ready-to-wear fashions, **1**:155–56; 1920s, **1**:104; 1930s, **1**:107; 1940s, **1**:109–11; 1970s, **2**:107; 1980s, **2**:111–12; 1990s, **2**:117–18

Sports radio broadcasts, 1920s, **1**:71

Sportswear: growth of ready-to-wear industry and, **1**:156–57; officially licensed, **2**:290; 1950s, **2**:165; 1960s and 1970s, **2**:167–68

Sportswear (children): 1900s, **1**:295; 1910s, **1**:303–4; 1920s, **1**:312–14; 1930s, **1**:322–23; 1940s, **1**:332–33

Sportswear (children to preteen): 1950s, **2**:314; 1960s, **2**:327; 1970s, **2**:341; 1980s, **2**:354–55; 1990s and 2000s, **2**:368–69

Sportswear (men): 1900s, **1**:252–53, **1**:252*f*; 1910s, **1**:259–60; 1920s, **1**:268–69; 1930s, **1**:276–77; 1940s, **1**:283–284; 1950s, **2**:253–54; 1960s, **2**:263–64; 1970s, **2**:273–74; 1980s, **2**:281–82; 1990s, **2**:291–92; 2000s, **2**:300–301

Sportswear (teen to college): 1950s, **2**:314–15; 1960s, **2**:327; 1970s, **2**:341–42; 1980s, **2**:355; 1990s and 2000s, **2**:369

Sportswear (women): 1900–1908,
  1:176–78; 1900–1914, 1:185–86;
  1914–1919, 1:193–94; 1940–1946,
  1:230–31; 1947–1949, 1:240–41;
  1920s, 1:203–5; 1930s, 1:217–19;
  1950s, 2:186–87; 1960s, 2:197–99;
  1970s, 2:210–11; 1980s, 2:220–21;
  1990s, 2:231–32; 2000s, 2:240–41
Sputnik I, 2:21, 2:28
St. Denis, Ruth, 1:69
St. Vincent Millay, Edna, 1:62
Star Spangled Banner, declared official
  anthem in 1931, 1:73
Steel, Danielle, 2:78
Steichen, Edward, 1:67, 1:73
Stein, Gertrude, 1:68
Steinbeck, John, 1:73
Steinem, Gloria, 2:70
Stella, Frank, 2:59
Stepanova, Varvara, 1:67
Stieglitz, Alfred, 1:66
Stimson Act, 1:43
Stock market collapse, 1949, 1:5, 1:20,
  1:36, 1:41, 1:134
Stock market drop, 1987, 2:38
Stonewall Riot, 1969, 2:137
Stoppard, Tom, 2:63
Strategic Defense Initiative (Star
  Wars), 2:35
Stravinsky, Igor, 1:67
Student Nonviolent Coordinating
  Committee, 2:25
Style with Elsa Klensch (TV show),
  2:82
Substance abuse prevention, 1980s,
  2:111, 2:134, 2:142, 2:154
Suits, women's business wear: 1900–
  1908, 1:173–74; 1909–1914, 1:183;
  1914–1919, 1:190; 1940–1946,
  1:225; 1947–1949, 1:238–39; 1920s,
  1:199–200; 1930s, 1:214–15; 1950s,
  2:182–83; 1960s, 2:194; 1970s,
  2:206–7, 2:206–7f; 1980s, 2:217;
  1990s, 2:228; 2000s, 2:237

Sullivan, Louis, 1:57
Sundblom, Haddon, 1:106
Supermodels, 1980s to present, 2:163
Surrealist movement, 1:54, 1:66, 1:73
Sustainable style, 2:177
Swanson, Gloria, 1:69
Sweater girls, 1:229f
Sweaters: men's casual wear, 1:251;
  1910s, 1:259; women's casual wear:
  1914–1919, 1:192; 1940–1946, 1:228
Swimwear (children): 1900s, 1:295;
  1910s, 1:303–4; 1920s, 1:312–14;
  1930s, 1:322–23; 1940s, 1:332–33
Swimwear (children to preteen): 1950s,
  2:314; 1960s, 2:327; 1970s, 2:341;
  1980s, 2:354–55; 1990s and 2000s,
  2:368
Swimwear (men): 1900s, 1:252; 1910s,
  1:259–60; 1920s, 1:268; 1930s,
  1:268; 1940s, 1:283; 1950s, 2:253;
  1960s, 2:263; 1970s, 2:273; 1980s,
  2:281; 1990s, 2:291; 2000s, 2:300
Swimwear (teen to college): 1950s,
  2:313–15; 1960s, 2:327; 1970s,
  2:341–42; 1980s, 2:355; 1990s and
  2000s, 2:369
Swimwear (women): 1900–1908,
  1:176; 1909–1914, 1:185;
  1914–1919, 1:193; 1940–1946,
  1:230; 1947–1949, 1:240–41; 1920s,
  1:203–4, 1:204f; 1930s, 1:217;
  1950s, 2:186–87, 2:186f; 1960s,
  2:197–99; 1970s, 2:210; 1980s,
  2:220; 1990s, 2:231; 2000s, 2:240
Synthetic fabrics: biodegradable, 2:178;
  fashion innovation of 1950s, 2:174;
  1960s and 1970s, 2:175; 1980s to
  present, 2:177

Tabloids, in the 1920s, 1:135–36
Taft, Robert A., Senator, conservatism,
  2:19
Taft, William H., 1:23, 1:28–30,
  1:250f

Tailor shops, early twentieth century, **1:**158

Teapot Dome scandal, **1:**33

Technologies: after WWII, **1:**46; family life in the 1900s, **1:**120–21; family life in the 1920s, **1:**133; innovations in the fashion business, **1:**150, **1:**165–67; 1910s, **1:**97; 1920s, **1:**35; 1990s, **2:**41; 1950s to present, **2:**10

Teddy Boys, **2:**203

Teen People (magazine), 1980s to present, **2:**173

Teenagers: as consumers, 1960s, **2:**132; defined after 1950, **2:**13; 1980s movies focused on, **2:**79; sexual intercourse, 1990s and 2000s, **2:**151; socializing in the 1950s, **2:**99

Television: cable, satellite and digital, **2:**91, **2:**150; children in the 1990s, **2:**155; conservative morality in the 1950s, **2:**123–24; early development, **1:**78; fashion communication, 1950s, **2:**170–71; news broadcasting, **2:**8; popular culture, 1950s to present, **2:**8, **2:**50; representation of minorities, **2:**73; 1940s, **1:**83–84; 1950s, **2:**57–58; 1960s, **2:**66–67; 1970s, **2:**73–74; 1980s, **2:**81–82; 1990s and 2000s, **2:**91–93

Tencel, 1980s to present, **2:**177

Tennessee Valley Authority, **1:**42

Tennis: men's sportswear: 1900s, **1:**252; 1910s, **1:**260; 1920s, **1:**269; 1930s, **1:**277; 1940s, **1:**283; 1960s, **2:**264; 1970s, **2:**273; 1980s, **2:**282; 1990s, **2:**291–92; 2000s, **2:**301; women's sportswear: 1900–1908, **1:**176; 1914–1919, **1:**193–94; 1940–1946, **1:**231; 1947–1949, **1:**241; 1920s, **1:**204–5; 1930s, **1:**219; 1950s, **2:**187; 1960s, **2:**198–99; 1970s, **2:**211; 1980s, **2:**221; 1990s, **2:**231; 2000s, **2:**240

Textile finishes, 1980s to present, **2:**177

Theater: 1950s, **2:**55; 1960s, **2:**63; 1970s, **2:**70–71; 1980s, **2:**78; 1990s and 2000s, **2:**88–89

Theater and movies: 1900s, **1:**60–61; 1910s, **1:**63–66; 1920s, **1:**68–70; 1930s, **1:**74–76; 1940s, **1:**82–83. *see also* Motion pictures

Théâtre de la Mode, **1:**154

Theyskend, Olivier, Goth looks, **2:**85

Thompson, Hunter S., **2:**63

Tiananmen Square, 1989, **2:**38–39

Tiegs, Cheryl, **2:**172

Till, Emmett, **2:**23

Tin Pan Alley, **1:**60, **1:**62

Titanic, **1:**99–100

Tobacco, 1920s, **1:**105

Tommy Hilfiger, **2:**41, **2:**164

Tops (children to preteen boys): casual wear: 1950s, **2:**310; 1960s, **2:**323; 1970s, **2:**339; 1980s, **2:**351; 1900s and 2000s, **2:**364

Tops (children to preteen girls): casual wear: 1950s, **2:**309; 1960s, **2:**322–23; 1970s, **2:**336; 1980s, **2:**350; 1900s and 2000s, **2:**363–64

Tops (teen to college boys): casual wear: 1950s, **2:**312; 1960s, **2:**325–26; 1970s, **2:**339; 1980s, **2:**353; 1900s and 2000s, **2:**367

Tops (teen to college girls): casual wear: 1950s, **2:**311–12; 1960s, **2:**324–25; 1970s, **2:**338–39; 1980s, **2:**352–53; 1900s and 2000s, **2:**366

Tournure drapery, **1:**181*f*

Transcendental meditation, **2:**107

Transistor radios, 1950s, **2:**57

Triangle Shirtwaist Factory tragedy, **1:**32

Trigere, Pauline, **2:**164

Trousers skirt, **1:**181*f*

Truman, Harry S., U. S. as the "world's policeman," **1**:49

Truman Doctrine, postwar U. S. foreign policy, **1**:49

Turkish-style trousers, **1**:182, **1**:182*f*

Turlington, Christy, **2**:163

Turrell, James, **2**:83

Twentieth century, historical landscape of early half, **1**:3–18

Twiggy, **2**:172

Undergarments (men): 1900s, **1**:253; 1910s, **1**:260–61; 1920s, **1**:269–70; 1930s, **1**:277–78; 1940s, **1**:284; 1950s, **2**:254–55; 1960s, **2**:264; 1970s, **2**:274; 1980s, **2**:282–83; 1990s, **2**:292–93; 2000s, **2**:301

Undergarments (women): 1900–1908, **1**:178; 1909–1914, **1**:186; 1914–1919, **1**:194; 1940–1946, **1**:231–32; 1947–1949, **1**:241–42; 1920s, **1**:206; 1930s, **1**:210–20; 1950s, **2**:187–88; 1960s, **2**:199–200; 1970s, **2**:212; 1980s, **2**:221–22; 1990s, **2**:232–33; 2000s, **2**:241

Unemployment, 1950s, **2**:21

Uniforms: military, men's business wear: 1910s, **1**:257–58; 1940s, **1**:280; 1980s, **2**:279; 1990s, **2**:289; women's business wear, 1940–1946, **1**:226–27, **1**:226*f*

United Auto Workers, 1930s, **1**:40

United Mine Workers, 1930s, **1**:40

United Nations, founded in San Francisco, 1945, **1**:45

United Service Organizations (USO), **1**:8, **1**:109

United States Motion Picture Production Code, **1**:55

Updike, John, **2**:87

Valentina, **1**:157

Valentino, Rudolph, **1**:65, **1**:69, **1**:270*f*

Valentino, 1960s fashion, **2**:162

Valley girls, alternative fashion movement, **2**:225–26

van Doesburg, Theo, **1**:66

Vaseline, origin of mascara, **1**:195

VH1, **2**:75–76, **2**:84

Video art, **2**:83

Video cassette recorder (VCR): cable, **2**:8–9; TV revolution, **2**:8

Video games, 1980s, **2**:147

Vidor, King, **1**:70

Vietnam War, **2**:4–5, **2**:18, **2**:25, **2**:28, **2**:32–33; effect on 1960s social occasions, **2**:101; effects on youth, 1970s, **2**:139–40; protests in 1960s, **2**:133

Viola, Bill, **2**:83

Violence: 1990s, **2**:41; schools in the 1990s, **2**:154

Vionnet, couturiere, **1**:152

Viscose (rayon), **1**:166

Vitamins and minerals, 1920s, **1**:103

Vogue (magazine): early 1900s, **1**:16; fashion communication, **1**:162; Hollywood stylists featured in 1920s and 1930s, **1**:153; photography, **1**:162; 1920s, **1**:67, **1**:103; 1950s, **2**:171; 1960s, **2**:171; 1980s to present, **2**:173; during WWII, **1**:164

Volstead Act, **1**:134

von Stroheim, Erich, **1**:70

Vonnegut, Kurt, **2**:63

Voting Rights Act, **2**:6

Walesa, Lech, **2**:38

Walker, Alice, **2**:77

Walking suit (men's), mid-1920s, **1**:266*f*

Wallis blue, **1**:213

Wang, Vera, **2**:164, **2**:166

War Advertising Council, 1942, **1**:47

War of the Worlds (radio), **1**:78

War Production Board, rationing during WWII, **1**:45

Warhol, Andy, **2**:59

Wartime silhouette, WWI, **1**:152

Wash-and-wear, fashion innovation of 1950s, **2**:174

Washington, Booker T., **1**:7, **1**:26

Watergate scandal, **2**:30, **2**:70

Webber, Andrew Lloyd, **2**:78

Wedding fashion: Diana Spencer and Prince Charles, 1981, **2**:108; Duke of Windsor and Mrs. Wallis Simpson (1930s), **1**:213; 1950s, **2**:96–97, **2**:121; 1970s, **2**:105

Weight loss craze, 1980s, **2**:110

Welles, Orson, **1**:78

Wells, Rebecca, **2**:87

West, Nathanel, **1**:74

Westinghouse Electric Company, first commercial radio station, Pittsburgh, **1**:70

Westwood, Vivienne, **2**:162

Wharton, Edith, **1**:62

Whistler, James McNeil, **1**:61–62

Whistler's Mother, **1**:62

White, George, **1**:74

White flight to suburbs, **2**:20

White slavery, the 1910s, **1**:128

Wiener Werkstatte, **1**:66

Wilder, Thornton, **1**:74

Williams, Tennessee, **1**:81, **2**:54–55

Williams, Thomas L., **1**:195

Wilson, August, **2**:78

Wilson, Lanford, **2**:78

Wilson, Woodrow: advances during first term, **1**:5; Clayton Antitrust Act, **1**:29–30; League of Nations, **1**:31, **1**:36; New Freedom reform program, **1**:29; U. S. entering WWI, **1**:19, **1**:28, **1**:31; Wilson's Fourteen Points, **1**:31

Winslow, Homer, **1**:56

Wolfe, Thomas, **1**:74

Wolfe, Tom, **2**:63, **2**:77

Woman's Day (magazine), during WWII, **1**:164

Women: after WWII, **1**:46; athletics in 1970s, **2**:106; athletics in 1990s, **2**:117–18; attractive wife, 1950s television, **2**:170; careers in the 1950s, **2**:123; changing role, 1900–1949, **1**:10–11, **1**:47; changing role, 1950s to present, **2**:11–12; college education, 1910s, **1**:129; education for girls in the 1900s, **1**:124; education for girls in the 1910s, **1**:128–29; entering the workforce, **1**:30, **1**:46, **1**:47, **1**:129; ready-to-wear industry and, **1**:156; family role in the 1950s, **2**:121; female artists, 1970s, **2**:67; forty percent of workforce, 1969, **2**:11; higher education, 1970s, **2**:104; marriage in the 1900s, **1**:117–21; new millennium called age of "new woman," **1**:120; right to vote, 1910s, **1**:28, **1**:97; right to vote, 1920s, **1**:131; roles and responsibilities, 1980s, **2**:144; in the 1960s, **2**:128; in 1900s literature, **1**:58; as targets of advertising in the 1900s, **1**:92; upper class, 1900s, **1**:90–91; well-dressed woman in the 1960s, **2**:128; in the workforce, 1970s, **2**:127

Women's Christian Temperance Union, **1**:58

Women's fashion, **1**:169–245, **2**:179–245; hat and gloves in the 1950s, **2**:122; 1950s entertaining, **2**:98

Women's International Terrorist Conspiracy from Hell, 1968, **2**:130

Women's organizations: movement in the 1960s, **2**:135–36; 1900s, **1**:120

Women's Wear Daily (magazine), **1**:161–62; 1980s to present, **2**:173

Wood, Grant, **1**:72

Woodstock Music and Arts Festival, 1967, **2**:7, **2**:102

Woodstock Music and Arts Festival, 1994 and 1999, **2**:84

Woodward, Bob, **2**:70

Woolworths, **1**:159–60

Working class families, depiction on TV, **2**:91–92

World Disarmament Conference, 1932, **1**:42

World War I (WWI): America in, **1**:4, **1**:7, **1**:19, **1**:31; couture houses shut down, **1**:151; immigration to America and, **1**:7; mass production techniques, **1**:9; men's fashions, **1**:256–63; ready-to-wear manufacturers, **1**:155; slacker marriages, **1**:127; U.S. as a world power, **1**:36; women in the workforce, **1**:11, **1**:96; women's fashions, **1**:188–97

World War II (WWII): collapse of haute couture during German occupation of Paris, **1**:153; economic growth after, **2**:3; effects on American life, **1**:44–45, **1**:140–41; ended Great Depression, **1**:46; fashion industry during, **1**:153; fashion magazines, **1**:164; Glenn Miller's "In the Mood," **1**:79; Hollywood films, **1**:82–83; mail-order catalogs, **1**:165; Marshall Plan, **1**:45; men's fashion, **1**:280–86; Pearl Harbor, **1**:20, **1**:44–45, **1**:48; racial discrimination during, **1**:50–51; scientific advances, **1**:10; treatment of Japanese Americans, **1**:45; United States in, **1**:5, **1**:6, **1**:20; women in the workforce, **1**:46, **1**:141–42; women's fashion, **1**:223–36

World Wide Web, **2**:10–11, **2**:41. **2**:43; catalog and home shopping, **2**:169–70; fashion communication, **2**:174; sexual content, **2**:151

Worth, Charles Frederick, **1**:151

Wright, Frank Lloyd, **1**:57, **1**:72

Yom Kippur War, 1973, **2**:33

Young Miss (magazine), 1960s and 1970s, **2**:171

YSL, 1960s, **2**:161

Yuppies, 79–80

Yves Saint Laurent (YSL), **2**:52

Ziegfeld, Florenz, **1**:64

Zimmermann telegram, **1**:28, **1**:31

Zippers, 1920s and 1930s, **1**:166–67

Zoot-suit riots, **1**:336

Zydeco, **1**:81